Research Methods
for Political Science

Research Methods for Political Science

Quantitative and Qualitative Methods

David E. McNabb

M.E.Sharpe
Armonk, New York
London, England

Library of Congress Cataloging-in-Publication Data

McNabb, David E.
  Research methods for political science : quantitative and qualitative methods / by
David E. McNabb.
    p. cm.
  Includes bibliographical references and index.
  ISBN 0-7656-1234-8 (cloth : alk. paper)
  1. Political science—Methodology. 2. Political science—Research.
I. Title.
JA71.5.M35 2004
320'.072—dc22   2003023975

Printed in the United States of America

The paper used in this publication meets the minimum requirements of
American National Standard for Information Sciences
Permanence of Paper for Printed Library Materials,
ANSI Z 39.48-1984.

∞

BM (c)   10   9   8   7   6   5   4   3   2   1

Dedicated to J.C., with everlasting affection, and
to the memory of my father, J.B. McNabb.

Brief Table of Contents

Detailed Table of Contents

List of Tables and Figures

Tables

Figures

Acknowledgments

Many people, known and unknown, helped with the preparation of this textbook. I wish to offer my special thanks to the consistently supportive members of the public administration graduate program faculty at The Evergreen State College, and to my present and former colleagues at Pacific Lutheran University and the Stockholm School of Economics in Riga. You have all given far more than I can ever return. The book could not have written without the support and encouragement of Harry Briggs at M.E. Sharpe. Finally, I wish to gratefully acknowledge the superlative assistance of Andrew Hudak and his great team at Westchester Book Services in Danbury, Connecticut.

Introduction

The purpose of this book is to provide in one location information about how to design, conduct, interpret, and report on research that is carried on by political scientists for increasing the body of knowledge in this social science discipline. The book has been written to serve as a guidebook for investigating and writing on any political or administrative science topic. While its focus is on research methods for students of political science, those already embarked on their careers in politics will also find it to be a valuable tool. The text can also aid students of other social science and education disciplines who have little or no experience in writing a scholarly paper for a class. Political science graduate students will find the book especially useful for designing and completing assignments in their research methods course, and for preparing their master's degree thesis or doctoral dissertation. Managers now employed in administrative and managerial positions in government, academia, and nonprofit organizations may also find the book useful as a step-by-step guide for designing and conducting a research project with their internal staff.

Scope of the Text

The text covers such important topics as research design, specifying research problems, designing questionnaires and writing questions, designing and carrying out various types of qualitative research approaches, and analyzing both quantitative and qualitative research data. Also included is a discussion of the evolution of political science research and some of the underlying disciplinary questions studied by political scientists. Changes in the philosophy of science from the positivist approach to postpositivist theory and critical research are discussed in some detail.

Research Methods for Political Science was researched and written to fill a need for a methods book that incorporates the latest thinking in the major subfields of political science, including comparative politics, international relations, and public administration, among others. It includes discussions and examples of research topics and research methods found in the current professional literature. A key advantage of the text is that it integrates *both* positivist and postpositivist approaches under one cover. It also provides specific instructions in the use of available statistical software programs such as Excel™ and the Statistical Package for the Social Sciences (SPSS)®. The text also illustrates many points by referring to some of the latest developments in social science research, management and organizational research, in addition to research in the political and administrative sciences.

The book is not a text on statistical methods. However, because of the continued heavy interest in positivist research methods found in most of major political science journals, the book does examine many of the statistical tools employed by today's political scientists. Both descriptive and inferential statistical methods are discussed, with step-by-step instructions for their use also included.

A Caveat

An important point must be made at this time. This is not a text about political science. It does not compare political systems, talk about declining voter activity, or provide instructions on how to run a political campaign. Certainly, it must and does cite examples of such topics and of the research approaches taken and data-gathering methods used by political scientists. It also draws extensively upon the findings, recommendations, conclusions, and intellectual creativity of many present and past political scientists. This work owes an unlimited debt to their scholarship. However, these examples should not be considered to be comprehensive nor fully representative of the scope of the discipline. The examples were chosen by the author, and reflect his own experience, education, and bias. Whatever errors exist, whether they are errors of omission or commission, they are entirely the responsibility of this author.

What this book *is* about is how anyone considering a career as either a practicing politician, a director of political campaigns, or a future academic researcher, as well as political scientists in general, can design and conduct research that meets the basic requirement of being "good science."

Structure of the Text

The book is organized into six major parts, each with two or more chapters. The first part, "Foundations of Political Science Research," contains seven chapters. Chapter 1, "The Systematic Approach to Political Science Research," presents an overview of the two important philosophical approaches to research and science: the *objectivist* and the *humanist* approaches—more commonly known as the *positivist* and *postpositivist* approaches. This discussion is followed by an overview of the purpose of social science research in general. Chapter 2, "The Foundations of Political Science Research," introduces the philosophical foundations that underlie research methodology. This chapter distinguishes the positivist and postpositivist approaches to research and describes a number of the philosophical approaches to the development of knowledge in the discipline. Chapter 3, "The State of Political Science Research," is an introductory review of the state of knowledge in political science, including a discussion of some of the current research in the discipline. It includes a discussion on the use of research for theory building, and on research in its practical, applied approach. Chapter 4, "The Political and Ethical Environments of Research," begins with an overview of the fundamental moral principles upon which political decisions are founded, and concludes with a discussion of the key moral concerns and ethical dilemmas encountered by researchers. Special emphasis is placed on research with human subjects.

Chapter 5, "Understanding the Research Process," introduces the reader to the seven-step process that all research activities should follow, regardless of the objectives, approaches, or methods followed by the researcher. This chapter begins with a discussion of the importance of thoroughly defining the problem before beginning the research, and concludes with a review of different ways to organize reports of research findings.

Chapter 6, "Focusing on a Research Topic," provides a more in-depth discussion of the first step in the research process: clearly and thoroughly defining the research problem. It also provides suggestions on how and where to begin the literature search, including carrying out detailed examinations of textbooks, journals, electronically stored and retrieved articles, and other materials in sources inside and outside of the researcher's organization. The early research proposals produced by most beginning political science researchers tend to be far too broad for the resources at hand (particularly time and money). Therefore, a discussion on the importance of *focus* is included in this chapter.

Chapter 7, the final chapter in the opening part is on "Understanding Research Design." Research designs are the specific data-gathering, data-processing, and data interpretation processes used by political science researchers; they are sometimes referred to as *research strategies.* This discussion includes step-by-step instructions for designing and conducting research projects.

Part 2, "Introduction to Quantitative Research Approaches," provides an overview of the fundamentals of designing and conducting research in the positivist tradition. Chapter 8, "Fundamental Concepts in Quantitative Research," begins with a discussion of the characteristics of measurements and includes an explanation of the types or categories of statistics used in research. Chapter 9, "Introduction to the Sampling Process," is a discussion of probability and nonprobability sampling methods. It includes instructions on the steps to follow during the sampling process. Sampling is an important concept in the use of inferential statistics, as is the nature of sample distributions.

The next three chapters in this part introduce researchers to the three chief quantitative research designs: exploratory, descriptive, and causal. Chapter 10, "Exploratory Research: The Probing Approach," is an introduction to the ways researchers use one-on-one and small-group interviews to collect information for insights and ideas that are used to design more detailed and rewarding research projects. This approach is often referred to as *small sample research.* It often employs probing methods to bring out information that can be used to design large sample survey studies. Chapter 11, "Descriptive Research: The Survey Approach," provides instructions on how to design and conduct large-sample field surveys. It includes step-by-step guidelines for writing questions and constructing questionnaires. This chapter is a practical guide to writing the many types of questions and scales that are used to measure attitudes and opinions. The chapter also includes instruction on how to put these questions into a logical sequence in the formal data-gathering instrument called the *questionnaire.* Chapter 12, "Causal Research: The Experimental Approach," the final chapter in this part, describes the experimental method and illustrates how causal research is conducted. Experiments and experimental design are concepts that are used to design and conduct *cause-and-effect* research studies. The discussion includes an introduction to single-factor and multiple-factor design methods.

In Part 3, "Applying Statistical Concepts in Research," readers are introduced to some of the ways political scientists analyze and display research data, and how they interpret statistical information. Chapter 13, "Interpreting Survey Results with Descriptive Statistics," is the first chapter in this part. The chapter examines a variety of the basic statistical tools used in research. The chapter provides simple-to-understand definitions of measures of central tendency, of variability, of relative position, and of correlation. Chapter 14, "Presenting Research Results with Tables, Charts, and Graphs," explains how these graphic tools can present descriptive statistical data to improve the readability of research reports, and goes on to describe specific steps needed to produce tables, charts, and graphs using readily available statistical software.

In Chapter 15, "Testing Simple Research Hypotheses," readers are shown how and why statistical tests are used to communicate information that relates to the validity of the results of the research. This is the first of several chapters dealing with *inferential statistics*. Inferential statistics are statistical tests used with samples and in which probabilities play an important role. Chapter 16, "Testing Hypotheses about Two or More Samples," is the second chapter dealing with hypothesis tests. It reviews the *t*-test and analysis-of-variance approaches to measuring for statistically significant differences between two or more groups or subgroups. The last chapter in this part, Chapter 17, is an "Introduction to Nonparametric Statistics." These are statistical tests used with measurements that do not meet the more stringent requirements of inferential statistics.

Part 4, "Advanced Quantitative Methods," introduces a number of advanced statistical processes and tests often used in political science research. Chapter 18, "Regression Analysis in Political Science," presents important concepts that underlie the statistical processes in association analysis, including correlation and regression analysis. These tests can now be quickly processed with modern statistical software for desk- and laptop personal computers. The text provides instructions and examples of those software applications.

Chapter 19, "Predicting the Future I: Time Series Methods," is the first of three chapters under the collective heading of "Predicting the Future." Time series models include various methods for smoothing out irregularities in the history of events in order to project trend lines forward in time. The next chapter in this sequence, Chapter 20, provides instruction on how to employ another tool, "Index Number Methods." Chapter 21 is about the third predictive statistical process, "Discriminant Analysis Methods." Discriminant analysis is also an effective tool for aggregating groups of like individuals together based on one or more distinctive characteristics. Applications include identifying groups of persons likely to vote in certain ways. Chapter 22, the final chapter in this part, presents instructions and examples on "Managing Large Databases: Factor and Cluster Analysis Methods." These statistical processes are used to group large amounts of data into logical and meaningful smaller concentrations of subjects or variables.

Part 5, "Introduction to Qualitative Research Methods," is the first of two parts on qualitative research strategies and methods. Chapter 23, "Introduction to Qualitative Research Methods," describes the development and purpose of qualitative research strategies. It also discusses how qualitative designs can contribute to understanding public organizational culture and its impact on the voting public and public agency employees. Chapter 24, "The Explanatory Approach I: Case Study Methods," describes both the single- and multicase approach to research. This is the first of two chapters that discuss the *explanatory approach* in qualitative research. The case method is considered by many to be the most-used qualitative design in political science, particularly in public administration and nonprofit organization research. Chapter 25, "The Explanatory Approach II: Historical Research Methods," is the second chapter in this section on explanatory approaches. For many political scientists, history plays a critical role in developing knowledge in the discipline. However, little, if any, instruction on the process of historiography is included in current political science curricula. This chapter is a small attempt at rectifying that error of omission.

Chapter 26, "The Interpretive Approach I: Grounded Theory Methods," is the first of two chapters on methods used in *interpretive approaches* to political science research. Interpretive research is becoming increasingly popular among researchers in education, sociology, and social psychology. This design is slowly being applied in some political science subfields, particularly in public administration research. In these studies, researchers approach a situation, event, or relationship with little or no preconceived theoretical bias. The researcher seeks to construct a theory only after in-depth analysis of the study data. Chapter 27, "The Interpretive Approach II: Ethnographic Methods," is a discussion on how this culture-based strategy can be used in political science research. Ethnography was originally developed by anthropologists to describe and explain phenomena in distant and what were considered to be "primitive" societies. It has been successfully adapted to research on modern political cultures and subcultures.

The final chapter in this section, Chapter 28, "The Critical Approach: Action Research Methods," presents an overview of action research methods as they are or can be used in political science research.

Part 6, "Analyzing Qualitative Research Data and Writing a Research Report," includes two chapters on several popular and easy-to-use methods used for analyzing qualitative data, a chapter on processing quantitative data with popular software programs, and a chapter on writing the research report. Chapter 29, "Analysis Methods for Qualitative Data," looks at the ethnographic, grounded theory, and action research methods of data analysis. The chapter also includes a brief introduction to the use of computers to analyze qualitative data.

Chapter 30, "Analyzing Texts, Documents, and Artifacts," describes several approaches to the analysis of data developed or collected by persons other than the researcher. Analysis of such data often involves probing for the symbolic meanings that people place on things, including written text. Researchers are interested in determining how events are interpreted and written about in narrative form. The content analysis method of researching published documents, internal memos, and other secondary sources is also examined. These strategies have evolved from historical analyses, and follow those procedures to a large degree.

Chapter 31, "Organizing and Writing the Research Report," provides tips on how to organize, structure, and write a political science research paper. It includes a discussion on the importance of following proven organizational procedures and dealing with citations and credits. Chapter 32, "Introduction to Statistical Software: Excel™ and SPSS®," describes how to use Microsoft Excel® and versions 9, 10, and 11 of SPSS® to conduct most, if not all, of the statistical tests used in public administration research.

Summary

The research activity can be defined as *the process of systematically acquiring data to answer a question or solve a problem.* A research method refers to the steps involved in a given approach. Two philosophical approaches underlie political science research: *positivism and postpositivism.* The positivist approach is the traditional scientific method that involves the following steps: selection of a hypothesis, observation, data collection, hypothesis testing, and acceptance or rejection of a hypothesis. The postpositivist approach is associated with qualitative research methods; it emphasizes understanding as well as description of phenomena.

The goal of this book is for students and professionals alike to know when and how to use a given research strategy and data-gathering method for a given information-need situation. Producing clear, cogent reports is an important ingredient in producing effective research. A variety of examples and exercises are included throughout the book that are designed to help the reader move beyond simple familiarization with the topic to achievement of full understanding and application.

Research and writing are important skills required of all political scientists. Researching means gathering, processing, and interpreting data of some kind. Research results must be communicated in intelligently and cogently written reports. Political scientists must also interpret and evaluate research reports that have been produced by other academics, administrators, or contract-research organizations.

Additional Reading

Finifter, Ada W., ed. 1983. *Political Science: The State of the Discipline*. Washington, DC: American Political Science Association.

———. 1993. *Political Science: The State of the Discipline II*. Washington, DC: American Political Science Association.

Katznelson, Ira, and Helen V. Milner, eds. 2002. *Political Science: The State of the Discipline*. New York: W.W. Norton.

Marsh, David, and Gerry Stoker, eds. 2002. *Theory and Methods in Political Science*, 2nd ed. Houndmills, UK: Palgrave Macmillan.

Plotkin, Henry. 1994. *The Nature of Knowledge*. London: Penguin Press.

Part 1

Foundations of
Political Science Research

1 The Systematic Approach to Political Science Research

The primary goal of all science is to expand human knowledge. The discipline of political science is the branch of learning that contributes to the growth of knowledge about politics and helps us learn about our political systems and the political behavior of our fellow human beings. Political science researchers face an almost unlimited number of research questions upon which to direct their investigative activity. This chapter examines some of the foundations of social science research in general and political science in the specific. This and the next chapter also look at some ways political scientists have attempted to define the appropriate scope of research in the field, including suggestions that have been made about what should constitute the topics in the discipline's major fields. This chapter is an introduction to the two major methodologies of scientific inquiry—the *positivist* and *interpretist* approaches. It also includes an introductory discussion on the use of these philosophical and methodological approaches in political science research.

The overarching objective of this chapter is to help students and researchers in all subfields of political science understand that they should not worry about deciding *what* to research when the need to conduct research arises. Politics is a big field and almost any aspect of political behavior is interesting. Deciding *how* to look at the problem will be suggested by the nature of the problem itself and the objectives spelled out by the researcher. Selecting which methodological tradition to adopt follows from, rather than precedes, the selection of a research topic.

What Is Research?

Research is an important skill required of all political scientists. "Research" means *gathering, processing,* and *interpreting* data. It also means intelligently and cogently communicating the results in a report that describes what was discovered from the research. Knowing how to interpret and evaluate research that has been done by academics, administrators, or contract research organizations is another important skill. To learn the skills needed both to conduct and to evaluate research, students of political science are often required to take one or more courses in *research methods.* Designing and conducting a research project is usually a requirement in those courses. This book has been developed to help students and practicing political scientists successfully complete their research projects.

3

When beginning political scientists embark on what too often seems to be an extremely daunting and thoroughly confusing task, they find themselves faced with such questions as these:

- What is the purpose for doing this research?
- What is a "research problem?"
- Who has the needed information?
- What is the best way to ask questions?
- Which research design should be followed in this situation?
- How should the data be gathered?
- How should data be processed?
- What does all this processed data mean?
- What is the best way to communicate these findings?
- And many, many more . . .

Equally important, researchers must decide what questions *not* to ask, what questions cannot be readily answered, and how much research can be conducted in the time allotted and with the people and money available. This book has been written to provide answers to both sets of questions. It is organized around a discussion of the major approaches taken in political science research. Students of science often use the terms *positivist and postpositivist* to discriminate between the two major approaches to scientific inquiry. In practice, researchers often refer to the techniques to gather and/or process data used most often in either approach as *quantitative* or *qualitative* research. However, today most political studies employ a research design that *combines* elements of both approaches. The book defines and explains some of the major variations and processes found in the political science research most often seen today.

Why Develop Research Skills?

There are at least five very good reasons for developing or expanding the skills needed to conduct research and prepare written research reports. The first reason is that it will help you to develop and hone your analysis and communication skills. These are problem-solving skills that can best be learned by doing research. This point was made by Dryzek (1986, 305), who noted, "The essence of scientific activity is solving problems." Academic employers, governments, and nonprofit organizations have long identified problem-solving skills as the most important characteristics of successful leaders and managers. A person who is able to gather information, to analyze and interpret data, and to communicate the findings effectively to others is a valuable asset in any organization.

A second reason is that by engaging in the research process, students of political science can become aware of what others in the career field are doing and saying about common problems. Every issue of the relevant periodical literature contains one or more articles about topical issues in public and nonprofit organization administration. In research terminology, the process of examining the literature of the field is called "reviewing the literature" and is a critical early step in every research project or program.

Conducting a literature review involves finding and studying information contained in both textbooks and journals. Textbooks are a good way to become introduced to a subject and to gain a broad awareness of an issue or a discipline; they are, however, often outdated by the time they reach the library shelf. It can take as long as four years for a textbook to move from the author's first draft to finally being published, and some texts are used year after year with little or no revision.

On the other hand, professional journals usually present the most current information available; they try to publish information on "the cutting edge" of the discipline. In this way, journals provide the "new" information needed for success in a discipline or career field. It is important to know which are the best publications in a field, why they are better, and what they stand for.

A third reason for learning how to do research has to do with the concept of *credibility*—which itself is founded on the ideas of *replicability* in scientific research. This reason is most applicable to methods that follow traditional positivist research approaches. For example, any theory that is developed under positivist scientific methods must be testable and, if necessary, correctable. Furthermore, conclusions from such theories must be repeatable, predictable, and supportable. Thus, conducting "scientific research" means that anyone reading a report of the research must be able to achieve the same or similar results by following the same research design. If not, the work may simply not be believed.

A fourth reason is the way new information is passed on to future generations; this occurs when the findings of research studies are published in scientific and professional journals. Research findings are also disseminated in papers presented at professional conferences and scholarly or professional meetings. Political scientists, sponsors of research, and educated people with an interest in the report of an author's research tend to consider the research incomplete or unfounded unless the findings are published (Gubanich 1991). Other researchers and administrators working in the field read these reports. Following long-established guidelines for research and report writing makes verification through publishing easier and more likely to take place. The role of published journal articles cannot be overstated; individual faculty members, researchers, and their departments in colleges and universities are increasingly being judged by the "quality" of the journals in which their papers appear (Norris and Crewe 1993). In their final study, Norris and Crewe reported rankings for 90 different journals in which political science articles appear.

Finally, in this era of superfast change and uncertainty in the political world, a key skill often needed by political scientists working in government, for political parties, and for special-interest organizations is the ability to make quick, intelligent decisions. The best decisions are almost always made after all the available information pertaining to the outcomes of the decisions is gathered, read, and weighed. This usually involves some research activity, whether it is conducted formally or informally, by the political scientist, by members of an internal staff, or by contract providers.

The Aims of Scientific Research

Martyn Denscombe (2002, 8–11) has identified five principal aims for all social science research. First, research is conducted in order to help scientists understand the properties of a phenomenon. This process enables the scientist to establish categories, classes, or types of phenomena based on identified properties or characteristics. In political science research an often-encountered set of categories is voter-nonvoter. The decision to place subjects in each category is based upon some discernible activity: the act of voting.

The second aim of research is to enable scientists to understand relationships between variables. Denscombe describes this as a "quest to present conclusive evidence (causal links) that a relationship exists between two or more phenomena." Until additional observations show that the cause and consequence occurs repeatedly, the research can only attribute the event to coincidence. The production of a theory or theories is the third aim, and it is considered by Denscombe to be the ultimate goal of all scientific research. In addition to describing things, theories offer explanations of why they occur. Theory generation is an integral component in both positivist and interpretist research, although Oakley (2000) suggested that theory production occurs in a different sequence in quantitative and qualitative research. In the former approach, the theory is established before testing. In the later approach, theory emerges from the researcher's analysis of the data; it is *grounded* in the findings.

The fourth principal aim of research is the prediction of outcomes. Prediction is based upon a thorough understanding of prior theory generation. The final aim of scientific research is the confirmation of the findings in one study by other researchers—replication. According to Denscombe, "scientific research is conducted so that it can be confirmed or refuted by a community of other scientists."

The Activities and Goals of Research

Research is the activity scientists do to gain a better understanding of how their world works. More formally, research can be defined as *the process of systematically acquiring data to answer a question or solve a problem* (Strauss and Corbin 1998). Achinstein (1970) defined the research activity as a *set of easily understood procedures for acquiring information,* and as a philosophical *mind-set* that people bring to any research activity. Rosenthal and Rosnow (1991) added that scientific research should not be considered simply a fixed procedure. Rather, it should be looked upon as a philosophical way of approaching all research, regardless of the problem addressed and approaches and methods employed. This scientific approach to research referred to by Achinstein and others means that researchers should approach a research problem without any preconceived answers; it requires avoiding any hint of subjective bias. It includes preparing comprehensive operational definitions, forming hypotheses and theories, and applying the appropriate quantitative or qualitative method of data analysis.

The goals that guide all research have been suggested as either to (1) *describe* some event, thing or phenomenon, (2) *predict* future behavior or events based on observed changes in existing conditions, or (3) provide for greater *understanding* of phenomena and how variables are related (Shaughnessy and Zechmeister 1994). Today there is a growing awareness of the need to use research to better *understand* as well as to describe human events and phenomena.

The first activity in researching the scientific way is the *recognition of a problem,* and forming a *theory* about that problem. As noted earlier, science is a problem-solving process. A researcher first recognizes that something is not known or understood about a problem or situation. A researcher must believe that the unknown information is important enough for an effort to be taken to search for the answer to the problem.

In the second activity of scientific inquiry, the researcher then formulates a hypothesis or hypotheses about the problem and its antecedents. Hypotheses are tentative explanations of a solution to the problem; they often take the form of an interpretation of the variables in a relationship, or the perception of a cause-and-effect situation. In scientific research, researchers use *inductive reasoning,* which means moving from the specific to the general. This reasoning

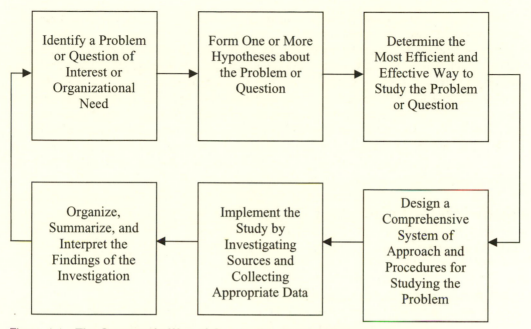

Figure 1.1   **The Systematic Way of Conducting Political Science Research**

process is involved in the act of making an *inference* from the information researchers observe to apply to what they cannot observe. In this way they use data from a *sample* for describing the characteristics or behaviors of a larger *population*. Or, the researcher may conclude that the facts in the case or situation speak for themselves. Theories that are formed in this way are considered to be *empirically grounded* (Manheim and Rich 1986).

The researcher may then test the hypothesis or hypotheses. In quantitative designs, *objective* statistical tests are used for this purpose. In qualitative designs, the researcher makes a *subjective* determination of the validity of the hypothesis. Next, the researcher examines or makes some type of observations and/or measurements of the "things" (variables) associated with the problem; this is data collection. The researcher then arranges the collected data in some meaningful order, looking for similarities and dissimilarities while doing so.

The process of gathering or accumulating data may require asking people to complete a survey questionnaire, personally interviewing a number of people, observing events or reading about them, reading and cataloging published documents, or preparing an in-depth study of one or more cases. However gathered, these data must be coded, tabulated, arranged, classified, analyzed, and interpreted if they are to become *information*. If after conducting an analysis of the data the researcher determines the hypothesis is valid, he or she may then see if there are other applications to which the hypothesis can be applied. The researcher proposes, for example, that "in this study, such and such was true; therefore, in further applications, the same must occur and also be true."

The final activity in this "scientific" approach to research is the verification of conclusions made from the research. This may entail replication of the design with a different sample. For example, the researcher asks, "If 'A' occurred once, will it occur in similar circumstances?" If it does, then the researcher may propose a *theory.* And if others accept the theory, the researcher may attempt to have it accepted as a *law.*

While there are other ways to go about conducting research, this scientific approach underlies them all. This approach emerged during the *Age of Enlightenment,* the explosion in scientific investigation and artistic creativity that began in Europe beginning in the seventeenth century. Early scientific investigators proposed the scientific approach to research as a way of maintaining "rigor" in scientific investigation. The method, simply put, meant not coming to a conclusion on a basis of preformed beliefs alone, but instead on only what can be observed or tested by the senses. Authority, custom, or tradition—the stuff of metaphysics—should not be the source of knowledge and understanding. Instead, knowledge should come from the reality of objects themselves (Richardson and Fowers 1983).

Knowledge, Logic, and Reasoning

Bernard Phillips described the scientific way of looking at the growth of knowledge and understanding this way:

> [It is] an effort to achieve increasing understanding of phenomena by (1) defining problems so as to build on available knowledge, (2) obtaining information essential for dealing with these problems, (3) analyzing and interpreting these data in accordance with clearly defined rules, and (4) communicating the results of these efforts to others. (Phillips 1976, 4)

Out of this "scientific" outlook emerged the idea that the world and everything in it was a giant collection of objects that could be mapped and understood by empirical observation. Scientists developed a faith in the formal, objective, or *positivist* method. Richardson and Fowers (1998) have described that faith as being "an almost boundless confidence." The positivists saw this "faith in method" as the only path to true knowledge. They concluded that this faith is exemplified by "mainstream social sciences' insistence on the use of correlational and experimental methods regardless of the subject matter being investigated."

Political scientists use research in order to add to the storehouse of knowledge about the political world, and to learn as much as they can about the processes of politics. While science, knowledge, and learning are clearly related, they are not the same. Lyotard spoke to this difference in the following way:

> Learning is the set of statements which, to the exclusion of all other statements, denote or describe objects and may be declared true or false. Science is a subset of learning. It is composed of denotative statements, but imposes two supplementary conditions on their acceptability: the objects to which they refer must be available for repeated access, in other words, they must be accessible in explicit conditions of observation, and it must be possible to decide whether or not a given statement pertains to the language judged relevant by the experts. (Lyotard 1984, 18)

Lyotard made the point that not all knowledge is scientific knowledge when he added, "Knowledge in general cannot be reduced to science." Some of our knowledge comes from human experiences, human beliefs, human values, and social interactions. This knowledge is called *common sense,* and is disseminated by *narrative.* Learning about politics and political behavior includes both scientific and common sense knowledge. Therefore, political science research can involve almost any method of learning available.

Logic is the subfield of philosophy that relates to how people make judgments. The word evolved from the Greek *logos,* which in its translation to English is generally used to refer to the activity of *reasoning.* Reasoning refers to how people come to various conclusions. In the fourth century B.C., Aristotle concluded that humans employ two types or methods of reasoning: *deductive* and *inductive.* Researchers working in the narrative tradition most often follow a *deductive* reasoning model, whereas researchers who follow a positivist model in their studies are said to be following an *inductive* reasoning process.

Deductive reasoning means arriving at a conclusion on the basis of something that you assume to be true—a general *law* that is assumed to apply to all similar phenomena. People use deductive reasoning to form theories that explain events that they encounter in their daily life. In practice, deductive reasoning is often demonstrated with a *syllogism.* A syllogism is an argument that includes two premises and a conclusion. For example: (1) Socrates is a man; (2) all men are mortal; therefore, Socrates is mortal (conclusion). The general law is: all men are mortal. Thus, the conclusion about the mortality of Socrates is based on belief or faith in the law, not from any empirical evaluation. In deductive reasoning, the conclusion *must* be true if the premises are true.

Deductive reasoning requires only that the premises be accepted as true as they are defined or assumed to be true. *Truth* is what the researcher decides it is, or what it has always been; it is based on a *faith* that does not have to be empirically tested or proved. For example, a cultural anthropologist might gather as much information as he or she can about the mating habits of young islanders in a primitive society by observing their actions over time. The researcher may then conclude that these are the mating habits of all young people in that society. This may not, in truth, be the case; it may be true only for the subjects observed by the researcher. Or, the subjects may have been playacting to fool the researcher. Thus, it can only be seen as a conclusion (or faith) of the researcher; it is not "Truth."

Inductive reasoning, on the other hand, is the quantitative paradigm of *positivism*—the "scientific research" approach that has dominated research in the natural and behavioral sciences. When following the scientific approach, researchers identify a problem, gather data from observation or through an experiment, and then draw an inductive conclusion from (and only from) the data. In this model an inductive conclusion is never thought to be final; it is always open to further question (verifiability). In inductive reasoning, the researcher uses a set of established facts (research data) to draw a general conclusion, but that conclusion remains open to revision if new facts are discovered. The defining characteristics of scientific inductive research have been explained in the following way:

> Scientific research is *explicit, systematic,* and *controlled.* It is explicit in that all of the rules for defining and examining reality are clearly stated. Nothing is hidden from view, and nothing is taken on faith. It is systematic in that . . . evidence is linked by reason or observation to other items of evidence. No ad hoc explanations are tolerated, and no carelessness of method is permitted. It is controlled in that the phenomena under analysis . . . are observed in as rigorous a manner as the state of the art allows. (Manheim and Rich 1986, 5)

The positivist tradition that dominated research methods until the late 1970s emerged in the early twentieth century in Vienna, Austria (Bernard 2000; Dusche 1994). A group of philosophers—the *Vienna Circle*—were concerned with what they saw as a rash of theoretical speculation in the new sciences that were appearing. These speculative concepts included evolution, natural selection, thermodynamics, molecular theory, and others. The Vienna Circle philosophers were worried that science was returning to its early metaphysical foundations. Their reaction was to propose a philosophy of science—labeled *logical positivism* in an early paper—that stressed the need for the researcher to follow a process that moves from observable evidence to accurate predictions.

The positivist approach to social science has as its primary goal application of the rigor of natural science methods to the study of social phenomena, including explanations of the "real" world. Denscombe (2002, 14–15) identified the following five basic premises of positivism:

1. Patterns and regularities exist in the social world just as they do in the natural world. Events do not occur at random, nor are they a result of fate. There is a logical cause-and-consequences sequence that researchers can discover or identify.
2. The patterns and regularities in the social world exist independent of their recognition; they constitute an objective reality that is "out there" waiting to be discovered.
3. Only empirical observation can be trusted to reveal the reality of cause and consequences, which results in a reliance on experimental methods.
4. Research in the social sciences must employ the appropriate tools and techniques—those used in the natural sciences—to discover and examine the patterns and regularities. These techniques must not have any effect upon the observed reality.
5. The neutral nature of research tools must be mirrored in the value-free position that the research must always hold.

The positivist approach follows the steps that are said to make up the standard *scientific method*. Thus, research conducted scientifically employs the following sequence of steps:

- Selection of a hypothesis,
- Observation,
- Data collection,
- Hypothesis testing,
- Acceptance or rejection of the hypothesis.

In a twenty-four-attribute comparison of the positivist and interpretist methodological paradigms, Ann Oakley (2000) began with a brief discussion on the ways that scientists have labeled the two camps. On one side is the "positivist/'scientific'/quantitative" group of supporters. On the other is the "naturalist/interpretist/qualitative" group. Researchers in the positivist camp believe that they are studying the "real world." Those in the interpretist camp argue that there is no single reality that can be known.

Summary

The study of politics is the science that contributes to the growth of knowledge about the institutions, behaviors, individuals, and groups that make up and influence the world of politics. Political science is one of the social sciences. The research that takes place in the discipline helps us learn about political systems and the political behavior of our fellow human beings. Political science research can involve almost any method of learning available; political science researchers face an almost unlimited number of research questions toward which to direct their investigative activity. This chapter examined some of the question topics addressed by political science research, and looked at some suggestions that have been made to distill the list down to a more-focused set of major fields. The chapter also introduced the two major methodologies of scientific inquiry—*positivism* and *postpositivism.* It concluded with a discussion on the application of these different philosophical and methodological approaches.

There are at least five very good reasons for developing or expanding the skills needed to use research methods and prepare written research reports. The first reason is that it will help develop and hone your analysis and communication skills. Second, by engaging in the research process, students of political science can become aware of what others in the career field are doing and saying about common problems. A third reason for learning how to do research has to do with the concept of *replicability* in scientific research; researchers who follow should be able to come up with the same results given the same methods and raw data. A fourth reason is the way new information is passed on to future generations. Research findings are published in scientific and professional journals and are disseminated at professional conferences and scholarly or professional meetings. Political scientists, sponsors of research, and educated people with an interest in the report of an author's research tend to consider the research incomplete or unfounded unless the findings are published. A fifth reason is that research information often helps improve the quality and efficiency of decisions.

Research can be defined as *the process of systematically acquiring data to answer a question or solve a problem. Research methodology* refers to the approach the researcher takes to acquire the information. Finally, *research techniques* or processes refer to the steps involved in a given approach. The research activity has been defined as a *set of easily understood procedures for acquiring information,* and as a philosophical *mind-set* that people bring to any research activity. Scientific research should not be considered simply a fixed procedure. Rather, it should be looked upon as a philosophical way of approaching all research, regardless of the problem addressed and approaches and methods employed.

The goals that guide all research have been suggested as either to (1) *describe* some event, thing, or phenomenon, (2) *predict* future behavior or events based on observed changes in existing conditions, or (3) provide for greater *understanding* of phenomena and how variables are related.

Logic is the subfield of philosophy that relates to how people make judgments. The word evolved from the Greek *logos,* which in its translation to English is generally used to refer to the activity of *reasoning.* Reasoning refers to how people come to various conclusions. Aristotle concluded that humans employ two types or methods of reasoning: *deductive* and *inductive.*

The first activity in researching the scientific way is the *recognition of a problem.* The researcher may then formulate a hypothesis or hypotheses. These are tentative explanations of a solution or interpretation of the variables or a relationship, or cause-and-effect perception of a situation. The researcher may employ inductive reasoning, which means moving from the specific to the general. This reasoning process is involved in the act of making an *inference,* that is, using data from a sample for describing the characteristics or behaviors of larger populations. Or, the researcher may use *deductive reasoning,* concluding that the facts in the case or situation speak for themselves. In this way, using deductive reasoning means moving from the general to the specific.

The researcher may then test the hypothesis or hypotheses. To do so, the researcher collects data about the phenomenon. The researcher then arranges the collected data in meaningful order, looking for similarities and dissimilarities. If after analysis of the data the researcher determines the hypothesis is valid, he or she may look for other applications to which the hypothesis can be applied. The final activity in research is verification of conclusions made from the research. The researcher may propose a *theory*. If others accept the theory, the researcher may attempt to have it accepted as a *law*.

Discussion Questions

1. In your own words, come up with a definition for research that you can use to explain the activity to people who have never done research.
2. Why is it important to develop research skills?
3. Martyn Denscombe (2002) identified five aims for research. What are they?
4. What is meant by the phrase "the scientific way of doing research?"
5. Come up with an explanation that connects knowledge, logic, and reasoning.
6. Compare inductive and deductive reasoning.
7. What reasons do positivist/scientific/quantitative researchers give for following their approaches to political science research?
8. What reasons do naturalist/interpretist/qualitative researchers give for following their approaches to political science research?

Additional Reading

Freedman, Paul. 1960. *The Principles of Scientific Research*. 2nd ed. London: Pergamon Press.
Golden, M. Patricia. 1976. *The Research Experience*. Itasca, IL: Iowa State University Press.
Hanson, N.R. 1958. *Patterns of Discovery: An Inquiry into the Conceptual Foundations of Science*. Cambridge: Cambridge University Press.
Hughes, John, and Wes Sharrock. 1997. *The Philosophy of Social Research*. 3rd ed. London: Longman.
Lastrucci, Carlo L. 1967. *The Scientific Approach: Basic Principles of the Scientific Method*. Cambridge: Schenkman Publishing.

2 The Foundations of Political Science Research

Political science is one of the *social sciences*. A social science is any discipline or branch of science that focuses on the behavior of humans in their social and cultural environments (*Encyclopædia Britannica* 2000). Because they are largely concerned with questions pertaining to human behavior in social situations, some of the social sciences are also known as the *behavioral sciences*. Examples of the disciplines included in the social or behavioral sciences include psychology, sociology, social psychology, social and cultural anthropology, and economics.

The constantly changing and expanding environment of the social science disciplines is also reflected in the study of politics. Political science includes the study of local, state, and national politics and governance, international relations, political theory and history, to name only a few of the wide variety of human endeavors included in the study of politics and political behavior. Chapter 1 provided a basic definition of political science. A more comprehensive way to define the discipline is as a *diverse and constantly changing field of inquiry into the political behavior of individuals and groups of human beings, the institutions with which mankind identifies and governs itself, and the values that underlie political thought and systems.* The research conducted by political scientists necessarily addresses the many questions that arise in this wide-ranging field of social science.

Purposes for Political Science Research

Research is conducted for many different purposes. At its most fundamental level, the purpose of research may be either *basic* or *applied*. Basic research, which is also called *pure* or *theoretical* research, is conducted to increase the general storehouse of knowledge. Basic research is concerned with coming up with theories about what things are and why events happen the way they do. An example of basic research is the study of the fossils of life forms that existed on earth millions of years ago. This is the science of paleontology, and is characterized by an emphasis on *theory building* rather than on the application of solutions to a real-life problem. A typical theory in paleontology may be concerned with why the dinosaurs disappeared. The findings of paleontologists are interesting indeed, but to many people they have little immediate, practical value.

Applied research, on the other hand, is conducted to help solve practical problems or to help researchers, politicians, and administrators understand past behavior in order to guide them in their attempts at predicting future behavior. Applied researchers are concerned with developing theories about why something happened; they look for *causal* relationships. They conduct research in order to describe in detail what caused something to happen. In this way, analysts seek to predict the same thing happening again in the future.

Political science research is more likely to be applied than it is to be basic, although pure research does play a large role in the discipline's academic community. Political scientists working in both basic and applied approaches use the same methodologies, follow similar research designs, and concern themselves with performing research tasks with scientific rigor, ethics, validity, and reliability. Researchers have used a number of different ways to characterize purposes for a research study. Neuman (2000), for example, has suggested that social science research is conducted for any one or more of four different purposes: one is to answer some practical question; a second is to gather information that will enable people to make better decisions; a third is to add to the body of knowledge about a topic or field; and a fourth is to change society in some way.

A number of authors have tried to develop a set of purposes that are specific to the topics and questions found in political science research. Babbie (2001), for example, identified the following three purposes for research in the social sciences, including political science: (1) the *exploration* of a topic, (2) the *description* of a topic, situation, or event, or (3) to *explain* some phenomenon. In their discussion of the comparative method in political science research, Jennings, Keman, and Kleinnijenhuis (1999), identified three purposes for research as being able to identify: (1) regularities regarding the relationship between societal and political actors, (2) the processes of institutionalization of political life, and (3) the changes in society that emerge from the first two forces.

Stallings and Ferris (1988) identified a three-category system to categorize the purposes for doing research, terming the different purposes *conceptual, relationship,* and *evaluative.* The purpose of a conceptual study is to establish the fundamental concepts that underlie a problem. Conceptual studies are designed to identify critical variables for further research, or to frame a problem for which another study can be developed. The purpose of a relationship study is to either describe relationships between variables or investigate the potential for causation resulting from a relationship. Evaluative studies are designed to explain or evaluate an event, a program, a policy, or some other phenomenon. A different approach was taken by Lathrop (1969), who described the following four purposes in his research methods text: (1) theory testing, (2) extending the range of applicability of existing research, (3) resolving conflicting research findings, and (4) replicating previous studies.

Another way to characterize the reasons for research is to look upon them as *research objectives.* In science, research objectives and research purposes are nearly interchangeable terms. For example, three often-stated objectives for research are: (1) to *explore* a topic for the purpose of gaining insights and ideas, (2) to *describe* a topic, which typically has the purpose of counting the occurrence of one or more phenomena, or (3) to establish and/or measure *causation;* in a causal *study,* the purpose is to determine the power of one or more independent variables to influence change in a dependent variable. These objectives could just as easily been termed *purposes.*

Philosophical Foundations of Research

Political scientists study the issues that they think should be examined, and conduct research the way that they believe knowledge is gained. Whether they are aware of it or not, researchers in all disciplines are guided in the way they conduct their studies by the underlying philosophical positions they bring to the research table (Marsh and Furlong 2002). The bases for these positions are cast from what in philosophy are known as *ontology* and *epistemology,* both of which are concerned with knowledge and the way scientists develop knowledge. Ontology is the field of philosophy that deals with what we can learn—what is "out there" that can be known. It has to do with what is the nature of the world we can experience. Epistemology, on the other hand, is concerned with questions about the *way* that we learn—the approaches used by humans to gain knowledge. It is also concerned with the validity of knowledge; it deals with questions about how we can know anything, and how we can be certain what we do know is true (Plotkin 1994).

The ontological question in political science deals with such issues as whether political scientists should study institutions, political behaviors, or other political phenomena. On the other hand, one of the major reoccurring issues in social science research for the past several decades has been an epistemological argument; it has to do with which research methodology is most appropriate. The meaning of *methodology* is confusing, and the term is often incorrectly used as a synonym for research methods. Raphael described this confusion in the following way:

> The term "methodology" means the study of method (though some people, rather foolishly, use it simply as a supposedly learned synonym for the word "method" itself). Scientists, including social scientists, often use the term to mean the study of particular kinds of investigation. (Raphael 1976, 24)

The two major methodological positions that guide political science researchers are the *positivist* and the *postpositivist.* The positivist approach is commonly referred to as simply *quantitative* research. The postpositivist approach is commonly referred to as *qualitative research.* Other names for postpositivist research include the *realist,* the *interpretist,* and the *hermeneutic* or *narrative* traditions. The positivist and postpositivist approaches are the chief methodological schools that political scientists follow to gain knowledge about the political world (Oakley 2000; Marsh and Furlong 2002).

This chapter introduces a few of the major ways that researchers who employ the positivist, postpositivist, or interpretist approaches to political science go about conducting that research. Positivist approaches examined include *institutional analysis, behavioralism,* and *rational choice theory.* Interpretist approaches include the *antifoundationalist, feminist, Marxist,* and *postmodern* approaches to political science. These different approaches to political science research are displayed in Figure 2.1.

The Positivist Research Tradition

The positivist approach to scientific inquiry emerged as a reaction to the metaphysically based philosophy of science that characterized science up to the Age of Enlightenment, which lasted from roughly 1600 to 1800. Before then, knowledge that was developed under ecclesiastical sponsorship was ascribed to supernatural or deific forces (Trochim 2002). The science was fashioned on a belief that the world was created in its entirety; it could only be observed and described by humans.

The positivist reaction to metaphysical science was *empiricism.* Empiricism means that all knowledge must be *sensed* to be real; faith alone—knowing that it is true because you believe

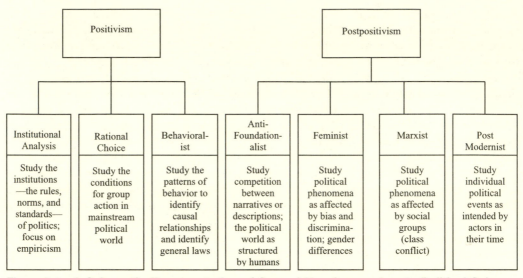

Figure 2.1   A Schematic Representation of Several Key Approaches to Political Science and Political Science Research
Sources: Stocker and Marsh 2002; Locher and Prügl 2001; Hodder 1989.

it to be so—is an insufficient basis for explaining a phenomenon or as a foundation for knowledge. The idea that if phenomena cannot be measured they should not be studied was a logical extension of this reaction to metaphysics. These early positivists also believed that the goal of all science—natural and social—is to describe everything that can be experienced. Positivists proposed cause-and-effect theories about phenomena, and then frame those theories in a way that they can be stated as *hypotheses,* which can then be tested. The preferred method of testing a hypothesis was to conduct an *experiment* in which variables are manipulated—that is, their values are changed—and the results are then observed and recorded. This pattern of inquiry is what we now call the *scientific method.* The scientific method relies on *logical reasoning,* an emphasis on *experience* (observation), and a commitment to *measurement.* While it was developed as a way of researching in the natural sciences, by the end of the nineteenth century the scientific method—with hypotheses, experimentation, observation, and quantification—was also being applied in the social sciences; it is the model of scientific inquiry that positivist researchers still follow today.

Political science researchers who follow the positivist tradition tend to study the formal operation of politics and the behavior of political actors. This includes studying all the institutions and organizations of government and those who try to influence it (Stocker and Marsh 2002). Marsh and Furlong (2002, 22–23) have identified the following four key concepts that characterize the positivist approach to political science research:

- The world exists independently of our knowledge about it; the world is real, not something socially created.
- Natural science and social science—including political science—are similar in outlook and require the same methods: forming hypotheses that can be tested by direct observation.

- The objective of political science is to identify causal relationships between social and political phenomena.
- The goal of social science is to focus on empirical—*what is* questions—with *what should be* questions relegated to the province of religion and philosophy.

Another fundamental tenet of positivism is that science must be objective, or *value-free;* scientific knowledge should be based upon what is observed, not on the opinion or beliefs of the researcher. Positivist researchers emphasize "precise quantitative data" that is gathered and analyzed using experiments, surveys, and statistics; they employ "rigorous, exact measures by carefully analyzing numbers from the measures" (Neuman 2000, 66). Neuman summarized positivism in the following way: "Positivism sees social science as an *organized method for combining deductive logic with precise empirical observations of individual behavior in order to discover and confirm a set of probabilistic causal laws that can be used to predict general patterns of human activity* [Neuman's emphasis]. The chief activity in positivist research is counting. The tools used are obtrusive and controlled measurements, with data gathered by surveys, experiments, case-control studies, statistical records, structured observations, content analysis, and other quantitative techniques" (Oakley 2000, 26–27).

Quantitative Methods

In political science in general, the traditional research approach has long focused on the employment of positivist research traditions with its emphasis on quantitative applications. Most social science research still follows a positivist approach (Boyte 2000). Researchers who remain detached from their subjects characterize positivist research; these political scientists are described as being "value-free" in their approach. They produce predictive theories based on experimentation, and emphasize mathematical and statistical methods in their analysis. The quantitative tradition in political science research was described this way more than a quarter century ago in the preface of a text on research methods:

> Political science has changed substantially in the last thirty years. Many textbooks and most professional journals cannot be understood fully without some minimal acquaintance with the philosophy of science or social science and a wide range of empirical and statistical methods including computer science, various forms of statistical analysis, content analysis, survey research, and many others. (Smith, Johnson, Paulsen, and Shocket 1976, xi)

Bartels and Brady (1993, 121) examined more than 2,000 articles in six of the most important political science journals and several different collections of papers. They concluded that quantitative methods still predominate in political science research. Their topic organization scheme is repeated in Table 2.1. Bartels and Brady had difficulty in achieving what they hoped would be a "logical way" of organizing the large collection of studies. Rather than continuing to try, they elected instead to follow what they called "a rough logical progression from data collection through modeling to estimation." One striking conclusion that may be taken away from the Bartels and Brady discussion is, not the wide range of types of studies found in the literature but, rather, that as late as 1993 a matching *qualitative* research methodology category was not considered important enough to be included in their collection of papers on theory and method.

Yan and Anders (2000) reviewed 634 research papers published over a three-year period in

Table 2.1

A Collection of Quantitative Methods Used in Political Science Research

1. Data Collection Methods
   a. Experiments
   b. Survey Designs
   c. Events Data
2. Time-Series Analysis
   a. Box-Tiao Intervention Methods
   b. Vector Autoregression
   c. Cointegration and Error Correction Methods
   d. The Kalman Filter
3. Time-Series of Cross-Sections, Panels, and Aggregated Data
   a. Aggregated Data and Ecological Inference
   b. Time-Series Crossectional, Panel, and Pseudopanel Methods
4. Techniques Tailored to Measurement Properties of Data
   a. Event Count and Event History Models
5. Measurement Error and Missing Data
   a. The consequences of Random and Nonrandom Measurement Error
   b. Guessing and Other Sources of Error in Survey Responses
   c. Nonrandom Samples and Sample Selection Bias
   d. Missing Data
6. Dimensional Analysis
   a. Voting Studies
   b. Perceptual Studies
   c. Legislative Studies
7. Model Specification
   a. Specification Uncertainty and the Perils of Data Dredging
   b. Sensitivity Analysis, Out-of-Sample Validation, and Cross-Validation
8. Estimation
   a. Maximum Likelihood Estimation
   b. Bootstrapping
9. Political Methodology and Political Science
   a. The Nature of Survey Response
   b. Economic Voting

Source: Bartels and Brady 1993.

eight public administration/political science professional journals. They found that most published research dealt with managerial issues relating to federal, state, or local government, with the emphasis on state and local levels. A smaller number dealt with public sector issues in general, while only a small portion addressed international issues. The primary emphasis of the examined research was on government in general or issues that concern the executive branches at all levels.

A Break with the Quantitative Tradition

Not every political science researcher accepts the emphasis on positivist methodology and quantitative research methods. Referring to the positivist mind-set of political science researchers as "a silent civic disease," Boyte offered the following example of their criticism:

Our implicit theories of knowledge assume the specific understanding of scientific inquiry that derives from positivism, for a time the dominant philosophy of science. This model delegitimates "ordinary knowledge" and depreciates the capacities, talents, and interests of the nonexpert and the amateur. It is antagonistic to common sense, folk traditions, and craft and practical knowledge mediated through everyday life experience. Of course, "common sense" is not always right, nor "science" always wrong. I argue only that many different kinds of valuable knowledge support public life and that conventional academic approaches slight the nonexpert. (Boyte 2000, 49)

Writing in the *Chronicle of Higher Education,* Smith (2001, B10) described why he joined a group of members of the American Political Science Association in protesting the positivist tradition of political science research. The goal of what he described as a group of several hundred scholars was to "restructure the profession." According to Smith, "We worry most of all that the enterprise of political science is becoming identified too exclusively with heavily mathematical work—either formal models or statistical analyses—that is often more about methods than substance (and still falls woefully short, methodologically, in the eyes of mathematicians). Too often, a project's chief claim to fame is its mere importation of new modeling or statistical techniques into political science, rather than its use of those techniques to say something new and significant about politics."

Criticisms of Positivist Research

There are a number of critics who attack the traditional positivist position followed by many political science researchers; they also find fault with the level of research that is being done in the discipline. One such view is that political scientists still place by far too great an emphasis upon *applied* research. As a result, political scientists are making few, if any, contributions to advancing the state of knowledge in the field. Moisés Naím, a *Foreign Policy* editor, summed up the perception of political science research during an interview with Dr. Larry Summers, president of Harvard University and a former Secretary of the Treasury. Naím compared what he called "the extraordinary progress in the revolution in technologies, biology and electronics, computer processing, and even astronomy" with what he then identified as "the dearth of comparable results in the social sciences, particularly in economics and political science" (Naím 2002, 38–39).

Smith offered a similar negative view in this criticism of political science research:

> [P]olitical scientists have, in recent years, put too much effort into trying to make the discipline more of a science, hence putatively superior to other sources of political knowledge, and not enough effort into making it a source of distinctive insights into substantive political questions. . . . I would have political scientists, political-science departments, university administrators, and providers of financial support for our research devote fewer resources to work that achieves greater methodological (usually mathematical) rigor in addressing minor questions, justified in the often vain hope that such efforts will serve as stepping stones toward more scientific work on larger questions. (Smith 2002, B10)

Richardson and Fowers (1998, 471) have echoed the critical view of social science research with the statement that "in spite of tremendous effort, enormous methodological sophistication, and many decades of efforts," social science has not achieved anything close to the type of "explanatory theory that counts as truth and is needed for precise prediction and instrumental control. Just describing interesting patterns of variables—which always have many exceptions—does not yield the sort of technical control over events we associate with modern physics, biology, or engineering."

It is important to know that today most political science researchers agree that no single method is the only appropriate way to conduct research. This includes positivism and postpositivism, the methodology that emerged in reaction to the strict empiricism of the positivist. Rather, there is a place and a purpose for all approaches and methods. The appropriate choice from among the growing variety of research traditions in political science must be, as Dryzek (1986, 315) has noted, "contingent upon time and place and a given set of socio-political circumstances."

The Postpositivist Reaction

Postpositivism emerged as a reaction to the strict *empiricism* of the positivists; "empiricism" refers to the observation-experimentation natural science model adopted for research in the social sciences. The theory of empiricism holds that humans can only know what their senses tell them (Jones 1971). Adoption of the postpositivist approach was a "radical shift" away from objective, value-free, universal knowledge that characterized the rationalist, positivist, and behavioralist approach to research (Locher and Prügl 2001). The research ethics based on human rights and justice that emerged after World War II also influenced the reaction against "value-free" positivist research, and helped to generate interest in a research methodology that no longer simply described what was, but that went beyond the obvious to interpret and explain why things are what they are. Hempel (1966, 15), an early critic of the positivist focus, identified what he saw as a problem in political science research of the period: "There is wide agreement today among philosophers of science that scientific hypotheses and theories are not derived from observed facts, but invented to account for them."

Empiricism is the way of learning things that says we can only know what our senses tell us. However, another way of learning is through a process of *mental reflection*—the investigative position that E. Terrence Jones (1971) called "rationalism." To make the jump to this rational way of learning, political scientists have increasingly been forced to adopt qualitative approaches for conducting their research. Because it involves rejection of the positivist tradition, the movement has been called "postpositivism." It is a way of thinking that occurs after rejection of the positivist tradition. Postpositivist political scientists apply rationalist or qualitative methods to study what governments choose to do and what they choose not to do. They are particularly interested in studying the distribution and exercise of power and domination, and the actions of individuals and groups who seek to gain power and hold on to it once they have it.

According to Pennock (1966), the aim of positivists, and particularly the behavioralists, has been "to apply the scientific method vigorously and rigorously to every nook and cranny" of political science. On the other hand, the rationalist goals of the postpositivists emphasize *ideas* more than constructs that must be observed and measured. In a critical paper on the position, Pennock explained:

> Empirical scientists have often made a fetish of measuring. Worse still, they have confused efforts to avoid bias caused by unconscious or uncritical values with the avoidance of all evaluation. They too have developed a crude positivism that most philosophers, if they ever held it, have long since abandoned. (Pennock 1966, 46)

From this small beginning in the early 1970s, research methodology has evolved into more than the one positivist way of approaching scientific inquiry in political science. In addition to the traditional *explanatory* approach taken by the positivists, two additional positions in research today are the *interpretive* and the *critical approaches* (Neuman 2000; White 1994). The interpretive research has been defined as "the systematic analysis of socially meaningful action through the direct detailed observation of people in natural settings and interpretations of how people create and maintain their social worlds" (Neuman 2000, 71).

Interpretive political scientists often employ the tools of anthropological research: participant observation, and field research. The major research activity followed in postpositivist/interpretist research approaches is observation. Interpretist observation is unobtrusive, however. The data-gathering techniques employed include participant observation, in-depth interviewing, action research case studies, life-history methods, focus groups, and similar qualitative tools (Oakley 2000, 27).

The critical approach to research is sometimes referred to as *emancipative* or *empowering* research. This approach has as its key objective helping research participants to identify and understand the causes of their circumstances, and then to empower them to bring about the change that they feel is required. The approach is "a critical process of inquiry that goes beyond surface illusions to uncover the real structures in the material world in order to help people change conditions and build a better world for themselves" (Neuman 2000, 76). Feminist and Marxist political science research are two of the major directions taken in critical research.

New Approaches to Political Science Research

Political science is an exceptionally dynamic discipline. Researchers have taken many different approaches to the study of political questions. At times, supporters of one approach or another have made strident claims that theirs is the only way to study politics. However, such chauvinistic attitudes are no longer as common as they once were. Today, political scientists are in general agreement that many different research methods and research topics are valid and appropriate. They are more likely than not to agree with the following conclusions: "there is no one method of acquiring knowledge about politics" (Stoker and Marsh 2002, 15); and "there now exist not only multiple approaches to empirical research, but also multiple agendas for the discipline as a whole" (Farr, Dryzek, and Leonard 1995, 2). Denscombe (2002) added that there is a growing tendency to combine the use of different methods and different research strategies within the same studies. Researchers eclectically select one or the other, drawing on their individual strengths and compensating for their weaknesses. It is an exciting time to be conducting research in political science!

In the following section, a brief introduction is made to what, in the early years of a new century, are some of what appear to be the approaches to research in political science (Marsh and Stoker 2002). These are not the only approaches extant by far. However, they do illustrate a representative cross-section of both the positivist and postpositivist positions in scientific inquiry. In what many see as a beneficial turn of events, political scientists are becoming eclectic in their approaches to research. Rather than stridently defending one or the other approaches, they are using parts of both, often in order to triangulate their findings.

Positivist Research Approaches

Positivist approaches examined include *institutional analysis, behavioralism,* and *rational choice theory.* A slightly disproportionate emphasis has been given to the discussion on Behavioralism because it is, as a review of the literature reveals, still the methodology of preference for a large number of political scientists.

Institutional Analysis

For most of its history as a discipline among the social sciences, the dominant methodological approach in political science was *institutionalism.* The institutional focus remained the direction of choice up until the 1950s, when it was replaced by the *behavioralist* approach. Prior to this change in focus, most political science research dealt with questions relating to the institutions that make up the polity, and the rules and conventions that emerged to allow political institutions to function. The chief research topics of political science were concerned with describing—often by the comparative method—such formal institutions as constitutions, legal systems, and government structures, and their changes over time. For more than a hundred years, "Institutionalism *was* political science" (Lowndes 2002, 90; Shepsle 1995, 277). The topic of political science research for that period was the concept of the state and the institutions that made the state possible. The concept of "the state" was of particular interest to nineteenth-century American political scientists; to discuss government meant to discuss institutions. According to Shepsle, "Government for the most part was conceptualized as the institutional manifestation of the state, and the agenda so set for political science carried on into the early decades of the twentieth century" (277).

The institutions that were the focus of institutionalist political science are not the *organizations* that make up the political world, but rather, the term refers to such concepts as the formal and informal rules, political standards, norms, and guides for accepted political behavior. The term "political" does not refer exclusively to party politics, but instead to the broader view of governance in general. Political phenomena are social phenomena; the rules that enable society to work are also necessary for government to work. *How* governments work—not how they *should* work—was the question that institutionalists sought, and still seek, to answer. One of the earliest examples of an institutional study is Woodrow Wilson's 1885 investigation of the American Congress. That study *(Congressional Government)* sought to explain the way Congress actually worked, instead of the way the Constitution says it should work (Shepsle 1995).

The influence of the institutionalist in political science began to wane as the twentieth century moved toward its halfway point. Arguments against the institutionalist approach centered on several points; one of these criticisms was that by retaining their attentions on the formal institutions of government, the focus of political science was too narrow to answer many of the larger issues of the discipline. Increasingly, institutionalists were studying the formal rules and organizations rather than informal solutions, and were spending more of their time attempting to define what it is that constitutes "good government," rather than looking for the causes of good and bad political behavior. Behavioralism was adopted largely because its focus was on individual behavior, rather than organizational behavior, which was far more difficult to pin down.

Today, institutionalism is enjoying a renewed popularity among political scientists, although in a format dramatically different from the institutionalism of the past; it no longer focuses only on the task of explaining political organizations by comparison. Instead, new institutionalists are interested in such concepts as the ways that power is gained, held, and exercised in political circumstances, in how values are shared and disseminated among members of political groups, and on the broader issues of organizational design. Institutionalism is still commonly used in some subfields of political science, including public administration and constitutional studies.

According to Lowndes (2002, 91), new institutionalists are no longer concerned with how political institutions affect individuals, but also with the "interaction between institutions and individuals." Lowndes (97) went on to identify six changes that she believed are helping to make the institutional approach more palatable. She was clear to point out that the changes are occurring on a sliding scale; they are points on a continuum, not one thing or the other. The points of change in focus for the new institutionalism in political science research are:

- From an old focus on organizations toward a new focus on rules.
- From a concentration of formal concepts to informal definitions of institutions.
- From a view of political institutions as static to a dynamic view.
- From submerged (or ignored) values to a position that sees values as critical to understanding institutional relationships.
- From a holistic view of institutions to one that focuses on their individual parts and components.
- From institutions as independent entities to one that sees them as embedded in societies and specific contexts.

A recent example of the application of the new institutionalist approach is Mark Aspinwall's 2000 paper on British (political) power-sharing institutions and British preferences on greater integration with Europe. Aspinwall refers to "classical institutionalist theory" in order to build greater understanding of why Great Britain is less prone to adopt a completely pro-European foreign policy, preferring instead to remain more closely attached to the United States and other "Anglo" nations, such as Australia and Canada, among others. According to Aspinwall, historical institutionalism theory explains that institutions structure political actions and outcomes; actions and outcomes are not simply mirror images of social activity and rational competition among diverse groups and organizations.

Institutions influence public policy and actions in three ways. The first is their structure. Institutional rules, norms, and procedures regulate behavior and limit choice. The second is via the concept of *path dependency*. Path dependency refers to the tendency for structure to not be easily altered; it resists change at all levels. In addition, decisions tend to have subsequent, often unintended, unanticipated and undesired, effects. The third influencing factor of institutions is what Aspinwall calls "appropriateness," which refers to action that is based upon rules, and is the product of norms and obligations. Moreover, institutions frame the environment in which political struggles take place. Institutional rules "structure the game and do so in ways that are not always anticipated when the rules are devised, thus leading to the notion of path dependency" (Aspinwall 2000, 426).

Behavioralism

Beginning in the middle to late 1950s, some political scientists began looking for ways to improve society by enhancing political institutions, increase public participation, and otherwise address politically based social problems. The institutional focus was unable to meet the needs of the new researchers, who felt that the purely descriptive approach of institutional methods was not able to successfully address the important issues of the discipline. A new political science was needed; the rigorous application of scientific principles of other behavioral sciences was seen to meet their need. This new way of studying political phenomena was, in the words of Shepsle (1995, 279), "tremendously important to the study of politics because it emphasized, in its many variations, precise observation, counting and measuring where possible, the clear statement of hypotheses, and unambiguous standards for accepting or rejecting them." Furthermore, it was a radical shift away from the rambling narratives that characterized much of the political science of the period.

To study political behavior and apply the same scientific rigor to their studies that the natural sciences use, political scientists looked to the behavioralist approach expressed in works of experimental psychologists like John B. Watson and B.F. Skinner. Behavioralism had taken hold in social science in the 1920s. By the 1940s, behavioralism was deeply entrenched in psychology and sociology. Researchers were beginning to move their data-gathering activities out of the laboratory or classroom and into the real world, which made it even easier to apply behavioralist research principles to political science research. For example, experimental social scientist William S. Verplanck (2002, 4), describing the lessons he learned while conducting research at the Naval Medical Research Lab during World War II, stated, "if you're really going to learn about behavior, unless you settle for a kind of myopia, you have to do research in the 'real' world, that is, the world in which we all live every day, and not solely in the restrictive environment of a laboratory. Neither what is theoretically best nor what works best in the lab is necessarily the best elsewhere."

The behavioralist approach continued to gain acceptance over the next several decades until by the late 1960s it had become the dominant way of conducting social science research. The primary focus of political science had shifted from the study of political institutions to the study of the political *behavior* of people in the "real world" described by Verplanck. However, acceptance of the behavioralist approach was not without a great deal of controversy. Somit and Tanenhaus described the acrimonious introduction of behavioralism to political science research this way:

> Political scientists have quarreled over many matters in the contemporary period but the most divisive issue by far has been behavioralism. If the controversy it has elicited is any measure, this latest quest for a more scientific politics is easily the paramount development in the discipline's entire history. (Somit and Tanenhaus 1967, 173)

According to Gunnell (1983, 15), the objectives of behavioral research were to be reached by "the formulation of systematic concepts and hypotheses; the development of explanatory generalizations that would raise inquiry beyond mere factual empiricisms; interdisciplinary borrowing; empirical methods of research; (and) direct observation."

Understanding behavior meant comparing the way people act in different cultures. This, in turn, brought about a strengthening of the *comparative method* as a research design and the emergence of comparative politics as a recognized subfield of political science. As the behavioralists turned their attention from political institutions to instead focus on understanding political behavior, they began thinking less about the way people *ought* to act and more about the way they really do act. In the process, controlling society gave way to understanding social behavior as the focus of political science research.

The following eight assumptions and objectives are characteristics of behavioralist concepts and methods in political science research that differentiate the approach from the traditional institutionalist approach (Easton 1962, 7–8; Somit and Tanenhaus 1967, 177–79):

1. *Regularities:* These are discoverable commonalities in political behavior. They are expressed as generalizations or theories. Political science is capable of prediction and should avoid the purely descriptive studies that characterized most of institutionalist research.
2. *Verification:* The validity of the generalizations must be testable and shown to be tied to relevant political behavior. Political science researchers should focus on observable phenomena—what is done, what is said by individuals. These data can then be studied together as "political aggregates." Institutional behavior is the behavior of individuals.
3. *Techniques:* The means for collecting and interpreting data about the generalizations and behavior must exist; they must be examined using rigorous means for observing, recording, measuring, and analyzing behavior. Research must be theory-oriented and theory-driven.
4. *Quantification:* Precise measuring requires quantification and application of mathematical (statistical) analysis. Data must be quantified; only quantification will make the discovery of precise relationships and regularities possible.
5. *Values:* Ethical evaluations are not empirical explanations, and their use should be kept apart. They require different methods of evaluation and interpretation. Extreme care must be taken not to mistake one for the other. The "truth" of such values as democracy, equality, freedom, etc. cannot be proven scientifically, and therefore should not be a part of political science research. Only observable, measurable behavior, not the "great issues" of society, is gist for the political science mill.
6. *Systemization:* Research ought to be systematic. Theory and research are closely associated parts of the orderly development of knowledge. "Research untutored by theory may prove trivial, and theory unsupported by data, futile" (Easton 1962, 7).
7. *Pure Science:* Although recognizing the importance of applied solving of real-life problems of society, political science research should focus on pure research that advances our knowledge of the political world. Behavioralists contended that applied research is an "unproductive diversion of energy, resources, and attention" (Somit and Tanenhaus 167, 178).
8. *Integration:* Political science research must not ignore the other social science disciplines; only by integrating all knowledge about human behavior will political science be brought back to its earlier high status and return the discipline where it belongs.

Sanders (2002) summarized the position that behavioralism finds itself in at the start of the new century by pointing out that, for behavioralists and postbehavioralists alike, the main objective for social scientific research is to explain the behavior of individuals and aggregates of individuals. The research question that they pose is: "Why do individuals, institutional actors, and nation states behave the way they do?" Referring to the central position that theory plays in the approach, Sanders added,

> Embedded in the behavioralist notion of explanation is the idea of causality. Although behavioralists are aware that causality may be as much a reflection of the way we think about the world

as it is of "reality," they none the less insist that, unless a theory makes some sort of causal statement, it cannot be deemed to explain anything. (Sanders 2002, 63)

Rational Choice Theory and Other Models

Rational choice-based models are among the most prevalent types of a group of model-based approaches that are now being used in political science. Other types include a variety of game theory models, psychological models and other choice-based behavioral models, and mathematical models (Morton 1999). Because of its popularity, only rational choice theory is discussed in some detail here.

Rational choice theory is an increasingly important direction that is being taken in political science. In her volume on the empirical analysis of formal models in political science, Rebecca Morton described this movement toward more theory-oriented research in the following manner:

> An important transformation has taken place in political science: a move from a focus on nonformal, largely inductive theorizing to formal deductive modeling using mathematics for theoretical purposes only—with no empirical testing or data analysis. . . . Also noticeable has been the growth of interdisciplinary journals publishing theoretical papers on political science questions. . . . Part of the rise in formal models in political science has been an increased focus on "rational choice" models from the discipline of economics. (Morton 1999, 9)

Morton went on to identify two main sources for the changes that have occurred recently in political science. The first is that researchers in other social sciences, particularly economics, have become interested in questions associated with the study of politics. This has meant the application of formal theorizing developed first in those other fields being applied to political questions. The second main force for change in political science has been a call for new ideas brought on as empirical research in the behavioralist tradition—such as the techniques of statistical estimation—has appeared to reach the end of its ability to expand the boundaries of knowledge in politics.

What Is Rational Choice Theory?

Rational choice theory is a way of explaining human behavior. It is based on the idea that people make decisions for the purpose of providing themselves the greatest possible benefits. In economics—where most of the principles of the theory were developed—this is referred to as the process of "maximizing utility." Political scientists began to employ rational choice theory during the 1960s and 1970s, partly in reaction to the behavioralist position that human behavior is not a matter of personal choice, but is instead shaped by psychological and social accidents to which humans are exposed, often against their will. In political science, the essential focus of choice theory research that has emerged is the analysis of the ways that groups of individuals respond to challenges in political institutions, public policy, and other political phenomena.

In the form it is used today, rational choice theory is probably closer to the institutionalist position than it is to behavioralism. Shepsle described how rational choice theory differs from behavioralism this way:

> In place of responsive, passive, sociological man, the rational choice paradigm substitutes a pur-
> pose, proactive agent, a maximizer of privately held values. A rational agent is one who comes to
> a social situation with preferences over possible social states, beliefs about the world around
> oneself, and a capability of employing these data intelligently. Agent behavior takes the form of
> choices based on either intelligent calculation or internalized rules that reflect optimal adaptation
> to experience. (Shepsle 1995, 280)

An additional key concept in rational choice theory is that all human behavior occurs for a purpose. Given a set of options and information about the costs and benefits of their choices, people will act in the way that provides them the greatest payoffs—they make the *rational* decision. Thus, all behavior is centered on the self. One of the underlying assumptions in rational choice theory is that people calculate their actions in the way games are played so as to win. Individuals make political decisions, not groups. Therefore, compromise occurs when it results in greater utility for the collected group. This helps to explain why political parties form.

Another key concept in rational choice theory is that all the players know—and generally adhere to—the rules of the game. "Rules" in this sense are similar to the standards and norms that are a focus in the institutionalist approach to political science. Additional conceptual underpinnings of the approach include the following (Turner 1991, 354):

- People are purposive and goal-oriented.
- People prioritize their preferences (utilities).
- People make rational calculations involving their prioritized utilities and the costs of alternative decisions, and make decisions that maximize their utility.
- Political behavior—just another form of social behavior—is ultimately the result of individual utility maximization.

Model-based political scientists also use such methods as game theory and mathematical models from economics in their research. They apply logic to sets of assumptions about human behavior in the attempt to develop basic laws and make predictions. According to Binmore, Kirman, and Tani (1993), game theorists have broad objectives for this approach to research: to develop a theory of conflict and cooperation that is universally applicable, and that covers much the same topics that are now addressed by the rest of the social sciences. Game theory is used for at least five general purposes: to predict future behavior and events, to explain phenomena, to investigate problems, to describe events, and for prescriptional purposes.

Interpretive Research Approaches

The many qualitative research approaches now finding their way into use in political science and the other social sciences have been grouped together under the label of *interpretive theory* (Bevir and Rhodes 2002). Interpretive approaches to research involve the use of what is essentially subjective narrative. Narrative methods are believed to produce knowledge that is different from knowledge gained by traditional (positivist) science. To interpretive researchers such as the *postmodernists,* for example, the things that citizens take for granted, such as the sovereignty of nature, are not "truth," but rather, simply a concept that has been constructed by humans. Some societies accept the premise that the natural environment is something that should be protected and preserved, while others do not. Neither view is inherently better than the other. This has been pointed out explicitly in research in international cooperation on environmental issues. Before progress can be made, negotiators must take care to ensure that everyone is working from the same basic assumptions (Wapner 2002).

Interpretive research involves the researcher intimately into the research process; there is no place for the detached, impartial, value-free investigator of the positivist tradition. Interpretive social science research—including political science—seeks to uncover the *sense* of an action, practice, or idea (Fay 1975). It does this by first discovering the intentions, desires, conceptual schemes, and experiences of the humans involved in the research, then attempting what Fay calls "seeing how they fit into a whole structure which defines the nature and purpose of human life" (79). While there is still a requirement for developing theory in qualitative research, it is derived from the findings, *grounded,* as it were, in the data and its interpretation by the researcher.

According to Denscombe (2002, 18), some writers use the term "constructionism" to categorize the same approaches that fall under the interpretist label. Constructionism means that the researchers do not hold with the idea that the world of reality is "out there," waiting only to be discovered. Rather, constructionists believe that humans construct all social phenomena, and that no single construction is better than any other. Denscombe found that most of the different approaches falling under this label all share a number of common points. First, all reality is subjective; it is constructed and interpreted by people. Second, humans react to the knowledge that they are being studied. When they become aware of this fact, their behavior changes, often in a subtle but real manner. Hence, the researcher can never know what is the "true" behavior of a group. Third, it simply is not possible to gain objective knowledge about social phenomena. Despite all their efforts, researchers cannot be objective. Fourth, there is little or no prospect of producing grand theories explaining the social world. All reality is subjective, created by individuals, and subject to change.

Interpretive approaches examined here include the *feminist, Marxist,* and the *antifoundationalist* or *postmodern* approaches to political science. A key characteristic of each of these three approaches is their narrative emphasis. They are typically small-sample studies, often analyzing a single case or a few cases, and place greater emphasis on qualitative methods than on mathematical tools. The first two positions discussed are offshoots of the critical approach; the last is a product of narrative description.

A Feminist Research Approach

Feminist issues appeared in political theory studies during the 1970s. Saxonhouse (1993, 15–16) has suggested that an initial goal of feminist research was to "document the dreadful history of misogynist statements by one male author or another, statements that have served to justify the exclusion of women from the political realm and confine them to the private world of the family."

The feminist approach to research and to science in general is based on the contention that women see things differently than men, have different ways of learning, and different ways of describing meaning. Because of centuries of being forced to accept a lesser status in the political sphere, feminist-oriented political science research was developed as a tool to aid women in their emancipatory efforts. Feminist researchers take issue with gender-based political theory and political writing that is both overtly and covertly gender-biased. Many feminists see traditional positivist research as resulting in a science with a gender bias that is potentially misleading at best, and insulting and derogatory at its worst. When feminist political science researchers examine such political phenomena as international relations and politics, state formation, war and peace, revolutions, international political economies, and global governance, they include in their analyses discussions about the role of gender in these events. Thus, gender is considered to be inherent in all international politics and other political writing (Locher and Prügl 2001).

Feminist research has been identified as one of four types of action-oriented research (Small 1995). The first of the three other models of action research is the traditional *action research* proposed by Kurt Lewin in the 1940s. The second model is *participatory research,* which, by breaking down barriers between researchers and the researched, enables people to identify the cause of their problems and to develop their own ways to deal with them. The third approach is *empowerment research*, which has its foundations in community psychology; empowerment research is seen as a tool to aid people to gain "mastery over their own affairs." Feminist research, according to Small (1995, 5), has as its primary goal "the promotion of the feminist agenda by challenging the male dominance and advocating the social, political, and economic equality of men and women." It has been described as "research for women rather than about women" (Allen and Baber 1992).

Feminist political science researchers share with their fellow social scientists what has been described as a concern for ethical issues, a belief in social justice, an ethic of compassion, and an awareness of the power of language to distort the experiences of research subjects (Small 1995). Typical of the types of themes approached in feminist research are these papers from the April 2002 issue of the *International Feminist Journal of Politics:* Prügl's "Toward a Feminist Political Economics," Peterson's "Rewriting (Global) Political Economy as Reproductive, Productive, and Virtual (Foucauldian) Economics," and "The UN Approach to Harmful Traditional Practices" (Winter, Thompson, and Jeffreys 2002).

Feminist research methodology has also been used extensively in public administration research. For example, two papers with feminist research foundations were published in the July/ August 2002, issue of *Public Administration Review.* These were "Gender Differences in Agency Head Salaries: The Case of Public Education" (Meier and Wilkins 2002) and "Sex-Based Occupational Segregation in U.S. State Bureaucracies, 1987–97" (Kerr, Miller, and Reid 2002).

The Marxist Approach

Classical Marxism may be the first of the critical approaches to research in the social sciences. This approach was based on the idea that conflict between the haves and have-nots, laborers versus owners, the worker class versus the capitalist ruling class, is at the root of all political behavior. Therefore, Marxist research focused on ways to highlight disparities, to identify the economic structures that form and restrict development of society, and on studies that foster egalitarian and emancipatory principles (Marsh 2002). Four main principles are associated with classical Marxism: economism, determinism, materialism, and structuralism. *Economism* refers to the concept that economic forces determine social conditions. The *determinism* principle holds that capitalist production methods determined the role men held in life; men were not free to choose their lot. *Materialism* refers to the materialism of the ruling class, the owners and operators of factories and the ruling classes they supported. Finally, *structuralism* refers to Marx's contention that economic and political structures established the actions of men. Modern Marxism is radically different from the classical version, however. According to Marsh:

> [W]hile modern Marxism is characterized by diversity, most of it rejects economism; rejects determinacy, emphasizing contingency; rejects materialism, acknowledging an independent role for ideas; rejects structuralism, accepting a key role for agents; no longer privileges class, acknowledging the crucial role of other causes of structured inequality; and, to an extent, privileges politics. (Marsh 2002, 161)

Marsh conceded that Marxism's influence on political science research is in decline. This decline may be attributed to several factors: the collapse of the Soviet Union, the renewed strength of conservative ideologies, and recent changes in capitalism, including widespread ownership, global economic development, and entrepreneurial activity, among others. Despite its decline, in Marsh's opinion, Marxism still has much to offer political science. Foremost of its potential contribution to the discipline is its tradition of critical analysis of existing social and political institutions. Because societies still contain inequalities and exploitation still dominates many Third World economic systems, the Marxist critical tradition is still relevant.

The Postmodern Approach

Among the postpositivist approaches that have gained some acceptance since they appeared in the last decades of the twentieth century are the *postmodern* or *antifoundationalist* positions. These approaches to political science research have their roots in the *critical theory* found in art, music, and literature that emerged during the 1960s. Several key principles of postmodernism are that no single fundamental political truths exist; there is no one absolutely certain way to gain knowledge; and no rules exist to guarantee the rationality of science. According to Oakley (2002), postmodernism refers to the extensive cultural changes that have taken place in Western societies since the end of World War II. Some of the salient phenomena include the emergence of a global economy, the weakening of radical politics and collapse of the Soviet Union, a lost faith in the power of rationality to bring about freedom, the rapid and all-pervasive spread of technology, the spread of popular culture, and other events and conditions. Postmodernist critics hold that, since social science is itself a part of the modernist condition, the changes in the philosophical foundations of political science research that are still evolving make it necessary to adopt a postmodernist approach to research in these disciplines.

The postmodern approach has been adopted by a variety of political scientists and philosophers who, according to Dwight Allman (1995, 69), "dispute the viability of modern civilization." They believe, in essence, that the positivist approach of searching for an all-encompassing "true" picture of a social event is a waste of time. Each event must be described individually, taking into consideration the intentions of the actors, the experience of the investigator, and the external event of the time of the event.

To determine the meaning of a political phenomenon, the postmodernist believes that the time, situation, and intent of the social actor must be considered in addition to the event or behavior itself. Furthermore, there is no one best way to describe or define a social or political event. Equally, there is no one best way to investigate or define a political behavior or event. Therefore, one of the most important tasks of the researcher is to interpret the phenomenon itself *before* it can be researched. The researcher must frame the act within a larger context that includes the objectives of the social actors and the specific circumstances existing at the time of the action (Fay 1975).

The postmodern researcher cannot simply progress from a known and accepted foundation of basic assumptions. To the postmodernist, the concepts we usually take for granted, such as democracy, the "sovereignty of nature," honesty, ethical behavior, and the like, do not really exist; they are, instead, human *constructs*. As such, the interpretations placed on these constructs are only one of many possible meanings. To postmodern researchers, the idea of a concept such as *nature* is not real; rather, it is a construction of the human intellect. For example, Wapner (2002, 167) adopted a postmodern approach in his discussion of the apparent lack of an international consensus in the importance of degradation of the natural environment, and how that lack limits public environmental policy. Thus, there is no *better* or *best* view of nature. Nature is what society makes of it, and people in different cultures, in different circumstances, have different points of view about nature that are equally legitimate. Wapner concluded that, "Postmodern critics have shown . . . that 'nature' is not simply a given, physical object but a social construction—an entity that assumes meaning within various cultural contexts and is fundamentally unknowable outside of human categories of understanding. This criticism raises significant challenges for global environmental politicians."

Four Strands of Postmodernism

Ian Hodder (1989) identified four strands of postmodern social science that may help to define this evolving approach to political science research. The first is what he describes as "the sense of disillusion" that social scientists and people in general have with the products and progress of scientific research. Science has not kept its promise of doing away with war, poverty, inhumanity, exploitation, and inequality. Second, "modernism" has resulted in detachment, alienation, and cynicism, rather than coming through with its promise of freedom, equality, and an enhanced quality of life for all of society.

Third, postmodernism has been shaped by a number of essentially revolutionary changes in society that have occurred since the end of World War II. Some of these have to do with advances in technology, such as computers, cellular telephones, high-speed data transmission, and similar developments. Others are founded in changes in the way people look at their world and society; examples include consumerism, world capitalism, planned obsolescence, very brief periods between alterations in fashion and style. According to Hodder, "There is little difference between 'high' and 'low' culture, or between fine art and *kitsch*. In contrast with modernism in which the meaning was in the functional form, now the façade is everything" (66).

The fourth defining strand of the postmodern approach is the way special-interest groups use the global press, fashion, and the arts to manipulate and manage the images of political events, economic issues, or social structure that modern society conceptualizes social and political phenomena. Together, these four strands provide a framework upon which to conduct research in political science with a postmodern focus. It is important to remember that these research approaches are only a representative sample of the current thinking in political science research methodology. No one paradigm defines political science research today. Rather, it has become an increasingly pluralistic discipline, in which its practitioners have exhibited a growing interest in combining the strengths of various methods (Marsh and Stoker 2002).

Summary

Political science, sociology, psychology, economics, and cultural anthropology, among others, are all disciplines in the *social sciences*. The methodologies that underlie political science research also direct inquiry in its sister social sciences. The topics of political science research are approached from several different methodological traditions, and framed with different conceptual elements that are found in other social science disciplines. In two different studies on American politics, for example, one researcher may have used a variable-based approach, with heavy emphasis on quantification and statistical analysis. This is the *positivist* research tradition. On the other hand, the second researcher may have elected to follow a comparative case study approach, in which the most-common themes are qualitatively compared.

Three often-stated purposes for research are: (1) to *explore* a topic for insights and ideas, (2) to *describe* a topic, which typically includes counting the occurrence of one or more phenomena, and (3) to establish and/or measure *causation.* Another way to describe the purposes for research includes: (1) theory testing, (2) extending the range of applicability of existing research, (3) resolving conflicting research findings, and (4) replicating previous studies.

Researchers approach their studies from several different *philosophical foundations,* each with its own preferred body of methods. The two major *philosophies of science* traditions are *positivism* and *postpositivism.* Positivist researchers emphasize quantitative data that is gathered and analyzed using experiments, surveys, and statistics. Postpositivism includes several different approaches, including explanatory, critical, feminist, and postmodern research. At one time a heated debate raged in the discipline over which of the approaches was the appropriate one. Traces of that debate still exist today, despite the growing acceptance that there is a correct time and place for both approaches to research in political science.

A number of observers are highly critical of the state of political science research. One view is that political scientists still place by far too great an emphasis upon *applied* research. As a result, political scientists are making few if any contributions to advancing the state of knowledge in the field. Others are critical of the continuing emphasis on quantitative methods, econometric methods, mathematical models, and similar mathematics based approaches. These critics urge a greater emphasis on interpretive approaches, including historical methods.

Despite the continuing turmoil, the discipline of political science clearly is alive and well—and probably better off for its differences of opinion and focus. Obviously, the research on politics, political institutions, and political behavior is not yet complete; much remains to be done. The good news is that there are many different topics to examine and many ways now to go about conducting the study.

Discussion Questions

1. In your own words, define political science.
2. Comment on the following statement: Political scientists study the issues that they think should be examined, and conduct research in the way that they believe knowledge is gained.
3. What are the two major methodological positions that guide political science researchers?
4. Describe the positivist research tradition.
5. Describe the criticisms of positivist research.
6. What was the postpositivist reaction?
7. Name and explain in some detail several of the new approaches to political science research.

8. Discuss the eight assumptions and objectives of behavioralist research.
9. What is rational choice theory? How is it used in political science research?
10. Explain the feminist approach to interpretive research.
11. What is the postmodern approach to political science research?

Additional Reading

Chalmers, A. 1985. *What Is This Thing Called Science?* Milton Keynes: Open University Press.
March, J., and J. Olsen. 1989. *Rediscovering Institutions.* New York: The Free Press.
Morrow, J. 1994. *Game Theory for Political Scientists.* Princeton, NJ: Princeton University Press.
Peters, G. 1999. *Institutional Theory in Political Science: The "New Institutionalism."* London: Pinter.

3 The State of Political Science Research

In 1983, the editorial board of the American Political Science Association (APSA) began a series of compendium publications in which a variety of political scientists were invited to submit papers that described the then-current state of intellectual activity in the political science discipline. Follow-on volumes appeared in 1993 and 2002 (Finifter 1983 and 1993; Katznelson and Milner 2002). A comparative summary of the major section headings in each of the volumes is displayed in Table 3.1. In the first edition of the *State of the Discipline* series, a major question that concerned researchers was whether research in the discipline should be *theoretical* or *applied*. This was taking place during the waning days of the *behavioral* focus in political science, when politics was considered first and foremost a behavioral system. The behavioral emphasis had reached its peak during the decades of the 1950s and the 1960s. Gunnell described the research of the period in this way:

> There was a distinct emphasis on pure or theoretical science and a turning away from the idea of liberal reform and social control as the rationale of social science. . . . The 1960s were a decade of optimism about the advance of scientific theory and the achievement of the behavioral goal of science of politics modeled after the [methodological rigor of the natural sciences]. . . . Paramount to all of these efforts was some notion of politics as a "system." (Gunnell 1983, 12)

Search for a New Paradigm

The 1970s were a period when many political science researchers were becoming dissatisfied with the behavioral/systems model; they felt that the discipline was in dire need of a new paradigm. This was also a time when the idea of political science as a policy science emerged, with much research focusing on policy questions. However, it was also becoming more and more difficult to clearly identify any limited set of core issues or a dominant research focus in the discipline, seen in this statement:

> Different interests and concerns would yield different distributions of emphasis. The important point is that the field was becoming too dispersed for there to be any core set of issues that would be readily agreed upon. . . . Although one could say that the field was vital, it could just as easily be said that it was without definite direction or focus. (Gunnell 1983, 33–34)

Table 3.1

State-of-the-Discipline Section Headings in Three Editions of a Survey Volume

Section	1983	1993	2002
1	Political Science: The Discipline and Its Scope and Theory	Theory and Method	The State in the Era of Globalization
2	American Political Processes and Policymaking	Political Processes and Individual Political Behavior	Democracy, Justice, and Their Institutions
3	Comparative Political Processes and Policymaking	Political Institutions of the State	Citizenship, Identity, and Political Participation
4	Micropolitical Behavior: American and Comparative	Nations and Their Relationships	Studying Politics
5	International Politics		
6	Addresses from the Lasswell Symposium: The Uses of Social Science		

Sources: Finifter, ed. 1983; 1993; Katznelson and Milner, eds. 2002.

The diversity of research approaches are exemplified by Apter's (1977) description of what he saw as the six dominant points of view held by political scientists: political philosophy, institutionalism, behavioralism, pluralism, structuralism, and developmentalism. Researchers in *political philosophy* focus on the issues pertaining to purposes, moral means, and intentions of political actors—this approach is still an important research direction today. The focus of *institutionalists* has been the study of government organizations, their interrelationships, norms, and governance patterns.

Behavioralists believe that the big questions in political science could best be answered by studying the political behavior, attitudes, and opinions of individuals. *Pluralism* is the study of the ways that groups compete and cooperate in the drive for power, and of the connections between these diverse forms of organizations. Pluralism is also concerned with the concept of growth and economic development.

Structuralists examine the structure that forms and frames society, exchange roles, classes, and the connections between individuals and their communities. Structuralism emerged from an attempt to include the best of behavioralism and institutionalism in political science. The final mode of political science investigation suggested by Apter is *developmentalism*. This approach examines the evolution of political institutions and organized political actions and behaviors over time. In this sense, it is a practical application of political philosophy and theory. Developmentalist issues include industrialization, economic development, growth and urbanization, and how government has evolved to meet these challenges.

The Global Influence of Behavioralism

The growth of political science in other parts of the world has been greatly influenced by the behavioralist tradition. In the view of Lisa Harrison (2001), the history of the growth of the two concepts mirrors each other; political science as a discipline is closely—but not exclusively—associated with the growth of the behavioral approach to research. By the middle of the last century, the behavioral approach had become the dominant way of conducting political research. The behavioralist influence on political science was not simply an intellectual focus; rather, it was even more a way of conducting research—what Harrison has referred to as the *methodological tools* of research. Perhaps the most important tool has been the use of the survey method for investigating the political attitudes and choices of citizens. Attitudes and choices are, therefore, among the most important issues in political science.

For some, this emphasis on attitudes and choices has stifled the acceptance of other methods in political science research. "The supremacy of quantitative methods as well as the academic success of rational choice theory [have] combined to discredit other approaches, especially more qualitative ones [in political science research]. . . . comparative politics and area studies are under assault" (Ruget 2002, 472).

The "Big Issues" in Political Science

At any given time, every discipline has a set of important questions that capture the minds and talents of those who carry out research in the field; these are the *big issues* of the discipline. These issues do not remain static; researchers lose interest in investigating the same questions time after time, or the issues are seen as inappropriate for the methodology then in vogue. Interest in the old questions wanes and new topics appear at conferences and in journals. Some researchers join what they see as the "cutting edge of thinking" in the field, and begin to conduct research on the new questions or application of new approaches or methods, even while many others remain focused on the older problems. As a result, this mix of the old and the new makes it difficult to identify the big issues in a discipline. This is clearly the situation in today's political science.

About the time that an issue trickles its way down through the many academic and practicing political scientists who might have an interest in the topic, it is outdated and something new has come along to pique the interests of researchers in the field. Heywood (2000) may have been guided by this fact when he avoided discussing specific questions in his book on *Key Concepts in Politics,* and instead enumerated seven different ways to look at questions and concerns in political science. He identified 15 key concepts, beginning with Authority and concluding with the State. Heywood next identified and defined 20 *ideologies* that drive human approaches to government and governance, and all of which are topics of extensive research. A few of the ideologies in his list included Anarchism, Christian Democracy, Communism, Ecologism, Feminism, New Left and New Right, and others. He then identified 19 different *approaches* employed in political science research, and 25 different *values* that are associated in one way or another with political science and research in the discipline. In addition, Heywood discussed 17 different governmental *systems,* 28 different *structures,* and 15 different *levels* of government institutions and issue focus. There are enough questions named in this small volume to supply political scientists everywhere with as many ideas for research questions as they will ever need.

Scott (1997, 137) discussed what he believed were the great issues in political science at the end of the twentieth century, admitting, however, that most people who call themselves political scientists still disagree widely on two vital and basic questions: (1) What is valid information (truth) concerning politics? And (2) how do we go about finding it? He saw the following topics as the eight great issues of political science:

1. How shall we get along with each other?
2. Politics and human nature.
3. Community and individuality.
4. Authority, order, and freedom.
5. Equality.
6. Justice.
7. Democracy.
8. Representation.

Research in Political Science Today

Most disciplines, including political science, have undergone substantial growth since the end of World War II. One of the unplanned consequences of this growth has been the expansion of interests in each of the various social science disciplines. While one result of the expansion has been a trend toward greater interdisciplinary research, many new researchers have wandered far from a limited core of questions to look at many different, unrelated questions with the goal of "finding something new to study." Like its sister social sciences, political science has become segmented into many separate and increasingly focused subfields (Abramson 1997; Barth 1994). Each of these subfields has at least one—and usually many more than one—journal dedicated to disseminating advances in its field.

A review of 2001 and 2002 issues of four important journals in the discipline—the *American Journal of Political Science, American Political Science Review, Journal of Politics,* and the *Political Research Quarterly*—found papers focusing on the traditional range of major themes, but with a wide variety of individual topics that did not fit into any of the key subfields. Most of the research papers in these four journals addressed questions in the following topic-areas: political theory, American politics, elections/voting, judiciary, comparative politics, international relations, research methodology, public administration, program evaluation, and a broad collection of unclassified topics. Currently, the *American Political Science Review* publishes research papers in five categories of inquiry: political theory, American politics, comparative politics, international relations, and public administration. The journal includes a sixth category, research methods and analysis, with an established focus on methodological issues, not on politics or political topics.

Lee Sigelman (2003), the new editor of the *American Political Science Review* (APSR), reported on the scope and quantity of papers submitted to the journal during 2001–2002, his first year in the post. The journal saw a 56 percent increase in the number of submissions of the previous year, from 425 to 615 (including invited resubmissions after editing). Sigelman identified six different research approaches in the new papers received by APSR from September 1, 2001 through August 15, 2002: formal (mathematical) models, quantitative, formal and quantitative, small studies, interpretive/conceptual, and another category. Table 3.2 compares the 2001–2002 single-year new submissions with those received during the previous five years.

Table 3.2

Distribution of Approaches Taken in Papers Submitted to APSR

	Approach					
Year	Formal Modeling	Quantitative	Formal and Quantitative	Small *n*	Interpretive/ Conceptual	Other
2001–2002	17	45	7	1	29	2
1995–2000	13	48	7	2	30	0

Source: Sigelman 2003, 114.

Table 3.3 displays the distribution of topic fields for submissions during four separate editorship periods from 1985 to 2002. Papers were grouped into six fields: American politics and policy, comparative politics, international relations, normative theory, formal theory, and methods. It is not clear whether the numbers chosen for classification were random samples of 100 for each of the four periods, or whether they represent the population for each period. However, because all but one period did contain 100 papers—the 1995–2000 period was missing just one, for an *n* of 99—the values may also be interpreted as percentages. As can be seen in the table, the largest proportions in every period were papers on American politics and policy topics; this percentage declined from 41 percent during 1985–1991 to 30 percent under Sigelman's 2001–2002 editorship. The proportions of papers on comparative politics and methods topics increased slightly over the four periods, while all others remained more or less constant.

Table 3.3

Distribution of Political Science Fields in Papers Submitted to APSR

	Field					
Year	American Politics and Policy	Comparative Politics	International Relations	Normative Theory	Formal Theory	Research Methods
2001–2002	30	25	14	17	8	6
1995–2000	38	23	12	18	6	2
1991–1995	35	22	12	21	10	0
1985–1991	41	17	10	19	13	0

Source: Sigelman 2003, 114.

In his attempt to provide some structure to the burgeoning field of political science, Fagan (2002) grouped a collection of working papers in political science into a little more than a dozen categories. The major topics listed on the Fagan's Web site are American politics, comparative politics, political communication, political theory, public administration, international relations, political economy, public policy, and methods and data. Superimposed upon these major focus areas are a number of subfields for which research is conducted on a regular basis. Cochran, Mayer, Carr, and Cayer (1995), for example, identified these nine topic areas that fall under the umbrella of studies in the *public policy* subfield: intergovernmental relations, the economy in general, economic issues such as taxation and spending, energy and the environment, crime and criminal justice, health care, education, legal and social equality, and diversity and tolerance.

Vanessa Ruget (2002) examined the political science discipline along what she called "four structuring dimensions." These included the status of the discipline in academia, the research fields addressed by political scientists, sociological characteristics of political scientists themselves, and their political allegiance. Together, these dimensions made up what Ruget saw as the *symbolic capital* of the discipline. An important conclusion of her research was that apparently, all fields in the discipline do not have the same "symbolic force":

> For historical and intellectual reasons, the study of American political phenomena has become dominant in the discipline, while other domains, like political theory . . . (which used to be considered the core of the field) . . . are implicitly considered to be less professionally promising. In 1991, for example, the course "American Government" was required by 80% of the political science departments in four-year colleges and universities, whereas a general introduction to the discipline was required in only 48% of them. (Ruget 2002, 472)

This emphasis on American government has not been accidental, and probably should not be considered denigrating. American political science has maintained its particular focus on developing specific kinds of knowledge about the American system of governance, while British political science, Indian political science, Russian political science, etc., have done the same for their countries. "The modifier *American* has to be taken seriously," according to Katznelson and Milner (2002, 3). The attempts of early political scientists to arrive at explanations for the emergence of the liberal democratic United States has naturally resulted in an emphasis on democracy and the features have enabled democracy to endure. However, if the papers commissioned for the third volume in the *State of the Discipline* series are any indication, dramatic changes in the focus of political science are taking place.

In addition to the domestic emphasis on American politics and policy, American political science is going global. Of the twenty-eight papers included in Katznelson and Milner's introductory article, nearly 30 percent have an international focus of some type. The papers that are explicitly international are identified in Table 3.4.

Research topics in political science range across the entire spectrum of the social sciences. Despite the widely diverse nature of the discipline, several common themes characterize the discipline (Katznelson and Milner 2002, 2). These include: (1) a pragmatic orientation to the concept of the state that incorporates the study of power and choice as integral features; (2) study of the nature of liberal political regimes and their stability, with an increasing focus on democracy; (3) a commitment to the study of the state in ways that are open and systematic.

The study of power is particularly interesting to political scientists; for many, it is the fundamental *raison d'etre* of the discipline. David Apter described the focus on power and power relationships as similar to what holds the attention of economics researchers: "Political science seeks to discover the ingredients of power in their concentrated and abstract forms. Power is to the political scientists what scarcity is to the economist. Scarcity assumes that something is valued, and that there is an insufficiency of it available. People will try to get something of value for themselves . . ." (Apter 1977, 6). Thus, political scientists study power and the ways that individuals and groups try to get power for themselves.

Table 3.4

Papers in Katznelson and Milner (2002) with a Global/International Theme

	Title	Authors
1	"The State of the State in World Politics"	Miles Kahler
2	"State, Society, and Development"	Atul Kuhli
3	"International Political Economy: Global and Domestic"	Jeffry Frieden and Lisa L. Martin
4	"International Conflict: Assessing the Democratic Peace and Offense-Defense Theory"	James D. Morrow
5	"The Great Transformation in the Study of Politics in Developing Countries"	Barbara Geddes
6	"The Political Economy of Business and Labor in the Developed Democracies"	Kathleen Thelen
7	"Political Theory and Political Membership in a Changing World"	Seyla Benhabib
8	"Constructionivism and International Institutions: Toward Conversations across Paradigms"	Thomas Risse
9	"Comparative Politics: The State of the Subdiscipline"	David D. Laitin

Source: Katznelson and Milner 2002.

Focus in Research Topics

How does the thematic focus of the discipline translate into topics for research? One way to discern what might be a legitimate topic for research in political science is to look at what other researchers are examining, and to see what is being funded and what is being published. Indicative of the variety of research topics is the following partial list of recent political science research studies that received National Science Foundation grants (NSF 2002). They include: bargaining processes; campaigns and elections, electoral choice, and electoral systems; citizen support in emerging and established democracies; and democratization, political change, and regime transitions. Other recent NSF-funded studies have included studies on party activism, political psychology, and political tolerance, advances in political and research methodology, and research experiences for students, to name only a few.

Another way to put a frame around the scope of work in political science is to look at how the discipline structures itself. Several attempts have been made to reduce the large and growing number of research topics to a smaller number of fundamental themes. The Social and Economic Sciences division (SBE) of the NSF, for example, reported that it supports political science research that expands the understanding of *citizenship, government,* and *politics.* Specifically, the foundation funds studies in, but not limited to, the following six topic areas: American government and politics, comparative government and politics, international relations, political behavior, political economy, and political institutions.

Laitin (2001) identified four branches of the discipline, but added two support areas in a paper presented at the 2001 American Political Science Association (APSA) conference.

> There are four substantive fields in political science: Political Theory, Comparative Politics, Political Institutions, and International Relations. [In addition] there is one field (methodology) that

develops tools to address the methodological problems in each of the substantive fields. There is also an applied field (Public Policy) whose practitioners address policy problems relying on the substantive knowledge and methodological skills developed in the non-applied part of the discipline. (Laitin 2001, 7)

The APSA conference literature identified the following five key thematic fields—political theory, political institutions, international relations, public policy, and methods—and three non-substantive areas, "arenas," "independent variables," and an "other" category. These fields and section subfields are listed in Table 3.5. Laitin did not identify public administration as one of the major subfields of political science, instead including it as part of the public policy applied field. Speaking to what he saw as the "increasingly fragmented" and "chaotic" nature of the

Table 3.5

Conference Fields and Topics, 2001 Annual APSA Conference

Field	Section
Political Theory	Foundations of Political Thought
	Human Rights
Political Institutions	Laws and Courts
	Legislative Studies
	Political Organizations and Parties
	Representative and Electoral Systems
	Presidency Research
	Elections, Public Opinion, and Voting Behavior
International Relations	Conflict Processes
	International Security and Arms Control
	Foreign Policy
Public Policy	Public Policy
	Public Administration
	Science, Technology, and Environmental Politics
Methodology	Political Methodology
Arenas	Politics and Society in Western Europe
	Urban Politics
	State Politics and Policy
Independent Variables	Politics and History
	International History and Politics
	Religion and Politics
	Race, Ethnicity, and Politics
	Women and Politics
	Ecological and Transformational Politics
	Political Communication
	Information Technology and Politics
Other	Political Economy
	Political Psychology
	New Political Science
	Politics and Literature
	Undergraduate Education

Source: Laitin 2001.

discipline, Laitin illustrated his point by referencing the organized sections and topics listed for the 2001 annual conference.

In their methods text, Johnson, Joslyn, and Reynolds (2001) included cases focusing on six central themes: American politics, public administration, the courts, international relations, comparative politics, and public policy. Abramson (1997) identified the four chief fields of research in political science as *national politics* (e.g., politics in America; politics in France, etc.), comparative politics, international relations, and political theory.

Research in the Subfields of Political Science

A sampling of some of the most important political science journals helps to bring closure to this problem of definition and structure. Most researchers in the discipline today appear to be focusing on questions in five broad fields of inquiry. These are (1) the history, theory and philosophy of politics, (2) national politics, (3) comparative politics, (4) public administration (including the judiciary, public law, and criminal justice), and (5) international relations and related geopolitical issues. Rather than limit the focus to American politics exclusively in the list, the second topic has been broadened here to *national politics* in recognition that significant research in political science is taking place throughout the world. Some of this research is comparative, while other studies interpret a specific national system. However, the research all focuses on issues that are idiosyncratically national in scope. Researchers in other nations substitute their own nation or region for American politics, of course, but generally follow a similar set of topic areas.

Still another way to get a handle on the huge scope of research on political science topics and themes comes from a review of the 102 journals in the discipline recognized by the American Political Science Association (APSA 2002). Two of these are official APSA journals: *American Political Science Review* and *PS: Political Science and Politics.* Others are grouped into ten categories, two of which are affiliated in some way with the association. One affiliated category includes three APSA section journals; sections are the large topic categories of the association, such as international relations, public policy, and others. The second category includes the fifteen journals of regional, state, and national political science associations. Other journal categories recognized by APSA include American politics, international politics, comparative politics, public administration and public policy, policy studies, political theory, women and politics, and a catchall *other* category.

Researchers in the area of the history, theory, and philosophy of politics study such questions as theories of political thought, the historical foundations of governance, and related philosophical and historical issues. APSA lists nearly twenty journals in this topic area. Among them are the *Critical Review of International Social and Political Philosophy, History of Political Thought,* and the *Journal of Political Thought.*

Researchers who address questions pertaining to the national politics and the political system often investigate such phenomena as development and evolution of political parties and political action. They also look at the conduct of campaigns for or against issues and candidates for elected office, the processes of forming public policy, the activities of lobbyists and special interest groups, and related topics. *American Politics Research, Party Developments,* and *White House Studies* are three journals in which studies on American politics can be found. Many of the journals in the area of comparative politics, such as the *British Journal of Political Science* and *Israel Affairs,* publish studies dealing with politics in other nations and areas.

Researchers who work in the area of comparative politics examine such questions as the similarities and differences in political systems and thought among two or more countries, regions, or ideologies. They also make in-depth analyses of specific functional areas in regions and nations. Examples of comparative functional studies can be found in the journals *Comparative Strategy* and *Electoral Studies*. Examples of regional comparison studies can be found in such journals as the *International Journal of Middle East Studies, West European Politics,* and the *Journal of Commonwealth and Comparative Studies.*

Researchers in public administration are typically concerned with studies that focus on problems in the administration of agencies, programs, and organizations in all levels of government, the management of nonprofit organizations, and specific functional areas of interest, such as finance or human resources. The research topics in this field include such questions as how to enhance public participation in government, how to foster ethical conduct by public administrators, the equitable distribution of services, improving public agency performance by applying relevant performance measurements, managing diversity in the public workforce, and others. Examples of articles in this field can be found in the *American Review of Public Administration* and *Public Administration Review,* to name just two journals serving this political science track.

Political scientists who study events and trends in international relations often adopt the case study method in their analyses. They describe in detail the politics, political systems, and public policies of other nations. They make comparisons of national governments and international institutions and policies such as global trade, monetary policy, defense, or environmental protection, for example. Other researchers in this field study the functions and policies of larger international bodies like the European Union, the United Nations, the North American Free Trade Agreement (NAFTA), and other issues of a bilateral, multilateral, or geopolitical nature. Examples of research in this area can be found in such journals as *Foreign Affairs, Foreign Policy, International Politics,* and the *Review of International Studies,* which are only a few of the nineteen journals specifically devoted to international politics.

The Continuing Legacy of Quantitative Methods

Obviously, political science research ranges across a wide range of methods and topics. However, despite what he saw as "great strides" occurring in efforts to integrate qualitative and quantitative approaches to research in political science, Abrahamson (2000, 675) was forced to conclude that "political scientists are still more likely to be influenced by developments in quantitative time series analyses." Despite what researchers would like to describe as the end of the emphasis on quantitative methods for data analysis, the tools associated with the behavioralist approach and economists' rational choice theory models remain strong in the discipline. According to Ruget (2002, 472), "the supremacy of quantitative methods as well as the academic success of rational choice theory combine to discredit other approaches, especially more qualitative ones." Research papers with a quantitative approach are still the mainstay in much of the political science literature. Sigelman (2003), for example, reported that quantitative approaches made up 48 percent of the papers received at the *American Political Science Review* in the five-year period from 1995 to 2000, and 45 percent of the papers received in 2001–2002.

Despite the continuing attention on quantitative research, qualitative approaches—the postpositivist, feminist, and postmodern approaches, among others—are continuing to gain greater acceptance. Furthermore, each of the subfields of political science still tends to have its own preferred methods and research designs. In American politics studies, for example, most of the work is conducted as case studies, while researchers in international relations look at conflicts and cooperation among nation states. Other subfields have similar traditions.

Different Answers for Similar Problems

Researchers in each subfield begin from a common starting point—the purpose statement upon which a research hypothesis is formed. From this beginning, they move in different ways to accomplish what on the surface may appear to be a common goal but, in reality, is something else entirely. Say, for example, that researchers in three different subfields find themselves interested in questions dealing with how issues influence voter behavior. A researcher in political activity might want to know whether voters in California react differently than Nebraska voters to the agriculture platform in the message of a presidential candidate. A researcher in the area of public policy might design a study to determine whether families from different ethnic groups respond differently to a candidate's stand on welfare reform training programs. Still another researcher working in the area of international relations might want to compare the way adults in the European Union vote after the introduction of a common currency. Similar differences occur in other subfields of political science.

These different researchers necessarily begin their studies with widely different assumptions. The first researcher might assume that different levels of industrialization influence the attitudes of voters in both states. The public policy researcher may assume that all ethnic groups feel the same about training and welfare reform. The research in international relations may assume that the citizens of all European Union nations have similar opinions about replacing their national currency with the *Euro*, the common currency of the European Union. Each one of these assumptions is a *hypothesis* that can be tested (Mattson 1976). In turn, each one becomes the starting point for identification of a research question.

Good political science research always follows a predetermined design and method. Any topic may be investigated in a variety of different ways. The two chief approaches to research were discussed earlier—the *positivist* and the *postpositivist* approaches. However, the researcher must remember that both the design of the study and the method followed are dictated by the nature of the research problem and the objectives for the research. Following a design means always beginning with a definition of a research problem, adopting a systematic plan for collecting, analyzing, and interpreting the data, and for reporting the study findings. Getting from the beginning to the end of a research project can take many different paths.

Katznelson and Milner provided a concise summary of the focus of political science research and the discipline itself at the close of their introductory chapter for the third edition of *The State of Discipline*. They wrote:

> Contested and methodologically diverse, political science nonetheless remains focused, as it has for a century, on a particular understanding of how to study the modern state and liberal democracy. Though there have been shifts, of course, in emphasis and method, attempts to periodize the discipline's history mislead if not grounded in these powerful continuities delineating the discipline. Moreover, though political science has not produced fixed findings in the strong sense of the term . . . , its intellectual debates have been cumulative and its disputations have grown more textured,

more variegated, and in many respects, though not all, more capable over time. (Katznelson and Milner 2002, 25)

Summary

Most political science research focuses on questions in five broad fields of inquiry: (1) the history, theory, and philosophy of politics, (2) American (or other national) politics, (3) comparative politics, (4) public administration (including the judiciary, public law, and criminal justice), and (5) international relations and related geopolitical issues. Each of the subfields of political science has its own set of common concerns and its own research traditions. However, in political science in general, the traditional research approach continues to be focused on the positivist approach and the use of quantitative methods.

A problem with identifying the big issues in political science is the constant change in the discipline. Heywood (2000) may have been guided by this fact when he avoided discussing specific questions in his book on *Key Concepts in Politics,* and instead enumerated seven different ways to look at questions and concerns in political science: basic concepts, ideologies, approaches to research, values, systems, structures, and levels.

A review of 2001 and 2002 issues of four important journals—the *American Journal of Political Science, American Political Science Review, Journal of Politics,* and the *Political Research Quarterly*—found papers focusing on the traditional range of major themes, but with a wide variety of individual topics that did not fit into any of the key subfields. Most of the research addressed the following topic-areas: political theory, American politics, elections/voting, judiciary, comparative politics, international relations, research methodology, public administration, program evaluation, and a broad collection of unclassified topics. A leading journal in the discipline, the *American Political Science Review,* publishes research papers in six categories: political theory, American politics, comparative politics, international relations, public administration, and, research methods and analysis. Researchers in each subfield begin from a common starting point—the purpose statement upon which a research hypothesis or hypotheses are formed. From this beginning, they move in different ways to accomplish what on the surface may appear to be a common goal but, in reality, is something else entirely.

Fagan (2002) grouped a collection of working papers in political science into the following categories: American politics, comparative politics, political communication, political theory, public administration, international relations, political economy, public policy, and methods and data. Superimposed upon these major focus areas are a number of subfields for which research is conducted on a regular basis. Ruget (2002) examined "four structuring dimensions" of political science research: the status of the discipline, the research fields addressed by political scientists, sociological characteristics of political scientists, and their political allegiance. These make up what Ruget saw as the *symbolic capital* of the discipline. An important conclusion of her research was that apparently, all fields in the discipline do not have the same "symbolic force."

Several common themes characterize the political science discipline. These include: (1) a pragmatic orientation to the concept of the state that incorporates the study of power and choice as integral features; (2) study of the nature of liberal political regimes and their stability, with an increasing focus on democracy; (3) a commitment to the study of the state in ways that are open and systematic.

Discussion Questions

1. What is behavioralism and what role has it played in political science research?
2. What are the main branches of political science?
3. What topics might someone interested in American politics choose to research?
4. What sorts of research topics might someone who is interested in the theory and philosophy of political science research?
5. What do political scientists engaged in the study of comparative politics research?
6. What do public administrators research?
7. Assume you want to specialize in international relations. On what sorts of topics might you conduct research?
8. What do you think will be the big issues in political science over the next ten years? Why?

Additional Reading

Finifter, Ada W., ed. 1983. *Political Science: The State of the Discipline*. Washington, DC: American Political Science Association.
———. 1993. *Political Science: The State of the Discipline II*. Washington, DC: American Political Science Association.
Heywood, Andrew. 2000. *Key Concepts in Politics*. Houndmills, UK: Palgrave Macmillan.
Katznelson, Ira, and Helen Milner, ed. 2002. *Political Science III: The State of the Discipline*. Washington, DC: American Political Science Association.

4 The Political and Ethical Environments of Research

All science, including political science, is increasingly subject to the influence of uncontrollable forces emanating from the political and ethical environments. Government legislators and administrators, the popular press, the general public, and a growing number of crusading social scientists are alike in their increasingly justified calls for moral reform, for passage of ethics laws and codes, and for greater education and training in ethical behavior for scientists working in all disciplines. Calls for ethics reform have been directed at every level of government, from the Office of the President of the United States to the smallest local special-service district. Ethical problems in government run the gamut from sexual harassment to embezzlement of millions. Citing a recent Gallup Poll, *USA Today* reporter Karen Peterson (2001) wrote that, for only the second time in half a century, ethics and morality are near the top of a list of the major problems that people believe are facing the nation. Gallup reported that 78 percent of the public feels that the nation's moral values are somewhat or very weak.

There has long been an ethical and a political aspect to the political world (Rohr 1998, 4). The problem of unethical behavior by researchers became an important political issue for Congress in the 1980s. According to LaFollete (1994, 264), scientists had "forged data, falsified experiments, and plagiarized before that time, but scientists and politicians alike had treated such behavior as isolated, deviant, irrelevant, or unrepresentative of normal science, and the news media only paid temporary attention when new cases were developed." Since then, however, legislators are quick to investigate and monitor the management practices of university administrators when they receive allegations of misconduct from constituents. In fulfilling their oversight responsibilities, Congress authorizes inquiries and holds hearings on issues of (1) expenditures of grant funds on research, (2) the qualifications of the scientists conducting the research, and (3) policies that guide and influence such processes as selection criteria for awarding research grants. Congress conducts oversight activities in three ways: by directly communicating with responsible agency personnel, by holding hearings, or by initiating investigative reports.

According to one widely cited author on the topic, Terry Cooper (1998), interest in political ethics appears to have mushroomed. This has resulted in a growing demand for in-service training, publication of many ethics articles, and professional conferences devoted solely to ethics problems in government. In addition, political science undergraduate and graduate education programs are requiring students to successfully complete a course in ethical behavior. This heightened interest in ethics has also included the practice of research. Every aspect of political research and analysis involves ethics (Mitchell 1998, 305). Mitchell included most types of research in his analysis, including "pure" social science, as well as more "applied" studies such as policy analyses, and program evaluations. He considered ethics to be an issue in research whether it is conducted to describe problems, predict outcomes, evaluate solutions, or measure agency performance.

The American Political Science Association (ASPA) has taken an active role in strengthening regulations dealing with research. For example, in 2001 the Consortium of Social Science Associations, to which APSA belongs, joined with other organizations to form a new research-accrediting group, the Association for the Accreditation of Human Research Protection Programs (AAHRPP). This group is expected to play a major role in improving the system of human subjects protection. But ethics is more than protecting human subjects; there are many ways to define this value-laden term.

The Meaning of *Ethics*

Ethics, a branch of philosophy, is the study of the *moral* behavior of humans in society. It has been further defined as the set of principles that govern the conduct of an individual or a group of persons, and briefly as the study of morality or moral behavior (Velasquez 1998). *Morality* refers to the standards that people have about what is right, what is wrong, what is good, or what is evil; these standards are the behavior norms of a society. *Moral behavior* is acting in ways that follow the moral standards that exist in society. *Moral standards* are the rules by which a society functions. Examples of moral standards include the moral commandments: *Do not kill, Do not steal, Do not lie,* etc. Standards are about what behavior is acceptable, what is "right" and what is "good" in society, and their opposites, of course. While moral standards often change from time to time, they remain relatively constant for at least a generation or more. When they do change, they tend to do so very slowly.

What do we mean when we talk about behavior that is *unethical?* In the specific sense of scientific research we are referring to the broad concept of *scientific misconduct.* Misconduct, in the words of Fox and Braxton (1994, 374), "encompasses acts of deception—alteration of data or materials, false representation of authorship or originality, and misrepresentation to advance oneself or to hurt the career or position of another."

Opinions about what is unethical behavior—moral standards—vary from society to society; there are few absolutes in ethics. However, the fundamental standards of behavior tend to be quite similar throughout the industrialized nations of the world. This is so because, if standards were wildly different, nations would have a difficult time cooperating in such value-laden areas as international relations, commerce, and other global activities. China's difficulty in achieving Most Favored Nation (MNF) status—valued in international trade because it provides lower tariffs—is a case in point. Some say that a key barrier was the Chinese government's behavior on certain human rights issues, a moral standard considered unacceptable in the West.

What distinguishes moral standards from standards that are not moral? Velasquez (1998) has identified five characteristics of moral behavior that make this distinction. First, moral standards are concerned with matters that people think can seriously injure or benefit human beings. Second, people absorb their moral standards as children, and revise them as they mature. Therefore, moral standards are not established or changed by the decisions of authoritative bodies; ethics cannot be legislated.

Third, by their very nature as fundamental norms of behavior in a society, moral standards are preferred over other values, including self-interest. Fourth, moral standards are based on impartial considerations; they apply equally to all persons in society. Finally, moral standards evoke special emotions, including guilt and shame, and are associated with a special vocabulary; words such as good, bad, honesty, justice, and injustice are examples.

Scientific research of all types is beset with ethical dilemmas, paradoxes, and ambiguities (de Laine 2000). This is particularly true when research involves human subjects, and when the research is conducted in social settings, as de Laine's following statement points out:

> Ethical and moral dilemmas are an occupational work hazard of fieldwork that the researcher cannot plan for, but nonetheless must be addressed on the spot, by drawing on the values, ideals, ethical codes, moral and professional standards, intuition and emotions. (de Laine 2000, 6)

Ethicists have identified a number of different theoretical foundations for the values, ideals, ethical codes, and moral standards that researchers draw upon when faced with these dilemmas; the foundations of our moral principles that have gained the widest acceptance are discussed in the next section of this chapter. Examples of the types of events that trigger ethical conflicts include the following behaviors cited by LaFollette (1994) who considered them to the cause of the increased oversight activity of Congress over the last two decades:

> The behavior in question ranged from fabrication of data, falsified experiments, or faked specimens and artifacts, to the deliberate misrepresentation or altering of data and theft of ideas from research proposals and published articles. Congressional attention concentrated on unethical or illegal activities that took place during the process of proposing, conducting, or communicating federally funded research in the biological, physical, and behavioral sciences (including political science), mathematics, and engineering. (LaFollette 1994, 270)

One of the agencies established by Congress to monitor research fraud is the Office of Research Integrity (ORI). Although ORI concern has been primarily directed at issues of ethical misconduct in health science research, the agency has proposed a list of critical topics that have applicability to research in all disciplines. The fourteen proposed topics are listed under three headings: *The Research Community, Professional Development,* and *The Research Process.* There are five subgroups in the Research Process category; these are concerned with issues on data management, publication of findings, authorship, peer review, and research misconduct specifically. A partial list of the topics proposed in the area of research misconduct includes the following (Office of Research Integrity 2002, 5):

- What factors affect the detection of research misconduct?
- What factors discourage the reporting of research misconduct?
- What factors motivate individuals to commit research misconduct?
- What happens to whistleblowers?

Sources of Moral Standards

Moral standards have evolved from a number of different philosophical traditions, some of which are as old as recorded time. Similar codes of behavior evolved some 5,000 years ago in both Egypt and Mesopotamia—present-day Iraq—for example. A key concept in those early codes was the idea of justice. It continues to underlie moral standards in many modern societies.

In the United States and Europe, codes of ethics have roots in the Judeo-Christian tradition. In the Middle East, behavioral standards are founded on the Koran. In parts of Asia, moral standards spring from the teachings of either Confucius or Buddha. In the last half of the twentieth century, a renewed interest in the rights of human beings has emerged as an integral part of modern ethical standards—it has been expanded to include the rights of animals as well, a point with great implication for medical researchers.

Today, at least five different ways to approach an ethical situation have evolved from these earliest guidelines for moral behavior. These include: *utilitarian, rights, justice, caring,* and *virtue ethics* (Velasquez 1998).

Utilitarian Ethics

Utilitarian ethics is based on the view that the "right" action or policy is the one that will result in the greatest benefit (or the lowest costs) to society. Thus, decisions on actions and policies must be evaluated according to their net benefits and costs. Utilitarian ethics is concerned with the *consequences* of an action, not the means to achieve the results. Today's cost-benefit analysis is based on this principle. Because it supports the value of efficiency, utilitarianism is often used in the resolution of political dilemmas. A key characteristic of utilitarianism is that the benefits need not be equally distributed; some people may not benefit at all, and some may be negatively impacted. What counts is the greatest good for all concerned—but the moral dilemma is determining who is to decide what is good (Malhotra 1999).

Rights Ethics

Rights ethics are another approach often seen in political science. A *right* is often defined as a person's entitlement to something. Because of its focus on the individual, it differs from the utilitarian approach, where the focus is on the greater good of a society. Rights have been classified in several different ways. In once classification system, two types of rights are included in ethics, *legal* rights and *human* rights. Legal rights are based upon laws; consumer protection and contract rights are examples. Human rights, on the other hand, are culturally based; they provide people with a way of justifying their actions; they are also associated with *duties.*

A second way to classify rights is whether they are first-generation or second-generation rights (Joseph, Schultz, and Castan 2000, 3–4). First-generation rights include civil rights and political rights. Civil rights are rights that apply to citizens' physical integrity, the procedural right of due process, and nondiscrimination rights. Political rights enable citizens to participate in the political life of their society. They include such rights as freedom of expression, assembly and association, and the right to vote. Civil and political rights are called first-generation rights because they are a large part of the content of the *Bills of Rights* that were written in the eighteenth and nineteenth centuries. Collectively, they are considered as rights to be free from government influence.

Second-generation rights embrace economic, social, and cultural rights. Among these are the right to an adequate standard of living, the right to an education, and the right to good health. Collectively, second-generation rights are considered to be rights that require positive government action. Of the two sets of rights, second-generation rights tend to be less developed than first-generation civil and political rights.

Today's basis for rights ethics comes from the writings of philosopher Immanuel Kant (1724–1804). Kant believed that all human beings possess some rights and duties, and that these exist regardless of any utilitarian benefit they might have for or against others in a society. Kant proposed moral principles he called *categorical imperatives* to make this point. Kant's first categorical imperative states that an action is morally right if—and only if—the reason for the action is one that the person would be willing for everyone to act upon in a similar situation. There are two parts to this concept: (1) *universalizability* (it applies to everyone), and (2) *reversibility* (people would be willing to have all others use the concept in the way they treat him or her). Kant's second imperative holds that an action is morally right if—and again, only if—when performing the action, a person does not use others as a means for improving his or her own interests. When making the decision, administrators must respect the right of others to choose freely for themselves.

Several key concepts in political science are founded upon Kantian rights theories. Among others, these include the idea that all people have positive rights to work, clothing, housing, and medical care; that everyone has a right to freedom from injury or fraud; and, that humans have the right to enter into contracts.

Justice Ethics

Moral standards based on the idea of justice include the concept of *fairness*. Together, justice and fairness contribute to three fundamental bases for moral behavior: *distributive justice, retributive justice,* and *compensatory justice. Distributive justice* is concerned with the "fair" distribution of society's benefits—and burdens. The idea of a just distribution based on a person's contribution to society is the value behind the *capitalist* system, whereas distributive justice based on needs and abilities underlies *socialism,* and justice, as freedom to do as he or she chooses, is the idea behind *libertarianism.*

Retributive justice is concerned with the providing of punishments and penalties that are "just." Thus, a person should not be considered to be morally responsible for an action under conditions of ignorance or inability. This principle is the idea behind the standard of enlightened consent for participation in research studies. *Compensatory justice* supports the idea of compensating people for what they lose when they are wronged by other individuals or by society (including government).

Caring Ethics

The ethics of caring means making a decision in the face of an ethical dilemma based upon a genuine caring for the best interests of another individual. Key virtues of the caring researcher include friendship, kindness, concern, and love for fellow human beings. As might be expected, these ethical standards are often employed in describing decisions made in social welfare agencies and activities.

The care ethic emphasizes two moral demands (Velasquez 1998, 122). First, because we all live in our own web of relationships, we should preserve and nurture the valuable relationships we have with others. Second, we must care for those with whom we are related by attending to their particular needs, values, desires, and concrete well-being as seen from their perspective. This also means responding to the needs, values, desires, and well-being of those who are vulnerable and dependent on our care.

Three different types of care ethics come into play in social situations: caring *about* something, caring *after* someone, and caring *for* someone. In the political world, the applicable ethic is caring for someone. It focuses on people and their well-being, not on things.

Virtue Ethics

Based upon the writings of Aristotle and others, virtue ethics refers to the idea of using society's virtues as the basis for making ethical decisions. Aristotle identified four "pivotal" virtues: courage, temperance, justice, and prudence. St. Thomas Aquinas added the following "Christian" virtues: *faith, hope,* and *charity.* In today's society, the virtues considered most important include *honesty, courage, temperance, integrity, compassion,* and *self-control*—terms often used to describe the "ideal" public servant. Vices are the opposite of virtues; they include such examples of "bad" behavior as dishonesty, ruthlessness, greed, lack of integrity, and cowardice. These are considered to be undesirable because of the way they can destroy human relationships. Velasquez described the thinking that shapes decision making in virtue theory in the following way:

> An action is morally right if in carrying out the action the agent exercises, exhibits, or develops a morally virtuous character, and is morally wrong to the extent that by carrying out the action the agent exercises, exhibits, or develops a morally vicious character. (Velasquez 1998, 137)

Which Approach to Follow?

Which, if any, of these ethical principles should guide the researcher when preparing, conducting, and reporting the results of research studies? Some of the underlying principles have resulted in the passage of laws that define specifically what a researcher can and cannot do. However, it is not enough to simply do what is legal; researchers have a moral responsibility that goes far beyond adhering to the letter of the law. Because there is no one comprehensive moral theory that is capable of stating exactly when a utilitarian consideration should take precedent over a right, a standard of justice, or the need for caring, the political science researcher is forced to "follow his or her conscience" when faced with an ethical dilemma. Ethical dilemmas that cause most difficulty for researchers in political science are not those associated with what Orlans (1967) described as outright "knavery—lying, bad faith, conscious misrepresentation to get money, or the deliberate breach of the terms on which it was obtained (i.e, research grants)." These are practical problems of a legal nature rather than problems of ethics. Although Orlans attributed the problems specifically to funded or sponsored research, his description remains applicable to all research:

> The persistent ethical dilemmas in . . . research are those in which the right course of action is *not* clear, in which honorable [researchers] may differ and no consistent rule obtains [*sic*]. They involve issues in what is reasonable to one [person] is ignoble to another; in which honesty must be reconciled with tact and effectiveness; in which the disinterested pursuit of innocent truth can abet the interested selection of useful knowledge; in which the judgment of the pragmatic [person] of affairs confronts that of the academic moralist. (Orlans 1967, 4)

Reynolds (1979, 43) identified five problem areas where research dilemmas occur most often:

1. *Research program effects*—the positive and negative effects of an overall research program.
2. *Research project effects*—the positive and negative effects that result from a specific research project.
3. *Participation effects*—how participation in the research project will affect each participant.
4. *Overall distribution effects*—how the key positive and negative effects of research are distributed evenly among different social groups (stakeholders).
5. *Consideration of participants' rights and welfare*—the features of the research program and project that ensure that the rights and welfare of participants are, or will be, respected.

Political Science Ethics

Is there a distinct ethics for political science and its subfields, such as comparative politics, international relations, or public administration, to name only three? Most professionals like to think that their profession is in some way unique, that it has an ethics or a morality of its own, and that their ethics takes precedence over the ethics of ordinary people (Goss 1996). Of course, political scientists feel the same about their profession. Like all professions, political science is affected by misconduct and is subject to social control (Fox and Braxton 1994).

Goss compared the attitudes of 100 elected state officials with those of 378 public administrators and a random sample of 250 voting citizens. Attitudes were measured across 12 dimensions arranged in two scales of six items each. One set of items referred to the service or democratic ethos; the second set of items covered the professional or bureaucratic ethos. Public administrators valued *Professional Competence* above all other eleven value characteristics, and rated *Being an Advocate of the Public Interest* as the least important characteristic. Clearly, practicing administrators were more concerned with their professional skills than they were with service to the public.

Both the elected legislator and general public samples rated *Trustworthiness* as the most important behavioral characteristic for public servants. If Goss' single state case study is valid, that is, if his results can be considered to be representative of administrators everywhere, it appears that many politicians may be out of touch with the publics they serve. Appointed political administrators apply their skills to the job at hand in ways that are different than the public and their elected legislators would have them do so; they are less sensitive to the public interest and individual rights than the public, directly or through their elected representatives, would prefer them to be.

This difference in moral focus has important implications for political science researchers. The academic community values competence, including knowledge, experience, and skill, above all things. If asked, political scientists would surely state that they believe that it is most important to conduct or purchase research that is, above all, competently conducted, informative, and skillfully presented. These are skills that can be readily learned. What is not so easily learned is research that is compassionate, caring, thoughtful, and above all, ethical. Caring, compassionate research may not be funded, and if it is, it may not reach its intended audience. It is critical, therefore, for researchers to strike a balance between the two points of view—but erring always on the side of ethics over expediency.

The Ethos of Politics

Ethics in politics functions on two dominant levels, or *ethos* (Garofalo and Geuras 1999; Woller and Patterson 1997; Goss 1996; Denhardt 1988). The term *ethos* refers to the characteristics that distinguish a particular person or group. First, workers in public agencies are faced with a professional or *bureaucratic* ethos. This has to do with the way people perform their jobs. According to Garofalo and Geuras (1999, 48), it is based "on hierarchical control and obedience to political superiors." In some ways, the ethics of politics are not much different than the ethics of any profession; the major distinguishing characteristic is the lack of a profit factor that motivates behavior in the private sector.

The second defining moral standard is the underlying belief and commitment to public service. This is the *democratic ethos*—possibly an unfortunate selection of names since it can exist in nondemocratic societies as well; a better choice might have been *service ethos*. These ideas deal with such values as liberty, justice, human rights, and equality (Garofalo and Geuras 1999). This is illustrated in Figure 4.1.

Political scientists and workers in government organizations face ethical questions in both

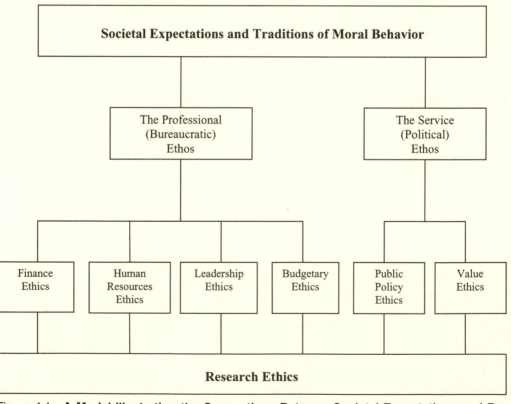

Figure 4.1   **A Model Illustrating the Connections Between Societal Expectations and Research Ethics**

of these areas of morality. For example, while maintaining a sense of fiscal responsibility and professional competence in their principle areas of administrative activity, administrators are also expected to live up to several distinctively service ethos characteristics in order to retain the public's trust. These include: (1) avoiding conflicts of interest, (2) maintaining impartiality toward the public and stakeholders with conflicting interests, (3) avoiding any appearance of impropriety, and (4) regularly submitting to public disclosure in most every detail of their existence (Petrick and Quinn 1997).

According to Ian McAllister (2000), in almost every advanced country with a democratic society, citizens' trust in their elected politicians has reached historic lows. In America, for example, voters' trust in politicians halved between the late 1950s and the early 1980s. The decline continued with airing of the White Water scandal and the alleged sexual misbehavior of President Bill Clinton. In 1994, almost two-thirds of British voters agreed with the statement that political parties favor their own financial contributors when making appointments. Moreover, in 1996, citizens' trust in government to put the nation before party was reported to have declined from 39 percent to 22 percent. Similar distrust of elected national and local politicians has recently been reported in Australia. The following partial list of attitudes of voters contrasted with opinions of elected federal officials further illustrates the difficulty. Responses are percentages of persons agreeing to a series of statements regarding federal politicians: Officials should respect the dignity and privacy of the public: voters 75 percent, officials 55 percent; political officials should use public resources economically: voters 74 percent, officials 50 percent; officials should put the public interest ahead of their personal interests: voters 73 percent, officials 59 percent; and officials should always tell the public the truth: voters 73 percent, officials 51 percent. Clearly, citizens perceive that a breakdown in the moral standards of our political leaders has taken place. If such is the case, political science researchers must take great care to ensure that they do not follow the same moral low road. Instead, researchers must always conduct their activities honestly, ethically, and legally.

The Meaning of *Research Ethics*

Research ethics refers to the application of moral standards to decisions made in planning, conducting, and reporting the results of research studies. The fundamental moral standards involved are those that focus on what is right and what is wrong. Beyond this, however, Mitchell (1998) has identified the following four practical ethical principles that shape morality in political research: *truthfulness, thoroughness, objectivity,* and *relevance.*

The *truthfulness principle* means that it is unethical for researchers to purposefully lie, deceive, or in any way employ fraud. Deliberately misrepresenting the purpose of a study, not informing subjects of the dangers of participation, hiding the identity of the sponsor of the study, or inflating or understating the findings of a research project are all examples of research that fails the truthfulness principle.

Despite the belief that truthfulness is a fundamental standard for all human endeavors, it sometimes gives way to expediency in research applications. When it does, a rationale for not telling the truth is usually provided. Some researchers believe that certain research cannot be conducted without deception of some sort. They believe that disclosing the true sponsor of a study will unnecessarily bias the findings. Researchers who use deception use two arguments to justify their actions: (1) they assume that participants will not suffer any physical or mental harm as a result of the deception, and (2) they take on the responsibility of informing the participants about the deception after the research study is completed (Zikmund 1994).

The *thoroughness principle* demands that researchers not "cut corners" in their designs. It means being "methodologically thorough" (J. Mitchell 1998, 312). It means "doing good science" by following all steps in a study. Researchers are morally obligated to include the following in the study reports:

1. Definitions for all key concepts used in the study.
2. Selection of appropriate samples or group participants, including full descriptions.
3. Identification of all limitations of the research design.
4. A description of the analysis design.

Furthermore, remaining methodologically thorough means that all results and findings are reported—good news and bad. It means guaranteeing that participants will not be physically harmed or emotionally distressed. Thoroughness is not a simple concept, however, and can cause a great deal of difficulty for a researcher. Mitchell summarized this difficulty in the following way: "In short, thoroughness is evidently at the core of methodology; the ethical problem is defining exactly what thoroughness means in the actual conduct of research" (J. Mitchell 1998, 313).

The *objectivity principle* refers to the need for the researcher to remain objective and impartial throughout all aspects of the study. The researcher should never interject his or her own personal feelings or biases into the design of a study, selection of participants, writing and/or asking questions, or interpreting results. "Doing good science" means that the researcher does not bias the study in any way. This means using probability methods to select a sample, wording questions is such a way as to avoid any hint of leading the subject to give a desired answer, and not allowing the researcher's own values to color the results.

Not all researchers believe that remaining neutral is the proper role for a researcher to take in conducting research for public organizations. Some say that it is impossible to do so. These researchers object to the positivist philosophy of science and instead purposefully place themselves as one with the study participants. These researchers typically follow a postpositivist approach and employ such methods as ethnography, case analysis, grounded theory, or action or participatory research methods.

The final ethical research principle discussed by Mitchell is *relevance*. Research should never be frivolous, or done because the researcher "has an axe to grind" and wants the study done to punish the persons or groups involved in the subject organization. According to Mitchell, in a democracy, research has a moral responsibility to be understandable to people and useful. Research that fails this test can be open to ridicule and worse. From 1975 to 1988, former Wisconsin Senator William Proxmire often used the press to disclose what he deemed to be wasteful, irrelevant, and often-childish government-funded research projects. He awarded the sponsoring government agencies his "Golden Fleece Award." An example was a $27,000 study to determine why inmates want to escape from prison (TFCS 2001).

Senator Proxmire's public ridicule of federally funded research that he called a "wasteful, ridiculous or ironic use of the taxpayers' money" should serve as a warning signal to all researchers in political science and political organizations. The phrase "if it sounds ridiculous, people will think it is" applies to all research. Kumar (1996, 192) has summarized the need for relevance in the following way: "[If] you cannot justify the relevance of the research you are conducting, you are wasting your respondents' time, which is unethical."

Hardwig (1991) has made the valid point that today teams of scientists conduct most research. The body of knowledge in most disciplines has grown so great and is evolving so rapidly that it has become increasingly difficult for any one investigator to have a complete grasp of everything going on in his or her discipline. This fact has contributed to the potential for scientific fraud. Although Hardwig was talking about research in the natural sciences, the following message applies equally to political science researchers as well:

> [R]esearch is increasingly done by teams because no one knows enough to be able to do the experiment by herself. Increasingly, no one could know enough—sheer limitations of intellect prohibit it. The cooperation of researchers from different specializations and the resulting division of cognitive labor are, consequently, often unavoidable if an experiment (or a field study) is to be done at all. . . . Specialization and teamwork are thus inescapable features of much modern knowledge acquisition. (Hardwig 1991, 695–6)

Hardwig went on to emphasize that the changing nature of research—from the idealized picture of the lone crusading investigator laboring away in an isolated laboratory to the realistic scene of a cooperative effort often involving many investigators working in different research sites around the globe but in instant electronic communication with one another—must not permit "defecting in the knowledge game—in other words, not cheating by fudging, fabricating, or otherwise publishing unreliable results."

Research with Human Subjects

The acceptance of ethical standards as a guiding principle for all human subjects research is based upon decisions made during the Nuremberg Military Tribunal on Nazi war crimes held after the end of World War II. The standards that emerged from those trials resulted in adoption of what is known as the *Nuremberg Code* (Neuman 2000; Neef, Iwata, and Page 1986). Although originally applied to medical experiments only, the principles in the Code are today used in all research that involves human subjects, including the research employed in political science. Included in the code are the following principles:

1. The requirement for informed, voluntary consent.
2. No unnecessary physical or mental suffering.
3. No experiments where death or disabling is likely.
4. Ending the research if continuation will cause injury or death.
5. Experiments should only be conducted by highly qualified researchers.
6. Results should be for the good of society and unattainable by any other method.

An example of a Human Subjects Research Application for use at the Evergreen State College in Olympia, Washington is included in Figures 4.2 through 4.4. Figure 4.2 describes the policy and its history; Figure 4.3 is the form required for all research involving human subjects; Figure 4.4 is an example of a human subjects review committee application form. The following instructions are included with consent forms distributed with each human subjects research application:

The Evergreen State College
USE OF HUMAN SUBJECTS

Background. The Human Subjects Review policy at Evergreen took effect in January 1979 to protect the rights of humans who are participants in research activities. If you are conducting a study using information from people or if you are recording them is some way for that study, you must complete this application with the collaboration of your faculty sponsor.

General Principles. All students, staff, and faculty conducting research at the college which involves the participation of humans as subjects of research must ensure that participation is **voluntary,** that **risks are minimal,** and that the **distribution of your study is limited.** All potential physical, psychological, emotional, and social risks should be considered, and explained to the participants in the study. This explanation must be clear, in letter form, and accompanied by a written consent form, which the participants sign. Similarly, the researcher must explain the benefits to the participant, the course of study, and intellectual inquiry. Participants must not be asked to expose themselves to risk unless the benefits to the participants or society are commensurate.

Please note that in most cases, keeping the participants' names confidential significantly minimizes risk.

Figure 4.2   **Background and Requirements for Human Subjects Review Form**
Source: TESC, used with permission.

- Prepare an abstract of your research project by summarizing the nature and purpose of your research.
- List the procedures to which humans will be subjected, i.e., questionnaires, interviews, audio or video recordings, etc. Explain when, where, and how these procedures will be carried out. In the case of questionnaires or interviews, please attach a copy of the questions you will be asking.
- Explain how subjects will be recruited for the proposed work, including your recruitment criteria and procedures.
- List the possible risks to the human subjects. Outline precautions that will be taken to minimize these risks, including methods to ensure confidentiality or obtaining a release to use attribute material. NOTE: The concept of risk goes beyond obvious physical risk. It could include risk to the subject's dignity and self-respect, as well as emotional, psychological, and behavioral risk. Risk could also include a potential for jeopardizing one's employment or standing in an academic program.
- List specific benefits to be gained by completing the project, which may be at an individual, institutional, or societal level.
- Describe how the information gained from this study is to be used, to whom the information is to be distributed, and how promise of confidentiality, if made, will be carried out in the final project.
- Prepare an Informed Consent Affidavit and a cover letter.

SAMPLE INFORMED CONSENT AFFIDAVIT
The Evergreen State College

I, _____, hereby agree to serve as a subject in the research project entitled _____. It has been explained to me that the purpose of this study is _____ and that the proposed use for the research obtained, now and in the future, is _____. I understand that the possible risks to me associated with this study are:

_____.

Medical treatment and/or compensations is _____ / is not _____ available for projects presenting physical risks; if available, treatment or compensation consists of _____.
I may not receive any direct benefit from participation in this study, but my participation may help

_____.
_____ has offered to answer any questions I may have about the study and provide me with access to the final report or presentation.

I understand that the person to contact in the event I experience problems as a result of my participation is _____ at _____.

I hereby agree to participate as a subject in the above-described research project. I understand that my participation in the project is voluntary, that I am free to withdraw from participation at any time, and that my choice of whether or not to participate in this project will not jeopardize my relationship with the Evergreen State College. I have read, understood, and agree to the foregoing.

Participant's Signature: _____ Date: _____

Parents' Signature, (required if subject is a minor): _____

Figure 4.3 **Sample Informed Consent Form**
Source: TESC, used with permission.

Applying Ethics in the Research Process

Political science researchers are most concerned with ethics at four times in the research process: (1) when they are planning to gather data, (2) while they are gathering data, (3) when they are processing and interpreting data, and (4) when they are disseminating the results of their research. The interrelated nature of these four situations is displayed in Figure 4.5.

Ethics When Planning Research

A key activity in planning a research project is deciding who will be the participants in the study. Use of the proper sampling design is a critical decision factor in planning a design. In all designs, special care must be taken to ensure that participants voluntarily agree to participate, that their privacy is protected, and that they are not physically or mentally harmed in any way.

When researchers follow a positivist (or quantitative) research approach, they often use the information gathered from a representative *sample* drawn from a larger *population* to imply or infer that the results apply to the larger body as well. Samples can be one of two basic types (with many variations): *probability* or *nonprobability.* Both have a place in research, but they

---

Human Subject Review Application
Please return this application to:

The Evergreen State College, Olympia WA 98505
The Evergreen State College (Revised Application 1/12/00)

Research Project Title: _____

Name of Project Director(s): _____

Mailing Address or Mailstop: _____

Phone Number: _____

Proposed Project Dates: _____

Date Application Submitted: _____

Immediate Supervisor, Faculty Sponsor, or Dean: _____

Funding agency/research sponsor (if applicable): _____

INDICATE IF THE PROJECT INVOLVES ANY OF THE FOLLOWING:

___ Minors   ___ Pregnant Women   ___ Developmentally disabled
___ Prisoners   ___ Abortuses   ___ Random sample
___ New drugs   ___ Fetuses   ___ A cooperating institution

Certification: We understand that the policies and procedures of the Evergreen State College apply to all research activities involving human subjects which are being performed by persons associated with the college and, therefore, that these activities cannot be initiated without prior review and approval by the appropriate academic dean and, as required, by the Human Subjects Review Board.

X _____
Signature of the Project Director   *Date*

X _____
Signature of the Supervisor or Project Coordinator   *Date*

Figure 4.4 **Sample Application for Human Subjects Review Board Approval**
Source: TESC, used with permission.

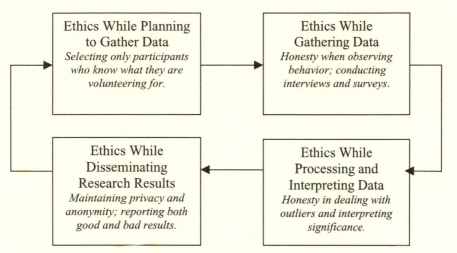

Figure 4.5   **The All-Pervasive Nature of Ethics in Research**

are not interchangeable. In a probability sample, all participants have an equal or known chance at being selected for the study. This is not the case with a nonprobability sample, where participants are usually selected for the convenience of the researcher or simply to fill a quota. Therefore, the results of a nonprobability sample study should not be used for inference; it is unethical to do so.

Sampling is also used in some postpositivist or interpretive designs, although typically not for inferential purposes. In case studies, for example, the sample might be a single person, some or all members of a group or organization, or from two or more groups or organizations. Thus, the sample ethics question may not be as critical; case study results are traditionally not used to extend the results to entire populations but, instead, to be a description of the case itself. The following six questions must be answered before involving a subject in a study; they must be addressed in the planning stage of the project.

1. Has the participant given his or her *informed consent* to be included in the study?
2. Has the subject *voluntarily agreed* to participate, or has some form of coercion been used to force the subject's participation?
3. Has the subject been *fully informed* of the right not to participate, and of any risks and/or benefits that might accrue from the study?
4. Will the subject be *harmed, either physically or mentally,* in any way as a result of participation in the study?
5. Is it necessary to use *deception,* to disguise the research, or to use covert research methods in order to collect the data?
6. Will a jury of external professional peers *validate* the study?

Informed Consent. The idea of "informed consent" is based upon Western society's ideas of individual freedom and self-determination, as spelled out in the body of common law (Neef, Iwata, and Page 1986). A person's right to be free from intrusion by others is supported by a number of court decisions, among which was the 1973 *Roe v. Wade* decision. From this and other court actions, the following components of the "Informed Consent" concept have been of particular interest:

- The capacity of the person to consent to participation,
- The free and voluntary giving of consent, and
- Consent that is informed and knowledgeable.

Courts have held that the capacity to consent requires that the person giving consent knowingly and rationally understand the nature of the experiment or study, any associated risk, and other relevant information. At the same time, researchers are not permitted to decide whether the subject is competent enough to make the decision; all people retain the right to manage their own affairs. In research involving children, parents have traditionally been allowed to give consent on their behalf, but Neef et al. (1986) noted that the courts have not always accepted that as a right. Therefore, researchers are advised to acquire the consent of the parents and the child, as well as that of relevant organizations (such as schools).

Voluntary Consent. There are two aspects to the concept of voluntary consent. First, the agreement must be entirely free of any coercion. Second, the subject must understand that the consent can be withdrawn at any time without any harmful consequence (Neef et al. 1986). Often, academic researchers use the students in their classes as participants in research studies. Students are not required to do so, and must know that their performance in the class will not suffer as a result of their not participating.

Knowledgeable Consent. All potential research participants must be made aware of all aspects of the study. This means that they must be told of their rights: (1) to not participate, (2) that they can withdraw at any time, (3) what risks might be involved, and (4) the potential benefits of the study, if any. If the study is an experiment, they must also know the risks and benefits of any alternative treatments.

Freedom from Harm. A fundamental ethical principle that must be followed in all research studies is that no harm shall fall on the participants as a result of their participation in the research. *Harm* is broadly defined; for example, it can mean physical, cultural, social, or psychological distress as well as physical pain (Neuman 2000; Oppenheim 1992).

Ethics When Gathering Data

Kumar (1996) identified five key points in the research when an ethical concern for respondents is particularly important: (1) when seeking consent from the subject, (2) when providing incentives to participate, if any, (3) when seeking sensitive information or information that might embarrass or otherwise cause discomfort to the subject, (4) when there is a possibility of causing harm, and (5) while maintaining confidentiality for the respondent.

Data-gathering methods used most often in political science research include observation, interviewing, and survey questionnaires. Which subjects to include in a research study and which to exclude is also affected by which of these methods are chosen. For example, personal interviews may take as long as two or more hours to complete. As a result, sample sizes may be quite small; researchers must be very selective in their choice of participants. However, if the design calls for use of a self-administered questionnaire, it is often relatively easy to add more subjects to the mailing list.

A number of ethical issues come into play when conducting interviews or writing questionnaires. The ethics of data gathering in all forms continue to raise controversial questions among researchers (Oppenheim 1992). The two problems that cause most difficulty are the potential for *bias* on the part of the interviewer or in the wording of the question, and the *response distortion* that such biases can cause. Most researchers concede that it is impossible to eliminate all interviewer bias; conscientious training of interviewers is the only way to reduce it.

Ethics in Processing and Interpreting Data

Researchers are sometimes asked to design and conduct a research study and analyze the collected data in order to provide "scientific credence" to pre-established conclusions. Other researchers have been asked to compromise their ethical standards as a condition for receiving a contract to conduct research. Both of these situations present ethical dilemmas. The researcher has three options in these situations (Neuman 2000): (1) The researcher may feel that loyalty to an employer or group overrides any ethical considerations and quietly go along with the request. (2) He or she may publicly oppose the request, making the opposition a part of the public record. This places the researcher in the role of a *whistleblower*, and may result in loss of credibility in the agency, elimination of future research opportunities, or even loss of a job. (3) He or she can simply refuse to make compromises and walk away from the request, aware that another researcher may be found to do the work.

Making the "right" moral decision in such situations is not an easy choice. Opting for the first path may not only cause the researcher undue personal stress, it may also open the door to criminal prosecution. On the other hand, refusing to go along with the request opens the researcher to accusations of disloyalty to the organization and disregard for the well-being of fellow workers.

Ethicists often encourage selecting the path of becoming a whistleblower; it is clearly the "most moral" of the three options. However, whistleblowers are seldom rewarded for their willingness to publicize unethical activity. The whistleblower must be in a position to prove his or her allegations in a court of law, where deliberations may take years to complete. In the intervening time, the whistleblower is often ostracized by fellow workers, removed from any meaningful work in the organization, eliminated from potential promotion, and ultimately forced to suffer loss of a job. The popular press has aired many reports of whistleblowers who have not only lost their job, but their home and other possessions as well. It takes a brave person to adopt this role; thankfully, many are still willing to do so.

Refusing to do the study may be the easiest way out of the dilemma. If morality can exist on a continuum, this path is less immoral than going along with the request and less moral than publicly disclosing the request. This does not mean to imply that it is an easy solution. Choosing to not do the research may mean loss of income or professional standing. On the other hand, complying with the request because someone else will do it anyway is never an acceptable justification. Neuman (2000, 103), discussing the conflict that often appears in such situations, concluded with the following statement: "Whatever the situation, unethical behavior is never justified by the argument that 'If I didn't do it, someone else would have.' "

Ethics in Disseminating Research Results

Researchers are faced with two broad classes of ethical considerations when disseminating their findings. First, ethical considerations come into play with the distribution and/or publication of the findings. Second, researchers have the moral obligation to protect the privacy of the participants in the research.

Researchers must consider several factors when communicating the results of their research. These include: (1) telling the entire story rather than just a few significant portions, (2) presenting insignificant, adverse, or negative findings, (3) and contributing to the general storehouse of disciplinary knowledge. Telling the entire story relates to the idea of methodological completeness discussed earlier. The obligation to include findings that reflect negatively on the sponsoring agency, the research method, or the researchers themselves, is based on the ethical standard of honesty. Telling only part of the truth is little different than not telling the truth at all. Contributing to knowledge in the field refers to the researcher's obligation to the ethos of the profession, both as administrators and as researchers. In addition to the ethical obligation to be truthful when preparing the research report, the researcher must also protect the rights of participants. Three participant ethical issues are of particular importance when disseminating the results of a research study. These are (1) protecting the privacy of participants, (2) ensuring the anonymity of participants, and (3) respecting the confidentiality of individuals involved in the study.

Protecting participants' privacy is a fundamental moral standard as well as a legal requirement affecting all researchers. While this is primarily a concern during the sample selection and data-gathering steps, the researcher must take great care to ensure that participants' identity cannot be deciphered from the findings. Participants must know that their privacy will not be invaded as a result of dissemination of the findings.

Ensuring the anonymity of participants is closely related to the privacy standard, except that it is primarily a concern during the preparation of the findings stage. An integral part of every study is, or should be, a description of the sample participants. This description should always be done in the aggregate, focusing on characteristics of the group, such as measures of central tendency, variation, and the like. The results of any single participant should never be made known, except in interpretive studies, which can focus on a single case. The confidentiality standard means that no one other than the primary researcher should know sample members' names and addresses. A single list must be kept by the researcher.

Researchers also have a moral obligation to avoid reporting incomplete research results, issuing misleading reports, and issuing biased reports (Malhotra 1999). Incomplete reports are more likely to be disseminated when the researcher uncovers adverse or negative information. Misleading results are released to intentionally mislead an audience, even if they are not an actual lie. For example, say that more than 90 percent of the citizens of a community prefer that a ten-acre parcel at the edge of town be left undeveloped, five percent want a new shopping center, three percent want an industrial park on the site, and two percent want it developed as a park with softball and soccer fields. It is unethical for the city planning commission to announce that more of the citizens prefer a shopping center to any other development scheme for the parcel without also saying that 90 percent want no development at the site. It is misleading not because it is false, but because it does not give all the facts: most citizens have no preference. It is equally misleading to simply say that by a margin of nearly two to one, citizens prefer a shopping center to a park on the site.

Biased research is often conducted to provide justification for a preconceived result or solution. It also occurs when researchers do not follow the required steps in a research process. It happens when the problem is incorrectly defined, the questionnaire is not pretested, or questions are written to almost force respondents to answer in a particular way. Bias can also occur when respondents are asked questions that they are unable to answer.

Finally, ethical decisions during dissemination of research findings arise with questions regarding disclosure of the limitations of the study. The sponsoring agency, respondents, and the recipients of the research report are justified in their right to know how much credence they can give to the findings.

Summary

The potential for unethical behavior is a universal problem; it affects academic political scientists and those working as administrators at all levels of government and nongovernment organizations. Political scientists, elected officials, public administrators, and the popular press have called for moral reform, passage of ethics laws and codes, and greater education and training in ethical behavior for everyone involved in science and in politics. These have been directed at every level of government, from the Office of the President of the United States to the smallest local special-service district.

Ethics, a branch of philosophy, is the study of the *moral* behavior of humans in society. *Morality* refers to the standards that people have about what is right, what is wrong, what is good, or what is evil. *Moral behavior* is acting in ways that follow the moral standards that exist in society. *Moral standards* are the rules by which a society functions. Moral standards have evolved from a number of different philosophical traditions.

Today, at least five different ways to approach an ethical situation have evolved from these earliest guidelines for moral behavior. These include: *utilitarian, rights, justice, caring, and virtue ethics.* Researchers draw upon these traditions when faced with ethical dilemmas. No one approach is more correct than any other. For example, because no one comprehensive moral theory is capable of stating exactly when a utilitarian consideration should take precedence over, say a right, a standard of justice, or the need for caring, the political science researcher is forced to "follow his or her conscience."

Ethics in political science functions on two dominant levels or *ethos.* First, researchers are faced with a professional or *bureaucratic* ethos. The second defining moral standard is the underlying belief and the commitment to public service. This is the *democratic ethos*—possibly an unfortunate selection of names since it can exist in nondemocratic societies as well; a better choice might have been *service ethos.* These ideas deal with such values as liberty, justice, human rights, and equality.

Research ethics refers to the application of moral standards to decisions made in planning, conducting, and reporting the results of research studies. The fundamental moral standards involved are those that focus on what is right and what is wrong. Four additional practical ethical principles shape morality in political science research: *truthfulness, thoroughness, objectivity,* and *relevance.*

Although originally applied to medical experiments only, the principles spelled out in the Nuremberg Code are today used in all research that involves human subjects. The key clauses of the Code deal with rules for ensuring that participants have the right to not participate, that they are informed of all risks, and that they will not be intentionally physically or mentally harmed.

Political science researchers are particularly concerned with ethics at four times in the research process: (1) when they are planning to gather data, (2) while they are gathering data, (3) when they are processing and interpreting data, and (4) when they are disseminating the results of their research.

Discussion Questions

1. In your own words, define what is meant by the term "ethics."
2. What are the different sources of our moral standards?
3. What are some of the reasons why the public has lost faith in the morality practiced by elected politicians?
4. Discuss in some detail your opinion on whether it is possible to discern an ethical tradition specifically for political science.
5. Four practical ethical principles that shape morality in political research are *truthfulness, thoroughness, objectivity,* and *relevance.* Describe how you will apply these principles in conducting research.
6. Distinguish between a *political ethos* and a *bureaucratic ethos.*
7. Discuss the major factors included in the international code for conducting research with human subjects.
8. How would you incorporate protection for the human subjects in your research on the politics of AIDS research?
9. Does asking people how they voted in the last election merit including provision for the protection of human subjects? Why or why not?

Additional Reading

Cooper, Terry L. 1998. *The Responsible Administrator: An Approach to Ethics for the Administrative Role.* 4th ed. San Francisco: Jossey-Bass.
de Laine, Marlene. 2000. *Fieldwork, Participation and Practice: Ethics and Dilemmas in Qualitative Research.* London: Sage.
Elliott, Deni, and Judy E. Stern, eds. 1997. *Research Ethics.* Hanover, NH: University Press of New England.
Garofalo, Charles, and Dean Geuras, 1999. *Ethics in the Public Sector: The Moral Mind at Work.* Washington, DC: Georgetown University Press.
Joseph, Sarah, Jenny Schultz, and Melissa Castan. 2000. *The International Covenant on Civil and Political Rights.* Oxford: Oxford University Press.
Rohr, John A. 1998. *Public Service, Ethics and Constitutional Practice.* Lawrence: University Press of Kansas.

5 Understanding the Research Process

All research activity takes place in a logical sequence of steps or stages. McDowell (2002), perhaps taking this concept to the extreme, identified a process for historical research that involves as many as twenty distinct steps. Regardless of how many steps are identified, most researchers would probably agree that research involves at a minimum the following distinct activities. First, someone is faced with a problem circumstance, question, event, or situation (a *study problem* is identified). Second, someone then designs a method of collecting information that promises effective resolution of the problem or question *(planning a research strategy)*. Third, information is then collected (*a data-gathering* activity); sometimes this means collecting quantitative data; at other times, qualitative data are collected. Fourth, once the information is collected, its meaning must be found (*data processing, analysis,* and *interpretation*). Finally, all the pieces must be put together in a report of the research findings—either written or oral or both—that either helps establish resolution of the problem or identifies a need for additional research. *How* these activities are put together is the subject matter of this and the remaining chapters. Together, the parts make up the whole that constitutes *the systematic process of research strategy and methods.* This chapter examines that process by explaining each of the steps in detail. The process has been compressed in order to be relevant for all types of research approaches. Research in political science takes many forms and approaches, and other authors may suggest a different process. However, if all the steps in the process presented here are followed, most researchers will successfully complete their projects.

There are few limits to the variety of choices of study questions, research strategies, data collection methods, data-processing, and evaluation approaches. There are also many different ways of interpreting the results. It is possible to put these together in many different combinations—no one of which is inherently more correct than another. Today, these different combinations are all seen as valid research strategies. Their selection and application is based upon the nature of the study question, the objectives for the study, the level of skill of the researcher, and his or her comfort with the research methods that are most appropriate for the objectives of the research.

Steps in the Research Process

Today, both quantitative and qualitative research strategies are considered to be legitimate designs for research in public administration and the other social and administrative sciences;

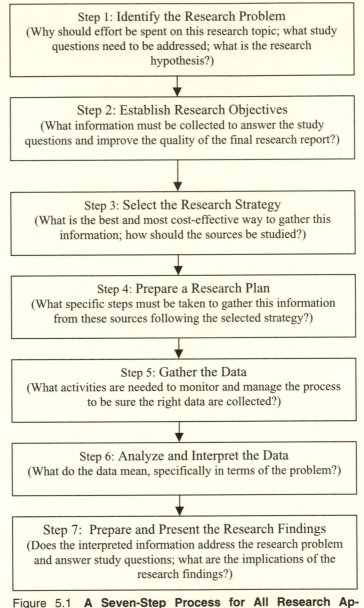

Step 1: Identify the Research Problem
(Why should effort be spent on this research topic; what study questions need to be addressed; what is the research hypothesis?)

Step 2: Establish Research Objectives
(What information must be collected to answer the study questions and improve the quality of the final research report?)

Step 3: Select the Research Strategy
(What is the best and most cost-effective way to gather this information; how should the sources be studied?)

Step 4: Prepare a Research Plan
(What specific steps must be taken to gather this information from these sources following the selected strategy?)

Step 5: Gather the Data
(What activities are needed to monitor and manage the process to be sure the right data are collected?)

Step 6: Analyze and Interpret the Data
(What do the data mean, specifically in terms of the problem?)

Step 7: Prepare and Present the Research Findings
(Does the interpreted information address the research problem and answer study questions; what are the implications of the research findings?)

Figure 5.1 **A Seven-Step Process for All Research Approaches, with Checklist Questions**

the different designs simply serve different purposes. Whichever approach is taken, all research takes place in a series of activities similar to the seven-step process shown in Figure 5.1.

This seven-step process has been used to guide research activities in the social, administrative, and natural sciences. The steps begin with identifying the research problem and proceed through establishing objectives and strategy, planning and collecting data, and analyzing and reporting the findings. The process is a composite of quantitative and qualitative methodologies.

Frankfort-Nachmias and Nachmias (1996, 20) suggested a model for social science research that closely follows the traditional plan for quantitative studies. Their model begins with identifying the problem, then goes on to include the writing of hypotheses, research design, measurement, data collection, data analysis, and generalization. Qualitative research process models vary with the methods employed. Among the methods used most often in the social sciences are participant observation, in-depth personal interviews, key informant and focus group interviews, case studies, and similar designs (Devine 2002). Each of these methods begins with identifying a research problem, and all include stating a goal for the study and planning the remaining elements, including data collection.

Step 1. Identifying the Research Problem

The first step in research is to clearly and succinctly *identify the research problem*. Frankfort-Nachmias and Nachmias (1996, 52) defined the research problem as "an intellectual stimulus calling for a response in the form of scientific inquiry;" they added that the problem is typically described in a set of concepts that have been identified or selected by the researcher. The problem concepts are, in turn, the *variables* evaluated in the study.

The label "study problem" is not always used to describe this initial activity in the research process. In the social sciences, it is often replaced with the phrase *defining the study question*. Other authors referred to it as a process of establishing a *rationale for the study*. The "question" has also been called the *research topic,* the *research situation,* the *information need,* and other things. The labels all mean the same: establishing a reason for expending the time and effort required to complete a research project before starting the process. Researchers agree that clearly identifying the study problem is among the most important steps in the entire research process (Berg 1998). If defining the study problem is not done correctly, it is likely that the remaining activities will be a waste of the time and labor of the researcher. Data will have been gathered, but the reason and meaning of that data will be lost. There are usually no simple answers to study questions; instead, each involves many subcomponents and antecedent factors.

The research problem often consists of two key components. It is important to not confuse one with the other. The first is a statement of the problem as it is seen by the researcher; the second is the set of research questions that will be addressed in the study. The following is an example of problem statement:

> This research examines some reasons why the governments and voter publics of the three Baltic States—Estonia, Latvia, and Lithuania—have different expectations of benefits and costs resulting from possible membership in the European Union. (Berg 1998, 23)

The research questions associated with this study problem might include the following:

- What are the cost and benefit expectations of each government?
- How have citizens in each country voted on European Union (EU) membership in the past?
- What changes have occurred in public opinion about EU membership?

- Which groups in each country support membership, and which oppose it?
- What conditions has the European Union made a price of EU membership?

Some of the key activities involved in the process of identifying the study problem include: (1) determining the unit of analysis for the study, (2) finding out what other researchers have discovered and reported about the issue, (3) identifying relevant concepts that are functions of the problem, and (4) translating the concepts into variables that can be stated in hypotheses and tested. The unit of analysis refers to the most basic, complete component part of the study concepts that can be investigated. The unit of analysis selected will affect the final research design, the data collection process selected, and the way the data are analyzed. A review of the literature will reveal what other researchers have discovered and help identify relevant concepts. Conducting a series of key informant interviews may also bring key concepts to light. The researcher or research team must translate these into study questions.

Key concepts that collectively constitute the study question may be determined by interpretive analysis of exploratory interview data or by conducting a small-sample pilot study—both of which should be augmented by a study of the problem as it has been experienced and examined by other investigators. Exploratory activities include conducting intensive interviews with persons with some knowledge of the problem; these persons are sometimes referred to as *key informants,* and the activity is known as *conducting key informant interviews*. A second way to identify potential concepts that influence the problem is by testing a preliminary data-gathering instrument on a small subsample of participants. Analysis of these findings will often reveal the underlying structure of the problem, including the concepts that frame the issues. Finally, research designs should always include a thorough reading of what other investigators have discovered. In the language of scientific research, this process is called a *literature review*. It is absolutely critical that the literature search be more than a simple spin through items found on the Internet. Certainly, electronic data sources are important, but they must be augmented with other sources. Examples of other sources include archival data, artifacts, symbols, historical narratives, and many other published and unpublished documents.

Conducting a Literature Review

An important part of the early development of a research project is carrying out a comprehensive *review* of the published literature on the topic. This examination of prior research on the topic is important for several fundamental reasons. First, it helps to define and delimit the study problem. Second, a review of the literature may reveal previous research that clearly answers the problem, thereby making further effort superfluous. It typically involves reading and analyzing material in published books, professional and academic journals, and government documents, among other sources.

The focus of the literature review should always be on the key ideas that may function as leads for further investigation. The literature typically builds on the work already done by other investigators, often including the authors of that work in the list of references. These references, in turn, become important contributors to the design of an appropriate research project. Previous investigators have often stated and tested some meaningful and enlightening hypotheses about the topic—very little in social science is really "new." The task of the research is to gather these previously published ideas, to evaluate their usefulness as they relate specifically to your research, and to determine whether they suggest new ways of looking at the problem that might have been missed (Selltiz, Wrightman, and Cook 1976).

Identifying Variables and Writing Hypotheses

The term *variable* is used to identify the characteristics or properties of the concepts that are to be studied. In a quantitative research design, variables must have two or more *values*—also known as *levels*. The characteristic must be able to take on any one of the values, and typically varies from subject to subject. The variation can be in quantity or in quality. For example, political party affiliations may have as many values as there are recognized parties. In U.S. presidential elections, the two traditional values of the variable *party* are Democrat and Republican. Periodically, third parties attempt to gain voter recognition, but as yet have not unseated the traditional two parties, despite millions of dollars in campaign spending. *Social class* is another variable often seen in social science research; traditionally, it has five levels: lower, lower middle, middle, upper middle, and upper (Frankfort-Nachmias and Nachmias 1996). The variable *gender* is what is known as a *dichotomous* variable, because it has just two possible classes: male or female. Other kinds of variables include the following:

- *Multichotomous:* A multichotomous variable provides a selection of more than two possible answers from which to choose. An example includes *multiple choice* questions (only one answer is correct). A question type that has a similar appearance, but one that is not multichotomous, is a list of items from which respondents may select more than one—these are called "check all that apply" questions. They are dichotomous rather than multichotomous in that the only possible coding for such responses is checked–not checked. In this sense, then, each item on the list is an individual variable with two values.
- *Continuous:* Continuous variables are not restricted to specific categories and can take almost any value within an upper and lower limit. Age in years; income in dollars, height in inches and fractions of inches, air pressure in pounds per square inch: these are all examples of continuous variables.
- *Discrete:* Also known as *categorical* variables, discrete variables are restricted to only a set number of possible values; discrete variables also have a minimum-sized unit. An example is the number of family members living in the same household.
- *Control:* Control variables are used in experiments in order to test the possibility that a relationship between two variables might be explained only in the presence of another variable. For example, to test whether gender influences party affiliation, control variables might include social class, education, occupation, or income.
- *Dependent:* Dependent variables are the variables that the researcher is attempting to explain. An example might be voting behavior.
- *Independent:* Independent variables are the variables that "cause" a change in the dependent variable. Causality is very difficult to prove in social and political research, however, so rather than "cause," researchers usually use the word "explain" instead.

Step 2. Establishing Research Objectives

Step Two in the research process is spelling out in advance and in detail what is to be accomplished by the research. These are the *objectives* for the study. This step is closely allied to the first step, identifying the research problem. Both address the reasons for doing the research. At this stage, however, the objectives may still be tentative; a final set of objectives may not emerge until after a review of the literature pertaining to the study question has been completed.

The research problem is a statement of the reason for doing the research; research objectives are statements of what the researcher wants the study to accomplish. Say, for example, that an appointed advisor to the State Governor manages a statewide program to collect ideas on ways to improve high-school students' awareness of the prevention of sexually transmitted diseases. The political advisor believes it is important to begin the study with a research project to identify students' current attitudes and awareness. A study question might be how to determine the best way to accomplish this task. Specific research objectives might include determining the students' current level of awareness of the diseases, their cause, spread, and methods of prevention. A second objective might be to determine where the students received their information. Another might be to establish their preferred medium of communication and its ability to effectively convey persuasive messages. And another might be to measure local public opinion about the plan in general. Finally, the researcher will also want to know who makes up the population at greatest risk so that in selecting the sample to study, the appropriate subjects are included.

Step 3. Deciding on a Research Strategy

Step Three of the research process is deciding on the research strategy that (1) provides the most cost-effective way of gathering the needed information, and (2) produces the best possible answers for the research or study questions. A partial list of the positivist and postpositivist strategies followed by political scientists today include institutionalism, behavioralism, and rational choice theory among the positivist approaches, and the feminist, Marxist, and a variety of other interpretive designs under the postpositivist umbrella. Each of these strategies provides the researcher with a wide variety of data-gathering approaches and specific methods and data-processing and analysis techniques from which to choose. Each strategy has its own advocates and critics as well, although the acrimony between the camps has become far less strident than it has been in the past. Peter John (2002, 216) described the irrationality of the disagreement between opposing schools of political science research methodology in the following way: "The current debate between quantitative and qualitative research is shallow and rests on stereotypes of the research process." He went on to add that researchers were correct in choosing a method that satisfies the objectives of their research. All researchers should design research projects capable of testing hypotheses, and that also allow them to apply their skills and knowledge to conduct "exciting and imaginative pieces of work." The selection of approach and method should be based on the first two steps in the research process.

Positivist strategies typically involve sample research, quantified data such as mathematical models and correlation and regression analysis, time-series, and other methods calling for statistical analysis. Postpositivist strategies may employ ethnographic methods common in anthropology, participant observation methods used in sociology, hermeneutic and symbiotic methods used in historical and literary approaches, or in-depth personal and focus group interviews found in psychological investigations. The key, of course, is to match the correct methods with the specified strategy.

Step 4. Preparing a Research Plan and a Research Proposal

The first three steps in the research process might legitimately be considered *preresearch activities.* The logical outcome of these first steps should be a detailed research proposal for achieving the research objectives, collecting and analyzing the data, and writing and presenting a comprehensive report of the research findings proposal. For this, the fourth step in the research process, the researcher begins by preparing a comprehensive *plan* that details each subsequent research activity. This means identifying in advance the research subjects or sample, the methods for gathering and processing data, and a time line for completing the project. Thus, designing an effective research plan requires decisions on (1) the data sources, (2) the research approaches, (3) the data-gathering instruments, (4) a sampling plan, and (5) methods of contacting study subjects. Each of these steps will be discussed in detail in subsequent chapters. Data sources are diverse and range from polling individual respondents in election night voting-booth-exit interviews, to archival data describing events leading up to the eighteenth-century French and Indian War on the American frontier of the time.

Step 5. Gathering the Research Data

Step Five is an action step; it involves gathering the data needed for meeting the study objectives and answering the study question. Depending upon the research strategy selected, data may be gathered by such activities as: (1) participating in a social situation and recording the findings, (2) overtly or covertly observing the behavior of subjects, (3) interviewing subjects one at a time or in groups, (4) administering a questionnaire to survey the attitudes of a sample of voters, (5) or reviewing documents of other information sources, among others.

The researcher may gather primary data, secondary data, or both. These data can come from internal sources, external sources, or both. A classification of data sources is displayed in Table 5.1. *Primary data* are original data that the researcher gathers from original sources. Examples of primary data include responses to a questionnaire, an interview, or some other type of measurement.

Secondary data are data that have been collected by someone else for another purpose. Examples of secondary data include government statistical reports, articles in professional journals, and city or agency records. Neither data type is inherently better than the other, but care must always be taken in the interpretation of secondary data to ensure that it meets the specific research objectives.

Researchers employ various tools in the data collection process. Examples include survey questionnaires, interview discussion guides, tape recorders, video cameras, and other recording devices. When the data are the behavior of individuals, simple paper-and-pencil recording is common. In such instance, the data collection process includes applying order and structure to the dataset. Researchers try various coding schemes and grouping categories of like phenomena.

Step 6. Analyzing and Interpreting the Data

Step Six is the payoff step; it is also the activity that may be the most difficult for beginning researchers to master. Once the data are in hand, the researcher must establish some order in

Table 5.1

A Classification of Data Sources

I. Positivist Research Data Sources
  A. Primary Data Sources
    1. Field Surveys
      a. Questionnaires
      b. Attitude surveys
      c. Lifestyle surveys
    2. Field Studies
      a. Observation studies
      b. Personal interviews
      c. Focus group interviews
      d. Videotaping and audio recording
    3. Experiments
      a. Laboratory experiments
      b. Field experiments
  B. Secondary Data Sources
      a. Organization internal reports
      b. Organization invoice and/or accounts payable records
      c. Registered voter lists
      d. Vote records
      e. Production and service records
      f. Human resource records
II. Postpositvist Research Data Sources
  A. Existing Documents
      a. Books, periodicals, published reports, films, unpublished literature
      b. Local, state, and federal government documents
      c. Professional association papers and reports
      d. College and university documents
      e. Consultants' research reports
      f. Meeting minutes
      g. Commercial databases
      h. Other
  B. Internal records
      a. E-mail
      b. Memoranda
      c. Policy papers
      d. Reports and other documents
  C. External Sources
      a. Interviews
      b. Life histories
      c. Case studies
      d. Observation and participant observation

the data, and determine their meaning and/or implications. This interpretation must be carried out so that the findings can be related to the original study question and research objectives.

Researchers are typically interested in knowing the following things about a data set. First, they want to know what is "typical" in the sample. This means getting some idea of the central values of the responses. In everyday language, they want to know what the averages are. Second, they want to know how widely individuals in the sample vary in their responses. In a legislative voting behavior study, for example, the researcher might want to know whether legislators have similar or widely diverse attitudes about a proposed law on achievement standards for primary school students.

Third, researchers want to see how subjects are distributed across the study variables. For example, is the number of people who prefer a new park for a ten-acre site the same as or greater than the number preferring a new shopping center, and those who want new single-family housing on the sites. A good way to display this type of information is to use charts or graphs showing the frequency of responses. What is the shape of the graph? Is one response category very much greater or smaller than the others?

Fourth, the analyst will want to show how the different variables relate to one another. It may be important to know, for example, that the preferences for different types of uses for the parcel seem related to certain characteristics of the population, such as age, gender, occupation, or annual income. Finally, the researcher will want to describe any differences among the two or more groups or objects. It might be important to know, for example, whether men in the sample respond differently about their preferences for the site than do women in the sample.

Tabulating Responses

The first activity in data analysis is to tabulate the responses to all items (the term "item" is used to mean the questions or categories of phenomena) in the study. In a quantitative study, this could mean counting all the answers to each question or schedule item. This count of responses is often referred to as a *frequency distribution*. Statistical software counts responses and prepares summary data for the researcher; frequency distributions and summaries are prepared for one variable at a time, producing *univariate statistics* for each variable. Counts of how many subjects answered "yes" to a question and how many answered "no" and the distribution of men and women in a sample are examples of univariate frequencies. Univariate statistics include measures of central tendency, variation, and location.

Once univariate statistical tabulations are done, the researcher then begins *bivariate* tabulations. In this process, responses to one variable are tabulated with a second variable. The information is usually presented in a table (called *crosstabulations* or "*crosstabs*" for short). For example, responses to a yes-no question are displayed broken down for men and women in the crosstabulation table displayed in Table 5.2. A bivariate crosstabulation is presented in Table 5.3.

In addition to simple counts of responses, crosstabulations can also display some summary information for each of the responses. The individual boxes with counts displayed are called *cells; rows* run across the page; and *columns* run down the page. Summary statistics include the percentage of the total represented by the number of responses in each cell, the cell's percentage of the row total, and the cell's percentage of the column. Row, column, and total percentage values are provided along the sides of the crosstabulation table. Finally, a wide variety of statistical tests for nominal, ordinal, and interval/rations data can also be produced

Table 5.2

A Simple Univariate Table, _n_ = 70

Gender	Count	Percent
Females	40	57.1
Males	30	52.9
Totals	70	100.0

Table 5.3

A Bivariate Crosstabulation Example

Political Party	Yes Responses		No Responses	
	Count	Percent	Count	Percent
Democrats	47	38.2	81	60.4
Republicans	76	61.8	53	39.6
Totals	123	100.0	134	100.0

with crosstabulation software. After analysis of relevant bivariate data, the analyst turns first to an analysis of variable correlations (hypothesis tests), and then proceeds to any of the many multivariate statistical processes needed to meet the objectives of the study.

For a qualitative study, researchers often begin the analysis by reviewing the data to establish a structural skeleton that will provide for meaningful interpretation and discussion. Analysis of qualitative data focuses on the _narrative text_ (Miles and Huberman 1984). This is often a comprehensive rewrite of the researcher's field notes, with the researcher's verbal interpretation and conclusions from the data. There are few agreed-upon styles and formats for the broad scope of qualitative analysis methods; selection is left up to the researcher, as the following suggests:

> Valid analysis requires, and is driven by, displays (i.e., narrative text and graphic presentations of qualitative research findings) that are as simultaneous as possible, are focused, and are as systematically arranged as the questions at hand demand. While such displays may sometimes be overloading, they will never be monotonous. Most important, the chances of drawing and verifying valid conclusions are very much greater. . . . The qualitative analyst has to handcraft all such data displays . . . each analyst has to invent his or her own. (Miles and Huberman 1984, 79)

Step 7. Preparing and Presenting the Research Findings

Step Seven is preparing the research report and presenting the findings. It is the final step in the process, but is second in importance only to clearly defining and focusing on a research problem/study question. The research report follows the same outline developed during the fourth step, preparation of a research plan. Some portions of the report, such as a description of the research problem, delineation of research objectives, the review of the literature, and the rationale for selecting the strategy employed, are often written as the researcher completes the earlier steps in the process.

There are many different ways to conduct a research project and many different ways of communicating the research findings. Ultimately, however, someone must sit down and write out the results of the study. These results must then be passed on to either a research team leader, a fellow researcher, members of a funding organization, or published in a brochure, report, or professional journal.

"Doing good science" means more than using good scientific methods to select the sample, gather data, and tabulate the results. It also mean interpreting what the data mean in terms of the study objectives and writing research reports that clearly and effectively communicate the findings of the research effort. Using an appropriate *style* is critical in all research writing. Style refers to the words, syntax, and punctuation that are used or not used. It includes the way these components are formed into sentences and paragraphs. It involves the structure and organization of the report, and whether it conforms to the traditions of the discipline. It also refers to the way that the author's sources are cited, identified, and credited.

As a researcher in political science, public administration, or any of the administrative or social sciences—present or future—it is important to remember that there is no one "best" writing style. Your style is your own. One or more may be more appropriate for a given discipline, but often that fact seems arbitrary. The "best style" to use in all research reports and organizational papers is writing that is *clear, concise,* and *readable.*

The processes necessary for producing a research report for the social and administrative sciences are similar to those that are used for research in chemistry, physics, biology, or any other natural science. Slightly different research, analysis, interpretation, and presentation processes are involved, however.

Following an accepted style enhances the readability of the research report, regardless of its discipline. Academicians (teachers) and practitioners (managers) are typically pressed for time. If a paper is written in a familiar format (style) it will be easier to read—and take less of the reader's time. This often results in greater acceptance of the research findings—an extremely important point for research that comes up with negative findings. This benefit alone should be a desired outcome.

Making professional writing difficult for researchers and students is the *lack of conformity* in formats required by different disciplines and their journals. The format demanded by the editors of an Academy of Management-sponsored journal, for example, will probably result in rejection of the paper by the editors of a political science, finance, accounting, or economics journal. Researchers must determine which style is used in their field, and which are unacceptable. The only thing consistent about writing styles is inconsistency!

Summary

The research activity can be defined as *the process of systematically acquiring data to answer a question or solve a problem.* Research is done to help political scientists, academics, and political consultants achieve a better understanding of how the political world works. Research *methodology* refers to the approach researchers take as they examine their study questions or problems. It includes the philosophical mind-set that researchers bring to the research activity as well as a set of procedures.

People use two types of reasoning when they come to conclusions about things: deductive reasoning and inductive reasoning. Deductive reasoning means arriving at a conclusion on the basis of something that you know, or that you assume to be true—a general principle or *law*. Inductive reasoning, on the other hand, is the logic model or paradigm normally followed in scientific research.

The research process involves seven steps, beginning with establishing what and why the research is necessary and ending with a comprehensive report of the findings that emerge from the research process. These steps are (1) identify the research problem; (2) establish research objectives; (3) decide on a research strategy; (4) prepare a research plan; (5) gather the data; (6) analyze and interpret the data; and (7) prepare and present the findings.

"Doing good research" means (1) using good scientific methods to select the sample, gather data, and tabulate the results, (2) interpreting what the data mean in terms of the study objectives, and (3) writing research reports that clearly communicate the findings of the research effort. Using an appropriate *style* is critical in all research writing. Style refers to the words, syntax, and punctuation that are used or not used. There is no one "best" writing style; your style is your own. The "best style" to use in all research reports and organizational papers is writing that is *clear, concise,* and *readable*.

Discussion Questions

1. Why is it so important to clearly define the research problem before gathering research data?
2. What is the purpose of a research proposal?
3. Give several examples of what you consider to be good research objectives.
4. What is a key informant interview?
5. What is the purpose for conducting a thorough review of the literature on the research topic?
6. What is a variable? Name four different types of variables.
7. What is a research strategy? What is a research plan?
8. Why do researchers use sample data?
9. What is the meaning of the phrase "do good science?"
10. Why is the research report so important?

Additional Reading

Babbie, Earl. 2001. *The Practice of Social Research*. 9th ed. Belmont CA: Wadsworth Thompson Learning.

Berg, Bruce L. 1998. *Qualitative Research Methods for the Social Sciences*. 2nd ed. Boston: Allyn and Bacon.

Kumar, Ranjit. 1996. *Research Methodology*. London: Sage.

Marsh, David, and Gerry Stoker. 2002. *Theory and Methods in Political Science*. Houndmills, UK: Palgrave Macmillan.

6   Focusing on a Research Topic

Beginning researchers often find themselves at the start of the research process struggling for answers to such questions as: *What shall I research? How shall I do it?* And, *once I've gathered my data, how can I make any sense of it; how can I know what it really means?* For some, simply choosing a subject to research and write about can be the most difficult part of the entire project. How political science students determine a topic to research, identify research problems, formulate study questions, and other related concerns are the subjects addressed in this chapter.

Research in political science is conducted for two very broad purposes: First, some research is to solve real problems in everyday political life; this is known as *applied, practical,* or, in the words of Catherine Hakim (2000, 4), *policy research.* Policy research is conducted in all subfields of political science except political theory. These studies are conducted to improve the way that politics works, with the unstated understanding that if we make it work better, we also make it work longer. Applied research is particularly important in the public administration subfield of political science. Much of the research in that subfield is conducted to provide information needed to make better administrative and managerial decisions. According to Hakim, policy research is concerned with "knowledge for action." As a result, it focuses on "actionable factors" or variables. The objective of this type of research can be expressed in the phrase: "It is more important to change the world than to understand it." Hakim concluded that the target audience for most policy research consists of policymakers in government, institutional decision makers, special-interest groups, managers and administrators of organizations, client groups, and similar political stakeholders.

As an example of policy research, a municipal administrator might want to discern the public's opinion about imposing a user fee for access to public parks. The administrator could conduct a public-opinion survey for this purpose before making the decision. In another example, an administrator of a program to provide financial assistance education to welfare recipients might find that the number of applicants for aid has declined precipitously in the last quarter. She would need to conduct research to find out the "cause" of the decline. In still another example, a public-health agency might conduct research to determine the most cost-effective way to communicate information about sexually transmitted diseases to teens and subteens in the central city. And, finally, another might be to help a new manager determine whether the morale, attitudes, and beliefs of the agency's personnel are affecting job satisfaction and performance. These are all examples of real research projects conducted by public-administration students for the organizations in which they were employed; they were real problems that needed real solutions.

The second type is research conducted for the purpose of advancing the body of knowledge about politics and the political world. This research is called *basic* or *pure* research. Studies of this type are called *theoretical research* (Hakim 2000). The long-term goal of social theoretical research is to build greater social science knowledge; in political science, the purpose is to produce greater knowledge and understanding of politics and the political process. It is directed at the following:

> The factors or variables considered [in theoretical research] are frequently abstract or purely theoretical constructs for which operational definitions and indicators of varying degrees of precision and validity are developed. (Hakim 2000, 4)

The methods employed in political science theoretical research are often aimed at identifying causal processes and coming up with explanations for them. Furthermore, policy research has an underlying goal of *prediction*. For this reason, political science researchers conducting policy research employ simulations, mathematical modeling, forecasting, time series studies, and other more advanced quantitative tools. The primary audience for theoretical research is other political scientists in the academic community. These fellow researchers have similar disciplinary backgrounds; they speak the same scientific language, and are familiar with the same sets of assumptions and operational definitions.

Defining the Research Topic

A key requirement for all research is beginning with a clear, concise, and thorough definition of the topic upon which the research is to be carried out (research topics are also called "study problems"). Defining the topic does not mean that answers are known before the questions are asked. Rather, it means that the researcher has a specific *goal* in mind for the research—before getting started. Having said this, it must also be said that choosing a valid research topic is hardly ever an easy process. Here are some examples:

Administrators are experiencing a decline in enrollments in programs designed to help welfare recipients gain the skills necessary for successful full-time enrollment. A recent state law mandates that all able-bodied recipients of public assistance receive aid for a maximum of five years. At the end of that period, they must be removed from the program, regardless of their employment or dependent status. The administrators of the program do not know the reason for the decline in the skill-development program, although they have some assumptions. Nor do they know what should be done to reverse the trend. Considering that people's lives are involved, making the wrong decision may be extremely costly.

Another example is the difficulties faced by law-enforcement agencies and administrators of federally mandated substance-abuse programs as they seek to halt growth in the use of controlled substances. Despite billions of dollars spent on public education and abatement programs, drug use continues to be a major problem across the nation. Demand for treatment facilities far outstrips the availability of tested and proved effective programs. Federal and state legislators, program administrators, and local law-enforcement agencies are all looking for the most effective way to apply their limited resources to deal with the problem. Each agency involved has a different mission, different information needs, and different objectives. Defining the research problem is a difficult task for every agency involved. The process of topic definition provided in Figure 6.1 may help researchers who face this often-difficult task.

Sources of Research Topics

Research topics can come from questions discovered in texts, in the professional literature, from classroom discussions, from reading the newspaper or watching a television news or talk program, and from other outside interests. Topics can also come from the life experience of the researcher. An example is the study of a hearing-impaired graduate student who learned that Native American children are more likely to have hearing problems than are children of other ethnic groups with similar socioeconomic characteristics. Determining why this is so and what can be done to alleviate the problem became the student's master's-degree program research project.

Bernard (2000, 82–83) identified the following five broad classes of research topics, based upon their relationships with various types of variables:

1. Internal conditions, which include attitudes, beliefs, values, lifestyles, and perceptions of participants in the political arena.
2. External conditions: these are primarily past, present, and predicted demographic characteristics of the political actors.
3. Behavioral characteristics: these include a wide variety of relevant behaviors, from how people vote or why they do not vote, where they get their information, with whom they communicate, how much they work and play, etc.
4. Artifacts: what Bernard described as the "physical residue" of human behavior.
5. Environmental conditions: these include the physical and social environmental characteristics—often referred to as *cultural factors*—that have some impact on the political and social world. They range from such items as the amount of rainfall and other geophysical features of a region to whether the society exists under a democratic or authoritarian regime. Working conditions, gender, and race factors are also sources of research topics that fall under this class.

While this list of topic sources may seem pedestrian in the extreme, Bernard warned researchers that they are not likely to find many, if any, "big issue" topics upon which to focus their efforts. In all of social science, there may be only four big-theory issues, not all of which may be applied to political science research. These issues include: (1) the nature-nurture problem, (2) the evolution problem, (3) the internal-external problem, and (4) the "superorganic" social facts problem. The nature-nurture problem refers to questions about the influences of inherited versus environmental factors on human behavior; the evolution problem refers to questions about how and why groups change from one kind of thing to another over time. The internal-external problem refers to questions about how behavior is influenced by values and environmental conditions; the social facts problem deals with questions of how people are influenced by social phenomena that emerge from the interaction of humans in social groups, but that are not reducible to individuals.

Sylvan Barnet made these statements about choosing a research topic: "No subject is undesirable," and "No subject is too trivial for study" (1993, 177–78). Barnet might have added: *No subject is inherently uninteresting*. It is the way subjects are researched and reported that

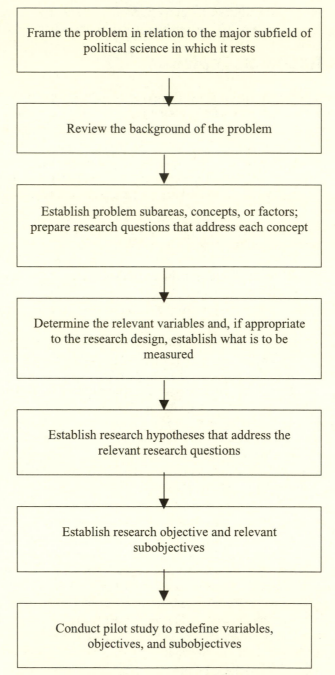

Figure 6.1   **Tasks in the Problem Definition Process**

makes them desirable or undesirable, interesting or uninteresting. Here are a few guidelines to think about when choosing a research project topic:

- Research and write about something that interests you.
- Be sure enough material about the topic is available to do a good job.
- Make sure that the topic is not so large that it is overwhelming.
- Be sure the topic fits your abilities and understanding.
- Make sure you take good notes once you start reading about the topic.
- Ask your reference librarian for guidance on your research topic.
- Run the topic by your instructor for his or her assistance.
- Focus, focus, and focus again!

Tasks in the Definition Process

The process displayed in Figure 6.1 has been designed to help researchers identify and define research topics and study problems. There are seven components in the definition process; each component is discussed is some detail below.

Task 1. Frame the Study Topic in Its Environment

The first step in the problem definition process is determining whether the proposed research project will produce information that is commensurate with the purpose, goals, and objectives of the organization, program, or agency. To do this, the researcher must frame the research problem within the broader field or subfield of political science in which it rests. For example, if the research is to be on an international relations topic, the researcher must identify the nations involved, the political history of the diplomatic relations between the nations, the past and current political and economic conditions, the point of conflict, if any, and similar important points. Moreover, the research project must be worth the effort, time, and money it will consume. The researcher must be absolutely sure of the relevance of the project; proper framing of the research question helps make this possible.

An organizational problem can usually be translated into many different types of study questions. Many of these questions may be intuitively interesting, but may also be beyond the scope of the particular research project. This does not mean that researchers should not "stretch" to increase or improve their level of awareness of their field of interests and of political science in its broadest scope, its institutions, actors, and the problems associated with political activity. It only means that they should first do what can be done. Answers to such questions as the following must be found before proceeding with the program:

- What is it specifically that I want to know?
- Who are the actors in this field of political activity, and why?
- What information do I need to improve my understanding of the topic and its underlying issues?
- Is the information I want to know readily available?
- Do I need this information for personal reasons, or is it needed for my research topic?

- Is this something I really need to know, or is it something I think I would like to know?
- Has someone else already researched this question? Am I just repeating something that has already been done?
- Could the resources necessary to complete the research be put to better use elsewhere?

Task 2. Review the Background of the Topic

Answers to such questions can often be found by conducting a thorough review of the background and published literature on the topic. Another way is to conduct a series of interviews with several key informants; these are people who have a greater than average familiarity with the problem and/or its associated antecedents or consequences.

There are two aspects to a problem's background. The first is the nature of the problem within the actors, institutions, organizations, or other entities involved in the study; this is called the *internal background.* The internal background includes the total body of knowledge on the topic that exists within the relevant topic entities. This knowledge may exist as published reports, operations records, or accounting data; it may reside in the memories of other participants or organizations. Or it may be stored in historical archives somewhere, such as the Library of Congress. Internal information is often easier to access than external sources or information. Internal data should always be the first place a researcher should look when conducting organizational research.

The second part is the body of research that already exists on the problem, its causes and cures, its extent and impact, and the way that other researchers have approached the issue. This is the *external background.* External information exists in the body of literature on the topic. Accessing this previous work is referred to as a *review of the literature.* It includes all the published and unpublished-but-available material on the question.

What to Do When Problems Appear

What happens when the researcher is unable to pinpoint a specific research problem before turning to the literature? Not surprisingly, this is often the case when students begin their research projects. The answer to the question is for the budding researcher to use the literature review to help with achieving a greater focus for the research.

It is a good idea to begin with an idea about some aspect of the general topic that seems particularly interesting. An example could be something from the student's life experience or the experiences of friends or family members. It could be an article in a newspaper or a story on a television news or opinion program. It could be something seen in a textbook or an issue discussed in a classroom. It could be a topic as broad as taxation, unemployment, the impact of technology on family life, workplace diversity, gender issues, disproportionate distribution of resources, environmental degradation, etc. All it takes is an interest in a topic.

The first step in the literature review is to examine a relevant index of articles or a library catalog. The researcher should then scan the several journal articles or books to see what parts of the broad topic are of most interest. It will not take long to go from just having a tentative interest in an unfocused topic to becoming focused on an interesting problem that can be researched. Searching the literature to break the larger problem down into subproblems can facilitate the remaining steps in the research process.

Task 3. Establish Topic Components or "Factors"

Once the researcher has settled on a problem or circumstance that requires more information, the next step is to break that broad problem into as many parts or subproblems as are feasible. Say, for example, the research problem decided upon is: "How can the level of service provided to outpatient disabled veterans be improved without raising hospital operating costs?" A partial list of some relevant subproblems of this question might be:

- The type of organization (e.g., hospital, outpatient clinic, field provider, etc.).
- Type of service patients require.
- Staffing levels.
- Queuing system in effect or not.
- Location of facility (urban, suburban, rural).
- Prescreening system.
- Attitudes of provider staff.
- Attitudes of service users.
- Expectations of service users.
- Operating costs, and others.

Normally, not all of the possible subareas can or should be included in the research study. Instead, they are prioritized, and only the most important are included. Limiting the final choice of factors to be included in the study are (1) what the researcher can do in the time allowed, and (2) what will give the greatest payback for the time and labor resources expended.

Task 4. Determine What Is to Be Measured or Evaluated

Once the researcher has identified the topic to study, the next step is to determine which relevant components should be measured. For example, say that a researcher is confronted with a problem pertaining to low voter turnouts. Should the researcher collect data on local economic conditions, on neighborhoods, on schools, on ethnic groups, on families, on peer groups, on former voters, students who have never voted, voters below a certain age or above that age, etc.? Each option will come up with very different information.

In another example, say that the research problem is concerned with the topic of gender abuse. Should the researcher gather data on men, women, children, family dyads, parents, or some other combination of subjects? If the research topic deals with problems faced by persons with a hearing disability, should the researcher study society in general, employers, service providers, persons with the disability, or persons without the disability?

Related to this question is one of *accessibility*. If the element or subject to be measured is a person, that subject must have the needed information, be willing to share the information with the researcher, speak the researcher's language, and be able to put into words why he or she behaved in a certain way. The same problems exist for all possible measurement elements.

Task 5. Determine Relevant Variables

Researchers study and test *variables*. A variable is anything that changes in value or varies in some way. Thus, variables are phenomena that can be "measured" in some way. Said another way, variables are study questions that have been rephrased into testable statements. For example, the high-school dropout phenomenon is a *study question,* whereas the annual rate of dropouts is a *variable* that can be measured. Another variable is the gender of the dropout; others are the dropout's age, ethnic group, the level of education of the dropout's parents, the location of the dropout's residence, and many more.

Another variable relating to this issue could be the dropout's attitudes or opinions about education in general. Others could be such things as the effectiveness of the dropout's teachers, the dropout's need to work in order to help support a family, or any similar measurement. A listing of some of the types of variables researchers use is displayed in Figure 6.2.

There are several ways to identify variables. One way is to divide variables into two categories based on the type of numerical measurements they provide. These are *categorical* and *continuous* variables. Categorical variables identify a limited number of possible categories. Gender is an example, with just two categories possible: female or male. Continuous variables, on the other hand, can have an unlimited number of values. Values for continuous variables can be measured on a continuous scale (such as weight, height in inches, etc.). They are not restricted to specific, discrete categories or values, as are categorical variables. Attitude scales that provide continuous data are often used in political science research. Researchers are concerned with mean (average) scores on a scale, not the response category (score) of any single subject.

A second way of looking at variables is whether they are *dependent* or *independent.* This dichotomy is important in causal research designs. Dependent variables are variables that are influenced in some way by another variable or variables. Independent variables are the variables that act upon or help explain change in a dependent variable. For example, the dependent variable *voting behavior* can be influenced by many different factors, such as the type of political contest involved, the income, education, occupation, or the age of the voters/nonvoter, etc. Each of these factors is an independent variable.

Task 6. Establish Research Hypotheses

The *hypothesis* is the fundamental building block of all scientific research. It defines the research topic and the researcher's ideas about it. Hypotheses can be defined in many different ways. One way is to look at the hypothesis as the researcher's ideas about a relationship between two phenomena (variables), while Shaughnessy and Zechmeister (1994) defined hypotheses as nothing more than a "tentative explanation for something."

Hypotheses are tentative answers to the 'How?' and 'Why?' questions about the research problem. No research should be started before one or more testable hypotheses have been written. There are two types of hypotheses: *causal* and *noncausal.* With causal hypotheses, the researcher proposes that *"event or activity A causes C to happen."* An example is: "Poverty *causes* juvenile crime." In this sense, the hypothesis is suggested as the reason for the occurrence of the phenomenon called "juvenile crime."

In a noncausal hypothesis, the researcher surmises that "A and B are caused by C." In this example, A and B can be said to be *correlated* (associated). However, in the absence of any

Variable:

A characteristic, quantity, or anything of interest that can have different values. Examples include such things as savings account amounts, stock prices, package designs, weight, monthly sales, gender, salaries, etc. The values of variables may be said to be either *continuous* or *categorical*.

Independent Variable:

A variable that functions as the causal element in a hypothesis. A change in the value of an independent variable is said to "cause" a positive or negative change in a dependent variable. An example is the independent variable "poverty" in the hypothesis "Poverty causes crime."

Dependent Variable:

The second part of a causal hypothesis, a change in the value of a dependent variable is hypothesized to have been "caused" by a change in the level of the independent variable. In the hypothesis "Poverty causes crime," the level of crime is the dependent variable.

Intervening Variable:

Sometimes referred to as a *control variable*, an intervening variable lies between an independent and a dependent variable. A change in the intervening variable must be "caused" by the independent variable; this change then "causes" the change in the dependent variable. For example, in the hypothesis "Workplace stress causes physical illness, which causes absenteeism," physical illness is the intervening variable.

Conditional Variable:

This variable establishes the antecedent conditions necessary for change in the dependent variable. The values of a conditional variable influence the level of impact that the independent and intervening variables have on a dependent variable. In the example "Poverty causes substance abuse, causing HIV-positive rates to increase, wherever needle exchange programs are proscribed," existence of needle exchange programs is the conditional variable.

Study Variable:

A variable whose cause or effect status the researcher is trying to discover through research. The study variable can be an independent variable, a dependent variable, an intervening variable, or a conditional variable.

Continuous Variables:

Quantities that can take any value within a range of measurements, such as weight or percentage of increase in the price of a stock, are said to be continuous.

Categorical Variables:

Categorical variables have values that can vary only in specific steps or categories (they are sometimes called *discrete* variables).

Figure 6.2 **A Partial Classification of Variables**

further proof, it is not possible to say that either A or B "causes" the other (Van Evera 1997). An example of this type of hypothesis might be: "High rates of high-school dropouts and high rates of teenage pregnancies are caused by poverty." This hypothesis does not say that dropping out of high school causes increases in the rate of pregnancies among teenage females. The high-school dropout phenomenon and teen pregnancies are related, but neither "causes" the other.

Hypotheses must be written in ways that no questions can be raised about the concepts that underlie the statement. This requires preparing clear and concise *definitions* for all variables, constructs and concepts, and spelling out all assumptions relating to the study. Hypotheses must always be written in ways that allow for their scientific testing. Such metaphysical concepts as beliefs or faith should never be used as the basis for a hypothesis because they cannot be empirically tested.

Task 7. Establish Research Objective and Relevant Subobjectives

Research objectives are statements of what the researcher wants to accomplish by completing the research activity. They are related directly to the study question. For example, the director of a program designed to help single parents receiving public assistance make the move to full-time employment might be concerned that the program participation rate is declining while the number of parents receiving assistance is not declining. Why enrollment is declining is a key study question. Identifying ways to reverse the decline might serve as the program director's main research objective. Subobjectives might include the following items. Clearly, the subobjectives are only a partial list of the possible factors the director may wish to include in the study; others are:

- Identify characteristics of clients who participate in the program.
- Determine reasons why they elected to participate.
- Identify characteristics of clients who do not participate in the program.
- Determine reasons why they elected to not participate.
- Identify barriers to participation.
- Identify what incentives might entice more qualified people to participate.
- Determine what successes other programs have had and whether they may be transplanted to the local program.

Pretest to Redefine Variables and Objectives

Pilot testing the study instrument or discussion guide is a critical step in the research process. No matter how close they might be to a problem, program, or issue under study, researchers are very different from their research subjects. They do not look at variables in the same way. The working definitions of variables and issues are also different. Without a thorough pretest of the data-gathering scheme, the probability of encountering a study error is significantly greater than it would be with a pretest.

Finding a Research Focus

Another problem that researchers often face is: *What part of this problem should I study* and *what parts should I ignore?* This is a question of *focus.* Making a few relatively easy decisions early about the focus of the study will make it easier to gather the data, interpret what is in the data, and then organize ideas into a meaningful research report later. One way to address the issue of *research focus* is to establish the *point of view* proposed for the topic and the research project. Making this determination early in the study establishes the method of gathering the required information. Narrowing the study's focus also makes it easier to organize the final report. *Organizing* the report means deciding what goes first in the paper, what goes second, etc.

Once the researcher has decided on a topic, there are many options on how to approach the study of the topic. According to Seech (1993), research studies and their reports can follow one of five different approaches:

- Thesis or "position" studies.
- Compare-and-contrast studies.
- Analysis studies.
- Summary studies.
- Basic research studies.

A *thesis* or *position* study is one in which the researcher begins by stating a position, either his or her own or some other person's or group's. This is then followed by arguments for or against the point of view. Various types of evidence are presented to support one viewpoint and/or refute the others. Political candidates regularly produce position papers in which they spell out their support or lack of support for such things as tax increases, school budgets, welfare expenditures, etc. The evidence presented in such papers is usually the product of a research project. Evidence can be acquired by using qualitative research methods to gather anecdotes, testimonials, or analogies, or quantitative research methods involving statistical analysis.

Compare-and-contrast studies are used to compare two or more ideas, methods, proposals, or positions. First, each of the approaches to be compared is defined. Research is usually necessary to fully develop each position. Several paragraphs in which key points that make up the differences are stated following the defining section. This portion of the study is then followed by a more detailed discussion of the differences. The arguments that can be used to explain the differences are then spelled out. The researcher then selects one argument and, using evidence found in the research to support the argument, explains to readers why that argument is "best."

Analysis studies are closely related to generic research reports, and often follow a similar structure. These studies require the researcher to carry out an in-depth analysis of an *idea.* Examples include such political science issues as characteristics of political parties, voting behavior, rules or standards that permit political institutions to continue to function, presidential policies, privatizing services, spending limitations, fiscal policies, foreign policy, and others. The researchers' opinions about the topic and its meanings or ramifications are typically included in analysis reports.

The investigator reviews and summarizes existing literature on a topic, then writes an analytical summary in which he or she interprets the information for the reading audience. For example, a researcher might be assigned to research and write a report about how passage of a people's initiative putting a cap on state automobile excise taxes affects a state highway department's plans to reinforce bridges to comply with federal earthquake damage requirements. The researcher will first go to the published literature to review trends and developments on all the topics. This could be followed by a series of interviews with department and budget administrators to establish their opinions about such things as delaying work on some bridges, finding cheaper ways to do the required work, or identifying other revenue sources.

Summary studies are detailed summaries of a topic or issue. They are much like an expanded version of the review of the literature section of other types of studies. These summary report studies include a brief introduction defining and describing the topic, then move immediately into a summary of what other researchers or practitioners have said about the topic. Unlike analysis studies, summary reports often do not require the author to subjectively interpret the previous research, but only to summarize what others have reported.

Seech's last style or approach to research studies is the *basic research study*. The form followed in research studies is rooted in the earliest traditions of scientific research. The scientific method approach to research evolved out of this tradition. Because of this, social science and administrative research usually follows a structure similar to research for such disciplines as chemistry or biology, for example.

When conducting a basic research study, the researcher designs and conducts a data-gathering project. To do this, the researcher may elect to follow a qualitative or a quantitative approach. In either approach, the data can be what is called *primary data,* or it can be *secondary data.* Collecting *primary data* means the researcher gathers "new" information. This might mean conducting a survey with a questionnaire, carrying out a series of personal interviews, employing content analysis to published documents, or conducting an experiment. Afterward, the gathered primary data are processed (often with computers) and interpreted. The researcher can then draw relevant conclusions and make recommendations.

Research to collect *secondary data* means getting most of the information from already published sources. These data can be found in libraries, on the Internet, or in internal publications, among other sources. Because this material has already been published, the researcher must use extreme care to report all the sources of material used in the report. The report must not be just a repeat of what others have written. Rather, the research report must include the researcher's *interpretation* of what others have written. In his book on writing, Barnet (1993, 176) said this about using secondary data in research reports: "A research report is not merely an elaborately footnoted presentation of what a dozen scholars have already said about a topic; it is a thoughtful evaluation of the available evidence, and so it is, finally, an expression of what the author thinks the evidence adds up to."

Finding Information about a Topic

Writing a research report means that the researcher must do research. There is no way to get out of it. There are a number of different ways to go about it, however. It can be done in a library, examining written, recorded, or filmed sources. The researcher can sit in front of a computer screen and do the research electronically. The researcher can interview subjects at work, at play, shopping, or anywhere it is possible to gain access to them. The researcher can use a telephone from a central location to ask respondents anywhere in the world questions from a survey questionnaire. Or, she can design and conduct either a laboratory or field experiment, or both.

Assuming that the topic has been narrowed down to something that sounds interesting, the researcher begins gathering information by conducting a comprehensive review of the published literature on the topic and its various subtopics. There are three ways to locate this literature:

1. Dive straight into the *library stacks* and begin the search by pulling out books, periodicals, reference materials, or government documents and other reference works that just might seem interesting.
2. Examine computerized, *on-line library catalog* lists. These catalog most library material, including books, journals, videos, and CD-ROMS, filing items by subject, author, or title. (Although highly unlikely, some or all of this information might still be stored in card catalog form. If so, the concepts and methods to follow are the same as if the data were available on-line.)
3. Refer to a *commercial database*; almost all will be found on-line.

Traditional Library Research

Researchers call all previously published information *secondary literature*—regardless of the form in which it is recorded. It is called *secondary* because it is information that has been gathered by someone else, usually for a different purpose. Published government statistics on aging, for example, is secondary data. Accounting information in an agency's annual report is secondary data. A report on regional economic conditions published by the federal government or by a local bank is secondary data. Tables, charts, and graphs from textbooks or city, county, or federal government documents or international organizations such as the United Nations are secondary sources. All information contained in previously published reports, magazines, and journals is secondary data.

It is the nature of academic research to find that, usually, more than one person is or has been interested in the same topic. Like fashions, researchers often follow "fads." This means that there will often be many possible sources of information about the chosen topic. Sometimes this means more sources than the researcher can deal with. Therefore, one of the researcher's first tasks will be to narrow the topic down to a manageable scope. For example, for an eight-page report on economics, a researcher cannot cope with 200 sources. Instead, examining something like eight to a dozen at most is manageable. In summary, researchers are encouraged to do what Lester and Lester (1992) recommended: "Start your research with a narrowed or *focused* topic—and, begin with a *plan*."

Efficient library research always begins with a plan. This means starting with a general topic, then focusing on relevant *parts* of that topic. The researcher must decide on what *key words* to begin with. Say that a student has been given a general assignment to research and write something about how computers have impacted ethical standards and practices in business. The student might start the search in the library catalog (cards or electronic) or in a special index of articles in a discipline looking up a general subject, such as organizational ethics. The *Business Periodicals Index* is an example of a comprehensive list of articles in a discipline; similar sources are compiled for nearly every discipline. These indexes (also called *indices*) are available either in CD-ROM or on-line databases.

Despite the phenomenal increase in the availability of information from electronic sources, libraries are still filled with books; they add hundreds, if not thousands, of new books to their collections each year. And, they still subscribe to many printed periodicals and other resource materials. Accessing much—but not all—of the information in the library has been made easier and faster through the use of computers and on-line databases. Most textbooks are not available as "e-books."

It is important to remember that a large database might return hundreds or even thousands of titles on a topic. The researcher should narrow the search down by using *qualifiers*. These limit the search to only topics that match the focus of the study. For example, a researcher could narrow down a broad topic like *ethics* to something like *ethics in government,* or *ethics and computers*. It can be focused even more this way: *government ethics and computers in Michigan.* Restricting the search to a specific year could make it even narrower.

Most library research begins with periodical literature. Periodicals are scholarly journals, magazines, or newspapers that are published *periodically* (daily, weekly, monthly, quarterly, etc.). Journals contain articles and research reports on relatively narrow topics, written by people who work in or know a lot about a particular career field. They are an excellent source of background information on most topics; many are now published only electronically.

Once the researcher has found an interesting article listing and its abstract (if available), the full article can usually be accessed from the library stacks, from microfilm, through interlibrary loan, or from the full-text provisions of many databases. Whatever else is done, it is always good to start the research with a visit with a *reference librarian!*

Research Using Electronic Sources

Electronic sources of information for research studies are often erroneously grouped under the single label the *Internet.* The Internet is just one of a wide variety of electronic sources. Other important electronic sources include on-line databases, CD-ROM databases, local-area networks, and library networks. Another important part of the Internet is the cooperative education and research network called *Bitnet* (today, Bitnets are used primarily for e-mail and electronic discussion groups or conferences, which are called *listservs*).

The Internet is a vast international network of computer networks. Hardware ranges in size from individual desktop computers to supercomputers used for complex scientific modeling. All kinds of information have been made available through the connecting of this huge network of computers; not all of it is true; not all of it is acceptable for research. Anyone, including private citizens, universities, research laboratories, companies, and government agencies, can place information on the Internet, change it at any time, or take it off. The information stored on those computers is accessed through the *World Wide Web* (www, or simply the *Web*). It is this complete accessibility that creates potential problems for users of the Internet. The Modern Language Association's (MLA) committee on new technologies for research had this to say about problems with Internet sources:

> We want researchers to look at more than the Web, for the sake of historical concerns. Many important things aren't on the Web. Also, researchers must learn how to cite Web sites. And we have to learn how to read Web sites critically. . . . How do you know if what you're reading is fact? What are the credentials of the person who posed the information? The very quality that makes the Internet an attractively egalitarian tool—anybody can say anything and send it anywhere—makes it problematic for researchers. (Keller 1998, C2)

An important first step in beginning an information search on the Internet is to differentiate between sites about politics and sites about political science (Pencek 2000). Sites dealing with politics address "real world" activities about governing and being governed. They include information about the activities of political parties, politicians, special-interest groups, political organizations, legislators and legislative bodies, and other related phenomena, including public policy. A valuable source for political information is *www.policy.com*. This site has a strong emphasis on political issues and organizations—the site is updated every Wednesday.

Political science sites, on the other hand, address issues in the academic discipline of political science. They include such information areas as political theory, methodology and methods, and historical and mathematical models, in addition to other topics of interest to academicians. Many college and university political science departments maintain sites that are accessible through the political science keyword. For example, California Polytechnic University maintains the following political science research methodology site: *www.cla.calpoly.edu/pols/html/study.html.*

Using Search Tools

Researchers use two tools to search for information on the *World Wide Web*. The first is what is known as *Internet directories*. These directories index information from many different sources. This is then stored in various databases. There are many different such collections of information; each deals with some particular aspect of research information. For example, one database indexes only economics literature; another index lists articles and papers from 375 life-science journals. For topical information about anything in the news, an on-line news and current affairs database is also available.

The second way to search for information on the Web is using what are known as *search engines*. Search engines allow researchers to search the Web for information on any subject, such as institutions, political parties, agencies and organizations, etc., by using keywords. If search engines cannot find the desired information, more powerful programs can often be accessed. They are particularly effective for search on obscure topics because they search multiple search engines at the same time, retrieving as many documents as possible with one search. Most eliminate duplicate listings as they search. A reference librarian can direct the researcher to these tools.

On-line Databases

Today, most literature search information is accessed using on-line databases. Until very recently, many, if not most, of these were available only in collections of CD-ROM files. Now, CD-ROMs are used almost exclusively for such resources as encyclopedias and special-interest compilations of sight and sound; the databases themselves are accessible on-line.

A number of different databases may be found in each of several different categories of information. For example, the business and economics areas are served by at least ten different databases; sixteen on-line databases are available in the natural and health sciences disciplines, and eight databases index articles and other information in the *News and Current Events* collection.

The following databases contain citations and full-text listings of scholarly and popular articles on public administration, economics, and business administration (Note: not all libraries subscribe to every possible source).

- *EBSCOhost* (Academic Search Full Text Elite): A comprehensive index to more than 3,100 scholarly (academic) journals and general periodicals in all subject areas.
- *EconLit:* This is the key database for economics information; it also includes reports on public administration and public policy issues.
- *ABI/INFORM* Global: A database covering U.S. and international professional publications, academic journals, and trade magazines.
- *Business & Industry:* This database indexes leading trade magazines, newsletters, the general business press, and international business newspapers.
- *Organizations, Agencies, and Publications Directory:* This is a global directory of new and established organizations, agencies, and publications.

Summary

Information about a research topic can come from already-published sources—what is called *secondary data*—or it can be gathered directly from the first, or "primary," source by the researcher or research team. When the second approach is used, the data are called *primary data.* Most research involves a combination of these approaches. The researcher first identifies a study topic and then looks to the published literature to gain more information or additional insights into the problem or issue.

A seven-step process can aid the researcher in defining the research problem. These steps are: (1) relate the problem to the program mission and objectives; (2) review the background of the problem, usually by conducting a literature review; (3) break down the problem into its subareas, components, or factors; (4) select the most relevant variables and determine what should be measured; (5) establish testable research hypotheses; (6) establish an objective for the research and establish relevant subobjectives; (7) conduct a pilot study to check on the validity of the variables, measurements, and hypotheses. The pilot study is also used to redefine any or all variables and hypotheses, if necessary, and to determine whether the objectives and subobjectives can be achieved.

Once the literature review is completed, the researcher decides which factors or components of the study question require more information. Then, the researcher either delves deeper into the published literature or designs a research project for acquiring the needed additional information.

Efficient library research always begins with a plan, identifying a general topic, then focusing on relevant *parts* of that topic. The researcher must decide on what *key words* to begin with. The researcher might start his or her search in the library catalog (cards or electronic) or in a special index of articles in a discipline looking up a general subject, such as international relations or public policy. Most library research begins with periodical literature. Periodicals are scholarly journals, magazines, or newspapers that are published *periodically* (daily, weekly, monthly, quarterly, etc.). Journals contain articles and research reports on relatively narrow topics, written by people who work in or know a lot about a particular career field. They are an excellent source of background information on most topics. Once the researcher has found an interesting article listing and its abstract (if available), the full article can usually be accessed from the library stacks, from microfilm, through interlibrary loan, or from the full-text provisions of many databases; start the research with a visit with a *reference librarian!*

Electronic sources of information for research studies are often erroneously grouped under the single label the *Internet.* The Internet is just one of a wide variety of electronic sources. Other important electronic sources include on-line databases, CD-ROM databases, local-area networks, and library networks. The Internet is a vast international network of computer networks. Hardware ranges in size from individual desktop computers to supercomputers used for complex scientific modeling. All kinds of information have been made available through the connecting of this huge network of computers; not all of it is true; not all of it is acceptable for research. Anyone, including private citizens, universities, research laboratories, companies, and government agencies, can place information on the Internet, change it at any time, or take it off. The information stored on those computers is accessed through the *World Wide Web* (www, or simply the *Web*). It is this complete accessibility that creates potential problems for users of the Internet.

Today, most literature search information is accessed using online databases. CD-ROMs are used almost exclusively for such resources as encyclopedias and special-interest compilations of sight and sound; the databases themselves are accessible online.

Discussion Questions

1. Explain the differences between basic and applied research.
2. Where might you go to find topics for a political science research project?
3. Do you agree or disagree with Sylvan Barnet's (1993) statement that no subject is too trivial for study? Why?
4. What is the meaning of framing a subject for research?
5. Why is it important to be familiar with the background of the topic you plan to research?
6. What is the purpose of breaking down the problem into smaller components or factors?
7. How do you know what to measure in a research topic?
8. Must all variables be measured? Why or why not?
9. Why should you write research hypotheses?
10. How do you know what to focus upon in the study?
11. Name and define four different focus approaches to research.
12. What is the difference between secondary and primary data?

Additional Reading

Adams, Gerald R., and Jay D. Schvaneveldt. 1985. *Understanding Research Methods.* New York: Longman.

Anastas, Jeane W., and Marian L. MacDonald. 1994. *Research Design for Social Work and the Human Services.* New York: Lexington Books.

Laurence, Helen, and William Miller, eds. 2000. *Academic Research on the Internet: Options for Scholars and Librarians.* New York: Hawthorne Information Press.

Shaughnessy, John J., and Eugene B. Zechmeister. 1994. *Research Methods in Psychology.* 3rd ed. New York: McGraw-Hill.

Wildavsky, Arron. 1993. *Craftways: On the Organization of Scholarly Work.* 2nd ed. New Brunswick, NJ: Transaction Publishers.

7 Understanding Research Design

The term "research design" refers to the way an investigator applies a logical structure to his or her research project. The function of this step in the research process is to make sure that the data gathered are sufficient and appropriate for answering the research questions completely and unambiguously (deVaus 2001). It is important to keep in mind that *research design* is not the same thing as *research methods*. Examples of quantitative designs include experiments, longitudinal and cross-sectional studies and surveys, content analysis, and cases analyses. Examples of qualitative designs include ethnography, action science, and grounded theory, among others. Methods, on the other hand, are the ways that data are collected. Some examples of methods used in quantitative studies include questionnaires, structured or semistructured interviews, observation, document and artifact analysis, and unobtrusive methods. Examples of methods used in qualitative studies include participant observation, unstructured interviews, and hermeneutic analysis of texts.

Researchers in the social and administrative sciences are no longer required to follow a single design for their investigations. Instead, today many different approaches are possible. For example, Hakim (2000, 9–10) identified eight types of study designs: (1) literature reviews, secondary data analysis, and meta-analysis of existing data; (2) qualitative research, including depth interviews and focus groups; (3) research based on administrative records and documentary evidence; (4) ad hoc interview surveys; (5) regular and continuous interview surveys; (6) case studies; (7) longitudinal studies; and (8) experimental social research. Bryman (2001, 32), on the other hand, felt that there were only five types of research designs in the social sciences: (1) experimental designs, (2) cross-sectional or social survey designs, (3) longitudinal designs, (4) case study designs, and (5) comparative designs.

To help clarify this great variety of options in research designs, here they are grouped into just two broad approach categories: *qualitative (positivist), and quantitative (postpositivist)* designs. Each approach supports a variety of designs and methods for gathering data; and each allows the researcher a variety of analysis and interpretation actions. A key task of the director of the research project is selecting the appropriate design for the research problem and study objectives. Figure 7.1 illustrates the design processes.

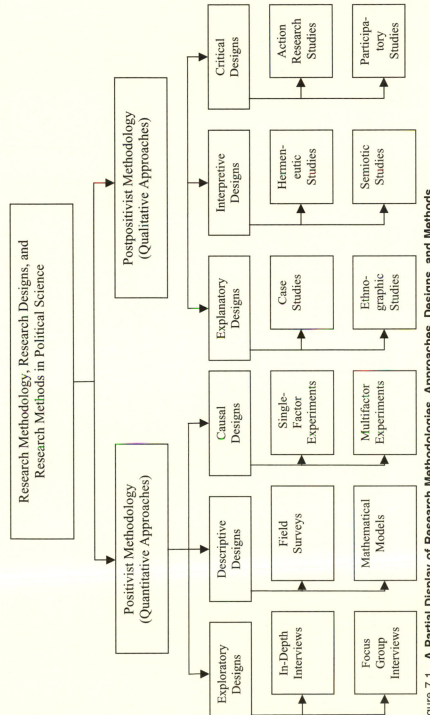

Figure 7.1 **A Partial Display of Research Methodologies, Approaches, Designs, and Methods**

The Importance of Research Design

An important thing to remember about research design selection is that the researcher is never locked into using any one "best" design. There are many acceptable ways to conduct research; the only selection criterion that ought to make sense is that the method chosen must provide the best possible conclusions. Phillips (1976) described the process of selecting a research design as a *Magna Carta* for the researcher, adding that,

> [The researcher] is not chained to a set of techniques simply because they have worked adequately in the past, nor must [he or she] defer to the supposedly superior methodological knowledge of other investigators because of their research reputation. It is not necessary for [researchers] to continually look back over [their] shoulder, wondering if others would consider [the] procedure to be "correct" or incorrect. . . . What counts is not what others think of those procedures but how well they work. (Phillips 1976, 5)

What Phillips and others like him mean with statements like this is that the key to good research results is "doing good science." This simply means selecting a research design that best meets the objectives for the study. It is the research question that drives the selection of a research design (Denscombe 2002).

Today, there are many acceptable research designs from which to choose; researchers are no longer required to slavishly adhere to one or more design, method, or approach:

> Increasingly, researchers are recognizing that scientific inquiry is a species of *research*. Research is not merely a species of social science. Virtually any careful, reflective, systematic study of phenomena undertaken to advance human understanding can count as a form of research. It all depends on how that work is pursued. (Eisner 1997, 261)

Researchers spend considerable time and effort in the design selection process. In making their decision, both positivist and interpretist political science researchers must give consideration to the following six key elements of research design (deVaus 2001, 47–50):

1. *The number of groups in the study.* For example, is it to be a study of a single case or will it require more than one case, as in comparative case study designs? Does the study need two or more groups, as in a test and a control group?
2. *The number of "pretest" measurement phases.* If the design is a cross-sectional design, extreme care must be taken with pretests. By their nature, cross-sectional designs are "one-shot" studies that provide a time-framed picture of phenomena; a pretest may bias the results of the final study. If, on the other hand, it is to be an experimental design, is more than one test of the variable in question required? Pre-tests are required for experiments.
3. *The number of "posttest" measurement phases.* These are measurements of the outcome variable—the dependent variable that is or is not affected by the "treatment." Does the design require a second measurement after some period to determine learning has been retained?
4. *The manner of assigning cases to groups.* For example, are probability or nonprobability sampling methods to be used? In qualitative research, what criteria dictate inclusion or exclusion of individuals into the group under study?

5. *The nature of the intervention.* If the study involves an experimental design, what treatment and treatment levels are to be employed? In a cross-sectional study, of course, no treatment is involved.

6. *The number of interventions.* Experiments often entail the application of two or more interventions or treatments. For example, in an experiment with university students to determine the amount of information retained after a period of time might involve two or more training sessions between pre- and posttesting.

As always, the nature of the study problem or topic to be researched and the data acquired will establish the researcher's options. For now, all that is necessary is for researchers to understand what their options are. Therefore, the following pages are devoted to an introductory discussion of the three basic forms of research designs: *quantitative, qualitative,* and *combined.*

The Quantitative Approach to Research

Quantitative research strategies are employed in the sequence of steps shown in Figure 7.2. Until recently, many research traditionalists maintained the opinion that quantitative research methods used in most physical or natural sciences research were the only appropriate approach to follow with any scientific research problem. Among these traditionalists, the watchword for "good science" is *measurement,* which was expressed in the following way: "If it can't be measured, it can't be studied." While the positivist emphasis of quantitative research may no longer be the overwhelmingly dominant opinion in political science research, quantitative studies still outnumber other approaches by far. For proof, an analysis of the collected body of political, social, or administrative science professional journals may provide support for the contention.

Questions and Statistical Tests

In deciding what strategy to follow in a quantitative design, political science researchers usually seek answers to these six basic questions (Miller 1991):

1. What characteristics of the people in my sample (such as demographic differences) distinguish them from other groups or subgroups of people who I might have included in my study?
2. Are there any differences in the subgroups contained in this sample that might influence the way the questions are answered or opinions that are offered?
3. Is there a statistically significant difference in the answers of any groups or subgroups in this sample, or did they all answer the questions in roughly the same way?
4. What confidence can I have that any difference that I do find did not occur by chance?
5. Is there any association between any two or more variables in my study? Is it relevant? Is it significant?
6. If there is any relationship between two or more variables, is it possible to measure how strong it is and whether it is a positive or negative relationship?

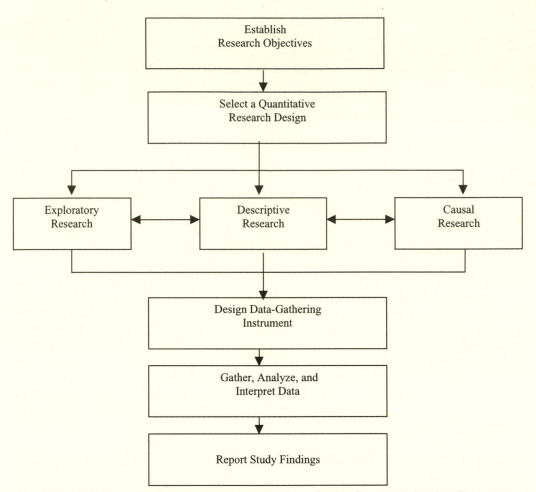

Figure 7.2   **A Schematic Representation of the Quantitative Research Design Process**

Types of Quantitative Designs

Depending on their research objectives, researchers select from three types of quantitative research designs: *exploratory, descriptive,* or *causal.* In each of these approaches, one or more of a variety of statistical tools are used to test ideas or concepts and to communicate research findings.

   The statistical tests typically used in quantitative political science research to answer questions such as these include, but are not limited to, the following:

   • Measures of central tendency, variability, and/or dispersion,
   • Graphic methods, such as tables, charts, and graphs,
   • Hypothesis tests,
   • Association (correlation) tests,
   • Regression analysis, and

- Some specific-purpose tools, such as time series, index numbers, and discriminant analysis, among others.

For more complex studies, a host of powerful multivariate statistical tools have been developed to aid the researcher. Some of these will be discussed in later chapters.

Exploratory Designs

Exploratory studies are small-sample designs used primarily for gaining insights and ideas about research problems and the variables and issues associated with those problems. These types of studies are sometimes referred to as "pilot studies." Exploratory studies are often employed as the first step in a multipart research project; because of their limited scope they seldom exist as stand-alone approaches. Exploratory studies help the researcher gain greater understanding of the problem for which more information is needed. They also help the researcher identify variables that may be only tangentially or marginally related, and thus, should not be included in a more extensive research effort.

Data gathering in exploratory research may involve quantitative, qualitative, or a combination of strategies. The data may come from either primary or secondary sources; that is, they may be gathered directly by the researcher, or may be gathered by someone else for a different purpose. Both primary and secondary data types have similar validity in exploratory research.

Descriptive Designs

Descriptive research designs are used to develop a "snapshot" of a particular phenomenon of interest. Descriptive studies typically involve large samples. They provide a description of an event, or help define a set of attitudes, opinions, or behaviors that are observed or measured at a given time and in a given environment. The focus of descriptive research is on the careful mapping out of a circumstance, situation, or set of events to describe what is happening or what has happened (Rosenthal and Rosnow 1991).

Descriptive studies may be either *cross-sectional* or *longitudinal.* The "snapshot" study is called a *cross-sectional* design. It is a one-shot assessment of a sample of respondents. Time is an important consideration because the "picture of the sample" usually varies—sometimes substantially—if the research is repeated at a later date or conducted with another sample taken from the same population. The purpose of a cross-sectional design is to determine to what extent different classes in the sample differ on some outcome (independent) variable. Categories could be gender, different age groups, income groups, social class groups, ethnic groups, and the like. The basic elements of a cross-sectional design are (deVaus 2001, 47–50):

1. The design measures variations in the responses to independent variables in the sample. An example is a survey to determine whether women and men have different attitudes toward a political candidate. Everyone is asked the same questions; their answers can be tabulated and compared.
2. At least one independent variable with at least two categories is used in the instrument. In the preceding example, the independent variable was attitudes; categories could be a simple approve/disapprove dichotomy, or more likely will be measured on something like a five-point scale.

3. Data are collected at one point in time. The cross-sectional design is a "snapshot" measurement, with results specific to that moment.
4. There is no random allocation of subjects to groups, although the total sample itself will most likely have been randomly selected from a known population.

Descriptive research that is repeated with the same sample over two or more time intervals is known as *longitudinal research*. Studies using panels of participants are longitudinal studies. The purpose of a longitudinal study is to identify and measure *change* in subjects' responses. The same elements in a cross-sectional design apply to a longitudinal study, except a follow-on measurement or measurements are taken after a period of time. *Cohort* studies, research projects that follow a sample over time to evaluate attitudes and behaviors, are longitudinal studies. They are popular for measuring changes in voter attitudes as a campaign progresses or as an administration serves its elected period in office.

Different Descriptive Research Approaches

Researchers use two related, but different, types of descriptive research approaches: *field studies* and *field surveys*. Field studies tend to go into greater depth on a fewer number of issues or items. To do so, they may use face-to-face or telephone personal-interviewing techniques for data gathering. Interviewing survey methods allow the research to employ "branching questions" that require a different set of questions for subjects who respond differently at a given place or "branch" in the instrument. They may also involve some open-ended questions. Although it is possible to later code open-ended responses, these types of questions require far more effort for coding and tabulating than is needed for the fixed-response items found in field survey studies. As a result, they are seldom used in survey research.

Field surveys are the most commonly encountered approach in political science; they make up more than 80 percent of all quantitative research. Surveys are popular because they are relatively easy to design and administer. The wide availability of powerful desktop computers and statistical software today has made them much easier to tabulate and interpret. It is now possible to use interactive surveying techniques, with the responses immediately entered into a database and tabulated.

Both field studies and field surveys produce data that are used as numeric *descriptions*. These descriptions may be of a *sample* of subjects or from an entire *population*. Many different types of variables can be used, including, but not limited to, demographic characteristics, attitudes, opinion, intentions, characteristics of organizations, groups, families, subgroups, etc. In essence, almost anything that can be measured can be a descriptive variable.

Causal Designs

Causal research studies are often the last step in a three-part approach to research in the administrative and social sciences. These designs typically involve planning and conducting *experiments*. Causal studies may be either *relational* or *experimental*. The purpose of relational studies is to identify how one or more variables are related to one another. They are sometimes called *correlation* studies. The purpose of an experimental study is to identify the cause or causes of *change* in a variable or event—that is, determining "what leads to what" (Rosenthal and Rosnow 1991).

The classic version of experimental design includes these five key components (deVaus 2001, 47–50):

1. One pretest measurement of the dependent (outcome) variable.
2. Two groups, one that is to be exposed to the treatment (intervention) and the other, the *control group,* which is not exposed.
3. Random assignment of subjects to the groups; this occurs prior to the pretest.
4. One treatment (intervention).
5. One posttest of both groups on the dependent (outcome) variable.

Designing an experiment is the key activity in a causal research project. Experiments involve subjecting two or more samples or subsamples to different *treatments* or *interventions.* Researchers may manipulate one, two, or more independent variables in the same treatment experiment. Treatments can be such things as:

- Different teaching methods (lecture vs. experiential)
- A new drug versus a placebo
- Tests of the impact of two different levels of expenditures on a social program
- Different communications media
- Any other relevant characteristic or phenomenon

Researchers must be careful in the design of experiments and interpretation of the findings so that potential intervening or confounding variables do not muddy the results of the study. The classic example of the need for careful attention to experimental design and how experiments are used to provide information about behaviors is the set of experiments conducted at the Western Electric manufacturing facility in Hawthorne, New Jersey. A random sample of assembly workers was selected, moved to a special location, and subjected to variations in working conditions, including varying the speed of the production line, different levels of lighting, rest periods, etc. Researchers measured performance under normal conditions, changed a working condition characteristic, and measured performance again. To their surprise, production increased with negative environmental changes just as they did with positive changes. The design did not consider the effect on workers of being singled out for attention. This unplanned change is what is known as an *intervening* or *confounding* variable.

Experiments can involve manipulating (making changes to) a single independent variable or two or more variables. The changes are referred to as *different treatments.* For example, a park administrator might want to know whether increasing the fee for campsite use will reduce or increase the need for maintenance personal at the campground. Two or three similar sites with comparable usage levels could be selected, with different fees charged in each test site (the "treatment" is the different fee rates). The administrator might use damage to campsites over the test period as a measurement of the need for more or fewer maintenance personnel. At the end of a designated test period, results at the three sites would be compared.

Manipulating two or more variables is also possible. For example, agricultural researchers often vary amounts of both fertilizer and irrigation, measuring the effects of different combinations on crop production. In a three-factor experiment, the researcher might also include different types of soil conditions (such as clay, sandy loam, etc.) as another of the test variables.

The Qualitative Approach to Research

Qualitative research is not based on a single, unified theoretical concept, nor does it require a single methodological approach. Rather, a variety of theoretical approaches and methods are involved (Flick 1999). All of these approaches and methods have one common underlying objective: *understanding* of the event, circumstance, or phenomenon under study. Thus, description is less important than the researcher's *interpretation* of the event, circumstance, or phenomenon. To achieve qualitative study objectives, researchers analyze the *interaction* of people with problems or issues. These interactions are studied in their context and then subjectively explained by the researcher.

According to Denscombe (2002, 18), some writers have used the term "constructionism" to cover the same group of designs that fall collectively under the qualitative designs label. All of the approaches seem to share the same common points:

1. Political reality is subjective; it is constructed and interpreted by researchers rather than something that exists independently.
2. Humans react to the knowledge that they are being studied. When they become aware that they are under investigation their behavior often changes. Thus, there is no one single truth; it is situation-specific.
3. It simply is not possible to gain objective knowledge about political phenomena; researchers cannot be objective, no matter how hard they try.
4. In light of the above three conditions, there is little prospect of ever producing grand theories that explain the political world.

Types of Qualitative Designs

Broadly speaking, qualitative strategies fall into three categories of study techniques. These are *explanatory, interpretive,* and *critical* designs (White 1999). These approaches can be applied to many different study approaches. Some include *ethnography, kinetics* (the study of movement), *atmospherics, phenomenology,* and *proxemics* (the study of space in social settings). Examples of data gathering techniques include *focus groups, elite-group interviewing,* and *unobtrusive measures,* among many others. Qualitative data are typically gathered in one of four ways: (1) by observation (usually, but not exclusively, *participant observation),* (2) in-depth personal interviews, (3) unobtrusive measures, and (4) a combination of these and other methods in what is known as a *triangulation approach* (Esterberg 2002).

Flick (1999) has identified the following features of qualitative research that help to differentiate these methods from positivist quantitative approaches:

- Diverse theories underlying the approach.
- Diverse perspectives of the participants.
- Reflexivity of the researcher and the research (i.e., responses to each other).
- Variety of approaches and methods.
- Reconstructing cases as a starting point.
- Construction of reality as a basis for the research.
- Text often serves as empirical data.

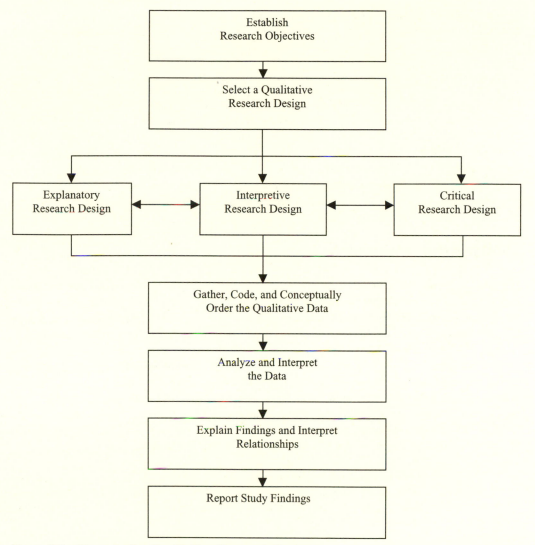

Figure 7.3 **Steps in the Qualitative Research Process**

Figure 7.3 displays the interconnected nature of the qualitative process. In all three approaches several different techniques may be employed for gathering data, including *observation, participation, interviewing,* and *document analysis.* In each, data are coded, placed in some intelligent order, interpreted, and used for explaining and/or predicting future interrelationships in similar circumstances.

Explanatory Research

Explanatory research is the approach taken in most mainstream qualitative research. In this way, its goal is to go beyond the traditional descriptive designs of the positivist approach to provide meaning as well as description. The purpose of explanatory research is also broader than that of descriptive research; it is conducted to build theories and predict events. According to White:

> Explanatory research strives to build theories that explain and predict natural and social events. Theory building requires the development of a collection of related and testable law-like statements that express causal relationships among relevant variables. The ultimate goal of explanatory research is the control of natural and social events. (White 1999, 44)

Typical objectives for explanatory research include explaining why some phenomenon occurred, interpreting a cause-and-effect relationship between two or more variables, and explaining differences in two or more groups' responses. The design is similar to the traditional positivist approach, and some numerical description and simple statistical analysis may be involved.

Interpretive Research

Interpretive research is characterized by a strong sense of connection between the researcher and the subjects who are part of an interpretive study. The goal of interpretive research is to build understanding between the participants and the researcher. Therefore, interpretive research often focuses on standards, norms, rules, and values held in common, and how these all influence human interactions (White 1999).

The primary objective of interpretive research is to establish the *meaning* of a circumstance, event, or social situation. It goes beyond simple description or explanation in aiming to enhance people's understanding of the symbols, artifacts, beliefs, meanings, feelings, or attitudes of the people in the study situation (White 1999). Interpretive research has much in common with the study of *phenomenology* in philosophy and the phenomenological approach to sociological research. Camilla Stivers provided this view of interpretive research:

> To me, interpretation entails sense-making: taking a more or less inchoate bundle of events and processes—what might be thought of as a situation or group of situations—and putting a frame around them based on more or less conscious assumptions about what is likely to be important, significant or meaningful. (Stivers 2000, 132)

Interpretive research also plays an important role in the third approach, critical research, and provides the common understanding that is necessary for successful attitude change. In this way, the interpretation of ideas that are associated with Freudian psychoanalysis has become an integral part of critical research.

Critical Research

Critical research is the least-used approach in political science research in general, although it is an increasingly important tool in public administration and sociological research. In addition, a growing number of applications are now seen in education research. The subjective nature of critical analysis makes it difficult for students to adopt in meaningful ways. While it has potential for application in political science, it has not yet been widely adopted. According to White:

> Criticism is the most radical of the three modes of [qualitative] research because it calls into question our most basic assumptions and asks us to evaluate them as a basis for action. Critical research does not always satisfy the critic, nor does it always change beliefs and values, but it has the potential to do so. (White 1999, 57)

Critical research in political science has been adapted mostly from sociology research methodology. It also has roots in the criticisms of social structures and the capitalist economic system that emerged in reaction to the excesses of the Industrial Revolution. It reached its highest influence in the studies of society's acceptance of tyrannical governments and the public's reactions to propaganda. This research was greatly influenced by the social scientists who fled Europe in the 1930s, and later helped build the New School for Social Research in New York City. The purpose of the critical research tradition that emerged from those early foundations was to help citizens overcome the constraints that an oppressive government placed on their freedom and development. "Thus, critical research assumes that people can misunderstand themselves and their situations and that people can be deceived about what is in their own interests" (White 2000, 54).

The overriding objective of critical research is to change people's beliefs and actions in ways that the investigator believes will better satisfy their needs and wants. The criticism points out inconsistencies that exist between what is true and false and what is good and bad. It aims to bring people to actions that are commensurate with accepted truth and goodness. The "truth" of critical research is only realized when people (through a process of self-reflection) finally take action to change their situation.

Gathering Qualitative Data

The three methods used most often for gathering qualitative data in political science research are *observation, participation,* and *interviewing.* A fourth method, *document analysis,* is also used, but less often than the first three approaches. A variation of document analysis—*hermeneutics*—is rapidly becoming a popular approach in qualitative research.

Observation

Observation research is the least intrusive of all research approaches. In this approach, the researcher simply watches and records the social behavior of subjects. This method came into wide acceptance with the growth of *cultural anthropology* and is used for the study of the behavior, beliefs, and customs of primitive cultures. It is still the predominant data gathering method in anthropology's ethnographic studies, and is also common in sociological field studies.

With data gathered by observation, researchers must interpret what they see in the light only of the conditions that exist in a culture at a given time. They cannot do so in terms of their own experiences within their own modern culture. The method is also gaining increasing acceptance in the study of organizations in both the private and public sectors (Gummesson 1991). For example, today political science researchers are using the method to come to a better understanding of the role organizational culture plays in organizational effectiveness.

Observation has very low impact on the social setting because the researcher only watches and records events in the study group or setting, remaining uninvolved in the group's activities or actions. The researcher's goal is to produce an unbiased record of the events, behaviors, etc. Extensive field notes must be maintained, however. Field notes have been described as the "systematic noting and recording of events, behaviors, and artifacts [objects] in the social setting chosen for the study" (Marshall and Rossman 1999, 107). Analysis of these descriptive records often occurs as an integral part of the data-gathering process (Miles and Huberman 1984).

Participation

Participation research studies are more intrusive than observation approaches. The researchers' involvement in the culture, subculture, clan, group, or organization under study cannot help but have some influence on the study target. Participation requires that the researcher become wholly immersed in the activities and environment of the study group. In this way the researcher experiences and senses the same reality that members of the study group do. The researcher's goal is to understand what individuals in the group see, feel, and hear. While acting as a participant, the researcher prepares field notes that include a description of the group members' experiences, reactions, and feelings (Marshall and Rossman 1999). For greater understanding, the researcher often includes personal experiences in the analysis.

Interviewing

Interviewing is the third primary data-gathering method used by researchers pursuing qualitative research strategies. Interviewing research is the most intrusive of all qualitative research approaches. Face-to-face or voice-to-voice (i.e., telephone) interviews may be *structured* or *unstructured.* Structured interviews follow a preplanned discussion guide in which answers are sought to specific questions. Unstructured interviews are more like conversations between friends. Respondents are left free to bring up whatever topic they wish. The researcher may then probe for more detailed information, but must be careful to avoid leading questions or communicating any value judgments. The researcher may, however, ask questions when the responses are terse or the respondent is unable to express needed information.

A single face-to-face interview typically takes up to two or more hours to complete. Care must be taken to be sure the respondent does not "ramble" excessively or use the interview to continually vent frustrations or anger—some such information is valuable, of course, but continual repetitions waste time and other resources.

Combination Research Designs

Combined designs entail using *both* qualitative and quantitative methods. The three broad classes of combined studies are *archival, media,* and *artifact* studies. Techniques used in these types of studies include content analysis, document analysis, and in situ analysis (also known as *within-site* analysis). Several types of multivariate statistical tools are also used in these designs, including *canonical correlation,* and *cluster* and *factor analysis.* These statistical tools all require some subjective (qualitative) interpretation of the data.

Flick (1999) is one of many writers on research and research methods who now report that good research often requires the use of a combination of quantitative and qualitative approaches:

It is well known that the juxtaposition "qualitative-quantitative" has sometimes led to not very fruitful controversies and is sometimes used as a schematic demarcation. But the combination of approaches is often truthful as well. (Flick 1999, 634)

Data-Gathering Methods

The first of the nontraditional designs, and one that is very often used in political science research, is the study of historical records. More commonly known as *archival studies,* this design involves the study of historical documents in order to establish an understanding of the circumstances that characterized an event or period. Archive researchers review the published and unpublished records of an organization, a community, or a culture. This design was used for a study in mass-communications history and persuasive communication (McNabb 1968). The design required analysis of historical documents dealing with the efforts by private power firms and public utilities from 1909 to 1939 to influence public opinion. Documents included pamphlets, press releases, annual reports, and newspaper articles published during the period.

Media analysis is a similar process, although in media analyses the items studied tend to be current rather than historical. Like archival studies, media analysis often employs *content analysis,* which is a way of organizing content into desired categories and "weighing" the results. In another example, the author once designed and led a study that involved comparative analysis of London's eight daily newspapers for editorial-content emphasis on the then-controversial plan of Britain's joining the European Union.

In a historical media analysis study, two hundred years of publications in the newspaper collection of the British National Library were surveyed (McNabb 1991). These included actual and microfilm copies of seventeenth- and eighteenth-century newspapers and other periodicals. The research resulted in a published report on the first one hundred years of the publication of one of Great Britain's first daily newspapers and consumer magazines as part of a larger description of the birth development of the modern consumer society.

Artifact studies (also called *object studies*) owe their emergence to the application of archeological methods to the study of modern societies and cultures. An example of a modern use of the method is the investigation and cataloging of items discarded in modern landfills. Researchers use this method to gain a greater understanding of the culture and values of groups.

Summary

This chapter has examined the different types of research designs employed by researchers in political science and other social science disciplines. All research strategies are employed in a sequence of steps. Three designs are possible with qualitative research; exploratory, descriptive, and causal. Quantitative designs usually begin with a small-sample, exploratory study to provide information for developing a questionnaire (also called a *survey instrument* or simply an *instrument*). The questionnaire will then be used in a large-sample, descriptive study. Or the exploratory study may be used to identify the key dependent and independent variables to be tested in an experiment (a *causal design*). Or the researcher may elect to use all three approaches, gaining insights into the problem with an exploratory study, following with a descriptive study to define the salient variables, and concluding with a causal design to test for cause-and-effect relationships.

Broadly speaking, qualitative strategies fall into three categories of research designs: *ex-*

planatory, interpretive, and *critical.* These approaches can be applied to many different research methods, including ethnography, kinetics, atmospherics, phenomenology, and proxemics, among others. The four principal data collection methods used most often for gathering qualitative data in political science research are unobtrusive observation, participant observation, personal interviewing, and archival analysis. A fifth method is artifact analysis, but it is not used nearly as often as are the first four approaches. Some of the methods that combine parts of both quantitative and qualitative approaches include archival studies, media analysis, and artifact studies. Content analysis is the quantitative method used in these studies, and hermeneutics is the predominant qualitative method.

Interviewing is the third primary data gathering method used by researchers pursuing qualitative research strategies. Interviewing research is the most intrusive of all qualitative research approaches. Face-to-face or voice-to-voice (i.e., telephone) interviews may be *structured* or *unstructured.* The researcher may probe for more detailed information, but must be careful to avoid leading questions or communicating any value judgments. The researcher may, however, ask questions when the responses are terse or the respondent is unable to express needed information.

Combined designs entail using *both* qualitative and quantitative methods. The three broad classes of combined studies are *archival, media,* and *artifact* studies. Techniques used in these types of studies include content analysis, document analysis, and in situ analysis. Several types of multivariate statistical tools are also used in these designs, including *canonical correlation, cluster*, and *factor analysis.*

Discussion Questions

1. What is meant by the term "research design?"
2. Why is research design important?
3. What are the six key elements in a research design?
4. What is an exploratory study? A descriptive study? A causal study?
5. What is an explanatory research design? An interpretive research design? A critical research design?
6. What are some of the ways to collect quantitative data?
7. What are some of the ways to collect qualitative data?
8. Describe a research design that incorporates both quantitative and qualitative components.
9. What is media analysis?
10. Is the artifact (object) study design appropriate for political science research? Why or why not?

Additional Reading

Folz, David H. 1996. *Survey Research for Public Administration*. Thousand Oaks, CA: Sage.
Kumar, Ranjit. 1996. *Research Methodology*. London: Sage.
Miller, Gerald J., and Marcia L. Whicker, eds. 1999. *Handbook of Research Methods in Public Administration*. New York: Marcel Dekker.
Schwab, Donald P. 1999. *Research Methods for Organizational Studies*. Mahwah, NJ: Lawrence Erlbaum Associates.

Part 2

Introduction to Quantitative Research Approaches

8 Fundamental Concepts in Quantitative Research

An underlying objective of most political science research is to uncover information needed to expand and improve the level of awareness and understanding of one or more political phenomena. Although they generally narrow their focus to more specific areas of interest, such as political theory, American government, international relations, or public policy, political scientists employ methods and techniques that are common to all the social sciences. In designing a research study, the political scientist must establish priorities, identify alternatives and choose options, set and manage budgets, and often hire, motivate, and, when necessary, fire research assistants. Researchers receive, give, or pass on instructions, develop and write research plans with objectives and strategies, monitor their staff's performance, and keep higher-level administrators and funding bodies informed about their progress toward achieving their research objectives. In turn, higher-level administrators, such as department heads and deans, are often called upon to communicate the progress of the researchers in their units to internal and external stakeholders.

In every one of these tasks, political scientists and administrators make decisions. In doing so, they compare two or more alternatives, weigh the costs and benefits of each, and then select and implement the better alternative. To improve the quality of their decisions, administrators must thoroughly understand the processes involved in conducting research.

To make effective decisions about their research proposals and research studies, political scientists more often than not apply quantitative research methods and interpret quantitative data. Often, the proper use of numbers—statistics—with words makes communicating easier, faster, and far more effective than the use of words alone. Statistics and statistical methods cannot be applied, however, until the fundamental nature of measurement is understood. Beginning with a discussion of the four types of measurements, the next several chapters are an introduction to some of the most-used quantitative research designs, looked at from a focus of how to use and interpret statistical methods, rather than on the theoretical aspect of statistical analysis. The purpose of this chapter is to help researchers and those involved in either approving, funding, monitoring, or evaluating research in political science. It begins with a review of the fundamentals of measurement and the nature of numbers.

Fundamentals of Measurement

The key to ensuring that everyone who reads a research report understands the measurements lies in the consistent use of the measurement scale appropriate for the task at hand. In the

Table 8.1

Measurements and Some Typical Applications

Class of Measurement	Typical Application
Ratio	Zero- or Fixed-Based Scales or Weights
Interval	Attitude or Opinion Scales, Equal Intervals
Ordinal	Rank Order of Items or Preferences
Nominal	Counts and/or Percentages of Frequencies

following discussion, the terms "measurement" and "data" will often be used interchangeably to refer to the same or similar idea: the numbers that are used to signify variable measurements. Variables are things that can be counted or measured. Different values of a variable can convey different meanings. Helping to establish this meaning is the nature of the measurement data. Measurements all belong to one of four classes, as shown in Table 8.1.

The four different types or levels of measurement found in political science research are: (1) nominal, (2) ordinal, (3) interval, and (4) ratio. Statisticians have developed different statistical tests that are used to analyze data of each different type (data types are also referred to as *scales* of measurement). In differentiating between the scale types, each level or type must meet one or more rules. Moving beyond nominal scales—considered to be the "least powerful" of the four scales in terms of meaning that can be conveyed—toward higher or more powerful scales, the preceding rules must also apply to each higher-level measurement. The discussion begins with nominal data. Nominal data are numbers assigned to a category or single counts of the times a category appears in the data.

Nominal Data

Nominal data, the least powerful of the four types of data, must comply with just one rule. This rule states that *different numbers must mean different things*. Thus, a nominal scale, as the term implies, is simply a *naming* or classification scale. With these scales, the differences in categories to which a number may be assigned are qualitative differences; this means they are not counts of something but a number that is subjectively assigned to one category in a class that contains more than one group.

With nominal-level data, numbers or labels are used only to differentiate between things. The numbers or labels serve no other purpose or function and supply no additional information. Furthermore, once a number has been assigned to a given category, all other items with the same characteristics must receive the same number or label. Just one attribute is singled out, such as gender, and that attribute, and only that attribute, dictates further classification. Typical examples of nominal or categorical scales

1. The values of "1" and "2" arbitrarily assigned to the categories of female and male.
2. The values "0" and "1" assigned to service user and nonuser groups.
3. Numbers used to denote different types of occupations, political party membership, class in college (freshman, sophomore, etc.), newspapers or magazines read by subjects, etc.
4. The counts of the number of times a head comes up when a coin is tossed.

When nominal-level data are presented in a table, they are said to be in *tabular form*. Tables are the most common way of presenting numerical information about a sample; tabular form is the most common way of presenting *descriptive statistics*—the summaries of the counts or frequencies found in the measurement. Once again, it is important to remember that, while only a single rule applies to nominal data—different numbers mean different things—it is a rule that cannot be broken.

Ordinal Data

An *ordinal* scale of measurement supplies more information than a nominal scale; *two* rules apply as opposed to just one with nominal data. The nominal scale rule, "different numbers mean different things," must first be passed. But the second rule must also apply. This rule states that *the things being measured can be ranked or ordered along some dimension*. With ordinal data (often simply referred to as *ranked* data), the differences between measures are *quantitative* rather than just qualitative. When things are ordered, they are arranged in some logical sequence—they may have more or less of a particular characteristic than others in the set. The primary limitation that exists with ordinal measurements is that the numbers seldom state precisely how *much more or less* difference exists in the sets of two or more collections of data; we know only that "more" or "less" of something is communicated by these numbers. We do not know *how much* more or less, however.

A typical use for ordinal scales is to measure people's preferences or rankings for candidates, services, or things. Much of the opinion data collected by political scientists is based upon ordinal scales. Examples include surveys of issue awareness, policy preferences, and preference rankings for political candidates.

Interval Data

The third class of measurement data is *equidistant interval*—more commonly referred to simply as "*interval*." To qualify as an interval scale, the measurements must now pass three tests. First, the different numbers must mean different things. Second, the things measured can be ranked or ordered on some appropriate dimension. And third—the most important rule—is that *the differences between adjacent levels on the scale are* (or are assumed to be) *equal.*

With interval data, in addition to determining that one scale item falls above or below another, it is now possible to determine "exactly" *how much* one item differs from another. The differences between levels on the scale can be any size but they must all be the same. The zero-point on the scale can be set anywhere on the scale that the researcher wants it to be. The key requirement is that a single-unit change *always* measures the same amount of change in whatever is being measured. The unit gradations within the scale may be as broad or as fine as need be. For example, on a five-point scale, the distance between "3" and "4" or "4" and "5" might be measured in tenths, hundreds, thousands, or even finer, but they apply to every part of the scale equally. Thus, one might see *mean* (the word "mean" refers to one type of average) measurements of 3.3, 3.33, or 3.333, depending on the accuracy desired. The distance between "3" and "4," or "1" and "2," etc., never changes, however. Only the *fineness* of the measurement is changed.

Measuring temperature using the Fahrenheit scale is a good example of interval-scale data. Fahrenheit scales have a zero point, but it is no more important than any other number on the scale. Other examples are grade point averages, dimensions, and IQ scores. Attitude scales using different levels of agreement are often assumed to provide interval-level data. This makes the attitude scale a highly desired measurement tool for all social and administrative science researchers. Interval scales provide more information than either nominal or ordinal scales because of the equal distance between measurement points. There are, however, still limitations to the information provided by interval data. For example, because the zero point is set arbitrarily, it is not possible to say that one measure is exactly twice as great or as small than another. We cannot say that 100 degrees Fahrenheit is exactly twice as warm as 50 degrees, nor that 35 degrees is half as warm as 70 degrees. We can only say that the differences between single points on the scale are equal. We must turn to the fourth level, ratio scales, to make such qualifying statements.

Many researchers still decry the practice of using attitude scale measurements as interval data, saying that the data are really ordinal. The criticism they put forward as a "law" is: *Do not make interval-level conclusions on ordinal-level data.* Despite this criticism, much published social and administrative science research continues to report statistical processing of attitude scales and their interpretations as interval data. The rationale is that, with large samples, the distributions of responses with the two data types are, or nearly are, equal.

Ratio Data

As with the other three scales or data types, lower-level rules also apply to ratio scales. Different numbers must still mean different things; the data can still be ranked or ordered on some dimension; and the intervals between adjacent points are of equal value. The ratio-required fourth rule is that *the measurement scale has an absolute or fixed zero point*—even if it is not used in the specific range of items being measured. Examples of ratio scales are time, distance, mass, and various combinations of these; units sold; number of purchasers; and temperature according to the Celsius scale. In applications of statistics in political science research, the distinction between interval and ratio is of little practical value. The same statistical tests can be used for either data type; they are also interpreted in the same manner. As a result, statistical software packages like the Statistical Package for the Social Sciences (SPSS®) have combined the two into a single category called "scale data," which includes statistical tests for both interval and ratio data.

Defining Statistics

The term "statistics" is used in a number of different ways. First, it is used to mean the numerical data in a report. Examples include such things as the number of clients served each day, week, or month, hours worked and employees' earnings, costs per unit, turnover rates, performance ratios, age and gender of citizens in the community, and many, many more. The term is also used to define the many mathematical techniques and procedures used for collecting, describing, analyzing, and interpreting data.

Statistical processes can include simple counts of events, or the determination of the central values of a group of counts. It can include conducting hypothesis tests, or determining relationships between two variables. In summary, statistics may be considered as both *numerical data* and the variety of *tools* or techniques that administrators and researchers use to process raw data to make them more meaningful.

Important Statistics Terms and Concepts

Like every discipline or management function, a variety of concepts and terms not part of our common language experience are to be found in the study of statistics. Definitions for some of these concepts are:

- *Descriptive Statistics*: Measurements or numbers used to summarize or describe datasets.
- *Inferential Statistics*: Statistical techniques used to make estimates or inferences about the characteristics of interest for a population using the data from a sample dataset.
- *Sample*: A portion of a population. The sample is chosen as representative of the entire population.
- *Population*: The set of all elements for which measurements are possible. A population can consist of products, workers, customers, firms, prices, etc., about which the decision maker or manager is interested. Another word used to identify a population is a *universe*.
- *Statistic*: A number used as a summary measure for a sample. For example, "The mean age for the 20 students in the sample is 20.3 years."
- *Parameter*: A numerical value used as a summary measure for a population or universe. For example, in the statement "The mean age for all entering college or university freshmen is 19.1 years," the mean age of all entering freshmen is a *parameter*.
- *Variable*: A characteristic or quantity that can have different values. Examples include such things as savings account amounts, stock prices, package designs, weight, monthly sales, gender, salaries, etc. The values of variables may be said to be either *continuous* or *discrete*.
- *Continuous Variables*: Quantities that are measured, such as weight or percentage of increase in the price of a stock, are said to be continuous. Values for continuous variables can be measured on a continuous scale such as weights, and are not restricted to specific, discrete categories or values.
- *Discrete Variables*: Discrete variables have values that can vary only in specific steps or categories (they are sometimes called categorical). Assuming that we assign in advance the value of "1" for female and "2" for male, the variable *gender* is an example of a discrete variable.
- *Univariate Statistics*: Univariate statistics are the statistics describing a single variable. They include such measures as the valid number of responses (frequencies), the mean, median, and mode, and standard deviation.
- *Bivariate Statistics*: These are measurements with which two variables are described or compared at the same time. A crosstabulation table is an example of bivariate statistics in use. Counts, percentages, correlations, difference tests, and many other statistical tests can be carried out with bivariate statistics.
- *Multivariate Statistics*: Multivariate statistics, such as *multiple regression analysis,* are statistics used when more than one independent variable influences one or more dependent variables. For example, votes for a particular candidate are probably influenced by the candidate's party, the platform, issues, make-up of the electorate, and advertising expenditures, among others.

Categories of Statistics

Statistics can be categorized in several different ways. One way is according to how they are applied. Statistics can be used to describe something or they can be used to infer similar measurements in another, larger group. The first of these applications is called *descriptive statistics;* the second application type is called *inferential statistics. Descriptive statistics* are used to numerically *describe* such things as events, concepts, people, work, or many other things. Another use of descriptive statistics is for *summarizing* a set of data. A *dataset* is simply a collection of a distinct set of measurements. A dataset can be as large as the combined total of all measurements of all U.S. residents taken every ten years for the *Census of Population.* Or, it can be as small as a dozen or so test scores from a midterm examination. *Inferential statistics* describes a class of statistics that are used for one or more of the following purposes:

1. To make generalizations about a larger group—called a *population*—from which the sample was taken,
2. To estimate or draw conclusions about a population, or,
3. To make predictions about some future event or state of affairs.

Note that these uses typically employ measurements of a smaller group (a *sample*) for making *inferences* about a larger group (a *population*). This is why they are known as "inferential statistics." The term "sample" is used to mean some portion of a population. Samples are usually chosen to be representative of some larger population. A *population,* on the other hand, is the set of all elements for which measurements are possible. A population can consist of voters, legislators, workers, customers, governmental units, prices, or anything else about which the researcher is interested. A survey of every unit in a population is called a *census.* Individually, each person, item, or thing in the sample, population, or universe is called a *population unit.* Another label sometimes used to identify a population is a *universe.* The labels "population" and "universe" are often used interchangeably to mean a complete set or group of people, items, events, etc. from which a sample is or can be drawn. If the population of interest is small—for example, all living ex-presidents—then no sample is necessary. Inferential statistics may still be used, however.

Parameters versus Statistics

Statisticians categorize measurement data based on whether they apply to a sample or to a parent population. A *parameter* is a numerical value used as a summary measure for a population or a universe. For example, consider the statement "The mean age for all entering college or university freshmen in California is 18.8 years." Because 18.8 years is the average of all entering freshmen—the population—it is a *parameter.*

A *statistic,* on the other hand, is a number used as a summary measure for a sample. For example, consider the statement "The mean age for a sample of 30 Benson College freshmen is 20.3 years." The mean for this sample is a *statistic.* In this case, the mean for the sample is larger than it was for the population of all college and university freshmen in the country, and statistical techniques have been developed to determine whether the two mean values are "statistically different" or not.

Parametric versus Nonparametric Statistics

Parametric statistics require that measurements come from a population in which the distribution of variances is normal. Parametric statistics require internal and ratio data. This does not mean that all the measurements are the same. Rather, it means that the differences vary in what we call a "normal" way. Take the measurements of the incomes of a randomly drawn sample of a thousand households, for example. If each of the measurements were plotted, it would be expected that the distribution of incomes for members of the sample would come close to the same distribution that occurred in the population—and this distribution would be expected to be "normal."

Plotting this distribution would result in a typical bell-shaped curve. There would be a few values at either end of the curve but the bulk would fall around the middle value—near what would be the mean for the sample. When discussing measures of central tendency, it would be appropriate to refer to the average or *mean* income of the group with this measurement. Inferential statistical tests could be used as well.

Nonparametric Statistics

Nonparametric statistical procedures must be used when working with nominal and ordinal-level data. No assumptions can be made about the distribution of these measurements, nor can any assumptions be made about the larger population. Rather, with nonparametric statistics, the distribution may be assumed to *not* be normal.

Testing a sample of new parts coming off a manufacturing line can be used as an example. The parts are examined to see if they work or don't work—often called a "pass or fail" test. Only one of two possible outcomes is possible. There is no way to establish if the distribution of "passes" and "fails" is normal or not. A mean or average score is no longer possible; instead, the researcher can only say something like "three out of a hundred failed," or that "97 out of a hundred passed." Both the "three" and the "97" are nonparametric statistics.

With this nonparametric example, the means must be replaced by the mode. The *mode* is the value that comes up most often. Here, the mode is 97. It is meaningless to talk about a "mean" score on a two- or three-category item. Rather, the category appearing most often, the "mode," is the relevant information.

Descriptive Statistics

One of the great advantages of using numbers instead of words to describe something is that it often makes it easier for both the sender and receiver to agree on what is being said. For example, one person might be described as being 6 feet tall, and a second person as being 5 feet, 9 inches tall. Clearly, when both people are standing on the same level surface, one is taller than the other. But how great is the difference? It is hard to tell by just looking at the two people. By *measuring* the differences in height, it becomes possible to know for sure. Because numbers were used instead of just saying "one is taller," it is now possible to know that one person is precisely three inches taller than the other person. Furthermore, in the English language the word "three" and the symbol "3" refer to the same amount. Three inches or three bananas is the same number (amount) as three oranges.

The same communication concept is true for fractions and percentages. Most people will comprehend the idea behind the phrase "one-third" and will know that 33.3 percent is very nearly the same thing as one-third. One-third of a gallon is the same *share* of the whole as is one third of a liter, or one-third of a pound, even though the absolute quantities are different. One-third of anything is always one-third of whatever is the unit of measurement. Numbers make it possible to communicate these ideas.

The same is true for other percentages. One hundred percent of anything can only mean all of it, a totality. One hundred and ten percent, on the other hand, is all of something plus ten percent more. And every time you use it or say it, it is the same. That's the beauty of using numbers when communicating; little or nothing is lost in translation. Because things can be measured, they can be described.

Using Descriptive Statistics to Summarize

Descriptive statistics are the sets of measurements (numbers) used to *summarize* a set of larger numbers, and *that have the same meaning for everyone.* The following example helps explain how descriptive statistics are used:

A public assistance program manager is interested in knowing the size (amount) of clients' allotments. In today's age of desktop computers, it would be a relatively simple task for the manager to call up a list of all client monthly totals, when the last payment occurred, and a host of other information about each client. However, the volume of data that such requests can quickly provide could soon become overwhelming. By themselves, the numbers for any individual would most likely provide little information about the total. What the administrator could use instead is a simple set of numbers that *summarize* specific features of all clients' accounts—in a word, produce a *summary* of the dataset. Such a summary uses descriptive statistics.

Inferential Statistics

As stated earlier, the second major use of statistics is for *inferential purposes*. With these tools, researchers assume or infer that measurements of some characteristics of a smaller group (the sample) are held in common by some larger group (the population). One example of inferential statistics is in the periodic testing of small portions of a production run (a sample or samples) to *estimate* the failure or error rate of the entire day's production (a population).

Another example of how inferential statistics are used is the now-famous experience of administrators who determined statistically that taking one aspirin a day may greatly decrease the likelihood of having a heart attack. In the aspirin experiment, some 10,000 medical doctors were recruited to participate in a 10-year experiment. Half were to take one aspirin a day; the other half, an inert placebo (colored chalk). Participants were assigned to their group randomly so that no one knew to which group he or she belonged. After just a few years, the incidence of heart attacks among the aspirin takers was found to be so much lower than among the placebo group that the experiment was called to a halt and the results announced. Taking one aspirin a day was deemed to be highly likely to reduce one's chance of (that is, lower the probability of) having a heart attack. Thus, the assumption (or inference) was made that the results (measurements) of the sample applied to the overall population as well.

Statistics and Measurements

As we have seen, *statistics* is a collective term used to denote the numbers used to communicate the *measurements* of something. The measurements of a particular *sample* are typically drawn from a larger body. The larger group is called the *population* or *universe*. As we have seen, only the numerical values that apply to the sample are known as "statistics," whereas the values of the population are known as "parameters." In learning about applying statistics to political science situations, this difference is seldom a problem; managers rarely deal with entire populations.

Measurement. Usually, the term "measurement" refers to numbers read from some measuring tool. The numerical values encountered in statistics are typically based upon some type of *scale* or other measuring device, such as a ruler, a questionnaire, or gauge. With such measurement or recording devices, the numbers are arranged according to some meaningful *scale* that has been determined to be appropriate by the person or persons reading the scale. Examples of scales include such measurements as inches and feet, millimeters and centimeters, foot-pounds of pressure, engine horsepower, computer chip memory capacity, miles per hour, and others.

Political science has followed the lead of the social sciences and expanded the concept of a scale to include such phenomena as responses to questions on an attitude or lifestyle questionnaire. Scales have also been established to measure levels or increments of awareness, agreement, desirability, rank order, preference, and many other similar concepts. In all applications, numbers are assigned to various "things" such as events, objects, characteristics, responses, qualities, and the like.

Statistics in Research

Political scientists use both descriptive and inferential statistics in their research. In both applications, the numerical information may be presented in tables, in charts, and as graphic illustrations. The most important of these statistics and some of the more commonly encountered uses of descriptive and inferential statistical tests are discussed in the following sections and illustrated by Figure 8.1.

Types of Descriptive Statistics

According to Lang and Heiss (1990), the four basic types of descriptive statistics used in scientific research are:

1. Measures of central tendency. This includes the mean, the mode, and the median values of a dataset.
2. Measures of variability in the dataset. The three variability values to be discussed are the standard deviation (SD), the range, and the interquartile range.
3. Measures of relative position in the set. Included are *percentiles* and *standard scores.* The most commonly used standardized score is the *Z-score.*
4. Measures of correlation between two or more variables. Correlation tests are used to show how strongly and in what direction two variables are related, if at all.

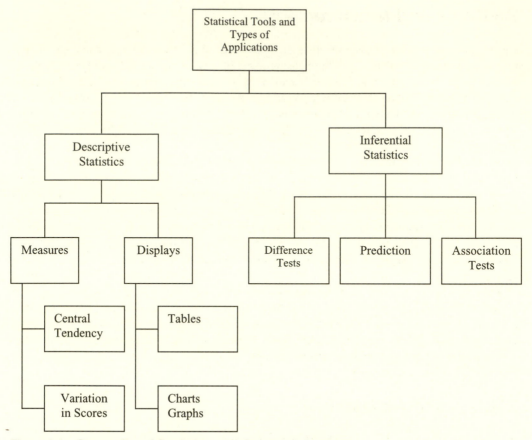

Figure 8.1   **Categories of Statistics with Some Applications**

A wide variety of inferential statistical tools have been developed for use in these four applications. Naturally, not all of these have application to the majority of decisions that face researchers or administrators. The tests discussed in later chapters have been selected for their extensive use in political science, public management, and organizational management literature, for their relative ease of application and clear interpretation characteristics, and for their availability in most general statistical software packages.

Types of Inferential Statistical Tests

Today, it is no longer necessary for anyone to memorize confusing statistical formulas or to work complex statistical calculations by hand. Most political science researchers have access to a personal computer. Powerful statistical software has been available almost from the desktop computer's introduction. However, much of the early statistical software was limited in scope because of hardware restrictions that resulted in slow processing speed and limited the number of variables and/or cases that could be contained in a working dataset. Efficient statistical processing of large datasets required far more memory than was available on early desktop computers. This is no longer a problem. Throughout the remainder of this book, a variety of statistical software will be referenced, primarily Microsoft's® Excel™ and the SPSS®.

The basic types of inferential statistics (i.e., procedures) used in political science research include, but are not limited to, the following:

1. The *t*-test for significant differences between means of dependent (uncorrelated) groups.
2. The *t*-test for significant differences between the means of paired or correlated groups.
3. Simple regression analysis for measuring the strength and the direction of relationships between variables.
4. Analysis of variance (ANOVA) tests for differences on one variable for two or more groups.
5. Analysis of variance (ANOVA) tests for differences on two or more variables between two or more groups, and for any *interaction* that might result from the two variables.
6. Analysis of covariance (ANCOVA) as used in pre- and posttest experimental applications.

Summary

Political scientists use words and numbers to communicate the results of their research and creative thinking about ideas and topics in the political world. Academic department heads, deans, college presidents, legislators, public administrators, and other organizational managers also use words and numbers to communicate with their staffs, supervisors, as well as with people and groups outside of their organization. Statistics are numbers and the results of tests conducted on sets of numbers. The results can be presented in either tables, graphs, or other illustrations, and help to ensure mutual understanding of the data at hand.

When the term "statistics" is used, it can mean one or more specific measures or values describing some thing, a sample of some type. Or the word can be used to refer to a body of mathematical tools and techniques invented for analyzing and giving meaning to sets of numbers. This latter use of the word is called *statistical analysis.*

The numerical values in statistics are typically measurements taken with some type of scale or measuring device. These scales provide different levels of information, based upon the type of data they are intended to acquire. The four types or levels of data (the terms apply to the data-gathering scales as well), from the "lowest" in power to the "highest," are nominal, ordinal, interval, and ratio. Each data type has a body of statistical tests that are appropriate for that level; lower-level tests should not be used on higher-level data.

Statistics are used in two main ways: (1) as *descriptive statistics,* they are used to summarize a larger set of numbers, called a "dataset"; (2) as *inferential statistics,* the measurements of a smaller group—a *sample*—are used for making assumptions about a larger group—the *population* or *universe* of interest.

Statistics may also be *parametric* or *nonparametric.* Parametric statistics require that certain assumptions be made of the host population, such as a normal distribution. These require universal and ratio data. With nonparametric statistics, no such assumptions need be made; ordinal and internal data are nonparametric.

It is no longer necessary for anyone to memorize confusing statistical formulas or to work complex statistical calculations by hand. Powerful statistical software has been available almost from the desktop computer's introduction. However, much of the early statistical software was limited in scope because of hardware restrictions that resulted in slow processing speed and limited the number of variables and/or cases that could be contained in a working dataset. Efficient statistical processing of large datasets required far more memory than was available on early desktop computers. Today, however, most personal computers can process nearly all the data that researchers can handle. Throughout the remainder of this book, a variety of statistical software will be referenced, primarily Microsoft's® Excel™ and the SPSS®.

Discussion Questions

1. Name the four levels of measurement and the rules that apply to each.
2. In your own words, define statistics.
3. Name six or more of the twelve major components found in the use of statistics.
4. What are descriptive statistics? Why and when are they used?
5. What are inferential statistics? Why and when are they used?
6. What is the difference between a statistic and a parameter?
7. What are nonparametric statistics?
8. What are the four basic types of descriptive statistics?
9. Name four or more of the basic types of inferential statistics seen in political science research.
10. What are statistical software packages?

Additional Reading

Berenson, Mark L., and David M. Levine. 1996. *Basic Business Statistics: Concepts and Applications.* 6th ed. Upper Saddle River, NJ: Prentice-Hall.

Einspruch, Eruch. 1998. *An Introductory Guide to SPSS® for Windows®.* Thousand Oaks, CA: Sage.

Green, Samuel B., Neil J. Salkind, and Theresa M. Akey. 2000. *Using SPSS.* Upper Saddle River, NJ: Prentice-Hall.

Lapin, Lawrence. 1993. *Statistics for Modern Business Decisions.* New York: Harcourt Brace Jovanovich.

Neufeld, John L. 1997. *Learning Business Statistics with Microsoft® Excel.™.* Upper Saddle River, NJ: Prentice-Hall.

Phillips, John L. 1996. *How to Think about Statistics.* 5th ed. New York: W.H. Freeman.

9 Introduction to the Sampling Process

Seldom, if ever, will researchers find themselves measuring entire populations. Rather, they are far more likely to draw a *sample* from the population and measure the elements in that sample. These results are then assumed to apply to the entire sample as well; researchers conclude that similar results would be found if every element in the sample were measured. Sample measurements are called *statistics;* population measurements are called *parameters.* Researchers acquire sample *statistics* to estimate a larger population's unknown *parameters.* The process is known as *inference,* and the statistical tests that are used for this purpose are called *inferential statistics.* If all possible information needed to solve a problem could be collected, there would be no need to sample. Political science researchers seldom have this luxury; they are typically limited in time and money. Therefore, people making decisions based on research use data gathered from samples, and make their decisions based on *probabilities* that the sample data mirror what could be expected if it were possible to survey an entire population (Fitz-Gibbon and Morris 1987).

For example, the author once conducted a series of focus groups at public recreation centers in ten different cities across the United States. The objective of the study was to determine which features of running shoes male and female recreational runners preferred. Obviously, the study did not require that all runners in the United States or even in a single state, town, or village be interviewed. Instead, a series of samples were interviewed in each of the most populous and urbanized states where large numbers of subjects engaged in the activity of interest. These data were determined by the number of shoes for each sport sold in the state and city (trade association data were used for this purpose). The results provided a consensus that greatly reduced the potential loss resulting from including less desirable features in new shoe models.

It must also be noted that sometimes it is, indeed, possible to take a census. The term "census" means that every element in the group or population of interest is measured. Surveys of industrial consumers or of consumer product distributors are frequently conducted as a census. For example, a manufacturer of commercial rainwear was able to purchase from the U.S. Coast Guard a list of all registered owners of commercial fishing vessels. In what later turned out to be a costly mistake, the firm wanted a questionnaire mailed to every name on the list. The mistake became apparent when it was learned that registered owners of commercial fishing vessels are not always fishermen. Banks and other investors own a majority of the vessels. These owners did not return the questionnaires sent to them—the study had no meaning for them. On the other hand, this same firm later surveyed a sample of just 165 active commercial fishermen to learn of their preferences in waterproof footwear. Subjects were randomly selected from participants at an off-season trade show. That information was exceptionally valuable.

This chapter begins with a discussion on why sampling is important. This is followed by a comparative description of several different types of samples, the meaning of bias and error in sampling, sample distributions, and concepts of sample size. It concludes with a review of several statistical procedures relating to sampling.

Why We Sample

The main reasons why samples are used in place of a census of a population involve considerations of cost, time, accuracy, and the "destructive" nature of the measurement process. Costs and time are closely related. In planning a statistical study budget, the researcher must address the following key concerns:

- How accurate must the final results be in order to make the type of decision required in the particular business situation?
- What is the cost to the organization if the wrong decision is made?
- How much more information must be added to reach that level of accuracy?
- What kinds of data are needed? How much does it cost to acquire the data?
- Can we afford the extra cost?

Sampling Precision

Researchers use measurements of the characteristics of a sample for inferring or forecasting similar characteristics about larger samples or populations. In a sense, they use the sample data to *predict* how a population will act or react under the same conditions in some future situation or event. However, researchers can control few, if any, of the intervening variables that might affect that future event; they are asked to measure the unknowable. The idea of *sampling precision* refers to how confident the researcher feels about using the sample data for inferences. The idea of using sample data this way is founded upon the fundamental concepts of *probability*. The researcher's level of confidence is typically stated in terms of probability, and typically stated as either a "0.10, 0.05, or 0.01 level of confidence." In the language of probability, a value of 1.0 indicates 100 percent confidence in a statistical result; 0.10 indicates that the researcher is 90 percent sure about the results; 0.05 means 95 percent sure; and 0.01 means 99 percent sure.

Achieving a high degree of precision is often difficult—if not impossible—to attain without greatly increasing the size of a sample. This is not the problem that it might seem to be, however. In most research in the social and administrative sciences, it is seldom necessary to achieve very high degrees of precision or reliability. Instead, researchers can most often deal very well with information that is only *relative*. The cost of acquiring additional information in order to improve the precision of a measurement is often prohibitive. Precision, and, hence, reliability, can be increased at a rate far more slowly than simply increasing sample size. Reliability grows at the square root of the increase in sample size. Thus, to double reliability requires making the sample four times as large!

Using very large samples can have other drawbacks as well. One is the *destructive nature* of the survey process. Simply by being asked questions, subjects begin to think about them. This can result in changes in their attitudes. Exposure to a survey questionnaire may help the subject to verbalize deeply seated attitudes that had lain dormant, but were brought to the fore during the study. There are a number of techniques that researchers can use to achieve greater reliability of a sample study. Among the most important of these is the type of *sampling method* employed.

Sampling Methods

Sampling method refers to the way the sample units are selected from a parent population. When deciding which combination of sampling characteristics to use, researchers must make decisions in five basic areas. These, when combined, allow for thirty-two different possible choice combinations. The five basic concerns are listed below; each is discussed in some detail in the following paragraphs:

- Probability versus nonprobability sample?
- Single unit versus cluster of units?
- Unstratified versus stratified sample?
- Equal unit probability versus unequal probability?
- Single stage versus multi-stage?

Probability or Nonprobability Sample?

This may be the single most important decision in sampling. Probability sampling is one of the fundamental bases upon which all inferential statistics is built. A *probability* sample is one in which the sample units (people, parts, groups, homes, cities, tribes, companies, etc.) are selected at random and all have an equal chance at being selected. Examples include the simple random samples (SRS) and systematic samples. A *nonprobability* sample is one in which chance selection techniques are not used. Examples include convenience samples (selected at the convenience of the manager) and quota samples, where only subjects with specific characteristics are added until some predetermined mix is achieved. A third example of a nonprobability sample often used in political science research is a judgment sample. Judgment sampling entails substituting experience or the judgment of an administrator or researcher for a more scientific approach at randomization. It often means deliberately picking a sample that is nonrepresentative of a population.

The choice between a probability and nonprobability sample is often based on the cost-versus-value principle. The researcher will pick the method that provides the greatest margin of value over cost. A worthwhile rule of thumb to follow in sample selection is that the more diversified the population, the greater the need to guarantee representativeness by following a probability sampling method.

Single-Unit or Cluster Sampling?

A *sampling unit* is the basic element of the population—such as a person or a thing—being sampled. When choosing whether to use *single-unit* or *cluster sampling* methods, the deciding factor is the nature of the sampling unit. In single-unit sampling, each sampling unit is selected independently. In cluster sampling, the units are selected in groups. If sampling units are households, single-unit sampling requires that households in the sample be selected without reference to any other characteristic. A cluster sample might change the sampling unit to the random selection of city blocks, with some or all households on each selected block then surveyed.

Cluster sampling usually costs less per sampling unit than does single-unit sampling. As a rule of thumb, whenever a study involves a low tolerance for error with a high expected cost of errors, and a highly heterogeneous population, single-unit sampling is favored over cluster sampling.

Stratified or Unstratified Sampling?

The third consideration is the *stratified* or *unstratified* sample question. A sample *stratum* is a portion of a population that has one or more characteristics of interest to the analyst. Examples include political party membership, income level, age, and many others. The final sample is selected so that it reflects the same percentages of the characteristic that are found in the larger population. A stratified sample may help to ensure representativeness and, thus, reduce potential for sampling error. Finally, to obtain the same level of sampling error, a smaller sample size is needed with a stratified sample than would be needed if a nonstratified sample were used. Opinion studies in political science often use stratified samples.

Equal or Unequal Unit Probability?

The question of *equal unit* or *unequal unit* probability sampling (that is, a greater or lesser likelihood of a sampling element's being included) is closely associated with strata in the population. The final sample drawn will include a disproportionately larger (or smaller) percentage of the characteristic of interest.

Although a key tenet of probability sampling is the concept of equal probability of being selected, researchers often find themselves in situations where following the equal probability rule will result in biased results. For example, a political campaign manager conducting a survey of local voting patterns will probably include more persons older than 50 years of age and fewer in the 18-to-24-years-of-age group in the sample because the older group tends to vote disproportionately more often than younger voters. The researcher's sample is more than likely to be heavily weighted in favor of relevant demographic and ethnic, socioeconomic, and gender groups because they are more likely to have a disproportionate influence on the outcome of the election.

Single-Stage or Multistage Sampling?

The final consideration has to do with *single* or *multistage sampling*. The number of stages included in a sampling process is usually dictated by the nature of the population and the sample frame (source of units). Sampling for a congressional attitude toward a particular bill may be a single-stage process; voters are randomly selected from the list of legislators. On the other hand, a study of citizens' opinions is typically a multistage sampling involving the three-stage process shown in Figure 9.1.

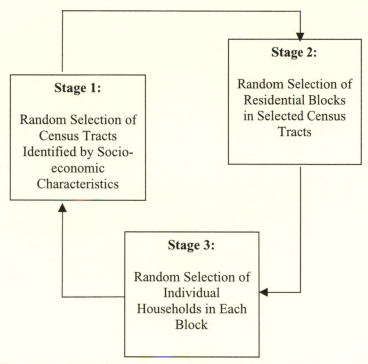

Figure 9.1 **Three Stages in a Multistage Sampling Process**

In a comprehensive survey of consumer attitudes across a large area, a multistage process will often be used. Multistage sampling is also the method of choice for needs analysis studies when sampling large populations and with population elements disbursed over a wide area.

Sample Bias and Sampling Error

The ultimate objective of all sampling is to select a set of elements from a population in such a way that the measurements of that set of elements accurately reflect the same measurements of the population from which they were selected. A number of potential pitfalls exist to make achieving this objective difficult. Among these are bias and several different types of potential error. These are characterized as *sampling error* and *nonsampling error*. Several types of non-sampling error can occur, including sampling frame error, nonresponse error, and data error.

Sample Bias

Bias in sampling refers to the sampling process itself; it is sometimes referred to as *systematic bias*. Bias can be intentional or unintentional. Intentional bias is used when a researcher has a particular point to prove and uses statistics to support the preestablished conclusion. For example, an agriculture researcher might intentionally select a better piece of ground to show more dramatic yield improvements from a new plant seed.

Unintentional bias can occur as a result of a researcher's best efforts to include relevant elements in the final sample. For example, in decision making to determine whether voters might approve a special bond issue for library construction, the researcher might telephone only registered voters. This results in a *double* bias. First, it includes only people with telephones, and second, it ignores the library users who have not voted in the past, but would in order to improve the library system. The best way to avoid or reduce any and all bias is to maintain random selection procedures.

Sampling Error

Sampling error occurs when a sample with characteristics that do not reflect the population is studied. It is almost impossible to specify a sample that exactly matches the parameters of a given population. Nor will the results of a second sample exactly match the first. More samples taken will not increase the likelihood of a perfect match occurring.

Two "laws of numbers" affect sampling error. First, the *law of large numbers* suggests that increasing sample size will reduce the size of the sampling error encountered. The *law of diminishing returns* also applies to error reduction. Recall that to reduce error by half requires making the sample *four* times as large. Using a statistically efficient sampling plan is clearly the best way to control sampling error.

Dealing with Nonsampling Error

Nonsampling error can result from many different sources. Several of these sources include problems with the *sampling frame,* with subjects' *nonresponse,* and errors in the *data* itself. Each of these sources of error is discussed in greater detail below.

Sampling Frame Error

The sampling frame is the source (such as a list or a telephone directory) from which the sample is drawn. If the study is a test of components provided by an outside supplier, the sampling frame is the collected total of all parts provided by the supplier. If the sample is to be drawn from voters who enter a particular polling place, the sample frame consists of the actual premises; the population in this example is all persons who enter the facility during the survey period.

For example, the author assisted in a study of the attitudes and concerns about terrorism among a group of regional airline passengers. The sampling frame for the study consisted of the list of passengers with reservations to fly on a specific route on a specific day. Individual passengers were randomly selected from those waiting in the boarding lounge before boarding their aircraft. The key to reducing *sampling frame error* is to start with as complete a sampling frame as possible. If the sampling frame is a list of clients, it should be up-to-date and include everyone. If the sample frame is "the voters in a given precinct or legislative district," it should include all citizens who are registered to vote, not just the voters who voted in the last one or two elections.

A way to adjust for potential sample frame error has been developed by researchers who gather data by telephone. Increasingly, private telephone numbers are not included in printed telephone directories. To deal with this problem, the survey operators modified their telephone book sample frames to include unknown, nonlisted numbers. In a process that is called *plus-*

one dialing, they do this by adding one number to the numbers taken at random from the directory.

Nonresponse Error

Nonresponse error is another problem encountered in survey research designs. When only small proportions of subjects respond, there is a strong probability that the results are not characteristic of the population. This type of error may be reduced through the use of incentives for completing and returning the survey instrument, and through follow-up telephoning, although there is no guarantee error reduction will occur.

Data Error

Finally, *data error* can occur because of distortions in the data collected or from mistakes in data coding, analysis, or interpretation of statistical analysis. Several different ways to reduce data error in research projects are:

- Ensure that survey instruments (questionnaires) are well prepared, simple to read, and easy to understand.
- Avoid internal bias (such as the use of leading or value-laden words).
- Properly select and train interviewers to control data-gathering bias or error.
- Use sound editing, coding, and tabulating procedures to reduce the possibility of data-processing error.

Sample Distributions

When researchers talk about *sampling distributions,* they are referring to the way a statistic would be distributed if computed for a series of samples taken from the same population. This concept has several uses: First, it provides the researcher a quick estimate of the validity of the results of the study. Second, it enables the researcher to estimate the values of some variable in a population of interest. Third, it produces a value that is associated with determining sample size.

Sampling distributions represents a fundamental concept in statistics (Zikmund 1994). It is sometimes a difficult concept to grasp, however. This is because it refers to a *hypothetical* distribution of something that will never take place: randomly selecting a very large number of samples (such as 5,000 or more) from a specified population, computing a mean for every sample, then examining the distribution of those means. The mean of all the 5,000 sample means is called the *expected value* of that statistic, and the standard deviation of the sampling distribution is the *standard error of the mean.*

When political science researchers draw two or more random samples of subjects or items from a given population, the statistics computed for each sample will almost always vary. Such variation is natural and expected. Drawing samples from the same population will produce summary measures that are also different from the first sample or samples drawn. Drawing more and more samples will also produce varying measurements. From this point on, assume that the statistic is the mean value on any relevant question, characteristic, or scale item.

If the value of the mean for each of the group of samples were displayed as a frequency distribution, the individual sample measurements would be typically distributed in such a way that the distribution of values would present a picture of a normal, symmetrical (bell-shaped) distribution. Most of the values would cluster around the center of the range, with smaller and smaller amounts drifting off toward the edges. A pictorial representation of the frequency distribution would be what is called a *bell-shaped curve.* A key requirement of most inferential statistical tests is that the data be normally distributed. Distributions that are not symmetrical are said to be *skewed.* Skewed distributions that have fewer values at the high end (right side) of a distribution are said to be *positively skewed,* or *skewed to the right.* When the values taper off toward the left side of the distribution, it is said to be *negatively skewed,* or *skewed to the left.* Distributions can also have more than one peak (in what is called a *bipolar* distribution).

The Standard Error of the Mean

The *standard error of the mean* provides an indication of how close the sample mean probably is to the mean of the population. This statistic is an estimate of the *sampling variability* in the sample mean. It is important to remember that the standard error of the mean is only an estimated standard deviation of a *hypothetical* series of samples. For example, in a study of public agency organizational climate, scale items consisted of such statements about the organization as: "Red-tape is kept to a minimum in this organization. The mean score on this seven-point agreement scale was 3.50; the standard deviation for the sample was 1.512. A *standard error* of .535 indicated that the sample mean was within a little more than half a point of what could be expected as the mean for the population from which the sample was drawn" (Sepic, Barnowe, Simpson, and McNabb 1998).

Central Limit Theorem

A rule of statistics called the *central limit theorem* states that as the number of sample subjects drawn from a population gets larger the distribution of the sample statistic will take on a normal distribution. At least thirty sample elements are necessary for the likelihood of the normal distribution to occur. In a normal distribution, the two sides of the curve are the same, with the *mean* and *median* both falling at the peak of the curve.

The central limit theorem applies for all sample statistics, but is usually applied to the value of the mean. The *sampling distribution of the mean* (sometimes referred to as the sampling distribution of the *average*) is nothing more than a distribution of the means of each of the samples that could be drawn from a population. The phrase *could be* is used instead of *is* because this is a theoretical concept; decision makers typically deal with just one sample. The problem at hand is how to know that the distribution of that sample statistic accurately reflects the same measurement that might be found in a census of the population.

Although it could happen, statisticians know that no single sample is likely to produce measurements that exactly mirror the measurements of population from which the sample is drawn. They also know that the measurements of another sample taken from the same population are highly likely to produce different values. The same is true for the third, fourth, fifth, and more samples. Therefore, they use probabilities that the sample comes close to mirroring the population to establish a level of confidence that such is the case.

Summary

Sampling in political science research is used because it is usually more efficient than studying a complete population. Sampling can lower the cost and improve the efficiency of measurement activities. Studying a sample rather than an entire population saves time and money. It is also thought to be less "destructive" of underlying attitudes (the process of measuring may influence future measurements). Decision makers must take care to avoid introducing bias and sampling or nonsampling error into the sample design and selection process.

The five fundamental considerations of the sampling process result in many different possible combinations in sample design. Sample design choices are based on the questions of: (1) probability versus nonprobability, (2) single-unit versus unit clusters, (3) stratified versus unstratified, (4) equal-unit probability versus weighted probability, and (5) single-stage versus multistage sampling.

Sampling distributions—the way each individual measurement clusters around some statistic—tend to reflect distinct patterns, with most following what is referred to as the *normal distribution.* In a normal distribution, the bulk of the measurements cluster around the mean value, with a few trailing off above and below the mean. When plotted, they appear in the shape of the familiar "bell-shaped curve." Most inferential statistics require that the data be from a normal distribution.

According to the *central limit theorem,* as the size of the sample increases, the distribution of the sample measurements tends to take on the shape of normal distribution, whereas small-sample studies may result in data that are not reflective of the parameters of the larger population.

Discussion Questions

1. What are the main reasons why researchers sample?
2. What does sampling precision mean?
3. What is the difference between a probability and a nonprobability sample?
4. What is the difference between stratified and unstratified samples?
5. What is the difference between equal and unequal probability sampling?
6. Why would a researcher use multistage sampling over single-stage sampling?
7. Differentiate between sample bias and sampling error.
8. Differentiate between Type I and Type II error.
9. What is sampling frame error?
10. Define the term "sampling distributions."
11. Define the term "sampling error of the mean."
12. What is the central limit theorem?

Additional Reading

Eddington, Eugene, 1987. *Randomization Tests.* New York: Marcel Decker.
Mattson, Dale. 1986. *Statistics: Difficult Concepts, Understandable Explanations.* Oak Park, IL: Bolchazy-Carducci.
Sincich, Terry. 1996. *Business Statistics by Example.* 5th ed. Upper Saddle River, NJ: Prentice-Hall.
Warwick, Donald P., and Charles A. Lininger. 1975. *The Sample Survey: Theory and Practice.* New York: McGraw-Hill.

10 Exploratory Research: The Probing Approach

Depending on their research objectives, researchers may select from three types of quantitative research designs: *exploratory, descriptive,* or *causal.* A research project may involve the use of just one or two designs, or it may involve all three. Typically, however, a research project begins with an exploratory study for preliminary identification of possible factors or variables, then moves to a descriptive study to define the salient or key variables, and concludes with a causal study such as an experiment to test the variables for strength of association or cause-and-effect relationships. For some unknown reason, exploratory research is not discussed in any great detail in many research methods textbooks, but it is an important approach that deserves greater attention. This chapter addresses some of the ways that exploratory designs are used in all the subfields of political science.

Most exploratory research is conducted for either one of two purposes: (1) a preparatory examination of an issue for gaining insights, or (2) for gathering information for immediate application to an administrative problem. In neither case is exploratory research intended to serve as an in-depth look into all the factors related to a political phenomenon. Because of their limited scope, exploratory studies seldom exist as stand-alone approaches. However, when exploratory research designs are also used to provide information for administrative decision making, the study may begin and end with only the exploratory study. The typical objective of these applied studies may be either to find an answer to a specific organizational question, or to provide information upon which to base a decision, such as gathering cost-benefit information for a proposed administrative action. Applied studies are typical in the public administration subfield of political science.

The great majority of exploratory research is conducted to investigate an issue or topic in order to develop *insight and ideas* about its underlying nature. Topics are often a problem or issue that requires additional research study for problem resolution. Designing and conducting a small-sample exploratory study, therefore, is often the first step in a more comprehensive or complex research project. Usually, the researcher has only a little or no prior knowledge about the issue or its components. As a result, exploratory research is often very flexible and unstructured. Because the research has few preconceptions even about how to study the problem, the first research steps usually involve qualitative methods (Aaker, Kumar, and Day 1998).

The objective of a typical exploratory research design is to gain as much information in as little time as possible, with the least amount of expenditure of money and effort. The wording of the objective will depend upon the reason for which the exploratory research is needed. For example, when the information is needed for developing a questionnaire—the *survey instrument*—for a large-sample descriptive study, the objective is to identify the variables and their constructs.

When the exploratory study precedes a social experiment of some type, a typical objective might be to determine which independent variables, treatments, or levels should be used in the experiment. In these applications, the exploratory study is also used to identify the key *dependent* and *independent variables* that will be tested in an experiment (a *causal design*). Exploratory studies also help the researcher identify which variables may be only tangentially or only marginally related, thereby telling the researcher what variables should not be included in the more extensive experimental research project.

Data gathering in exploratory research may take place in several different ways. Hakim (2000) identified three approaches: (1) prior research reviews, (2) in-depth interviews and focus group, and (3) administrative records and documentary evidence. Aaker, Kumar, and Day (1998) suggested a similar list of approaches: (1) literature reviews, (2) individual depth interviews, (3) focus group unstructured interviews, and (4) case studies. The four techniques suggested by Aaker, Kumar, and Day plus a fifth method, the pilot survey, are discussed in greater detail below.

The Literature Review

Exploratory research designs, like all research, usually begins with a study of the reported findings of other researchers. The process is called a *literature review,* and is one of the first steps in any research project. While it is recommended that all research include a review of the literature, the technique is especially applicable as an exploratory research technique. A six-step process for conducting a literature review is presented in Figure 10.1.

Among other reasons, researchers use the literature review to gain knowledge about what they should be looking for in their own data gathering, as well as for weighing the applicability of their proposed research methods. In doing so, they look for major themes in the research, which they may later incorporate into their research questions. According to Knight (2002), some major themes in a review of the literature include: What is the point of concern with this topic? Why is it important, and to whom is it important? On what points do other researchers agree and on what and why do they disagree? Out of all this literature, what research question has been missed or treated too lightly? What research question or questions, then, should I focus on? What research methodology and methods have been used to study this problem?

The next step in the process is to establish objectives for the review. Hart (1998, 27) identified nearly a dozen purposes or objectives for a literature review, including, but not limited to, the following (these are not in any prioritized order, nor will all apply for any one review):

1. The literature review can inform the researcher what has been done and what needs to be done on the research topic.
2. It provides a means for discovering important variables that are relevant to the topic.
3. It can make it possible to identify relationships between ideas and practices.
4. It provides a means for synthesizing various takes on the topic, often allowing the researcher to gain a new perspective.
5. The literature review permits framing of the topic or problem by establishing the topic in its context.

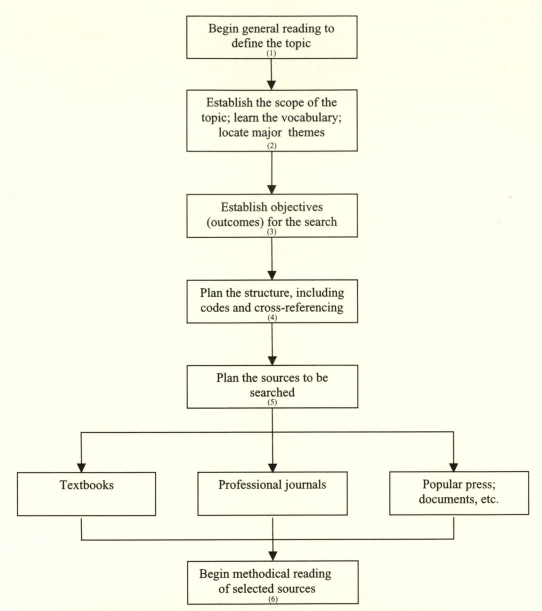

Figure 10.1   A Flowchart of a Six-Step Process for a Review of the Literature
Source: After material in Hart 1998.

6. The extent and quality of existing research can help rationalize the significance of the topic.
7. Gaining a familiarity with what others have discovered can result in enhancing or gaining the vocabulary of the topic.
8. It helps to gain understanding of the structure of the topic.
9. It provides a means for relating the researcher's ideas and theory to actual application of the theory's concepts.

10. The literature review informs the researcher of the main methodologies and research techniques that others have used to study the topic.
11. It describes the historical development of the topic and changes in its significance.

The exploratory literature review can become an integral part of the research report, or it can simply provide the researcher with background information, only some of which may find its way into the body of the study. Although they are not specifically exploratory studies, the following two examples of how the exploratory literature review can be woven into the final research paper help to illustrate the value of the technique. The first example is an illustration of the way the review is used as a distinct section in the paper; the example can be seen in the Summer 2002 issue of *Political Science Quarterly* (*PSQ*) in a paper on Senate scrutiny of Federal Court nominees (Hartley and Holmes, 259–78). The analysis of the literature was incorporated into the *Background and Review of the Literature* section in the paper. The review was organized into four main themes or constructs: (1) lower-court nominees and institutional change, (2) institutional changes in the Senate, (3) a historical review of the current controversy, and (4) Senate scrutiny on nominations. It is likely that the decision to use these constructs came after a review of the literature. As with the majority of exploratory studies, Hartley and Holmes used the most basic of descriptive statistics in their paper—two bivariate line charts and five simple frequency distribution tables. No measures of central tendency (averages) or of variation or correlation were included with the tables.

A different approach can be seen in the paper "Human Rights and Domestic Violence" (Hawkins and Humes, 231–57), in the same issue of *PSQ*. This paper followed a combined approach, using parts of two of the three qualitative approaches described by Hakim (2000): a research review combined with analysis of administrative records and documentary evidence. Hawkins and Humes examined two competing theories pertaining to differences in the willingness of nations to intervene in domestic violence issues. One theory focused on social movements; the second on international socialization. Their review of the literature was interwoven throughout the paper. The nature of the research design of Hawkins and Humes did not provide for any tables or graphs, or any statistics in their paper.

Conducting Personal Interviews

Exploratory research designs often involve conducting personal interviews with knowledgeable individuals. In policy studies, these subjects may come from within and/or outside of the organization. In theoretical studies, the subjects are often other professionals in the discipline, including professors and political practitioners. Whatever their source or affiliation, these individuals are collectively referred to as "key informants," and the process is known as *key informant interviews*. Key informant subjects are selected because they are likely to be better informed about the study problem and the issues associated with that problem.

The Interview Process

Gaskell (2000, 51) defined the personal interview process: The interview should be like a conversation between two (or more) friends. It may last as long as two hours or more, but normally lasts for one to one-and-a-half hours. The interviewer begins the session with some introductory comments about the research, thanks the subject for agreeing to participate, and asks permission to tape the session. The information-gathering session should start with some straightforward, interesting, and unthreatening questions. The interviewer must remain attentive and show interest in what the respondent is saying; eye contact is encouraged; proper body language should be used—respond with nods when appropriate, smile when you should, and remain serious and sympathetic when you are expected to be so. Always try to end the session on a positive note.

When used in an exploratory research project, the personal interview is used to collect the basic data for gaining an understanding of the relationships between the people in the study and the larger social group about which the study is focused. An objective for interviews in these situations is to amass the "thick description" that characterizes much qualitative research.

The focus group, on the other hand, is used to develop an understanding of the beliefs, opinions, attitudes, values, and motivations for behavior of people in the social group. If they are not used specifically for developing instruments for additional research, focus group interviews are a good way to frame the study in its context and to form hypotheses for descriptive or experimental research designs (Gaskel 2000).

An example of how interviews were used in an exploratory study is the team of faculty and students engaged to design and conduct an extensive community needs analysis for a regional general hospital. The team's first step in the study was to conduct a series of in-depth interviews with key local employers, community leaders, hospital administrators, and senior medical staff. These data were then developed into a comprehensive needs-analysis questionnaire administered throughout a three-community region. In its presentation to the hospital district board of directors, the hospital administrative staff used the findings of the exploratory study to justify further research. The exploratory research report provided concrete evidence that a larger, in-depth survey was needed to provide information necessary to complete the district's ten-year development plan.

To be effective an interviewer must begin an interview session by establishing rapport with the subject (Johnson 2002). This is done by developing and building on a sense of intimate association such as found between two close friends in a conversation. The goal of the interview is to ferret out "deep" information, knowledge, and feelings. Johnson suggested that interviewers use the following four-step process in a semi- or fully structured interview:

1. Begin with two or three introductory "icebreakers" to get the ball rolling.
2. Once the subject appears comfortable with the process, employ several transition questions. These may help to explain the purposes of the research. It is also a good time to secure the subject's permission to use a tape recorder, if appropriate.
3. Now start asking the key questions that address the heart of the research question. This may involve as few as four or five questions, but in a typical in-depth interview, there is no set limit to the number of questions that should be used. The goal is to continue asking questions until the desired information objectives are met.
4. The interview session typically ends with the interviewer summarizing some of the main points that were brought up. The interviewer may also take this time to share with the informant some of the points raised by other subjects.

Good interview research calls for researchers and participants developing a trust in each other. When this trust exists, participants are free to speak openly and often work with the researcher to "tease out fresh understanding and bring some embodied or embedded things into words" (Gubrium and Holstein 2002; Knight 2002). Once this rapport is established, the interviewer can proceed with the rest of the process, which occurs in the following six steps:

1. *Prepare the conversation guide.* The guide is a list of topics that the researcher wants covered in the interview. It should be followed as a guide, not addressed in any mandated order. Interviews, if conducted correctly, can be freewheeling open-ended conversations, with important topics that the researcher had not even considered coming to the fore. Certainly, there is a core of items that must be covered, but the key idea in interviews is to maintain your flexibility.
2. *Select the way the interviews are to be conducted.* Three options are possible: individual interviews, group interviews, or a combination of the two.
3. *Determine how to select the respondents.* Will they be randomly selected subjects, anyone willing to participate, or only a specific group of key informants whose opinions are necessary to meet research objectives?
4. *Conduct the interviews.* A large body of literature exists on how to successfully conduct personal interviews. Three of the key points in this literature are: (1) be friendly, unthreatening, and empathetic, (2) be a good, attentive listener, and (3) remain flexible and uncritical.
5. *Transcribe the interviews* just as they took place.
6. *Analyze the body of information collected.* Some researchers feel that it is a good idea to wait a week or two after collecting the data before beginning the analysis; others begin right after their collection. No method has been proven to be best.

An important point to remember in scheduling and conducting personal interviews is that informants do not always move on the same schedule that drives the researcher. Informants often have topics that they want brought open and discussed, and will remain focused on them until they are satisfied. In addition, the interview will often take what Johnson (2002) described as "unexpected turns or digressions" that the informant is interested in and knows about. He also noted that these unexpected shifts in the interview process can be very productive. Therefore, the interviewer should be willing to depart with the planned discussion guide, going along with the informant to see where the discussion leads.

Collecting Focus Group Data

Focus group interview sessions are another often-used exploratory research technique (Kitzinger and Barbour 1999). The focus group is a good way to develop an understanding of key issues before writing questions, and can also help by enabling the researcher to gain a sharper focus on the way that questions are worded. Focus groups can also be used to develop story scenarios ("vignettes") to be used in in-depth interviewing designs. Respondents are asked to react to the scenarios, usually responding to a structured question list in a quantitative study and an unstructured list in qualitative designs. Kitzinger and Barbour also point out that focus groups may be used after completion of a survey in order to help explain response outliers. Outliers can only be identified, not explained, in survey research.

A focus group is a group discussion in which six to ten (more or less) subjects explore a specific set of ideas or issues under the guidance of a moderator or session leader. The focus group has been a staple research technique in business for many years; they are particularly useful in marketing and advertising research. However, in the past decade or two they have come to be recognized as a valuable contributor to developing political science—and all social science—knowledge (Knight 2002; Bloor, Frankland, Thomas, and Robson 2001; Wilkinson and Kitzinger 2000; Kitzinger and Barbour 1999). Politicians in both Canada and the United States have long used focus group sessions to provide data for strategy formulation and, according to Wilkinson and Kitzinger (1999), focus group research is now a common feature in political research in all of North America and Great Britain.

Types of Focus Groups

Focus groups can be classified in several different ways. One way is according to the structure of the session. Some sessions are highly structured, whereas others are only lightly structured (Knight 2002). A second way of classifying focus groups is according to whether the session is conceived of as a group interview or as a focus group. In the opinion of David Morgan (2002), rather than the traditional dichotomy of structured-unstructured sessions, all focus group sessions *must* have some structure. Otherwise, they are nothing more than a mob gathering with no reason for being. Instead, Morgan preferred to categorize focus group sessions as either "more structured" or "less structured." The distinguishing features of the two structure approaches are compared in Table 10.1.

A major benefit of group interviews is the potential interaction among participants. This interaction is impossible to achieve in one-on-one interviews. Focus groups are also more efficient than a series of individual in-depth interviews, in that a group of subjects are interviewed in the same amount of time interviewing one subject would entail. A major disadvantage of focus groups is the fear of public embarrassment, which sometimes makes it difficult, if not impossible, to bring up sensitive issues.

Interview sessions with groups can also be classified as either *group interviews* or *interactive focus groups* (Bloor, Frankland, Thomas, and Robson 2001). With group interviews, the researcher asks interview subjects to respond to a preestablished sequence of the questions, in much the same way as if the researcher were interviewing a single subject. The advantage of the group interview is simply one of convenience and efficiency. With all subjects together in the same location, the researcher can collect large amounts of data in a short period of time.

The second type of group session is the traditional interactive focus group. While the re-

Table 10.1

A Comparison of Focus Groups according to the Level of Structure in the Session

More Structured Sessions	Less Structured Sessions
Objective of the session is to collect answers to the researcher's questions	Objective of the session is to gain an understanding of what participants are thinking
Focused on the interests of the researcher	Focused on the interests of the participants
Question guide keeps discussion focused	Questions are only guides for discussion
Many specific questions asked	Fewer, more general questions asked
Time limits for each question	Flexibility in time allocation
Group leader asks questions of each subject	Leader is moderator, seeking subject interactions
Leader stops off-topic comments	Leader permits exploring new directions
Subjects speak to the moderator	Subjects talk among themselves

Source: Morgan 2002, 147.

searcher may, indeed, use a structured question guide, the objective for the focus group is not to collect a series of individual answers, but rather to generate interactive discussion among the group members. When subjects respond and react to the comments of other group members, the resultant discussion can often bring to light the meanings, opinions, and norms that underlie attitudes and behaviors. Table 10.2 illustrates how these different classification schemes affect the role of the researcher.

In the highly structured group interview, the researcher is simply an interrogator, asking each subject the same questions. There is little room for creative thinking in this type of session; the researcher does not probe for deeper responses. Typically, the interviewer has little or no knowledge about the reasons and objectives for the study, and did not have any role in the development of the question guide. On the other hand, in the less structured group interview the research takes on a somewhat more active role, serving much as a teacher employing the Socratic method. In this approach, the session leader continues to ask a prescribed set of questions, but allows more flexibility in the responses, often probing for more information when the respondent stumbles or is unable to put a response into words. The leader may rephrase the question, or go so far as to state it in the form of a projective, sentence-completion statement. Regardless of the approach taken, the point of the session is to generate answers to every question on the list from every subject. Application of structure to the gathered data takes place in the editing of the transcript.

Most focus groups are lightly structured sessions. In fact, the structure may be so slight that it is all but invisible. The research uses the question list only as a tool to generate discussion and only partially as a list of items that must be answered. In a focus group session with more structure, the leader serves as a moderator, allowing discussion to proceed as it may and encouraging interaction, but eventually bringing the group back to the point in question. The moderator-leader is less concerned how the group gets to its conversation destination, and more concerned that it continues to move in the desired direction. In a lightly structured focus group, the goal of the session is not to secure answers to questions, but to generate interactive discussion. In this situation, the session leader takes on the role of a conversation catalyst. This is the most difficult of the four roles that a session leader may take. The leader must take great pains to keep the conversation moving, while not allowing any one or two members to dominate the discussion. Often, the greatest difficulty is gaining the participation of the one or two reticent session members who sit quietly taking it all in but refraining from offering their own comments. Sometimes, however, the objective of the session is to investigate the way that the group members interact, who leads and who follows, who forces as issue and who is will-

---

Table 10.2

The Role of the Group Leader in Group Interviews and Focus Group Sessions

Question Guide	Session Type	
	Group Interview	Interactive Focus Group
Highly Structured	Leader as Interrogator	Leader as Moderator
Semistructured	Socratic Leader	Leader as Catalyst

Source: After Morgan 2002.

ing to compromise. In these sessions, the discussion is of less interest than the interaction process.

Focus groups have been shown to be an ideal way to explore peoples' opinions, concerns, desires, and experiences. However, they may be most valuable when the researcher wants to determine *how* these opinions, etc. are expressed, influenced, formed, and counterformed in a social situation (Kitzinger and Barbour 1999). In an effective focus group session, subjects develop their own questions, frames of reference, and ideas. They follow their own priorities, and do so on their own terms, using their own vocabulary. Bloor et al. (2001) discussed how focus groups are used for such purposes. In such applications, the focus group is used to (1) bring out background or contextual information, (2) identify salient issues that appear to be held in common among sample members, (3) discern the everyday language—including slang—that subjects use when talking about the topic, and (4) gather respondent opinions about previous research that has been done on the topic.

A Focus Group Example

An example of how focus groups are used along with traditional survey research can be seen in Rosenthal's 2000 study of gender styles among committee chairpersons in state legislatures. Rosenthal conducted a series of three group sessions over the 1994 and 1996 National Conference of State Legislators conferences. The design also included ethnographic observations of legislative committees in action, and concluded with a mailed survey to committee chairpersons. More than 300 usable instruments were returned, for response rates of 39 percent for women legislators and 30.5 percent for male respondents.

Stratified, equal unit sample methods were used to form the focus groups. One group was made up exclusively of female committee chairs; a second group consisted of only male committee chairs; and the third group contained a mix of males and females. Respondents were from twenty-four different U.S. state legislatures. During the legislative sessions, participants were asked to define "consensus" and to describe the functioning of committee business during their tenure as committee chair. Rosenthal coded and combined the responses into two broad sets of characteristics. Comments were coded as either *destructive* or as *integrative*. Variables in the destructive classification included comments pertaining to winning and losing, interest group competition, bargaining, and majority votes. Variables coded as integrative included comments pertaining to deliberation, discussion, and overall participant satisfaction in the outcome.

Using the Case Study to Collect Data

The case study is another exploratory research technique, although case study designs may also be complete in themselves. This is not because the case study is not appropriate for exploratory research. Rather, case studies typically go into too much depth for the objectives of an exploratory design. The case study is not a *methods* choice, but rather, is a choice of *what* is to be studied. By whatever method of data collection is used, the researcher elects to study the case or cases because of what can be learned (Stake 2000).

The case study is, according to Knight (2002), the study of one of something (although case studies may involve more than one item, they are investigated individually; hence Knight's "one at a time" statement). In political science research, the case can be a party, a candidate, a state legislature, a political office, a domestic or foreign policy decision—the list includes, essentially, any single event, person, organizational unit, site, or whatever is applicable to the world of politics.

The case study may be simple, or it may be complex. This great applicability of the case is also one of its greatest detractions. A problem that researchers often face with case studies is the difficulty of defining the boundaries of the case. Despite this difficulty, case studies do have a number of advantages. First, they tend to bring out information that might be ignored, forgotten, or not even brought to mind in a different study method. Second, because they are usually descriptions of what the research sees in the case, they are not artificial constructs such as what a survey or an experiment might produce. No variables are controlled in a case; what you see is what you get. Third, by their very nature, case studies push the researcher to work in depth, to go beyond the surface indications to get at reasons why things happen as they have. The fourth advantage is closely related to the third—case studies force researchers to look for meanings, not simply descriptions. The goal with a case is to establish understanding. The purpose of the case is to define and describe the case, not to use the case as a representation of the world (Stake 2000).

The fifth advantage associated with the case study approach is that it helps the researcher remember that the political world is as complex and variable as any social institution. Political phenomena are not, usually, simple, single-faceted events; they are as complex as the people who exist and function in this world. A survey, no matter how complex or sophisticated, provides only a snapshot of the phenomena; a case study can be like a master's oil painting: deep, with many nuances and a variety of meanings. The sixth advantage is that, because of its complexity, the case research can be what Knight (2002) termed "a powerful antidote to determinism and over generalization." Finally, case studies tend to be person-centered, a fact that further adds to their informative underpinning.

Structure of the Case Study

The case study, like all research designs, is constructed around a distinct structure (Stake 2000, 440). While the case may be built upon only a few research questions, the issues in the case tend to focus on complex relationships. Stake identified six major conceptual issues that are typically addressed in a case study:

1. Framing the case; setting its boundaries, and identifying the object of the case study.
2. Selecting the issues to address; the phenomena, themes, constructs, or issues that result in formation of research questions.
3. Close analysis of the case material in order to identify the relevant data patterns that frame the issues.
4. If appropriate, triangulating key observations and interpretations through the use of other research methods.
5. Examining the data and its literature in order to identify interpretations that differ from the one adopted by the researcher.
6. Developing the conclusions that can be drawn from the case, including what general-izations may be applied in similar situations.

As a recent illustration of a case study, Bryant (2002) studied the indigenous populations of a group of islands in the Philippines. He followed an ethnographic data-gathering approach, using the case study to illustrate nongovernment organization (NGO) conflicting influences on development and conservation. The objective of the case was to reveal that, despite their different agendas, the NGOs shared a common objective: to help local residents internalize state control over their environment through self-regulation.

Collecting Data with a Pilot Survey

Another approach used in exploratory research studies is to survey a small random sample drawn from the same population of interest—what is called a *pilot survey.* A commonly used purpose of a pilot study is for pretesting a draft of a survey questionnaire. Results of the exploratory study are used only to test the validity and reliability of the study design and the instrument questions. Problem words, phrases, and entire questions may be edited, deleted, or replaced. Results of such pilot studies should never be included with the findings of the final study.

Pilot studies are often nothing more than small-sample applications of a standard questionnaire survey. The questions included in the pilot study instrument are usually generated through the use of one or more of the other exploratory methods: literature reviews, interviews, focus groups, or case studies. Pilot studies are extremely important in survey research. They are used to pretest the proposed questionnaire, check the wording, and ensure that the researcher and respondents have the same definitions of key words, phrases, and, if used, acronyms. The pilot survey is also a good opportunity to test whether the respondents have the knowledge necessary to answer the question. People will often answer questions simply because they think that they must, whether they really know the answer or not.

Beginning researchers often ask two questions in one, believing they are being more efficient in the use of time and space. But double-barreled questions are not only difficult for subjects to answer, they are next-to-impossible to code and tabulate. The researcher is never sure which half of the question was answered. Consider this example of a poorly written demographic question: "How many children do you have and what are their ages?" This is really a series of questions. First, "Do you have any children?" (It says nothing about the gender of the children). Second, it asks, "How many children do you have?" (It says nothing about whether they live with you or elsewhere.) A better wording might be: If you have children, "What is the age of your first child?" "What is the age of your second child?" and so on.

Pilot studies can be conducted with a small sample drawn from the same population from which the final sample will be drawn, or if this is not possible for some reason, pilot studies are also carried out on a sample of persons with some knowledge of the subject, the study objectives and methods, and a willingness to contribute their time and effort. In academic situations, professors often use a sample of their students to pretest the instrument designed for use in the outside social environment—a nonprobability convenience sample. Care must be taken in using students in the pilot study, however, particularly with undergraduates. Not only are younger students likely to have little knowledge of the situation under study, they may not grasp the relevance of certain items in the instrument. They often use very different terms for phenomena than researchers and the eventual study subjects employ. About the only justification for using students to pretest a survey instrument designed for nonstudents is that conducting some type of pretest is better than no pretest at all.

Analyzing Exploratory Research Data

Data in exploratory research may involve quantitative, qualitative, or a combination of forms. The data may come from either primary or secondary sources; they may be gathered directly by the researcher, or may be gathered by someone else for a different purpose. Both data types have similar validity in exploratory research. Their analysis occurs in different ways, however.

Analysis of Quantitative Data

In general, only descriptive statistics and graphic presentations of data are employed in the analysis of exploratory research data. This statement is qualified because some researchers may employ inferential statistical tests on the data in something like a "dry run," in which the methods are tested for applicability, not the data itself. The most commonly used descriptive statistics include measures of central tendency and measures of variability, although measures of correlation are also used. Little credence should be given to associations found in small-sample data, however. Small-sample correlations should only be used as indicators of variables that might be included in follow-on descriptive or experimental research designs. Nonparametric tests, such as the chi-square test of independence, are often used to analyze exploratory research data, but they, too, have sample size minimum limits. The general rule is that in a crosstabulation of two (or more) variables, each cell in the crosstabulation table should have at least five responses. Often, this rule cannot be met in exploratory studies, where samples are small and random selection of subjects cannot always be guaranteed.

Tables, charts, and graphs are also considered to fall under the category of descriptive statistics. A first analysis step the researcher takes when establishing order and meaning from raw, unprocessed data is to construct either a *frequency distribution table,* a *stem-and-leaf diagram,* a *histogram,* or any combination of these graphic devices. Stem-and-leaf diagrams can often be more informative than simple frequency tables in that none of the underlying data are lost in the analysis; all values are displayed in the diagram. Histograms also present summary data, but they do not display individual values for a class in the same way that a stem-and-leaf diagram does.

Analysis of Qualitative Data

Probably the single greatest advantage of employing qualitative research methods in exploratory studies—and possibly the greatest disadvantage as well—is the richness of the information gained. *Richness* refers to the large number of topics that may surface in an interview, for example. As Gaskell (2000, 53) has pointed out, "The broad aim of [all qualitative data] analysis is to look for meanings and understanding of what is said in the data, but the researcher must interpret [all of] this."

Because most exploratory research data is generated by interviews with key informants, researchers are most concerned with analyzing qualitative interview data. As noted earlier, there are basically three types of interviews: highly structured, lightly structured, and unstructured. However, Knight (2002) pointed out that it is really impossible to have a valid interview that is totally unstructured, although most methods texts continue to use this terminology. Therefore, data analysis methods for only highly and lightly structured interviews are discussed here.

Data from highly structured interviews are the easiest to deal with. Respondents simply answer researcher-created questions, often responding to a selected list of answer categories. These responses can be quickly counted and recorded. However, with lightly structured (and unstructured) interviews, the reverse is true. Respondents are free to come up with their own answers and justifications. Certainly, not all respondents will give the same answer to a question, nor will they all give complete answers. The researcher must devise categories and codes in order to overlay a structural framework onto the data so that it can be meaningfully interpreted.

Planning codes, constructs, cross-referencing, and other structural activities, as well as the actual process of evaluating the textual material, follow a normal process for evaluating and interpreting qualitative data. Knight (2002, 182) reduced this process to just two steps: (1) indexing or coding the data and (2) reflecting upon and interpreting the data. As Knight so aptly pointed out, "Qualitative data are easier to code if you know what you're looking for."

Three points must be made before reviewing a method of analyzing qualitative data. First, it must be remembered that it is possible to analyze qualitative data at different levels of complexity; researchers may analyze the data deeply, with "thick description" in mind, or they may take a broad-brush approach, not mining the data for every ounce of information. Qualitative data used in exploratory studies are far more likely to be analyzed less deeply than would be the case in a comprehensive qualitative design. Qualitative data in an exploratory study provides background information that gives the researcher insight and ideas into what will be needed to conduct the larger quantitative study.

Second, despite what many quantitative researchers desire, qualitative data are seldom value-free. The researcher will find it difficult to remain objective for the following reasons: the unit of analysis is selected by the researcher; the codes, themes, and constructs are assigned by the researcher; and the researcher constantly makes judgments about the data and the meanings to be drawn from the material.

The third point is that data analysis is a continuous process in qualitative research. It begins with the selection of the study design, data collection, and during continual thinking about the meanings embedded in the data. Codes and constructs are identified, evolve, and sometimes disappear. Categories, patterns, and themes are always subject to modification. The process is different from quantitative research, where once the data collection instrument is established, it is printed and administered. Arbitrary changes cannot take place; if they are, a separate study is required. Without boundaries, quantitative researchers would find it difficult to design a research study that replicates a previous project. Replication is one of the cornerstones of the positivist tradition.

The Analysis Process

The analysis of qualitative data takes place in a two-stage process. First, the researcher must establish a coding system for the data, and second, by contemplating on what is revealed in the data, the researcher develops a plausible set of explanations and meanings. Knight (2002) suggested a list of six ways to avoid becoming artificially restricted or donning blinders during the analysis. They include the following:

1. Early in the analysis, open your mind to broader theoretical possibilities, propositions, or points of view that might be applied to the analysis.

2. Ask a colleague or someone you know to examine some of the data, then to talk with you about what he/she reads therein.
3. Ask other knowledgeable people to look at your indexing or coding scheme, and how you are applying it.
4. Keep your eyes open for examples that run opposite to the trend—"counter-examples," or "discordant evidence."
5. Stop, take a break, and get away from the data for a while. Come back to the analysis after a week or two. Does the coding system still seem appropriate?
6. Pace your analysis; don't try to do it all at one sitting. Do other things in-between sessions so that your mind is fresh again when you return to the data.

Finally, consider using Computer-Assisted Qualitative Data Analysis Software (CAQDAS) to aid in the analysis. Many different programs are available. Most have the following functions in common (Gaskell 2000, 54):

- Memoing: This allows the analyst to add comments during the process of analysis.
- Coding, tagging, and labeling: These enable the researcher to identify similar units in the text material.
- Retrieving: This process makes it possible to find units in the same category, wherever they are in the body of the text material.
- Linking: A number of different linking systems are possible, including text-text, code-text, memo-text, memo-code, code-code, etc.
- Boolean searching: this function enables the researcher to find specified combinations of codes, using such links as "and," "or," "nor," etc.
- Graphic interfacing: This feature permits the researcher to develop tables, charts, and graphs that show the relationships between codes and texts.
- Comparisons between texts of different origins: This permits comparing such sources of data as social categories, time series, etc.

Summary

The purpose of exploratory research studies is to provide the researcher with greater insight into the study problem and ideas about the variables that should be included in a larger or more comprehensive study to follow. In addition, the findings of an exploratory study can often be used to train data gatherers and help the researcher design and test a data-processing plan. Equally important, the findings of an exploratory study can often provide guidance to the researcher in rephrasing the study question. It can also require the imposition of totally new variables into the study.

Among other reasons, researchers use the literature review to gain knowledge about what they should be looking for in their own data gathering, as well as for weighing the applicability of their proposed research methods. They look for major themes in the database, which they may later incorporate into their research questions.

A major advantage of employing qualitative research methods in exploratory studies—and possibly the greatest disadvantage as well—is the richness of the information gained. It is an advantage because it often goes beyond simple description or numeration, to also include some level of deeper understanding of the underlying motivations, attitudes, justifications for interactions and behaviors, etc. This greater understanding can be a disadvantage in a quantitative study because of the underlying objective of the study: to either describe phenomena with measurements and counting, or to identify causal relationships between dependent and independent variables.

Data gathering in exploratory research takes place in three or more ways. Hakim (2000) identified three approaches: (1) prior research reviews, (2) in-depth interviews and focus group, and (3) administrative records and documentary evidence. Aaker, Kumar, and Day (1998) suggested a list of four approaches: (1) literature reviews, (2) individual depth interviews, (3) focus group unstructured interviews, and (4) case studies. These four techniques plus a fifth method, the pilot survey, were discussed in this chapter. Also discussed was the use of CAQDAS to aid in the analysis. Many different programs are available; most have seven important functions in common.

The analysis of qualitative data takes place in a two-stage process. First, the researcher must establish a coding system for the data, and second, the researcher develops a plausible set of explanations and meanings. In the analysis stage, becoming artificially restricted or donning blinders can be avoided using these six techniques; they include (1) be open to broad theoretical possibilities, propositions, or points of view; (2) ask a colleague to examine some of the data, then to talk with you about what he/she sees in the data; (3) ask other knowledgeable people to look at your indexing or coding scheme, and how it is applied; (4) look for examples that run opposite to the trend—"counter-examples," or "discordant evidence;" (5) stop, take a break, and get away from the data for a while; come back to the analysis in a week or two to see if the coding system still seems appropriate; (6) pace the analysis; don't try to do it all in one sitting. Do other things in-between sessions so that your mind is fresh again when you return to the data.

Discussion Questions

1. What is the primary objective for exploratory research studies?
2. Explain the role of a literature review in an exploratory study.
3. Name and define the six steps in the literature review process.
4. How would you use personal interviews in an exploratory study?
5. How do structured and unstructured interviews differ?
6. What is a conversation guide?
7. What is a focus group? Explain the different ways that they can be classified.
8. What is the role or roles of the researcher in a focus group situation?
9. What is a case study? Name the different types of case studies.
10. How should case studies be structured, if at all?
11. What is a pilot survey, and what is its major purpose?

Additional Reading

Bryman, Alan. 2001. *Social Research Methods*. Oxford: Oxford University Press.
Hart, Chris. 1998. *Doing a Literature Review*. London: Sage.
Jennings, Paul, Hans Keman, and Jan Kleinnijenhuis. 1999. *Doing Research in Political Science*. London: Sage.
Wengraf, Tom. 2001. *Qualitative Research Interviewing*. London: Sage.

11 Descriptive Research: The Survey Approach

The year 1997 was the last year in which the British Election Study (BES) was conducted in England, Wales, and Scotland. The 1997 survey was the tenth study in a series of national cross-sectional surveys, having been conducted every election year since 1964. This survey had become, according to Elinor Scarbrough (2000), the closest that British political scientists could consider as "institutionalized empirical research." The BES, while seldom the source of open debate, did have many critics, however. The survey was attacked for being biased electoral research, for its lack of theoretical grounding, paucity of robust findings, lack of originality, "propagation of a theoretical orthodoxy," methodological conservatism, and its systematic bias in focusing primarily on the fortunes of the two major parties—Labor and Conservatives. In addition, some political scientists criticized the study for its basis in three sociological and social psychological concepts: class, socialization, and party identification (partisanship)—concepts that many saw as no longer relevant. The survey was also criticized for showing little or no interest in the cultural pressures on the nonvoting behavior of Asian and black females. Finally, rational choice political scientists criticized the survey for not investigating the "cost" of voting—not determining what costs might be relevant.

This brief introductory example illustrates some of the problems political science researchers face when designing a comprehensive survey instrument for postelection surveys of the national electorate. It is clearly a problem everywhere, not only in the United States.

Different Approaches in Quantitative Research

Researchers use two different approaches when gathering data in quantitative research studies; they may collect data by *observing* and *counting* overt acts of behavior, or they may use a *questionnaire* to generate responses to specific questions, including questions about attitudes, opinions, motivations, knowledge, demographics, and many more categories of data. Questionnaires are the most popular way to gather primary data—it has been estimated that questionnaires are used in 85 percent or more of all quantitative research projects. They are particularly appropriate when the research problem calls for a descriptive design. This chapter discusses the process of descriptive research design, and the steps involved in questionnaire preparation, including the nature, limitations, and wide variety of ways to write survey questions. For the survey approach, the researcher must first prepare or acquire either a list of topics to cover or a number of questions to ask. The observation method uses what is known as a *schedule,* which is nothing more than a list of items, events, characteristics, or behaviors that the observer wants to be sure are counted. A questionnaire is a set of open-or closed-end questions that respondents are asked to answer.

Questionnaires can be used to gather information about large numbers of respondents (populations) and from small groups (samples). Most often descriptive research is conducted using *samples.* The sample method used most often is the *probability* or random *sample.* Samples that are representative of the population are surveyed; the researcher then makes inferences about the population from the sample data. Within some known margin of error, the sample *statistics* are assumed to be a reflection of the population's *parameters.* Careful planning and construction of the questionnaire is, therefore, a critical step in descriptive research.

Advantages of Using Questionnaires

Questionnaires have many advantages. The greatest of these is the considerable *flexibility* of the questionnaire. Questionnaires can be custom-designed to meet the objectives of almost any type of research project. Researchers may develop their own or purchase the rights to employ many different types of preprepared questionnaires, which are instruments that have been developed by other researchers. They have typically been thoroughly tested with a variety of different samples. In this way, they are applied enough times to warrant strong belief in their ability to effectively measure some phenomenon. These preprepared questionnaires are called *standardized instruments* and may be ordered from a wide variety of test catalogs.

Questionnaires may be designed to gather information from any group of respondents. Questionnaires can be short or long, simple or complex, straightforward or branched. They can be rigidly structured or be a loosely organized list of topics for discussion. They can be administered face-to-face, over the telephone, by mail, and over computer networks. Usually, respondents' answers are relatively easy to code and tabulate, which can reduce turnaround time and lower project costs.

Questionnaires can be designed to determine what people know, what they think, or how they act or plan to act. They can measure subjects' factual knowledge about a thing or an idea, or they can be used to measure people's opinions, attitudes, or motives for behaving in certain ways. They can be used to measure the frequency of past behaviors, or to predict future actions. When subjects are from different cultures, response alternatives in the form of pictures or symbols may be substituted for words.

This flexibility of the questionnaire results in very few rules to follow in development of the instrument. However, constructing an effective questionnaire does demand a high degree of skill. Questions must be arranged in a logical order; they must be worded in such a way that their meaning is clear to people of all backgrounds, ages, and educational levels. Particular care must be taken when asking questions of a potentially controversial or personal nature to not embarrass or offend respondents. Folz has summarized the concerns associated with questionnaire construction this way:

> Know what you want to ask and why you want to ask it; compose clear, unambiguous questions; keep the survey [questionnaire] as brief as possible; and have a plan for analyzing the result before the instrument is administered. (Folz 1996, 79–80)

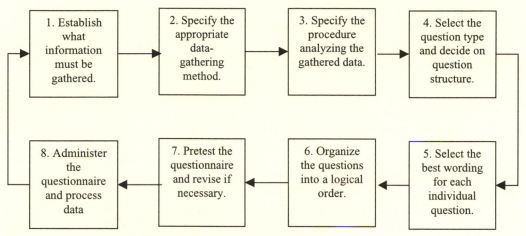

Figure 11.1 **The Eight-Step Questionnaire Construction Procedure**

Questionnaire Construction Procedure

When preparing a questionnaire, the researcher must follow a systematic procedure in order to be sure that it fulfills three broad objectives (Malhotra 1999). The questionnaire must:

1. Successfully gather information that answers each study question.
2. Motivate respondents to answer all questions to the best of their ability.
3. Keep all potential error to a minimum.

The eight-step procedure displayed in Figure 11.1 has been shown to help in the preparation of effective questionnaires and questions. Because questionnaire construction is as much an art as it is a science, the list should be considered as a guide, rather than a checklist of steps that must be followed in the order and content presented.

Determine What Information Is Needed

Before any questions are written, the researcher must be absolutely certain that the objectives for the research are clearly spelled out. It is never enough for a researcher to just "think" that he or she has an idea of what it would be "nice" to know. Rather, only questions that contribute to the overall research objective should be asked. This begins with an understanding of the scope of the proposed research: Is the research being done to solve a particular problem in a public administration or nonprofit organization, or is it "pure" research designed to identify or test some theory? This is the applied-theoretical research dichotomy question that appears periodically in the literature on public administration research.

The bulk of public administration research is applied research. However, over the past several decades, a growing body of research on public administration theory has emerged. Today, a loosely organized group of academics and practitioners are joined in an effort to advance theoretical knowledge. The *Public Administration Theory Network (www.PAT-Net.org)* allows interested persons to share their ideas on political and social theory, philosophy and ethics, theory of institutions and organizations, and other related concepts, problems, and issues. The group publishes a quarterly journal, *Administrative Theory & Praxis* (ATP).

Specify Data-Gathering Method

The three primary ways to collect data with questionnaires are: (1) in-person or *face-to-face* interviews, (2) telephone interviews (also called *voice-to-voice* interviews), and (3) mailed survey instruments that are *self-administered*. In what is the latest method of data collection, today data may also be gathered over computer networks. Self-administered questionnaires may be mailed to respondents, handed out in public locations such as shopping malls, or dropped off at homes or offices. Each of these approaches has its own advantages and disadvantages.

Face-to-face Interviews. The primary advantage of conducting in-person interviews is that they usually make it possible to gather large amounts of information in a relatively short period of time. Also, people who might not otherwise participate in the survey can often be encouraged to do so by a persuasive interviewer or researcher. Another advantage of the personal administration approach is that the data gatherer can often help respondents who might not understand a word or a question.

In-person administration is particularly helpful when branching questions are used in the questionnaire. This involves asking people questions that only they should answer, based on their response to one or more screening questions. Other respondents are instructed to move to a different section or set of questions. There are four major disadvantages associated with the use of in-person interviews. These are:

1. They take longer to administer than any other method.
2. They tend to be the most costly method of collecting survey data.
3. The changing demographic makeup of the country means that fewer adults of working age will be at home during the day.
4. Interviewers are subjected to potential personal harm when interviewing takes place in some urban areas.

One way that researchers get around these problems is by conducting interviews in public places, such as shopping malls or recreational facilities. While this tends to eliminate the poor and older citizens from the sample, it does allow a large number of completed questionnaires to be gathered in a short time.

Telephone interviews. The major advantages of telephone surveys are (1) the relative speed with which the data can be gathered, (2) their lower cost, and (3) the opportunity for the researcher to ask questions that might not be answered in a face-to-face situation. To reach people at home, most interviews are conducted on weekday evenings or on Saturdays; this allows public administration researchers to use public agency or office telephones after the working day, further cutting the costs of data gathering. Today, telephone interviews are usually conducted from a central location, thus reducing researcher travel time and its related cost.

The major disadvantages of telephone interviewing are the inability to make eye contact with respondents and to know that people with the desired demographic profiles are answering the questions. Another disadvantage is the limited length of time that the respondent is willing to give to the interview. Also, many respondents are leery of providing personal information to strangers over the telephone. They may assume that the caller is a telemarketer rather than someone who is conducting legitimate research. Or they fear that the caller has sinister motives. Finally, no one is as yet aware of the effect the wide use of cellular and car telephones will have on response rates for telephone interviewing. Researchers do know that it is becoming increasingly difficult to acquire the desired number of completed instruments in the time allowed for data gathering.

Mailed questionnaires. Mailing questionnaires is often the least expensive of all data-gathering processes. On the other hand, this method often results in the lowest return rates of all data-gathering methods. *Return rates* are referred to as *response rates* when applied to face-to-face and voice-to-voice interviewing. They all mean the number of completed questionnaires received by the researcher. It is important to plan for return rates when planning the sample size. For example, it is not uncommon to achieve return rates of 10 percent or less in a mailed questionnaire, although the typical rate is closer to 25 to 40 percent. This means that for a sample of 100, the researcher may have to mail out from 400 to 1,000 survey instruments!

Determine Analysis Procedure

The way that the gathered data will be coded, tabulated, analyzed, and interpreted plays a big role in the way the questionnaire and individual questions are developed. Today, computers using readily available, easy-to-use statistical software tabulate almost all survey results. For this reason, most questionnaires are *precoded* (classification numbers appear beside each question and each possible response), making data entry simple and less error-prone. The increasing use of machine-readable answer forms further improves the data entry process. Responses to open-ended questions are grouped into categories and classes are then translated into numerical form for counting and additional statistical analysis.

Select Question Type and Structure

There are many different ways to classify question types. The most common way is by the type of measurements they produce: *nominal, ordinal, interval,* or *ratio* data. Another is by the character of the measurement values, such as: "are the values *discrete* (as in 'yes' or 'no' answers) or are they *continuous* (such as incomes, weights, attitude scale data, etc.)?" A third classification system is based on the form of the responses; that is, are the answers *open-ended* or *closed-ended*?

A fourth way to classify question types is based on the *objective* of the generated response, that is, on the cognitive level of the information produced. Folz (1996) has identified these six broad categories of objective-based questions: *factual, opinion, attitude, motive, knowledge,* and *action* or *behavior* questions. Each question type delivers a different type of information, and must be worded in such a way that this objective is achieved.

Table 11.1 displays the question types alongside respondents' level of cognitive activity addressed by each type. These three stages are (1) the *cognitive* (knowledge) stage, (2) the *affective* (attitudinal) stage, and (3) the *action* (or behavioral) stage. Examples of the information each type of question produces are also shown.

Table 11.1

A Classification of Question Types by Content

Cognitive Awareness Stage	Type of Question	Information Acquired
Cognitive Stage:	Factual	The facts about people or things.
	Knowledge	What people know about things.
Affective Stage:	Opinions	What people say about things.
	Attitudes	What people believe about things.
	Motives	Why people act the way they do.
Action Stage:	Behavior	How people act, what they do; how they will respond to certain stimuli.

Source: Folz 1996.

Select Best Wording for Each Question

Very great differences in responses can occur with small variations in the wording of a question. As a result, extreme care must be taken in developing questions. The key things to look for when writing questions are *clarity, brevity, simplicity, precision, bias,* and *appropriateness.*

Clarity. Questions must be worded so that everyone completing the questionnaire understands what is being asked. Each question should address a single topic. Trying to include too much in a question often results in what is called *a double-barreled* question. Double-barreled questions result when two or more questions are included under a single answer. They are confusing not only to the respondent, but also to the researcher; it can be difficult, if not impossible, for the researcher to know what part of the question generated the response.

Brevity. Questions should always be as short and to the point as possible. Never ask two questions in one—avoid the use of "and" in a question. Somewhat longer questions can be included with in-person interviews and mail surveys, but shorter questions—less than twenty words—should be used in telephone interviews (Folz 1996).

Also, be sure that the questionnaire itself is not too long. A rule of thumb to follow is that interviews should not take longer than an hour or so to complete. Phone surveys should be kept to less than twenty minutes. Mailed, self-administered instruments should be kept to four standard pages or less.

Simplicity. Never ask complex or difficult-to-answer questions. Make sure the question is one that subjects can answer knowledgeably. Use short words and simple sentences. This is not to say that respondents should be given the idea that they are being looked down upon. Rather, focus on words that are in common everyday use while avoiding the use of slang.

Precision. The wording of every question must be as precise as possible (focus, focus, focus!). Never use ambiguous words in the body of the question. Examples of words with ambiguous meanings include "sometimes," "possibly," "maybe," etc. And always make sure that each question asks just one thing.

Freedom from Bias. Avoid asking questions that arouse strong emotions, generate resistance, or result in a refusal to answer. If you must ask these questions, place them at or near the end of the questionnaire, so that they do not result in only partly completed instruments. Such questions will often cause respondents to simply stop answering all questions, resulting in an incomplete instrument.

Do not ask "leading" questions—avoid questions that direct or influence the response toward one point of view. These, too, will often cause subjects to not respond to the survey.

Large numbers of refusals to answer can greatly influence the results of a survey by introducing what is known as *nonresponse error* or *bias*. Often, subjects who do not complete the questionnaire would respond far differently than those who do respond.

Appropriateness. As has been said, be sure that each question is one that needs to be asked. Avoid "fishing expeditions." Relate each and every question to the study objectives. This point is related to the bias issue, as well.

Today, many persons have very strong opinions about what should be asked and what shouldn't. Federal privacy laws also confound this issue. This is particularly true with classification or demographic questions. Gender, marital status, ethnicity, income, and the like are potential stumbling blocks in any questionnaire. It is important to remember to ask such questions only if they are critical to the study. If they are not absolutely needed, they are inappropriate and should be left out of the questionnaire.

Organize Questions into a Logical Order

The sequence of items in a questionnaire can also unintentionally influence or bias answers to questions that occur later in the instrument (an *item* is just another word for a *question*). Therefore, the researcher needs to carefully organize the questionnaire in such a way that subjects are encouraged to follow through with answers to all questions.

Questions are usually arranged in an order that begins with the broad and easy-to-answer questions placed before the more focused in-depth questions. The latter often require a significant effort on the part of the subject to answer. If the task is too difficult, respondents will often skip the question. This format is called the *funnel sequence* of questioning (Oskamp 1977).

Every questionnaire is composed of five distinct parts: (1) the title and identification of the survey's sponsors, (2) instructions to respondents, (3) warm-up questions, (4) the most important body of the survey, and (5) a section containing classification questions (Figure 11.2).

Title, Purpose, and Sponsor Identification. Questionnaires should have a title; they should indicate the purpose of the survey, including how the information will be used. The public likes to know who is sponsoring the survey and to know that individual anonymity is guaranteed. These items should all be included at the top of the first page of the questionnaire, although in mail surveys it is also acceptable to include some of this information in a covering letter attached to the questionnaire.

Instructions. Instructions are particularly important for self-administered questionnaires. They should be clear and easy-to-follow. Care must be taken to clearly spell out what is expected of the respondent. It is also a good idea to introduce early in the questionnaire information about potential points of confusion that might appear later, such as who is expected to answer sections of questions after a screening or branching point in the questionnaire. These instructions should be repeated right before the branching occurs.

Warm-up Questions. These are simple, easy-to-answer questions that subjects can answer quickly and with a minimum of effort. They are often dichotomous or, at most, simple multiple-

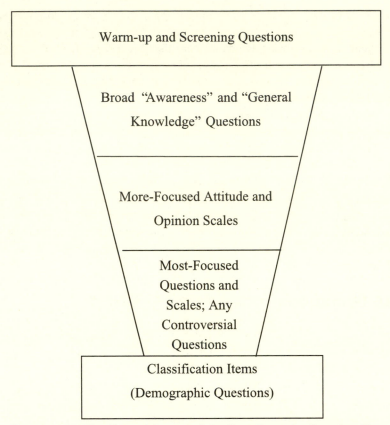

Figure 11.2   **The Funnel Approach to Questionnaire Construction**

choice questions. These are usually questions designed to discern factual or knowledge information; they seldom dive right into gathering attitudinal data.

Items in this section of the questionnaire are often *screening questions,* that is, questions to determine whether the respondent qualifies as a primary target subject. Examples of screening questions include the following three items:

1. Do you consider yourself to be a   Democrat   ☐
   Democrat or a Republican voter?   Republican   ☐
2. Do you drive your personal car to   Yes   ☐
   work more than three times a week?   No   ☐
3. Do you own a bicycle?   Yes   ☐
                                            No   ☐

The objective of this section is to ease respondents into the questionnaire and to bring them to a level of comfort with the questions and the question-answering process. Therefore, questions that are potentially contentious, controversial, or personal in nature should never be included early in the instrument. The best place for potentially controversial questions is right after the most important body of the questionnaire and just before the classification questions.

In the past, some researchers have tried to use warm-up questions that have no connection whatsoever to the study, but which were asked only in an attempt to capture subjects' interest in the survey process. There have not been any convincing reports in the literature on the effectiveness of this ploy, however. Because of the already existing difficulty of gaining subjects' willingness to participate in yet another survey, it is probably a good idea not to waste a question this way. Researchers are encouraged to stick to the point and focus all their attention on gaining only meaningful data.

Body of the Questionnaire. This is where the most important questions should be placed. Again, the easiest of these questions should appear before the more difficult or complex questions. The questions should be placed in a logical order that does not require the respondent to leap from one idea to another. When changes in direction are necessary, a line or two of additional instructions or words calling the shift to the respondent's attention should be considered.

The first third of this section is sometimes used as a transition section between the introduction and ultimate core section of the questionnaire. Researchers use this section of the questionnaire to ask questions to determine subjects' awareness of the survey issue. Other questions can serve to "test" their knowledge of component factors, indicators, and possible causal factors. These are usually broad questions that help build an overall view of the study for the researcher.

In the second third of the instrument, researchers often employ more focused attitude, opinion, or other types of scales—*if* scales are included in the design. Because they often require the subject to *think* about the question before answering, this is often where nonresponse error creeps into the survey. Another type of question that is sometimes included in either the second or last third of the body of the instrument is for gathering what is called *lifestyle* information. These data are often grouped together into a category of information called *psychographics*. Lifestyle information is used to develop a more in-depth profile of the respondents, adding *attitude, opinion, value, and activity* information to the traditional demographic profile.

The final third of the body of the questionnaire is where the most focused questions should be placed, as should all potentially controversial or personally embarrassing questions. The reason for this is that while subjects might skip a threatening question because it appears near the end of the questionnaire, they will have already provided answers for the bulk of the instrument. Questionnaires that are *mostly* completed are almost as valuable as those that are completely answered.

Classification Items. Classification items are questions that enable the researcher to describe the sample in some detail and to compare the responses of one or more subgroups of subjects with responses of other subgroups. Classification information is sometimes referred to as *demographic data* because it usually consists of demographic statistics about the subjects themselves.

These data are, indeed, important to the research results, but not as critical as the information contained in the body of the questionnaire. This occurs because researchers are seldom interested in any one subject's responses, but instead, want to know the mean (average) scores for the entire group. Thus, missing some classification data does not render the instrument completely useless.

Pretest and Revise the Questionnaire

Every questionnaire should be pretested on a group of subjects that as closely as possible reflects the same characteristics as the study sample. This is the critical "debugging" phase of questionnaire construction. No matter how many times the researcher or members of the research team go over the instrument, some problems are almost sure to surface. Typographical errors and misspellings are the least of these potential problems.

People in a career path will often share a particular sense of meanings for words and phrases that are not likely to be shared by everyone else. Thus, subjects who share the experience and characteristics of the study sample, not the research team, must look at question wording. The best way to do this is to administer the questionnaire to a random sample of subjects from the population of interest. The results from questionnaire pretests should not be included with the findings of the final study sample.

Developing and Wording Questions

Responses to questions produce what are called *raw data*. Only when coded, tabulated, and interpreted, do raw data become information. The way in which questions are formed influences the way they are coded, tabulated, and interpreted. Questions may be written in many different ways; they may include a limited set of responses from which the respondent must choose (closed-ended), or they may allow respondents to provide answers freely and in their own words (open-ended).

Most survey questions used in descriptive research designs are closed-ended. These questions "force" respondents to choose from only those alternatives provided by the researcher. While this results in survey instruments that tend to be more objective than open-ended questions, it can also work as a disadvantage. Closed-end questions force subjects into using the same ideas, terms, and alternatives that the researcher uses—thus following the potential bias of the researcher (Oskamp 1977).

Open-ended questions are far more difficult to code and tabulate than are closed-ended questions. Therefore, open-ended questions are usually reserved for small sample, exploratory research designs, or as a small component in an otherwise completely qualitative design.

Closed-End Questions

Closed-end questions can be organized into two broad classes: *structured answer* (dichotomous and multiple choice), and *scales*. Structured answer questions are used for warm-up, introductory and classification portions of the questionnaire, while scales are more commonly found in the body of the instrument. The types of scales used most often in political science and other social science research are: (1) attitude scales, (2) importance scales, (3) rating scales, and (4) readiness-to-act scales.

Structured Answer Questions. Structured answer questions are the easiest type to write and easiest for respondents to answer. There are two types of structured answer questions: *dichotomous* and *multichotomous*. For both types, the data provided are *discrete* (also known as *categorical data*).

The examples of dichotomous and multichotomous questions in Figure 11.3 were used in a public safety agency survey of organizational climate and culture. Dichotomous questions require respondents to select from just two alternative answers. Examples include gender (female/male), behavior (do/don't), intentions (will/will not), status (employed/unemployed), and any number of such two-alternative answer forms. Multichotomous questions allow for more than two possible answers (they are also called *multiple-choice* questions).

63.	Where do you work most of the time?	Field	Jail				
		[2]	[1]				
64.	Your gender:	Male	Female				
		[2]	[1]				
65.	Years with the department:	1—5	6—10	11—15	16—20	20+	
		[5]	[4]	[3]	[2]	[1]	
66.	Highest level of education you have attained:	Graduate work or degree	4-year college degree	2-year college degree	Some college	High school graduate	Not an HS graduate
		[6]	[5]	[4]	[3]	[2]	[1]
67.	Do you have supervisory responsibility?	Yes	No				
		[2]	[1]				

Figure 11.3 **Example of Dichotomous and Multichotomous Questions**
Source: McNabb, Sepic, and Barnowe. 1999. *Organizational Climate Survey.*

Open-End Questions

Open-end questions can also be divided into two broad types: *completely unstructured-response* and *projective techniques.* Unstructured-response questions are entirely the subject's own responses to a question. The researcher provides no clues or direction for the response, although subsequent questions may involve probing for more information. The subject may answer the question in any way desired, with a short or a long answer, and with or without qualifying statements. Projective techniques also allow subjects to respond to some stimulus in his or her own words. The stimulus can be words, pictures, or symbols. The questions are structured in such a way that the respondent unconsciously projects hidden feelings or attitudes into the response. It is believed that in this way projective questions can produce answers that might not otherwise surface.

Projective Techniques

Five different types of projective techniques are used in social and administrative science research. These are: (1) association, (2) construction, (3) completion, (4) ordering, and (5) expressive techniques. Each is discussed in more detail below.

Association Techniques. With association techniques, subjects are asked to react to a particular stimulus, such as a word, an inkblot, or other symbol, with the first thoughts or ideas that come to mind. The technique is believed to be a good way to discern the underlying values that certain words or symbols convey.

Construction Techniques. With construction techniques, subjects are asked to create a story, about either themselves or others, or to draw a self-portrait. The idea is that even though subjects are not told that the story is about them, their underlying values and attitudes will be reflected in the general sense of the subjects' stories.

Completion Techniques. These techniques require the subject to finish an already started stimulus, such as a sentence or a picture. In the sentence completion version, subjects are asked to finish the sentence with any statement that they wish. The rationale for this approach is that the subjects' responses will not emerge from a vacuum; rather, the words chosen for the sentence completion will reflect the subjects' subconscious attitudes.

In the "picture" version of this process, a photograph or a drawing of two characters is shown to the subject. One of the characters is portrayed making a statement. Subjects are asked to put themselves in the other character's shoes and respond in the way that the second character or characters would. Again, the belief is that without consciously doing so, the subject will interject his or her own feelings or opinions into the created response.

Ordering Techniques. Also called "classifying" or "choice" techniques, these require the subject to arrange a group of stimuli into some order or to choose one or more items from a group of items. The item(s) selected are supposed to be most representative of the idea or thought involved. This method can also measure what is called *salience,* which is another way of indicating the importance that a respondent places on each of the items.

Expressive Techniques. In these techniques, subjects are asked to creatively express themselves in some way, such as by drawing a picture, cartoon, finger painting, etc. The method is often used in conjunction with the construction technique. The two are considered to reinforce each other. The picture will reveal an underlying attitude, with the subject's description of the events or components of the picture often indicating salience.

It is important to recognize that projective techniques require skilled and empathetic interpretation that goes far beyond the abilities of most undergraduate students. On the other hand, in the hands of a trained professional, they can and do provide valuable information that might not otherwise surface in a traditional, scale-driven attitudinal research study.

Developing and Using Scales

As noted earlier, the types of scales that are used most often in political science research are: (1) attitude scales, (2) importance scales, (3) rating scales, and (4) readiness-to-act scales. Each is discussed in more detail in the following pages.

Attitude Scales

Attitude scales are the scales used most often in public administration research. An attitude has been defined as a *relatively enduring, learned disposition that provides motivation to respond in a consistent way toward a given attitude object* (Oskamp 1977). Political scientists are interested in people's attitudes for any number of reasons. Just a few examples are:

- Voters' attitudes toward candidates and issues directly influence the outcome of elections.
- Citizens' attitudes influence the formation and adoption of public policies.
- Peoples' attitudes influence their behavior and the consistency of that behavior.
- Attitudes determine group support for issues and programs.

Many different types of scales for measuring attitudes have been developed. The types of attitude scale that are used most often today include: (1) Thurstone scales, (2) Likert scales, (3) semantic differential rating scales, and (4) a related semantic differential approach, the Stapel scale. Each is discussed below.

Thurstone Scales. The Thurstone scale is as much a method as it is a scale. More formally known as "Thurston's Method of Equal-Appearing Intervals," it was developed in the late 1920s as a way of measuring the precise amount of difference between one subject's attitudes and another subject's.

With the Thurstone process, the researcher collects a hundred or more opinion statements about a subject. These should be positive, negative, and neutral. The next step is to have a large number of "informed judges" rate the degree to which each statement is favorable or unfavorable. Judges then sort the statements into eleven equally spaced categories based on this favorable-unfavorable continuum. When judges disagree widely about a statement, it is discarded.

The remaining statements are then assigned scale values based on the median favorable value assigned by the panel of judges. The statements with highest panel agreement are then included in a final attitude scale that is administered to the sample of interest. While Thurston's method does a good job of scale development, the fact that it is so time-consuming and tedious is the reason it is seldom used outside of the laboratory or classroom.

Likert Scales. By far the most favored attitude-measuring tool in use today is the Likert scale, developed in the early 1930s. Likert scales do not require a panel of judges to rate the scale items. The researcher prepares a pool of items that express an opinion about a subject or one of its contributing aspects. Items are individual statements. While the resulting data are most appropriately considered to be *ordinal-level data,* some researchers treat groups of Likert items as *interval-level* and process Likert data with interval-scale statistics. O'Sullivan and Rassel summarized the argument this way:

> The level of measurement of a Likert-type index is ordinal. The items do not really measure the quantity of a characteristic, but we can use the items to rank the cases. However, by adding together the numbers assigned to the response categories for each item, we are treating the measurement as if it were interval. This practice allows us to use more statistical techniques for analysis. Many analysts feel that treating Likert-type scales as if they were interval measures provides more advantages than disadvantages. (O'Sullivan and Rassel 1995, 274)

Objective of Likert Scales

The objective of the Likert scale is to measure the extent of subjects' agreement with each item. The extent is measured on a five-point scale: *strongly agree, agree, undecided, disagree,* and *strongly disagree.* The items are assigned values running from "1" through "5," respectively. Depending on how the statements are worded (positively or negatively, approving or disapproving, etc.), the researcher can use low mean scores to equate with either positive or negative attitudes, while using high mean scores to reflect the opposite attitude.

Researchers are typically not concerned with subjects' responses to any one item on the scale. Rather, an attitude score is established by summing all ratings of items in that scale. Reverse scoring must be used when items are stated in positive and negative terms used together in the same Likert scale. An example of a six-item Likert scale designed to measure subject's attitudes or opinions about one aspect of an organization's climate is shown in Figure 11.4.

		Very Definitely Describes ⇓						Does Not Describe ⇓
18.	The philosophy of our management is that in the long run we get ahead fastest by playing it slow, safe, and sure.	[1]	[2]	[3]	[4]	[5]	[6]	[7]
19.	You get rewarded for taking risks in this organization.	[7]	[6]	[5]	[4]	[3]	[2]	[1]
20.	Decision making in this organization is too cautious for maximum effectiveness.	[1]	[2]	[3]	[4]	[5]	[6]	[7]
21.	You won't get ahead in this organization unless you stick your neck out and take a chance now and then.	[7]	[6]	[5]	[4]	[3]	[2]	[1]
22.	We do things by the book around here; taking risks is strongly discouraged.	[1]	[2]	[3]	[4]	[5]	[6]	[7]
23.	We have to take some pretty big risks occasionally to make sure the organization meets its objectives.	[7]	[6]	[5]	[4]	[3]	[2]	[1]

Figure 11.4 Statements to Measure Attitudes toward Risk in an Organization
Source: McNabb, Sepic, and Barnowe. 1999. *Organizational Climate Survey.*
Notes: Low values = negative attitudes; high values = positive attitudes. Positive statements are reverse-scored.

Responses are coded in reverse order for the first two questions in that scale. Because low scores are assigned to negative attitudes, agreeing with the statement in question 18 is coded with low values. Question 19 is assumed to register a positive attitude toward the company. Positive attitudes are assigned with high values. Hence, agreeing with the statement is coded with high values.

Individual attitude statements to be used as statements or items in the Likert scale are often generated by an exploratory study that uses series of in-depth interviews with key informants in the organization or sample.

Semantic Differential and Stapel Scales. Two additional scales are often used to measure attitudes and opinions. These are the *semantic differential* and its close relative, the *Stapel scale.* The Stapel scale is almost identical to the semantic differential, except that only *one* of the polar adjectives is used instead of both; the scale is *unipolar* rather than *bipolar.*

Semantic differential scales are *pairs* of opposing adjectives, with spaces between each for subjects to mark their opinion. A seven-point scale typically separates the adjectives. Subjects are asked to make a personal judgment about a characteristic or a complete concept. For example, adjective pairs can be used to help researchers build a picture of how subjects rate the service they receive at a particular agency. Or, the adjective pairs could pertain to the agency as a whole.

In the following example, subjects are asked to rate the overall effectiveness of a brochure describing any program or agency. Subjects are first asked to read the brochure, then asked to

Clear	[ ]	[ ]	[ ]	[ ]	[ ]	Confusing
Simple	[ ]	[ ]	[ ]	[ ]	[ ]	Difficult
Quick	[ ]	[ ]	[ ]	[ ]	[ ]	Slow
Complete	[ ]	[ ]	[ ]	[ ]	[ ]	Incomplete
Realistic	[ ]	[ ]	[ ]	[ ]	[ ]	Phony
Valuable	[ ]	[ ]	[ ]	[ ]	[ ]	Worthless

Figure 11.5   **An Example of a Semantic Differential Scale**

rate it on the five-point scale. Subjects are to check the box that most closely matches their perceptions of the document. Figure 11.5 includes adjectives that could be used to describe a public service announcement proposed for an AIDS prevention campaign.

In practice, many researchers consider the points on both the semantic differential and Stapel scale to be equidistant, thus providing interval-level data. However, because the assigned differences are arbitrarily assigned, other researchers feel that the scale provides only ordinal data. This conflicting interpretation has resulted in a reduction in the use of the scales in social and administrative science research.

Other Types of Scales

Other types of scales include *ordinal* (ranked) *importance scales, comparative and noncomparative rating scales,* and *ratio scales.* Example questions are included to illustrate these several types of scales.

1. Ordinal Scale Importance Ranking

Please rank each of the following public transportation methods in terms of how important it is to reducing traffic congestion in this region. (Use "1" for most important, "2" for next in importance, etc. Do not give any two items the same value)

    _____ Freeway buses
    _____ Light-rail system
    _____ Vehicle ferry boats
    _____ Passenger-only ferryboats
    _____ Heavy rail commuter trains
    _____ Commuter pool vans

In your opinion, would you say that patient waiting time at the veterans' hospital you visit is?

    _____ Shorter than most
    _____ About the same as most
    _____ Longer than most
    _____ The longest I have ever encountered

2. *Comparative Rating Scale (single attribute)*

Compared with Microsoft® Excel™, how do you rate SPSS® in ease of use? (Check the appropriate bin)

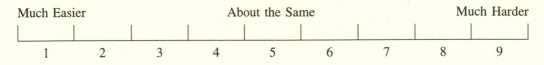

Much Easier				About the Same				Much Harder
1	2	3	4	5	6	7	8	9

3. *Noncomparative Rating Scale*

How would you rate this brochure on its ability to inform you of the disadvantages of using tobacco products? (Circle the appropriate number)

Very Good				About Average				Very Poor
1	2	3	4	5	6	7	8	9

Summary

Researchers use two different approaches when gathering primary data in quantitative research studies; they may collect data by *observing* and counting overt acts of behavior, or they may use a *questionnaire* to generate responses to specific questions. Questionnaires are the most popular way to gather primary data. They are particularly appropriate when the research problem calls for a *descriptive* design. Questionnaires have many advantages. The greatest of these is their *flexibility*. Questionnaires can be custom-designed to meet the objectives of almost any type of research project.

Eight steps are followed in questionnaire construction: (1) establish what information is needed, (2) specify the data-gathering method, (3) specify procedures for analyzing the data, (4) select question type and structure, (5) select the best wording for each questions, (6) organize the question in a logical order, (7) pretest and revise the questionnaire, if necessary, and 8) administer the questionnaire and collect the data.

Questions may be written as a limited set of responses from which the respondent must choose (closed-ended), or they may allow respondents to provide answers in their own words (open-ended). There are two types of closed-end questions: *structured answer* (dichotomous and multiple choice), and *scales*. Structured answer questions are used for warm-up, introductory, and classification portions of the questionnaire; scales are usually found in the body of the questionnaire. The types of scales used most often in political science research are: (1) attitude scales, (2) importance scales, (3) rating scales, and (4) readiness-to-act scales.

Open-ended questions can also be divided into two broad types: *completely unstructured response* and *projective techniques*. Unstructured-response questions are entirely the subject's own responses to a question. Projective techniques also allow subjects to respond to some stimulus in their own words. The stimulus can be words, pictures, or symbols. The questions are structured in such a way that the respondent unconsciously *projects* hidden feelings or attitudes into the response. Five different types of projective techniques are used in research: (1) association, (2) construction, (3) completion, (4) ordering, and (5) expressive techniques.

Many different types of scales have been developed for measuring attitudes. The attitude scale methods that are used most often today are: (1) Thurstone scales, (2) Likert scales, (3) semantic differential rating scales, and (4) its related approach, the Stapel scale.

Discussion Questions

1. What are some of the benefits researchers gain with the use of questionnaires?
2. Name the eight steps followed in questionnaire construction.
3. Why are researchers concerned with brevity and clarity in questionnaires?
4. What are "classification items," and why are they important? Give some examples.
5. What are dichotomous questions? What are multichotomous questions?
6. Describe the difference between open-ended and closed-ended questions.
7. What is a scale?
8. Distinguish between Thurstone and Likert scales.
9. Define the bipolar adjectives scale.
10. What are "projective techniques," and how are they used in questionnaires?

Additional Reading

Alreck, Pamela L., and Robert B. Settle. 1995. *The Survey Research Handbook.* 2nd ed. Boston: Irwin McGraw-Hill.

DeVellin, Robert F. 1991. *Scale Development: Theory and Applications.* Newbury Park: Sage.

Folz, David H. 1996. *Survey Research for Public Administration.* Thousand Oaks, CA: Sage.

Oskamp, Stuart. 1977. *Attitudes and Opinions.* Englewood Cliffs, NJ: Prentice-Hall.

O'Sullivan, Elizabethann, and Gary R. Rassel. 1995. *Research Methods for Public Administrators.* 2nd ed. White Plains, NY: Longman.

12 Causal Research: The Experimental Approach

Experimental design (ED) is the term used in the social, behavioral, and natural sciences to identify the processes involved in designing, conducting, and evaluating the results of all types of experiments. Researchers conduct experiments when they want to determine whether a *causal relationship* exists between two or more variables. ED also enables researchers to measure the strength—and sometimes the direction—of the possible relationship.

Experiments are characterized by three distinguishing components (Greeno 2001). First, at least two groups of similar subjects are selected; one group is administered a "treatment" of some kind. The second group—usually referred to as the *control group*—gets either no treatment or an alternate treatment. This treatment is referred to as the *independent variable*. Second, the researcher determines what activity, behavior, or result to measure after application of the treatment(s). This variable that is altered as a result of the experiment is the *dependent variable*. The measured change in the dependent variable is the *outcome of the experiment*. The researcher observes the dependent variable to discern the amount of shift, if any, that might have occurred after application of the treatment. In an early example of experimental design, the independent variable treatment was the application or no application of fertilizer; the dependent variable measured outcome was variation in crop yields on plots with and without the treatment (Cochran 1977).

The third distinguishing characteristic of experiments is the requirement that subjects be *randomly assigned* to all test groups. Randomization ensures that the researcher does not influence who receives the treatment and who does not. It is a method for controlling for the possible effects of extraneous, or *confounding*, factors that might influence the outcome.

Key Concepts in Experimental Design

As we have seen, quantitative research can have as its fundamental focus either (1) the illumination of concepts and themes, (2) the description of events or phenomena, or (3) the determination of causal effects that the manipulation of one or more factors may have on some variable of interest. These three different approaches are called *exploratory, descriptive,* and *causal.* Causal research is called experimental research because it follows an experimental design. In exploratory and descriptive designs, the researcher is a collector of data that already exist. In an experiment, however, the researcher becomes an active participant in the data-generating process by manipulating different treatments to examine their effects on a variable of interest.

A number of important concepts play a role in experimental design. Some of the key concerns involved in the design, conduct, and interpretation of experiments and the statistical tests employed in experimental design are probability and confidence levels, sample factors, and inference. Some of these factors are discussed below.

Probability. Probability is the level of confidence a researcher holds in implying that a causal relationship exists; it is also a numerical indication in the researcher's belief in the reliability of a prediction that X is a cause of Y, or if the occurrence of X makes Y more likely.

Confidence Levels. Confidence levels are closely related to the concept of probability. Before widespread acceptance of the *p*-value approach to hypothesis testing, managers were required to compute acceptance and rejection levels and to look up decision values in tables. Today, most statistical packages, such as SPSS® and Excel™, compute critical *p*-values along with *t*-test, *z*-test and *F*-test results. The decision whether to retain or reject the null hypothesis can now be made by comparing the computed *p*-value with the confidence level, or *alpha*. Confidence levels used most often in all social sciences include the .01, the .05, and the .10 probability levels.

Statistical Significance. Statistical significance is the term used to describe the point or value beyond which analysts accept or reject a null hypothesis; decisions are made in accordance with preselected levels of confidence. Hypotheses tests are themselves sometimes called *significance tests*. In the past, the critical values of a statistic had to be read from a table of values found at the end of most statistics texts. These were then compared with a value that was found by following steps in a formula for calculating the statistical test. Today, the value at which the decision can be made appears as a *probability* value in the results of most, if not all, inferential statistical tests. This is called the p-*value approach.*

Alpha Levels. In statistical notation, the lower-case Greek letter alpha (α) is used to represent the confidence value; *p*-values the same or greater than the selected alpha result in retaining (or accepting) the null hypothesis; *p*-values less than the significance value require that the null hypothesis be rejected. Most researchers in the social sciences, including political science, make hypothesis acceptance decisions at the .05 level of confidence. However, the nature of the study and required level of confidence in the results often require that a level of .10 or of .01 be employed. This decision is made by the researcher or sponsoring agency.

The Confidence Coefficient. When analysts use the .05 level of confidence they are in fact saying they are 95 percent sure about a hypothesis decision. This "95 percent" is what is known as the *confidence coefficient,* and is the probability that a null hypothesis is retained when it should be retained.

Experimental Validity. Experimental validity means making sure that the experiment and statistical analysis measures what the researcher wants to measure. There are two types of validity: internal and external. Internal validity refers to the effectiveness of the design at limiting possible explanations for the outcome to the treatment applied. This means controlling external or confounding factors. External validity refers to the degree to which the researcher can make inferences to larger populations from the results of the sample experiment. Over time, field experiments have been shown to provide a greater level of external validity and a lower level of internal validity than laboratory experiments (McDaniels and Gates 1993).

Independent Variable. Also called the explanatory or experimental variable, this is the changed or manipulated factor in an experiment. It can be anything that the researcher believes might influence a change in something else.

Dependent Variable. This is the phenomenon that the researcher observes in order to check for a change as a result of application of the treatment. The observed and measured change is called the *outcome.*

Treatment. Treatment refers to the changes the researcher makes in the independent variable or variables. Different instructional methods, communications methods, prices, models, designs, and issues are examples of variables that are manipulated in the experiment.

Randomness. The random assignment of subjects to treatment and control groups is a fundamental assumption of experimental design.

Degrees-of-Freedom. Degrees-of-freedom (abbreviated as *d.f.* or simply *df*) refers to the number of observations in an experiment that are free to vary. The degrees of freedom must be known when using a statistical table, such as the *t*-table or *F*-table, to determine a critical value in hypothesis testing. Modern statistical software eliminates the need for using statistical tables, but *df* are still reported when making hypothesis decisions using the p-*value approach.* Degrees-of-freedom are reported for either columns (variables) or rows (cases) or both, depending on the test in question. When a statistics calculation is concerned only with description, the degrees-of-freedom is *n*, the full sample size (Phillips 1996). However, when the statistical calculation is concerned with inference, the *df* is always smaller than *n* (e.g., $n-1$, $n-2$, etc.).

Inference. Researchers can never prove beyond all doubt that for a given population, X is a cause of Y. Rather, they can only *infer* from the observation of sample results that a causal relationship exists for the population from which the sample was drawn. In all science, causality is always inferred; it is never proven conclusively.

Approaches to Experimental Design

Experiments can take any one of three different approaches. The first is a group of approaches known as *pre-experimental designs.* A second type is one that is used often in political science research, the *quasi-experimental* design. The third group consists of two types of true experiments, *laboratory experiments* and *field experiments.* Laboratory experiments are seldom used in political science research.

Pre-experimental designs are the least scientifically rigorous of all experimental designs. They provide little or no control over confounding variables. As a result, they are considered to be only slightly better than simple descriptive studies when the results are used to make inferences. The advantages that make them so desirable in political research are that they are far less costly to administer than classical experiments, and they typically take far less time to administer. A pre-experimental design may produce results in a week or less—a fact that makes them popular with campaign managers in the midst of a heated political race. Three of the most commonly used pre-experimental designs are the *one-time, single case study*, the *one-group pretest, posttest design*, and the *base-group comparison design* (McDaniels and Gates 1993).

In a quasi-experimental design researchers follow most of the requirements of true experiments. They employ treatments, outcomes, and sample units, but do not use random sampling methods to assign subjects to sample groups (Cook and Campbell 1979). The groups usually already exist, and are chosen because of this existing structure or cohesiveness. Examples might be the registered voters of two different communities, groups of lobbyists supporting a controversial issue and groups of lobbyists who support an opposite point of view, or elected government officials in two different cities, states or nations.

Laboratory experiments are one of the two main types of classical experimental designs. They take place in controlled environments, such as classrooms, university laboratories, research centers, and similar locations. In this type of experiment, the researcher creates a situation that mirrors as much as possible external conditions; he or she then manipulates the independent variable(s) and measures changes in the dependent variable. In political science research, most studies tend to be empirical. Therefore, laboratory experiments are seldom seen outside of academic settings.

In field experiments, the research is conducted in a realistic situation—often in one or more communities. Although the researcher attempts to control conditions as much as possible, the potential for bias from intervening or confounding variables is always a possibility in these situations. Both laboratory and field experiments involve two principal components: (1) the actual process of designing the experiment, and (2) determination of the statistical tests to use in evaluating the results of the experiment. These two principal components of ED incorporate a number of connected activities (Kirk 1995, 1–2). As in all research, these begin with establishing a valid research question and end with interpreting the results of the research. Activities involved in experimental design include the following:

1. Selecting a valid research question and forming a hypothesis or hypotheses that can be scientifically tested using proven ED methods.
2. Identifying the treatments (i.e., the independent variable or variables), establishing what changes in the dependent variable will be measured as a result of the changes in treatment, and identifying the variables and conditions that might confound or bias the results.
3. Identifying the population from which a sample will be drawn, the characteristics or constraints that limit the sample alternatives, and determining the sample size needed for validity in the experiment.
4. Determining the approach for assigning units to test and control groups. This involves selecting from several experimental designs. Although as many as fourteen and more designs have been developed, the four basic designs used most often are the *one-sample, two-sample, factorial,* and *Latin Square designs.*
5. Planning the appropriate statistical analysis processes to be used for analyzing and interpreting results of the experiment.

Pre-experimental Designs

Pre-experimental designs are used primarily because of their ease of application and speedy turnaround. Pre-experimental designs are little better than standard descriptive studies in their use for inferences to larger populations. They typically take any one of three different approaches, ranging from the least scientifically rigorous to the nearly so.

One-Time Single Case Study

In this design, the researcher selects a convenience sample that he or she expects is similar to the population of interest. This could be a group of students, a neighborhood, a group of House or Senate employees, or any convenient group. The researcher administers a treatment of some kind, and then measures the previously identified dependent variable. No pretests are taken, so the researcher never knows if the treatment induced any change. The design does not control for confounding variables, nor is a control group included in the research.

The Single Group, Pretest and Posttest Design

This design adds the validity safeguard of establishing a benchmark to measure against, after the treatment. This is a very common design, used extensively in tests of public acceptance of political strategies and other types of attitude and opinion research, for example. However, the research does not include a control group. Elimination of a control group makes the results of the experiment potentially suspect. There is no way of controlling for maturation or other confounding variables.

Base-Group Comparison Design

In this type of pre-experimental design, the researcher uses two groups—an experimental and a control group—but does not use random assignment of subjects to either group. Treatments are applied to the entire sample, so it is not possible to randomly assign treatment to sample subjects. No pretests are used, thus making it possible only to infer causality from the results of the treatment.

Quasi-experimental Designs

Quasi-experimental designs are similar to true experiments. The major difference is that the researcher randomly assigns subjects to groups, but does not use random application of treatments to the groups. They are often used in large-scale studies and in circumstances where it might be impossible to make random applications. Kirk (1977, 6–7) described an example quasi-experimental study in which whole communities were selected to receive different levels of fluoride in the water supply. The measured outcomes were levels of tooth decay in children. The results were compared with tooth decay rates in a community with high levels of fluoride naturally occurring in the water supply.

True Experimental Designs

In all true experimental designs the researcher randomly assigns treatments to randomly selected sample subjects. The use of randomization in subject selection and treatment application has the benefit of controlling for the effects of many intervening variables. These designs are particularly appropriate for use for inferences. The three types of experiments include *randomized two-sample designs, randomized block designs, factorial designs,* and *Latin Square designs.*

Randomized Two-Sample Designs

The most typical of a number of two-sample designs is the *experimental/control groups, before and after tests.* Because subjects are randomly assigned to both groups, they are considered to be equivalent. Of the several different variations of this design, the simplest to use and the best known is the t-*test for independent samples design* (Kirk 1995). The *t*-test is used to test for differences in the mean values for both the experimental and control groups after application of the treatment. The hypothesis is often expressed as: the difference between the two statistics is equal to some value, which is usually zero. This approach is also known as the *before and after with control group* design (McDaniels and Gates 1993).

Randomized Block Designs

This design is similar to the randomized two-sample design, except that it can be used to test for the effects of two variables at the same time—it is a two-factor experiment with a one-factor focus (Hildebrand and Ott 1998, 458). The two factors are *treatments* and *blocks*. The term "block" refers to the environment in which the treatment is administered. In this design, the researcher is concerned with measuring treatment effects, but controls extraneous or "nuisance" block factor. The following example will help to clarify the design.

A political strategist wants to know which is the best message to use to influence voter attitudes in her state. She has three different strategies that might be effective. She decides to test the messages on three types of voters—Democrats, Republicans, and Independents—in each of three legislative districts. The legislative districts are the blocks in her experiment, whereas the different messages are the treatments. She is not concerned with which legislative district the voter resides in, but rather, in assuring that all voter groups are exposed to all different messages (treatments). The strategist might simply randomly assign the messages to each district. The problem with that approach is that the random assignment by itself could result in a design where all Democrats receive only the first message, all Republicans receive only the second message, and all Independents receive only the third. That type of assignment might look like the display in Table 12.1. Note that each column receives the same treatment (message). Clearly, this would defeat the purpose of the randomized experiment.

To control for the block variable, the researcher requires that every message be used in every legislative district. In each district, voter groups are randomly assigned one of the three messages, until each of the three messages is represented by each category. The appropriate randomized block design will look like the distribution in Table 12.2. In this design, each of the nine experimental groups receives one block assignment and one treatment assignment, thus improving validity by ensuring greater randomization to the study.

Table 12.1

Example of a Random Design Affected by the Nuisance Variable "Block"

Legislative District	Party Affiliation		
	Democrat Voters	Republican Voters	Independent Voters
First District	Message 1	Message 2	Message 3
Second District	Message 1	Message 2	Message 3
Third District	Message 1	Message 2	Message 3

Table 12.2

Example of a Random Design with a Nuisance Variable (Block) Controlled

Legislative District	Party Affiliation		
	Democrat Voters	Republican Voters	Independent Voters
First District	Message 1	Message 2	Message 3
Second District	Message 2	Message 3	Message 1
Third District	Message 3	Message 2	Message 1

Factorial Designs

In a factorial design, two or more independent variables are studied simultaneously in the same experiment. All possible combinations of each level of treatment are tested together in this design. In this way, they also allow the researcher to test for any *interaction* that a combination of factors might have. According to Kirk (1997, 364), they are the most widely used designs in the behavioral sciences. They are also very popular in political science research, and are the principal experimental design employed in business and education research.

In the following example of how a factorial experiment might be designed: Suppose that the managing director of an environmental lobby in Washington, DC wants to know what messages might be best to use for influencing members of Congress to vote for legislation to protect Arctic wildlife habitat. The director wants to test whether to use an appeal based on reason, an appeal based on emotion, or an appeal based on economic considerations. In persuasive communications, these are called *head, heart,* and *pocketbook* appeals, respectively.

In addition, the researcher wants to test which communications method will have the greatest impact on recipients of the message, a four-color brochure produced and distributed by the organization's home office or a letter-writing campaign by the organization's members directly to members of Congress. Together, these allow for six possible combinations, as shown in Table 12.3. In one approach, the researcher could plan a number of independent experiments of a single variable, such as one concerned only with which appeal to use. In any one such experiment, all other relevant variables would be held constant. However, a much better procedure would be to vary all factors in a single experiment. This would permit the manager not only to accomplish the purposes of single-variable experiments, but also to test for possible interactions among the factors.

To conduct the experiment, the lobbyist might test the combinations on members of several state legislatures, randomly assigning legislators to each of the six groups. Referring to the diagramed experiment in Table 12.3, the design allows the researcher to test for the following in one statistical operation:

1. The main effects of the communications *appeal* altogether,
2. The simple effects of each *appeal* separately,
3. The main effects of communications *method* together,

Table 12.3

Example of a Two-Factor Factorial Experimental Design

	Type of Appeal and Treatments		
Communication Method	Head Appeal (A$_1$)	Heart Appeal (A$_2$)	Pocketbook Appeal (A$_3$)
Home Office Brochure (C$_1$)	A$_1$ C$_1$	A$_2$ C$_1$	A$_3$ C$_1$
Membership Letter-Writing Campaign (C$_2$)	A$_1$ C$_2$	A$_2$ C$_2$	A$_3$ C$_2$

4. The simple effects of each communications *method* separately, and
5. The *interaction* effects of *appeal* times *method*.

In this example, a simple analysis of variance (ANOVA) procedure would test the significance of each of the four main and simple effects, while also providing a bonus test for interaction. ANOVA procedures are discussed in the next section.

Latin Square Designs

The Latin Square design is similar to the randomized block design in that it allows the researcher to control for the effects of nuisance factors. However, this design lets the researcher control for two or more nuisance variables at the same time. The key characteristic of the Latin Square design is the assignment of each level of treatment to every combination of nuisance variables. If rows and columns are levels of the nuisance factors, each level of treatment appears once in each row of the design and once in each column.

For example, in the following Latin Square design scenario, the Tribal Council of a Native American tribe is interested in expanding income enhancement opportunities for tribal members. The funding for the program would come from development of a gambling center and/ or resort on tribal lands. Three types of opportunities have been identified as levels for the treatment variable *(treatment)*: promises of service jobs now (T$_1$), technical job training with low monthly stipends (T$_2$), transportation to nearby colleges for academic education with stipends replaced by tuition grants (T$_3$). A layout of the experiment is shown in Table 12.4. The Tribal Council is running the experiment to see if enough support for gambling exists to proceed with planning the development.

Three groups of tribal members have been identified: modernists, traditionalists, and externally focused *(status)*. Modernists (S$_1$) want to bring gambling to the reservation; traditionalists (S$_2$) will accept a resort, but do not want gambling; and externally focused members (S$_3$) live off the reservation and consider themselves integrated into the larger, nontribal community. Three levels of development *(develop)* are identified: no change (D$_1$), gambling center only (D$_2$), or gambling center and resort (D$_3$). The three test hypotheses for this Latin Square are (1) there is no difference in the means of the treatment groups, (2) there is no difference in the means of the social orientation groups (rows), and (3) there is no difference in the means of the development preference groups (columns).

Table 12.4

Example of a Two-Factor, Three-Treatments, Latin Square Experimental Design

Status	Development Type Supported and Treatments		
	No Development (D_1)	Gambling Only (D_2)	Gambling and Resort (D_3)
Modernists (S_1)	T_1	T_2	T_3
Traditionalists (S_2)	T_2	T_3	T_1
Externally Orienteds (S_3)	T_3	T_1	T_2

Steps in Planning and Conducting Experiments

Step 1. Determine the Research Question

Research questions are the concepts the researcher wants to study. The question selected then dictates which research design, data collection method, and analysis approach satisfies the objectives spelled out for the selected study question. Political scientists typically examine questions that fall under the categories of either political theory, the philosophy and/or history of politics and political institutions, American politics, comparative politics, elections and voting behavior, all levels of the judiciary, public policy, public administration, program evaluation, international relations, research methodology, and other related topics.

Step 2. Select Research Treatments

The concept of treatments originated with the founder of experimental design and methods, agricultural researcher Sir Ronald A. Fisher. Fisher developed ED techniques in order to test the influences of such factors as water, fertilizer, soil type, and other variables on improving yields of farm crops (Antony 1998). Classical experimental design follows the procedures set forth by Fisher and William D. Gosset, who published his statistics research under the pen name of "Student" (Cochran 1977). The design involves the random assignment of subjects or units to experimental and control groups, pretesting to establish benchmarks, variations in treatments, and posttesting after treatment application.

Selection of a treatment variable also involves identifying and controlling for potentially confounding variables as well. Confounding or extraneous variables threaten internal validity. They range from the effects of being tested, history, changes that subjects may undergo over the time from pretest to posttest (called *maturation*), to any variations that might creep into the measuring instrument (such as leading questions and unintentional bias).

In political science research, treatments have included such examples as different types of messages and different types of communication media (such as television vs. newspaper), testing of different issues or appeals to voters, comparisons of different policy scenarios with various groups, and similar variables that may be manipulated in experimental situations. Examples of how treatments are employed include two papers published in the July 2000 edition of the *American Journal of Political Science*. In the first paper, Bottom, Eavy, Miller, and Victor described a laboratory experiment on the institutional effect on majority rule instability. Subjects were assigned to forty six-person groups. Groups were assigned to one of four different treatments, which involved different meeting arrangements to represent bicameral or unicameral formats for policy decisions. In the second paper, Gilliam and Iyengar (2000) used as their treatment different versions of a hypothetical television news script. In one version, the crime was described as violent and the perpetrators as nonwhite males; in other versions these descriptions were changed. The hypothesis tested was that inflammatory news stories influence citizens' attitudes toward minorities.

Step 3. Identify the Population and Select a Sample

Researchers must be certain that the population they are studying is one that is appropriate for the research question and study hypotheses. Samples are smaller groups or research subjects that are drawn from larger populations. The sample selection process begins with determining who are the appropriate subjects for the study. This decision is based upon the research question selected by the investigator. The researcher must take care to ensure that the sample is representative of the population of interest, and is large enough to enable the researcher to apply the level of precision necessary in measuring the effects of the independent variable(s).

Sample size has an influence on the level of Type I and Type II errors acceptable to the researcher (Wyner 1997). "Error" refers to making right or wrong decisions based on the evidence established in the analysis of the data. Type I error means deciding that the null hypothesis is false when, in reality, it is true. Type II error is the opposite: concluding that a null hypothesis is true when it is actually false. While neither can be eliminated entirely, establishing more rigid confidence levels and random selection of subjects can control Type I error. Type II error may be controlled by increasing the sample size. A rule of thumb often followed in establishing sample size for empirical research is that the sample must consist of at least 30 subjects or 10 percent of the total population size; small samples typically do not exceed 100. When researching with larger populations, such as the entire population of a state or of the nation, most sample sizes seldom exceed 1,000 subjects. Nearly any statistical textbook will have a formula for sample size determination.

Randomness in Sample Selection

Randomness refers to the way subjects are assigned to experimental and control groups. The principle of random selection and assignment of cases was introduced in 1925 by Fisher, one of the fathers of experimental design and the statistical techniques used to evaluate results of experiments. The principal gains from random assignment are that it allows the researcher to control for any bias that might originate from treatment effects or from confounding variables because applications are averaged across all possible groupings (Yates 1977).

The most common approach to selecting a random sample is called a *simple random sample* (SRS). The key characteristic of this type of sample is that every potential sample member has an equal chance at being selected. Often, subjects are numbered sequentially, then either a table of random numbers or a computer-generated random table is used to select individual subject numbers from the list. The total list is called the *sample frame*. Randomly generated telephone numbers (called *random digit dialing*) are another method used in random sample selection. When the sample frame is large, as with a telephone directory, the researcher often simply opens the directory at random, randomly decides on a starting point on the page and a number of pages to turn each time, then continues through the directory from either front to back or the reverse, following the same selection system.

Step 4. Select Experimental Design

Three major categories of experimental designs used most often by political science researchers today include *pre-experimental designs, quasi-experimental designs,* and *true experimental designs.* Of a wide number of applications of these three basic approaches, the most commonly used designs include one-sample pre-experimental designs, quasi-experimental designs, randomized two-sample designs, randomized block designs, factorial designs, and Latin Square designs. Each of these is discussed in greater detail below, beginning with the three types of pre-experimental designs.

Step 5. Plan the Appropriate Statistical Analysis

The underlying concepts of one-sample hypothesis testing also apply to a body of statistical techniques designed to test hypotheses with two or more samples. These tools permit managers to test whether the different values found in two or more samples are statistically significant or whether they could have occurred by chance. Another way to look at a hypothesis test is to consider it a *significance test,* the results of which help the researcher evaluate certain characteristics in measurements. *Differences* are one class of characteristics; *relationships* are another. In experiments, the researcher is almost always testing for differences in the outcomes of a set of treatments.

Researchers want to know if the differences seen in test measurements are "real" or if they are simply chance-related variations that are seen every time a new measurement is made and that would fall within the range of a normal distribution of the statistic. They are looking for differences that are *statistically significant.* A difference that is statistically significant is one with a high probability that the differences did not occur through chance alone. It is important to remember that the analyst never knows if the differences are, indeed, "real." Rather, within a predetermined acceptable *level of confidence,* such as 90, 95, or 99 percent, the procedure entails only rejecting or accepting a hypothesis or hypotheses about a difference.

Many statistical techniques exist to test for differences with all levels of measurements. Managers will most likely find themselves using the several tests for comparing differences in means, a statistic that requires interval or ratio data. However, other data types can also be tested for differences. The choice of a particular statistical test for differences between measures depends upon the nature of the measurements themselves. A statistic based on two groups' categorical measurement (nominal data) should not be measured with the same statistic used for a continuous (nominal or ratio level data) variable, for example.

As can be seen in Figure 12.1, an extensive body of statistical tools has been developed for testing hypotheses about statistics for two or more groups. Various tests exist for use with *parametric* and *nonparametric* statistics. Parametric statistical tests can only be used with data at

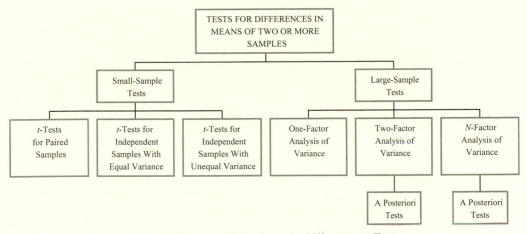

Figure 12.1   **Commonly Used Two or More Sample Differences Tests**

the equidistant-interval or ratio level. When the data are either ordinal (ranked data) or nominal (categorical), a body of tests known as *nonparametric* statistics must be used. In addition, parametric statistics require that the data be from random samples, with a normal distribution. When these assumptions cannot be met, nonparametric tests must be used in place of parametric tests. Some parametric tests require that the samples be independent from one another, while other tests have been developed for use with dependent or paired samples. Separate-but-related statistical tests have been developed to meet either independence requirement.

Two of the statistical tests often used when comparing the mean values for independent samples are the Student's *t*-test for independent samples, and the one-way, two-way, and *n*-way *analysis of variance* (ANOVA) tests. When the decision maker has any doubt about the independence of the samples, testing a null hypothesis for dependence with the SPSS® *Levene test for independence* can be done before selecting either of the difference tests.

Once the researcher is assured the samples are independent, he or she must then decide whether the *t*-test or ANOVA is appropriate. The *t*-test has more limitations than ANOVA, and is usually used for comparisons between the means of two (and only two) relatively small samples, and with each sample having about the same number of observations or cases.

Testing Differences with Student's *t*-Test

The *t*-test is used to compare the means of two groups with approximately equal variances. This could be the test scores of two groups of employment applicants. Scores from a group of trainees gathered prior to a training program might be compared with scores for the same group after completion of the training. Another might be comparing different sample means in production line situations, such as filling boxes or bottles. Many similar such uses are possible. Minimum required assumptions for using the *t*-test include the following: (1) the measurements are of at least interval level data, (2) the samples are randomly selected, and (3) the scores are randomly distributed.

The *t*-tests in Microsoft® Excel™ programs are to be used only when the researcher has all the raw data (individual measurements) available. When this is not the case, when the researcher has only the means at hand, it is possible to make a similar comparison using just summary data and the Excel™ mathematical formula capability. ANOVA, which compares variances between samples, also requires that the raw data be available.

As in one-sample hypothesis testing, the first step must be to prepare the null and alternate hypotheses. It is possible to perform both a one-tailed test and a two-tailed test with the pooled variance *t*-test in Excel™. A typical two-tailed test hypothesis pair, to determine where the means are different in any way, would be:

$$H_O: \quad \mu_1 = \mu_2$$
$$H_A: \quad \mu_1 \neq \mu_2$$

If a one-tailed test is desired, either a greater or lesser hypothesis pair must be written as follows:

$$\mu_1 \text{ Greater than } \mu_2 \qquad \mu_1 \text{ Lesser than } \mu_2$$
$$H_O: \mu_1 \geq \mu_2 \quad H_0: \qquad \mu_1 \leq \mu_2$$
$$H_A: \quad \mu_1 < \mu_2 \quad H_A: \qquad \mu_1 > \mu_2$$

The difference between *one-tailed* and *two-tailed* tests is that in one-tailed tests the researcher specifies the direction of the difference: it is either greater or lesser. The probabilities calculated with the *t*-test on a one-tailed test are half of the probabilities for a two-tailed test. It should be noted that deciding whether to select either the one- or two-tailed tests cannot be done arbitrarily. If the manager has no specific reason to expect a difference in one direction, it follows that no prediction can be made in advance. The manager is obligated to use the two-tailed test.

Different Approaches for the *t*-Test

Several different approaches to difference tests are possible with the *t*-test. The major differentiating characteristic between these tests is the nature of the samples for which measurements are available: are they paired or independent? This question must be answered before selecting one of the several different *t*-test computational methods. At the heart of this issue is what are known as *degrees of freedom*. Degrees of freedom refer to the limits to which a set of measurements may vary. The concept is rooted in physics, where an object that can move on a flat plane is said to have *two degrees of freedom*. If it can move in only a straight line, it has just one degree of freedom.

In statistics, this idea is used to mean the number of independent comparisons that can be taken between sets of data. For example, if we have two observations, we are limited to just one independent comparison. Two "observations" means two independent measurements, such as would be taken from a sample of just two individuals. If there are three observations, then we have two independent comparisons, and so on. In statistical notation, this is written as "$n - 1$" degrees of freedom, with *n* meaning the total number of observations.

Degrees of freedom are computed differently depending upon whether the data are collected from the same individuals, as in a pretest and a posttest situation, or whether they are collected from different sets of individuals (two independent samples). Data collected from the same individuals at different times are called *correlated data*. Data collected from separate samples are called *uncorrelated data*. To determine the degrees of freedom for *correlated* data, one is subtracted from the total number of cases. To compute the degrees of freedom for *uncorrelated* data, one is subtracted from each sample. In statistical notations, this is shown as: $df = n_1 + n_2$. The various *t*-tests contained in Excel™ include these different values in their computations; all the manager needs to do is to select the correct option.

Both the Excel™ *Function Wizard* and *Tools: Data Analysis* include different *t*-test options: a test for paired samples and two tests for independent samples. The two independent sample tests vary in that one assumes the samples were taken from populations with equal variance, while the second test assumes two populations in which the variance is unequal. In practice, this means the manager should select the equal variance option when comparing the means of two samples, both of which were randomly selected from the same larger population. The unequal variance option is to be used when the populations are different. An example would be comparing the means of samples taken from two separate production lines or processing machines.

All two-sample *t*-tests compare sample (or group) means by computing a Student's *t*-value, and comparing the significance of whatever difference is found between the means. Considered to be only slightly less "robust" than the *F*-test statistic used in ANOVA procedures, it can be used to test the means for either different (independent) samples or paired samples. "Different samples" refers most often to different groups within a larger sample.

For example, the attitudes of nonsupervisory personnel might be compared with attitudes of agency management; the responses of women in a sample might be compared with those of men, etc. Paired sample testing refers to testing for differences between two separate variables. Examples include comparing the mean scores on a pretest given before a training activity variable with the mean of a second test given after the training session. Table 12.5 displays data from a paired-sample, pre- and posttest example.

To summarize *t*-test applications, the paired-sample *t*-tests in Microsoft® Excel™ will compare the means for the two variables (pretest and posttest), report the difference in the means, and calculate a *p*-value for the *t*-statistic. The samples may be paired, or independent; inde-

Table 12.5

Individual's Scores before and after Computer-Assisted Training

(Variable 1) Pretest Scores	(Variable 2) Posttest Scores
20.7	19.3
21.7	23.9
17.2	19.9
18.0	24.0
15.1	17.7
21.1	21.5
24.5	25.9
17.8	19.1
23.6	24.0
19.0	19.5

pendent samples may be from one population with equal variance, or from different samples with unequal variance.

Comparing Scores of More than Two Groups

ANOVA is a powerful tool for comparing the differences in means between any number of groups, and of doing so at more than one level. With ANOVA, it is possible to test the role of each of several variables independently, and then to determine whether two or more variables *interact* to influence differences between groups' scores. A classical example often cited is that of testing the influence of farm plot location (or any other variable, such as amount of water applied) and the amount of fertilizer on crop yields. Each variable can be tested by itself. The two are then tested for interactive influence on the yield result. ANOVA is also regularly used in market research studies to compare mean attitude scores of potential customer groups.

In all applications, ANOVA uses the *F*-ratio to calculate *variances* of the mean scores and compares this variance to the overall variance found in the total sample. Decisions about the null hypothesis are based on these comparisons.

To make its comparisons, ANOVA compares the means of two samples or two groups within a sample. Furthermore, ANOVA statistical program results include summary statistics for each sample or group, an *F*-ratio, and a probability value. This makes interpretation simple. The means are "statistically different" if the *p*-value is less (smaller) than the analyst-selected confidence level. Interpretation is a little more difficult when more than two groups or levels are compared. The results of another test—a *post hoc* test—must be used. Post hoc tests are available in SPSS®, but not in Excel™.

Another way to interpret the test is to refer to the "critical *F*-value" produced along with the *F*-ratio and *p*-value. The critical *F*-value is compared with the computed *F*-statistic; if the computed *F* is smaller than the critical value, the null hypothesis is rejected.

The *p*-value of the *F*-ratio will indicate whether the null hypothesis is to be rejected, but it will not indicate where the differences lie. When a *post hoc* test is selected, actual differences will be highlighted, while those that are statistically "the same" will not be so marked.

Three Versions of ANOVA

Researchers have three different versions of ANOVA to choose from: a one-way version, a two-way version, and an '*n*-way' version. One-way ANOVA is the basic procedure; it is used when two or more groups' means are being compared across a single factor. For example, the manager of a political action committee (PAC) might want to know if men or women voters respond differently to an advertisement for new donations to counter a legislative threat against the members' best wishes. The response variable must be at least interval level; the "grouping variable" can be any level data; in this case it is the nominal-level gender. Each of the several different types of ANOVA is discussed in greater detail below.

One-Way ANOVA

The following example represents the method used for testing differences in the mean scores of two groups. A new manager was hired at a manufacturing firm. Employee morale has declined dramatically, product quality and customer service were ranked very poor by the

Table 12.6

Organizational Climate Scales Scores, Staff and Management

		Staff Scores					Management Scores	
3.0	5.0	3.0	4.0	5.0	2.0	2.0	3.0	4.0
5.0	6.0	5.0	5.0	3.0	4.0	3.0	4.0	2.0
3.0	3.0	4.0	6.0	3.0	4.0	2.0	2.0	1.0
7.0	4.0	5.0	6.0	2.0	1.0	1.0	3.0	2.0
3.0	5.0	6.0	4.0	5.0	3.0	2.0	3.0	1.0

ANOVA: Single Factor

Summary

Groups	Count	Sum	Average	Variance
Column 1	24	105	4.375	1.722826
Column 2	20	49	2.45	1.102632

ANOVA

Source of Variation	SS	df	MS	F	P-value	F-crit
Between Groups	40.425	1	40.425	28.02889	0.000004	4.07266
Within Groups	60.575	42	1.442262			
Total	101	43				

Figure 12.2 **Results of an Excel™ One-Factor ANOVA Test**

company's customers, and employee absenteeism was becoming a major problem. The manager wanted to determine if both managers and staff workers perceived the company climate in the same way. A seven-point composite organizational climate scale was administered to a random selection of twenty workers and fifteen managers. Individual scores on the scale are shown in Table 12.6.

The manager's null hypothesis was "there is no difference in the way managers and staff employees rate the organization's climate." To test this hypothesis, a one-way ANOVA procedure can be used. The results of that procedure are presented in Figure 12.2.

To interpret these results, refer to the p-value of .000004 printed along with the F-ratio of 28.02889. The large F-value alone would indicate that the difference in the two groups' means is likely to be statistically significant. This is supported unequivocally by the very small p-value. In this case, the null hypothesis must be rejected.

Two-Way ANOVA

Two-way ANOVA designs are the simplest example of a class of statistical tests developed for what are called "factorial experiments" or "factorial designs." In all such cases, the goal of ANOVA is to test the means of two or more groups on two or more variables or factors at the

Table 12.7

Daily Sales by *Position* and *Day of Week*

Position	Sales by Day of the Week			
	Wednesday	Thursday	Friday	Saturday
1	$ 933	$ 979	$1,240	$1,610
1	1,004	1,112	1,299	1,020
1	933	1,003	1,353	1,003
1	979	980	1,222	1,900
2	1,217	1,172	1,175	1,945
2	1,171	1,034	1,371	1,837
2	1,178	1,011	1,421	1,958
2	1,230	1,021	1,314	1,851
3	1,021	1,871	1,889	1,835
3	1,015	1,735	1,948	1,631
3	1,041	1,642	1,872	1,500
3	995	1,675	1,919	1,720

same time. In addition, the procedure tests to see if two or more of the variables working together may have had an impact on the differences, in what is known as the *interaction effect.*

In this example of a two-factor ANOVA procedure, the advertising manager for the state lottery wants to establish which is the best day to advertise in a newspaper, and in which section of the paper the ad should appear. The two factors are *day* and *position.* Four days are selected: Wednesday, Thursday, Friday, and Saturday. Three positions are tested: general news (the first two sections of the paper), the sports section, and the family section (which includes the entertainment pages). Outcomes to be compared are daily sales totals. In setting up the experiment, *position* is to be the manager's grouping variable. The two factors being tested are *position* and *day* of the week. Four levels of the *position* variable are included in order to match the four *days* of the levels, making it necessary to record forty-eight total observations. ANOVA will compare the mean of the four levels of each of the three positions with the four days in each position.

This ANOVA procedure will compute an *F*-ratio with *p*-values and critical *F* values for each of the three positions, the four days (labeled as "columns" in the ANOVA summary table), and a measurement of the effect of any interaction between *position* and *day.* Table 12.7 displays the two factors and sales totals; Figure 12.3 displays the results of an Excel™ two-factor ANOVA procedure.

There are three results to interpret in the ANOVA results produced in this Excel™ application of this test: The first null hypothesis is that there is no difference in the *position* factor. These are the groups in the table; each includes four iterations of sales results. The second null hypothesis is that there is no difference in the days of the week the advertisement is placed. The final null hypothesis is that there is no interaction between the two factors as they relate to the differences, if any. We can interpret these results in two ways. First is the traditional *p*-value approach. Since these are less than the .05 level of confidence, we reject all three of the null hypotheses.

Another way is to compare the *F*-ratio with the critical value of *F.* In the past, analysts had

ANOVA: Two-Factor With Replication

SUMMARY	WEDNESDAY	THURSDAY	FRIDAY	SATURDAY	Total
GENERAL NEWS (1)					
Count	4	4	4	4	16
Sum	3849	4074	5114	5533	18570
Average	962.25	1018.5	1278.5	1383.25	1160.625
Variance	1244.916667	4008.333333	3548.333333	198328.9167	74228.38333
SPORTS (2)					
Count	4	4	4	4	16
Sum	4796	4238	5281	7591	21906
Average	1199	1059.5	1320.25	1897.75	1369.125
Variance	836.6666667	5713.666667	11287.58333	3912.916667	112788.3833
FAMILY (3)					
Count	4	4	4	4	16
Sum	4072	6923	7628	6686	25309
Average	1018	1730.75	1907	1671.5	1581.8125
Variance	358.6666667	10224.25	1124.666667	20045.66667	127379.3625
Total					
Count	12	12	12	12	
Sum	12717	15235	18023	19810	
Average	1059.75	1269.583333	1501.916667	1650.833333	
Variance	11807.29545	121749.9015	94174.81061	108985.9697	

ANOVA

Source of Variation	SS	df	MS	F	p-value	F-crit
Sample	1419238.042	2	709619.0208	32.67190463	.000000008	3.25944427
Columns	2431282.229	3	810427.4097	37.31327129	.000000000	2.866265447
Interaction	1502755.958	6	250459.3264	11.53151619	.000000360	2.363748308
Within	781903.75	36	21719.54861			
Total	6135179.979	47				

Figure 12.3   **Two-Factor ANOVA Results for Sales/Advertising Media/Day of Advertisement**

to look this up in a table of values for various degrees of freedom and values for the .05 and .01 levels of confidence. This is no longer necessary. The critical value for the data and degrees of freedom is presented alongside the *p*-value. If the *F*-statistic is smaller than the critical value from the *F*-table, the null hypothesis is retained. In this example, the *F*-statistic is larger than the critical *F* for all three hypotheses. Hence, all three null hypotheses must be rejected. The samples (newspaper locations) are statistically different from one another.

Three-Way ANOVA and More

This design is very much like two-way ANOVA. The principal effects of each factor are examined to see if it makes a difference between groups. This is followed by tests for inter- actions among the variables. However, now these interactions are expanded; two-way interac- tions, three-way interactions, and more are evaluated. The results are interpreted in the same way as one- and two-way analyses.

Designs have been developed to test the impact on differences for more than two sets of groups at the same time. These tests compare all factors against each grouping variable at the same time, then test for interaction, and then test for combinations of groups. These are known as *multivariate analysis of variance* (MANOVA). Finally, a technique has been designed that combines regression analysis with ANOVA: analysis of covariance, known as ANCOVA. To learn more about MANOVA and ANCOVA, refer to a recent edition of a multivariate statistics text.

Summary

This chapter has looked at a number of the ways researchers design experiments and test for differences in the results of different levels of a treatment. Two broad classes of tests were discussed. The first class included the various types of two-sample *t*-tests. Minor variations in portions of the computation formulas are necessary for paired or independent samples—cor- related or uncorrelated data. Microsoft® Excel's™ analysis programs (*Function Wizard* and *Data Analysis Tools*) both take these differences into consideration, enabling the analyst to specify which computation procedure to follow.

Typically, *t*-tests should be used for smaller sample sizes (around a total of thirty cases), and preferably with groups that are equal in size. The *t*-test can only be used to compare the means of two groups at a time.

The second major category of differences tests discussed in this chapter was analysis of variance (ANOVA) procedures. These all use the *F*-ratio to compare variances across two or more samples or groups. ANOVA procedures do not limit the number of groups being com- pared. Thus, three, four, and more levels or groups' scores can be compared at the same time. Equally, ANOVA can test for differences with more than one factor at a time. One-way ANOVA tests a single factor for differences. Two-way tests two factors individually, and then tests whether the two factors interact to influence the differences. More than two-factor ANOVA procedures, together with tests that permit testing a number of factors with more than one grouping variable (MANOVA) have been developed. Finally, a procedure that combines ANOVA with regression analysis, ANCOVA, makes it possible to do all these tests at one time.

Discussion Questions

1. Identify some of the key concepts in experimental design.
2. How do quasi-experimental designs differ from true experimental designs?
3. Name the five steps involved in planning and conducting experiments.
4. Distinguish between association and causality.
5. When should Student's *t*-test be used to test for statistically significant differences?

6. What are the several different *t*-test models that researchers can use to compare group means?
7. What is analysis of variance (ANOVA)? How does it differ from the *t*-test?
8. When should ANOVA procedures be used in place of the *t*-test?
9. Discuss the three different types of ANOVA designs presented in the chapter.
10. Describe a situation when a political science researcher might elect to employ a causal (experimental) research design.

Additional Reading

Collier, Raymond O., Jr., and Thomas J. Hummel, eds. 1977. *Experimental Design and Interpretation*. Berkeley, CA: McCutchan Publishing.

Cook, Thomas D., and Donald T. Campbell. 1979. *Quasi-experimentation: Design and Analysis Issues for Field Settings*. Chicago: Rand McNally.

Fairweather, George W., and Louis G. Tornatzky. 1977. *Experimental Methods for Social Policy Research*. New York: Pergamon Press.

Kirk, Roger E. 1995. *Experimental Design: Procedures for the Behavioral Sciences*. Pacific Grove, CA: Brooks/Cole Publishing.

Levine, David M., Mark L. Berenson, and David Stephan. 1997. *Statistics for Managers Using Microsoft® Excel™*. Upper Saddle River, NJ: Prentice-Hall.

Part 3

Applying Statistical Concepts in Research

13 Interpreting Survey Results with Descriptive Statistics

Researchers use *descriptive* statistics for such tasks as describing a sample, providing a quantitative summary of a variable, summarizing a dataset, and similar purposes. Four classes of descriptive statistics are used to describe and convey summary information. The four categories of descriptive statistics are:

1. Measures of central tendency.
2. Measures of variability.
3. Measures of relative position.
4. Measures of correlation.

These four types of measurements make it possible to reduce a large dataset to a smaller amount of meaningful numbers that everyone can understand. They provide essential information about the internal structure of the raw data (Lang and Heiss 1990).

The main purpose for measurements of location (also called *measures of central tendency*) is to identify the value in the dataset that is "most typical" of the full set. This "typical" value may then be used as a summary value. Several different numbers can be used as measures of location. These include the *mean* (algebraic, geometric, and trimmed mean), the *median*, and the *mode*.

Measurements of variability (sometimes referred to as *measures of dispersion*) tell how the individual measurements vary within the dataset. Variability measures include the range, the variance, and the standard deviation in a set of measurements.

Percentiles and distributions in general are used to indicate *position* and variation within a range of data, while measures of *correlation* help to describe relationships between two or more variables. Each of these descriptive measures is discussed in some detail below.

Measures of Central Tendency

The easiest way to quickly summarize a set of measurements is to identify the most typical value in the set. This value is sometimes called "the most representative score." Most people refer to this most typical value as the *average value*. Five types of averages can be used to show central tendency. They are:

- *The Arithmetic Mean.* Also known as the "average of all scores," the *mean* is the number arrived at by adding up all the values of a variable and then dividing by the number of items or cases in the set. It is used when the distribution of scores is fairly symmetrical about the center value. When plotted, a symmetrical distribution produces the typical bell-shaped curve.
- *The Median.* This quantitative measure is the halfway point in a dataset. Exactly one-half of the values lie above the median value and one-half fall below that point. The median should be used when the scores are not symmetrical, such as when they are closely grouped but with a few very high or very low scores. These very high or very low values might have a disproportionate influence on the arithmetic mean.
- *The Mode.* The mode is simply the value for a variable that appears most often. It is the value with the greatest frequency of occurrence. The mode can be used for a quick estimate of the typical or representative score.
- *The Geometric Mean.* This is the root of the product of all items in the dataset. It is particularly appropriate when computing an average of changes in percentages. For some reason, not all statistics texts include a discussion of the geometric mean. However, it has many uses in statistics used by researchers. It is easy to calculate with the Microsoft® Excel™ statistics package.
- *The Trimmed Mean.* This average value is used when the dataset includes one or more outliers. It trims the top and bottom values of the sample by some percentage. A new arithmetic mean is then calculated from the truncated dataset.

The Arithmetic Mean

The term "central tendency" refers to a point in a dataset that corresponds to a typical, representative, or central value. The measurement used most often for this is the *arithmetic mean.* Means are valid for use with ratio or equidistant interval (i.e., continuous) data; a mean should not be computed for categorical data. Average scores for attitude and opinion scales are typical examples of the appropriate use of means. In attitude and opinion scales, a mean (or "average") score for the total sample conveys far more information than the exact response for any one subject in the sample. For example, assume that 100 voters are asked their opinions about a proposed national health insurance plan. An individual subject might respond with any value from 1 to 5 on a five-point attitude scale. The researcher uses low scores for negative attitudes and high scores for positive attitudes. While any one subject's score might be interesting to know, by itself it does not tell the research much. However, a *sample mean* of 1.2 on the scale clearly suggests a negative attitude interpretation of the attitude held by members of this sample.

Arithmetic means are calculated for both populations and samples. Their computation is similar, but separate notation or symbols differentiate them. Below are symbols used to signify sample sizes and means for samples and populations:

N = the total number of cases in a population
n = the total number of cases in a sample
μ = the mean of a population (pronounced "mew")
$\bar{X}$ = the mean for a sample (pronounced "X-bar")
σ = the standard deviation of a population (lower case Greek letter sigma)
s = the standard deviation of a sample

Mean scores or values are generally not valid for use with qualitative measurements such as rankings or numbers assigned to categories (ordinal and nominal data). For example, political polling firms might ask citizens to rank a number of different gubernatorial candidates in their order of preference. The research firm wants to know which candidate is the one most preferred, which is second, etc. A mean rank value has no meaning in this case. In the following example, say that voters are asked to note their occupation from a list of eight or nine categories. In this case, the total number for each category is informative; determining the mean or average occupational category is nonsense. Despite this limitation, it must be noted that computing mean ranks is often done with certain nonparametric statistical tests, and may be encountered on some statistical program printouts.

The Median

The *median* is the halfway point in a set of numbers. Half of the values are above the median value; half are below. The median is appropriate for all data types, but is particularly useful with ranking (ordinal) data, or when the dataset contains outliers, which would disproportionately influence the mean. Because the median deals with structure or order in the dataset, it can be used with ordinal and interval/ratio data, but it is meaningless with nominal (categorical) data.

For a small-sample example of how the median is computed, say that during the first half-hour of a fund-raising event, a public broadcast radio station received donations in the following amounts:

$$\$25, \$18, \$20, \$22, \text{ and } \$100$$

The mean donation value is $185 divided by 5 ($185/5), or $37. However, a mean of $37 is misleading, since the $100 *outlier* unduly disproportionately influences the result. A more meaningful measure of location in this case would be the median. This is arrived at by rearranging the data in ascending order ($18, $20, $22, $25, and $100). Then, by selecting the value that falls in the center. The median for the five values is $22. For larger datasets, the median is computed by subtracting one from the total number of cases and then dividing by 2. A formula for computing the median is:

$$\text{Median} = (n - 1)/2.$$

The Mode

The *mode* is the only measurement that makes sense when dealing with nominal-level variables. It is defined as the value that appears most often in a collection of all counts for a variable. The example below was obtained in a focus-group study conducted for a political campaign. Subjects were asked which of four candidates they preferred. Individual candidates were assigned identifying code numbers ranging from 1 to 4. The final tally of subjects' preferences was:

$$3, 2, 1, 1, 3, 4, 2, 3, 1, 2, 1, 1, 1$$

The category value "1" appears most often in the dataset: six times. This gives the researcher the maximum amount of information. Since the numbers represent specific candidates and are not quantitative, both the mean and the median clearly are inappropriate measures of location in this example. Political campaign finance managers are also often interested in the modal distribution, the distribution of donation amounts within a total range of amounts.

The Geometric Mean

Not all statistics texts include a discussion of the *geometric mean*. This is a mistake, for there are many instances where a geometric mean is far more appropriate than an arithmetic mean. A commonly encountered use is when a campaign manager wants to know the average of a series of percentage changes, such as voter approval rate changes. The changes are measured by the number of votes over her closest opponent the candidate has received during the past four biannual elections. Vote plurality is converted to percentages and reported as the relative change from the previous total. The manager has the following gross percentages for a four-year period and wants to know the overall average percentage change. The data are displayed in Table 13.1.

Either the arithmetic or geometric mean can be used to summarize the changes over time. The arithmetic mean for the 1996–2002 period is 7 percent [(12 + 7 + 2)/3 = 21/3 = 7]. Computing the geometric mean, however, arrives at a more appropriate measure. This mean is computed by multiplying each percentage change in sequence, then calculating the root of the sum. Note that each change is the new change plus the base 100 percent (which is the previous value). The number of measurements in the sequence determines which root is appropriate. In this example, three periods of change are measured; therefore, the cube root must be used:

$$G = X_1 * X_2 * X_3 * \ldots * X_n$$
$$G = 112 \times 107 \times 102$$
$$G = \sqrt[3]{1{,}234{,}352}$$
$$G = 106.9221, \text{ or } 6.92\%$$

Thus, a more accurate average rate of plurality increase over the four-election period is 6.92% (106.9221), not the 7 percent of the arithmetic mean.

Excel Example. Computing the geometric mean is a quick and simple process with Micro-

---

Table 13.1

Annual Candidate Pluralities in the 35th District, 1996–2002 (in thousands)

	Election			
	1996	1998	2000	2002
Gross votes	4,000	4,800	4,940	4,890
% Change	—	12%	7%	2%

Table 13.2

Excel™ Worksheet Setup for the Geometric Mean

Variable	Election Year				Gmean
	1996	1998	2000	2002	
Sales	4,000	4,800	4,940	4,890	
% Change		112	107	102	106.9221

soft® Excel™. The data are arranged in a column array, as displayed in Table 13.2; the GEOMEAN option is then selected from the *Function Wizard*. All computations are conducted in the Wizard, which produces a geometric mean to four decimal points. Use the following Excel™ seven-step process:

1. Insert all labels and values into a new worksheet. Cell A1 contains the label for column 1, "variable."
2. In Cells B1 through E1, insert the years 1993 through 1996. Type the label "Gmean" in Cell F1.
3. Insert the labels and data. Percentage changes must be written as hundreds; e.g., a 7 percent increase must be inserted as "107."
4. In Cell F4, insert an equals sign (=).
5. Select the Function Wizard (*fx*). Scroll down to GEOMEAN. "=GEOMEAN" will appear in the worksheet formula bar for that cell.
6. Hit **Return** to begin the calculation.
7. The value for the geometric mean will appear in Cell F4, alongside the last inserted percentage change value.

It should be noted that roots of different power may also be used, thus allowing extension to the time series data. Excel GEOMEAN automatically computes the root that is appropriate for the dataset.

Trimmed Mean

The trimmed mean is a mean computed from a truncated set of values rather than the entire set of measurements. It is particularly useful when one or more extreme measurements have the potential to produce misleading summary statistics. It is calculated by deleting some percentage of responses at both ends of the distribution before calculating the mean for the remaining values. For example, to establish a 30 percent trimmed mean, remove the bottom 15 percent and top 15 percent and calculate the mean for the remaining 70 percent. The TRIMMEAN function in the Excel™ *Function Wizard* makes it simple to make this calculation.

Measures of Variability

Once the researcher has determined which is the appropriate measure of location, the next concern is to determine how the distribution of numbers in the data varies around the central value. The researcher asks how and to what extent the scores or values differ from one another, and how this variability can be summarized. The three most common ways to express variability are the *range,* the *variance,* and the *standard deviation;* these all provide information about the distribution of responses within the range.

The Range

The range is the easiest statistic to compute. It is determined by subtracting the lowest value from the highest value in a distribution. It can be misleading, however, and is not used very often by itself. By itself, the range does not take into consideration the variability within a distribution; it is only a crude approximation of variability. For example, consider the following two sets of data:

>   Dataset A: 65, 80, 81, 82, 83, 84, 98
>   Dataset B: 65, 69, 74, 78, 87, 89, 98

Both sets have the same range: $98 - 65 = 33$. However, a closer look at the two sets reveals that Set B clearly has more internal variability than Set A.

Also limiting the uses for the range is that it uses only two values in the set of measurements: the highest and lowest values. As a result, percentiles (or fractiles) are often used with the range to give more meaning to this measurement. Percentiles are values below which some proportion of the total scores or observations fall. The most commonly used percentiles divide the data into quartiles. These divide the data into roughly 25 percent segments. A quarter of the values fall below the first (or 25 percent) quartile; half are below the second (or 50 percent) quartile; and three-fourths are below the third quartile. The second quartile value is the same value as the median.

One important application of quartiles used in political science is the interquartile range. This includes all values above the first quartile and below the third quartile, which is the same as the range for the central 50 percent of all cases.

The Variance

The variance is an index of how scores or values in a dataset vary from their mean or average value. Because it is only an index of variation, interpreting the variance is more art than science. Statistically, the variance is defined as the average of the squared deviation of all values in the range, divided by the number of cases in the dataset (minus 1). Larger variance values indicate the data is more spread out, whereas smaller variances mean the values are more concentrated around the mean.

Many comprehensive statistics texts distinguish between the variance of a set of scores for a sample (S^2) and the variance of a set of values for a population (r^2). The formulas for computing each are slightly different: for a population, the divisor is $N - 1$; for a sample, the divisor is $n - 1$. Similar differences occur with the standard deviation of populations and samples. Because researchers are most often dealing with samples rather than total populations, researchers almost always work with the variance for a sample.

The Standard Deviation

Because the variance is only an index or rough indicator of variation and, thus, somewhat abstract, it is far more common to find variability stated in terms of the standard deviation rather than as the variance. The standard deviation is nothing more than the square root of the variance. Rather than a squared value, which suggests or implies variation, the standard deviation is a more exact measurement, stated in exactly the same units as the original data.

Because the standard deviation focuses on variation from the true mean, it is probably the most reliable of all the measures of variability. It is certainly the one used most often. As with the variance, standard deviations for samples and for populations vary slightly in their computation formulas. The divisor for the standard deviation of a population is the total number of cases (N); for a sample, it is $n - 1$.

Excel™ Example. Excel™'s procedure for obtaining the variance or standard deviation for samples and populations is included under the statistics function found in the *Function Wizard* (f_x on the main toolbar). The subcommand for the sample variance is VAR; for the variance of a population, it is VARP. To obtain the standard deviation for a sample, the function command is STDEV; for the standard deviation of a population, it is STDEVP.

SPSS® Example. Instructions for determining the variance and standard deviation in a variable or dataset are found in two *analysis* processes under the *descriptive statistics* subprogram. These subprograms are *frequencies* and *descriptives*.

Table 13.3 displays the amounts that lobbyists for companies, labor unions, and other organizations spent on lobbying activities in Washington, DC from 1997 to 2000. The expenditure information was reported on their Web pages by the Center for Responsive Politics, May 5, 2002. Table 13.4 displays summary statistics for this data.

Table 13.3

Total Lobbyist Spending, 1997–2000 ($ millions)

	Year			
Sector	1997	1998	1999	2000
Agribusiness	86	119	83	77
Commun/Electronics	154	186	193	200
Construction	17	22	24	23
Defense	49	49	53	60
Energy/NatResources	143	149	158	159
Financ/Insur/REstate	177	203	214	227
Health	136	165	197	209
Lawyers/Lobbyists	13	19	18	16
Misc. Business	15	169	193	223
Transportation	112	115	117	138
Ideol/Single Issue	73	76	76	85
Labor	21	24	24	27
Other	66	69	87	102

Source: Lobbyists Database. *Influence Inc.* 2000. Center for Responsive Politics. www.opensecrets.org/lobbyists.

Table 13.4

Summary Descriptive Statistics of Lobbyist Data Produced by SPSS® *Frequencies*

Statistics YR2000

N	Valid	13
	Missing	0
Mean		118.92
Median		102.00
Mode[a]		16
Std. Deviation		78.57
Variance		6173.41
Range		211
Minimum		16
Maximum		227
Percentiles	25	43.50
	50	102.00
	75	204.50

[a]Multiple modes exist. The smallest value is shown.

Measures of Relative Position

Measures of relative position are used to compare one measurement against other measurements in the dataset. Two types of statistical processes can be used for this: *percentiles* and *standard scores;* standard scores are also called Z-scores.

Percentiles

Percentiles are points or values used to indicate the percentage of subjects or measurements with scores below that point. Percentiles are not often found in political science statistics, but can be very useful in selected situations. A well-known example of the use of percentiles is students' scores on the Standard Aptitude Test (SATs). SAT results include an indication of how the set of scores for one student compares with all other scores for that test set. Similar applications exist for the *Graduate Record Examination* (GRE), the *Law School Aptitude Test* (LSAT), and the *General Management Aptitude Test* (GMAT).

Say, for example, a graduate business school applicant scores 580 on the GMAT. This might be reported as falling in the 85th percentile (P_{85}) of all scores for persons taking the test at that time. This means that 85 percent of all applicants had lower scores than the applicant's 580. If the applicant had scored, say, 450, this might have fallen in the 65th percentile (P_{65}), and so on. The 50th percentile (P_{50}) is always the median value for that set of scores.

Excel™ Example. Microsoft® Excel™ includes procedures for obtaining any-level percentiles as well as standard quartiles. These functions are incorporated into the "STATISTICS" toolbox of the FUNCTION WIZARD (*fx*). When the Function Wizard is selected, two lists appear in the window. The left-hand list shows categories of functions, one of which is "STATISTICS." Within the statistics master-category function are a variety of specific functions. These appear in the right-hand window. Scroll bars must be used to display all the choices included.

The commands for Excel's™ percentile function are slightly different from most applications. In Excel™, a value between 0 and 1 must be entered. For example, to arrive at the 90 percent percentile value, the user must enter "9" (without the quotation marks, of course). In most other applications, the values to be entered are a number between 0 and 99. Thus, to have a statistics program compute the 90th percentile value, the user enters "90" (again, without the quotation marks).

With the Excel™ *quartile* function, the user may set the "QUART" value from 0 to 4. Setting it to 1, 2, or 3 will return the corresponding quartile values. Setting it to 0 or 4 will return either the minimum or maximum values in the dataset range. Excel uses the median value for the second quartile.

Standard Scores

Standard scores are the original, "raw," scores of the dataset that have been transformed in some way. When the scores are all transformed in the same way, it becomes possible to compare any two or more scores against one another on an equal basis. The standard-score transformation process used most often is the Z-score. Z-scores are raw scores that have been converted into standard deviation units. The Z-score indicates how many standard deviation units any one score is from the mean score for the total group.

Z-scores also make it possible to compare a single subject's scores on two different scales. For example, the SAT includes a communications skills and a mathematics skills component. The mean score for each of these components serves as the common reference point for the test population; standard deviations are the common unit used to measure variability, thus providing a clear picture of how each score compares with the total group's scores.

Excel™ Example. Standardized scores (Z-values) are easy and quick to compute with Microsoft® Excel™. All that is required is to highlight the dataset. Data from a hypothetical set of scores on a political awareness survey taken in six separate samples drawn from the population in four different wards of the city are shown in Table 13.5.

Table 13.5

Weights of Sample Units, AM Dataset

| Ward | Awareness Scores | | | | | |
	Sample 1	Sample 2	Sample 3	Sample 4	Sample 5	Sample 6
1	18.4	17.9	18.6	19.0	17.8	18.7
2	18.2	18.0	18.5	19.1	17.4	19.0
3	18.0	18.1	18.4	19.2	16.9	18.8
4	17.9	18.2	18.6	19.1	17.6	18.5

Source: Example data.

To calculate Z-scores with Microsoft® Excel™, follow these simple steps:

1. Arrange the raw data into a one-column data array.
2. Calculate the mean and standard deviation for the total sample using the Excel™ Function Wizard.

NOTE: To calculate the mean, use the AVERAGE option in the set of statistical applications. To find the standard deviation for the sample, use the Function Wizard's STDDEV option in the same set of applications. The formula for standardization requires three numbers:

> (1) The value to be standardized.
> (2) The mean for the sample.
> (3) The standard deviation (SD) for the sample.

3. Using the STANDARDIZE option in the Function Wizard applications, insert the three appropriate values.
4. For a shortcut, type the mean in the cell below the cell where it was calculated using an Excel™ Wizard formula. Do the same thing for the standard deviation value.
5. Now, click and hold on the small fill capability box in the lower-right-hand corner of only the cell in which you copied the mean. Drag down to the bottom of the data array. The repeated formula calculates the appropriate value in each cell. Do the same for the standard deviation column.

NOTE: If you include the cell that contains the formula for the mean and/or the SD in this click and fill, Excel™ will calculate a new mean and a new SD formula for each raw score, but using one less raw value each time. All the subsequent means and SDs will be wrong.

6. Now, click on the second, empty Z-score cell, click and hold the drag button, and drag to the bottom of the array. Correct Z-scores will be calculated for each raw data value.
7. Now go back and use the Format—Cells—Numbers selections and format for the number of places after the decimal point desired.
8. Add lines, boldface, or other options as desired.

The results of a standardization of the measurements in Table 13.5 can be seen in Table 13.6. Beginning at the left, the first column contains the recorded raw measurements. The column on the right contains the Z-score conversions for each raw measurement.

Measures of Correlation

Measures of correlation are used to reveal the relationships or associations between two or more variables or subjects. In many statistics texts, correlation is discussed under the umbrella of inferential statistics. However, since measures of correlation are commonly included in the preliminary section of reports, together with other descriptive statistics, it is not inappropriate to include them as descriptive statistics as well. Different correlation measures are used with different types of data, as indicated in Table 13.7.

The data types in Table 13.7 can also be grouped into just two categories, depending upon the type of measurements they represent—*discrete* (sometimes referred to as *categorical*) and *continuous* data. Nominal and ordinal data are discrete or categorical measurements. Interval

Table 13.6

Standardized Values for Political Awareness Scores in Four City Wards (sample mean = 18.3; sample standard deviation = 0.583)

Raw Score	Z-score
18.4	0.1216
18.2	−0.2164
18.0	−0.5694
17.9	−0.7682
17.9	−0.7365
18.0	−0.5148
18.1	−0.3432
18.2	−0.1716
18.6	0.5148
18.5	0.3432
18.4	0.1716
18.6	0.5148
19.0	1.2013
19.1	1.3729
19.2	1.5445
19.1	1.3729
17.8	−0.8581
17.4	−1.5445
16.9	−2.4026
17.6	−1.2013
18.7	0.6865
19.0	1.2013
18.8	0.8581
18.5	0.3432

and ratio data can vary within a set of ranges; thus, they are considered to be continuous. However, it is more appropriate to apply the appropriate statistical test as indicated.

The *chi-square test for independence* should be used to determine whether two nominal-level variables are related or independent. The null hypothesis for the test is the two variables are independent. Table 13.8 displays the results of a crosstabulation (crosstabs) table for two variables in a hypothetical survey of political behaviors and attitudes of a sample of 60 registered voters. In this hypothetical sample, 20 subjects reported they considered themselves to be affiliated with the Republican Party, 29 said they were affiliated with the Democrat Party, and 11 indicated they were Independents. The researcher wants to know whether there is any association between party affiliation and voting behavior.

Because both variables are nominal-level measurements, the chi-square test in the Descriptive Statistics/Crosstabs option is the appropriate test. The results of that test are shown in Table 13.9. The chi-square test for independence produces a Pearson chi-square value, the

---

Table 13.7

Data Types and Their Appropriate Correlation Statistics

Data Type	Measurement Statistic
Nominal	Chi-square (X^2)
Ordinal	Spearman's rank order coefficient (*rho*)
Interval/Ratio	Pearson's correlation coefficient (*r*)

Table 13.8

SPSS®-Produced Crosstabulations Table for Sample Data, *n* = 60

	Voted in Presidential Election		
Political Party Affiliation[a]	Did Vote	Did Not Vote	Totals
Republican	14	6	20
Democrat	10	19	29
Independent	4	7	11
Totals	28	32	60

[a]Political party affiliation, voted in presidential election crosstabulation count.

---

degrees of freedom for the dataset, and a "two-sided" (more often referred to as "two-tailed") significance value. Two-sided tests mean that the researcher looks at the correlations for both variables, from either direction, that is, regardless of which variable is dependent and which is independent. The easiest way to interpret the results of the test is to compare the significance value with the level of confidence established by the researcher; the .05 level of confidence is used most often in all social science research.

In the Table 13.9 example, the calculated significance level of .037 (the Pearson chi-square value) is less than the researcher-set .05 level of confidence. The null hypothesis is that these two variables are not related; or, said another way, the two variables are independent. The alternate hypothesis is that the two variables—party affiliation and voting behavior—for this sample are related. Therefore, the null hypothesis must be rejected and the alternate hypothesis accepted. The two variables are not independent.

Note that only the lower half of the correlation matrix is shown in Table 13.10. The upper half simply duplicates the same information. SPSS® Correlations/Bivarate with the ordinal test (Spearman's) option selected produces both the upper and lower part of the matrix as a default (the duplicated information has been omitted here). Excel™ produces a lower-half matrix as its default output.

Only two of the correlation coefficients in this example were significant at the .05 level of confidence: the relationship between attitudes toward rail travel and travel abroad (*r* = .345, sig. = .007), and the attitude of the sample toward tour group travel and travel abroad (*r* =

Table 13.9

Chi-Square Test for Independence on Party Affiliation and Voting Behavior, $n = 60$

Chi-Square Tests

	Value	df	Asymp. Sig. (2-sided)
Pearson Chi-Square	6.574	2	.037
Likelihood Ratio	6.693	2	.035
Linear-by-Linear Association	4.483	1	.034
N of Valid Cases	60		

[a]0 cells (.0%) have expected count less than 5. The minimum expected count is 5.13.

Table 13.10

Spearman's Correlation Coefficients for Variables in Hypothetical Travel Survey

Spearman's rho (r) Correlations

		Toward travel in U.S.	Toward travel abroad	Toward travel this year	Toward cruise travel	Toward rail travel	Toward tour group travel
Toward travel in U.S.	Correlation Coefficient	1.000					
Toward travel abroad	Correlation Coefficient	−.168	1.000				
	Sig. (2-tail)	.198	.				
Toward travel this year	Correlation Coefficient	−.096	.060	1.000			
	Sig. (2-tail)	.466	.650	.			
Toward cruise travel	Correlation Coefficient	.150	−.164	.212	1.000		
	Sig. (2-tail)	.252	.210	.104	.		
Toward rail travel	Correlation Coefficient	.154	.345	.039	.061	1.000	
	Sig. (2-tail)	.239	.007	.769	.646	.	
Toward tour group travel	Correlation Coefficient	.011	.363	.010	−.089	−.131	1.000
	Sig. (2-tail)	.931	.004	.940	.500	.317	.

Source: Example data.

.363, sig. .004). They are shown in boldface type in the table. Thus, the research can assume that there is a low to moderate relationship between the two variables. The Pearson's-scale-level data correlation matrix in both SPSS® and Excel™ are identical to the ordinal-level Spearman's tests. It is only necessary to request the appropriate test option.

Understanding Frequency Distributions

Understanding the information contained in a given set of scores or values requires looking at the ways frequency distributions of scores can be distributed around their mean value. We are most familiar with what are called "normal distributions." These are the typical bell-shaped curves that enclose what we call a "normal distribution." Normal distributions tend to be symmetrical, with the mean and median falling near one another at the middle or high point on the curve. This is often the *modal value* as well.

Most distributions encountered for samples larger than 30 subjects are more or less *normal*. That is, the bulk of the responses or scores cluster around the mean, with the rest trailing off toward the ends. The following information about *normal distributions* has been found to be true so often that it is now accepted as a "rule" (Table 13.11). Sometimes, the distribution of scores does not cluster around the mean. Instead, it may be either grouped at either end of the scale, or even has more than one mode. These distributions are known as "skewed" or *asymmetrical,* and somewhat different distribution rules prevail.

In normal distributions, one standard deviation above the mean will include some 34 percent of all the cases in the dataset. Similarly, one standard deviation below the mean will include another 34 percent of the sample, for a total of 68 percent falling within a range of plus or minus one standard deviation. Another 27 percent of the cases will be included if one more standard deviation above and below the mean is included. Together, some 95 percent of all cases will fall within two standard deviations above or below the mean. Finally, when three standard deviations are included, 99.7 percent of all cases will be included under the curve (this makes the normal distribution *six standard deviations wide*).

Not all distributions are normal. Some have a majority of the values gathered at either the low or high end of the scale. Other distributions have the great majority gathered at the center, whereas others may bunch up in two or more points or modes. The three most commonly encountered nonnormal distributions are *positively skewed, negatively skewed,* and *bimodal* distributions.

Positively skewed distributions have their peak nearer the *left-hand* end of the graph, with the line stretched out toward the lower-right-hand corner. Negatively skewed distributions have greater concentrations at the *right-hand* side, with the left line stretched toward the lower-left-hand corner. Bimodal distributions have two concentrations of scores, and have curves resem-

---

Table 13.11

Empirical Rules for Normal Distributions

Approximately 68% of all the items will be within one standard deviation of the mean.
Approximately 95% of the items will be within two standard deviations of the mean.
Almost all items will be within three standard deviations of the mean.

bling a two-humped camel's back. Multimodal distributions have three or more concentrations or peaks.

Calculating Descriptive Statistics with Excel™

The Microsoft® Excel™ *Data Analysis* package contained in the *tools* subprogram will produce a complete set of summary statistics with very little effort. To begin, the first step is to establish a "data array," a spreadsheet table in which all data are arranged in columns and rows. The data array shown in Table 13.12 is public information published in 2002 by the Center for Responsive Politics. Table 13.13 shows Excel™-produced descriptive statistics for donations by individuals, PACs, and soft money.

Steps for using Excel to produce Descriptive Statistics:

Step 1. Arrange the data in a spreadsheet data array.
Step 2. Highlight the data only (do not highlight the hours or sample numbers).
Step 3. Select the *tools* option, followed by the *data analysis* option.
Step 4. In the *data analysis* option, select *descriptive statistics*.

Table 13.13 shows the Excel™-produced descriptive statistics for the categories of political donations (individuals, PACs, and soft money) shown in Table 13.12.

Similar summary statistics are produced by SPSS®. The commands are *tools, data analysis, descriptive statistics, and descriptives*. The variables for analysis must be moved into the proper analysis box, with desired statistical options selected. The information supplied by the Center for Responsive Politics was accessed on the Internet.

Table 13.12

Political Donations by the Communications/Electronics Industry, 1990–2002 ($ millions)

Election Cycle	Total Contribs	From Individuals	From PACs	Soft Money	To Democrats	To Republicans	% to Dems	% to Reps
2002	35.9	8.6	6.4	20.9	18.5	17.0	51	47
2000	132.7	50.1	14.7	67.8	71.0	60.3	54	45
1998	52.7	19.5	11.6	21.7	26.0	26.3	49	50
1996	58.2	22.3	10.8	25.1	29.1	28.3	50	49
1994	28.5	12.5	8.7	7.3	16.5	12.0	58	42
1992	36.5	18.6	10.2	7.7	21.7	14.6	59	40
1990	16.1	6.8	9.2	0.0	9.1	6.9	57	43
Totals	360.6	138.4	71.6	150.5	191.9	165.4	53	46

Source: Center for Responsive Politics. *Communications/Electronics: Long-Term Contribution Trends.* From data released by the Federal Election Commission on May 11, 2002; donations are of $200 or more.

Table 13.13

Descriptive Statistics Produced by Microsoft® Excel™, 1990–2002

From Individuals		From PACs		Soft Money	
Mean	19.7714	Mean	10.2286	Mean	21.5000
Standard Error	5.5067	Standard Error	0.9790	Standard Error	8.4676
Median	18.6000	Median	10.2000	Median	20.9000
Mode		Mode		Mode	
Std Deviation	14.5693	Std Deviation	2.5902	Std Deviation	22.4031
Sample Variance	212.2657	Sample Variance	6.7090	Sample Variance	501.8967
Kurtosis	3.8470	Kurtosis	1.0780	Kurtosis	3.6521
Skewness	1.8070	Skewness	0.4214	Skewness	1.7404
Range	43.3000	Range	8.3000	Range	67.8000
Minimum	6.8000	Minimum	6.4000	Minimum	0.0000
Maximum	50.1000	Maximum	14.7000	Maximum	67.8000
Sum	138.4000	Sum	71.6000	Sum	150.5000
Count	7	Count	7	Count	7

Source: Center for Responsive Politics. *Communications/Electronics: Long-Term Contribution Trends.* From data released by the Federal Election Commission on May 11, 2002.

Summary

Descriptive statistics are used to summarize data and describe samples. Four categories of descriptive information can be used for these purposes: measures of central tendency, measures of variability, measures of relative position, and measures of correlation. All of these statistics can be quickly calculated with Microsoft® Excel™.

The main purpose for measurements of location (also called *measures of central tendency*) is to identify the value in the dataset that is "most typical" of the full set. This "typical" value may then be used as a summary value. Five measures of central tendency are used at different times. They include the mean (sometimes called "the average"), the median, the mode, the geometric mean, and the trimmed mean.

Measurements of variability (sometimes referred to as *measures of dispersion*) tell how the individual measurements vary within the dataset. The three measures of variability include the range, the variance, and the standard deviation. The range is the distribution of scores from the highest value to the lowest. The variance is an index of how scores or values in a dataset vary from their mean or average value. Larger variance values indicate the data are more spread out, whereas smaller variances mean the values are more concentrated around the mean. The standard deviation is simply the square root of the variance. Because the variance is a squared value, it is more convenient to work with the standard deviation, which is a more exact measurement than the variance; it is stated in exactly the same units as the original data.

Two measures of relative position make it possible to compare one score against any other in the dataset. They are percentiles and standard scores. Percentiles are values below which some proportion of the total scores or observations fall. The most commonly used percentiles divide the data into quartiles—segments containing 25 percent of the cases. One-quarter of the values are below the first quartile; half are below the second quartile; and three-fourths are below the third quartile. The most commonly used standard score is the Z-statistic; Z-scores are expressions of variation stated in values of standard deviations from the mean. For most datasets, almost all scores fall within plus or minus three standard deviations of the group mean.

Measures of correlation are used to numerically identify the level of relationships between variables. Care must be taken to avoid unsubstantiated cause-and-effect relationships from correlation values. The chi-square test for independence should be used to determine whether two nominal level variables are related or independent. The Pearson's *r*-correlation should be used with interval and ratio data (*scale* data in SPSS); the Spearman's *rho* statistic is used with ordinal-level data. Both programs produce a correlation matrix for ordinal and scale data.

Discussion Questions

1. Name and define the four measures of central tendency discussed in the text.
2. Why are researchers concerned with measures of variability in a dataset?
3. Define the range, variance, and standard deviation.
4. What are the measures of relative position, and what do they tell the researcher?
5. What are percentiles? What are quartiles?
6. What are standard scores? Why and how are they used?
7. Measures of correlation are used for what purpose?
8. Frequency distributions are often the first step in the statistical analysis design. What are they, and what purpose do they serve?
9. Explain the Excel™ process for producing summary statistics.
10. Explain the SPSS® process for producing summary statistics.

Additional Reading

Brightman, Harvey J. 1999. *Data Analysis in Plain English, with Microsoft® Excel™*. Pacific Grove, CA: Duxbury Press.

Field, Andy. 2000. *Discovering Statistics using SPSS® for Windows*. Thousand Oaks, CA: Sage.

Neufeld, John L. 1997. *Learning Business Statistics with Microsoft® Excel™*. Upper Saddle River, NJ: Prentice-Hall.

Phillips, John L. 1996. *How to Think about Statistics*. 5th ed. New York: W.H. Freeman.

Salkind, Neil J. 2000. *Statistics for People Who (Think They) Hate Statistics*. Thousand Oaks, CA: Sage.

Witte, Robert S., and John S. Witte. 1997. *Statistics*. 3rd ed. Fort Worth: Harcourt Brace.

14 Presenting Research Results with Tables, Charts, and Graphs

When first collected, "raw" data usually make little or no sense. Raw data are simply a loose collection of numbers; they have no intuitive meaning of their own. Data must be put into some kind of order or structure; they must be grouped together into sets that have logic and structure. Numbers do not speak for themselves; they acquire meaning only when they are organized in terms of some mutually understood framework (Wasson 1965). This chapter describes graphic tools to accomplish this task.

Nearly all research reports contain statistical data presented in tables, graphs, or charts. Descriptive statistics particularly are almost always presented in some sort of tabular or graphic form (such as bar charts and pie charts). The type of table, chart, or graph used often depends upon the preference of the manager presenting the information. There are many different styles from which to choose. While the nature of the data has some influence on the structure selected for presentation, the choice is mostly a matter of user preference. For example, summary data is usually presented in the form of a table. However, other ways exist to graphically communicate this same information, including scatter plots, histograms, bar charts, pie charts, relative-frequency polygons, among other forms of graphic presentation.

Most good research reports make maximum use of graphic communications tools. Remember the old saying "A picture is worth ten thousand words"? This is true for research reports as well. Graphics and other illustrations make reports more readable and, in the process, more effective in meeting their communications objectives. According to Wasson (p. 176), tables, summaries, graphs, and other illustrations have but two purposes. First, they make it easier for the researcher to capture the meaning of the data and more clearly apply the data to the decisions or actions that are going to be made based on the results of the study. Second, they make it easier for the readers of the report to see how the researcher arrived at the conclusions and interpretations that are presented in the report.

This chapter describes three ways that researchers use structure and graphic representations to better discover meaning in their studies, while also improving the communications quality of their decision-making reports. It begins with a discussion on how to make sense of ungrouped or "raw" data. This is followed by a discussion on how to make and use tables and discusses several ways of developing charts and graphs with statistics software.

Making Sense out of Ungrouped or "Raw" Data

A principal objective of descriptive statistics is to summarize the information contained in a dataset. A collection of raw data by itself typically contains very little information; further analysis and bringing of order to the set is required. Researchers use tables and graphs to present data about a single variable, about two variables at the same time, and about more than two variables. In statistical parlance, these are called univariate, bivariate, and multivariate statistics.

Univariate Statistical Presentations

One of the first analysis steps the researcher takes to establish some meaning from raw data is to construct a graphic presentation of the underlying structure. This can be in the form of a *frequency-distribution table,* a *stem-and-leaf diagram,* or a *histogram,* or any combination of these tools. Nearly all statistical-analysis reports include frequency distribution tables. However, analysts often bypass stem-and-leaf diagrams. Stem-and-leaf diagrams can often be more informative than simple frequency tables in that none of the underlying data are lost in the analysis; all values are displayed in the diagram. Histograms present summary data, but they do not display individual values for a class in the same way that a stem-and-leaf diagram does.

Before any analysis occurs, raw data are typically entered into a *spreadsheet-based* data file. Examples include Microsoft® Excel™ and the Statistical Package for the Social Sciences® (SPSS). In all spreadsheets, individual variables are entered as separate columns, while "cases" are entered in rows. A different value is assigned to each category of a variable; each value is then assigned a definition. Examples of statistical software-ready values for the variable *gender* might be the number 1 assigned to all women and the number 2 assigned to all men. Statistical software programs count the frequency of occurrence for each value, compute summary statistics and percentages, calculate measures of central tendency and variation, and conduct a host of other tests appropriate for the type of data. Collections of data are maintained in *datasets.* Statistically processed data are maintained in *data files* or *output files.*

Frequency-Distribution Tables

Preparing frequency distribution tables is typically the first step in applying structure to a collection of raw data. Frequency tables present the *frequency of occurrence* for each class or category included in the data structure. The data in a frequency table are presented as counts and as percentages. Percentages are easily understood, and typically convey more meaning than simple frequencies. Statistical software programs that produce tables, charts, and graphs usually include a procedure for producing summary statistics as well. Summary statistics include relative frequencies, which are usually presented as percentages, measures of central tendency, and variation, among others. Usually, the researcher will want more information than just the counts of occurrences in a frequency-distribution table. Therefore, statistical software programs such as SPSS® also allow the researcher to print the row, column, and total percentage of the total that each class represents.

Four guidelines to think about when arranging data in a table are: (1) the total number of classes or categories to include, (2) the upper and lower limits of each category, (3) the titles, captions, headings, and legends you want in the table, and (4) any additional explanatory information to include, such as the relative percentage each number of occurrences represents.

Establishing Categories or Classes

Preparing a frequency table begins with determining how to group the table data into meaningful categories. The total number of categories or classifications that cover all possibilities for the dataset is called a *category set*. The category set should be identified as the data-gathering instrument is prepared. The number of classes or categories in the set—that is, the level of precision employed—depends on the purpose of the research. Decisions that involve large sums of money or potential loss of life, for example, will require greater precision than decisions that deal with routine activities. The number of categories or classes selected for such measures depends first on the nature of the data. For example, dichotomous data (male-female, yes-no, pass-fail) requires two and only two classes. With multichotomous data (data with more than two categories), the analyst's choices are more complicated.

In the final analysis, the researcher who prepares the dataset is the one who establishes how many classes to include in a table. Despite the assumed "scientific" nature of statistics, there is little agreement on the number of classes. Recommendations can be found that vary from a range of from low five with a high of fifteen classes, up to a range of from a low of ten to a high of twenty.

When working with ranked data (ordinal measurements) such as candidate or program preferences or needs priorities, the most commonly used number of classes ranges from around six to a maximum of twelve subjects. Experienced data analysts are convinced that most people experience difficulty when asked to rank more than six to eight items. When asked to rank large numbers of items, people are usually able to quickly rank a few at the top and a few at the bottom, but distinctions tend to blur when they face items in the middle rankings. Because a key purpose for presenting data in tables in the first place is to communicate patterns in the data, it is best to keep the number of categories to a number that makes most sense to the people reading the tables. This usually means using the fewest meaningful categories or classes possible. Convention suggests using no more than ten classes, and preferably something closer to six or seven, at most.

The information in Table 14.1 is a hypothetical count of the number of visas for entry into the United States processed at a U.S. embassy each week over a quarter. Numbers are smaller on Saturdays because of a shorter workday. The visa officer recorded processing an average of a little more than 95 visas per day during the quarter, with a standard deviation of almost 21. The embassy officer wants to display the data in a table that best explains the underlying structure of the data.

The data in Table 14.1 are shown organized into rows and columns. The rows are weeks 1 through 13; each week is considered a case. Each column is a different day's total number of visa applications processed (these values are known as the "frequency of responses"). The width or inclusiveness of each class in a table is influenced by the nature of the data, the frequencies of occurrence, and the guidelines for the maximum number of classes to include. A formula to help establish class width follows:

$$\text{Class Width} = \frac{\text{Range of the Data}}{\text{Preferred Number of Categories}}$$

Table 14.1

Daily Applications for Entry Visas, Quarter 1 Data

Week	Monday	Tuesday	Wednesday	Thursday	Friday	Saturday
1	110	83	95	112	110	72
2	99	121	115	105	112	59
3	120	80	92	103	111	61
4	121	95	87	125	103	63
5	73	113	78	92	93	64
6	91	83	122	107	93	71
7	107	130	85	111	112	56
8	99	69	74	104	106	57
9	123	105	111	101	117	66
10	85	105	109	88	109	55
11	108	99	117	106	109	61
12	102	75	74	128	116	54
13	64	124	91	118	85	63
Totals	1302	1282	1250	1400	1376	802
Mean	95.03					
SD	20.92					

Source: Hypothetical data.

The range is determined by subtracting the lowest value from the highest measurement. The analyst has complete freedom to choose, again guided by the previously mentioned rules of thumb, the number of classes or categories to use. By scanning through the data, the analyst can see that the highest number of sales applications processed (130) occurred on Tuesday of Week 7. The lowest number (54) occurred on Saturday of Week 12. Therefore, the range is 130 minus 54, or 76. The embassy officer thinks that he would like to present the data after they are grouped in six or so classes. To establish class width, the officer substitutes the range and desired number of classes numbers in the formula, and comes up with a class width of 12.66.

$$W = \frac{76}{6} = 12.66$$

Class widths of 12.66 will, of course, be very difficult to work with. However, since the nature of the data seems to lend it to groupings of 10, and because 12.66 is about as close to 10 as it is to 15, it is much more likely that the officer would use a class width of 10 rather than the cumbersome 12.66. If a class width of 10 is selected, the number of classes must be increased from the desired 6 to 9. This is still below the convention-imposed upper limit of 10. The important thing to remember is that all the classes must be the same size (equal in width), and that all measures can fall into one and *only* one class. Thus, the 10-wide ranges for each class should be 50–59, 60–69, and so on. Table 14.2 was produced by the *Data Analysis: Histograms* capability in Microsoft® Excel™. Note that only one value of the class width range needs to be identified for the table bin-width requirement.

Additional guidelines for presenting data in tables begin with numbering each table and

Table 14.2

**Excel™ Frequency Table
Showing 10-Wide Bins, Table
14.1 Data**

Bins	Frequency
50	0
60	5
70	8
80	8
90	7
100	11
110	18
120	13
130	8
More	0
Total:	78

Source: Example data from table 14.1.

Table 14.3

Gender Distribution of Responses, Satisfaction Study Sample

Gender	Sample *n*	Count	Percent of Responses	Percent of Total Sample
Females	500	456	58.6	45.6
Males	500	322	41.4	32.2
Missing	—	222	—	22.2
Total	1,000	778	100.0	100.0

Source: Experimental data.

including a caption. Most often, it is easier to read the table when the data are arranged downward, as opposed to having it spread across a page. Columns and rows must be identified, with qualifiers placed under the table in the form of footnotes. The caption and figure number of a table is always printed above the table; captions for graphs, charts, and other illustrations are presented below the figure. Almost any type of data can be presented in a table. In addition, tables may display information about one, two, or more than two variables. That is, they may be *univariate, bivariate*, or *multivariate*. Table 14.3 is a *univariate* table; it displays data only for the variable *gender*.

Table 14.4 is a *bivariate table,* in which responses for two variables are included. The variables are *sex of respondent* and *political party membership*. Table 14.5 is a *multivariate* table, in which the distribution of frequency responses for three variables, *gender, height,* and *weight,* is displayed.

Table 14.4

A Bivariate Table Produced with SPSS® *Crosstabs* Program

Sex of Respondent, Political Party Membership, Crosstabulation

		Political Party			
Gender:		Democrat	Republican	Independent	Totals
Female	Count:	28	6	16	50
	% within Sex of Respondent	56.0%	12.0%	32.0%	100.0%
Male	Count:	12	26	12	50
	% within Sex of Respondent	24.0%	52.0%	24.0%	100.0%
Totals:	Count:	40	32	28	100
	% within Sex of Respondent	40.0%	32.0%	28.0%	100.0%

Source: Experimental data.

Table 14.5

Physical Characteristics of Fitness Group A-1, Week 1

Gender	Sample *n*	Mean Height (inches)	Mean Weight (pounds)
Females	456	66.6	129.50
Males	322	71.3	177.00
Total	778		

Source: Example data.

Relative-Frequency Distribution Tables

A type of table often seen in research reports is the *relative-frequency distribution table.* In a frequency-distribution table instead of reporting every measurement or response separately, as is required for a stem-and-leaf diagram, all scores are grouped into classes, their occurrence counted, and converted to proportions and percentages. Relative frequency refers to the proportion of the total that each group or value represents. Knowing the relative frequency of responses can be important for several different types of comparisons of the distribution of responses. The researchers compare counts and percentages. The relative frequency of responses for each class can also be read as a *probability of occurrence* for that class. Table 14.6 is an example of a simple frequency-distribution table that shows responses to a scale of exercise participation.

Table 14.6

Weekly Exercise Rates, Total Sample (Hypothetical Data)

Weekly Hours of Exercise	Frequency	Relative Frequency	Cumulative Percent
3 hours or less	5	.156	15.6%
4 to 6 hours	7	.219	37.5%
7 to 9 hours	10	.312	68.7%
10 to 12 hours	8	.250	93.7%
13 hours or more	2	.063	100.0%

Rules for Frequency-Distribution Tables

Researchers must be aware of the important rules to follow when preparing frequency-distribution tables. First, the table must exhibit *internal consistency*. That is, groups or classes must be equal in size. In Table 14.6, except for the upper level, all classes consisted of three-hour levels. Although the highest category appears to be open-ended, it is not. It includes the highest count while making it possible for the researcher to deal with *outliers*. Outliers are "abnormal" counts that fall outside of the normal distribution confidence interval. That is, they are either excessively high or low. Because they fall outside of the assumed normal distribution, ignoring them results in loss of the information about the case. Therefore, if the outlier is abnormally high, it is grouped with the highest class; if it is abnormally low, it is grouped with the lowest class. An example for the data in Table 14.6 would be if one member of the employer-sponsored fitness program was an "exercise freak," working out more than 3 hours a day, 6 or 7 days a week, or a total of 21 hours. The gap between 13 and 21 hours would require two blank classes. By including the outlier in the highest "normal" class, its ability to excessively influence the group average has been alleviated.

Second, frequency distribution tables should include the *relative frequency* and often, but not necessarily always, the *cumulative frequency* of occurrences. Relative frequency is the proportion of the total each class represents. It can be stated as a decimal or as a percentage. In decimal form the total must always equal 1; in percentages, the total must equal 100 percent. In Table 14.6, the relative frequency of the lowest category is .156, or 15.6 percent.

Table 14.7 is an expanded version of a relative-frequency table. The final column on the right displays the *cumulative relative frequency*. This is simply the sum of a class and all preceding classes. For example, the cumulative relative frequency for the second level, 4 to 6 hours, is its value (21.9 percent) plus the value of the 3 hours or less class (15.6 percent), for a total of 37.5 percent.

Finally, some statistical software packages include provisions for computing relative frequencies when the data contain missing values. A missing value might occur when a subject refuses to answer a particular question on a survey. When this occurs, the relative frequency distribution column will include the proportion of the total represented by the missing values. A separate column labeled *Valid Percent* will appear in the table alongside the relative frequency column. Table 14.7 displays data from a fitness program study. In this example, the sample includes 35 workers instead of 32; 3 subjects did not respond to the question of how many hours they exercised each week. The new table would look like this:

Table 14.7

Weekly Exercise Rates, Total Sample

Weekly Hours of Exercise	Count	Percent	Valid Percent	Cumulative Percent
3 hours or less	5	14.3%	15.6%	15.6%
4 to 6 hours	7	20.0%	21.9%	37.5%
7 to 9 hours	10	28.6%	31.2%	68.7%
10 to 12 hours	8	22.8%	25.0%	93.7%
13 hours or more	2	5.7%	6.3%	100.0%
Missing	3	8.6%	—	
Totals	35	100.0%	100.0%	

Table 14.8

Weights of Sample Pharmaceutical Research Packages (in ounces), Example Data

			Package Weights (in ounces)					
Sample	Hour	Quarter	Package 1	Package 2	Package 3	Package 4	Package 5	Package 6
1	1	1	8.04	7.95	7.87	7.90	7.98	8.07
2	1	2	8.02	8.04	7.93	8.11	7.94	8.98
3	1	3	8.00	8.11	8.04	7.99	7.97	8.08
4	1	4	7.90	8.02	8.06	7.98	7.96	8.05
5	2	1	8.06	8.13	7.97	8.09	7.88	7.97
6	2	2	8.05	8.04	8.04	8.07	7.89	8.00
7	2	3	8.04	8.07	8.11	8.06	7.94	8.01
8	2	4	8.06	8.06	8.02	8.11	8.04	8.02
9	3	1	8.05	8.04	7.99	8.06	7.99	8.01
10	3	2	8.20	8.03	8.06	8.05	8.00	8.00
11	3	3	8.00	8.03	8.01	8.10	8.01	8.00
12	3	4	8.00	8.12	8.02	7.89	8.01	7.90
13	4	1	8.01	8.13	8.05	7.88	8.00	8.01
14	4	2	8.02	7.99	7.07	7.79	8.00	7.89
15	4	3	8.01	8.05	8.24	7.78	7.90	7.99
16	4	4	8.03	8.04	8.11	7.77	8.01	8.00

Preparing a Stem-and-Leaf Diagram

A *stem-and-leaf diagram* is a convenient way to display at one glance every measurement for each major value. As a result, it is appropriate for use with relatively small samples. In the dataset shown in Table 14.8, the first value in the stem is the whole number of ounces in the package: 7, 8, or 9. The second value in the stem is the first digit after the decimal point, the tenths-of-an-ounce measurement. The leaves are the hundredths-of-an-ounce measurement (the second number after the decimal point).

The following example of a pharmaceutical researcher at a research hospital is provided to illustrate how data might be presented in a stem-and-leaf diagram. The researcher is responsible for ensuring that the package-filling equipment loads 8 ounces of a new pain-killing product into each package. The product is distributed as part of a medical experiment to determine whether the new drug is more effective than aspirin at treating arthritis pain. It would not be cost-effective to weigh every single package; instead, with the approval of supervising medical staff, the researcher randomly selects six sample packages from the package-filling line. Over a four-hour morning shift, packages are pulled and weighed every quarter-hour, until a total sample of 96 packages (4 * 4 * 6) in 16 samples of 6 packages each is collected. The researcher must present a summary of the measurements to the experiment supervisor. The summary can be presented as a *stem-and-leaf diagram,* a *frequency-distribution table,* or a *histogram.* Before any of these communications tools can be processed by statistical software, however, the data must first be entered as a raw dataset. The data file will appear as seen in Table 14.8. Rows are measurements; columns are variables (in this case, each sample is a separate variable). Each row is a "case," which comprises a sample of 6 packages. The three variables are (1) hour, (2) quarter, and (3) unit.

Preparing a Stem-and-Leaf Diagram with SPSS®

Excel™ does not include a special function or "wizard" for creating stem-and-leaf diagrams. However, with several simple intermediate steps, it is possible to come up with a satisfactory diagram. SPSS® does have this capability to quickly produce a stem-and-leaf diagram for each variable in the dataset. Figure 14.1 is an SPSS-produced stem-and-leaf diagram for all 16 units in the Package Design Two set. The first column registers the number of measurements in that category. For example, there were two observations in the 7.95 to 7.99 category (7.95 and 7.99), seven observations in the 8.0 to 8.49 class, and four observations in the 8.00 to 8.19 category (8.11, 8.12, 8.13, and a second 8.13).

Frequency	Stem	Leaves
0.0	79 .	0
2.0	79 .	5 9
7.0	80 .	2 3 3 4 4 4 4
3.0	80 .	5 6 7
4.0	81 .	1 2 3 3

Stem width: 10
Each leaf: 1 case(s)

Figure 14.1 **An SPSS®-Produced Stem-and-Leaf Diagram for Package Design Two**

Communicating with Charts and Graphs

Charts and graphs are used to pictorially present numerical data. They are most often used to display summary information about a dataset, although they are not limited to this application alone. With today's increasingly powerful spreadsheet and statistical software programs, together with color ink jet printers, these pictorial devices are easy and quick to produce and use.

Charts

Among the more commonly used types of charts and graphs are *bar charts, histograms, frequency polygons, line-and-area charts, scatter plots*, and *pie charts.*

Bar charts. Bar charts show how many measurements or observations fall into each class or category of each variable. Printers may use asterisks (stars) or shading to represent the extent of the relative frequencies. It is important to remember that the bars are not accurate measures; they are symbolic. The bars in any one chart may not appear to exact scale, but they do give a clear visual impression of the variation among the values in the class. Bar charts may be displayed either vertically or horizontally; charts with many classes should typically use the horizontal form (page width limitations may otherwise force the chart into an overlap, confusing the viewer). Bar charts are often used to show changes or trends over time. In this application, the horizontal line is always the time line, while the vertical line represents the data values. Figure 14.2 is a vertical bar chart (column chart) of the visa-processing example data; it is based on ten-wide bin sizes.

Histograms. A second way to graphically display a frequency distribution is with a *histogram.* A histogram has a visual appearance much like a bar chart, except that in histograms the bars often touch one another (gaps always separate the bars of a bar chart). And while bar charts should only be used when displaying discrete data (that is, data in distinct categories such as occupations), histograms can be used to display both discrete and continuous data.

The Excel™ *Tools/Data Analysis/Histogram* wizard was used to construct the bin frequency table in Table 14.9 and the histogram in Figure 14.3. Recall that a computed class width using the mathematical formula resulted in a value of 12.666, which is a cumbersome span. Bin widths of 10 or 15 measurements could have been used with similar results. The histogram above was calculated using a bin width of 15, whereas 10-wide bins were used in Table 14.2 displayed earlier.

Examples of continuous data include incomes, height, weight, and other similar measures. As with frequency-distribution tables, continuous data categories or classes used in histograms must exhibit internal consistency; all classes must be of the same width. In histograms, the horizontal line (X axis) displays the measurement values of the data, while the vertical (Y axis) represents the frequencies or counts of how often the values occur.

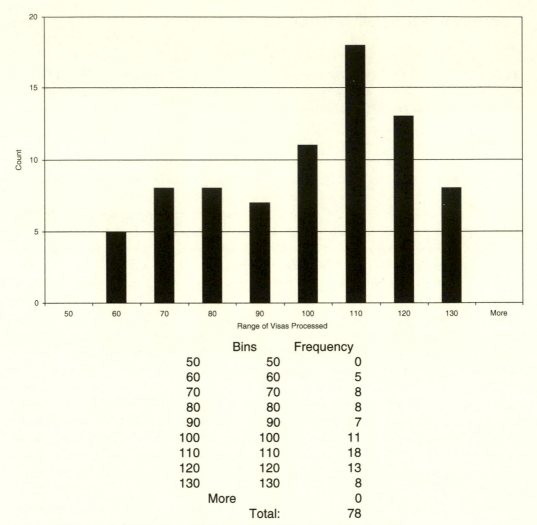

Bins		Frequency
50	50	0
60	60	5
70	70	8
80	80	8
90	90	7
100	100	11
110	110	18
120	120	13
130	130	8
	More	0
	Total:	78

Figure 14.2 **Vertical Bar Chart (Column Chart) Produced by Excel**™

Table 14.9

15-Wide Bins and Frequencies for Visa Applications Data

Bin	Frequency
60	5
75	14
90	9
105	19
120	23
135	8
More	0

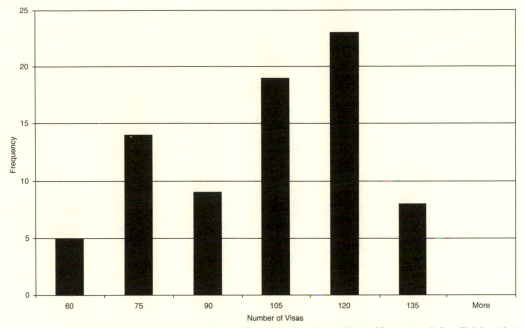

Figure 14.3   **Histogram of Hypothetical Visa Applications Data (Quarter 1) for Table 14.9 Data**

Graphs

Graphs are another good way to present a visual summary of data. The types used most are *line graphs, frequency polygons,* and *pie-graphs* (also known as "pie-charts").

Line graphs. Line graphs are used to show how values of a variable change over time. The time periods are always shown on the horizontal axis, while the vertical axis displays the values of the variables being examined. When continuous data are plotted, the points at each time period represent the middle level of the class. Simple line graphs are used this way to display trend lines of single variables. Compound line charts displaying the component values of a larger sum are often used to visually display comparisons over time. A line chart is shown in Figure 14.4.

Frequency polygons. Frequency polygons show much the same data as histograms: the counts of occurrences of each value of a variable. In appearance, however, they look almost identical to line graphs. For many years, when statistical computations were done by hand or, at best, with a hand calculator, the frequency polygon was probably the most-often-used method for graphically displaying frequency distributions. This was because they are extremely easy to construct. However, today they are not encountered as often as bar charts and histograms.

With all frequency polygons, two axes are needed. The vertical axis almost always represents the frequencies; the horizontal axis displays the measurement or class values. With grouped data, the midpoint of the interval is used. When plotting specific data such as individual scores,

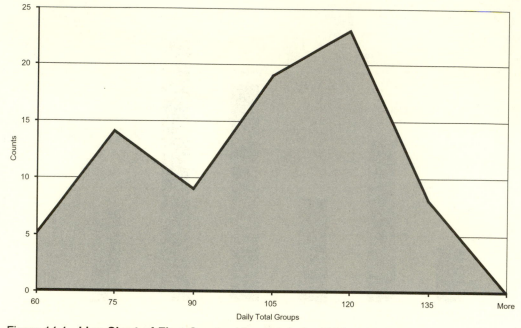

Figure 14.4   **Line Chart of First-Quarter Visa Totals for Table 14.9 Data**

the actual score value is used. Lines connect all total-frequency values. The polygon's lines are often extended to one value above and one below the observed data so as to "close off" the polygon instead of leaving it hanging in midair.

Frequency polygons can also be used to plot and compare two or more sets of scores or values that are based on separate scales. In this case, use the *relative frequency distribution* in place of actual frequency distributions.

Pie charts. In pie charts, the data are presented as portions of a 360-degree total. Each portion of the "pie" is a representation of its proportion of the total (100 percent). Figure 14.5 is a pie chart of the data presented in Table 14.10. It was produced with the Excel™ *Chart Wizard*.

Scatter Plots

Scatter plots are a separate category of ways to visually present data. Scatter plots are used to display a series of points of two (or more) related or associated variables. In one sense, they might be considered to be somewhat similar to line charts, except that no lines connect the various points on the scatter plot. Measurement units for one variable are marked on one axis; units for the second variable are marked on the other axis. For example, a quality scatter plot

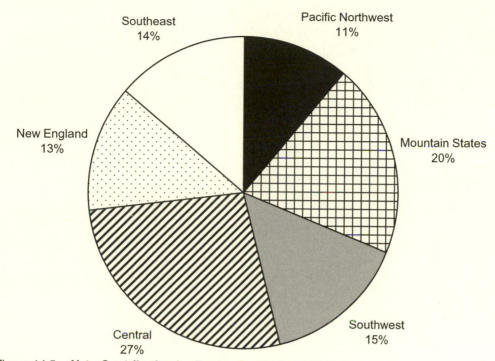

Figure 14.5. **Vote Contribution by Region for Table 14.10 Data**

Table 14.10

Vote Contribution by Region

Region	(%)
Pacific Northwest	11
Mountain States	20
Southwest	15
Central	27
New England	13
Southeast	14
Total	100

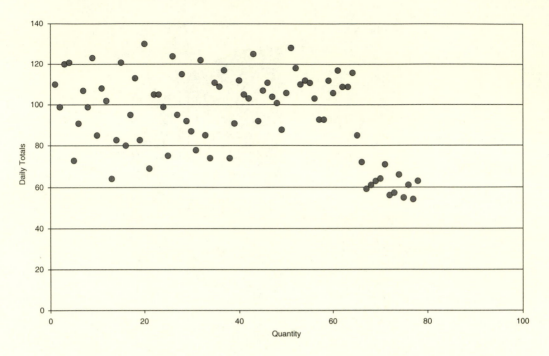

WEEK	Sales Orders	TUESDAY	WEDNESDAY	THURSDAY	FRIDAY	SATURDAY
1	110					
2	99					
3	120					
4	121		60			
5	73		75			
6	91		90			
7	107		105			
8	99		120			
9	123		135			
10	85					
11	108					
12	102					
13	64					
	83					
	121					
	80					
	95					
	113					
	83					
	130					

Bin	Frequency
60	5
75	14
90	9
105	19
120	23
135	8
More	0

Figure 14.6   **A Scatter Plot Example**

might list machine production rates on one axis and part failures on another. Each point represents a single measure of both variables.

When all measures are plotted, a visual picture of the relationship between variables can often be seen (Figure 14.6). When scatter plots are used to display dependent-independent variables, the horizontal axis is the independent variable.

An example of an independent variable could be various levels of advertising expenditures; the dependent variable might be sales levels associated with different levels of advertising spending.

Summary

When first collected, "raw" data make little or no sense. Raw data are simply a loose collection of numbers; they have no intuitive meaning of their own. Data must be put into some kind of order or structure; they must be grouped together into sets that have logic and structure. Numbers do not speak for themselves; they acquire meaning only when they are organized in terms of some mutually understood framework. To begin with, data must be ordered and classified into a structure that has meaning and pertains to the decision problem. Often, the first step in this process is the preparation of simple *univariate, bivariate,* and/or *multivariate* tables that present the data in summary form. "Tables" are nothing more than sets of numbers—and their identifying labels—that are presented in some organized, logical way. When quantitative information is arranged in tables, it is easier for persons reading the report to spot trends, relationships, and differences in the data. Examples of data almost always presented in the form of a table include demographic data, such as family incomes, subjects' occupational categories, geographic dispersion of voters, and size or performance measures that fall within researcher-determined tolerances.

An early step in the analysis and interpretation of statistical data is arranging the collected numbers in some logical sequence; this is often done by reorganizing the data into ascending or descending order, or transforming it into standardized values, which can then be organized into logical tabular form.

Graphic displays of data also improve the researcher's ability to communicate meaning to readers. Bar charts, histograms, line-and-area charts, scatter plots, and pie charts are used to graphically display the information mined from datasets.

Discussion Questions

1. Why do most good research reports make maximum use of graphic communication tools?
2. What is a frequency-distribution table? What is a relative-frequency-distribution table? What are the rules for forming a relative-frequency-distribution table?
3. What is a stem-and-leaf diagram?
4. What is the procedure for establishing class widths for tables, charts, and graphs?
5. Seven different types of charts were mentioned in the chapter. Name and describe at least five of them.
6. Name three different types of graphs used to display numerical information.
7. How can tables be developed with Microsoft® Excel™?
8. Explain how Excel™ is used to prepare charts.

Additional Reading

Brightman, Harvey J. 1999. *Data Analysis in Plain English, with Microsoft® Excel™*. Pacific Grove, CA: Duxbury Press.

Carver, Robert H., and Jane Gradwohl Nash. 2000. *Doing Data Analysis with SPSS® 10.0*. Pacifc Grove, CA: Brooks/Cole.

Field, Andy. 2000. *Discovering Statistics Using SPSS® for Windows*. Thousand Oaks, CA: Sage.

Green, Samuel B., Neil J. Salkind, and Theresa M. Akey. 2000. *Using SPSS® for Windows: Analyzing and Understanding Data*. 2nd ed. Upper Saddle River, NJ: Prentice-Hall.

15 Testing Simple Research Hypotheses

Before data are gathered, processed, and interpreted someone must have established a purpose for the study. All subsequent analysis follows from this purpose. In scientific research, the reason is typically expressed as a *hypothesis* or a set of *hypotheses*. A hypothesis is a statement that describes some assumption of the researcher. Hypotheses also explain or suggest a researcher's conclusions about some phenomena of interest. For example, the statement "people over 50 years of age vote more often than do people 30 years of age and younger" is a testable hypothesis about the behavior of two defined groups of people. The testable research assumption is that age influences voting behavior.

In addition to setting the stage for a research project, hypotheses guide further research action; hypotheses dictate the appropriate research design to follow. For example, hypotheses written about the mean score for a group on an attitude scale dictate the type of data-gathering methods to be followed; subjects must answer questions that reveal their attitudes. This usually means development of a questionnaire that the researcher administers in a survey research design. The voting-age hypothesis above calls for collecting data that can be analyzed with correlation statistics. Equally, a hypothesis that calls for comparing the responses of a subgroup with that of another group drawn from the same population dictates analysis that allows the researcher to compare group responses.

Finally, the type of research hypothesis largely influences selection of the appropriate statistical method or methods for a research project and the way that the alternative explanation is formed. This chapter addresses the fundamentals of hypothesis testing, techniques for one-sample hypothesis tests, and concludes with an introduction to the ideas behind using *p*-values to make decisions about hypotheses.

Fundamentals of Hypothesis Testing

Hypotheses can be written in many different ways and for many different purposes. For example, they can be formed to address *relationships* between variables, or as *differences* between values. They can be stated as facts or as the way responses are distributed. They can be written as predictions and as comparisons. They can refer to a sample statistic, a population parameter, or a proportion. In all approaches, they are usually written as pairs, a null hypothesis and its obverse, the alternate. In political science, researchers typically form one or more of three main types of hypotheses: predictive, comparative, or association.

1. *Predictive Hypotheses*. These are predictions about the future value of a measurement. Examples include predictions about tax revenues in the next several quarters, predictions about the movements of stock prices, and the government's predictions of annual growth in the deficit, productivity, or unemployment.
2. *Comparative Hypotheses*. These make comparisons between groups of voters, political parties, countries, products, and the like. These are often used in hypotheses about differences between scores of one group compared with another. Examples include differences in mean product preference scores between two samples of beer drinkers, and production-rate differences encountered after a change in environmental conditions (sometimes called a *treatment*).
3. *Association Hypotheses*. These deal with the levels of relationship or association between two or more variables. Examples include measuring whether new advertising, a shift in policy announced at a series of press briefings, or modifications in issue focus influence attitudes among voters.

It is important to remember that hypotheses are statements about events or things that researchers *believe* are true or not true. They are assumptions, not facts. Statistical tests are carried out to verify the statement or assumption. Hypotheses are always employed in pairs. The first of the pair is typically stated in status quo terms; that is, a predicted change in attitudes will not take place; variables are not related; groups' scores on political awareness surveys after a public opinion campaign will not differ from scores gathered before the campaign. This is called the *null hypothesis,* and is represented by the notation H_O. Null hypotheses are also said to exist as "negative statements." Examples include: "There is no association between the age of a machine and its production-error rate." "There is no difference in a sample of voters' preferences for candidates seeking office in the 35th legislative district." "There is no disproportionate distribution in the frequencies of responses among different age groups to a question on political issues."

An alternate hypothesis is always paired *with* the null hypothesis. Alternate hypotheses are stated in terms exactly opposite from null hypotheses. They are represented by the notation H_A. Researchers gather data to support the alternate hypothesis, and to decide against the null hypothesis.

The null hypothesis is what is being "tested" in a statistical procedure. For example, a researcher first computes the mean value of some variable for a sample. Because it is a sample mean, it is called a *statistic*. She could then conduct a one-sample hypothesis test to establish whether this statistic is "different" from the mean of the larger population. The mean for a population is always called a *parameter*. The question she faces is: *does this sample statistic fall in the acceptable range of possible sample means for this population?* The researcher must decide whether to accept or reject the null hypothesis. If the sample mean falls within an acceptable range of values, she determines that the statistic is not different; it falls within the *sample distribution of the mean*.

Statistical processes exist to test hypotheses about all types of measurements: categorical (nominal), ordered (ordinal), and continuous (interval and ratio) data. Hypothesis tests exist for a single case, a single sample, for two or more groups, differences in a statistic or parameter, about a single proportion, and for differences between two or more proportions. A commonly encountered use of hypothesis tests is for testing for differences between sample statistics that are known by the researcher and of parameters that are unknown (inferred).

In statistical notation, hypotheses stated as recognizing no difference or change are signified by the notation: $H_O = H_A$. The alternate hypothesis to this null hypothesis is that the two are not equal, and is signified by the notation $H_O \neq H_A$. Change in one direction only is indicated by the notations: $H_O < H_A$, or $H_O > H_A$. This type of hypothesis may also be stated as one is "equal to or less than" the other, or that one is "greater than or equal to" the other; these statements are signified by the notations $H_O \leq H_A$ and $H_O \geq H_A$, respectively.

One-direction changes (either greater or less than) are called a *one-tailed test*. When the test involves difference in any direction, it is called a *two-tailed test*. Statistical-processing programs often print out test statistics for both one- and two-tailed tests for the same data. The choice of which result to use, either a one-tailed, two-tailed, or both test, is dictated by the pre-established null hypothesis.

Classes of Hypothesis Tests

Researchers must deal with three different classes of hypothesis tests: (1) tests concerning a single subject, (2) tests for a single group or sample, and (3) tests of hypotheses about two or more groups. A variety of different hypothesis tests have been developed for use with each of these three classes of hypotheses. Among the most commonly used in political science research are Z-tests, *t*-tests, and analysis of variance (ANOVA) tests. Single-subject tests are used to establish whether the subject statistic falls within the accepted range of all possible statistics for the sample or a population. One purpose of one-sample tests is to establish that the sample is, indeed, representative of the population; another is to determine whether the sample distribution is normal. Two-sample tests are typically used to test for statistically significant differences in a test statistic between sets of samples or groups. Generally—but not always—the statistic used for such tests is the mean or a proportion. Because decisions on hypothesis tests are so closely intertwined with probability rules, a brief description of the topic follows.

Probability and Hypothesis Testing

Research decisions based on inferential statistics are made on the basis of what is *probably* true, not on what is actually true. Probabilities are, in fact, the basis of all statistical inference. Researchers seldom, if ever, have perfect information before them when they are required to make a decision. To gain information and reduce uncertainty, researchers typically use the results of a sample as an *approximation* of what is or what might be true of a population. They make *inferences* about the population from the sample data.

However, a major limitation of sample research is that a study based on another sample taken from the same group will almost always produce results that are entirely different from the results of the first sample data. One way that researchers lower the risk of this happening is by increasing the size of their sample; larger samples lower the influence of extreme values—called *outliers*—in a dataset. However, collecting data costs money and takes time, both of which are limited resources; increasing the sample size is often simply not possible. What researchers do instead is to change the acceptable level of confidence they have in the results of the hypothesis test.

Hypotheses are statements *or predictions* by someone that explain or suggest some conclusion, event, or thing. Hypotheses are suggestions or beliefs about something; they are not "true" statements. Researchers can have varying amounts of confidence in the veracity of their predictions. They can hope to be 99 percent sure, 95 percent sure, or 90 percent sure—or any other amount. This degree of faith in the truth of the hypothesis statement is the *level of confidence;* confidence levels are typically stated as *probabilities,* and abbreviated as p-*values.* Probabilities and *p*-values are typically stated as decimals; they range from .0 to 1.0. For example, when a researcher is 99 percent sure that a statement is true, the probability of truth is .01. A probability of 1.0 refers to a perfect level of confidence; it means that the researcher is 100 percent sure about the statement. Probabilities can only be positive values.

Confidence Intervals and p-Values

A *confidence interval* is the researcher's estimate of the probability of all possible random samples drawn from the same population falling within a range of values that contains the mean of the population. The Greek lower-case letter for m (μ) is the symbol used to signify the population mean. The decision to accept or reject a null hypothesis is based upon a level of probability that is acceptable. The researcher-established probability is called the *confidence level;* it is the degree of confidence the researcher has that the decision to accept or reject the null hypothesis not be in error. Confidence levels are also considered to be the probabilities that the results of the test could not have occurred by chance. For example, a confidence level of .05 means that the statistic values for 95 out of 100 samples will fall within the range that contains the population parameter. This range is also referred to as the *sample space.*

No two samples drawn from the same population can be expected to have the same mean or variation. With normal distributions, roughly half of the possible values of a sample statistic will fall above the mean, and half below. Thus, sample space refers to a range of statistics that fall to either side of the population mean, and that are considered to be statistically the same. Acceptable ranges refer to the proportion of possible values of the statistic that fall between the mean and a cutoff point some distance from the mean. The range includes values greater and less than the central mean. Values falling outside of this acceptable range are those that call for rejection of the null hypothesis.

The entire set of possible values within this range is called the *confidence interval.* The confidence interval is the range of values within which the "true" value of the population (mean) parameter is expected to fall. The researcher's expectation is stated as some chosen level of probability that the statistic falls in the accepted range. The values delineating the confidence range are known as the *upper* and *lower confidence limits;* together they form the bounds of the confidence interval. That is, with a 95 percent confidence value and a normal distribution, 2.5 percent of the values are expected to be above (outside) the upper confidence value and 2.5 percent are expected to fall in the lowest portion or *tail* of the normal curve.

The statistical test to determine whether a sample statistic falls within the acceptable sample space is called a *significance test.* Significance tests are important decision tools with uses in all inferential statistics.

Testing Hypotheses Using Confidence Intervals

Researchers use sample statistics as the basis for making inferences about populations. These inferences are based on confidence levels or confidence intervals established by the manager, or from the results of significance tests. In most research situations, confidence levels are predetermined at either one of three standard points: the 99 percent, 95 percent, or 90 percent level, which is another way of saying the *.01, .05, or .10 level of confidence.* These confidence level values are called "alphas." The Greek symbol for "a" is alpha, which is indicated by the Greek lower-case α. Because hypothesis testing is founded in probability theory, most decisions about hypotheses are made on the basis of some level of probability concerning the acceptance region of a statistic; this is called the p-*value approach* to hypothesis testing.

When a statistical test of the null hypothesis fails to support the belief statement, researchers can only say that the null hypothesis must be rejected. They cannot say that the statement is "true." For example, say that a statistical test is carried out for differences between the mean scores on an attitude scale for two groups of voters. The null hypothesis is that there is no (statistically significant) difference between the two means. The alternate hypothesis is that the two mean scores are not the same. If the difference is great and the probability that the difference did not occur by chance is lower than a preset confidence level, the null hypothesis must be rejected and the alternate hypothesis retained (or accepted).

Error in Hypothesis Testing

Regardless of what confidence level is selected or computed, several errors of analysis may confound the results of a study (Mattson 1986). The two types of errors associated with hypothesis tests are *Type I* and *Type II* errors. Both error types and indications of when they occur are illustrated in Figure 15.1.

Political science researchers are more concerned about making Type I errors than they are about Type II errors. Type I errors occur when a null hypothesis that is actually true is rejected. This is called *falsely rejecting the null hypothesis.* Type I errors are related to the confidence level adopted for a decision. Thus, with a 90 percent level of confidence, the researcher can falsely reject the null hypothesis 10 percent of the time. Lowering the confidence level to 95 percent (an alpha of .05) means the researcher can expect to be wrong only 5 percent of the time. Thus, tightening confidence levels lowers the likelihood of Type I errors occurring. Remember: rejecting a null hypothesis does not mean that something is "true"; it only means this hypothesis must be rejected and the alternate hypothesis retained.

Type II errors occur when a researcher does *not* reject the null hypothesis when it is, in fact, false. Type II errors occur less often than Type I errors; procedures for computing their possible occurrence are usually found in comprehensive mathematical statistics texts, and will not be covered here. In general, researchers reduce the likelihood of Type II errors occurring by increasing the size of the sample.

DECISION

		Reject the Null	Accept (Retain) the Null
	Null is False:	Correct Decision	**Type II Error**
REALITY:	Null is True:	**Type I Error**	Correct Decision

Figure 15.1 **Type I and Type II Error in Hypothesis Testing**

One-Sample Hypothesis Tests

One-sample hypothesis test applications are tests of a sample statistic, usually the mean or a proportion, in order to establish that the sample measurement is representative of the population from which it is drawn. One-sample tests are also available to determine whether the test statistics have a normal distribution. These tests for normality are important because two key assumptions in most interval and ratio data hypothesis tests are random samples and a normal distribution.

How hypotheses are formed and which statistical tests are used depend upon specific decision circumstances facing the researcher. These circumstances include the level of measurement, the data-collection process followed, whether the variance is known, and whether the test is one-tailed or two-tailed, among others. Researchers must also consider the concept of *error* as they form and test their hypotheses. Two types of error are associated with hypothesis testing.

Basic Concepts in One-Sample Hypothesis Testing

Inferential statistics involves using measurements of a sample to draw conclusions about the characteristics of a population. Researchers never know with complete certainty that the sample statistics match the population parameters. On the other hand, researchers do know that drawing another random sample or samples from the same population will usually produce similar, but different, values for their statistics. It will not happen every time, however. The researcher wants to know how likely it is (with what degree of probability) that the sample statistic will fall within an *acceptable range* of possible values. This acceptable range is called the *confidence interval*.

A Single-Case Hypothesis Test

In a single-case hypothesis test, a researcher is typically interested in knowing if the case statistic, such as a mean score on a test of issue awareness, falls within a defined range of values for a population. The null hypothesis for this example is that the case statistic is the same as that of the sample from which it is taken (i.e., there is no difference). The alternate hypothesis is that the statistic for the case is not in the acceptable sample space. The one-sample Z-test is used to test this hypothesis. The following steps explain how to use Microsoft® Excel™ for the procedure.

1. Using the STANDARDIZE procedure from the Excel™ *Function Wizard,* convert the single-subject statistic to a Z-score. (Note: the terms Z-score and Z-value are often used interchangeably.)
2. Select a confidence level for deciding whether the score falls within the acceptable range. The .05 level of confidence has long been the level used in most social-science research, including political science. The normal distribution table found in most statistics texts refers to the proportion of area under the bell-shaped curve of a normal distribution that corresponds to the Z-value. A check of the table reveals that the .05 level of confidence coincides with a Z-score of 1.96. This value represents the number

of standard deviations from the population parameter. The larger the Z, the farther it falls from the center of the curve; the smaller the Z, the closer it is to the center of the sample space.

3. Determine whether the standardized (Z-score) single-case test statistic value is greater or less than the confidence value. If it is the same or smaller than 1.96, retain the null—the case does belong to the group. If it is greater—that is, if the Z-value is larger than 1.96—reject the null and accept the alternate hypothesis; the case does not belong to the group.

The Excel™ CONFIDENCE Test

Researchers often want to know what percentage of all possible samples would include the parameter for the population somewhere within the interval (range) of their statistic values. Since the *actual* parameter value is seldom known, an estimate for this number must be made. The sample statistic is substituted for the unknown parameter. The sample statistic usually used for this purpose is the sample mean.

Microsoft® Excel's™ CONFIDENCE test function can quickly establish an estimate for the range of values above and below the hypothesized population mean. Three values are needed to complete the CONFIDENCE test:

1. *Alpha* (the researcher-determined significance level to be used to compute the confidence level; a number greater than 0 and less than 1).
2. The standard deviation (SD) of the population (since this is seldom known, the SD for the sample is substituted).
3. The total of sample items involved (n).

The data in Table 15.1 can be used with the CONFIDENCE function test in the Microsoft® Excel™ *Function Wizard* to illustrate how to establish a confidence interval. A researcher is interested in determining whether the size of donations to a campaign for an initiative to establish class-size limits in the state's elementary schools is representative of donations received in other weeks of the campaign. Because of the variation in individual income of the supporters of the initiative, some donation variation is expected to naturally occur. The researcher wants to know whether the mean donation amount received in the critical fourth week of the campaign is within the acceptable range of possible mean amounts. To conduct the one-sample hypothesis test, the researcher randomly selects a sample of twenty mailed donations received on a randomly selected day of the week over a period of eight weeks prior to the election. Table 15.2 displays the Excel test results for the data. A significance value of .05 is established at the decision value or cutoff point for accepting the null hypothesis. The mean for this sample of forty observations is \$52.09; the standard deviation is \$28.62. The null hypothesis is: *the mean amount donated in Week 4 is the same as the overall mean.* The alternate hypothesis is that the mean for Week 4 is not the same. They can be written as:

$$H_o : \bar{X}_{week4} = \mu$$
$$H_A : \bar{X}_{week4} = \mu$$

Table 15.1

Variations in Initiative-Campaign Donations

Sample:	Week 1	Week 2	Week 3	Week 4	Week 5	Week 6	Week 7	Week 8
	40	50	50	25	75	40	30	25
	25	35	40	50	50	75	100	75
	20	25	45	40	50	75	100	75
	20	20	50	30	25	75	60	50
	35	40	100	75	30	100	75	35
	30	50	80	50	40	75	40	35
	25	10	40	75	50	100	25	100
	20	25	50	80	80	40	20	30
	35	60	45	90	100	75	20	50
	40	15	40	100	30	75	35	45
	40	20	75	150	50	75	150	40
	45	25	50	100	45	100	100	75
	30	40	100	75	40	50	30	125
	50	20	30	75	75	40	100	45
	35	30	50	75	40	25	30	30
	10	50	45	50	25	20	50	100
	20	35	40	45	20	20	45	30
	30	25	75	40	20	35	40	50
	15	20	30	30	35	10	75	45
	40	40	40	25	25	50	50	40
Mean:	30.25	31.75	53.75	64.00	45.25	57.75	58.75	55.00
StdDev:	10.70	13.60	20.83	31.61	22.03	28.31	35.46	27.67

Population Mean: 49.56
Population StDv: 27.26

The three pieces of information needed to establish the confidence interval are (1) the selected significance value, (2) the standard deviation for the total sample, and (3) the total number of cases in the sample. These values must be inserted in the appropriate windows in the Excel™ Function Wizard *CONFIDENCE* test.

The Excel™ Confidence test produces a value that is exactly one-half of the confidence interval. The eight-week campaign period sample standard deviation of 27.26, the researcher specified alpha of .05, and a sample size of 160 together produce a confidence value of 4.22 (Table 15.2).

Table 15.2

Confidence Interval for Initiative-Campaign Donations

Confidence:	$4.22
Upper Limit:	$53.79
Lower Limit:	$45.34

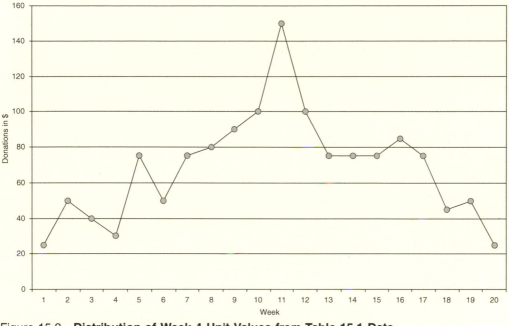

Figure 15.2   **Distribution of Week 4 Unit Values from Table 15.1 Data**

Thus, any mean falling within the range of $4.22 above the total sample mean and $4.22 below results in a rejection of the null hypothesis and acceptance of the alternative hypothesis. The mean for the total sample, $46.96, is the center value of the range of the means. The range of acceptable means extends from $45.34 to $53.79. When a sample mean falls outside this range, the alternate hypothesis is accepted. The mean value for Week 4 donations is $64.00; the standard deviation is 31.61. Clearly, $64 is larger than the upper limit, $53.79. Donations for Week 4 are significantly greater than the mean for the entire eight-week campaign period. Thus, the null is rejected for this sample. Figure 15.2 is a *line graph* of the twenty-donation sample for Week 4; Table 15.3 is a frequency distribution table of the donations classified by $15 increments. They are both included to illustrate how graphic elements can help in the interpretation and presentation of data.

Normal Distribution Tests

A key condition of many statistical tests is the requirement that the samples be drawn from a population with a normal distribution and normal variance. Therefore, one of the firsts tests carried out on a sample dataset is often a test for *normality*—that is, a test to see if the population parameter has a normal distribution. It is important to remember that this test should only be done with a probability sample, that is, one that meets requirements for random selection.

Researchers are often required to compute the area under a normal curve and/or to establish probabilities associated with the normal distribution. Microsoft® Excel's™ statistical analysis capabilities under the *Function Wizard* (f_x) include five functions that pertain to normal distributions. An illustration of the five tests and the purpose for each is displayed in Table 15.3.

The first of the five tests is the STANDARDIZE function, which computes standardized Z-

Table 15.3

Frequency Distribution of Contributions, 8-Week Period

Class	Frequency	Relative %	Cumulative %
0–15	5	3.13	3.13
16–30	46	28.75	31.88
31–45	43	26.88	58.75
46–60	24	15.00	73.75
61–75	22	13.75	87.50
76–90	3	1.88	89.38
91–105	14	8.75	98.13
106–120	0	0.00	98.13
120–135	1	0.63	98.75
136–150	2	1.25	100.00
More	0	0.00	0.00
Totals	160	100%	100%

Table 15.4

Normal-Distribution Tests in Microsoft® Excel™ 2000

Excel Test	Purpose
STANDARDIZE	Computes standardized Z-values for given raw scores
NORMSDIST	Computes the probability that an area under the curve is less than a given Z-value
NORMSINV (Opposite of the NORMSDIST test)	Computes a Z-value that corresponds to a given total area under the normal curve
NORMDIST	Computes the probability that an area under the normal curve is less than a given measurement value $(\bar{X})$
NORMINV	Computes the measurement value $(\bar{X})$ that corresponds to a given area under the normal curve.

Source: Excel™ 2000 HELP function.

values for given raw scores. The second function related to the normal distribution is the NORMSDIST test. This function computes the area under the curve (probability) that is less than a given Z-value. The third function, NORMSINV, computes a Z-value that corresponds to a given total area under the normal curve. This function is the opposite of the NORMSDIST function.

The fourth Excel™ normal distribution function, NORMDIST, computes the probability that an area is less than a given measurement value ($\bar{X}$). The last function in this family of tools is the NORMINV function. This function—the obverse of the NORMDIST function—computes the measurement value of X that corresponds to a given area under the normal curve.

In addition to these five specific normal-distribution-related tests, Excel™ also conducts one-tailed and two-tailed tests, one-sample t-tests, a two-tailed (only) Z-test, and a confidence interval test.

A "Normality" Test Using SPSS®

The popular social science statistical package SPSS® provides additional possibilities for dealing with questions that deal with distributions. For example, the *Explore* procedure in the descriptive statistics set of processes includes the following normal distribution-associated tests among its capabilities:

- Stem-and-leaf-diagrams
- Box plots
- The Levene test for normality
- A normal probability plot
- The Lilliefors test for normality
- The Shapiro-Wilks test for normality

The Lilliefors Normality Test provides a convenient way to test for the normality of a distribution. The results of an SPSS® *Explore* analysis of the data from Table 15.1 political campaign donation data are shown in Table 15.5.

The Lilliefors normality test produces results for two normalcy tests: the Kolmogorov-Smirnov (K-S) and the Shapiro-Wilks (S-W) test. The K-S test is used most often, although the S-W test results tend to be somewhat more accurate (Field 2000). Output for the two tests includes a test statistic, the degrees of freedom (which should be the same as the sample size),

Table 15.5

SPSS® Normalcy Test Results for Table 15.1 Data

Tests of Normality

	Kolmogorov-Smirnov Statistic	df	Sig.	Statistic Shapiro-Wilk	df	Sig.
WEEK1	.131	20	.200	.967	20	.693
WEEK2	.190	20	.056	.945	20	.296
WEEK3	.305	20	.000	.799	20	.001
WEEK4	.171	20	.127	.909	20	.061
WEEK5	.215	20	.016	.889	20	.026
WEEK6	.209	20	.022	.846	20	.005
WEEK7	.197	20	.040	.878	20	.016
WEEK8	.272	20	.000	.849	20	.005

[a]This is a lower bound of the true significance.
[b]Lilliefors significance correction.

and a significance level. If the significance value is .05 or greater, the null hypothesis (the distribution is not a normal distribution) must be rejected and the alternative hypothesis—the sample distribution is not different from a normal distribution—accepted. In the Week 4 example in Table 15.5, the significance is .127, which is larger than a *p*-value of .05.

In a sample drawn from a population with a normal distribution, both the sample statistic and the population parameter are expected to have the same variance. The Lilliefors test is based upon an evaluation of this assumption. Using the tools in *Explore,* the researcher first produces a normal probability plot. Probability plots provide only a visual indication of a normal distribution of variance. In a normal distribution individual values appear clustered on a straight line. A "detrended plot" shows the distribution of deviations around a horizontal line through zero. If the variances are not normal, the points will not cluster along the straight line, nor will they be randomly distributed around the zero line. Because they are only visual suggestions of the level of normalcy, the plots are not shown here.

Summary

This chapter dealt with the theory and procedures of hypothesis testing. Hypotheses are statements or predictions by someone that explain or suggest some conclusion, event, or thing. They are only suggestions or beliefs; they are not statements of truth.

Researchers deal with three main types of hypotheses: predictive hypotheses, comparative hypotheses, and association hypotheses. Hypotheses are usually stated as pairs: a hypothesis that is to be tested, and an alternative hypothesis, which is the obverse of the test hypothesis. In practice, most test hypotheses are stated in "null" form. That is, they refer to a status quo situation. The alternative hypothesis is stated in terms opposite from null hypotheses. When hypothesis tests are interpreted, they are said to be either *retained* or *accepted* if they are true, and *rejected* or *not accepted* if they are found to be false.

Two types of errors are associated with hypothesis tests—*Type I error* and *Type II error*. Type I errors occur when a null hypothesis that is actually true is rejected. Type II errors occur when a null hypothesis that is false is not rejected. In practice, hypothesis tests are often associated with confidence intervals for sample statistics. Normal distribution tests in Excel™ compute the area under a normal curve that falls below a test statistic. SPSS® includes several tests for normality; Excel™ does not.

Researchers often want to know what percentage of all possible samples would include the parameter for the population somewhere within the interval (range) of their statistic values. Since the *actual* parameter value is seldom known, an estimate for this number must be made. The sample statistic is substituted for the unknown parameter. The sample statistic usually used for this purpose is the sample mean. Microsoft® Excel's™ CONFIDENCE test function can quickly establish an estimate for the range of values above and below the hypothesized population mean.

Researchers are often required to compute the area under a normal curve and/or to establish probabilities associated with the normal distribution. Microsoft® Excel's™ includes five functions that pertain to normal distributions. The social science statistical package SPSS® provides additional possibilities for dealing with questions about distributions. For example, the *explore* procedure in the descriptive statistics set of processes also includes normal distribution-associated tests among its capabilities.

Discussion Questions

1. What are the three major purposes for which hypothesis tests are formulated?
2. What is the difference between a null hypothesis and an alternate hypothesis?
3. The chapter identified three classes of hypothesis tests. What are they?
4. What role does probability play in hypothesis testing?
5. What is a confidence interval?
6. Discuss the concepts of Type I and Type II error in hypothesis testing.
7. What are the different ways that researchers use one-sample hypothesis tests?
8. What are normal distribution tests?

Additional Reading

Berenson, Mark N., and David M. Levine. 1998. *Basic Business Statistics*. 6th ed. Upper Saddle River, NJ: Prentice-Hall.

Brightman, Harvey J. *Data Analysis in Plain English with Microsoft® Excel™*. 1999. Pacific Grove, CA: Duxbury Press.

Levine, David M., Mark N. Berenson, and David Stephan. 1997. *Statistics for Managers Using Microstoft® Excel™*. Upper Saddle River, NJ: Prentice-Hall.

Morrison, Denton E., and Ramon E. Henkel. 1970. "Significance Tests Reconsidered." In *The Significance Test Controversy: A Reader*. D. E. Morrison, and R. E. Henkel, eds. Chicago: Aldine Publishing. 182–98.

Neufeld, John L. 1997. *Learning Business Statistics with Microsoft® Excel™*. Upper Saddle River, NJ: Prentice-Hall.

16 Testing Hypotheses about Two or More Samples

In addition to the one-sample tests discussed in the last chapter, social scientists and statisticians have developed a body of statistical techniques designed to test hypotheses about two or more samples. As we have seen, hypotheses are used to test for differences and for relationships. Techniques for testing for differences permit political science researchers to apply experimental design methods in which they test whether the differences in mean scores for two or more samples are statistically significant or whether they could have occurred by chance. This chapter examines some of the statistical procedures used to test hypotheses about differences. The procedures discussed require parametric data; similar tests have been developed for use with nonparametric data. Those nonparametric techniques will be discussed in the next chapter.

Statistical procedures for two types of research situations are discussed here: small-sample tests for two groups, and large-sample tests for two or more than two groups. The two-groups tests are several versions of *t*-tests; tests for large samples or for more than two groups are *analysis of variance* (ANOVA) procedures. Two-groups tests are based upon the *t*-distribution, a special distribution that is shaped by the degrees of freedom with the dataset. These procedures are most appropriate with small samples—that is, when the total number of cases is thirty or less (Anderson, Sweeney, and Williams 2002). However, because the difference between the *t*-distribution and a normal distribution is made nearly insignificant as the number of degrees of freedom increases, this size limitation is typically ignored, and *t*-tests are often used for comparing the means of any-size samples. The three situations in which the *t*-test is applied include: (1) when the samples are paired, (2) when the samples come from a population or populations with equal variances, and (3) when the samples come from populations with unequal variances.

Political science researchers are highly likely to find themselves using one or more two-sample procedures very early in their research careers. The several tests for comparing differences are among the most commonly reported statistical results found in research literature. Techniques exist to test for differences with all levels of data.

Fundamentals of Two-Sample Hypothesis Tests

Several basic concepts underlie interpretations of two-sample hypothesis tests, and must be examined before moving ahead with applications instructions. The first is what is known as *degrees of freedom;* the second is the concept of significance and its associated *p*-value method of interpreting test results.

Degrees of Freedom

In statistics, the term "degrees of freedom" is used to refer to *the number of independent comparisons that can be taken between sets of data.* For example, if you have two observations, you are limited to just one independent comparison. Two observations require two independent measurements, such as from a sample of two individuals. If there are three observations, then there are three independent measurements, and so on. Degrees of freedom are computed differently depending upon whether the data are collected from the same individuals, as in a paired sample or a pretest and a posttest situation, or whether it is collected from different sets of individuals (two independent samples). Data collected from the same individuals at different times are called *correlated data.* Data collected from separate samples are called *uncorrelated data.* To determine the degrees of freedom for correlated data, one is subtracted from the total number of cases. In statistical notation, this is written as "$n - 1$" degrees of freedom, with n meaning the total number of observations. To compute the degrees of freedom for uncorrelated data, one is subtracted from each sample. The various *t*-tests contained in Excel™ include these different values in their computations; all the researcher needs to do is to select the correct option.

Looking at Test Results

The *t*-test procedures produce a value for *t* and a *p*-value for use in interpreting the results of the test. ANOVA procedures produce an *F*-ratio and a *p*-value (some software programs label the *p*-value the *significance* value, or *sig.* for short). In the past, the calculated *t* or *F* had to be compared with a table of values established for various sets of degrees of freedom and two researcher-elected levels of confidence (alphas). Today, however, hypothesis decisions are made on the basis of the *p*-values produced by the statistical software. Both of these sets of procedures require at least interval-level measurements.

Statistical Significance in Hypothesis Testing

Statistical significance is the term used to describe the point or value beyond which researchers accept or reject a null hypothesis. They are stated as probabilities and/or percentages. For example, the .05 level of confidence is the same as saying a 95 percent confidence level. Decisions on hypotheses are made in accordance with preselected levels of confidence, which are typically .01, .05, or .10; the .05 level of confidence is the most commonly applied level in all social sciences, including political science. In the past, to interpret the results of the test, the values of a calculated statistic had to be compared with a critical level for the statistic in a table of values found at the end of most statistics texts. The calculated value was found by following steps in a formula for mathematically computing the statistical test. Today, statistical software quickly computes the test statistic and provides a true probability value along with the results of the statistical tests. Hypothesis decisions are made on the basis of the calculated statistic and/or the probability or *p*-value. Using the probability value for interpretation of procedure results is called the p-*value approach.*

Significance and Importance Are Not the Same

It is important that significance levels not be confused with importance. The two concepts are not related in any way. Importance refers to the weight or values the decision maker places on the information received from a statistical study. Statistical significance is a product of a selected confidence level. Just because the result of a statistical test is found to be *statistically significant,* it does not automatically mean that it is socially, culturally, administratively, or even logically, important (Poister and Harris 1978). A result can be statistically significant and totally irrelevant or trivial at the same time. On the other hand, there are many times when a small difference has great practical importance. It is up to the researcher to make these determinations.

Interpreting Results with p-Values

Most social science researchers make hypothesis-acceptance decisions at the .05 level of confidence. However, the nature of the study and required level of confidence in the results often require that a level of .10 or of .01 be employed. The lower-case Greek letter *alpha* (α) is used to indicate the confidence value. When analysts use an alpha of .05, they are in fact saying that they are 95 percent sure about a hypothesis decision. This "95 percent" is called the *confidence coefficient.* Researchers are never 100 percent sure about a hypothesis decision; they can only accept or reject a null hypothesis or its alternate.

Two-Group Hypothesis Tests

As can be seen in Figure 16.1, an extensive body of statistical tools has been developed for testing hypotheses about statistics for two or more groups. These procedures are to be used with *parametric* statistics. Parametric statistical tests require the measurements to be at the equidistant-interval or ratio level. Parametric statistics also require that the data be from random samples and have a normal distribution. When these assumptions cannot be met, nonparametric tests must be used in place of parametric tests. In addition, some parametric tests require that the samples be independent from one another, while other tests have been developed for use with dependent or paired samples. Separate-but-related statistical tests have been developed to meet each independence requirement. Whether the samples are independent (as most are) or are dependent (as with samples that are paired), some minor differences will be found in the computational formulas, although their interpretation is identical. Finally, the *t*-tests and ANOVA procedures discussed here should be used only when the researcher has all the raw data (individual measurements) available; the tests should never be used with data that are already summarized.

Two of the statistical tests often used when comparing the mean values for independent

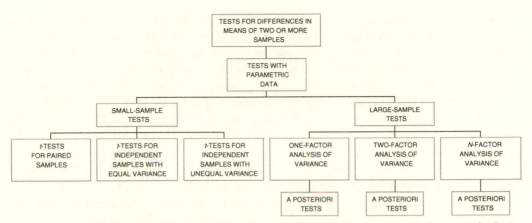

Figure 16.1   **A Schematic Display of Two-Sample Hypothesis Tests with Parametric Data**

samples are the *Student's t-test* for two samples, and the one-way, two-way, and *n*-way *analysis of variance* (ANOVA) tests. Although the *t*-test has more limitations than the *F*-test, it is well suited for comparisons between the means of two, but only two, relatively small samples (typically around thirty cases), and with each sample having the same or nearly the same number of observations or cases. ANOVA, on the other hand, is considered to be very robust. It can be used with two or more samples, large or small samples, and samples of unequal sizes. Whenever three or more samples are to be compared with ANOVA, a body of post hoc or a posteriori tests may also be employed to pinpoint the differences. Post hoc tests are not included in the basic set of procedures in Excel™. Instead, they must be calculated using mathematical procedures; they are not discussed here. More powerful statistical software, such as SPSSR, includes a wide variety of post hoc tests from which to select.

Comparing Two-Group Differences with the *t*-Test

The *t*-test is used to compare the means of two groups; variations of the test exist for use with paired samples, with samples with unequal variances, and with samples with approximately equal variances. The test might, for example, be used to compare scores from a group of voters tested prior to a political campaign information program. These scores might then be compared with scores for the same group after completion of the information program. In another use, the mean scores are compared on political attitudes for two groups of voters, with the groups determined by gender, age, income, political party, or ethnic group (two groups with assumed equal variances). Another application might be comparing attitudes about political parties held by university sophomores with the attitudes of juniors at the same university (two groups with unequal variances).

Minimum required assumptions for all applications *t*-test are: (1) the measurements are of at least interval-level data, (2) the samples are randomly selected, and (3) the scores are randomly distributed. Only two sets of means can be compared at any one time using the *t*-test. As in one-sample hypothesis testing, the first step must always be to establish a null and alternate hypothesis for testing.

The major differentiating characteristic is the nature of the two samples for which measurements are available: are they paired or independent? This question must be answered before selecting one of the several different *t*-test computational methods. The *tools* ⇒ *data analysis* feature in Excel™ includes three different *t*-test options: a test for paired samples and two tests for independent samples. The two independent sample tests vary in that one assumes the samples were taken from two separate populations, while the second test assumes two populations in which the variance is known to be either equal or unequal. Because researchers seldom, if ever, know the variance of a population, this usually means the researcher selects the unequal variance option. Regardless of which option is used, both samples should always be randomly selected from the population or populations. The unequal-variance option should be used when the samples are drawn from different populations. An example would be comparing the means of samples taken from two separate cities or different states.

All two-sample *t*-tests compare sample means by computing a Student's *t*-value, and comparing the significance of whatever difference is found between the calculated *t*-statistic and a critical *t*-statistic for the number of degrees of freedom in the dataset. Considered to be only slightly less "robust" than the *F*-test, the *t*-test is very easy to use and interpret and is, therefore, a popular tool for comparing the mean scores of two samples or groups.

A Paired-Sample Example

A typical example of a paired two-sample hypothesis test application is the standard pre- and posttest research design used in education, training, and public opinion measurements. Researchers use this design when they want to know if the differences between the first and second measurements are "real," or if they are simply chance-related variations encountered every time a new measurement is made. This type of design is often used during an experimental test of a "treatment," such as different instructional methods or different communications media.

In all these applications, the researchers are looking for differences that are *statistically significant*. A difference that is statistically significant is one with an acceptable level of probability that the differences did not occur through chance alone. It is important to remember that the analyst never knows if the differences are, indeed, "real." The procedure calls for accepting or rejecting a hypothesis with the possibility of making the wrong decision held to a level within some acceptable *level of confidence*. This means that the research must accept the possibility that the correct decision is made—that is, avoiding making a *Type I error*—90, 95, or 99 percent of the time.

Table 16.1 displays data from a paired-sample, pre- and posttest example. In this example, a political science researcher wanted to know if a white paper prepared by the staff of a state senator changed a sample of voters' attitudes toward a proposed change in funding for the state's portion of elementary school teachers' salaries. A group of community leaders completed a twenty-five-item opinion questionnaire, and were then asked to read the white paper. The group was administered the same opinion survey one week later. Scores for the pre- and posttest survey are displayed in Table 16.1. Table 16.2 displays the results of a Microsoft® Excel™ paired-sample *t*-test.

The researcher's null hypothesis for this study was that the mean of the group before reading the white paper was the same as the mean for the group after reading the white paper. An

Table 16.1

**Subject Attitude Scores before and after
Reading an Issue White Paper**

PRETEST SCORES (Variable 1)	POSTTEST SCORES (Variable 2)
20.7	19.3
21.7	23.9
17.2	19.9
18.0	24.0
15.1	17.7
21.1	21.5
24.5	25.9
17.8	19.1
23.6	24.4
19.0	19.9

Table 16.2

Excel™ Output of a Paired Two-Sample *t*-Test

t-Test: Paired Two Sample for Means

	Variable 1	Variable 2
Mean	19.87	21.56
Variance	8.8134	7.7671
Observations	10	10
Pearson Correlation	0.776726572	
Hypothesized Mean Difference	0	
df	9	
t Stat	−2.768013281	
P (T<=*t*) one-tail	0.010912144	
t Critical one-tail	1.833113856	
P (T<=*t*) two-tail	0.021824288	
t Critical two-tail	2.262158887	

alpha of .05 was selected as the test confidence level. In statistical notation, the null and alternate hypotheses for this example are:

$$H_O: \mu_{pre} = \mu_{post}$$
$$H_A: \mu_{pre} \neq \mu_{post}$$

Because no direction—neither greater nor lesser—in the change was specified, this was a two-tailed test. The important information in the Excel™ procedure results is included in the information displayed in Table 16.3.

Interpretations of the information in the above output include the following:

Table 16.3

Selected Information in Excel™ *t*-Test Output

	Pretest	Posttest
Mean	19.87	21.56
df	9	
t Stat	−2.768013281	
P(T<=*t*) two-tail	0.021824288	
t Critical two-tail	2.262158887	

- The mean for the presample was 19.87; after reading the white paper, the score increased to 21.56 for the postsample.
- The calculated *t*-statistic was −2.77, with 9 degrees of freedom.
- The critical *t*-statistic for 9 degrees of freedom was 2.26, which is less than the critical *t* of −2.77.
- Using this information alone, the null would be rejected and the alternate hypothesis accepted.
- The calculated *p*-value for the data was .022, which is less than the alpha of .05.
- Using the *p*-value approach, the null would also be rejected and the alternate hypothesis accepted.

The difference between *one-tailed* and *two-tailed* tests is that in one-tailed tests the researcher specifies the direction of the difference: the mean is either larger or smaller than the mean of the second group. The probabilities calculated with the *t*-test on a one-tailed test are half of the probabilities for a two-tailed test. It should be noted that deciding whether to select either the one- or two-tailed tests cannot be done arbitrarily. If the researcher has no specific reason to expect a difference in one direction, it follows that no prediction can be made in advance. The analyst is then obligated to use the two-tailed test. A typical two-tailed test hypothesis pair, to determine where the means are different in any way, would be:

$$H_o: \mu_1 = \mu_2$$
$$H_A: \mu_1 \neq \mu_2$$

If a one-tailed test is desired, either a greater or lesser hypothesis pair must be written; these would appear as follows:

μ_1 greater than μ_2	μ_1 lesser than μ_2
$H_o: \mu_1 \geq \mu_2$	$H_o: \mu_1 \leq \mu_2$
$H_A: \mu_1 < \mu_2$	$H_A: \mu_1 > \mu_2$

A Two-Sample, Unequal Variance Example

In the following example, a political scientist was interested in the percentages of voters who said they supported a bill to limit increases in property taxes to no more than 5 percent per

Table 16.4

**Percentages of Voters Supporting a
Tax-Limit Bill**

Urban Counties	Rural Counties
22.20	33.30
19.90	29.89
42.09	59.76
26.12	35.22
41.11	51.98
46.44	54.66
63.67	69.09
44.12	45.24
44.22	47.93
44.23	53.22
60.56	61.12
33.12	42.90
51.07	58.43
43.07	
43.55	

Table 16.5

**Excel™ Results of a *t*-Test on Urban/Rural Support of a Proposed
Tax-Limit Bill**

t-Test: Two-Sample Assuming Unequal Variances

	Urban Voters	Rural Voters
Mean	41.698	49.44153846
Variance	153.2067886	138.7881641
Observations	15	13
Hypothesized Mean Difference	0	
df	26	
t-Stat	−1.694229869	
P(T<=*t*) one-tail	0.051084648	
t Critical one-tail	1.705616341	
P(T<=*t*) two-tail	0.102169296	
t Critical two-tail	2.055530786	

year. Data were collected in 28 counties; 15 counties were considered to be predominately urban, while 13 counties were predominately rural. The results of the telephone survey are shown in Table 16.4.

A one-tailed *t*-test was conducted using Microsoft® Excel™ on the data to test the hypothesis that voters in rural counties were more likely to support a bill to limit increases in property taxes than were voters in urban counties. The results of that test procedure are shown in Table 16.5. The null and alternate hypotheses for this study problem can be written as follows:

$$H_O: \mu_1 \geqslant \mu_2$$
$$H_A: \mu_1 < \mu_2$$

The null hypothesis for this study was that rural voters are no more likely to support the tax-limit bill than are urban voters. The alternate or test statistic was the opposite of the null: rural voters are more likely to support limits on property taxes than are urban voters. Because this was a one-tailed test, the *p*-value for the one-tailed test is used for decisions on the hypotheses. The decision rule is: reject the null and accept the alternate hypothesis if the *p*-value for the one-tailed test is equal to or less than .05. The critical one-tailed *p*-value calculated by the procedure is .05, with a .05 level of confidence. Therefore, there is enough information to conclude with a 95 percent level of confidence that a statistically significant difference exists in the preferences reported in the survey. Therefore, the null hypothesis must be rejected and the alternate accepted.

Comparing Group Scores with ANOVA

The second set of tests for differences are based on differences in the variances in group means; these tests are conducted using *analysis of variance* (ANOVA). The two most commonly encountered versions of the test are *one-way ANOVA* and n-*way ANOVA*. The first version involves testing differences in a single factor; these differences can be tested with any number of groups during the same procedure. The second version tests differences in two or more factors across any number of groups. *Factors* are what are known in experimental design as *treatments*. Both versions of ANOVA involve analysis based on what is referred to as the *F-test*. The *F*-test is a ratio developed from calculating the value computed for the variances in means for each group, and the value calculated as an estimate of the variation caused by the measurements for individuals in the group.

ANOVA is typically the test used for comparing the differences in the variation between means of any number of groups, and of doing so at more than one factor level. With ANOVA, it is also possible to test the role of each of several variables independently, and then to determine whether two or more variables *interact* to influence any differences in groups' mean scores. In all applications, analysis of variance uses the *F*-statistic to compare the variances in each group's mean scores. The process compares the variance of each mean to the overall variance found in the sample. In statistical notation, the overall variance is referred to as "error," and relates to the distance from the mean for each individual case. A large "error" score infers that the scores are widely disbursed; a small "error" score means little variation in the set of scores.

To make group comparisons, ANOVA compares the means of two samples or two groups within a sample. The procedure produces summary statistics for each sample or group, an *F*-ratio (also called an *F*-statistic), and a probability value (called a *significance value* in some software's printed output). Interpretation of the results is a one-step process: The means are "statistically different" if the *p*-value is the same or less than the analyst-selected confidence level.

Interpretation becomes a little more complicated when more than two groups or levels are compared. The *p*-value of the *F*-ratio will indicate whether the null hypothesis is to be rejected, but it will not indicate where the differences lie. Another test, called an *a posteriori* test or a *post hoc* test, is required. When one of these is selected, actual differences will be indicated, while those that are statistically "the same" will be so indicated. None of these "after the fact" tests are available in Microsoft® Excel™, but are available in more powerful statistical packages such as SPSS®.

Three-Way ANOVA

Researchers have three different versions of ANOVA to choose from: a one-way or one-factor model, a two-factor model, and an "*n*-way" or three or more factor version. One-way ANOVA is the basic procedure; it is used when two or more group means are being compared across a single factor. For example, a political campaign manager might want to know if married female voters and unmarried female voters respond differently to an advertisement for a presidential candidate. The response variable must be at least interval-level; the grouping variable can be any-level data.

One-Way ANOVA

One-way ANOVA compares the variance on a scale variable across two or more categories of a single categorical variable. The groups of cases or subjects that make up each category are referred to as *subsamples* or *subgroups*. The categorical variable is called a *grouping variable*. Grouping variables are often demographic characteristics, such as gender, marital status, ethnic group, education level, occupation, or some similar social characteristic.

Three different ways of estimating variance are possible: (1) a total estimate of the variance of all cases, (2) a between-group estimate based on the variation of the subgroups' means around a "grand mean," which is nothing more than a mean of the means, and (3) a within-group estimate that is based on the variation of subgroup cases around their subgroup mean. ANOVA divides the between-group variance by the within-group variance to come up with a value that is called the F-ratio, or F-statistic. The total group variance model is not used in ANOVA.

When using one-way ANOVA to compare group means, the null hypothesis should be that the means of the subgroups are the same. This hypothesis can also be stated in the following ways: *the groups are equal, the groups are not different,* or *the two groups are from the same population.* The most common way of stating the null hypothesis is: There is no statistically significant difference in the means of the two (or more) groups. The alternate hypothesis is always the opposite of the null hypothesis.

Degrees of Freedom in One-Way ANOVA

The number of degrees of freedom affects estimates of population variance in ANOVA tests. A different F-distribution has been calculated for nearly every combination of degrees of freedom, and is included in the appendices of almost all statistics textbooks. Until the advent of powerful desktop computers, researchers were forced to manually calculate the three different variances and an F-ratio. This F-ratio was then compared with the appropriate statistic in the F-tables. Tabular F-values were available for both the .05 and .10 levels of confidence. Null-hypothesis decisions were based on these comparisons. Today, however, most statistical packages calculate an F-ratio and a significance value for every set of variables. Hence, it is no longer necessary to determine the number of degrees of freedom. Since they are identified for the researcher, it is still traditional to include the number of degrees of freedom in the results of ANOVA analysis.

When the researcher-selected alpha is .05, if the calculated significance value is the same or less than .05 the null is rejected; the group means are (statistically) different. When reporting the results of a *F*-test, researchers should report the value of the *F*-statistic, the degrees of freedom involved in the test, and the associated probability or significance value.

A One-Way ANOVA Example

The following example represents the method used for testing differences in the mean scores of two groups. A new office administrator was hired to manage the office of a U.S. congress-woman. Under the leadership of the former manager, staff morale had declined dramatically, the overall quality and quantity of the staff's work had dropped, customer service was ranked very poor by the visitors to the congresswoman's office, and staff absenteeism was becoming a major problem. Before making sweeping changes in the office, the new manager wanted to determine if supervisors, staff workers, and visitors to the congresswoman's office perceived the office climate in the same way. A 7-point composite organizational climate scale was administered to a random selection of 12 supervisors, 25 members of the staff, and 20 regular visitors to the office. Individual scores on the scale are shown in Table 16.6.

Table 16.6

Organizational Climate Scales Scores for Supervisors, Staff, and Visitors

Supervisors	Staff	Visitors
2.9	3.2	3.8
4.8	5.6	4.1
4.0	3.0	3.0
2.8	5.7	2.5
3.3	3.1	2.1
2.6	5.0	5.6
3.7	6.0	1.8
4.2	3.3	1.6
4.8	4.4	2.3
4.4	5.4	3.1
2.9	3.4	2.0
1.9	4.9	9.0
	4.1	1.9
	5.3	3.3
	6.0	2.3
	4.1	1.3
	5.0	4.1
	6.4	2.1
	6.7	3.2
	4.7	2.0
	5.0	
	3.5	
	3.9	
	2.9	
	5.1	

ANOVA: Single Factor

SUMMARY

Groups	Count	Sum	Mean	Variance
Supervisors	12	42.3	3.525	.8711
Staff	25	115.7	4.628	1.2813
Visitors	20	61.1	3.055	3.0658

ANOVA

Source of Variation	SS	df	MS	F	P-value	F crit
Between Groups	29.03795088	2	14.51897544	7.9530	**.00094**	3.1682
Within Groups	98.5824	54	1.8256			
Total	127.6203509	56				

Figure 16.2 Results of an Excel™ One-Factor ANOVA Test (*p*-value emphasis added)

The manager's null hypothesis was: "There is no difference in the way staff employees, office supervisors, and outside visitors rate the organization's climate." The alternate hypothesis was: "Supervisors, staff, and visitors have different views of the climate at this organization." To test this hypothesis, a one-way ANOVA procedure and a 95 percent confidence level was used to analyze the survey data. The results of that procedure are presented in Figure 16.2.

To interpret these results, refer to the *p*-value of .00094 printed along with the *F*-ratio of 7.9530. The large *F*-value alone would indicate that the difference in the three groups' means is statistically significant. This is supported by the very small *p*-value. In this case, the null hypothesis is rejected and the alternate hypothesis accepted; the groups do view the office climate differently. The *F*-test is always multidirectional, testing for differences in either direction; therefore, it is always a two-tailed test.

Two-Way ANOVA

Two-way ANOVA designs are the simplest example of a class of statistical tests developed for what are called *factorial experiments* or *factorial designs*. In all such cases, the goal of ANOVA is to test the means of two or more groups on two or more variables or factors at the same time. In addition, the procedure tests to see if two or more of the variables working together may have had an impact on the differences; this is what is known as the *interaction effect*.

In the following example of a two-factor ANOVA procedure, an advertising manager for a mayoral candidate wanted to establish which was the best day of the week to advertise in the city newspaper, and in which section of the paper the ad should appear. The two factors are *day* and *position*. Four levels of the day variable were selected: Wednesday, Thursday, Friday, and Saturday. In the language of experimental design, these four days are referred to as *four levels of treatment*.

Three positions within the newspaper were also a part of the test design: general news (the first two sections of the paper), the sports section, and the family section (which includes the entertainment pages). These are the levels of the treatment variable *position*. Measurements to be compared are daily readership totals, as reported by the newspaper's circulation manager. To avoid the results bias that just one measurement might create, readership figures were collected from four randomly selected weeks. In setting up the experiment, *day* was to be the manager's grouping variable, and was represented by row data in the data setup. *Position* treatments were

Table 16.7

Daily Readership by Position and Day of the Week

	Readership by Day of the Week (000s)			
Position	Wednesday	Thursday	Friday	Saturday
1	933	979	1,240	1,610
1	1,004	1,112	1,299	1,020
1	933	1,003	1,353	1,003
1	979	980	1,222	1,900
2	1,217	1,172	1,175	1,945
2	1,171	1,034	1,371	1,837
2	1,178	1,011	1,421	1,958
2	1,230	1,021	1,314	1,851
3	1,021	1,871	1,889	1,835
3	1,015	1,735	1,948	1,631
3	1,041	1,642	1,872	1,500
3	995	1,675	1,919	1,720

represented in columns. Table 16.7 displays the two factors and readership totals; Figure 16.3 displays the results of an Excel™ two-factor ANOVA with replication procedure. There are three treatment levels for the *position* variable and four samples drawn for each treatment level. Each sample consists of four measurements for each of the four levels of the *day* factor. Therefore, it was necessary to record forty-eight separate observations.

ANOVA compares the mean of the four levels of each of the three positions of the four days in each position. This procedure computes an *F*-statistic with *p*-values and *critical F* values for each of the three positions, the four days (labeled as "columns" in the ANOVA summary table), and an *F*-statistic with *p*-values and critical *F*-values for the entire sample.

Interpreting Two-Factor ANOVA Results

There are three sets of values to interpret in the ANOVA results produced in this Excel™ application; all results are included in the last block of numbers near the bottom of Figure 16.3, and headed by the label "Source of Variation." The first null hypothesis was that newspaper readership is the same for all four days. These are the three groups in the table; each includes four iterations of sales results. The first result in the ANOVA output addresses this null hypothesis, and is presented in the row labeled "Sample."

The first level of the interpretation of this test is presented in the row labeled "Sample." The null hypothesis for this portion of the study was: readership is the same in each of the three sections of the newspaper on each of the four days of the week. This *F* statistic is the first in the ANOVA table, and is labeled "Sample." The calculated *F* of 32.672 is much larger than the critical *F* of 3.259; the *p*-value for this portion of the test is .0000. Therefore, the null hypothesis must be rejected. There is a difference in readership by section. But where did the differences occur? To make this determination, a closer examination of the table is necessary. Average readership for the general news section for the four four-day samples was 1,160.6 million; average readership for the sports section was 1,369.1 million; and average readership

ANOVA: Two-Factor With Replication

SUMMARY	WEDNESDAY	THURSDAY	FRIDAY	SATURDAY	Total
GENERAL NEWS (1)					
Count	4	4	4	4	16
Sum	3849	4074	5114	5533	18570
Average	962.25	1018.5	1278.5	1383.25	1160.625
Variance	1244.916667	4008.333333	3548.333333	198328.9167	74228.38333
SPORTS (2)					
Count	4	4	4	4	16
Sum	4796	4238	5281	7591	21906
Average	1199	1059.5	1320.25	1897.75	1369.125
Variance	836.6666667	5713.666667	11287.58333	3912.916667	112788.3833
FAMILY (3)					
Count	4	4	4	4	16
Sum	4072	6923	7628	6686	25309
Average	1018	1730.75	1907	1671.5	1581.8125
Variance	358.6666667	10224.25	1124.666667	20045.66667	127379.3625
Total					
Count	12	12	12	12	
Sum	12717	15235	18023	19810	
Average	1059.75	1269.583333	1501.916667	1650.833333	
Variance	11807.29545	121749.9015	94174.81061	108985.9697	

ANOVA

Source of Variation	SS	df	MS	F	P-value	F crit
Sample	1419238.042	2	709619.0208	32.67190463	0.000000008	3.25944427
Columns	2431282.229	3	810427.4097	37.31327129	0.000000000	2.866265447
Interaction	1502755.958	6	250459.3264	11.53151619	0.000000360	2.363748308
Within	781903.75	36	21719.54861			
Total	6135179.979	47				

Figure 16.3   Excel™ ANOVA Results for Two-Factor Readership Study

for the family section was 1,581.8 million. This difference was statistically significant; the campaign manager would be advised to place the advertisement in the family section, all other things being equal.

The second step of the ANOVA table that must be interpreted is the day variable—the "Columns" section of the table. The section just above the "Source of Variation" portion of the Excel™ output contains summary data for each of the four days. Average readership was nearly 1,060,000 on Wednesdays, nearly 1,270,000 on Thursdays, close to 1,502,000 on Fridays, and nearly 1,650,800 on Saturdays. The calculated F-statistic of 37.313 with a *p*-value of .0000 indicates that these differences were statistically significant. However, considering the lack of a post hoc test, the location of the difference(s) is somewhat difficult to determine. Readership on Wednesdays and Thursdays seems close enough to be considered the same; readership on Fridays and Saturdays is also close enough to be considered the same. Therefore, the campaign manager could feel safe that an advertisement placed on either Friday or Saturday would produce similar results.

The final test result in the table is the "Interaction" line in the ANOVA table. This *F*-test was also statistically significant; the day and position variables work together to influence final readership figures. The "Interaction" *F*-statistic of 11.532 and *p*-value of .0000 calls for rejecting the null hypothesis, which was stated as: *no interaction is present.* The results of these three tests can be interpreted in two ways: the first is the traditional critical and calculated critical and calculated *F*-ratio approach; the second is the *p*-value approach.

Three-Way ANOVA and More

The three-way ANOVA design is very much like two-way ANOVA. The principal effects of each factor are examined to see if it makes a difference between groups. This is followed by tests for interactions among the variables. However, now these interactions are expanded; two-way interactions, three-way interactions, and more are also evaluated. The results are interpreted in the same way as one-and two-way analyses.

Designs have been developed to test the impact on differences for more than two sets of groups at the same time. These tests compare all factors against each grouping variable at time, then test for interaction, and then test for combinations of groups. These are known as *multivariate ANOVA* designs; refer to a text on multivariate analysis techniques for more information.

Summary

This chapter has looked at some of the ways political science researchers test for differences in datasets. Differences tests are among the statistical tools used most often by political science researchers, along with correlation and regression analysis procedures. Two sets of procedures for testing differences between the means of groups were discussed in this chapter: First, *t*-test applications for two-sample tests were explained. Then, analysis of variance (ANOVA) procedures for testing differences with two or more groups were examined.

The paired-sample *t*-test in Microsoft® Excel™ compares the means for two related groups, as in a pretest and posttest research design. The procedure then reports both the calculated and critical *t*-statistic for the means, and calculates a *p*-value for the *t*-statistic. Results for both a one-tailed and a two-tailed test are produced. In addition to the procedure for comparing paired samples, Excel™ includes a similar procedure for testing independent samples; independent samples may be from one population with equal variance or from different samples with unequal variance.

Typically, *t*-tests are used with smaller sample sizes (around a total of thirty cases), and they should be used with groups that are equal in size. In addition, *t*-tests can only be used to compare the means of two groups at a time.

ANOVA (which is based upon the *F*-test) is used for samples of any size and with any number of groups or subgroups. Three different levels of ANOVA tests were also discussed:

one-factor, two-factor, and three- or more factor designs. All ANOVA procedures produce a calculated and a critical F-statistic and a p-value that can be used for quick interpretation of the test results.

Discussion Questions

1. What role does degrees of freedom play in interpreting hypothesis tests?
2. What is meant by statistical significance?
3. Are significance and importance the same? Why or why not?
4. What are the different ways that the t-test can be used to compare the means of two groups?
5. When must analysis of variance (ANOVA) be used instead of the t-test? Why?
6. What is one-way ANOVA? What is n-way ANOVA?

Additional Reading

Brightman, Harvey J. 1999. *Data Analysis in Plain English with Microsoft® Excel™*. Pacific Grove, CA: Duxbury Press.

Johnson, Richard A., and Dean W. Wickern. 1988. *Applied Multivariate Statistical Analysis*. 2nd ed. Englewood Cliffs, NJ: Prentice-Hall.

Krzanowski, W.J. 1988. *Principles of Multivariate Analysis: A User's Perspective*. Oxford: Oxford University Press.

Levine, David M., Mark L. Berenson, and David Stephan. 1997. *Statistics for Managers Using Microsoft® Excel™*. Upper Saddle River, NJ: Prentice-Hall.

17 Introduction to Nonparametric Statistics

Quantitative research results may be grouped into two broad classes of measurements: *parametric* and *nonparametric* statistics. Parametric statistics are measurements about samples and populations. Sample measurements are called *statistics;* population measurements are called *parameters.* Most quantitative political researchers work with parametric statistics. Parametric statistics are also called *inferential* statistics because the statistical results are *inferred* to apply to a population from which the sample or samples were drawn.

Measurement data can be either *continuous* or *discrete.* The measurements in inferential statistics are almost always from variables that produce *continuous* measurements. Continuous variables can have many different possible values; they are not restricted to a specific number of categories as are categorical variables. An example of a continuous variable is a test score. An example of a categorical variable is the answer to a yes-or-no question. Because only two answers are possible, this type of categorical variable is sometimes called a *dichotomous* variable. Another common form of a categorical variable is the multiple-choice question. Multiple-choice questions usually have from three to five possible answers, but are not limited to any number of categories. Multiple-choice questions are also known as *multichotomous* variables. Because categorical statistics cannot be used for inferential purposes, they are known collectively as *nonparametric statistics.* Categorical data may be either *nominal- or ordinal-level* measurements (Lehmkuhl 1996).

A large collection of nonparametric statistical tests have been developed for use with *categorical* variables. In fact, Lapin (1993, 605) considered the many choices to be one of the major disadvantages of the body of nonparametric test: there are almost too many from which to choose. It is hard to be sure that exactly the best test has been chosen for the dataset being investigated. Nonparametric statistics use *rank* and *frequency* distribution information (Lehmkuhl 1996). Means are not appropriate for these data. Instead, measures of central tendency are likely to be either the median or the mode.

Parametric statistics must meet several basic assumptions. These are: (1) the samples must be randomly selected, (2) the data are assumed to come from samples with equal variances, (3) the distribution of responses must be normally distributed, and (4) the samples are assumed to be independent from one another. Another assumption often cited is that researchers must be able to replicate the results with other studies. Except for a few examples, parametric measurements must be *interval-* or *ratio-level* data; they use *mean* scores in their computations.

These required assumptions cannot always be met. Distributions are often not normal; they may be all gathered around one value or the other, becoming what is known as "positively or negatively skewed." They may be bipolar, or evenly distributed across all possible scores. When only two answers are possible, it is meaningless to talk about a "normal distribution" or a "bell-shaped curve." In addition, researchers often draw samples from two or more very different populations. Therefore, no assumptions can be made about the population parameters. When this happens, there is no way of assuring that the samples have equal variances. In these cases, nonparametric statistics may be more appropriate for analyzing research results.

Parametric statistics are typically used for making inferences about some population parameter or parameters. With nonparametric statistics, however, the assumption of a normal distribution does not apply; that is, nonparametric statistics are those that are considered to be "distribution free." In a dichotomous variable, for example, the distribution can only be binomial (have only two answers); this is the same type of data developed by flipping a coin.

Because nonparametric statistics do not require the assumptions necessary for parametric statistics, one might wonder why they are not always used. In fact, nonparametric statistical tests *can* be used with higher levels of data. They are not done so because they typically provide less information than parametric statistics. They are sometimes described as being "less powerful" or "not as robust" as parametric tests. However, these accusations are not really relevant; there are times when nonparametric statistics are the only appropriate choice. Lehmkuhl summarized the position of when parametric statistics should and should not be used in the following way:

> Nonparametric tests should not be substituted for parametric tests when parametric tests are more appropriate. Nonparametric tests should be used when the assumptions of parametric tests cannot be met, when very small numbers of data are used, and when no basis exists for assuming certain types of shapes of distributions. (Lehmkuhl 1996, 106)

Thus, nonparametric statistics are entirely appropriate for use when the researcher cannot make any assumptions about distributions, when the sample size is small (less than 100), and measurements are nominal or ordinal level. Such applications occur when the data are categorical (nominal level) or ranked or ordered (ordinal level). An illustration of a manifestly appropriate application of a nonparametric statistical test is the chi-square based *Cramer's V*-test for relationships between nominal-level variables. This statistic, with its table-shape variant the *phi* statistic, provides an index of the strength of a relationship, although it does not tell the direction of that relationship. While nonparametric tests for differences will provide information about differences in measurements between two or more groups, they are unable to include information about possible *interaction* between two or more influencing variables.

Nonparametric Analogs of Parametric Statistics

At least one nonparametric equivalent test exists for each type of basic parametric statistical test (StatSoft 2002). Table 17.1 displays a variety of the available nonparametric and parametric tests. This chapter discusses some of the most commonly used nonparametric statistical tests in each of four general categories of statistical analysis:

- Tests for location.
- Tests for statistically significant differences between groups (independent samples).

Table 17.1

Selected Nonparametric Analogs to Parametric Statistical Tests

Test Type	Nonparametric Analog	Parametric Tests
Tests for Location	Chi-square one-sample tests	*t-test* for small samples
	Kolmogorov-Smirnov one-sample test	*z-test* for samples of 30 or more
Differences tests with independent samples	Mann-Whitney *U*-test	*t-test* for independent samples
	Kolmogorov-Smirnov two-sample test	*F*-test of variance (ANOVA)
	Kruskal-Wallis *H*-test	
	Kruskal-Wallis ANOVA	
Differences tests with dependent samples	Friedman's two-way analysis-of-variance test	*t-test* for dependent [paired] samples
	McNemar's chi-square test	ANOVA
Tests for association between two or more variables	Spearman's *R, X², phi,* and Cramer's *V*	Pearson's correlation coefficient

- Tests for differences between variables (dependent samples).
- Tests for associations between variables.

Only some of the nonparametric tests listed above are included in Microsoft® Excel™. However, provision for the majority of the nonparametric relationship and differences tests are included in the more comprehensive and powerful statistical software package SPSS®. For additional information, a standard statistical methods textbook should be consulted. One or more nonparametric procedures for tests of *location,* for *differences,* and for *association* are discussed in the following pages.

Nonparametric Tests for Location

Tests of location are designed to determine whether a sample or samples could have come from a known population (Siegel 1956). The procedure is to compare a sample's measurement of central tendency with a known or hypothesized parameter. When the researcher is dealing with parametric data, the one-sample *t*-test or *Z*-test is the preferred procedure. The *t*-test is used to compare a sample mean with a hypothesized population mean; the *Z*-test is used with large samples, and the unknown population standard is replaced by the sample standard deviation. In both these applications the scores are assumed to have come from a population where the distribution is normal. Because both tests compare means, the data must be either interval or ratio. When these assumptions cannot be met, the nonparametric chi-square test of location may be substituted for the *t*-test or the *Z*-test.

Both one-sample and two-sample models nonparametric tests of location compare actual with expected distributions. In the one-sample test, the researcher draws a sample and then attempts to determine if there is any significant difference in the location (central tendency) between the sample and the population. Because the data are nominal or ordinal, the central tendency measurement in these tests is usually the median. In a two- (or more) sample test, the researcher wants to know if there is a statistically significant difference between the actual (observed) distribution of responses and an expected distribution. Modified versions of the chi-square test are appropriate for one-, two-, and three- or more sample situations.

Tests based on the chi-square statistic (X^2) are extremely versatile statistical tools. (Greek letters are used throughout statistics and mathematics; in English, the Greek letter X is written as "chi," and pronounced "ki." Because the final statistic is squared, the test and distribution are called *chi-square,* and written as X^2.) Chi-square has important applications with both parametric and nonparametric statistical tests. The statistic is based on the X^2 distribution, which was originally developed for use with small samples where the assumptions of normality could not be upheld. Small-sample results, simply because of the limited number of responses available, seldom resemble a normal distribution, for example. The one-sample location test is just one of many tests based on the X^2 distribution. Several other X^2-based nonparametric tests are discussed below. This simple-to-use and easy-to-understand test has become a popular one-sample test for making decisions about the distribution of responses in one-sample situations. The inclusion of this test in the majority of statistical software packages has increased its popularity such that it has replaced many other tests, such as the *one-sample sign test,* in many empirical research applications. Although it is used with all types of measurements, the test is particularly at home with all types of categorical measurements.

One-Sample Nonparametric Tests

Of the many statistical tests that are available for testing hypotheses about a single sample, two of the most popular are the chi-square test for use with nominal data and the Kolmogorov-Smirnov one-sample test for ordinal data. One-sample tests are conducted to test hypotheses that the sample in question came from an identified population. One-sample tests use a goodness-of-fit model, in which they test for a disproportionate or unexpected distribution of scores across the various categories of a variable.

The One-Sample Chi-Square Test

The X^2 one-sample test should be used when a researcher has questions about the distribution of responses in data taken from a sample. Specifically, the research has questions about the distribution of responses that fall into the spread of possible responses. For example, say that the county clerk of a rural county in a Western state has reported that for the past decade, the number of registered voters in the county has remained stable. County records reveal that 45 percent are registered Democrats, 38 percent are Republican, 12 percent are Independent, and 5 percent are members of the Socialist Labor Party (Table 17.2). In these types of applications, the one-sample test is similar to the *goodness-of-fit test* because it compares the set of *observed* cases against an *expected* distribution (Siegel 1956). The null hypothesis for this test is that the proportion of cases that make up a sample of county voters will not differ from the known distribution. The alternate hypothesis is that the distribution does not mirror the expected distribution of responses.

The Excel™ chi-square test (CHITEST) in the *Function Wizard* looks at differences within the sample, computes a chi-square distribution, and compares the actual distribution of responses with the expected distribution. The only required assumptions for the X^2 test are: (1) the sample is randomly selected, and (2) each observation must fit into one and only one class.

Table 17.2

Distribution of Registered Voters in a Population and a Sample

Party Affiliation:	Number of Registered Voters (n = 131,687)	Expected Percentage	Number in Sample (n = 250)	Observed Percentage
Democrat	59,260	45	128	51
Republican	50,041	38	80	32
Independent	15,802	12	37	15
Socialist Labor	6,584	5	5	2
Totals:	131,687	100.0%	250	100.0%

Source: Example data.

CHITEST only returns the two-tailed *probability* for a X^2 statistic with the appropriate degrees of freedom (rows $-$ 1); it does not return a calculated chi-square value. The syntax for this simple test is: CHITEST = (actual range, expected range). For the data in Table 17.2, the test returned the probability of 0.2311 that the actual proportion of voters in the four categories is representative of the known population parameter distribution. As with the parametric tests discussed earlier, decisions regarding nonparametric hypotheses are made based on the size of the p-value. If the researcher elects to use a 0.05 confidence level for the test, the null hypothesis cannot be rejected; the computed p-value of 0.2311 is greater than 0.05. The research must conclude that the sample is not representative of the population.

The Logic Behind the Chi-Square Test of Location

In the following one-sample example, a media buyer planning a political advertising campaign in a given state or community wants to know which Wednesday and Thursday evening prime-time television programs are preferred by a target audience of adult registered voters. The media buyer will use this information to place advertisements for her candidate. Data are gathered from a sample of 200 subjects. Local advertising can be purchased on eight programs over the two evenings. The variable of interests is *preferred television program*. The null hypothesis is that the distribution of preferred programs is equal; no one program is preferred above any other program. The data are *categorical* (preferred, not preferred). The data are presented in Table 17.3. The number of *expected* cases was determined by dividing the total number of cases by the number of classes or categories (100/8 = 12.5); degrees-of-freedom refers to the number of categories (rows) minus 1 (8 $-$ 1 = 7). Table 17.4 displays the information and steps needed to calculate a chi-square value.

Using the chi-square distribution (CHIDIST) capability in the Excel™ *Function Wizard,* a one-tailed p-value of 0.0853 is found for the distribution of 12.5 observed cases per cell and 7 ($n - 1$) degrees of freedom. Since this is a two-tailed test, the one-tailed probability of 0.0853 must be doubled, for a final value of 0.1706. The null hypothesis cannot be rejected; the distribution of responses is statistically disproportionate. The null hypothesis for both a

Table 17.3

Frequencies for Wednesday-Thursday Preferred Television Programs

Program Type	Program Code	Observed Cases	Percent	Expected Cases
Situation Comedy	1	22	12.5	25
Medical Drama	2	28	12.5	25
News Magazine	3	14	12.5	25
Sports Show	4	30	12.5	25
Variety Musical	5	22	12.5	25
Slice-of-Life	6	30	12.5	25
Ethnic Comedy	7	26	12.5	25
Childrens' Omnibus	8	28	12.5	25
Totals		200	100.0%	200

Table 17.4

Calculations for Determination of a Chi-Square Test

Code	Actual Count (A)	Actual Percent	Expected Count (B)	Expected Percent	Actual minus Expected (A-B)	(A-B)/25
1	22	0.110	25	0.125	−3	0.36
2	35	0.175	25	0.125	10	4
3	28	0.140	25	0.125	3	0.36
4	18	0.090	25	0.125	−7	1.96
5	32	0.160	25	0.125	7	1.96
6	25	0.125	25	0.125	0	0
7	21	0.105	25	0.125	−4	0.64
8	19	0.095	25	0.125	−6	1.44
	200	1.00	200	1.00	0	10.72
					X^2 (table)	14.067

Source: Sample data from Table 17.3.
Computed chi-square = 10.72
Degrees of freedom $(r - 1) = 7$
Table X^2 value = 14.067

one-tailed and a two-tailed test would be rejected at the 0.05 level of confidence. The alternate hypothesis is retained (or accepted) for both.

The K-S One-Sample Test for Ordinal Data

The Kolmogorov-Smirnov (K-S) one-sample test for ordinal-level data is different in concept than the nominal-data (Chi-square) test for location. Instead of comparing a sample median with a population median, the K-S test compares the distribution of a sample dataset with a theoretical *expected distribution*. The K-S test is used when the researcher wants to determine whether the sample rankings can be assumed to be from a population theoretically with the same rankings.

The K-S one-sample test tests for differences among the rankings of classes within one sample. The only two assumptions that must be met are: (1) that the data are at least ordinal-level (rankings), and (2) they are from a randomly selected sample. A null hypothesis for this test is that there is no difference in the way groups in the sample have ranked a given set of objects. Therefore, the K-S one-sample test may be said to be a test that follows the *goodness-of-fit* model (Siegel 1956).

The K-S test is included in the SPSS® Nonparametric Tests group, listed as "1-sample K-S." The test computes a mean rank for each group, a Z-score, and a two-tailed probability. It requires selection of a test distribution (either normal, uniform, or Poisson). In almost all cases (unless the manager knows specifically that another distribution is present), the normal distribution option is selected even though this a distribution-free test. The test results are interpreted by comparing the two-tailed probability value with the desired confidence level; *p*-values equal to or greater than the chosen alpha result in retaining the null hypotheses.

Nonparametric Tests for Differences

A number of nonparametric statistical tests have been developed to measure the significance of differences in variables that are measured in either nominal- or ordinal-level data. Table 17.5 displays a small sample of the better-known nonparametric differences tests between more than one group. The table lists dependent and independent group nonparametric tests that have been developed for two-, and more-than-two samples comparisons.

Not all of the differences tests identified in Table 17.5 are regularly used in standard political science research situations. The following discussion looks at only those tests that might be seen in political science, administrative science, and public administration journals, and which are easy to employ and interpret. The following two-sample tests are discussed first: the K-S Z-test for nominal data, and the Mann-Whitney (M-W) *U*-test for ordinal data. For three or more samples the following procedures are discussed: the Kruskal-Wallis *H*-test for nominal data, and the Kruskal-Wallis one-way ANOVA procedure for ordinal data.

Table 17.5

A Partial List of Nonparametric Tests for Statistically Significant Differences

	Independent Samples		Related Samples	
	2-Sample Tests	3+-Sample Tests	2-Sample Tests	3+-Sample Tests
NOMINAL DATA:	Kolmogorov-Smirnov Test	X^2 Test for Independent Samples	McNemar Test	Cochran's *Q*-Test
ORDINAL DATA:	Mann-Whitney *U*-Test	Kruskal-Wallis One-way ANOVA	Wilcoxon Rank Sum Test	Friedman Analysis-of-Variance Test

Source: After Siegel 1956.

Two Independent-Sample Tests

SPSS® includes four two-independent-sample test procedures in its powerful *Nonparametric Tests* subprogram. Two of these independent sample tests are often used in organizational research, including studies in political science and public administration. They are the *K-S Z*-test (K-S), which is used with categorical (nominal-level) data, and *the M-W U*-test, which should be used with ordinal-level data.

The nominal-data K-S Z-test compares the observed distributions counts of numeric variables across categories for two samples or groups. A Z-value and a two-tailed probability value are produced. The test results are interpreted by comparing the *p*-value with the desired confidence level (either .01, .05, or .10). The only required assumption is that the samples are randomly selected.

The Mann-Whitney *U*-test ranks all responses to an ordinal-level variable and computes a *U*-score and its significance level, which is used for interpreting the results of this test. It tests the hypothesis that two independent samples come from populations having the same distribution. The Mann Whitney *U*-test requires that the samples are randomly selected and that data are ordinal-level. The U-test converts the observed data to ranks and compares the differences.

In the following example, suppose that a state elections board is evaluating the effectiveness of two different vote-recording systems. One, the existing system, is a manual process that requires voters to use a small metal stylus to punch out partially perforated windows in card-like ballots. The finished ballots are then counted at the end of the day by equipment resembling old IBM punch-card readers.

The second system is an electronic touch-screen that allows voters to record their votes, erase or change any mistakes, and electronically counts all ballots as they are completed. A random sample of thirty voters is selected to test both systems, with the time to complete the voting in seconds recorded for each voter. Half of the sample is randomly assigned to the existing system (the *control group*), and half is randomly assigned to the new electronic system (the *experimental group*). The time (in seconds) for each sample member to complete the voting process is shown in Table 17.6.

Two Related-Sample Nonparametric Tests

In political science research, nearly all of the applications of differences tests involve independent samples. Tests with related samples are used primarily in laboratory-based experimental research. The setups and test results for dependent sample tests are nearly identical to those of independent tests. In the SPSS® Nonparametric Tests statistical program, for example, four types of related-sample tests are grouped under the "two-related-samples tests" set of procedures. Two of these tests for related samples are the McNemar test for dichotomous (nominal) data, and the Wilcoxon rank sum test for ordinal data. McNemar's test is designed to test hypotheses about pairs of variables, such as spouses or in before-and-after designs. Norušis (2000, 344) defined the McNemar procedure as one that "tests whether the two possible combinations of unlike values for the variables are likely." In a before-and-after experiment, subjects are tested before a treatment, such as being exposed to a communication, and again after the treatment.

The Wilcoxon rank sum test performs a similar function for data at the ordinal level, but data do not have to be dichotomous. The test computes differences between pairs of variables,

Table 17.6

Time (in seconds) and Rank Order for Two Voting Procedures

	Control Group		Experimental Group	
Sample No.	Time (in seconds)	Rank Order	Time (in seconds)	Rank Order
1	217	20	239	22
2	256	24	198	12
3	285	27	201	14
4	192	10	204	15
5	191	9	187	7
6	175	2	162	1
7	268	26	211	18
8	261	25	213	19
9	380	30	183	6
10	292	28	176	3
11	189	8	207	16
12	210	17	182	5
13	244	23	177	4
14	220	21	200	13
15	360	29	195	11

ranks the differences, and computes a Z-statistic and a significance level for interpretation. The null hypothesis for this test is there is no difference in the way the related samples ranked the variables. It is interpreted using the *p*-value approach.

Three or More Independent Sample Tests

Nonparametric tests are also available to test for differences in more than two independent samples. When three or more independent samples are involved and the data are categorical, a choice of three-sample tests are included in the SPSS® Tests for Several Independent Samples capability (called *k Independent Samples* in the dialog box menu).

The X^2 k-Independent-Samples and Fisher's Exact Probability Tests

The k-sample X^2 test for three or more independent samples compares the medians of three or more independent samples, computes a chi-square and a significance value (*p*-value). This test is included in the SPSS® crosstabs procedure in the Descriptives Statistics section, and has been described thus:

> When frequencies in discrete categories constitute the data of research, the X^2 test may be used to determine the significance of the differences among [3 or more] independent groups. The X^2 test for *k* independent samples is a straightforward extension of the X^2 test for two independent samples. . . . In general, the test is the same for both two and *k* independent samples. (Siegel 1956, 175)

Table 17.7

Data Distribution for a Survey of Attitudes Regarding Cuba

Subject	15–29 years of age	30–44 years of age	45–59 years of age	60 years of age or older
1	1	1	2	2
2	1	2	2	1
3	2	1	2	1
4	2	1	2	2
5	1	2	1	2
6	1	1	2	2
7	1	1	2	2
8	2	2	2	2
9	1	1		2
10		2		

Key: 1 = Yes; 2 = No

Table 17.8

Age Group Membership: Should the United States Normalize Relations?

		Should US normalize?		
		Yes	No	Total
Age group:	15–29	6	3	9
	30–44	6	4	10
	45–59	1	7	8
	60 or older	2	7	9
Total		15	21	36

In the following example, a researcher is interested in determining whether Cuban-Americans of different ages support or do not support normalizing relations with Cuba. The researcher identified four age-group categories, 15 to 29 years, 30 to 44 years, 45 to 59 years, and 60 years and older. Subjects were asked to answer either *Yes* or *No* to the question "Should the United States normalize diplomatic relations with Cuba as long as Castro still leads the country?" Subjects were surveyed at random on a street in a Cuban-American community in Miami, Florida. The data from a small-sample attitude survey are shown in Table 17.7 Table 17.8 is a crosstabulation table produced by the SPSS® descriptive statistics procedure. Table 17.9 displays a table of the results of the chi-square test.

Two results of interest are presented in Table 17.9. One is the result of the X^2 test. The calculated X^2 value is 7.897, with 3 degrees of freedom (rows-1). A two-tailed probability of 0.048 indicates that at the .05 level of confidence the hypothesis that the age groups are not from the same population must be rejected.

Table 17.9

Chi-Square Test Results, Age Group Membership: Should the United States Normalize?

	Value	df	Asymp. Sig. (2-sided)
Pearson Chi-Square	7.897	3	.048
Likelihood Ratio	8.421	3	.038
Linear-by-Linear Association	5.812	1	.016
N of Valid Cases	36		

5 cells (62.5%) have expected count less than 5. The minimum expected count is 3.33

Kruskal-Wallis Analysis-of-Variance Test

The Kruskal-Wallis (K-W) analysis-of-variance test is used to test differences in the way that three or more groups respond to one or more ordinal-level variables, such as the way subjects rank a set of statements or other items in terms of their perceived importance. The test computes an H-statistic similar to a chi-square distribution (a chi-square value is also printed as the default). This test also provides a significance value that can be used in the same way as a p-value for interpreting the results. If there are a large number of ties in raw data, a second chi-square and significance value corrected for ties is also computed.

The K-W procedure tests for differences in the way that three or more independent groups or samples rank a variable in order to establish whether three or more independent samples are from the same population (Seigel 1956). In much the same way as the K-W H-test, it computes a chi-square and a significance value, and repeats these results corrected for ties in the data. This test is also included in SPSS® Nonparametric Tests.

In the following example, a researcher is interested in determining the best appeal to use in order to influence citizens' attitudes about constructing a new wastewater treatment facility in the community. The city and county must float a bond issue in order to pay for the facility; property taxes are expected to increase if the bond issue passes. Table 17.10 displays the data for the hypothetical test of three independent groups exposed to different advertising appeals and a control group that does not get the treatment. All subjects were asked to rank the importance of a proposed community bond issue by awarding up to 100 points; the more points awarded, the greater the perceived importance.

To prepare the data for an SPSS® K-W analysis of variance test procedure, the data in Table 17.10 must be rearranged into three columns, as displayed in Table 17.11. Column 1 is the subject number variable, with subjects numbered sequentially from 1 to 21. Column 2 is the grouping variable. Groups are numbered from 1 to 4, with 1 assigned to the control group, 2 to the reason group, 3 to the emotion group, and 4 to the financial appeal group. The third column is the rank value given by each subject. The SPSS® procedure requires entry of the rank variable as the test variable and the group assignment variable as the grouping variable. The default selection for the test is the K-W H-test, so this box should already be checked. Table 17.12 shows mean rank calculations for this test.

The SPSS® procedure produces a summary table in which the calculated mean rankings for each group are displayed, and a test statistics result for the test (Table 17.13). In this example,

Table 17.10

Data for a Kruskal-Wallis ANOVA Test

		Important Rankings		
Subject	Group 1	Group 2	Group 3	Group 4
1	20	25	65	30
2	25	10	40	70
3	60	40	15	70
4	80	30	25	40
5	50	90	35	95
6	40	20	75	100
7	45	50		20
8		50		15

Table 17.11

Importance Data Reformatted into Column Form

Subject	Group	Importance Score
1	1	20
2	1	25
3	1	60
4	1	80
5	1	50
6	1	40
7	1	45
8	2	25
9	2	10
10	2	40
11	2	30
12	2	90
13	2	20
14	2	50
15	2	50
16	3	65
17	3	40
18	3	15
19	3	25
20	3	35
21	3	75
22	4	30
23	4	70
24	4	70
25	4	40
26	4	95
27	4	100
28	4	20
29	4	15

Table 17.12

Mean Rank Calculations for SPSS® Kruskal-Wallis *H*-Test

Ranks

	Group	N	Mean Rank
IMPRANK	Control Group	7	7.93
	Appeal to Reason	8	13.38
	Appeal to Emotion	6	14.50
	Financial Appeal	8	23.19
	Total	29	

Table 17.13

Calculated Chi-Square Value, Degrees of Freedom, and *p*-Value for K-W *H*-Test

Test Statistics

	IMPRANK
Chi-Square	12.602
df	3
Asymp. Sig.	.006

Kruskal-Wallis test.
Grouping variable: group

the computed chi-square is 12.602, with 3 degrees of freedom, and a significance of .006. There are only 6 chances in 1,000 that a Type I error will occur. The null hypothesis—the distribution of rankings is not the same in all groups—must be rejected and the alternate hypothesis, the distribution is similar in all groups, accepted.

The nonparametric test for differences in three or more related samples is the Cochran Q-test for nominal data. For differences between three or more related samples where the data are ordinal, the Friedman analysis of variance test for ordinal-level data may be used. Neither of these tests is included in the standard edition of SPSS® for Windows™, version 10.0 and below. Readers are encouraged to consult a standard nonparametric statistics text for instruction on the manual methods for conducting these two tests. The tests are included in more powerful editions of earlier desktop and mainframe versions of the software.

Nonparametric Relationship Tests

In the previous chapter on parametric statistical tests for relationships it was brought out that two different statistical techniques are needed to provide information on whether a significant relationship existed, and about both the strength and the direction of a relationship. Regression

Table 17.14

A Summary of Some Nonparametric Relationship Tests

Nominal Data Tests	Ordinal Data Tests
X^2 Test for Independence	Spearman's Rank Order Coefficient R (rho)
Cramer's *V*-Test (for square tables)	Kendall's *tau-b* (for square tables)
Phi Statistic (for rectangular tables)	Kendall's *tau-c* (for rectangular tables)

analysis measured the way in which variables might be related; correlation analysis provided a numerical measure or index of the strength of the relationship. These tests are listed in Table 17.14.

Tests for Nominal-Level Data

The first step often used to test for associations between nominal-level data is to employ the chi-square test for independence. This test provides a coarse measurement of association in that it allows the manager to test a null hypothesis that the two categorical variables are independent (that is, they are not related). The chi-square test is included in two separate categories of statistical tests in SPSS® for Windows™ *Crosstabulations* and *Nonparametric Tests.*

Crosstabulations, which are two-way frequency-distribution tables, include a number of other relationship or association tests for categorical data. Among the two most useful of these are tests for the *phi*-statistic and for Cramer's *V.* Both of these tests compute a nonparametric correlation coefficient index number that ranges from 0 (no relationship) to 1.0 (a perfect relationship). This means they can only provide a one-directional measure of relationship; it is impossible to determine whether the relationship is positive or negative. The samples can be of any size with either of these tests.

The only difference between these two tests is the way they are structured for comparing responses to different numbers of categories. The *phi*-statistic is used with tables that are "square," that is, a table with the same number of categories in both rows and columns. For example, a "two-by-two table" is one with just two possible classes for each variable. Examples include such dichotomous variables as gender, yes or no, read or don't read, member or non-member, use or don't use. The Cramer's *V*-test, on the other hand, measures association for all tables that are rectangular in shape; rows and columns do not have the same number of categories. They may be 2 by 3, 2 by 4, 3 by 4, 4 by 6, etc. Both tests are included under the same statistics option in the SPSS® crosstabs procedure.

The crosstabs procedure prepares tables and measures of association for two or more non-scale-level variables. Crosstabulations may be prepared with any level of data, but are particularly appropriate for use with categorical data. The association measures are grouped in three categories: for nominal data, for ordinal data, and for tables where one variable is nominal and the other is interval level. Among the options for inclusion in the table are row percentages, column percentages and the percentages of the total represented by each cell count. Counts (or "observed") frequencies for each category are always printed. It is also possible to have the expected frequencies counted for goodness-of-fit applications.

The data will dictate which of the two tests is carried out by the statistical software (they are included in the same selection option). Interpretation of both of these chi-square-based tests is identical. Each produces a relationship value (correlation coefficient) ranging from 0 to 1.0. This can be interpreted in the same way as the parametric coefficient of determination's percentage of association.

Among other applications, the X^2 statistic is used as a test of *independence* between variables, as a test for *normality* (normal distribution), or as a *one-sample relationship test*. Another important use for the chi-square statistic is the X^2 *goodness-of-fit test,* which is a nonparametric test for evaluating the distribution of responses for a categorical variable. It is called a *goodness-of-fit* test because it looks at the data to determine whether the distribution of responses "fits" the allowable distribution of categories, or is *disproportionate*. Basically, the idea of the goodness-of-fit test is to compare the actual frequency results against a hypothetical distribution, referred to as an "expected" distribution. While most nonparametric tests were developed for nominal- and ordinal-level data, the X^2 goodness-of-fit test can be used with interval and ratio data as well, although other, more powerful tests are used for the higher-level measurements.

The goodness-of-fit test compares two sets of data. One set is the actual collected data (called the *observed data*); the second is a hypothetical dataset (called the *expected data*). The hypothetical data represent what the data would be if the null hypothesis of *no difference* were really true. For a goodness-of-fit test, the null hypothesis might be "the distribution of responses found in the collected data is not different from the expected distribution." If the collected data differ significantly from the expected distribution, the null hypothesis is rejected.

The expected distribution may be established by the researcher or estimated by the statistical software program. Statistical software packages calculate a chi-square, the degrees of freedom, and a *p*-value—the significance level. Large chi-square values usually suggest that the null hypothesis must be retained. Small chi-square values usually mean the null hypothesis must be rejected. A computed *p*-value is used to make the final decision; *p*-values of the same or less than the selected significance value (typically 0.05, although 0.01 and 0.10 levels are also used) call for rejecting the null hypothesis.

Finally, when carrying out a goodness-of-fit test, there must be at least five responses in each category or cell; if not, the results of the test are considered to be *spurious*; that is, they are considered more likely to have occurred by chance.

Ordinal Data Association Tests

Ordinal-level measurements, like nominal data, are considered to be measures of *category* rather than quantity. With nominal data, the numbers mean how many cases fall into each specific and discrete category, such as "male" or "female" in the variable "gender." With ordinal data, the numbers also refer to how many observations fall into each of the descriptive categories. But now they also mean that the various categories may be placed in some kind of order. Examples included voters' preferred presidential candidates, the perceived importance of how a set of factors influence determination of public policy, or the possession of more or less of a characteristic, such as a "liberal attitude." Each level in ordinal measurement is a statement of order for the category. It is not possible to tell from the rankings how far apart the levels are, but simply that one level is higher (or lower) than others.

Researchers often want to know how ordinal-level variables are related to one another, if at all. For example, a public administrator might want to know if there is any relationship between the importance ranking citizens give a civic service with the way the public ranks the perceived quality of the service.

When at least one of the variables in a crosstabulation test is ordinal level, the SPSS® crosstabs procedure allows a choice of several different tests. These include the *Spearman correlation coefficient* (Spearman's *rho*), *zero-order Gammas, Somer's d-tests,* and *Kendall's tau-b* and t*au-c tests.* Spearman's *rho* is perhaps the most-used measure of correlation between two ordinal-level variables. It is the nonparametric analog of the parametric *product moment correlation coefficient* (Pearson's *r*) and is interpreted in the same way as the interval-level test. It also identifies whether the relationship is positive or negative. Spearman's *rho* can be used with samples of any size, with equal or unequal size groups, and with any table shape.

The Kendall tests are also simple to use and interpret; each is appropriate for slightly different situations. Tau-b should be used for square tables (when the number of columns equals the number of rows in the Crosstabulations table); a tau-b corrected for ties tests is also computed. Tau-c is to be used when the tables are rectangular rather than square.

Summary

A number of nonparametric statistics procedures were discussed in this chapter. A few are included in Microsoft® Excel™, and all are included in SPSS® and SPSS® for Windows™ software. Nonparametric tests, which are also known as *distribution-free* tests, are appropriate when a researcher must deal with categorical or ranked data. Nonparametric statistics are to be used when the researcher cannot make any assumptions about distributions, when the sample size is small (less than 100), and when measurements are nominal or ordinal level. Such applications occur when the data are categorical (nominal level) or ranked or ordered (ordinal level).

There are many different uses for nonparametric tests. They begin with several different versions of chi-square tests, and extend across a variety of independent and paired-sample applications for one, two, and three or more samples or groups. They include tests for differences and tests for relationships. At least one nonparametric equivalent test exists for each type of basic parametric statistical test. Nonparametric statistical tests have been developed for each of three general categories of statistical analysis: tests for location, tests for statistically significant differences between independent and related samples, and tests for associations between variables.

Two of the most popular one-sample nonparametric tests are the chi-square test for use with nominal data and the Kolmogorov-Smirnov one-sample test for ordinal data. One-sample tests are conducted to test hypotheses that the sample in question could come from an identified population.

Two of the independent sample tests in SPSS often used in political science are the *Kolmogorov-Smirnov* (K-S) *Z-test*, which is used with nominal-level data, and *the Mann-Whitney* (M-W) *U-test*, which is used with ordinal-level data. For two, related-samples tests the McNemar test for dichotomous (nominal) data, and the Wilcoxon rank sum test for ordinal data should be used.

The SPSS® crosstabs procedure prepares tables and measures of association for two or more non-scale-level variables. When at least one of the variables in a crosstabulation test is ordinal-level, Spearman's *rho* is the most appropriate measure of correlation between two ordinal level variables.

Discussion Questions

1. What is meant by the term "distribution-free statistics?"
2. When and why do researchers use nonparametric tests for location?
3. When should the X^2 one-sample test be used? Why?
4. What is the appropriate test to use when comparing two related samples with nominal data?
5. What is the appropriate test to use when comparing two related samples with ordinal data?
6. Name at least one nonparametric relationship test for nominal data.
7. Name at least one nonparametric relationship test for ordinal data.
8. Describe the SPSS® procedures for developing tests for nonparametric data.
9. Describe the Microsoft® Excel™ procedures for nonparametric tests.
10. Is it ever possible to use a parametric test on nonparametric data?

Additional Reading

Fitz-Gibbon, Carol T., and Lynn L. Morris. 1987. *How to Analyze Data*. Newberry Park, CA: Sage.

McCall, Robert B. 1986. *Fundamental Statistics for the Behavioral Sciences*. San Diego: Harcourt Brace Jovanovich.

Neufeld, John L. 1997. *Learning Statistics with Microsoft® Excel™*. Upper Saddle River, NJ: Prentice-Hall.

Siegel, Sidney. 1956. *Nonparametric Statistics for the Behavioral Sciences*. New York: McGraw-Hill.

Sincich, Terry. 1996. *Business Statistics by Example*. 4th ed. Upper Saddle River, NJ: Prentice-Hall.

Part 4

Advanced Quantitative Methods

18 Regression Analysis in Political Science

There are many instances when researchers are interested in determining either (1) how two or more variables are associated or related to one another, or (2) how a change in one variable or variables affects another variable. In the broadest terms, these are called *multivariate association tests*. They include correlation and regression analyses. Identifying and measuring the strength of relationships is, in fact, one of the most fundamental tasks of data analysis. Measuring relationships also defines the type of research design selected by the researcher. For example, a researcher might have "a feeling" that the public's use of a state park is directly related to the price charged for access to the facilities. Or a highway maintenance researcher might believe that maintaining consistent quality on patchwork paving is related to employee job satisfaction. Another researcher might want to know whether the level of service provided citizens by her agency is related to staff workload, or if the productivity of staff members is related to the amount or type of training they receive.

Other researchers might look at other problems and have other questions. For example, one might want to know if voting behavior is related to amount and type of advertising about candidates' qualifications. Another researcher might want to know if legislator-voting patterns are affected by party strength or weakness in the home district. A human resources director in a large city might have an idea that the level of service provided in an agency is affected by the announcement of a deferred pay increase, while another researcher might want to determine whether employee productivity varies with changes in the weather. In every one of these examples, a regression analysis research design is often used in an attempt to find answers to political questions.

It is important to note that the relationships described in these examples have alternative conclusions. The point is that a variable relationship is not always what it appears to be. Variables may only seem to be associated, or they may be only a "confounding" factor in the issue. Researchers test many different variables before selecting what seems to be the most probable answer.

Obviously, it would be irresponsible behavior on the part of a researcher to make major economic decisions based on how he or she "feels" about a relationship between two or more variables. Before making such a decision, the researcher would propose a hypothesis about a relationship, write an alternate hypothesis, collect data, and then test the hypotheses statistically. The correct procedure is to assume that associations do not exist until they are "proven" statistically. Fortunately, an extensive body of easy-to-use statistical tools exists to help researchers identify and weigh evidence about relationships. This process is often described as proving that the relationship is "statistically significant." The phrase "statistically significant" means that the identified relationship did not occur because of chance alone, and that there is some measured degree of probability that it does exist.

It is possible to carry out statistical tests for associations with all levels of data. Because each test employs different assumptions, measures, and calculations, it is particularly important that the appropriate test statistic be selected for the type of data collected. Tests for nominal- and ordinal-level tests were covered in the chapter on nonparametric statistics. Tests for interval and ratio data are covered here.

Measures of relationship between two interval- or ratio-level variables involve two closely related measurement concepts: regression analysis and correlation analysis. Regression analysis measures the way in which two or more variables are related to one another, whereas correlation analysis provides a measure of the strength of the relationship. Together, these constitute what may be the most heavily used statistical tests in political science, public administration, and economics.

Relationship Test Applications

Relationship tests have two broad applications. They can be used to examine the way in which variables vary together; this is called a *covariational* relationship. Or they may be used to test whether a *causal* relationship between two or more variables exists. An example of a covariational relationship is the statement "Wisdom increases with age." The hypothesis is that as people get older, they get smarter. An example of a causal relationship is a prediction that if advertising expenditures are increased, more people will vote for a candidate for Congress. The hypothesis is that advertising "causes" votes.

In organization applications, covariational relationships are seldom studied. Rather, managers are always on the lookout for cause-and-effect relationships. We will discuss only causal relationships here. All causal relationships have three key characteristics in common. First, the variables always vary together (either positively or negatively). Second, a time factor is always involved. One variable must change in order to "cause" a commensurate change in the other. The *independent* variable always changes first, followed by the *dependent* variable. In the advertising and voting example above, advertising expenditures were the independent variable; votes for a candidate was the dependent variable. And finally, the relationship is statistically significant; it did not appear through chance alone. In other words, it is not a "fake" relationship.

An example of a fake or "spurious" relationship occurred some forty or more years ago when it was reported that more families were using pots and pans made of aluminum. It was also reported that more people were being diagnosed with cancer. Reporters assumed a cause-and-effect relationship between these two in-dependent social factors. Knowledgeable scientists quickly debunked this spurious relationship.

The analytical techniques used to test relationships fall into two families of tests: regression analysis and correlation analysis. Regression analysis identifies *the way* in which two or more variables are related to one another. Correlation analysis, on the other hand, is concerned with providing a mathematical measurement of the *strength* of any relationship between variables.

Regression analysis and correlation analysis are most appropriate for interval- and ratio-level measurements. When dealing with categorical or ranked data, other, somewhat less powerful, relationship tests have been developed. However, it is possible to create what are called *dummy variables* from nominal and ranked data in order to test relationships with the lower-level measurements.

Correlation Analysis

Because of the many similarities and common terms used in both correlation and regression, a brief overview of correlation analysis is important. Correlation is a test for association; regression also reports association, but is primarily used for predictive purposes. Correlation analysis enables us to measure the degree to which the two variables are related by measuring the strength and direction of the relationship. Regression analysis, on the other hand, provides a way of estimating the value of one variable from the value of another, or of visually determining the way in which two or more variables are associated. Correlation analysis can also indicate how well a regression line explains a relationship between variables. Correlation analysis should be used instead of regression when the only question the manager has is "How strongly are the two variables related?"

The concept of correlation analysis is closely linked to regression analysis in another way. That is, if all the paired points of X and Y lie on a straight line, then the correlations between the variables would be "perfect": the coefficient value would be 1.0. The value 1.0 represents a perfect positive correlation; -1.0 is the value for a perfect negative correlation; 0.0 refers to no association whatsoever between the two variables. A negative correlation means that as the X-axis values *increase,* Y-values would *decrease,* and the obverse, as X-axis values decrease, Y-values would increase.

This numerical value for correlation analysis serves as a mathematical summary measure of the degree of correlation between two variables, X and Y. The summary number is called the *correlation coefficient;* it is expressed in statistical notation as the lower-case Greek letter r.

The Coefficient of Determination

The *coefficient of determination* is the square of the correlation coefficient value; it is probably the most useful measurement in correlation analysis. It provides a clear, easy-to-understand measurement of the explanatory power of a correlation coefficient. In addition, r^2 can help show how close the computed r describes a relationship between two variables. For example, say that a correlation coefficient (r) of 0.667 is found to exist between the variables n-votes results and advertising expenditures. If we square this value, we get an r^2 of 0.44. We are then able to use this coefficient of determination for an interpretation that everyone can understand: 44 percent of the variation in votes is "explained" by variation in spending on advertising, while 56 percent is "unexplained," or due to other, unidentified, factors.

An important caveat to keep in mind when making such interpretations of the results of correlation analysis is that we are never able to say for certain that a dependent variable or variables actually "causes" a change in the independent variable (that "X causes Y"). Instead, we can only report the existence and strength of a statistical relationship.

The Standard Error of the Estimate

One of the key concepts of statistics is measurement of variability. These measurements included the *range,* the *variance*, and the *standard deviation.* The point of these measurements is that data seldom fit neatly into values or categories that researchers would like to see. Instead, most often the data vary, either positively or negatively, from some middle point of a range of data. The central point used most often in analysis is the average score. A similar variability concept applies in regression analysis, although in regression, the central point is not an average, but is instead the computed *best line of regression.* Because the observed data points usually do not all fall on the regression line, the regression equation is not a perfect indicator of association; rather, it is an estimate. How close it comes to estimating the association can be judged by computing one additional value, the *standard error of the estimate.* In statistical notation, the standard error of the estimate is indicated by the symbol S_{yx}. When calculated, the standard error of the estimate provides a measure of the variation around the fitted line of regression. It is measured in the same units as the dependent variable (Y) in much the same way that the standard deviation measures variability around the mean.

In application, the standard error of the estimate is used to make inferences about the predicted value of Y. For example, a "small" standard error suggests that the data points cluster relatively closely to the plotted regression line; in a word, the data are homogeneous. A "large" standard error suggests that data points are widely disbursed on either side of the regression line, and that a high degree of variability exists. What is "small" and what is "large" is a judgment of the researcher.

A second inference statistic is produced with the standard error of the estimate, this is the *p*-value. The *p*-value is a confidence measure, in that it suggests with what degree of probability the regression equation can be relied upon. In this way, it is used to make decisions about the statistical significance of the relationship between the two variables.

Three quick steps can provide most of the information a manager needs to have about the potential relationship between a set of values. In Excel™, these are the *XY SCATTER* plot in the Chart Wizard, and the *CORREL* and *RSQ* calculations in the Function Wizard.

Interpreting Correlation Values

Researchers have developed many different ways of interpreting correlation values in order to describe relationships in terms that have meaning for everyone. The following defining model is a purely subjective suggestion. Many other models can be found in the research literature. In this model, values range from 0 to 1 in units of 10 percentage points for each level. Since the coefficients of determination are the squares of the *r*-values, it is not necessary to use positive or negative values; squaring a negative number produces a positive number. The labels and their respective values are:

> 0.0 = No relationship
> .01 to .19 = Weak relationship
> .20 to .39 = Low but definite relationship
> .40 to .59 = Moderate relationship
> .60 to .79 = Strong relationship

.80 to .99 = Very strong relationship
    1.0 = Perfect relationship

Interpretations of the correlation coefficient (r) and the coefficient of determination (r^2) are slightly different. For example in the two test-score data, the r-value could be interpreted as: "The more than .99 correlation coefficient suggests that the relationship between the two test scores is nearly perfectly linear." To interpret the r^2, use the above interpretation labels. For example: "The r^2 of 0.95 suggests that there is a very strong relationship between the two tests."

Simple Regression Analysis

Regression analysis is a statistical procedure developed to determine whether two or more interval- or ratio-level variables are related. To put it another way, regression analysis allows the manager to determine how different values of one variable (called the *dependent variable*) might or might not help to *explain* variation in an independent variable. This is the methodology underlying experiments that are specifically designed to determine whether changes in one variable will influence changes in another variable. The test marketing of a new campaign platform is an example of an experiment. In such an experiment, a campaign manager might take the proposed platform to three or more similar districts. In each, one or several variables will be changed, with all other variables kept as constant as possible. At the end of the test period, opinion results in each test district will be compared to see if platform content had any impact on voter opinion.

In addition to measuring the way in which variables are related, regression analysis also enables political scientists to predict responses or reactions to changes in independent variables. Such predictions are often needed before making expenditure decisions. From the above example, a researcher will be able to predict with some level of certainty voters' acceptance of the party platforms. Prediction is one of if not the most important uses of regression analysis results.

The Regression Procedure

The regression analysis procedure begins with collecting a dataset that includes pairs of observed values or measurements. One set of measurements is needed for each variable to be included in the analysis. The idea of *pairs of measurements* may be somewhat misleading. It does not mean regression analysis is restricted to analyzing just two variables at a time. With multiple regression analysis, many variables can be included. The term "pair" refers instead to measurements for a dependent and one or more independent variables.

The usual next step in the procedure is to produce a scatter plot of all measurements. Value pairs should be plotted as points on a *scatter diagram* (also called a *scatter plot*). A scatter diagram has two axes: a vertical line (the Y-axis) and a horizontal line (the X-axis). The vertical line represents values on the dependent (or changed) variable. The horizontal (X) axis identifies increments of the independent variable or variables. Regression analysis evaluates all recorded data points and computes a regression equation. A *regression function,* or numerical value, is produced. When multiplied with independent variable values, this function enables the researcher to predict the value of a corresponding measurement of the dependent (Y) variable, given any value of *X*. The final step in the regression analysis procedure is interpretation of the findings.

The Regression Equation

Interpretation of the findings of a regression analysis procedure begins with fitting the sample data into a best-fit line. The regression analysis statistical procedure in statistics software packages does this through a process called the *method of least squares*. This process measures the amount each point varies from a proposed line, squares each deviation, and then sums the squares. After computing these values, the minimum squared value of all differences establishes the slope of the regression line. At the same time, the regression process determines the point at which the *Y*-axis (the vertical line in the scatter diagram) and the computed regression line would meet. This point is called *the intercept*. Once this point is known, the regression equation is used to predict additional points along the line, given a value for the X-axis. In statistical notation, the regression equation is expressed thus:

$$Y = a + bX$$

where

  $Y =$ the value of *Y* calculated from the estimated regression equation
  $a =$ the point on *Y* where the regression line intercepts on *Y*
  $b =$ the amount of change in *X* required for a corresponding change in *Y* which, when plotted, represents the slope of the line
  $X =$ a measured value for the independent variable (X)

In some statistics texts, the statistical symbol for the *Y* intercept point is given as b_o, and the symbol for the regression slope value as b_1. The regression equation for straight-line regression (linear) then is depicted as:

$$Y_i = b_o + b_1X_i$$

where

  $Y_i =$ the predicted value of *Y* for measurement *i*
  $X_i =$ the value of *X* for measurement *i*

In general terms, we would interpret the $Y = a + bX$ equation in this way: "As *X* changes, *Y* also changes by *b* times the change in *X*." Once the regression equation has been obtained, predictions or estimates of the dependent variable can be made. For example, say that we have computed the following regression equation:

$$Y = 4.0199 + .00896 * X$$

This is interpreted to mean that the regression line begins at that point on the vertical axis that coincides with the value of 4.0199. Then, any subsequent increase in a value on the X-axis, multiplied by 0.00876, will equal a corresponding change in *Y*. By moving along the X-axis and periodically plotting the increases to both *X* and *Y*, connecting each point, we get a graphic impression of the regression line. The regression equation indicates how steep the line must be, whether it slopes to the right or left, or whether it is curvilinear. When very little or no relationship exists, the scatter plot will show the data points distributed haphazardly around the space, with no connection visible.

Researchers usually look for a *linear* relationship, one that shows a definite relationship between the variables. However, not all relationships will be linear. Some will be curvilinear, some will be more or less flat, showing no relationship whatsoever, some may be U-shaped, and others may take on S-like patterns. Techniques are available for dealing with nonlinear relationships, but are not part of most introductory research texts, and are not discussed here.

A Simple Regression Example

The caucus secretary of the legislature wanted to know the relationship between the number of bills introduced per week and the number that made it out of committee. Data were collected for the twenty weeks that the legislature was in session. He decided to use Microsoft® Excel™ (1) to see if a relationship existed, (2) to determine the strength and direction of the relationship, and (3) to determine whether it would be possible to predict committee productivity at future legislative sessions. A regression analysis was conducted on the data. The data are shown in Table 18.1.

In this simple example, three Excel™ Wizard applications are applied to the data. First, the

Table 18.1

**Bills Introduced and Passed Out of Committee,
20-Week Legislative Session**

Week	Bills Introduced	Out of Committee
1	53	2
2	91	8
3	59	6
4	72	10
5	45	11
6	44	16
7	31	22
8	55	37
9	68	92
10	71	66
11	88	58
12	90	73
13	79	64
14	67	52
15	44	24
16	31	15
17	22	16
18	14	7
19	4	2
20	1	0

Source: Hypothetical data.

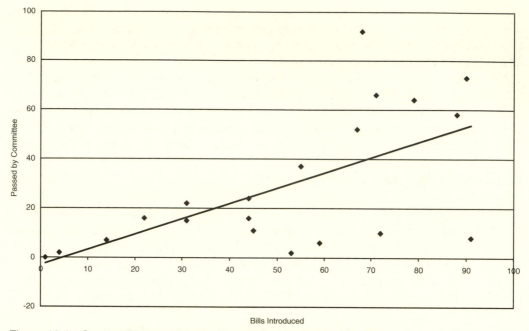

Figure 18.1   **Scatter Plot and Linear Trend Line for Table 18.1 Data**

Chart Wizard's *XY Scatterplot* program is used to graphically display the type of relationship between the two variables. Next, using the *Add a Trendline* option from the *Tools* menu, a linear trend is fitted to the scatter plot. Because the scatter diagram revealed a linear relationship, the next step is to call up the *CORREL* (Correlations) program in the Function Wizard. The value produced is the correlation coefficient (also referred to as the *Pearson Product Moment Correlation Coefficient* after the statistician who first reported its application).

The third step is to interpret the relationship findings using the *RSQ* (R-Square) capability in the Function Wizard, which makes it much easier to make an interpretation. The R^2 value produced is the coefficient of determination; it's used to express the relationship as a *percentage.*

The scatter plot and trend line are shown in Figure 18.1. The Excel™ result for the CORREL test was 0.61. The results for the RSQ test was 0.3761, which can be interpreted as "Nearly 38 percent of the change in the dependent variable, bills passed by committee, is explained by the independent variable, the number of bills introduced each week." Figure 18.2 is a line chart comparison of bills introduced and passed during the eight-week session.

Some Key Regression Concepts

When carrying out a regression analysis procedure, two approaches are possible. They differ only on the number of variables used in the regression equation. The first is called "simple regression" and includes just one independent variable to explain one dependent variable. The second approach is known as "multiple regression analysis" and, as its name implies, involves more than one independent variable in the regression equation. Both simple and multiple regression produce a regression equation that helps explain the shape and direction of the rela-

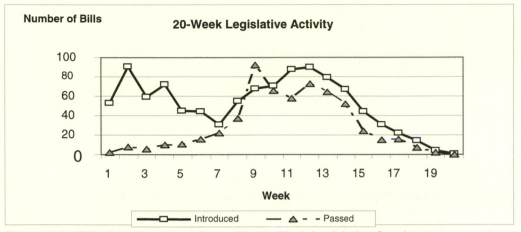

Figure 18.2 **Bills Introduced and Passed in 20-Week Legislative Session**

tionship between variables. Multiple regression is nothing more than expanding simple regression to consider two or more independent variables at the same time. Adding more variables to simple regression in order to conduct a multiple regression analysis is often far more efficient and effective than conducting a series of sample regressions.

When measuring association of one variable at a time with simple regression analysis, too often much of the variation in Y cannot be explained by any X alone. Doing two, three, or more simple regression analyses may still not explain the source of a majority of the variation. However, when two or more variables are tested *together* in a multiple regression procedure, an *interaction*-like effect may come into play. Thus, more information becomes available for the analysis, often resulting in more effective and informative results.

Correlation analysis, when extended for use with multiple X variables, calculates a multiple correlation coefficient. As in simple regression, the direction of the association may be either positive or negative. This makes it possible to judge both the strength and direction of the association explained by the set of X variables. The test statistic for interval and ratio data for both simple and multiple regression analysis is Pearson's r. This r-value can range from -1.0 (a perfect negative relationship) to $+1.0$ (a perfect positive relationship).

The square of Pearson's r (r^2) is called the *coefficient of determination*. This value represents the *proportion* of the variation in the Y variable that can be explained by linear regression in the X variable. The coefficient of determination in simple regression becomes the *coefficient of multiple determination* in multiple regression analysis (MRA). This last value is used as an index of association for the combined set of independent variables, in exactly the same manner as r^2 in simple regression.

The Excel™ *regression* procedure in the data analysis option in the tools menu produces a set of summary statistics for both simple and multiple regression. The information in Figure 18.3 was produced in this way from the data in Table 18.1.

Multiple Regression Analysis

MRA, a popular multivariate statistical method, has wide application in political, economic, social, and educational research (Kerlinger and Pedhazur 1973). An extremely robust procedure,

SUMMARY OUTPUT								
Regression Statistics								
Multiple R	0.6132							
R Square	0.3761							
Adjusted R2	0.3414							
Std. Error	22.7864							
Cases	20							

ANOVA								
	df	*SS*	*MS*	*F*	Sig. of F			
Regression	1	5633.01655	5633.02	10.8490	0.0040			
Residual	18	9345.93345	519.219					
Total	19	14978.95						

	Coefficients	*Standard Error*	*t Stat*	*P-value*	*Lower 95%*	*Upper 95%*	*Lower 95.0%*	*Upper 95.0%*
Intercept	-2.91571	10.96107	-0.26601	0.79326	-25.9440	20.1126	-25.94408	20.11266
Introduced	0.62130	0.18863	3.29379	0.00404	0.2250	1.01759	0.22501	1.01759

Figure 18.3   **Excel™ Regression Procedure Output for Table 18.1 Data**

it can be used with either continuous (interval and ratio) measurements or categorical (nominal and ordinal) data. In addition, theoretically there is no limit to the number of independent variables it can handle.

Multiple regression is a method of analyzing the contribution that more than one independent variable makes to the relative change in a dependent variable. It is used to explain and predict future events from measurements of a variety of independent variables. For example, political science researchers use multiple regression analysis to study how such phenomena as gender, age, education, party affiliation, ethnic status, income level and occupation, place and type of residence, and similar characteristics influence such behaviors as registering and voting. University admissions personnel use multiple regression to predict successful completion of advanced-degree programs from such independent variables as graduate aptitude tests and college grade-point averages, among other factors. Medical personnel use multiple regression to predict the likelihood of contracting a disease from such factors as weight, exercise, and diet factors.

In an example of a typical use of the method, say that the manager of the copy center in a government agency is interested in determining whether existing cost controls are effective at lowering costs and improving productivity. She elects to measure productivity by the gross revenue earned per individual copy made. Records are kept of each copying order, including the time to produce each copy in seconds, the labor cost per sheet, the number of bad copies in each order, and a measure of gross profit per sheet in cents per sheet. The manager randomly selects a sample of twenty jobs and comes up with the data presented in Table 18.2.

The independent variables in this example include: the n*umber of copies, time to produce, cost per copy,* and the n*umber of errors.* The number of errors is particularly important because the researcher has just completed a training program designed to improve productivity by eliminating waste caused by errors in copying. A simple regression analysis procedure can be conducted on each independent variable in order to establish what impact each variable has on gross revenue. However, the more appropriate statistical test to use for evaluating the relationships between these values is MRA.

The multiple regression programs in SPSS® and Microsoft® Excel™ allow the researcher to conduct both linear and curvilinear regression analyses, and to produce several different statistical-test results for the data in Table 18.2. Options in SPSS® include a table of descriptive statistics for all variables in the analysis (Table 18.3).

Both programs produce a correlation table for the variables included in the equation. Table

Table 18.2

Variables with Potential Impact on Gross Revenue

ROWS			COLUMNS		
Job Number	N of Copies	Time (minutes)	Cost (dollars)	Errors	Gross Revenue
1	150	4.0	1.75	2	1.50
2	310	15.5	1.35	5	1.00
3	450	11.0	1.10	6	0.90
4	1,150	19.5	0.80	9	1.20
5	800	16.0	0.99	3	0.80
6	200	6.0	1.30	2	1.00
7	300	8.5	1.35	4	1.10
8	250	6.0	1.30	2	0.80
9	910	14.5	1.05	3	1.20
10	100	14.0	2.00	5	1.10
11	500	14.0	0.95	2	0.20
12	225	10.0	1.30	1	0.50
13	50	4.0	1.75	0	0.60
14	920	17.0	0.90	5	1.50
15	5,000	49.0	0.70	10	1.25
16	600	13.0	1.10	2	1.50
17	1,400	22.5	0.95	6	1.00
18	2,750	28.0	0.90	2	1.25
19	410	12.5	1.25	1	1.00
20	2,500	29.0	0.95	2	1.50

Source: Personal data, 2002.

Table 18.3

Descriptive Statistics for the Variables in Table 18.2

Descriptive Statistics

	Mean	Std. Dev.	*n*
Gross Revenue	1.05	.350	20
n of Copies	948.75	1208.779	20
Time in Minutes	15.70	10.495	20
Cost in Dollars	1.19	.339	20
n of Errors	3.60	2.644	20

18.4 is a *correlation matrix* produced by Excel™. The most relevant information is the moderate and low correlations for each of the independent variables and the dependent variable, gross revenue: .35 for Copies, .32 for time, −.13 for cost, and .27 for errors.

Correlations measure the strength and direction of the relationship between any two pairs of interval or ratio-scale variables. Other relationship tests, such as Spearman's rank-order correlation, are available for ordinal and nominal-level data. Excel™ produces a lower-half

Table 18.4

A Correlation Matrix for the Independent Variables in Table 18.2

	Copies	Time	Cost	Errors	Revenue
Copies	1				
Time	0.96058259	1			
Cost	−0.63637334	−0.650999	1		
Errors	0.50486879	0.600563	−0.41956	1	
Revenue	0.35267705	0.320736	−0.12931	0.276613	1

SUMMARY OUTPUT

Regression Statistics

Multiple R	0.6132
R Square	0.3761
Adjusted R2	0.3414
Std. Error	22.7864
Cases	20

ANOVA

	df	SS	MS	F	Sig. of F
Regression	1	5633.01655	5633.02	10.8490	0.0040
Residual	18	9345.93345	519.219		
Total	19	14978.95			

	Coefficients	Standard Error	t Stat	P-value	Lower 95%	Upper 95%	Lower 95.0%	Upper 95.0%
Intercept	-2.91571	10.96107	-0.26601	0.79326	-25.9440	20.1126	-25.94408	20.11266
Introduced	0.62130	0.18863	3.29379	0.00404	0.2250	1.01759	0.22501	1.01759

Figure 18.4   **Regression Analysis Output Produced by Microsoft® Excel™**
Source: Excel™ output from data in Table 18.2

correlation table, not repeating the same table on the upper half. The values printed in a correlation table are correlation coefficients that indicate the strength and direction of the relationship between variable pairs. For example, the coefficient for the variables *errors* and *time* is 0.60, and the variables are positively related. *Errors* and *cost* display a negative correlation of −0.42. The strongest relationship in the table is the nearly perfect positive relationship (0.96) between the variables *time* and *number of copies.*

Excel™ regression program results are shown in Figure 18.4. They include a summary output for the regression analysis procedure and significance tests for the full regression equation for individual variables in the equation.

The regression analysis procedure produces summary regression statistics, an analysis-of-variance (ANOVA) table with the results of an F-test, and a t-test for each independent variable. Summary regression statistics include a solution for the regression equation, and both a regression coefficient (r) and a regression coefficient of determination (r^2), and an adjusted r^2.

The three sets of statistics shown in Figure 18.4 are: (1) the set of regression statistics, (2) an ANOVA table, and (3) the coefficients, standard error, t-statistic, p-value, and confidence intervals for the coefficients. The coefficients are the calculated values that, with the computed Y-axis intercept value, are values included in the computed regression correlation. These values are the data needed to calculate a future value for Y given new values for the independent variables.

The model summary produced by SPSS® is shown in Table 18.5. It includes (1) the re-

Table 18.5

Model Summary Produced by the SPSS® Regression Procedure, Table 18.2 Data

Model Summary

Model	R	R^2	Adjusted R^2	Std. Error of the Estimate
1	.414	172	−.049	.358

[a]Predictors: (constant), n of errors, cost in dollars, n of copies, time in minutes.

Table 18.6

ANOVA Table for SPSS® Regression Analysis

ANOVA

Model		Sum of Squares	df	Mean Square	F	Sig.
1	Regression	.399	4	.100	.777	.557
	Residual	1.925	15	.128		
	Total	2.325	19			

[a]Predictors: (constant), n of errors, cost in dollars, n of copies, time in minutes.
[b]Dependent variable: gross revenue.

gression coefficient (r), (2) a regression coefficient of determination (r^2), (3) an adjusted r^2, and (4) the standard-error value. The strength of the computed r^2 tells the researcher how effective the set of independent variables are at "explaining" the variation in the dependent variable Y. In the copy-center-example data, the r^2 of 0.17 suggests that the model is only marginally successful at explaining the variation in gross revenue. The adjusted r^2 is an estimate of how well the model would fit a different dataset from the same population; the adjusted r^2 is always less than the r^2. The standard error of the estimate is a measure of the variability of the distribution of values of the dependent variable. The smaller this value is in real terms, the less variability in the Y values. Normally, close to 95 percent of all Y values will fall within two standard errors of the estimate.

The ANOVA table shows results of a hypothesis test on the regression equation. The purpose of the test is to determine whether a linear relationship exists between the set of independent variables and the dependent variable. The null hypothesis for this test is that a set of independent variables does not predict Y. Table 18.6 shows results of an ANOVA test on the data in Table 18.2. The large significance (.557) and the small F (.777) indicate that this regression model is clearly not a good predictor. There is a probability of more than 55 percent that the variables cannot predict changes in Y any better than could random prediction.

Table 18.7 displays the individual coefficients for each of the independent variables in the regression equations. In the equation, the value for the slope (a) plus the measurements for each of the X variables multiplied by their corresponding coefficients is necessary in order to

Table 18.7

Regression Coefficients Produced by the SPSS® Regression Procedure

Model		Coefficients				
		Unstandardized Coefficients B	Std. Error	Standardized Coefficients Beta	t	Sig.
1	(Constant)	.767	.534	1.438	.171	
	n of copies	2.359E-04	.000	.815	.910	.377
	time in minutes	−1.645E-02	.032	−.494	−.507	.619
	cost in dollars	.170	.321	.165	.531	.603
	n of errors	3.051E-02	.041	.231	.741	.470

[a]Dependent variable: gross revenue.

compute future values of Y. The corresponding t-tests are results of significant tests for each of the independent variables. Since all significance values are greater than the normal cutoff of .05, none of the variables are significant. The overall conclusion that must be drawn from this regression equation is that the four independent variables of number of copies, cost, time, and number of errors are not a good predictor of gross revenue.

Multiple Regression with Dummy Variables

Multiple regression is generally employed with continuous dependent and independent variables. However, it is also possible to use categorical data for either the dependent or independent variable, or both. This requires creating what is called an *indicator,* or *dummy,* variable out of the categorical variable (Siegel 2002). For example, say that the variable gender—with two categories, female and male—is an important factor in a regression equation. To create a dummy variable, the research simply assigns a value of 0 to the first category of gender and a value of 1 to the other category. The multiple regression equation uses one category as the baseline against which to compare the presence of the second category. Dummy variables can be used by themselves in a regression equation, or in conjunction with continuous variables.

Values for dummy variables are assigned according to the number of alternative categories and are named for a variable. The general rule is to assign one fewer categories than the total number of values. Thus, for a two-category variable such as gender, dummy variables of 0 and 1 are assigned. For a three-category variable, dummy variables are 0, 1, and 2.

Multiple regression models have also been developed for those times when the researcher wants to use a categorical variable for the dependent or Y-axis variable. If the categorical dependent variable has only two categories, either a *multiple logic regression* or a *probit regression* model can be used. If the dependent variable has more than two values—as in *yes, no,* and *maybe*—then the *multinomial logit* or *multinomial probit* model should be used. None of these models is available in the standard Excel™ or SPSS® software packages, but may be found in extensions of these two commonly used software programs.

The probit model is used extensively in political science research. According to Norušis (2000), probit analysis is used when the researcher wants to estimate the strength of a stimulus variable or set of variables that are needed to produce a certain proportion of dichotomous responses. Examples of a set of stimulus variables are television advertising, newspaper advertising, voters' perceptions of a candidate's performance during a televised debate, and political party affiliation; an example of a response that these stimuli might influence is the proportion of voters who are likely to vote for a particular candidate. In a logit analysis procedure, the dependent variables are always categorical, while the independent variables can be factor scores. Factors are composite variables that are composed of one or more individual items or variables. The program allows the researcher to use from one to ten dependent and factor variables combined.

Summary

When researchers are interested in determining either (1) how two or more variables are associated or related to one another, or (2) how a change in one variable or variables affects another variable, they carry out what are called *association tests*. These tests include correlation and regression analyses. Identifying and measuring the strength of relationships is one of the most fundamental tasks of data analysis.

Variable relationships have alternative conclusions; they are not always what they appear to be. Statistical tests may indicate that variables are associated, whereas in truth, they may be only a "confounding" factor in the behavior of a variable of interest. Researchers test many different variables before selecting what seems to be the most probable answer, and even then they may not have a true measurement.

It is possible to carry out statistical tests for associations with all levels of data. Because each test employs different assumptions, measures, and calculations, it is particularly important that the appropriate test statistic be selected for the type of data collected. Measures of relationship between two interval- or ratio-level variables involve two closely related measurement concepts: regression analysis and correlation analysis. Regression analysis measures the way in which two or more variables are related to one another, whereas correlation analysis provides a measure of the strength of the relationship. Together, these constitute what may be the most heavily used statistical tests in political science, public administration, and economics.

Relationship tests have two broad applications. They can be used to examine the way in which variables vary together (called a *covariational* relationship), or they may be used to test whether a *causal* relationship exists. The analytical techniques used to test relationships fall into two families of tests: regression analysis and correlation analysis. Regression analysis identifies the *way* in which two or more variables are related to one another. Correlation analysis, on the other hand, is concerned with providing a mathematical measurement of the *strength* of any relationship between variables.

Regression analysis and correlation analysis are most appropriate for use in interval- and ratio-level measurements. When dealing with categorical or ranked data, other, somewhat less powerful, nonparametric tests must be used. However, it is possible to create what are called *dummy variables* from nominal and ranked data in order to test relationships using the more powerful parametric techniques.

Discussion Questions

1. What are the two broad applications for relationship tests?
2. What does correlation analysis tell the researcher about two variables?
3. What is the coefficient of determination?

    4. Describe how correlation values are subjectively interpreted.

    5. What is simple regression analysis, and what does it tell the researcher?

    6. What is the difference between dependent and independent variables?

    7. What is a multiple regression analysis?

    8. What is a slope?

    9. What is the intercept?

   10. What is a dummy variable?

Additional Reading

Field, Andy. 2000. *Discovering Statistics Using SPSS® for Windows™: Advanced Techniques for the Beginner*. Thousand Oaks, CA: Sage.

Kerlinger, Fred N., and Elazar J. Pedhazur. 1973. *Multiple Regression in Behavioral Research*. New York: Holt, Rinehart, and Winston.

Neufeld, John L. 1997. *Learning Business Statistics with Microsoft® Excel™*. Upper Saddle River, NJ: Prentice-Hall.

Norušis, Marija J. 2002. *SPSS® 11.0 Guide to Data Analysis*. Upper Saddle River, NJ: Prentice-Hall.

19 Predicting the Future I: Time Series Methods

Political science researchers, organization managers, and agency administrators are often required to use information gathered in the past as their guide to the future. This is particularly true in the process of forecasting. Typically, the data needed for a forecast are measured at regular intervals in the past and kept as part of the organization's historical record. Examples include client service levels, usage rates, error histories, incremental changes in social behavior, production records, complaint history, and many others. To forecast future events, researchers examine these historical records in order to identify trends in the measurements. They then try to extend the identified trends forward in time as forecasts of the way the variable will change in the future. This process of extending a trend forward as a forecast is called *time series analysis.*

A number of statistical processes are involved in these efforts at predicting future events. Collectively, these statistical techniques are known as "predictive" or "forecasting" statistics. They include time series analysis, regression analysis, index numbers, discriminant analysis, experimental design and hypothesis testing, and certain descriptive statistics. All these predictive statistical tools require that a sequence of pairs of measurements be taken. These measurements include the value of the variable of interest (such as the price of a product), and a record of the time the measurement was made. The various statistical techniques process these measurements in different ways to produce information about trends that can then be extended into the future as forecasts. Obviously, these forecasts are only estimates; there is never a guarantee that the predicted state of nature will come to pass as predicted. The statistical techniques used in these predictions were developed in order to improve the validity and the reliability of the forecasts. Time series analysis is one of the most commonly used management forecasting tools. This chapter examines several approaches to time series analysis.

The Time Series Approach to Data Analysis

As more government agencies, political parties, and nonprofit organizations adopt strategic planning processes, many researchers and administrators are finding that a large portion of their daily management activities involve some degree of forecasting. Strategic planning means that they must predict future events over a five-year or longer planning horizon. They are asked to forecast the actions of clients, manpower needs for normal operations and research, and financial needs for new equipment, workers, facilities, and supplies. The ability to forecast well—and to critically interpret forecasts made by others—has become one of the most important skills needed by researchers and administrators in all types of organizations. Because forecasts inherently force researchers to deal with the unknown—and with all the risk and uncertainty that the unknown entails—forecasting is one of the most difficult tasks a researcher can face.

What Is a "Time Series"?

The time series process has been defined in the following manner:

> Time series are sequences, discrete or continuous, of quantitative data assigned to specific moments in time and studies with respect to the statistics of their distribution in time. They may be simple, in which case they consist of a single numerically given observation at each moment of the . . . sequence; or multiple, in which case they consist of a number of separate quantities tabulated according to a time common to all. The closing price of wheat at Chicago, tabulated by days, is a simple time series. The closing price of all grains constitutes a multiple time series. (Weiner 1966, 1–2)

What Does Time Series Analysis Do?

Time series analysis measures variations in a series of events over time. These measurements are taken at fixed time periods; these periods can be days, weeks, months, quarters, years, or even multiyear cycles. When these data are collected, time series analysis attempts to uncover fundamental patterns in the data. Such patterns may then be extended or projected into the future. Researchers use these future trend projections to predict future movement of the variable. Since these movements are all to happen at some time in the future, the predictions must be seen as *extrapolations* of a trend rather than statements of fact. They are estimates of future change and, naturally, neither estimates nor predictions always come out the way they are projected.

Uses for Time Series Information

Information obtained from a time series analysis has two major uses. First, it provides the researcher a detailed picture of the underlying structure of change in a variable, including certain reoccurring trends or cycles that may be present in the change. Such information about the structure of the change helps explain *why* as well as *how* changes have occurred over time. In this way, the information helps the researcher to explain the "cause" of unexpected fluctuations. Second, time series analysis enables researchers to trace the historical behavior of past change, which, in turn, allows for extrapolating from the data to make predictions about future changes. It is these extrapolations that are the foundation of the planning process.

Most time series analyses are based on the assumption that the changes that occur over the time period do so in a *linear* manner. That is, the changes are projected to continue at a regular rate. Of course, this is not always the case. Therefore, just as with regression analysis, time series analysis models have been developed to deal with data relationships that may or may not be linear. Only linear time series analysis is discussed in this chapter.

Linear changes occur in a more or less straight line. When this is not the case, when a straight-line model fails to fit the data, nonlinear or exponential trend curve time series methods should be used. These methods are encountered far less often than linear relationships and are not discussed here. Most theoretically oriented statistics texts provide an introduction to non-linear methods.

The Components of a Time Series

There are four components or factors involved in time series analysis. These components affect overall change over different time periods. The first of these components is the underlying *trend* in the movement over time. The letter "T" is used to indicate trend in calculations. Trend is also known as the "secular" or long-term trend that the variable follows over a relatively long period of time. An example is the ten-year tendency for the Dow Jones stock price averages to increase, regardless of daily, seasonal, or cyclical fluctuations.

The second component in analysis models is a measurement of *cycles* within the trend; the letter "C" is used to indicate cyclical movement. Cycles may be positive or negative changes. While they typically tend to offset one another over long time periods, they do have an impact on the overall tendency of the trend, and must be included in the analysis. An example is the business cycle of inflation-recession-inflation. Cycles follow longer periods than *seasonal* changes, which make up the third component of the analysis.

Seasonal changes occur with the regularity of seasons in the year or from month to month. They tend to occur with the same regularity year after year. The seasonal effect is expressed in mathematical notation as "S." Finally, a *randomness* component is included in the analysis. The random factor, indicated by the letter "R," is sometimes called an "irregular" component or a "residual effect." It refers to unexpected changes or "blips" that appear at random in the overall trend, and for which there is no other explanation.

Models of Time Series Analysis

Several different methods or models of linear time series analysis have been developed. One of these is known as the *additive model*. This model assumes that the relationship between the factors in the model is equal and, therefore, is simply added to the effects of earlier events or components. The second approach to time series analysis is the *multiplicative model*. This model assumes that the effect of each factor amplifies the effects of previous factors. The multiplicative model is used far more often than the additive today. However, because of its ease of use and interpretation, the additive approach is still encountered today. Therefore, both models are discussed here.

The Additive Time Series Model

In the additive model, the four components of time series are expressed in the following equation, with Y_t signifying the value of the changing variable at any given point in time:

$$Y_t = T + C + S + R$$

where

> Y = the value of the changing variable
> t = the time period measured or forecast
> T = *trend*
> C = *cycle*
> S = *season,* and
> R = a *random* factor

In this model, *trend* may be defined as the observed long-term movement of the Y variable; it is usually measured over time periods as long as ten years or longer. *Cyclical* movement refers to the wider swings of the change trend that take place over time periods. They are shorter than the overall trend period, but occur for periods that are longer—at least one year or longer—than regular seasonal movements. The *season* component is the regular positive or negative patterns of change that take place on a more or less regular time period, such as quarters or, in some cases, monthly. Finally, *random* variations are the up or down "spikes" in the trend line that are totally unpredictable. Examples of random events include strikes, wars, climatic disasters, terrorism attacks, and the like. Because all of these four components are considered to have equal impact on the overall trend in the additive model, their effects are simply added together to produce a predicted Y value for any given point of time.

The additive model was developed for use when the components are considered to be completely independent of one another. Because such circumstances seldom occur in the real world, the additive model is seldom used.

The Multiplicative Time Series Model

Also called the "classical" approach to time series analysis, this model assumes that the effect of each component in the model significantly amplifies the effect of the previous component. This model requires multiplying the components rather than simply adding them to each other. This is the preferred model for forecasting. Managers believe it produces a more realistic picture of the effects of the various components on the trend. The model is expressed by the equation:

$$Y_t = T * C * S * R$$

The additive model's interpretations for each component apply to the multiplicative model as well.

Developing a Time Series Equation

To develop a time series equation for either of the two major models, the four components of a time series must be identified, measured or estimated, and evaluated in all time series models. This process is discussed in some detail in the following section.

Measurement of Trend (T)

The trend component of the time series equation is perhaps the most critical for making forecasts with time series data. This step involves finding a trend line that best summarizes the movement of the series over a period of at least as long as one year (although shorter periods are possible, if necessary). Trend may move in an upward or a downward direction, or may remain constant or "flat" for fairly long periods of time. The objective of trend analysis is to identify the line that best explains its historical shape and direction. The process is similar to that employed in regression analysis. Three statistical procedures or methods may be used for identifying trend: a *linear* method, *exponential smoothing,* and a *moving average* method.

The linear method uses the sum of least squares to come up with the best "fit" for the trend line. The sum of least squares refers to the mathematical fitting of a line that passes through or near all points over the time period that results in the lowest square of the distance from each point to the line. Exponential smoothing goes a step beyond the least-squares method to apply one or more constants to "smooth out" positive or negative variations in the trend. This constant is both positive and negative; it applies to values above and below the trend line, thus reducing the distance of the point from the line by limiting the power of "outriders" to influence the direction of the trend line. Finally, the moving average method controls for seasonal and/ or cyclical variations by using averages of several measurements rather than individual measurements in its calculation.

The Linear Trend Method

Usually at least ten and preferably more than ten years of data are needed to determine a reliable basic trend pattern. Time series data measured over shorter periods can lead to conclusions that have the potential for being spurious. When longer periods are used, the data can often be fitted to a linear, straight-line solution. The model used for establishing a trend line is very similar to that used in regression analysis. The linear trend procedure uses what is known as a "least squares" method almost identical to the regression procedure. The objective of the process is to identify the starting point of the trend line, which is the point where the trend line and *Y*-axis intercept. The process measures the distance of points, selecting the path that results in the smallest squares of the variation.

The equation for computing Trend is expressed as:

$$T_y = a + bX_t$$

where

T_y = the underlying trend value of the variable *Y* under consideration, measured at regular intervals

a = the Y intercept point

b = the amount of change in T per unit of time

X_t = the measured period of time (numbered consecutively)

A Linear Trend Example

In the following hypothetical example, Diane Williams is the purchasing agent for the Streets and Sanitation Department of the City of Houndstooth, Nebraska. As she prepares her annual budget plan, she must estimate how much to budget for road salt purchases for the coming year. She begins by checking past records to determine the overall trend of road salt purchases

Table 19.1

Gross Values Data for Road Salt Purchases, 1992 Base Year

Unit Number	Year	Gross Amount ($ millions)
1	1992	106.2
2	1993	108.7
3	1994	109.5
4	1995	110.2
5	1996	105.4
6	1997	110.7
7	1998	115.1
8	1999	117.2
9	2000	119.4
10	2001	122.5
11	2002	

Sources: Example data 2002.

over a ten-year period beginning in 1992. The purchase data for each year of the ten-year period is shown in Table 19.1.

Because time is always used as the X or independent variable in the linear trend series model, it is possible to simplify the computation process by changing the time periods to a simple consecutive series. In the Houndstooth data, zero may be substituted for the base year 1987, with the remaining years numbered sequentially, beginning with one, then two, etc. Or, the measurement years may be displayed as they are in Figure 19.1, which is a scatter diagram produced by Microsoft® Excel™ *Chart Wizard* with a trend line superimposed on the data. This chart shows the trend for time periods as the independent (X) variable, and for purchase levels as the dependent (Y) variable. Purchases can be forecast for five or more years into the future.

Trend values for any given year or partial year in the series may be extrapolated by examining the intercepts of each value at each consecutive unit of X (years). This procedure calculates a predicted Y value for a single X value. To project sales out five years in the future, the researcher may use the Excel™ Function Wizard's GROWTH procedure. The known data for years 1992 through 2001, together with linear model forecasts computed with the GROWTH procedure, are shown in Table 19.2. The model predicts that salt purchase sales in the year 2006 will be in excess of $130.44 million.

Smoothing the Trend for Better Forecast Accuracy

Trend smoothing refers to a family of time series analysis tools in which one or more constants are used to "smooth out" variations in the data. Various smoothing techniques are employed to revise the estimates of trend measurements based on earlier observations. The most commonly used smoothing techniques include using *constants* and using a *moving average*. Using

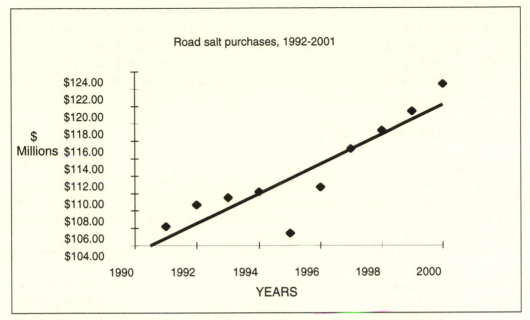

Figure 19.1   **Road Salt Purchases by the City of Houndstooth, 1992–2001**

Table 19.2

**Ten-Year Known and Five-Year
Projected Road Salt Purchases**

Year	Sales
1992	$106.20
1993	108.70
1994	109.50
1995	110.20
1996	105.40
1997	110.70
1998	115.10
1999	117.20
2000	119.40
2001	122.50
2002	123.80
2003	124.47
2004	126.43
2005	128.42
2006	130.44

constants is also known as *exponential smoothing*. The moving average method spreads the unit measurements across a wider range, with an average for all measurements in the wider range substituted for individual measurements. Constants and moving averages tend to erase the effects of wide swings in the data. Measurements that are far from the general trend are known as *outliers*. If outliers are allowed to remain in the equation they can have a significant distorting effect on the overall trend.

Exponential Smoothing

Using constants produces forecasts with built-in adjustments for past fluctuations, such as when a researcher's forecast varies from actual values. Over a number of these *forecast-versus-actual* situations, increasing or decreasing values in the direction opposite from previous fluctuations smooths out the variations. For instance, if the actual values are greater or smaller than forecast values in one period, a constant in the amount of the variation between the two values is subtracted from that point. In this way, potentially more accurate forecasts can be made for future periods.

A typical application of exponential smoothing uses one or more constants to smooth data with shifting linear trends. Constant values can only range from 0 to 1, although they seldom exceed 0.3. Forecasts are then made using the *weighted average* of the data. Exponential smoothing may use one or more smoothing constants. One-value smoothing is used most often, however. In two-constant smoothing, the first constant smoothes the data to more closely identify the trend shape, while the second constant is used to smooth the slope in the trend. Forecasts with more than two constants are seldom encountered.

An exponential smoothing procedure is included in Microsoft® Excel's™ data analysis tools. This procedure requires that the value of the constant be selected by the analyst and inserted when called for on the program menu. The value of the constant can be any number ranging from 0.0 to 1.0. It is important to remember that the value of a constant is data-specific; a new constant must be established for every dataset. Exponential smoothing programs do not set the value of a constant. The analyst must do this.

Moving Average Smoothing

Because of potential difficulty in selecting a valid constant for the smoothing process, many researchers use the *moving average* method instead. With this method, a trend line is adjusted for the fluctuations in the time series that are caused by repeated changes in the measurements. A major advantage of this method is that sets of data that have irregular variations may still be fitted to a linear trend line.

The moving average procedure controls both the trend and within-trend fluctuations by a process similar to the *smoothed* time series method cited earlier. However, rather than applying a constant value, trend smoothing by moving averages is done by selecting regular sets of time periods (such as four quarters) within the larger set and computing an average for the smaller set. The set is then advanced a determined amount and another average computed. The final trend is built upon the values of the averages rather than the initial data points.

The process works easiest when odd numbers of observations (such as 3, 5, etc.) are selected for averaging; the middle period of the first set is used as the starting point for the second set

Table 19.3

Ten-Year Record of Police Department Vehicle Auction Sales, 1993–2002

Year	Value of Vehicles Sold ($ Thousands)
1992	31
1993	35
1994	38
1995	46
1996	48
1997	50
1998	61
1999	61
2000	73
2001	75

Table 19.4

Actual and Moving Average Values for Vehicle Auction Sales (Excel™ Output)

Year	Sales ($ thousands)	Moving Average
1992	31	
1993	35	34.67
1994	38	39.67
1995	46	44.00
1996	48	48.700
1997	50	53.00
1998	61	57.33
1999	61	65.00
2000	73	69.67
2001	75	

for averaging. In the following hypothetical example, agricultural equipment exports to Chile are recorded for 10 years. To compute moving averages for the data, simply add 3 years' data and divide by 3. Then move to the next 3 measurements, beginning with the midpoint of the first set (Tables 19.3 and 19.4).

Microsoft® Excel's™ *moving average* procedure in *data analysis tools* produces the following set of moving averages for the annual sales data. The procedure returns the message "#N/A" for any period for which a moving average does not apply or cannot be computed. Note that in Table 19.4 the first average value appears in 1994, which is the middle year of the first three-year set. Table 19.5 displays both actual and moving average values. The trend for actual sales data is displayed in Figure 19.2a; the moving average adjusted line is displayed in Figure 19.2b.

Actual Data

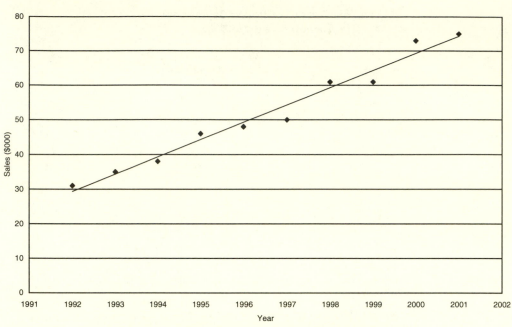

Figure 19.2a   **Scatter Plots and Trend Lines for Actual Sales Data**

Moving Average

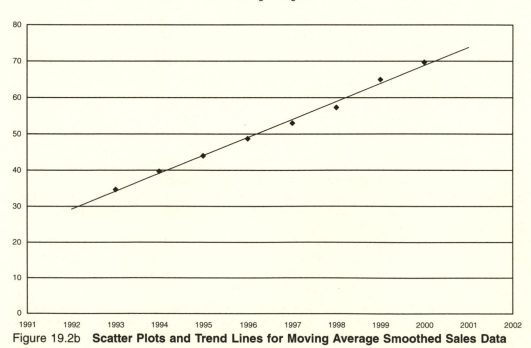

Figure 19.2b   **Scatter Plots and Trend Lines for Moving Average Smoothed Sales Data**

Table 19.5

Actual and Moving Average Values

Year	Sales	Year	Moving Average
1992	31	1992	
1993	35	1993	34.67
1994	38	1994	39.67
1995	46	1995	44
1996	48	1996	48.7
1997	50	1997	53
1998	61	1998	57.33
1999	61	1999	65
2000	73	2000	69.67
2001	75	2001	

Dealing with Seasonal Variations

Data recorded at relatively short periods, such as monthly or quarterly, will often exhibit strong variations from period to period. As a result, conclusions drawn from the data may differ widely with regard to when the data are measured. For example, the number of unemployed workers goes up in winter when jobs are not available for many seasonal occupations. These include logging, farming, fishing, construction, and similar jobs. Despite such increases in unemployment, the longer-term unemployment rate for the region or nation may actually be decreasing. Equally confounding the long-term trend are the measures taken during the summer months when seasonal workers are back on the job. To account for these seasonal or "inter-trend" fluctuations, many time series reports appear in two forms: seasonally unadjusted and seasonally adjusted. "Deseasonalizing" is the term used to describe the process during which adjustments are made for seasonal fluctuations.

Of course, government administrators are concerned about short-term employment fluctuations. However, what is typically far more important is the overall trend of unemployment. Therefore, for any given month reports on labor statistics are adjusted to account for seasonal variations. For these reports, the greater questions might be: "Is the overall trend of unemployment greater or less than would be expected, given the normal seasonal effect of farm labor?" For an answer, the data must be adjusted to remove the seasonal effect. The statistical process to do this is called the ratio-to-moving-average method of time series analysis.

The ratio-to-moving-average method isolates both the trend (*T*) and seasonal (*S*) components together in one smoothing procedure. For the simple smoothing procedure the averages are superimposed upon the basic time series data; in the ratio procedure, however, seasonal averages are instead embedded within the basic trend series data. This may be made clearer in the deseasonalizing example that follows.

A Seven-Step Process for Producing Deseasonalized Trends

STEP 1:   Gather average values for each seasonal period.

STEP 2:   Add the values for the first four quarters; divide by 4 to get the first *four-quarter moving average* (one full year).

STEP 3.   Repeat the quarterly averaging process, dropping the first quarter each time and adding the next in the sequence of four. Repeat until you have run out of quarters.

STEP 4:   Compute a *centered moving average* by adding each successive pair of four-quarter averages and dividing by 2 for the average.

STEP 5:   Divide the original value for each quarter by its appropriate *centered moving average*. This will produce a *percentage of moving average* for that quarter. Continue until a percentage of moving average is computed for all quarters.

STEP 6:   Compute a *seasonal index* for each quarter by finding the average percentage of moving average for each of the quarters. Note that for the first two quarters, no data are available for the first year, and that for the last two quarters, no data are available for the last year. If the sum of the four quarters does not equal 400, make proportional adjustments until it does.

STEP 7:   Deseasonalize the data by dividing the original values of each quarter by the seasonal index for that quarter, then multiplying each by 100.

Table 19.6

Four-Quarter Averages, 1993–1995

Year	Quarter	Sales ($ millions)
1998	1	90
	2	110
	3	115
	4	112
1999	1	111
	2	118
	3	200
	4	160
2000	1	250
	2	300
	3	320
	4	300
2001	1	280
	2	350
	3	400
	4	360

Source: Example data 2002.

Table 19.7

Information Necessary for Deseasonalizing Data, 1998–2001

Year	Quarter	Sales ($ Mil)	4-Qtr Moving Average	Centered Moving Average	Original as a % of Moving Average	Seasonal Index	Deseasonalized Data
1998	1	90				99	90.90
	2	110				98	112.25
	3	115	106.75	110	105	111	103.60
	4	112	113.00	114	98	91	123.07
1999	1	111	114.00	125	89	99	112.12
	2	118	135.25	141	84	98	120.41
	3	200	147.25	165	121	111	180.18
	4	160	182.00	205	78	91	175.82
2000	1	250	227.50	205	122	99	252.53
	2	300	257.25	276	109	98	306.12
	3	320	292.50	296	108	111	288.29
	4	300	300.00	306	98	91	329.67
2001	1	280	312.50	323	87	99	282.83
	2	350	332.50	340	103	98	357.14
	3	400	347.50			111	360.36
	4	360	91				395.60

Table 19.8

Procedure for Establishing Seasonal Indexes by Quarters, 1998–2001 Data

Year	1st Quarters	2nd Quarters	3rd Quarters	4th Quarters
1998	—	—	105	100
1999	89	84	121	78
2000	122	109	108	98
2001	87	103	—	—
Average	99	98	111	92*

*The four quarterly averages must sum to 400 to provide the four quarterly seasonal indexes. If they do not do so naturally, make proportionate adjustments until they do sum to 400. Each quarter index value represents 100% of the value for that quarter. Thus, 4 times 100% = 400%.

In an example of the process, assume that Step 1 produced the quarterly averages presented in Table 19.6 for each of four years:

The data calculated for each of the remaining steps in the procedure is displayed in Table 19.7. The final step in this procedure would be to plot the "deseasonalized data" in a time series plot.

To produce the "seasonal index," compute an average of the "original as a percentage of moving average" values for each of the annual quarters. This procedure is shown in Table 19.8.

Summary

Time series analysis measures variations in a series of events over time. Measurements are taken at fixed time periods; these periods can be days, weeks, months, quarters, years, or even multiyear cycles. When the data are collected, time series analysis attempts to uncover fundamental patterns in the data. Such patterns may then be extended or projected into the future. Most time series analyses are based on the assumption that the changes that occur over the time period do so in a *linear* manner. That is, the changes are expected to continue at a regular rate.

Researchers use these future trend projections to predict future movement of a dependent variable. Since these movements are projected to happen at some time in the future, the predictions must be seen as *extrapolations* of a trend rather than statements of fact. They are estimates of future change and, naturally, neither estimates nor predictions always come out the way they are projected. Two types of time series are used: the price index and the quantity index.

Four components or factors make up both models of time series analysis. These components affect overall change over different time periods. The first of these components is the underlying *trend* in the movement over time. The second component in analysis models is a measurement of *cycles* within the trend. Cycles may be positive or negative changes. Cycles follow longer periods than *seasonal* changes, which make up the third component of the analysis. The fourth component is a *randomness* factor. The random factor *r* refers to changes or "blips" that appear at random in the overall trend, and for which there is no other explanation.

Discussion Questions

1. Define what is meant by "time series." What does a time series do?
2. Why are political scientists interested in time series analysis?
3. Name the four components of a time series equation.
4. Define what is meant by the term "trend."
5. What are cycles in a time series?
6. What role do random variations play in a time series?
7. How and why do seasonal variations influence a time series?
8. Which are more important to a time series, long or short-term changes? Why?
9. Describe the additive time series model.
10. Define the multiplicative time series model.

Additional Reading

Hair, Joseph F., Jr., Rolph E. Anderson, Ronald L. Tatham, and William C. Black. 1992. *Multivariate Data Analysis with Readings*. New York: Macmillan.

Johnson, Richard A., and Dean W. Wickern. 1988. *Applied Multivariate Statistical Analysis*. 2nd ed. Englewood Cliffs, NJ: Prentice-Hall.

Krzanowski, W.J. 1988. *Principles of Multivariate Analysis: A User's Perspective*. Oxford: Oxford University Press.

Manheim, Jarol B. 1986. *Empirical Political Analysis: Research Methods in Political Science*. 2nd ed. Englewood Cliffs, NJ: Prentice-Hall.

Stevens, James. 1992. *Applied Multivariate Statistics for the Social Sciences*. 2nd ed. Hillsdale, NJ: Lawrence Erlbaum.

20 Predicting the Future II: Index Number Methods

Index numbers (plural, *indexes* or *indices*) are descriptive measurements that are based on time series data. Index values are used to express change in a sequence of different measurements. An index is a common unit of measurement of change over time, thus eliminating the need for subjective interpretation for a variety of variables. Because of this wide applicability, index numbers have many different uses in many different disciplines. This chapter illustrates some examples of the many uses for index numbers and describes procedures for constructing the more commonly used index number types.

Political and labor economists have long sought a simple system to compare economic and political systems. Kenworthy (2001) has described an example of comparative analysis in his article on the level and type of political influence and participation in domestic wage-setting agreements. Over the past several decades, more than a dozen indexes have been proposed to fill this need. Kenworthy examined eight different indexes developed to measure wage-setting centralization, and evaluated another seven proposals for measuring wage coordination. Like all indexes, the variations studied by Kenworthy employed time series data and some simple composite or weighted index value. Many, however, relied on subjective assigning of measurements, rather than adhering to more reliable quantitative measures.

Another example of the use of index numbers was reported by a small Northwest state college. The school's Office of Research and Planning has employed a standardized instrument, the *College Student Experience Questionnaire* (CSEQ), as a measurement tool for meeting accountability performance requirements mandated by the state legislature and higher-education coordinating board. A portion of the instrument measures students' rating on eleven individual items. Responses are recorded on a four-point scale. Mean scores are reported for the freshman, sophomore, junior, and senior classes. Class means are then summed across the eleven items. The sum of all means is reported as a *lifelong learning index* (LLLI). The LLLI numbers range from a low near 29, to highs that are greater than 32, making interpretation of any change difficult. However, producing traditional index numbers from the raw scores solves that problem. It also makes it possible to communicate the measured changes as percentages.

The first step in preparing an index is to group means for each item. The mean scores on each of the eleven items for seniors are shown in Table 20.1. The final column in the table contains the sums of all mean scores. The index numbers displayed below the table were computed from the composite mean scores.

This chapter presents the rationale and development of index numbers; it also illustrates

Table 20.1

Lifelong Learning Index for Senior Class, 1997–2001

Year	SFE	BGE		WC	FWC	UO	TM	UST	TA	QT	SU	LOO	Total
1997	3.12	3.02		3.10	2.91	3.07	3.00	2.40	3.25	2.54	3.39	3.49	33.29
1998	3.01	3.03		3.11	2.54	3.28	3.28	2.26	3.31	2.15	3.53	3.53	33.03
1999	2.75	3.15		3.08	2.59	3.27	3.15	2.29	3.24	2.31	3.36	3.61	32.80
2000	2.78	2.94		2.75	2.31	3.16	2.94	2.13	3.03	2.06	3.41	3.50	31.01
2001	3.11	2.93		2.97	2.55	3.34	3.13	2.32	3.02	2.24	3.37	3.54	32.52

Year			
1997	: 33.29/33.29*100 =	100 [Base Year Index]
1998	:	99.2
1999	:	98.5
2000	:	93.2
2001	:	97.7

their use in a variety of applications. The goal of the chapter is to help researchers avoid misusing the concept. No special statistical knowledge is required. All mathematical processes in the chapter are conducted with Microsoft® Excel™, using simple, "point-and-click" division, multiplication, and summing techniques.

In another example of an index application, Robson, Deas, Bradford, Wong, and Anderson (2002) developed an index for application in the 760 wards, local divisions, in the 32 boroughs that constitute Greater London. Their *London Index of Deprivation* was based on seven multi-item "domains." The domain constructs included (1) poverty in and exclusion from the labor force, (2) dependency, (3) education, (4) health, (5) housing, (6) crime, and (7) environmental conditions. An eighth scale on affordability was measured but left out of the index because of problems with interpreting the data; the team was unable to identify a robust measure of affordability. Each of the domains (except for housing) included two or more indicators. From these, after initial analysis of the data one individual "headline" indicator was chosen to represent the domain. The indicator choice was made on the basis of correlation coefficients and the reliability and interpretability of the indicator. The composite index was constructed by adding these headline indicator-values together. The team considered, but rejected, the application of any weights to index items.

Final index values for the London index of deprivation were applied to three measurements: degree of deprivation, extent of deprivation in the ward, and intensity of deprivation for ward residents. Scores were added for each of the 32 boroughs, with the results then ranked. Each borough received 6 final scores: a composite value each for all wards in the borough on degree, extent, and intensity, respectively, and a rank order for each measure. For example, the final scores for the borough of Tower Hamlets (with 19 wards) were 66.8 for degree, 74.3 for extent, and 2.4 for intensity. Adding the three scores results in an index of 143.5. These scores were the lowest for all 32 boroughs. Therefore, the researchers concluded that Tower Hamlets has more deprivation than any other London borough, as measured by its rank on all bases.

The Meaning of Index Numbers

An index number is one or more values of a variable or variables that is expressed in relation to some value of the same variable(s) that was reported at an earlier period. A commonly encountered example is the cost of an item today compared to its cost in an earlier year. For example, an index number for the purchasing power of $100 today when compared to the purchasing power of the same amount ten years earlier can be expressed as a single comparative number. Used in this way, the index number is an indicator of the positive or negative change that occurred over the ten-year period.

The purpose of any index number is to communicate in a quick and easily understood way information in quantitative terms about the *amount of change* in a variable. It may then be converted to a percentage value, or left as a single-number indicator.

Typically, index numbers are used to indicate changes in either *prices* or *quantities*—or both. A well-known index number is the U.S. Labor Department's Consumer Price Index (CPI). The CPI is based on changes in some 400 goods and services. This important index comes in several different forms. One is the Consumer Price Index for all urban consumers, the CPI-U. Another is the CPI-W, which includes only purchases by wage earners. A few other index numbers often used in politics and government includes the Wholesale Price Index (WPI), the Index of Leading Economic Indicators (ILEI), the Dow Jones Industrial Average (DJA), and many others.

When to Use an Index Number

Zeisel (1968) has provided the following extensive list of examples in answer to the brief question "When should an index number be used?"

> When does one need an index? Whenever one wants to measure or, at least, rank a complex phenomenon; whenever one must decide how to rank performance in a contest or in a class; whenever one wants to predict which ones among several children promise to be the better students in years to come; whenever one wants to know by how much living expenses have risen as, for instance, to adjust wages to the change; whenever one wants to know whether the nation's health has improved or deteriorated. (Zeisel 1968, 76–77)

A Key Limitation of Index Numbers

Despite their many uses, index numbers do have limitations. An index should not be used to infer that a change that has occurred in the past would continue in the same way in the future; index values are not reliable predictive tools. The change displayed in an index value is a descriptive measure rather than an inferential statistical process; it describes only a specific change that has occurred over a specific time period.

Index numbers can be produced for any variables that can be recorded over time. As a result, they are widely used in political science, public administration, economics, and business and nonprofit management. Examples often seen in political studies include crime statistics, housing starts, population changes, energy produced and/or consumed, economic changes, climatic changes, air or water pollution levels, and many others.

Types of Index Numbers

Index numbers come in a variety of types. They can be simple or complex, weighted or unweighted, and can be used with many different types of characteristics and variables. Simple index numbers indicate change in a single characteristic of a single variable, such as the changes in the price of housing. Complex index numbers indicate change in two or more variables over the same period. An example might be an index made up of the cost of several components needed to produce a product or service.

Index numbers are often used to indicate changes in either one or more of the following characteristics of a variable: (1) the *price* of one or more items, (2) changes in the *quantities* produced, used, or consumed, or (3) a *value-based* index, which is formed by multiplying the price of an item by the quantity used. Each of these index types can reflect changes in a single product or item, or they can be a composite index that is built up of the prices and/or quantities of many different items. The composite index is sometimes called an *aggregate index*.

The value-based index can take any one of three different forms. The differences in the three types of value index numbers are based upon which quantity levels are used in the calculation, the base year, the index year, or both. The three types are:

1. The standard *weighted composite* index, in which the price and quantity for the base year and the price and quantity for the given index year are used in calculating the index value.
2. The *Paasche index,* in which the prices for each of the base and index years are used, but they are applied to only the final- or index-year quantities.
3. The *Laspeyres index,* in which both the base-year and final-index-year prices are used, but they are applied to only the base-year quantities.

Of these three forms, the *Laspeyres index*—sometimes called the *classical* approach—is the method seen most often. Each of the types of index numbers is illustrated in the following sections.

Developing a Simple Index

A simple index number is based on changes in just one characteristic of a single variable. Examples include such important economic indicators as the number of persons unemployed, the cost of energy, the interest rate for thirty-year mortgages, mileage rates for new automobiles, and many, many more. Table 20.2 displays quantities consumed and a simple index number for the number of vehicles powered by liquefied petroleum gases (LPG) in the United States for the years 1992 to 2000. In all index variants, the base year is always assigned the value of 100.

Calculating a simple index number is accomplished by dividing the value for the current year of interest by the value for the base year, then multiplying the product of this division by 100. In Table 20.2, the index value for 1993 was determined by dividing 269,000 by the base-

Table 20.2

Simple Annual Indexes of Vehicles Fueled by Liquefied Petroleum Gases

	1992	1993	1994	1995	1996	1997	1998	1999	2000
Number	221,000	269,000	264,000	259,000	263,000	263,000	266,000	267,000	268,000
Index	100	122	119	117	119	119	120	121	121

Source: U.S. Dept. of Energy. *Annual Energy Review.* 2002.

year amount, 221,000. In the next step, the product of this division (1.22) was multiplied by 100. This resulted in an index value of 122. The index of 122 may be interpreted as a 22 percent increase in the number of vehicles fueled by LPG from 1992–1993. Similarly, the index value for 1995 is 117. The increase is 17 percent over the same year. The index for 2000 is 121; the increase is 21 percent.

Developing a Simple Composite Index

Adding the measures of two or more variables, rather than the one variable used in the simple index, produces a simple composite index. Table 20.3 displays a set of items that might be included in a simple composite index. Table 20.4 is a complete index table with conversions. Commodities purchased by consumers are listed in the first or left-hand column. Current-year prices for the package sizes included are next. These are followed by prices for the same amounts in the base year. The fourth column is the computed current-year index for each item. The final, or right-hand, column is the index number converted to percentage increases for each item over the time period.

The first step in developing the composite index is to calculate an index for each of the items to be included in the set. Next, add the individual index numbers and calculate a mean (average) value. The mean index value is for the basket of commodities.

Table 20.3

Simple Composite Index for Seven Commodities in a Price Basket

Commodity	2002 Price	1998 Price	Item Index
Bread (1-lb loaf)	1.35	0.75	180
Ground Beef (lb)	1.49	1.09	137
Oleo (1 lb tub)	0.91	0.75	121
2% Milk (1 gal)	2.39	2.09	114
Coffee (14 oz)	3.49	2.99	117
Sugar (lb)	0.65	0.39	167
Grade A Eggs (doz)	1.19	0.79	151

Table 20.4

Price Changes in a Basket of Seven Consumer Products, 1998–2002

Commodity	Size	2002 Price	1998 Price	Index Product	Percent Changes
Bread	1-lb Loaf	$1.35	$0.75	180	80.0
Ground Beef	1 lb	1.49	1.09	137	36.6
Oleomargarine	1-lb Tub	0.91	0.75	121	21.3
2% Milk	Gallon	2.39	2.09	114	14.4
Coffee	14-oz Can	3.39	2.99	113	16.7
Sugar	1 lb	0.65	0.39	167	66.6
Grade A Eggs	Large, Doz	1.19	0.79	151	50.6

Table 20.5

PAC and Soft-Money Political Contributions of the NRA, 1989–1998

Party and Type	Period				
	1989–1990	1991–1992	1993–1994	1995–1996	1997–1998
Democrats:					
PAC Money	$263,708	604392	377920	26200	285700
Soft Money	0	0	0	0	0
Total	263,708	604,392	377,920	262,600	285,700
Republicans:					
PAC Money	475,135	1,129,104	1,475,118	1,303,221	1,347,511
Soft Money	100,000	300,000	308,000	87,725	350,000
Total	575,135	1,129,404	1,783,118	1,390,946	1,697,511
Grand Total:	838,843	1,733,796	2,161,038	1,653,546	1,983,211
Index Numbers:	100	207	258	197	236

Source: Common Cause. *National Rifle Association (NRA) Political Spending Factsheet 1989–1998.* 1999. www.commoncause.org/publications/june99/061599/htm.

The individual items and their 2002 index values are displayed in Table 20.3. Prices are shown for the current or index year, and for the base year. Dividing the base-year prices into the current year, then multiplying by 100, gives the index shown in the right-hand column. Table 20.4 shows how the commodity price index numbers are calculated for each of the items in the basket of goods. The last column in this table is the index converted to the percent change indicated by the index number.

Table 20.5 is another example of simple composite index numbers developed from time series data. The table displays political contribution data reported to the Federal Election Commission by the National Rifle Association. Data are presented for five annual periods, beginning in 1989–1990 and ending in 1997–1998. Both Political Action Committee (PAC) money contributions to candidates and "soft money" contributions to political parties are reported.

Voting records are another form of time series data that lend themselves to the use of index numbers to show change. The data in Table 20.6 are records published by the Mississippi Historical Society; they represent votes by party affiliation in fourteen presidential election years. Index numbers for the two major political parties are shown in the two right-hand columns.

In Table 20.6, index numbers for each year are included in the two right-hand columns. The year 1952 was selected as the base year instead of 1948 because of the very large (87.2 percent) vote by a local "Dixiecrat" group. This was an isolated event that would have caused misinterpretation of the actual trend. As presented in Table 20.6, the index numbers suggest declining votes for Democrat candidates and continued strength in the numbers casting votes for Republican candidates. In addition, note how anomalies in the years 1948 and 1968, if included as outliers in a time series analysis, could corrupt the overall trend that individual-year index numbers reveal.

Table 20.6

Voting History by Political Party for the State of Mississippi, 1948–2000

Year	(%) Democrat	(%) Republican	(%) Other	Democrat Index	Republican Index
1948	10.1	2.5	87.2		
1952	60.4	39.6		100	100
1956	58.2	24.5		96	62
1960	36.3	24.7	39.0	60	62
1964	12.9	87.1		21	220
1968	23.0	13.5	63.5	38	34
1972	19.6	78.2		32	197
1976	49.6	47.7		82	120
1980	49.2	50.8		81	128
1984	37.5	61.4		62	155
1988	39.3	59.7		65	151
1992	40.8	49.7	8.7	68	126
1996	44.1	49.2	5.8	73	124
2000	40.7	57.6	1.7	67	145

Source: Mississippi Historical Society. *Mississippi's Voting History.* 2001–2002.

A Simple Quantity Index

Table 20.7 is the type of simple composite index that uses *quantity* time series data. The table displays rates of consumption for several different forms of renewable energy by residential, commercial, industrial, and transportation users. While the table contains a large amount of data, the processes for developing both simple and simple-composite indexes remain the same: divide the index-year value by the base-year value and multiply the product by 100. The selected base year is 1990; the data are recorded for all years until 2000. An index has been calculated for consumption of all energy forms for each of the four sectors. For example, the index for consumption of all three forms of renewable energy by residential users for 1995 is 104; the index for the commercial sector for the same year is 125. Comparing the two index numbers indicates that growth in the use of renewable energy by residential users lags behind that of the rate of growth by commercial-sector users.

Index numbers can also be plotted to show the relationship of the values to one another over the time period. For example, Figure 20.1 is an Excel-produced scatter plot of the composite index data in Table 20.7, the U.S. Department of Energy's data on the consumption of selected types of renewable energy (missing from the data is wind-generated energy).

A Simple Price Index

A price index is based wholly upon changes in the price of a product, good, or service over some specified period of time. There are many uses for price indexes, and many ways to construct them. As in all indexes, the first-year price in the designated period is the starting

Table 20.7

An Index of Renewable Energy Consumption by End-Use, 1990/2000 (trillion Btu)

Sector	1990	1991	1992	1993	1994	1995	1996	1997	1998	1999	2000
Residential:											
Wood	581	613	645	548	537	596	595	433	387	414	433
Geothermal	6	6	6	7	6	7	7	7	8	8	9
Solar	56	58	60	62	64	65	66	65	65	64	62
Total	642	677	711	616	607	667	668	506	459	486	503
Index	*100*	*105.5*	*110.7*	*96*	*94.5*	*103.9*	*104*	*78.8*	*71.5*	*75.7*	*78.3*
Commercial:											
Wood	37	39	42	44	45	45	49	47	47	51	52
Geothermal	3	3	3	3	4	5	5	6	7	7	8
Total	40	42	45	47	49	50	54	53	54	58	60
Index	*100*	*105*	*112.5*	*117.5*	*122.5*	*125*	*135*	*132.5*	*135*	*145*	*150*
Industrial:											
Wood	1254	1190	1233	1255	1342	1402	1441	1513	1564	1711	1702
Waste	271	275	289	288	318	322	363	338	312	291	287
Geothermal	2	2	2	2	3	3	3	3	3	4	4
Total	1527	1467	1525	1546	1663	1727	1801	1854	1879	2007	1993
Index	*100*	*96.071*	*99.869*	*101.24*	*108.91*	*113.1*	*117.94*	*121.41*	*123.05*	*131.43*	*130.52*
Transportation:											
Alcohol Fuels	63	73	83	97	109	117	84	106	117	122	139
Index	*100*	*115.87*	*131.75*	*153.97*	*173.02*	*185.71*	*133.33*	*168.25*	*185.71*	*193.65*	*220.63*
TOTAL:	2272	2259	2365	2307	2248	2561	2612	2518	2509	2673	2695
Composite Index:	100	99.428	104.09	101.54	98.944	112.72	114.96	110.83	110.43	117.65	118.62

Source: U.S. Dept. of Energy. *Annual Energy Review.* 2002.

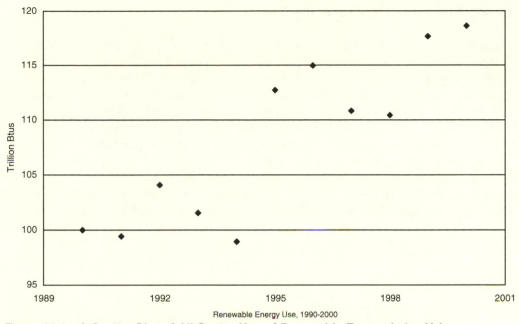

Figure 20.1   **A Scatter Plot of All-Sector Use of Renewable Energy Index Values, 1990–2000**

point and is assigned an index number of 100. This first year is the *base year* for the price index.

For example, say 1998 was designated the starting point—the base year—for a price index. If prices rose 3 percent in 1999, an index of 103 would be assigned to the year 1999. If in the year 2000 prices were 10 percent higher than they were in the 1998 base year, the index value for 2000 would be 110. Each year after the base year has its own index value; this value is always based on change from the base year, regardless of what occurs in years between the base and index year.

Index numbers can also be used to indicate declines in prices. If prices were 6 percent lower in 2000 than they were in the 1998 base year, the index value for 2000 would be 94. Index numbers can also be applied as reference indicators of earlier prices. If 1990's prices were 60 percent lower than 1998 base-year prices, the 1990 index would be 40.

The base year remains in effect until a new base year is established. Base years are selected by the researcher, and are usually selected because they have some meaning or point of reference. For example, the base year 1990 in Table 20.5 was selected because it was the first year that all data were recorded by the Department of Energy. Fuel price index numbers are often pegged at 1974 prices, after the price of crude petroleum quadrupled in a single year, 1973. Base years vary with the goals and objectives of the manager establishing an index, but when selected, they are seldom changed.

Developing a Composite Index

While it is important to know how individual commodity prices have performed, it is more likely that an *overall* or *composite* index value will have more value when planning for decision making. There are three ways to develop a composite price index: the *weighted-index* method, the *Laspeyres index* method, and the *Paasch index* method. The weighted-index method uses prices and quantities of both the base and index years. The weighted-average-of-prices method produces the same value as the Laspeyres method. The Laspeyres method uses a weighted-price index that is founded on quantities used during the *base* year. The Paasch index method uses quantities used during the current or *index* year.

Most political, public administration, and economics index numbers use the Laspeyres method, with all values constructed from base year quantities. Therefore, the example included here follows the Laspeyres procedure. The statistical formula for the Laspeyres procedure is:

$$I = \Sigma P_{it} Q_{ib} \; \Sigma P_{ib} Q_{ib} * 100$$

where

$I_t =$	the index number for the year t
$P_{it} =$	the price of each item in the current or index year
$Q_{ib} =$	the quantity of the item used in the base year
$\Sigma P_{it} Q_{io} =$	the sum of price of each item times its base year quantity
$P_{io} =$	the price of each item in the base year
$Q_{ib} =$	the quantity of the item used in the base year
$\Sigma P_{ib} Q_{ib} =$	the sum of price of each item times its base year quantity

The information needed to create either price or quantity-based index numbers is presented in Table 20.8. It includes price and quantity information for 1998, the base year, and for 2002, the current or index year. The computations necessary for establishing the agency's commodity price index are shown in Tables 20.9 and 20.10. Table 20.9 uses the Laspeyres method; Table 20.10 uses the Paasche method. For both, the two value columns must be summed to establish the all-commodity price index for 2002. The current-year total is then divided by the base-year total, and the index computed by multiplying by 100.

For both methods, the two value columns must be summed to establish the all-commodity price index for 2002. The current-year total is then divided by the base-year total, and the index computed by multiplying by 100. An interpretation of the Paasche index is that for the same amounts of commodities used in 2002, the price for this basket of goods has risen 53 percent from 1998 to 2002.

Developing a Quantity-Based Composite Index

A similar procedure is used to establish an index for changes in *quantities* of goods or services. These indexes are often used as an indicator of the health and productivity of an economy, and its growth. An example is the index of industrial production. Just as for developing a price

Table 20.8

Relative Prices and Quantities for Basic Commodities, Family of Three, 1998–2002

	Prices per Unit		Quantities Used	
COMMODITY	1998	2002	1998	2002
Bread (1-lb loaf)	$0.75	1.35	80 loafs	300 loafs
Ground Beef (lb)	1.09	1.49	150 lbs	200 lbs
Oleomargarine (lb)	0.75	0.91	40 lbs	120 lbs
2% Milk (gal)	2.09	2.39	75 gals	140 gals
Coffee (14 oz)	2.99	3.49	30 cans	45 cans
Sugar (lb)	0.39	0.65	25 lbs	30 lbs
Large Eggs (doz)	0.79	1.19	52 doz	65 doz

Source: Personal data 2002.

Table 20.9

Laspeyres Computations for a Consumer Commodity Price Index (Base Year Quantities)

	Base Year			Index Year		
Item	1998 Price	1998 Quantity	Base-Yr Value	2002 Price	1998 Quantity	Index-Yr Value
Bread (1-lb loaf)	0.75	280	210.00	1.35	280	378.00
Ground Beef (1 1b)	1.09	150	163.50	1.49	150	223.50
Oleomargarine (1 lb)	0.75	40	30.00	0.91	40	36.40
2% Milk (1 gal)	2.09	75	156.75	2.39	75	179.25
Coffee (14-oz can)	2.99	30	89.70	3.49	30	104.70
Sugar (1 lb)	0.39	25	9.75	0.65	25	16.25
Grade A Eggs (doz)	0.79	52	41.08	1.19	52	61.88
		Sum:	700.78		Sum:	999.98

1998 Index = 100

Laspeyres price index = 999.98/700.78 * 100 = 1.42 * 100 = 142.70, or 143

Table 20.10

Paasche Computations for a Consumer Commodity Price Index

	Base Year			Index Year		
Item	1998 Price	2002 Quantity	Base Yr Value	2002 Price	2002 Quantity	2002 Value
Bread (1-lb loaf)	0.75	300	435.00	1.35	300	783.00
Ground Beef (1 lb)	1.09	200	381.50	1.49	200	521.50
Oleomargarine (1 lb)	0.75	72	264.00	0.91	72	443.52
2% Milk (1 gal)	2.09	140	456.10	2.39	140	558.10
Coffee (14-oz can)	2.99	42	335.58	3.49	42	524.58
Sugar (1 lb)	0.39	30	175.20	0.65	30	243.00
Grade A Eggs (doz)	0.79	65	261.35	1.19	65	455.35
		Sum:	2308.73		Sum:	3529.05
1998 Index = 100			152.856			

Paasche index = 3.529.05/2,308.73 * 100 = 1.52 * 100 = 152.86, or 153

index, the Laspeyres (base-weighted) method is also used most often for establishing a quantity index. With quantities, however, the base-year prices are used rather than base-year quantities.

Table 20.11 displays a simple quantity-change index for individual commodities. The data are the estimated quantities purchased over a one-year period by a family of three. The base year is 1998; the index year is 2002. A base-weighted table of computations for a quantity index follows this table.

Developing a Weighted Quantity Index

The procedure for producing a weighted quantity index using base-year quantities begins with the following formula:

$$\text{Price-Weighted Quantity Index} = \Sigma Q_{it} P_{it} / \Sigma Q_{ib} P_{ib} * 100$$

Table 20.11

Percent Changes in Quantities of Selected Commodities, 1998–2002

	Quantities		Quantity Changes
Commodity	2002	1998	1998 to 2002 (%)
Bread (1-lb loaf)	300	280	+7
Ground Beef (lb)	200	150	+33
Oleo (1-lb tub)	72	40	+80
2% Milk (1 gal)	140	75	+87
Coffee (14-oz can)	45	30	+50
Sugar (lb)	30	25	+20
Grade A Eggs (doz)	65	52	+25

Table 20.12

Data for a Base-Weighted Quantity Index

	1998 Price	1998 Quantity	BP*BQ	2002 Price	1998 Quantity	CP*BQ
Bread (1-lb loaf)	0.75	280	210.00	1.35	280	378.00
Ground Beef (lb)	1.09	150	163.50	1.49	150	223.50
Oleo (1-lb tub)	0.75	40	30.00	0.91	40	36.40
2% Milk (1 gal)	2.09	75	156.75	2.39	75	179.25
Coffee (14-oz can)	2.99	30	89.70	3.49	30	104.70
Sugar (lb)	0.39	25	9.75	0.65	25	16.25
Grade A Eggs (doz)	0.79	52	41.08	1.19	52	61.88
		Sum:	700.78		Sum:	999.98

Price-Weighted Quantity Index = 999.98/700.78*100 = 142.6953, or 143

The index is the sum of the base-year quantities (1998) times the base-year prices (1998), divided by the sum of the base-year quantities (1998) times the index-year price (2002), multiplied by 100. The index for the data in Table 20.12 is (700.98 divided by 999.98) times 100, or 143. In index terms, this means that the costs of all items in the basket in 2002 were 43 percent higher than they were in 1998.

Summary

Index numbers are descriptive statistics. They are practical answers to practical problems. Their purpose is to provide an easy-to-understand measurement of change. They can be developed as indicators of changes in prices or quantities or both. They are all based on time series data. Change recorded as time series is considered in relation to some previously established base period.

There are at least three different ways to calculate price and quantity indexes; the most commonly used method is the Laspeyres base-weighted procedure. The Laspeyres method uses quantities from the base year for its calculations. Another is the Paasche method. The Paasche Index used quantities consumed in the index rather than the base year. A third method is to use a weighted approach. Weights can be based on any relevant factor.

For most price index numbers, base-period *quantities* in the Laspeyres approach are used. For a quantity index, base-period *prices* are used. The index value of a price series always uses the value 100 to represent the *base*-period level. Percentage changes for subsequent years are stated in relation to this base value. For example, if prices in Year 2 of a time series are 25 percent higher than they were in the base period, the index value for Year 2 is 125. If they are, say, 13 percent lower than in the base year, the index number is 87.

While it is important to know how individual commodity prices have performed, often an *overall* or *composite* index value will have more value when planning for decision making. There are three ways to develop a composite price index: the *weighted-index* method, the *Laspeyres index* method, and the *Paasche index* method. Most political, public administration, and economics index numbers use the Laspeyres method.

Quantity-based composite indices are often used as an indicator of the health and productivity of an economy, and its growth. An example is the index of industrial production.

Discussion Questions

1. What are index numbers; how can they be used in political science?
2. Changes over time in what two factors are commonly shown as index numbers?
3. When is it appropriate to use an index number?
4. What is a value-based index?
5. What is an aggregate index?
6. What is a weighted composite index?
7. What is a Paasche index?
8. What is a Laspeyres index?
9. Give an example of a simple price index.
10. Give an example of a quantity-based index.

Additional Reading

Allen, R.G.D. 1975. *Index Numbers in Theory and Practice*. Chicago: Aldine Publishing Co.

Brown, Robert G. 1963. *Smoothing, Forecasting and Prediction of Discrete Time Series*. Englewood Cliffs, NJ: Prentice-Hall.

Fischer, Franklin M., and Karl Shell. 1972. *The Economic Theory of Price Indices*. New York: Academic Press.

Fleming, Michael C., and Joseph G. Nellis. 1991. *The Essence of Statistics for Business*. Englewood Cliffs, NJ: Prentice-Hall.

Garner, Theresa, David S. Johnson, and Mary F. Kokoski. 1996. "An Experimental Consumer Price Index for the Poor." *Monthly Labor Review*. 119 (September): 32–42.

21 Predicting the Future III: Discriminant Analysis Methods

Discriminant analysis is one of a series of statistical techniques designed to analyze relationships among two or more variables; it belongs to the multivariate statistics family of tests (Bennett and Bowers 1976; Maxwell 1977; Klecka 1980). Other often-encountered multivariate techniques include multiple regression analysis, multiple dimensional scaling, factor analysis, cluster analysis, multiple analysis of variance and multiple analysis of covariance, among others. Discriminant analysis has been defined as a mathematical technique that weighs and combines a set of measurements in a way that their ability to discriminate between two or more groups is maximized (Cooper 1987). When more than two grouping variables are used in the design, the discriminant process is considered to be *multiple discriminant analysis* (MDA). With MDA it is possible to assign subjects to two or more groups on the basis of their scores or measurements on two or more tests or scales (Kerlinger and Pedhazur 1973).

The underlying research problem in discriminant analysis is how to establish a decision rule that enables assigning (or predicting) a subject whose group membership is not known to only one of the categories that make up a complete group. Although assigning is done on the basis of measurements on a set of descriptor variables, selection of these loading items is the province of the researcher. Thus, it is difficult, if not impossible, to know if the selected items constitute the best combination of items.

A set of measurements can be any number of different types of descriptive variables, including such descriptors as demographics, attitude scales, lifestyle characteristics, behavioral measurements, preferences, and others. Group assignment or prediction is made upon the basis of subjects' scores on these characteristics. A group can be any two or more distinct sets in a sample. Examples of two-group sets include Republican/Democrat; committed/noncommitted voters; legislators who, regardless of their party affiliation, traditionally vote for legislation on social issues and those who vote against such legislation; nonprofit organizations that either support or ignore environmental issues; patients with one or more symptoms who are likely to develop or not develop a disease, etc.

Discriminant Analysis Applications

Regardless of the application, discriminant analysis requires that several important assumptions be met. First, the distribution of measurements for the descriptive (independent) variables must be approximately normal. Second, the sample must be relatively large; samples in the range of 250 to 300 are considered to be of minimum size, although the process works with smaller samples. Third, independent variable measurements must be at least nominal-level (or transformed into dummy variables). Fourth, it must be possible to distinguish between two or more known categories among the sample. And fifth, there should be no missing values on either the dependent or independent variables for any subject included in the analysis; most statistical packages provide for elimination of cases with missing data with a simple instruction.

In practice, discriminant analysis can be used in at least five different types of applications. First, the technique may be used as a way of *classifying* and *describing* subjects in two or more respective relevant groups at the same time. Second, political scientists use discriminant analysis as a tool for improving the quality of their *predictions* about which subject belongs with which group and why. Third, researchers often use the technique to determine which descriptive variables have the greatest *power to discriminate* between two or more groups of people. Fourth, the method may be used as a *post hoc* test, in which it serves as a check for diagnoses or predictions made on the bases of other types of evaluations. And fifth, discriminant analysis may be used to gauge how far apart the groups are located on a set of descriptive characteristics. In this application, which is somewhat similar to the discrimination test, the distance between groups is based upon the location of the central tendency values (called *centroids*) for each group in two-dimensional space established by computer-generated functions. Each of these applications is discussed in greater detail in this chapter, beginning with the use of discriminant analysis to classify or predict groups.

Two Discriminant Analysis Models

In their review of the capacity of discriminant analysis procedures contained in three different statistical software packages, Huberty and Lowman (1997) distinguished between two fundamental types of discriminant analysis: descriptive (DDA) and predictive (PDA). In the DDA model, it is the *grouping variable* that serves as the predictor variable, with the responses on the descriptive-characteristics variables taking on the role of the outcome variables. The DDA model is used less often in political science research than the PDA model, but enough to warrant greater explanation here. The role of each set of variables is reversed in the predictive model; in the PDA model, characteristic variables serve as predictor factors.

The Descriptive Discriminant Analysis Model

For an example of a DDA application, a researcher might want to know if differences in a set of descriptive characteristics—the outcome variables—can be used to make the differences between groups distinct, logical, and understandable. The research question in descriptive designs is centered, not on the differences themselves, but instead on *how* the groups differ on some set of descriptors. For example, discriminant analysis may be used to test whether voters and nonvoters are the same or different on a set of lifestyle characteristics. The same model could be used to develop descriptive profiles of several candidates for political office, or of adults who are politically active or politically inactive, for example. The DDA method tests of the grouping variable(s) to differentiate among the characteristics of group members.

Most applications of discriminant analysis in political science use the predictive approach. In predictive applications the grouping variable is simply the categorical variable that signifies group membership; in these circumstances, the set of characteristics variables serve as the predictor variables. The predictive model is discussed in greater detail below.

The Predictive Discriminant Analysis Model

In an example of the PDA application, Cooper (1987) first used cluster analysis to group nations according to the type and size of their debt to foreign banks. After developing a profile of nations that had failed in the past, he then used discriminant analysis to predict which debtor nations were most likely to fail in their repayments of the debt.

Roberts (1992) used discriminant analysis in a voter prediction study. She employed panel information gathered in three waves leading up to the 1990 Texas gubernatorial elections. The data consisted of measurements of subjects' attitude changes over time. In her sample of 283 subjects, 52.5 percent were male, 47.5 percent female; 49.6 percent were registered Republicans, and 50.4 percent registered as Democrats. The dependent variable in the study was exit interviews in which subjects reported for which candidate they voted. Independent variables— the descriptive scales—consisted of multi-item variables measuring partisanship, gender, degree of media reliance, and closeness of their attention in following the race. After editing for missing data, Roberts resulted with 160 valid cases. Using the set of independent variable measurements, discriminant analysis revealed that they correctly grouped 84 percent of the male voters and 91 percent of the female voters.

In another example of a predictive application, Kim (1995) used a discriminant analysis design in a comparative study in which he tested the power of selected scales to predict the voting behavior of uncommitted voters in 1992 presidential elections in North Carolina and in the Republic of South Korea. Kim then used the same scales to predict how voter behavior would change after a third or minority party dropped from the race late in the campaign period. Kim found that in political polls, analysts are often uncertain as to how to treat uncommitted voters in the findings. That uncertainty has resulted in at least four different ways of looking at uncommitted data:

1. Eliminate the group from the analysis entirely.
2. Assign the uncommitted group on the basis of another discrete descriptive variable, such as the party affiliation of the respondent.
3. Predict the group assignments on the basis of an attitudinal variable, such as the respondent's attitude toward candidates, parties, and/or their position on key political issues in the campaign.
4. Use qualitative information gathered from intensive personal interviews with a small sample of respondents, then classify the uncommitted group according to how similar they are to the interviewed sample.

Kim was convinced that neither of the four approaches used took full advantage of the collected information. Also, they often resulted in grossly inadequate prediction results—a fact that could have serious effects on a political campaign strategy. Instead, Kim proposed using a discriminant analysis design upon which to base the uncommitted voter classifications. Kim concluded that discriminant analysis is particularly useful for the following purposes: (1) to identify the election issues and the demographic variables with the greatest power to discriminate between groups, (2) to predict how many of the uncommitted voters would vote for each

Table 21.1

An Example of Discriminant Results for a Prediction Application

Country Sample	Prediction Power with 3rd-Party Candidate in the Race	Prediction Power, 3rd-Party Candidate out of the Race
United States	73.0% of grouped cases correctly classified	87.0% of grouped cases correctly classified
Korea	82.9% of grouped cases correctly classified	87.2% of grouped cases correctly classified

of the candidates, and (3) to judge the effect one candidate withdrawing from a race with more than two candidates will have on the distribution of votes for the remaining candidates.

Kim's comparison of possible Korean voter reaction with third-party candidates in a race and their reaction when the third-party candidate withdraws was particularly insightful. The results of his analysis with seventeen predictor variables are shown in Table 21.1; the data were collected from nationwide polls.

Predicting Organizational Commitment: An Example

Discriminant analysis was also used to determine whether responses on the Organizational Climate Assessment Survey (OCAS) instrument could predict the level of commitment to an organization. The test took place as part of an organizational development study conducted for a large public agency (McNabb and Sepic 2002). The organization provides public-safety serices in a county with a population of 1.5 million, and also provides several municipalities within the county with contract police services. The department also manages the regional correction facility. The study began after an acrimonious internal debate over management philosophy resulted in the departure of the chief executive officer. The data were gathered during the search for a new department administrator. The research began in 1998 and concluded in late 1999.

The Assessment Instrument

The OCAS instrument was developed over nearly a decade of trial and revisions. Items with low reliability scores after several applications were deleted or integrated into other items. A review of thirteen different approaches to climate assessment resulted in a grouping of items into nine separate climate-dimension scales (Sepic and McNabb 1992; Sepic, Barnowe, Simpson, and McNabb 1998). These dimensions are *structure, responsibility, risk, rewards, warmth and support, conflict, organizational identity, values,* and *approved practices.* Definitions for each dimension follow.

- *Structure:* The feelings that employees have about structural constraints in the organization.
- *Responsibility:* The feeling of being "your own boss," of not being forced to double-check all decisions with higher authority.

- *Risk:* The sense of risks and challenge encountered in the organization.
- *Rewards:* The feeling of being rewarded for a job well done. An emphasis exists in the organization on positive rewards for personnel, rather than punishments.
- *Warmth and support:* The feeling of good fellowship that prevails in the work group atmosphere; emphasis on mutual support from above and below.
- *Conflict:* The feeling that managers and other workers are open to hearing different opinions; emphasis on getting problems out in the open.
- *Organizational identity:* The extent to which members of the group identify with the organization.
- *Values:* The extent to which members of the organization believe that ethical principles are important, that the organization's core values and codes of conduct can and should be upheld in all circumstances.
- *Approved practices:* The perceived importance of implicit and explicit goals and performance standards; emphasis on doing a good job.

Data-Gathering Methods

The survey instrument included multiple items designed to assess the above nine dimensions. Responses to all items were made on a seven-point scale. For items assessing the first eight dimensions, a value of "1" indicated that the item "very definitely describes" the way things are in the organization, and a value of "7" indicated that the item "does not describe" the way things are. A number of items were worded so that the response category "very definitely describes" indicated a negative meaning (i.e., a negative or unfavorable aspect of climate). These items were reverse-scored so that a low score indicated a more favorable climate, and a high score indicated an unfavorable climate.

Full-Sample Scores

Dimension summary (index) scores for the sample are compared in Table 21.2. They are listed in ascending order by mean score (most favorable index scores are listed first).

Two discriminant tests were run on the data. The first run excluded the ethics scale from the set of predictive variables. Table 21.3 shows the success rate for the scale without the ethics items. The model successfully predicted ethical group membership nearly 78 percent of the time.

The ethics scale was retained in the second discriminant run. Those results are displayed in Table 21.4. As expected, including the ethics scale specifically developed for this organization greatly increased the predictive power of the composite instrument; the percentage of cases correctly classified increased from 77.6 percent in the basic instrument to more than 96 percent correct classification with the composite instrument. This measure of effectiveness is called a "hit ratio." It is presented as a percentage, with 100 percent meaning that all cases were correctly predicted in their respective group (Bennett and Bowers 1976).

In the discriminant analysis run with the ethics scale included, the distances between group centroids increased from the 1.649 points on the computed factor to 3.297 points on the function. Those results are shown in Table 21.6. Inclusion of the ethics scale greatly increased the predictive power of the composite instrument; not only did the percentage of cases correctly classified increase, the differences between the groups were determined to be nearly twice as distant from one another, suggesting the superior power of the composite scale to discriminate between groups.

Table 21.2

Dimension Index Scores for Government Agency Study

Dimension	Mean	Standard deviation
Approved Practices	3.50	0.94
Values	3.54	0.68
Responsibility	3.70	1.17
Organizational Identity	4.13	1.33
Warmth and Support	4.15	1.23
Structure	4.41	1.09
Risk	4.57	0.99
Conflict	4.64	0.98
Rewards	5.36	1.25

Source: Unpublished study by McNabb and Sepic 2002.
Note: A low mean score (1.0) indicates a favorable climate, a high mean score (7.0) an unfavorable climate (midpoint = 4.0).

Table 21.3

Results of Classification Test on Data without the Ethics Items

	Classification Results[a]		
	Predicted Group Membership		
Personal-Ethics-Group Membership	More-Ethical Group	Less-Ethical Group	Total
More-Ethical Group	104	26	130
Less-Ethical Group	25	73	98
Ungrouped Cases	2	4	6
More-Ethical Group	80.0	20.0	100.0
Less-Ethical Group	25.5	74.5	100.0
Ungrouped Cases	33.3	66.7	100.0

Source: Unpublished study by McNabb and Sepic 2002.
[a]77.6% of original grouped cases correctly classified.

Group-Classification Applications

The group-classification use process can be described in the same way that the ethics scale was employed. Consider the following example: Suppose that a researcher is working with two equal-size groups of politically aware people, of whom 160 consider themselves to be liberals at heart and 160 say they are conservatives. Each of the 320 subjects is measured on several describing characteristics. The researcher wants to know whether the variables can be used as a tool for distinguishing between the two political groups. Discrimination analysis, by com-

Table 21.4

Results of Classification Test on Data with the Ethics Scale Included

Classification Results[a]

Personal-Ethics-Group Membership	Predicted Group Membership		Total
	More-Ethical Group	Less-Ethical Group	
More-Ethical Group	126	4	130
Less-Ethical Group	5	93	98
Ungrouped Cases	0	1	1
More-Ethical Group	96.9	3.1	100.0
Less-Ethical Group	5.1	94.9	100.0
Ungrouped Cases	0.0	100.0	100.0

Source: Unpublished study by McNabb and Sepic 2002.
[a]96.1% of original grouped cases correctly classified.

Table 21.5

Centroids for Groups with the Complete OCAS Instrument

Functions at Group Centroids

	Function
Personal-Ethics-Group Membership	1
More-Ethical Group	−.709
Less-Ethical Group	.940

Source: Unpublished study by McNabb and Sepic 2002.
Note: Unstandardized canonical discriminant functions evaluated at group mean.

Table 21.6

Centroid Values for Composite OCAS Instrument

Functions at Group Centroids

	Function
Personal-Ethics-Group Membership	1
More-Ethical Group	−1.417
Less-Ethical Group	1.880

Source: Unpublished study by McNabb and Sepic 2002.

paring known with predicted group membership, will give the analyst a numerical measure of the prediction effectiveness of the scale.

Testing the Discrimination Power of Scales

In another application, discriminant analysis was used in a study conducted to test methodology for segmenting groups of high school students according to their interests in postsecondary education (McNabb 1980). This study compared different scales of measurement on the basis of their power to discriminate between pre-identified segments. The study first grouped a sample of 195 secondary-school students into different groups according to their stated intent to attend one of five different types of postsecondary institutions, together with a sixth group that did not plan to continue their education immediately after high school. This enabled determination of which of the demographic, social, economic, and attitudinal scales had the greatest power to classify subjects into their preidentified groups.

Post Hoc Validation of Other Diagnosis Models

In a fourth application, Runyon, Faust, and Orvaschel (2002) used discriminant analysis to determine whether scales developed to diagnose children with posttraumatic stress disorder (PTSD) were effective in distinguishing between children who were or were not suffering current depression. The researchers tested the Children's Schedule of Affective Disorders and Schizophrenia (K-SDAS) and the Children's Depression Inventory (CDI) on a sample of 96 children, ranging in age from 5 to 17 years. Their discriminant analysis found that, overall, the items they selected after analysis of variance for statistically significant differences were able to successfully classify children with both disorders 81.8 percent of the time (see Table 21.5).

Discriminant Analysis Software

The Statistical Package for the Social Sciences (SPSS) contains a discriminant analysis capability. Discriminant analysis is possibly best known in political science as a tool for predicting which individuals will fall into two or more separate groups based upon the measurements taken from a similar sample of subjects. This is the method that SPSS defines in Version 11 (2001) of the package: "Discriminant analysis is useful for situations where you want to build a predictive model of group membership based on observed characteristics of each case. The procedure generates a discriminant function (or, for more than two groups, a set of discriminant functions) based on linear combinations of the predictor variables that provide the best discrimination between the groups."

How Discriminant Analysis Works

The discriminant-analysis model calculates distances between measurements of central tendency for each group. These central measurements are termed "centroids," and are plotted by SPSS® on what is called a "territorial map." The map displays the position of correlation coefficient in two-dimensional space. The axes of the territorial map are the functions that are computed by the discriminant algorithm. SPSS ® for Windows ® computes the centroids values for the previously established groups. The centroids table was produced by SPSS ® from the organizational development study data cited earlier. These centroids were developed for the OCAS instrument.

The following example information is contained in the "help" section of the program: On average, people in temperate-zone countries consume more calories per day than those in the tropics, and a greater proportion of the people in the temperate zones are city dwellers. A researcher wants to combine this information in a function to determine how well an individual can discriminate between the two groups of countries. The researcher thinks that population size and economic information may also be important.

If these variables are useful for discriminating between the two climate zones, the values of D will differ for the temperate and tropical countries. If you use a stepwise variable-selection method, you may find that you do not need to include all four variables in the function.

Statistics. For each variable: means, standard deviations, univariate ANOVA. For each analysis: Box's M, within-groups correlation matrix, within-groups covariance matrix, separate-groups covariance matrix, total covariance matrix. For each canonical discriminant function: eigenvalue, percentage of variance, canonical correlation, Wilks' lambda, and chi-square. For each step: prior probabilities, Fisher's function coefficients, unstandardized function coefficients, Wilks' lambda for each canonical function. Tables 21.7 and 21.8 are examples of the information produced by the discriminant-analysis program.

Table 21.7

Eigenvalues for Composite OCAS Instrument

Eigenvalues

Function	Eigenvalue	% of Variance	Cumulative %	Canonical Correlation
1	0.672[a]	100.0	100.0	0.634

[a]First 1 canonical discriminant functions were used in the analysis.

Table 21.8

Wilks' Lambda Values for Composite OCAS Instrument

Wilks' Lambda

Test of Function(s)	Wilks' Lambda	Chi-square	df	Sig.
1	0.598	103.566	49	0.000

Summary

Discriminant analysis, a multivariate statistics application, analyzes relationships among two or more variables. Other multivariate techniques include multiple regression analysis, multiple dimensional scaling, factor analysis, cluster analysis, multiple analysis of variance, and multiple analysis of covariance, among others. Discriminant analysis is a mathematical technique that weighs and combines a set of measurements in a way that their ability to discriminate between two or more groups is maximized.

Classifying groups with cluster analysis uses a set of classification correlations between each scale item and the composite functions. Item contribution is measured by the size of correlation value; higher correlation coefficients mean greater contribution.

Two different types of discriminant analysis have been identified: descriptive (DDA) and predictive (PDA). In the DDA model, it is the grouping variable that serves as the predictor variable, with the responses on the descriptive characteristics variables taking on the role of the outcome variables. In the PDA model, characteristic variables serve as predictor factors. The PDA model is used most often in political science research.

The research problem in discriminant analysis is how to assign a subject to membership in a particular group, or to predict in which group a subject belongs. Assigning and/or predicting is done on the basis of measurements on a set of descriptor variables. Measurements can be any type of descriptive variables, including demographics, attitude scales, lifestyle characteristics, behavioral measurements, preferences, and others. Group assignment or prediction is made upon the basis of subjects' scores on the characteristics.

Discriminant analysis is used for at least four purposes. First, it is a way of *classifying* subjects into relevant groups. Second, it is a tool for improving the quality of *predictions*. Third, it is used to determine which descriptive variables have the greatest *power to discriminate* between two or more groups of people. Fourth, it is used as a *post hoc* test, serving as a check for diagnoses made on the bases of other types of evaluations.

Discussion Questions

1. Define discriminant analysis.
2. What role do classification correlations play in discriminant analysis?
3. Describe the descriptive discriminant model.
4. Describe the predictive discriminant model.
5. How does discriminant analysis classify subjects into groups?
6. How does discriminant analysis improve the quality of predictions?
7. How does discriminant analysis determine the discrimination power of scales?
8. How can discriminant analysis be used as a post hoc test for diagnoses?

Additional Reading

Bennett, Spencer, and David Bowers. 1976. *An Introduction to Multivariate Techniques for Social and Behavioral Sciences.* London: Macmillan.
Huberty, Carl J. 1994. *Applied Discriminant Analysis.* New York: John Wiley.
Klecka, William R. 1980. *Discriminant Analysis.* Beverly Hills: Sage.
Maxwell, Albert E. 1977. *Multivariate Analysis in Behavioral Research.* London: Chapman and Hall.

22 Managing Large Databases: Factor and Cluster Analysis Methods

Much research in political science involves analyzing just one or two variables at a time. The techniques used for this research are known as *univariate* (one variable) and *bivariate* (two variables) statistics. However, there are many times in a research project when it is necessary to analyze more than two variables at once. The procedures used in these situations are referred to as *multivariate* statistics. With affordable personal computers available and present at nearly everyone's desk, the use of multivariate processes has increased dramatically. This chapter looks at two multivariate techniques, *cluster analysis* and *factor analysis*. These two procedures are used in the management and analysis of large databases. Large databases are those datasets that consist of measurements in the neighborhood of 300 and more subjects and/or 100 or more variables.

Multivariate statistical analysis is often used to determine and explain how groups of variables are related, and ultimately to develop theories of causation that can be traced to those relationships (Bernard 2000; Eber 1975). Cluster and factor multivariate analysis procedures are based on the results of this type of relationship testing.

Database Reduction and Management

Data reduction is one of the processes applied in database management. Factor analysis is one of the most common data reduction tools. However, cluster analysis, image analysis, and component analysis are additional tools used for dataset reduction purposes (Eber 1975). Factor analysis serves many different purposes, the most important of which are the reduction in the number of variables and for testing of hypotheses. Factor analysis techniques include *principal-component analysis* (PCA) and *standard-factor analysis* (SFA). PCA is similar to SFA in concept and application; it is one of the seven different ways that the SPSS® statistical software package provides for extracting the factors that underlie a set of measurements. However, the principal-components model does not result in a direct reduction in the number of variables. Instead, the model lists components in the order of the amount of variation they explain in all the variables (Cattell 1978; Goddard and Kirby 1976). PCA transforms an original dataset of variables into a set of uncorrelated variables. The new composite variables (components) include most of the information in the original dataset, but does so with fewer variables. (Dunteman 1994, 157).

The SFA model, which is also known as *common-factor analysis* (CFA), is used more often than PCA. With SFA the observed variables are considered to be causal influences on the underlying factors as well as influences on factors that are unique to each observed variable (Lance and Vandenberg 2002). SFA examines the variance in a set of variables and then groups together the variables or subjects that show the smallest amount of variance among themselves, while showing larger variation from other groupings. The things that go together is this way are then considered to be a "type," or a *factor*. Examining a smaller number of factors results in a reduction in complexity. This makes it much easier to deal with large volumes of data (Eber 1975, 555).

Cluster analysis results in a reduction in the amount of data with which the researcher must work, but involves more subjective decision making than factor analysis. However, cluster analysis is a popular tool for grouping people into similar categories or classifications; it has become an important statistical tool for identifying and describing voter segments in political campaigning, and even more important as a tool in business for segmenting markets for products and services. PCA, SFA, and cluster analysis are discussed in greater detail in this chapter.

Factor Analysis

Factor analysis is one of a family of statistical techniques for summarizing interrelationships among a set of variable measurements, identifying underlying structure in a dataset, and reducing the number of variables with which the researcher must work. The techniques all produce a smaller number of artificial variables, called *factors* or *components*. Factors are artificial constructs generated by the statistical program that are based on measures of intercorrelations; they represent what is common among the original variables (Babbie 2001; Cattell 1978; Lance and Vandenberg 2002). Bernard (2000) called these underlying constructs "super variables" because they are made up of more than one initial variable. The initial variables that make up the factors do so on the basis of the strength of their *similarity correlation* with the factor. The variables included in the factor, in turn, help the researcher find meaning in and subjectively explain the composition of each factor.

A factor is nothing more than a variable that is a composite of other variables. By examining the commonality of the initial variables and the strength of their factor correlations (called *factor loadings)*, factor analysis helps make it possible to explain portions of the variance in a dependent variable. An arbitrary number of important variables (importance is determined by the size of the factor loadings) are determined to make up the composite factor. Interpretation of the factor is a subjective determination of the researcher. The cutoff point in the number of variables loading on a factor is also at the discretion of the researcher. Traditionally, only variables with correlation values of .60 or greater are always included, with loadings of from .30 to .59 are considered as possible contributors. According to Bernard, however, some researchers use .50 as the cutoff point in factor loadings, with values from .30 to .49 considered as possibly worth including.

Many researchers feel that the subjective interpretation of factors is one of the greatest advantages of factor analysis. Subjective interpretation makes it possible to interject an aspect of reality to the process; it is an attempt to decipher meaning from simple numerical description. However, Babbie (2001) saw this subjectivity as the root cause of several disadvantages of the technique, including the following:

- The factors themselves are generated mathematically, with no meaningful assistance of the researcher; interpretation occurs *after* establishment of the factors and factor loadings of the individual variables.
- Factor analysis does not provide a means for disproving a hypothesis; therefore, it is more a qualitative analysis technique than a scientific, positivist research approach.
- No matter what data the researcher includes in the analysis matrix, factor analysis will generate a factor solution. The algorithm ignores the form and content of the initial variables. Therefore, the factor result may be nonsense.

Factor analysis processes data that are in a standard matrix format; that is, the rows are individual cases (subjects); each column is the score for each subject on the specific variable. The data may be of any level of measurement: nominal, ordinal, interval, or ratio, and may be discrete or continuous. If, however, the data are measured in many different ways—for example, if some in dollars, yen, and euros; some as demographic characteristics; and some as attitude scales, etc.—it is a good idea to standardize the data into similar units so that meaningful comparisons can be made between the distributions (Goddard and Kirby 1976). The most frequently used standardization involves converting to standardized (Z) scores. Z-scores have a mean of zero (0) and a standard deviation of one (1). There are some problems with standardization, however. Chief among these problems is that with Z-score standardization all variables are given equal weight, whereas in reality, some variables are inherently more important than others in a particular application. In such cases, weights should be assigned to the more important variables. However, the factor analysis algorithm does not allow for assigning weights. Therefore, the problem of when to use standardization is left to the researcher (Alenderfer and Blashfield 1984; Kaufman and Rousseeuw 1990). The decision should be made on a case-by-case basis, and researchers must know that the solution after standardization may be different than the solution without standardization.

Factor analysis requires that the data meet a few simple assumptions: a normal distribution, a large sample size (an *n* of at least 300, although some researchers reduce this to a minimum of 150 cases), at least nominal-level (or standardized) data, a linear relationship, and outliers screened and omitted. When and how to use factor analysis, together with its two main approaches, is discussed below.

Applications of Standard Factor Analysis

Factor analysis is used in two major applications. One, *exploratory factor analysis* (EFA), identifies relationships among variables. The relationships are not always obvious in the data, but show up as a pattern of correlations with artificial factors. The purpose of EFA is to summarize, group, and explain the data. The research interprets the meaning of the factor according to its correlated items. The second chief application for factor analysis is called *confirmatory factor analysis* (CFA). CFA is the newer of the two uses, but is rapidly gaining acceptance by researchers.

Exploratory Factor Analysis

In EFA, the researcher uses the method to determine the minimum number of hypothetical factors or components that account for the variance between the variables; it also is used to *explore* the data for ways to reduce the number of active variables. Well into the 1990s, exploratory models remained the chief factor analysis application in the social sciences (Kim and Mueller 1994). The following steps are presented to guide the researcher through the EFA process:

1. Collect the data from a representative sample.
2. Determine which of the observed variables should be included in the analysis.
3. Determine which method of extraction to use in the analysis.
4. Specify how many factors to include in the solution.
5. Interpret the patterns of factor loadings, variances, and covariances.
6. Rotate the matrix to test for alternative factor structures.
7. Interpret the final EFA solution.

In an example of the EFA method, data acquired by Lee, McNabb, and Barnowe (1999) were subjected to an EFA to identify the underlying structure of an international environmental awareness database. The study assessed awareness and perceived importance of risk associated with a number of environmental and social concerns among a sample of 295 university students in the United States and Taiwan. The researchers combined portions of several instruments available in the research literature to produce a topical and comprehensive instrument. The final instrument was pretested in several undergraduate and graduate classes in private and public universities.

The instrument contained a list of forty-five issues that the researchers believed were naturally classified into three broad groups: items pertaining to the natural, social, and technological environments. Results of an exploratory analysis revealed that the issues logically fell into three major groupings as follows: natural-environment issues, social-environment issues, and technological-environment issues. The natural-environment scale consisted of 24 items often cited as pressing environmental problems. These ranged from ozone depletion and acid rain to Ebola and dioxins. The scale was developed from items focusing on five broad categories of environmental problems: air, water, waste, climate, and disease.

The social environment issues scale contained 13 items associated with the quality of life and health and welfare in modern society. Example items range from tobacco and drug use to AIDs and crime and violence. The scale was constructed from six items in each of two subscale categories: social issues and health issues.

The technological environment scale contained eight items that ranged from nuclear waste to cloning and irradiation of food. These items were subjectively assigned to the technology scale. The scale was constructed from four items each in two subscale categories: technology in science and energy.

Confirmatory Factor Analysis

The purpose of the CFA model is to test hypotheses, about either the number of underlying factors or the variables or items that load on any single factor or component. Having made the assertion in advance which items belong to which factor, the researcher can test his assertion (hypothesis) by examining factor loadings. While describing the difference between the two approaches is relatively simple, Kim and Mueller point out that in practice, the distinction is not always this clear; some of both models is found in many studies.

Table 22.1

A Comparison of EFA and CFA Factor Analysis Approaches

Issue	EFA	CFA
Mathematical Model	Either standard factor or principal components	Standard-factor model
Selection of Measures	Wide variation	Determined by hypothesized factor format
Number of Factors	Determine from the data	Specified before the analysis
Interpretation of Factors	Interpreted from items loading on each factor	Specified before the analysis
Factor Pattern Matrix	Fully free; no constraints	Constrained; a fixed set of elements
Factor Correlations	Established after rotation	Estimated before the analysis
Goodness of Fit	Not an issue	A key, controversial issue

Source: After material in C.E. Lance and R.J. Vandenberg 2002.

Factor analysis methods have been traced back to the initial development of the principal-components model developed by Charles Spearman in 1904. Nearly all of the factor analysis literature from that date, and especially through the 1970s, was concerned with exploratory applications. However, from the 1980s onward, there has been significantly more interest in the CFA model. The objective of CFA is related to hypothesis testing. The researcher hypothesizes that a number of items or variables are collectively related. He or she can run a factor analysis on the data to test whether the relationships exist as they were hypothesized.

In his monograph on confirmatory factor analysis, Long (1984) identified a number of hypotheses that may be established for a CFA analysis. These include specifying the number of factors to be included in the solution, deciding what variables to include, what variances and covariances to expect among both common and unique factors, and what relationships between variables and underlying factors and/or between unique factors and initial variables to expect.

Lance and Vandenberg (2002, 223) developed Table 22.1 to display the major differences between the EFA and CFA approaches.

Today, researchers agree that CFA should be considered a tool for testing the validity of an underlying structure using prior identified variables, whereas EFA should be used as a technique for identifying which variables are related with which other variables. The following seven steps were proposed by Lance and Vandenberg (2002, 221) to lead the researcher through the process of conducting a confirmatory factor analysis:

1. Define the theoretical factors or components to be used in the CFA.
2. Determine what observed variables should load on each theoretical factor.
3. Collect the data from a representative sample.
4. Specify in advance the patterns of factor loadings (which variables should have higher

loadings, etc.), together with amounts of variances and covariances (which factors ought to account for the greatest amount of variance).

5. Propose alternative, competing theoretical factor structures.
6. Estimate model parameters and assess goodness of fit.
7. Interpret the CFA solution.

A Second Confirmatory Factor Analysis Example

Sepic, Barnowe, Simpson, and McNabb employed the sixty-five-item core *Organizational Climate Assessment Survey* (OCAS) scale developed in 1992 as a diagnostic tool used in testing for disequilibrium in organizations. The OCAS was developed over nearly a decade of trial and revisions; it has been tested in both public and private organizations, and is currently being used in several applications is South Korea. Responses to all items on the scale are made on a seven-point scale. In their latest application of the scale, the authors studied the organizational climate of a large, multitask public-safety organization.

A review of thirteen different approaches to climate assessment resulted in a grouping of items into nine separate climate-dimension scales (Sepic and McNabb 1992). These dimensions were labeled and defined as follows: Structure, responsibility, risk, rewards, warmth and support, conflict, organizational identity, values, and approved practices.

The CFA conducted upon all sixty-five items largely confirmed the researcher-imposed structure of the internment.

Analysis Procedure

Descriptive statistics were calculated for each individual item and, following the required item reversals, descriptive statistics computed for each item. Items that make up each dimension were intercorrelated, and the internal consistency reliability (coefficient alpha) of each dimension was examined. Alphas for all but one of the nine scales exceed the .40 alpha value; the four-item *risk* scale failed the test (Table 22.2).

Dimension index scores were developed by computing the mean of all the items that make up each dimension. This provided a single score for each dimension. For example, the ten items that comprise the dimension structure were averaged so that a single summary score represents this dimension. The same calculation was repeated for each of the other dimensions. Index scores allow comparisons to be made between dimensions, to see which represent strengths and which represent weaknesses in the organization's climate.

The major part of the findings reported below consists of comparisons between subsample groups within the department. A series of one-way analyses of variance were conducted to make comparisons between subsample groups. These analyses allow comparison of mean scores on items and indexes, computation of *F*-statistics, and *post hoc* comparisons to identify statistically significant differences between specific subsample groups when more than two groups exist.

Table 22.2

Reliability Coefficients for the Nine Scales in the OCAS

Scale	Scale Items	Reliability Coefficient (Alpha)
Rewards	19–26	.8777
Warmth and Support	27–33	.8063
Structure	1–10	.8007
Approved Practices	57–65	.7485
Values/Ethics	41–56	.5789
Responsibility	11–14	.5471
Organ. Identity	39–40	.4800
Conflict	34–38	.4786
Risk	15–18	.2005

Conducting a Factor Analysis with SPSS®

The SPSS® factor analysis program procedure is highly flexible: it provides seven methods of factor extraction and five methods of rotation. Three methods of computing factor scores are included, and factor scores can be saved as variables for additional analysis. The following example is contained in the help file of SPSS® for Windows®: factor analysis:

> What underlying attitudes lead people to respond to the questions on a political survey as they do? Examining the correlations among the survey items reveals that there is significant overlap among various subgroups of items—questions about taxes tend to correlate with each other, questions about military issues correlate with each other, and so on. With factor analysis, you can investigate the number of underlying factors and, in many cases, you can identify what the factors represent conceptually. Additionally, you can compute factor scores for each respondent, which can then be used in subsequent analyses. (SSPS® Version 11.0, 2002)

SPSS® produces the following statistics for each variable: the number of valid cases, the mean, and the standard deviation. Among many other test results, the SPSS® factor analysis program produces a correlation matrix of variables, including their significance levels; an initial solution, with communalities, eigenvalues, and percentage of variance explained; an unrotated solution, including factor loadings, communalities, and eigenvalues; a rotated solution, including rotated pattern matrix and transformation matrix; a factor score coefficient matrix and factor covariance matrix.

In addition, the SPSS® factor analysis program produces two plots: a "scree plot" of eigenvalues and a loading plot of the first two or three factors. The scree plot shown in Figure 22.1 was produced from PCA results in a report on the *London Deprivation Index* published in 2002 by the Greater London Council. The summary data are displayed in Table 22.3. Scree plots are simply the value of the eigenvalue plotted on a *Y*-axis (vertical), with the number of the factor (the composite variable) plotted on the *X*-axis (horizontal). The term "scree" is a word from geology that is used as the name for the rubble and other debris that collects at the bottom of a rocky slope (Child 1990). The SPSS®-produced table in which eigenvalues and

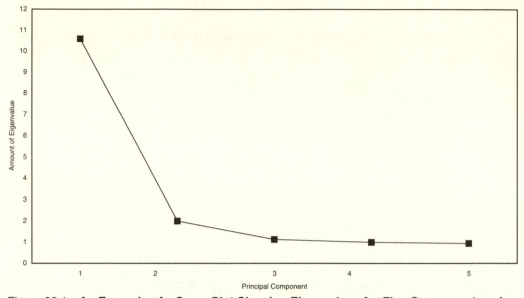

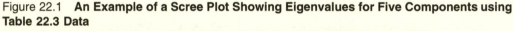

Figure 22.1   **An Example of a Scree Plot Showing Eigenvalues for Five Components using Table 22.3 Data**

Source: From material in Greater London Council. *London Index of Deprivation.* 2002.

amount of explained variance are displayed serves as a visual cue for deciding which factors to include and which to omit. There are no set rules for establishing the optimum number of factors in the final solution, but several different methods are used for making this decision. One is the scree plot discussed earlier; another is the Kaiser-Guttman rule of thumb, which specifies that only factors with an eigenvalue larger than 1.0 should be retained (Cattell 1978; Hutcheson and Sofroniou 1999).

To determine how many factors or components to include in the final analysis using the scree method, simply use the point where the curve straightens out as the maximum number of factors to include. In the example in Figure 22.1, the curve begins to flatten out convincingly at the third component. Therefore, the London Index included three components in its PCA. As can be seen in Table 22.3, three components account for more than 65 percent of the variance in the model.

The term "eigenvalue" (also known by the label *characteristic root* and other names) in the above example is an important mathematical concept in factor analysis; it is particularly important as a component in deciding how may factors or components to retain in the final analysis (Kim and Mueller 1994), and in determining how much variance is explained by each factor. Eigenvalues are simply *the sum of the squares of the factor loadings on each independent factor.* This is the total amount of variance for that factor. A glance at the computed factor-loading matrix will reveal that variables load on more than one variable at the same time. This is not a problem, for it is the sum of all (squared) loadings—the "similarity coefficients—that is of interest. The larger the eigenvalue, the more variance is explained by the factor.

Table 22.3

Summary Data for 2002 London Deprivation Index

Component	Eigenvalue	Percent of Variance	Cumulative Percent
1	10.587	50.414	50.414
2	1.991	9.48	59.894
3	1.121	5.339	65.223
4	0.983	4.681	69.914
5	0.934	4.446	74.36

Source: Greater London Council. *London Index of Deprivation.* 2002.

Cluster Analysis

Cluster analysis is a generic label for a number of statistical processes used to group objects, people, variables, or concepts into more or less homogeneous groups on the basis of their similarities (Lorr 1983). Bernard (2000, 646) defined the cluster statistical technique as "a descriptive tool for exploring relations among items—for finding what goes with what." The result of a cluster analysis is a set of classes, types, categories, or some other type of group. One of the difficulties researchers have with using cluster analysis is the lack of consensus on the terms used for cluster parts and processes. For example, some of the names used in the past for cluster techniques include *typological analysis, numerical taxonomy, pattern recognition,* and *classification analysis.* Other terms that are used interchangeably in applications of cluster analysis include the following terms used to mean the "things" being classified: subject, case, entity, object, pattern, and operational taxonomic unit (OTU). Entity seems to be used most often, but certainly not by any meaningful majority. Terms used to mean the "things" that are used to assess the similarities among entities include: variable, attribute, character or characteristic, and feature, among others. Finally, the following terms are used interchangeably to mean similarities: resemblance, proximity, and association (Aldenderfer and Blashfield 1984).

Classifying groups with cluster analysis is based upon a set of *classification correlations* that are mathematically generated between each scale item and the composite functions. Contribution is measured by the size of correlation value; higher correlation coefficients mean greater contribution (Dalgleish and Chant 1995). The functions are then interpreted by the strength of the individual items that contribute most to the function. While several authors have examined mathematical rules for determining cutoff points for including an item in the interpretation (see, for example, Glorfeld 1995), most analysts resort to rules of thumb to set their cutoff values—coefficients of less than .40 or .50 are often left out of the analysis, but this is only a subjective decision. Too many retained items greatly increase the difficulty of the required subjective interpretation of functions. Too many items retained increase the difficulty of making subjective interpretations; too few and the function often lacks intuitive sense.

Cluster analysis can be used for many different tasks, including, but not limited to, data reduction, identification of natural groupings or types, development of classifications systems, and testing hypotheses. There are at least six objectives for a cluster analysis process (Lorr 1983, 3–4):

1. To identify natural clusters of independent variables.
2. To identify some number of distinguishable groups or clusters of cases.
3. To construct a rationale for classifying subjects or items into groups.
4. To generate hypotheses within the data by uncovering unexpected clusters.
5. To test hypothesized groupings that the researcher believes are present in a larger group of cases.
6. To identify homogeneous subgroups that are characterized by the patterns of variables upon which the classification reveals.

Cluster analysis is not without its disadvantages, a number of which were pointed out by Aldenderfer and Blashfield (1984). Foremost of these may be the fact that cluster analysis, unlike much of our statistical knowledge, is constructed upon rather simple mathematical procedures; the techniques are not yet supported by a large body of statistical reasoning. As a result, a great deal of subjective interpretation is required in the identifying underlying structure and the selection of distinct clusters from the output. A second problem is that cluster analysis methods have been developed in many different disciplines, including anthropology, sociology, psychology, political science, and others. Thus, the conventions that have been built up over the years reflect the biases extant in those disciplines. Furthermore, as more applications occur, new users seem intent upon adding their own contributions to the process, as is evidenced by the lack even of a standard terminology.

A third disadvantage of cluster analysis is the problematic nature of replication—a key requirement for scientific analysis. Different cluster methods regularly result in different cluster solutions from the same dataset. A fourth disadvantage has to do with the strategic rationale for grouping in the first place: the reason for doing a cluster analysis is to identify the structure within a dataset, whereas the technique itself imposes a structure upon the data.

Like all statistical processes, the cluster analysis procedure progresses through a logical series of steps. A graphic representation of these steps is presented in Figure 22.2. Not included in the flowchart, but a vital preliminary step just the same, is the establishment of *objectives* for the research. The researcher must always determine in advance what is the desired outcome of the statistical procedure. Once this is determined, the researcher then develops or selects an appropriate data-gathering instrument, for which there are an adequately large sample of subjects and a representative set of attributes or characteristics for collecting measurements.

Cluster analysis works with all types and levels of data, but it is usually best to standardize the scores so that a common measurement is used in the final analysis. If the database is too large, if there are too many variables and too many branches in the cluster tree for logical interpretation, the researcher may wish to reduce the number of active variables. One way to do this is by conducting either a SFA or a PCA first, and then using the results of this secondary analysis as input for the cluster analysis procedure.

Some Different Clustering Methods

Selecting the right algorithm refers to the many different types of clustering methods that are available from which to choose. Aldenderfer and Blashfield (1984) identified seven different clustering methods: hierarchical agglomerative, iterative, and factor analytic are the three most

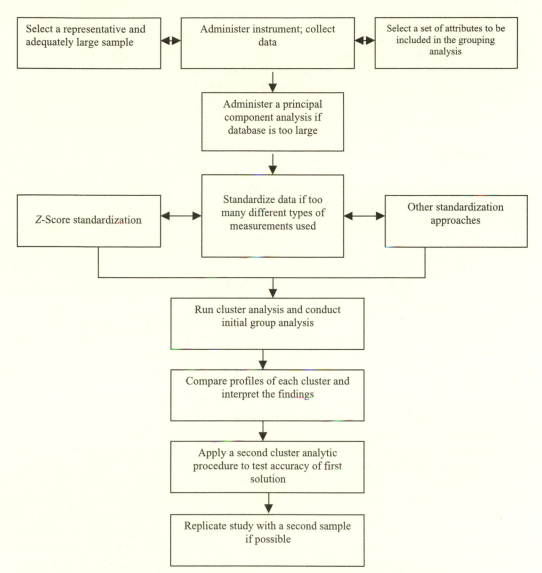

Figure 22.2   **A Flowchart of the Steps Involved in a Cluster Analysis Procedure**

popular methods used in social science. Of these three, hierarchical cluster analysis is most common. Other types of cluster algorithms include hierarchical divisive, density search, clumping, and graph theoretic. Researchers interested in knowing more about these models should consult one of the many books written specifically on the cluster analysis method.

Within the hierarchical agglomerative model, researchers can choose from several different linkage models—linkage refers to the way that dendograms (cluster analysis trees) are used to identify groupings: single linkage, complete linkage, average linkage. Because of its simplicity and ease of interpretation, single linkage may be the more popular model.

Cluster analysis may have any of or more of the following goals: (1) to develop a typology or classification system, (2) to investigate methods for grouping subjects, (3) to generate hypotheses through data exploration, and (4) to test hypotheses by comparing cluster analysis groupings with groups identified another way. Of these uses, the creation of classifications is by far the most common use for cluster analysis. However, in applied cluster analysis, two or more of these uses are likely to be combined in the study (Aldenderfer and Blashfield 1984, 9).

Summary

Many multivariate analysis techniques or methods have been developed for the analysis of large databases—datasets that consist of measurements in the neighborhood of 300 and more subjects and/or 100 or more variables. Among these techniques are *principal component analysis* (PCA), *standard factor analysis* (SFA), and *cluster analysis* (CA). PCA is similar to SFA in concept and application. In fact, it is just one of the many different ways that statistical software packages extract the factors that underlie a set of measurements. PCA transforms an original dataset of variables into a set of uncorrelated variables that include most of the information in the original dataset, but are fewer in number.

Factor analysis serves many different purposes, the most important of which are the reduction in the number of variables, and testing of hypotheses. SFA model, which is also known as *common factor analysis,* is used more often than PCA. In SFA the variables are considered to be causal influences on the underlying factors as well as on factors that are unique to each observed variable.

Cluster analysis also results in a reduction in the amount of data, but involves more subjective decision making than factor analysis. Cluster analysis is a tool for grouping people into similar categories or classifications; it is used for identifying and describing voter segments in political campaigning, and as a tool for segmenting groups of citizens who desire particular types or forms of governmental services.

Factor analysis is one of a family of statistical techniques for summarizing interrelationships among a set of variables, identifying underlying structure in a dataset, and reducing the number of variables with which the researcher must work. The techniques all produce a smaller number of artificial variables, called *factors* or *components*. Factors are artificial constructs generated by the statistical program that are based on measures of intercorrelations; they represent what is common among the original variables. A factor is a variable that is a composite of other variables. By examining the commonality of the initial variables and the strength of their factor correlations (called *factor loadings),* factor analysis helps make it possible to explain portions of the variance in a dependent variable.

Many researchers feel that the subjective interpretation of factors is one of the greatest advantages of factor analysis. Subjective interpretation makes it possible to interject an aspect of reality into the process; it is an attempt to decipher meaning from simple numerical description. However, others see this subjectivity as the root cause of several disadvantages of the technique.

Cluster analysis is a generic label for a number of statistical processes used to group objects, people, variables, or concepts into more or less homogeneous groups on the basis of their similarities. The result of a cluster analysis is a set of classes, types, categories, or some other type of group. One of the difficulties researchers have with using cluster analysis is the lack of consensus on the terms used for cluster parts and processes. Terms used to mean the things that are used to assess the similarities among entities include: variable, attribute, character or characteristic, and feature, among others. These terms are used interchangeably to mean similarities: resemblance, proximity, and association.

Cluster analysis can be used for many different tasks, including, but not limited to, data reduction, identification of natural groupings or types, development of classification systems, and testing hypotheses.

Discussion Questions

1. Describe several different statistical techniques for managing large databases.
2. What is the primary purpose of factor analysis?
3. Define principal component analysis (PCA).
4. Define standard factor analysis (SFA).
5. What are factor loadings? What are they used for?
6. What is a standard matrix format? How is it used in factor analysis?
7. What is the difference between exploratory factor analysis (EFA) and confirmatory factor analysis (CFA)?
8. How are the results of a factor analysis interpreted?
9. What is cluster analysis? What is it used for?
10. Name four or more of the six objectives for cluster analysis.
11. Name several different clustering methods.
12. How are the results of a cluster analysis interpreted?

Additional Reading

Aldenderfer, Mark S., and Roger K. Blashfield. 1984. *Cluster Analysis*. Beverly Hills: Sage.
Hutcheson, Graem, and Nick Sofroniou. 1999. *The Multivariate Social Scientist*. London: Sage.
Kerlinger, Fred N., and Elazar J. Pedhazur. 1973. *Multiple Regression in Behavioral Research*. New York: Holt, Rinehart, and Winston.
Long, J. Scott. 1983. *Confirmatory Factor Analysis*. Beverly Hills: Sage.
Lorr, Maurice. 1983. *Cluster Analysis for Social Scientists*. San Francisco: Jossey-Bass.
Rummel, R.J. 1970. *Applied Factor Analysis*. Evanston, IL: Northwestern University Press.

Part 5

Introduction to Qualitative Research Methods

23 Introduction to Qualitative Research Methods

The term "qualitative research" is used to describe a set of nonstatistical inquiry techniques and processes used to gather data about social phenomena. *Qualitative data* refers to some collection of words, symbols, pictures, or other nonnumerical records, materials, or artifacts that are collected by a researcher and is data that has relevance to the social group under study. The uses for these data go beyond simple description of events and phenomena; rather, they are used for creating understanding, for subjective interpretation, and for critical analysis as well.

Qualitative research differs from quantitative research in several fundamental ways. For example, qualitative research studies typically involve what has been described as "inductive, theory-generating, subjective, and nonpositivist processes." In contrast, quantitative research involves "deductive, theory-testing, objective, and positivist processes" (Lee 1999, 10). Creswell (1994) identified five ways these two approaches differ, based upon these five philosophical foundations: *ontology* (researchers' perceptions of reality); *epistemology* (the role or roles taken by researchers); *axiological assumptions* (researchers' values); *rhetorical traditions* (the style of language used by researchers); and *methodological approaches* (approaches taken by researchers). The differences identified by Creswell are displayed in Figure 23.1.

Differences in Epistemology, Methodology, and Method

A key difference lies in the *epistemology* of the two approaches. Epistemology refers to the different positions in the philosophy of science researchers take about the ways that valid knowledge can be developed and acquired. Two additional key issues are included in the distinction between positivist (scientific) and postpositivist (interpretive) epistemology. One is *methodology;* the other is *method*. Methodology refers to the strategies researchers follow in gaining knowledge. Quantitative and qualitative research strategies are examples of methodologies. Method refers to the research tactics that are used in the conduct of a research effort. Examples include drawing samples, conducting questionnaire surveys, engaging in participant observation, and the like. Epistemology has a direct influence upon methodology, whereas methodology/strategy influences method/tactics (Bowen and Balch 1981).

In qualitative research designs, researchers must often interact with individuals in the groups

RESEARCH STRATEGIES

Philosophical Foundations	Qualitative Research Designs	Quantitative Research Designs
ONTOLOGY *(Perceptions of Reality)*	Researchers assume that multiple, subjectively derived realities can coexist.	Researchers assume that a single, objective world exists.
EPISTEMOLOGY *(Roles for the Researcher)*	Researchers commonly assume that they must interact with their studied phenomena.	Researchers assume that they are independent from the variables under study.
AXIOLOGY *(Researchers' Values)*	Researchers overtly act in a value-laden and biased fashion.	Researchers overtly act in a value-free and unbiased manner.
RHETORIC *(Language Styles)*	Researchers often use personalized, informal, and context-laden language.	Researchers most often use impersonal, formal, and rule-based text.
METHODOLOGY *(Approaches to Research)*	Researchers tend to apply induction, multivariate, and multiprocess interactions, following context-laden methods.	Researchers tend to apply deduction, limited cause-and-effect relationships, with context-free methods.

Figure 23.1   **Five Ways Qualitative Research Differs from Quantitative Research**
Source: Creswell 1994.

they are studying. Researchers record not only what they see, but also their interpretations of the meaning inherent in the interactions that take place in the groups. Quantitative researchers, on the other hand, maintain the position that a deliberate distance and objectivity from the study group is necessary. They are careful to avoid making judgments about attitudes, perceptions, values, interactions, or predispositions.

Another way to describe the differences between qualitative and quantitative research methods has been proposed by Cassell and Symon (1994). The most fundamental of these differences is a bias against using numbers for qualitative research, whereas quantitative research is biased heavily toward numerical measurements and statistical analysis—the *positivist* approach to scientific analysis (White 1999). The objective of the positive approach to research is to control events through a process of *prediction* that is based on explanation. In doing so, it employs inferential statistical methods (White and Adams 1994).

The second difference is what is referred to as the *subjective-objective dichotomy*. Qualitative researchers "explicitly and overtly apply" their own subjective interpretations of what they see and hear—often, they are active participants in the phenomenon under study. On the other hand, a foundation stone of the quantitative, positivist research approach is researcher *objectivity*. The researcher is expected to function as an unbiased, unobtrusive observer, reporting only what happens or what can be measured (Lee 1999, 7).

These two approaches also differ in a third way: qualitative researchers tend to approach the research process with a willingness to be flexible, to follow where the data lead them. Qualitative researchers often approach a topic with little or no preconceived assumptions; these are expected to appear out of the data as they are collected and studied. Quantitative research, on the other hand, tends to be guided by a strict set of rules and formal processes. Typically, specific hypotheses are established prior to the data gathering and tested during the analysis.

Variables are identified and explicitly defined beforehand. Searching for cause-and-effect relationships between defined variables that can be measured is a hallmark of quantitative research studies.

A fourth way that the two approaches differ has to do with the aim of the study. Qualitative researchers seek understanding of social interactions and processes in organizations, whereas quantitative studies are more often concerned with predicting future events and behaviors. To make these predictions, they often apply inferential statistical analyses to measurements taken from representative samples drawn from a population of interest. Another difference is associated with the context of the study. Qualitative research is usually concerned with a situation or event that takes place within a single organizational context. A major goal of much quantitative research, however, is to apply the study results to other situations; thus, quantitative research is what Lee (1999) termed "more generalizable."

A sixth way that these two approaches to research differ is the emphasis that qualitative researchers assign to the research process. The way that subjects interact with, and react to, the researcher during the qualitative study is of as much interest as the original phenomenon of interest. Quantitative researchers tend to take great pains to avoid introducing extraneous influences into the study, and seek to isolate subjects from the process as much as possible by controlling for process effects.

Classes of Qualitative Research Strategies

Qualitative research strategies can be grouped into three broad strategic classes. These are (1) *explanatory research studies,* (2) *interpretive research studies,* and (3) *critical research studies.* These strategies and the four key approaches that are followed in much political science research are displayed in Figure 23.2. These roughly correspond to the exploratory-descriptive-causal categories of quantitative research designs.

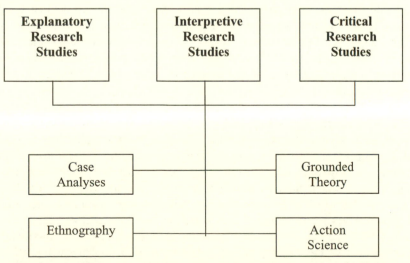

Figure 23.2 Some Interpretive Research Strategies Used in Political Science Research

Explanatory Research Studies

Explanatory research was described by Schwandt (1997) in his dictionary of terms and concepts encountered in qualitative research as studies that are conducted to develop a *causal explanation* of some social phenomenon. The researcher identifies a specific social event or circumstance (a *consequence*)—such as crime in the inner city—that he or she wants to investigate. The researcher then seeks to identify the social, economic, climate, practice, or other such characteristic (variable) in the social environment that can be explained as a *cause* of the consequence of interest.

One of the major objectives of explanatory research is to build *theories* that researchers can then use to explain a phenomenon, and that can then be used to predict future behavior or events in similar circumstances. The ability to predict responses allows investigators a measure of control over events. Therefore, the ultimate goal of all explanatory research is the control of natural and social events (White 1999). Explanatory research is the easiest approach to understand and apply, and is often used simply for this reason.

In addition to this controlling aspect of explanatory research, this strategy is seen by many as the fastest way to produce a cumulative stream of knowledge in a field or discipline. Possibly because of this and their relationship to control, studies that are designed to explain a phenomenon are still the strategy seen most often in public administration research. Explanatory strategies fulfill much the same role in qualitative research that exploratory research does in quantitative research; they are used as a means of gathering fundamental information about the topic, its contributing factors, and the influences a phenomenon might have on various outcomes. This process can be described as *gaining insights and ideas* about a study problem. These studies are seldom complete in themselves; they are conducted as preliminaries to additional, follow-on research.

Interpretive Research Studies

Not all research theorists agree that human events or actions can be defined by the causal explanations that are part and parcel of explanatory research. Instead, these critics argue that human action can never be explained this way. It can only be understood by studies that follow the second approach in the triad of qualitative approaches, which is *interpretation.* The researcher arrives at an interpretation of a phenomenon by developing (subjective) meanings of social events or actions.

According to White (1994), interpretive research helps us achieve understanding of actions of people in social circumstances and situations. White cites as an example the way an interpretive researcher goes beyond describing why a job-enrichment program is not working, using established hypotheses of motivation and job design. Instead, the interpretive research might circulate among employees in their job setting, ask them what they think about the program, the meaning it has for them, and how it conflicts or reinforces their existing attitudes, opinions, and behaviors. In this way, the research seeks to "discover the meaning of the program; how it fits with [the workers'] prior norms, rules, values, and social practice" (45).

Schwandt (1997, 73) has offered this definition of interpretation: "A classification, explication, or explanation of the meaning of some phenomenon." Thus, interpretive studies require the researcher to go beyond simply describing or explaining what a phenomenon is to also "interpret" the phenomenon for the reader. This entails providing an interpretation of what it *means,* as well as what it *is.* Schwandt concluded that the term "interpretation" is used as a synonym for *hermeneutics* or *Verstehen. The Oxford English Dictionary* (OED) defines the term "hermeneutics" as the "art or science of interpretation," and the term "hermeneutical" as "belonging to or concerned with interpretation." *Verstehen,* a German word, defines an approach to the social sciences that is committed to providing understanding of human actions.

Research can be classified as interpretive when it is builds on the assumption that humans learn about reality from the meanings they assign to social phenomena such as language, consciousness, shared experiences, publications, tools, and other artifacts. The task is made difficult because a fundamental tenet of interpretive theory is that social phenomena are constantly changing. Thus, the meanings that people assign are in constant flux. At the same time, interpretive research is always *context-laden.* Thus, interpretation is like shooting at a constantly moving target. In political science, the interpretive approach assumes that laws and generalizations—the hallmarks of the positivist approach—are not really necessary for arriving at an understanding of human political actions and political institutions (Moon 1975).

A primary goal of the interpretive research approach is to provide many-layered descriptions and interpretations of human experiences (Meacham 1998). To achieve this goal, interpretive research looks at the way humans make sense out of events in their lives—as they happen, not as they are planned. Therefore, to thoroughly understand an event or an organization, the researcher must also understand its historical context.

Interpretive research is particularly important for the study of government organizations and agencies. The fundamental objective for interpretive research that makes this approach particularly relevant in applications is described by White as:

> The basic aim of the interpretive model is to develop a more complete understanding of social relationships and to discover human possibilities. Recent studies of organizational culture demonstrate the importance of interpretive methods for properly understanding norms, values, and belief systems in organizations. (White 1994, 45)

Seven Principles of Interpretive Research

Klein and Meyers (1999) developed a set of seven fundamental principles to help researchers conduct and evaluate interpretive research studies. The first and most fundamental of these principles is the *hermeneutic circle,* derived from document and literary analysis. The hermeneutic circle was devised to illustrate a phenomenon of the learning/understanding process. People develop understanding about complex concepts from the meanings they bring to its parts, such as words, and the way that these parts relate to one another. Interpretations of the larger whole moves from a preliminary understanding of the parts, to understanding the whole, and then back again to a better understanding of the parts, and on and on. The process of understanding thus moves continuously in an expanding circle of greater and greater understanding.

The second principle of interpretive research is the importance of the *contextual nature* of the studied phenomenon or organization that was mentioned earlier. The researcher's "meaning" is derived out of the particular social and historical context in which the phenomenon is embedded; at the same time, all patterns that can be discovered within this embedded context are constantly changing. The organization that is interpreted is thus time- and situation-specific.

The *interactions between researchers and the subjects* they study constitute the third of the seven principles of interpretive research; the information is not something inherent in the phenomenon. Rather, it is developed as a result of the social interrelations of both subjects and researcher. Gummesson (1987) likens this to the interaction that often results in the researcher metamorphosing into an "internal consultant" role during case study research. The researcher, by interacting with participants, becomes one with the members of the group under study.

Abstraction and generalization together make up the fourth principle of interpretive research. This principle deals with abstractions as it attempts to bring order to disunited parts by categorizing them into generalizations and concepts with wider application. The inferences drawn by the researcher that are based on his or her subjective interpretation of the single case are seen as theoretical generalizations.

The fifth principle of interpretive research is *dialogical reasoning.* In this intellectual process, the researcher explicitly weighs all preconceptions and/or biases brought to the planned research activity against the information that actually emerges from the actual research process. This principle forces the researcher to begin by defining the underlying assumptions that guide the research and the research paradigm upon which the study is based. By a process of dialog with participant actors, the researcher defines and redefines the assumptions and research questions in light of the data that emerge.

The *principle of multiple interpretations* demands that the researcher aggressively compare his or her historical and contextual interpretation of the phenomenon against all other available interpretations and the reasons offered for them. Thus, the researcher subjects his or her own preconceptions and biases to comparison against competing interpretations, including those of the participants in the organization under study. Even if no conflicting interpretations are found during the study, the researcher is expected to probe for them, and to document the fruitless process. In this way, the researcher strengthens the conclusions and interpretations derived from the analysis.

The final principle of interpretive research is *suspicion.* This requires the researcher to not accept an interpretation at face value. To avoid making false interpretations, the researcher must examine every personal preconception, conclusion, definition, and derived meaning with a healthy dose of skepticism.

Critical Research Studies

Critical qualitative research is a third approach to investigations of social phenomena adopted by the public administration researchers. Critical research has evolved from approaches exemplified in Marxian *critical sociology* and Freudian *psychotherapy* traditions (Argyris, Putnam, and Smith 1984). According to Klein and Meyers (1999), a study can be considered to be *critical* in nature if it is a social critique that exposes harmful or alienating social conditions. Furthermore, the purpose of the critique should be to emancipate members of the society from the harmful conditions, thus eliminating the causes of the alienation. Members of the society are not told how to change their conditions, but are instead helped to identify on their own alternative ways of defining their society and for achieving human potential.

According to White (1994), the primary objective of critical research is to help people *change* their beliefs and actions as part of a process of helping them become aware of the often-unconscious bases for the way they act or their beliefs. By becoming aware of *why* they live and think the way they do, "critique points out inconsistencies between what is true and false, good and bad; it compels [people] to act in accordance with truth and goodness" (46).

Critical public administration research begins with the assumption that a crisis exists in some aspect of society. The researcher approaches the study of this crisis from a deeply personal and involved commitment to help the people involved. Recognition of a "crisis," then, is one of the key concepts of the approach. The role of critical research in these circumstances is explained in the following quote:

> From [the crisis] perspective, society is seen as [torn] by social and political divisions which make the process of social reproduction . . . prone to actual or incipient breakdown. Society [is not] a harmonious, self-regulating system. Rather, it must be seen as a field of complex and contradictory possibilities for social actors who would . . . assume command of these possibilities and produce new social realities which would express their ability to act as empowered, autonomous agents. The task of critical research involves identifying these possibilities and suggesting what social actors might do to bring their lives under their conscious direction. (Hansen and Muszynski 1990, 2)

Schwandt (1997, 24–25) identified a number of structural themes that characterize critical research. The two that seem to appear most regularly in the literature of critical research methodology are distortion in the perceptions held by members of a group, and rejection of the idea of the disinterested scientist. With the first theme, the goal of critical research is to integrate social theory and application or practice in such a way that the members of social groups become cognizant of distortions and other problems in their society or their value systems. Then, the group members are encouraged to propose ways to change their social and value systems in ways that improve their quality of life.

The second key theme in critical research is the refusal to accept the traditional idea that called for the social scientist to remain objective or "disinterested," and replacing this with the concept of the active, change-oriented researcher whose emphasis is on motivating change processes in social groups and individuals.

Nancy Blyler (1998) addressed the issue of adopting a critical perspective in "professional communication" in general, defining the critical approach thus:

> The critical perspective aims at empowerment and emancipation. It reinterprets the relationship between researcher and participants as one of collaboration, where participants define research questions that matter to them and where social action is the desired goal. (Blyler 1998, 33)

Is One Strategy Inherently Better?

No; one is not inherently better than the others. The choice of which strategy to adopt when designing a qualitative study will depend upon what objectives the researcher has identified for the study. These must be clearly stated prior to going into the field to embark on the collection of data.

Often considered the easiest of the three strategies to carry out, and possibly because of this, by far most public administration research studies follow an *explanatory* design. However, according to White (1999) and others, there is a strong movement among researchers in all the social and administrative sciences to go beyond a simple descriptive explanation of a phenomenon to also explore whatever meaning underlies the behavior, event, or circumstance. Professionals, administrators, sponsoring agencies, and the public at large are asking researchers to explain what things *mean,* rather than simply describing them as they appear.

An even smaller number of researchers are extending the range of research even greater by designing studies that begin with a critique of a social phenomenon and end with the design and introduction of subject-sponsored new ways of addressing old problems (Robinson 1994). The *critical* approach in political science is still in its infancy, however (White 1999). The critical approach has been employed often enough, however, to result in a reputation for making it difficult to transform research results into meaningful program applications. The method requires subjects to form alternative concepts or courses of action; the role of the researcher is to assist the group to first identify and then resolve their social problems themselves. Despite this difficulty, the critical approach is seen as an important way of addressing single-case studies.

The Changing Research Paradigm

One important consequence of this push to extend the scope of research has been a widespread increase in the use of subjective qualitative methods to augment, if not replace, the once-prevalent emphasis on objective, positivist research principles. Lan and Anders have described this change in emphasis as a major paradigm shift (2000). Building their argument on Thomas S. Kuhn's *The Structure of Scientific Revolutions* (1970), Lan and Anders concluded that more than one approach to research is not only possible, it is desirable. If science does progress by shifts in paradigms, as their interpretation of Kuhn's work suggests, and if it is indeed true that more than one paradigm can exist within a single discipline, then the question of which research approach to take is moot. Researchers are not required to follow the same set of rules. White and Adams (1994, 19–20) have summarized this point in reaching this conclusion:

> We are persuaded by the weight of historical and epistemological evidence that no single approach—even if accorded the highly positive label *science*—is adequate for the conduct of research in public administration. If research is to be guided by reason, a diversity of approaches, honoring both practical and theoretical reasons, seems necessary. (White and Adams 1994, 19–20)

Qualitative Research Methods

Many different types of research methods are employed for conducting qualitative research. The four methods most often followed in political science and management are *case studies, grounded theory, ethnography,* and *action science.* These are not the only approaches seen in research in the administrative and social sciences, however. Others include *phenomenology, hermeneutics, ethnomethodology, atmospherics, systems theory, chaos theory, nonlinear dynamics, grounded theory, symbolic interactionism, ecological psychology, cognitive anthropology, human ethnology,* and *holistic ethnography,* to name only a few (Patton 1990; Denzin and Lincoln 1994; Morse 1994; Marshall and Rossman 1999).

There are few limits to what may be researched or how researchers go about conducting their research activities; researchers are not limited to one or even a few different approaches in their scientific investigations. Just as there are no restrictions on research topics, there are no rules that limit any of these to any one-application focus. Case studies or ethnography may be appropriate for research with an exploratory focus. Grounded theory and hermeneutics, on the other hand, are approaches that are typically employed in interpretive research strategies. Phenomenology, hermeneutics, and action science are most applicable for research that follows the critical model. Clearly, these approaches and applications often overlap, just as different observers may see different approaches taken in any individual research study.

Figure 23.3 displays six popular research approaches, their disciplinary traditions, some

Qualitative Research Approach	Disciplinary Traditions	Typical Data-Gathering Methods	Types of Research Questions
Ethnography	Anthropology	Participant Observation; Un-structured Interviews; Analysis of Cultural Artifacts	*"Culture" questions:* What are the values of this group? What is accepted behavior? What is not acceptable?
Phenomenology	Philosophy	Personal Experience Narratives; Video/Audio Taped Discussions; In-depth Interviews	*"Meaning" questions:* What is the meaning of a person's experience? How do group members cope with various phenomena?
Case Studies	Psychology; Public Administration	Observation; Personal Interviews; Organizational Studies	*"Explanatory" questions:* What is distinct about this group?
Hermeneutics	Biblical Studies; Literary Analysis	Content Analysis; Narrative and Discourse Analysis	*"Interpretation" questions:* What meaning does this text hold?
Grounded Theory	Sociology; Social Psychology	Personal Interviews; Diaries; Participant Observation	*"Process" questions:* What theory is embedded in the relationships between variables? Is there a theory of change?
Action Science	Social Psychology; Education	Discourse Analysis; Intervention Studies	*"Critique" questions:* How can we emancipate group members? What behaviors inhibit change?

Figure 23.3 **Various Approaches to Qualitative Research: Foundations, Methods, and Focus**

common ways data are gathered, and a suggestion of some of the types of research questions addressed. The disciplinary approaches compared include (1) *ethnography,* (2) *phenomenology,* (3) *the case study approach,* (4) *hermeneutics,* (5) *grounded theory,* and (6) *action science.*

Ethnographic Research

Anthropologists developed the approach to research known as ethnography as a method for studying different cultures and how members of different societies develop and employ coping mechanisms for social phenomena. A differentiating characteristic of this approach is its emphasis on specific ways to prepare field notes and rules for writing about cultural events.

The primary data-gathering technique used in ethnography is *participant observation.* Ethnographers often live, work, and play with the members of the group under study for long periods of time. Their aim is to be absorbed into the group, with the underlying objective of becoming "accepted" as a nonthreatening or nonintrusive member of the groups so that events and interrelationships unfold as they would naturally, as if the observer were not in attendance.

Ethnography methods are used in the administrative sciences to analyze and diagnose organizational cultures (Wilson 1989; Schein 1992). However, the rules for conducting fieldwork and the preparation of field notes tend to be less rigorously applied than is the case in anthropology research.

The Phenomenology Approach

The phenomenological approach to qualitative research has its roots in such traditions of philosophy as existentialism and the meaning of language and other symbolic behaviors. In political science, it is used to establish "meanings" social actors apply to events, works, symbols, and the like. Data are typically gathered through collection of narratives, personal experiences, and by in-depth personal interviews.

The underlying concept of interest is the *life history* of individual persons. Researchers often employ taped discussions and other narrative recording tools to study the everyday personal experiences of subjects. Examples include narrative personal histories of gang members, participants in the drug culture, and other, similar social aberrative behaviors. The goal of the researcher is for the subject to define the meaning of the behavior. Phenomenology researchers use participant observation, in-depth interviewing, and passive recording of life histories as data-gathering methods.

The Case Analysis Approach

The case analysis approach to research in political science focuses on the agency, organization, person, or group under study, rather than dealing with variables (Schwandt 1997). The objective of the case is to serve as a defining description of the organization. In this way, the case description serves as an example of similar groups.

Today, case studies are used extensively in many of the human sciences, although their disciplinary roots are centered in psychology. They are one of the most often used approaches to conducting research public administration. The following examples are taken from a single issue of the public administration journal *Public Productivity and Management Review* (23:3, March 2000):

- "The dual potentialities of performance measurement: The case of the Social Security Administration."
- "Organizational change issues in performance government: The case of contracting."
- "Comprehensive management and budgeting reform in local government: The case of Milwaukee."
- "Implementing performance accountability in Florida: What changed, what mattered, and what resulted."

Each of these articles describes in some detail the organization and its experiences with some aspect of administration. They are intended to serve as examples for other administrators or agencies to follow.

The Hermeneutic Approach

Hermeneutics is an approach to qualitative research that focuses on the *interpretation* of such social phenomena as texts, tools, objects, works of art, documents, statements of other people, and particularly, the actions of humans in social environments. Developed at the end of the eighteenth century, it was originally concerned with interpreting biblical, legal, and classical texts. Today it is often used as an approach in investigating social phenomena, such as statements and behaviors in government groups and agency settings. The hermeneutic view of social science—including political science—begins with the assumption that human behavior is different from the natural sciences, and requires a different approach to understanding. The phenomena studied in the natural sciences are considered to exist without intention and without inherent meaning. A primary goal of the researcher is to observe, describe, and create theories. With the hermeneutic approach, the political scientist is faced with the task of understanding the actions and phenomena of the world of political behavior and events—as seen and recorded by participants. Only by interpreting the actions, beliefs, norms, and standards of political actors in the sense of the meaning that the actions, beliefs, norms, and standards have for the actors themselves can the political scientist make them intelligible. "Political science, like economics, sociology, and anthropology, is not only concerned to understand particular events and traditions, it also aspires to compare and to generalize about social phenomena" (Moon 1975, 182).

Some Uses for Hermeneutic Techniques

Researchers in many different disciplines have discovered they use a number of similar hermeneutic techniques, methods, and principles in arriving at their interpretations. This type of interpretation may be applied to the study of social action because of an "assumption that social situations display some of the features of a text and that the methodology for interpreting social action develops some of the same procedures of text interpretation" (White 1999, 130).

The principal analysis technique in these studies involves the *hermeneutic circle*. This is the method of relating parts of the text or conversation to the whole, and then back again to the parts. Analysis proceeds in this circular way until the entire text is interpreted. Furthermore, every interpretation is connected to earlier interpretations and understandings; nothing exists outside of interpretation.

The following four laws guide all hermeneutic interpretation processes (White 1999, 143–45):

(1) social actors and their beliefs and actions must be understood on their own terms, and not imposed by the investigator; (2) the interactions of all actors in the social setting must be understood within their own context; (3) the researcher must have some pre-existing experience with the group members—some common experience must bind them together; (4) the interpretation arrived at by the investigator must conform to the intentions of the actors.

The Grounded Theory Approach

The *grounded theory* approach to research in the administrative and social sciences has its roots in sociology and social psychology. According to Strauss and Corbin (1998), this approach to research has as its primary objective to develop theory out of the information gathered, rather than the testing of predetermined theories through a process of experimentation. Grounded theory researchers approach their study organization by gathering all possible facts pertaining to the problem. These data are gathered through personal interviews, analyses of participants' diaries, and participant observation. Once the data are collected they are analyzed and interpreted by the investigator, who finally develops a theory from that analysis and interpretation.

As developed by Strauss, grounded theory employs a detailed list of rigorous steps and processes for developing theory out of social situations. Insights and ideas are generated only after in-depth analysis of the data, during which the analyst searches for commonalties and differences in the data. These are compared and contrasted as the analyst weighs possible theories against opposing interpretations. Ultimately, a theory that is grounded in the data emerges.

The Action Science Approach

The action science approach has been defined as a way of changing social systems by studying the way they function. It has also been described as "an informal, qualitative, formative, subjective, interpretive, reflective, and experimental model of inquiry in which all individuals involved in the study are knowing and contributing participants" (Gabel 1995, 1).

Chris Argyris and others developed this approach from the earlier contributions of John Dewey—who proposed separating science and practice—and Kurt Lewin in field group dynamics, an area of study in social psychology. Dewey's contribution led to Lewin's separation of the idea of *diagnosis* of an organization or other social group from the idea of *intervention,* which is the concept of working to bring about change (Argyris, Putnam, and Smith 1984; Schein 1995). Action theory research has been described in the following manner:

> The evaluation of social situations is the point of any action theory, which strives to help actors understand their situations in a different light and to make value judgments about whether or not their situations should be changed. (White 1999, 142)

Although Lewin never explicitly defined the action science method as such, his early work in developing approaches to interventions and change in social organizations led Argyris to give him credit for development of most of the techniques involved in the approach (Argyris 1985; Schein 1995).

Five Themes in Action Research

The following five themes in action research were used by Argyris in developing the approach as it is used today: First, the approach entails applying change experiments to real problems in existing social systems, with the goal of helping the organization or system resolve the problem. Second, the research method involves a cyclical process of problem identification, planning, acting, and evaluating—over and over again.

Third, a major component of the proposed change is reeducation to change the way group members think and act. The fourth theme is an emphasis on participation and free choice in the problem resolution. Finally, there is a dual purpose or goal to action research; research results should contribute to basic social science knowledge, while also improving everyday life in social groups (Argyris 1985, 8–9).

Action research can be used to test two kinds of statements: *dispositional attributions* and *theories of causal responsibility.* The first of these is an assertion by an actor in the social group about the perceived mental outlook, tendency, or characteristic of another action in the group. Examples of a dispositional attribution are the statements: "John is insensitive [to my feelings]," and "Mary is a thoughtful, caring supervisor." An example of a theory of causal responsibility is: "Our supervisor's insensitivity to minorities is causing discomfort and dissatisfaction in our work group."

Two additional important points about action research are: (1) the *domain of* action research, and (2) the *data of* action research. "Domain" is another way of describing what is the appropriate area of application for the approach, whereas "data" refers to the type or form of information gathered. Action science should be used when the researcher is concerned with *actions* and *interpretive understandings.* To better understand what is meant by "action," Argyris saw that the data of action research are the *actions* taken by members of the social group under study; the most important of these actions is *talk:*

> The first point to note is that talk *is* action . . . talk is meaningful . . . when people talk they are performing such actions as promising, justifying, ordering, conceding, and so forth. Using talk as data for the empirical testing of theory forces us to deal with the issues raised by interpretation. (Argyris 1985, 54–57)

In practice, action research activities should follow a circular process that begins with an initial review of the situation, then proceeds to development of a plan, introduces the intervention, and ends with monitoring and reflecting upon the results of the intervention to make revisions whenever necessary (Gabel 1995). The steps and their primary activities are:

- *Reconnaissance:* An understanding of the problem in the organization is developed through a study of its whole.
- *General Plan:* Plans are developed for an intervention to resolve the problem.
- *Introducing the Intervention:* Introducing desired elements of change into the organization.
- *Monitoring the Intervention:* Observations of the process are collected.
- *Reflection and Revision:* New intervention strategies are implemented, if necessary, with the cycle beginning anew. It is continued until a satisfactory understanding or change is reached.

Analyzing and Interpreting Qualitative Data

All qualitative research strategies and approaches involve three basic components: (1) collection of data, (2) analysis and interpretation of that data, and (3) communicating research findings in one or more communications media, such as producing a written report (Strauss and Corbin 1998).

The major methods used to collect qualitative data include: (1) *participation in the group setting or activity,* (2) *personal and group interviewing,* (3) *observation,* and (4) *document and cultural artifact analysis.* There are also many secondary methods of collecting information (Marshall and Rossman 1999). These include historical analysis, recording and analysis of live histories and narratives, films, videos and photographs, kinesics, proxemics, unobtrusive measures, surveys, and projective techniques.

Some researchers collect qualitative data by actually participating in a social situation and writing down what they see, while others do so by unobtrusively observing social interrelationships and behaviors. Researchers also gather qualitative data for analysis by video or audio tape recordings of narrative accounts of life histories, events, perceptions, or personal values; they question subjects using structured or unstructured, personal or group interviews.

Still others collect qualitative data by examining collections of printed documents, past and present artifacts, or by examining cultural or artistic creations, including the media. And some use a combination of these and other methods.

Analyzing Qualitative Data

The analysis and interpretation of qualitative data begins with bringing the raw data into some level of order. First, the researcher identifies and selects a set of relevant *categories* or *classes* in which to sort the data. Comparing the data across categories—a step that is typically used in the testing of hypotheses—often follows the initial comparing phase of the analysis. This is the process of *conceptualizing* (Strauss and Corbin 1998). Conceptualizing means reducing the often-bulky amounts of raw data into workable, ordered bits of information that the researcher can manage with confidence. Kvale (1996) described this act of data categorization as a key qualitative research activity, and one that most distinguishes qualitative strategies from quantitative research.

Another procedure sometimes used for this purpose is what is known as *power* or *influence analysis.* In this process, the researcher first collects data observing the way people interact or by questioning them on their perceptions of such factors as power or influence in the organization. The researcher can then draw a diagram or chart to illustrate the interactions and responses to others within a group or other social setting. Examples of graphic displays of this type include context charts, linkage patterns and knowledge flowcharts, and role and power charts (Miles and Huberman 1984).

Interpreting Qualitative Data

The next step in analysis of qualitative data is *interpreting the patterns and connections* that are revealed by bringing the data into order. Interpretation occurs when the researcher draws conclusions from whatever structure is revealed in the data. If graphic diagrams are used, the interpretation requires the researcher to explain the connections and interfaces that have been recorded by examining and describing the personal connections, misconnections, interfaces, relationships, and/or interplay of behaviors. These explanations become the gist of a *cogent and meaningful report,* which is the third step in the process. These three steps must be followed in all studies, regardless of in which underlying discipline the study falls, which approach the researcher follows, or which technique is used to gather and analyze the data.

Summary

Qualitative research describes a set of nonstatistical inquiry techniques and for gathering data about social phenomena. *Qualitative data* are words, symbols, pictures, or other nonnumeric records, materials, or artifacts collected by a researcher. The uses for these data go beyond simple description of events and phenomena; they are used for creating understanding, for subjective interpretation, and for critical analysis as well.

Qualitative research differs from quantitative research in several fundamental ways. Qualitative research studies employ inductive, theory-generating, subjective, and nonpositivist processes, while quantitative research uses deductive, theory-testing, objective, and positivist processes. Creswell (1994) identified five ways these two approaches differ, based upon these five philosophical foundations: *ontology, epistemology, axiological assumptions, rhetorical traditions,* and *methodological approaches.*

Qualitative research strategies can be grouped into three broad classes: (1) *explanatory research studies,* (2) *interpretive research studies,* and (3) *critical research studies.* These roughly correspond to the exploratory-descriptive-causal categories of quantitative research designs. The choice of which strategy to adopt when designing a qualitative study will depend upon what objectives the researcher has identified for the study. These must be clearly stated prior to going into the field to embark on the collection of data.

Many different types of research approaches are employed for conducting qualitative research in political science. Among the disciplinary approaches often followed are *ethnography, phenomenology, case studies, hermeneutics, grounded theory,* and *action science,* among others. All qualitative research strategies and approaches involve three basic components: (1) collection of data, (2) analysis and interpretation of that data, and (3) communicating research findings in one or more communications media, such as producing a written report.

The major methods used to collect qualitative data include: (1) participation in the group setting or activity, (2) personal and/or group interviewing, (3) observation, and (4) document and cultural artifact analysis. There are also many secondary methods of collecting information, including historical analysis, live histories and narratives, films, videos and photographs, kinesics, proxemics, unobtrusive measures, surveys, and projective techniques.

Discussion Questions

1. What is epistemology?
2. Differentiate between epistemology, methodology, and methods.
3. Is qualitative research a strategy or a tactic? Explain your answer.
4. What is meant by the changing paradigm?
5. What is ethnology? How can it be applied in political science research?
6. What is hermeneutics? How can it be applied in political science research?
7. What is grounded theory? How can it be applied in political science research?

8. What is action science? Does it have a place in political science research?
9. Explain how participant observation works.
10. Explain the purpose of proxemics.

Additional Reading

Cassell, Catherine, and Gillian Symon. 1997. *Qualitative Methods in Organizational Research*. Thousand Oaks, CA: Sage.

Denzin, Norman K., and Yvonna S. Lincoln, eds. 1994. *Handbook of Qualitative Research*. Thousand Oaks, CA: Sage.

Lee, Thomas W. 1999. *Using Qualitative Methods in Organizational Research*. Thousand Oaks, CA: Sage.

Marshall, Catherine, and Gretchen B. Rossman. 1999. *Designing Qualitative Research*. 3rd ed. Thousand Oaks, CA: Sage.

Strauss, Anselm, and Juliet Corbin. 1998. *Basics of Qualitative Research: Techniques and Procedures for Developing Grounded Theory*. 2nd ed. Thousand Oaks, CA: Sage.

24 The Explanatory Approach I: Case Study Methods

The case method has long been one of the most popular approaches in political science. Whelan (1989) traced the approach as far back as 1948, when a planning committee was formed at Harvard University to develop guidelines for applying the method to research in political science and public administration. Under the leadership of Harold Stein, the original committee became the *Inter-University Case Program* (IUCP) in 1951. The IUCP published a text with twenty-six cases just a year later (Stein 1952). In the introduction to that casebook, Stein defined the case as "a narrative of the events that constitute or lead to a decision or group of related decisions" (xxvii).

A number of now-classic case studies were published beginning about the same time as the method was evolving at Harvard. Philip Selznick's *TVA and the Grass Roots* appeared in 1949; Herbert Kaufman's study of the forest service, *The Forest Ranger*, was published in 1960. A third classic case study, Michael Lipsky's (1980) study of city bureaucracies, *Street-Level Bureaucracy*, helped the case approach to achieve recognition as a valid and important research methodology.

These larger case studies were mirrored in miniature by acceptance of the approach in the discipline's professional literature. For example, in his detailed overview of the state of research methods, Yeager (1989) found that one or more case studies appeared in every issue of *Public Administration Review* (PAR) for more than forty years. If their continuing appearance in PAR—this political science subfield's leading publication—and if other political science journals are any indication, case studies are just as popular today as they were when Yeager examined the field in the late 1980s.

The popularity of the case study approach lies in the great flexibility of the method. The primary purpose of the case is to identify what in the event or group of interest is common to the group and what is specific to the case under study. In this light, cases serve to inform all political scientists about what is going on in their field; Through the study of cases, political scientists are able to learn about political events, agencies, parties, and levels of government and politics around the globe. Cases are also written to serve as examples of approved management practices.

Defining the Case Study Approach

Many different definitions for case studies have been proposed. Yeager traced most of them to Harold Stein, who, in an article published in 1952, was one of the first to promote the method as a way to do research in the public sector. Yeager based the following definition of the case on the work of Stein:

> A case is a description of a management situation based on interview, archival, naturalistic observation, and other data, constructed to be sensitive to the context in which management behavior takes place and to its temporal restraints. These are characteristics shared by all cases. (Yeager 1989, 685)

Today, most scholars consider the writing of Robert K. Yin as the key contribution in the development and use of the social and political science case study. In the first edition of his important book, Yin (1984) wrote: "As a research strategy, the distinguishing characteristic of the case is that it attempts to examine (a) a contemporary phenomenon in its real-life context, especially when (b) the boundaries between phenomenon and context are not clearly evident." In the 1994 edition, Yin described the case study as "an empirical inquiry" that (1) investigates a contemporary phenomenon within its real-life context, and particularly when "the boundaries between phenomenon and context are not clearly evident" (13).

Case studies are often intensive studies of one or a few exemplary individuals, families, events, time periods, decisions or set of decisions, processes, programs, institutions, organizations, groups, or even entire communities (Lang and Heiss 1990; Arenson 1993). Discussing the case method as one of three qualitative approaches for research in organizational communications, Arneson (1993) saw it as an appropriate research method when some noteworthy success or failure in a case is present, adding: "Qualitative case studies most appropriately address programs directed toward *individualized* outcomes" (164). The subject selected as a case example typically is chosen for study because it points out some underlying problem, or because it represents a successful solution to a problem. It is hoped that publishing the successful experience can provide a model for others to emulate.

Another way to classify case studies was proposed by Stake (2000). He identified three different types of case studies: *instrumental, intrinsic,* and the *collective* case study. Stake saw the case as playing a secondary or supporting role; it is studied because it improves understanding of something else.

An instrumental case is the type used in exploratory research designs. It is conducted mainly because it promises to provide insight into an issue, not for any specific interest in the case itself. An intrinsic case study design is chosen when the researcher just wants more and better information about the case. The objective is not to study the case because it illustrates some specific characteristic or problem. Rather, the study is undertaken just because the researcher thinks that it is interesting or because it will provide better understanding of the phenomenon. In these situations, the subject case is expected to contribute to a greater understanding of a topic of interest, such as *performance measurement,* but not to serve as a design for applying performance measurement in the agency serving as the case.

The third type of case design is the collective case study. Other authors have used different names, most referring to this design as a *multiple-case* or *cross-case* study; Yeager (1989) called this type of case *multisite qualitative research.* This design is one of the major research approaches taken in comparative political studies. A group of similar cases, say conservative parties in several different countries, are studied in order to study a particular phenomenon. The design is also used to suggest whether a characteristic might be common to a larger population of similar cases. The cases selected may be chosen because they are similar or because they are different. They are selected because the researcher believes that understanding what is going on in those cases will result in better understanding about a larger group of cases. Stake added that understanding the cases under study might also lead to "a little theorizing."

When to Use the Case Study Approach

Van Evera (1997) proposed the following five different situations for when the case study method is a particularly appropriate design: They can be used when (1) the researcher wants to establish a theory or theories, or (2) for testing theories that already exist; (3) they can be used for identifying a previous condition or conditions that lead or contribute to a phenomenon (what Van Evera called *antecedents*), or (4) when the researcher wants to establish the relative importance of those contributing conditions. And finally, (5) they can be used to establish the fundamental importance of the case with regard to other potential examples.

Establishing a theory upon which to base predictions of future events is an important reason for much of the published research in the administrative sciences. In his review of works that used the case study method to examine city planning and planners, Fischler (2000) noted that case studies are uniquely suited for exploring the interaction of personal behavior and collective institutions, and the interplay of agency and structure. In this way, the cases were seen as contributing to the development of a theory of government planning practices. Fischler also called cases "the most essential tools" in theory development.

Developing theory from case studies occurs through a four-phase process: (1) formulation of research questions and hypotheses, (2) selection of the case and definition of units of analysis, (3) data gathering and presentation, and (4) analysis and theory building. Finally, Fischler concluded that case studies should remain an important study approach:

> Case studies that explore the behavior and experience of innovative practitioners and innovative organizations, be they public, private, or not-for-profit, should therefore be placed high on our agenda. (Fischler 2000,194)

Bailey (1994) also identified a variety of purposes for the case study. They can be *descriptive, interpretive, critical, for solving administrative problems,* or used for the purpose of forming a theory. They can have a purely practitioner-oriented focus, or they can be "esoteric scholarly studies." For maximum value, however, Bailey concluded that the ideal case study was one that had value for *both* practitioners and academics.

Because political science researchers have used the case study for so long and in so many different ways, it is not surprising that so many different purposes for the method have surfaced. However, most authors agree with Lang and Heiss, who contend that the following fundamental principle underlies all case studies:

> The basic rationale for a case study is that there are processes and interactions . . . , which cannot be studied effectively except as they interact and function within the entity itself. Thus, if we learn how these processes interact in one person or organization, we will know more about how the processes [serve] as factors in themselves and perhaps apply these [what we have learned] to other similar type persons or organizations. (Lang and Heiss 1990, 86)

Features of Case Studies

For both the single-case and multicase approaches, the purpose of the study is not to be a representative picture of "the world," but rather simply to represent the specific case or cases.

While this is certainly true, it is also true that good case studies do include features of the case or set of cases that are uniform and generalizable, as well as those that have the appearance of being relatively unique to the case(s) under study (Bailey 1994, 192).

Single-Case Study Design

Most case studies that are conducted in each of the subfields of political science except comparative politics are single-case studies. They are also used in all the social and administrative sciences, making them what Miles and Huberman (1998, 193) called the *traditional mode of qualitative analysis*.

An early example of the single-case study is the 1951 Elliott analysis of the Glacier Metal Company in London. The report was described as a case study of developments in the social life of one industrial community. Moreover, the study was not intended to serve as a statement of precise and definite conclusions; rather, it was written to show how managers and employees in one company deal with change.

Nunez (2001) provided an example of a recent case-study design. His *Political Science Quarterly* paper examined the history and current methods of dealing with family homelessness in New York City. He began his analysis with a demographic profile of the "typical" homeless family—a single mother in her late 20s—and went on to briefly review how this composition has changed over several decades. The case concluded with a brief review of actions taken by city government to alleviate the problem. A different single-case approach was followed by Hoddie (2002). The Hoddie case focused on one group of indigenous people, aboriginal Australians. His research question was how preferential policies and ethnic boundaries blurred over the decade of the 1980s. The unit of analysis used by Hoddie was the fifty-nine statistical divisions in Australia. Neither the number nor the boundaries of the units changed in the ten-year period.

An example of a public administration single-case study is Soni's (2000) study of a regional office of the U.S. Environmental Protection Agency. The study focused on workplace diversity and the attitudes of agency personnel toward mandated awareness initiatives. Soni first determined how employees valued workplace diversity, and then looked at whether the staff supported the agency management-development program. That program was designed to enhance worker acceptance of racial, age, and gender diversity in the organization. This included requirements for diversity-management initiatives in five-year strategic plans, and diversity goals at the local or agency group level.

Analysis of this single case led Soni to conclude that workers accept and support diversity to a far lesser extent than the ideal published in the literature. In addition, diversity-management programs appeared to have only minimal effects in changing workers' sensitivity of differences, their acceptance and valuing of diversity, reducing stereotyping and prejudice, or any of the other goals established for the program.

Case studies such as that carried out by Soni should not be used to infer similar behaviors or conditions in other or related organizations. The results of a case study are applicable only to the organization or group examined. No inferences can be made from the results. Soni reflected on this possible limitation of the method by adding the following caveat at the conclusion of the paper:

> The racial and gender effects found in this case study may be a consequence of the many specific organizational characteristics and cannot be assumed to be representative of other organizations. (Soni 2000, 407)

In another example of a single-case study in the political science literature, Poister and Harris (2000) examined a "mature" total quality management program in the Pennsylvania Department of Transportation. The program began in 1982 with the introduction of quality circles and evolved into a major strategic force in the department, with quality concepts incorporated into all levels of the culture of the organization.

Poister and Harris (175) point to the experience of this department as an example for other agencies to emulate—one of the key purposes of the case study. They concluded their study with the statement that the department "has indeed transformed itself over the past 15 years around core values of quality and customer service. Hopefully, its experience along these lines will be helpful to other public agencies that have embarked on this journey more recently."

Multicase Study Method

Ammons, Coe, and Lombardo (2001) used a multicase approach to compare the performance of three public-sector benchmarking programs. Two of the projects were national in scope, while the third was a single-state program. The first project was a 1991 program sponsored by the Innovation Groups to collect performance measurement information from cities and counties across the country. This information was eventually incorporated into a national performance-benchmarking information network, eventually named the *PBCenter*. Participants were charged a $750 fee to join the project, which was designed to measure forty-three programs. However, both participation and enthusiasm among potential users of the information was disappointing.

The second project in this multicase study, the *Center for Performance Measurement,* was a national program sponsored by the International City/County Management Association (ICMA). This program was established in 1994 by a consortium of 34 cities and counties with populations over 200,000. Performance measurements were collected and shared in these four core service areas: police services, fire services, neighborhood services, and support services. Neighborhood services included code enforcement, housing, libraries, parks and recreation, road maintenance, garbage collection, and street-lighting services.

The third program examined in this three-case study was a state project that began in 1994 in North Carolina; its purpose was to provide performance statistics to the state's city managers. By 1995, it had evolved into the *North Carolina Local Government Performance Management Project,* and was run by the Institute of Government at the University of North Carolina–Chapel Hill. By 1997, thirty-five cities and counties were participating. Overall, the Ammons, Coe, and Lombardo analysis concluded that all three programs had failed to deliver results that even closely approached the expectations of their participants, and many felt that program costs exceeded any benefits. On the basis of their comparative analysis of the three cases, the authors recommended that administrators of similar projects in the future should make sure that participants have realistic expectations for benchmarking before they buy into their programs.

In another multicase design, Fernandez and Fabricant (2000) examined two cases from Florida's experience with privatization of child support programs in an effort to make comparisons of efficiency and effectiveness between public and private service providers. Their analysis concluded with recommendations on ways to avoid problems encountered in the evaluation process.

The primary objective of the Florida study was to compare the relative efficiency of the research methodologies of private firms versus government-agency providers. The topic was collection of delinquent child support payments from an absent parent. The initial report issued by the state indicated that in one case, the state agency produced a collection rate that was 307 percent greater than that of the private or contracted group. The authors revealed that the study design was fatally flawed. The agency success report was based on a sample that represented the total population of cases, whereas the sample worked on by the private firm represented only those cases that had been delinquent for longer than six months, and that the state agency had been working on unsuccessfully for the six-month period. A suggestion offered by the authors was that a negative correlation probably existed for the period of time a case is delinquent and the probability of collecting owed child support. Had similar samples been used, the researchers would most likely not have replicated the heavily biased results they produced with the faulty design.

Steps in the Case Study Method

The model presented in Figure 24.1 illustrates various steps in the selection and preparation of a case study. The model can be considered a flowchart; case study activities should begin at the top and proceed downward. The concepts included in the model owe much to Robert Stake's 1994 synopsis of the case method. Additional contribution to the model came from the five components of a case study design identified by Yin (1994, 20): (1) the study question, (2) its propositions (others call these *hypotheses*), if any, (3) the unit or units of analysis, (4) the logic that links the collected information to the propositions, and (5) the criteria selected by the researcher for interpreting the case.

Step 1. Frame the Case

The first step in researching a case study is to establish a *frame* for the research. Framing goes beyond identifying the basic research problem. Instead, when framing the case, the researcher must answer three questions: First, why should the case study method be used in preference to any other research method in this situation? Second, why should this particular case be studied? Are there more representative cases available for study? And, third, why choose the specific behaviors or phenomena to study?

Step 2. Operationalize Key Constructs

Operationalizing relevant themes, issues, research questions, and variables is the second step in the process. "Operationalizing" describes the process of *defining* or *conceptualizing* the key constructs or themes that form and shape the research. Operationalizing also requires the researcher to identify any limitations and assumptions for the research. Depending upon the research approach followed, operationalizing activities can take place before or after the data are collected. The process occurs before data collection in the case study approach. However, when it is done after the data are collected, the study is more appropriately a "grounded theory study." In the grounded theory approach the structure and order emerges from the collected data; in these studies *all* data are "right."

Regardless of when it takes place, its purpose is the same: to impose *order and structure* on the data, and to identify any limitations or assumptions. Order and structure imposed by the researcher beforehand helps to ensure that the needed data will be collected during case

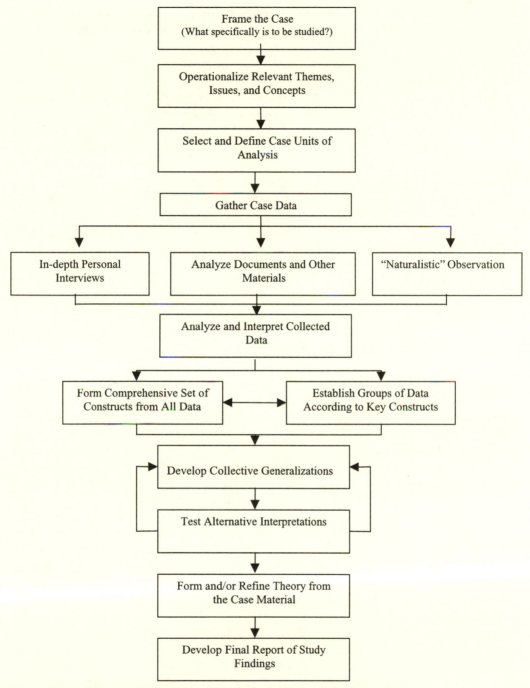

Figure 24.1 **Steps in Case Study Planning, Analysis, and Presentation**

interviews and observations. Finally, when a researcher "operationalizes" the salient themes or constructs for a case study, he or she makes it much easier to organize the data as they are collected.

Defining the categories also involves providing some amount of descriptive information in any number of ways. Strauss and Corbin (1998) defined it as the process of applying order to collected data by placing them in discrete categories, adding that researchers are almost certain to include some amount of descriptive material along with the code descriptions and category definitions. Gathered information must be coded and assigned to its proper category. Coding is based on a researcher-selected set of general properties, characteristics, or dimensions. In their discussion on coding of qualitative data, Strauss and Corbin (103) added that conceptualizing is also the first step in theory building. A concept is the researcher's description of a significant event, object, or action-interaction. Naming the researched phenomena and organizing them into logical categories is necessary so that the research can group similar events, things, etc. into common groupings, classifications, or categories that share some common characteristic or meaning. Thus, "a labeled thing" is something that can be located, placed in a class of similar objects, or classified in some way.

Finally, operationalization requires that the researcher identify each of the procedures that will be followed, in both data collection and analysis, identify the coding plans and methods that will be used, and prepare a preliminary list of categories for the analysis.

Step 3. Define Units of Analysis

The third step in case study analysis is defining the *units of analysis*. This critical step hinges upon how the researcher has defined the problem to be studied. As noted earlier, case studies can focus on many different types or amounts of phenomena; they can be either single-case or multicase studies. Most case studies typically focus on individuals, pairs (dyads), small or large groups, processes, or organizations (Marshall and Rossman 1999). They can also be about a decision or set of decisions made by administrators, supervisors, or work teams. They can focus on programs, agencies, small subunits of agencies, or groups of agencies that address a similar problem or service. They can even be about entire communities.

These subjects of case studies are all what is meant by the term "unit of analysis." Deciding on the unit of analysis is what Yin (1994) referred to as *a narrowing of the relevant data*. Narrowing the data allows the researcher to focus the study on topics identified in the research objectives. Taking the unit-of-analysis decision to the next level depends first on the way the researcher has defined the study question. For example, a study designed to bring to light the effects of a reduction in the number of beds available at a state mental health hospital could be addressed from several points of view.

First, the study could chronicle the effects that inability to access treatment might have on one or a category-group of patients. Another study might focus on the impact the closures will have on community-based treatment centers. An even more focused study could limit the investigation to locally funded charitable organizations treating the client base. A broader view might look at the economic impact that funding the services locally will have on other community-based programs competing for shares of the same funding pool. Clearly, defining the unit of analysis is a critical first step that must take place before moving to the next step, collecting information.

Step 4. Collect the Data

The fourth step, *data collection,* can take place in a variety of ways. The techniques used most often in social science research include (1) interviews, (2) simple (also called *naturalistic*) observation, and (3) analysis of internal and external documents. One of the hallmarks of a good case study is the selection of two or more of these methods (Arneson 1993).

Interviews. Gathering data by interview may take one of several different forms. The method used most often in public administration research is the in-depth personal interview. An approach that is becoming increasingly important in political science research is the *focus group interview.* Individual interviews occur as conversations between a researcher and a subject or respondent. To keep the conversation focused, the researcher uses a conversation guide in which are listed the key points that are to be covered in the interview. The respondent is free to provide any answer that comes to mind. Another type of interview is the more structured type, in which respondents must reply to specific open-ended questions.

Observation. Naturalistic or simple observation is another way data are gathered for case studies. Marshall and Rossman (1999, 107) described this method as "the systematic noting and recording of events, behaviors, and artifacts in the social setting chosen for study." The researcher records events and behaviors as they happen, collecting the written records into compilations of impressions that are similar if not identical to the field notes that characterize data collection in ethnographic studies. In this type of observation, however, the researcher does not seek to be accepted as a member of the group, staying, instead, an outsider.

It is a toss-up as to which is more important in the case study approach to research: personal interviewing or simple observation. Each has its own advantages and disadvantages. Interviews, for example, allow researchers to delve deeply into a subject, encouraging respondents to provide the reasons for their behavior or opinions. Interviews are time-consuming, however, and require interviewers with special questioning and listening skills.

Observation has long been an important data-gathering technique used in social science research. While it may indeed be called "simple observation," it is not an easy process to employ, as the following statement indicates:

> Observation is a fundamental and highly important method in all qualitative inquiry: it is used to discover complex interactions in natural social settings.... It is, however, a method that requires a great deal of the researcher. Discomfort, uncomfortable ethical dilemmas and even danger, the difficulty of managing a relatively unobtrusive role, and the challenge of identifying the "big picture" while finely observing huge amounts of fast-moving and complex behavior are just a few of the challenges. (Marshall and Rossman 1999, 107)

One way that researchers try to get around the time and skills limitations of in-depth interviewing is with the use of group interviewing, what marketing and advertising researchers call *focus groups.* A focus group is a group of from six to a dozen individuals with similar interests or characteristics who are interviewed together in the same room. The researcher functions as a moderator, keeping any one or a few subjects from monopolizing the conversation or intimidating other subjects. As each participant is called upon to contribute, group interaction often begins to appear, thus providing for a richer, more meaningful discussion of the topic.

Document Analysis. The study of documents and archival data is usually undertaken to supplement the information the case study researcher acquires by interview or by observing in a situation. These may be official government records, internal organization reports or memos, or external reports or articles about a case subject. The technique that is usually used in document analysis is called *content analysis.* This process may be either qualitative or quantitative, or both. One of the key advantages of document analysis is that it does not interfere with or disturb the case setting in any way. According to Marshall and Rossman, the fact that document and archival analysis is unobtrusive and nonreactive is probably the greatest strength of this research activity.

As well as providing a means for *triangulation,* the use of more than one approach helps ensure that relevant data are not missed. Triangulation is studying a phenomenon in two or more ways to substantiate the *validity* of the study findings; it is an important concept in the postpositivist approach to political science research. This term, taken from land surveying, map making, and radio direction finding, refers to the use of several different research methods to get a better handle on a phenomenon by looking at it in more than one way.

There are three different ways to employ triangulation in a research study (Northrop and Kraemer 1982). The first is to use different research methods independent of one another and to then compare the findings as a check of the external validity of the data. This has been the approach used most often in political science. The second is to use different data collection techniques within either the qualitative or quantitative approaches, but not mixing the overall approaches. The third is what has been termed the "holistic approach" (Denzin 1978). The holistic approach includes the planned mixing of qualitative and quantitative methods into a single broadly based research design. For example, random sampling might be used in selecting sites for in-depth fieldwork.

Looking at a problem in more than one way is considered necessary because of the postpositivist stand that researchers can never be sure that their findings are not biased by their own experiences, culture, or worldviews. Triangulation permits a wider acceptance of qualitative research methods. In the view of Trochim, the application of triangulation in the postpositivist approach to research can be summed up in the following way:

> Where the positivist believed that the goal of science was to uncover the truth, the postpositivist . . . believes that *the goal of science is to hold steadfastly to the goal of getting it right about reality, even though we can never achieve that goal!* [Trochim's emphasis] Because all measurement is fallible, the postpositivist emphasizes the importance of multiple measurements and observations, each of which may possess different types of error, and the need to use triangulation across these multiple errorful sources to try to get a better bead on what's happening in reality. The postpositivist also believes that all observations are theory-laden and that scientists . . . are inherently biased. (Trochim 2002, 2)

Step 5. Analyze the Data

The analysis of all qualitative data takes place in a progression of six separate phases. Figure 24.2 displays a slightly different version of the progression of analysis steps. An important requirement inherent in all data analysis is that the data be reduced in volume at each stage. Unless this occurs, the researcher may be inundated with reams of unrelated information that make logical interpretation impossible. Organizing the data into sets of mutually exclusive categories is one way that data reduction can be achieved.

Raw data in the case study method can be any or all of the collected information. The primary responsibility of the analyst is to remain focused on information that sheds light on

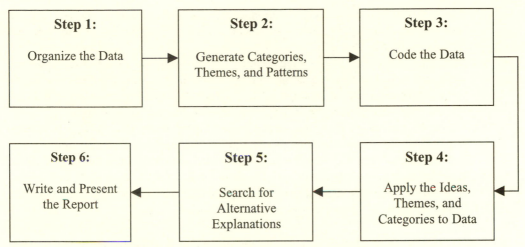

Figure 24.2   **A Six-Step Procedure for Analysis of Case Study Data**

the study question. This may mean ignoring or leaving to a later review highly interesting but extraneous data. Analysis of case data involves looking at and weighing the collected data from a number of different viewpoints before writing the final case narrative.

Data analysis does not always take place in the logical sequence illustrated in Figure 24.2. Rather, two or more of the activities may be occurring at the same time. In addition, data analysis does not simply end with the first set of conclusions; it occurs in a *circular* process. Parts of the analysis may be moved forward to the next step or steps, while other parts, even whole sections, may butt up against conclusions with dead ends. When this happens, the researcher must search for alternative explanations, test these against the themes that evolved in the operationalization phase, and then either reach new and different conclusions or adjust the themes and categories to reflect the reality of the data.

The analysis process involves five activities: (1) grouping the data according to key constructs, (2) identifying bases for interpretation, (3) developing generalizations from the data, (4) testing alternative interpretations, and (5) forming and/or refining generalizable theory from the case study.

Step 6. Prepare and Present a Report of the Findings

The final step in the process is producing a comprehensive narrative of the case, in which the connections between key concepts and study objectives are addressed. The *narrative* is a descriptive account of the program, person, organization, office, or agency under study. It requires that all the information necessary to understand the case be included in the narrative. It typically revolves around the researcher's *interpretation* of the behaviors and events observed in the case during the study period.

Patton (1980, 304) referred to the final case narrative as "the descriptive, analytic, interpretive, and evaluative treatment of the more comprehensive descriptive data" collected by the researcher. He saw the report-writing phase taking place in a series of three distinct phases:

- Phase 1: Collecting and categorizing the raw case data. This is all the information that can be gathered by interviews, in observing, and by reviewing any relevant documents and/or literature.
- Phase 2: Constructing a preliminary record of the case. A case record is the researchers' coded and subsequent distillation of the mass of raw case data. It involves establishing categories and assigning the data to them in a logical order. A draft of the report eventually emerges from completion of this and the first step.
- Phase 3: Producing a case study narrative. This is the final written (or other presentation form) narrative that presents the case information in a readable, informative, and evaluative form that communicates how the case meets the original objectives for the research. It includes all the information that readers need to fully understand the subject. It can be presented in the form of a chronological record of events, or according to a set of themes—or as both approaches.

The case study report must clearly show that the researcher has accurately explained what he or she perceived to be the "facts." In addition, it must contain a discussion of what the researcher believes are relevant alternative interpretations, as well as an explanation of why the researcher chose not to accept those alternatives. Finally, all case studies should end with a conclusion that is soundly based in the interpretation adopted by the researcher (Yeager 1989).

Important Guidelines for Case Studies

A number of guidelines have been offered for preparing case study reports. Five key characteristics are found in the best, most informative case studies. These are:

The case study must be significant. Cases that are "significant" are those that stand out either as superior examples or the "best in their class." They illustrate a particular point in a better or more succinct way than others that could have been chosen. In this way, the researcher indicates that selection of the case or cases was not only appropriate, but that the study adds to the body of knowledge about the topic or issue; the study makes a *significant* contribution. Researcher problems that are trivial do not make good case studies. Yin (1994, 147) concluded that the best case studies are those in which:

- The single case or sets of cases are unusual and not "mundane."
- The case or cases are what the public would be interested in reading about.
- The fundamental issues brought to light in the case have wide appeal—they are "nationally important," either as theory, as policy, or in practical application.
- Or they are all of the above.

The case study must be "complete." Cases that are "complete" leave the reader with the feeling that all relevant evidence has been collected, evaluated, interpreted, and either accepted or rejected. The operative word here, of course, is *relevant*. In Yin's opinion (1994) a case is not complete unless it is so on three distinct dimensions. First, a "complete" case is one in which the phenomenon of interest in the case is explicitly addressed. Second, all the relevant information is collected; no information that fits this dimension should be left ungathered or, if collected, left uninterpreted and discussed in the final narrative. Third, the researcher/case author must not impose any artificial conditions during the analysis or evaluation of the collected data. This means, for example, that the researcher must not stop collecting relevant information because he or she ran out of money or time, or for any other constraint.

The case study must consider alternative perspectives. It is important that the researcher not limit the analysis of case data to a single point of view. Alternative explanations for a social phenomenon *always* exist (Marshall and Rossman 1999). Throughout the analysis of the case data, the researcher is obligated to identify alternative explanations or interpretations of the "raw" data, and to show why these are rejected in favor of the adopted explanation. Evidence that supports the selected interpretation must also be presented.

The case study must display sufficient evidence. Data reduction solely for the sake of brevity in a case analysis is not desirable. All the relevant evidence must appear in the final narrative. Certainly, condensing, distilling, and combining data takes place at each step of the analysis; otherwise, the final report would end up little more than a motley collection of unrelated, disjointed, hodgepodge of unrelated raw data. The researcher must analyze the data in order to fully interpret and evaluate what was collected. In this process, some data reduction naturally occurs. However, the researcher should probably err on the side of including *too much* material rather than finding out later that he or she has omitted important evidence from the final case report.

The case study must be written in an engaging way. While this does not apply directly to the concept of completeness in a case report, it is relevant because it has a great influence on whether the case will ultimately be read, understood, and, where appropriate, used in policy development. It is a question of *style.* According to Yin, a complaint that is often heard about case studies is that they are often too long, they are cumbersome to read and interpret, and they are simply boring. He suggested that the writer of cases strive to engage readers' intelligence, entice their interest by early hinting at exciting information to come, and seduce readers into accepting the underlying premise.

Summary

The case method has long been one of the most popular approaches followed in public administration research. The popularity of the case study approach lies in the great flexibility of the method. Case studies can be written to serve as examples of what ought not to be done, as well as what should be done, and for pointing out what other people or organizations are doing.

Case studies are often intensive studies of one or a few exemplary individuals, families, events, time periods, decisions or set of decisions, processes, programs, institutions, organizations, groups, or even entire communities. The case method is one of three qualitative approaches for research in organizational communications. This application has been described as appropriate when some noteworthy success or failure in a case is present.

There are three types of case studies: (1) intrinsic case studies, (2) instrumental studies, and (3) collective studies. *Intrinsic* case studies are done when the researcher wants to provide a better understanding of the subject case itself. *Instrumental* case studies are used when the public administration researcher wants to gain greater insight into a specific issue. The *collective case* is a multiple-case design; a group of individual cases are studied together because it is believed that they can contribute to greater understanding of a phenomenon, a population, or some general organizational condition. Another name for this type of case is *multisite qualitative research.*

Five purposes for case studies have been identified: (1) when the researcher wants to establish a theory or theories, or (2) for testing theories that already exist; (3) for identifying a previous condition or conditions that lead or contribute to a phenomenon; or (4) when the researcher wants to establish the relative importance of those contributing conditions, (5) they can be used to establish the fundamental importance of the case with regard to other potential examples.

Case studies can be single-case or multicase designs. Most case studies that are conducted in the behavioral and administrative sciences are single-case studies. Multicase designs can be used to compare two or more cases, or for gathering extended evidence across a group of like cases.

Designing and preparing a case study takes place through a series of interlocking steps. In Step 1, the case must be *framed,* which means that the researcher must determine what should be studied in what case, and why. In Step 2, key constructs, variables, terms, etc. are operationalized so that no confusion occurs later in the analysis process. Step 3 is when the researcher selects and defines the unit(s) of analysis: Is the case about individuals, groups, neighborhoods, etc.? The researcher collects data in Step 4. This usually involves conducting in-depth interviews, performing naturalistic or simple observations, and examining any relevant documentation. The data are analyzed in Step 5, with a final case report prepared during Step 6.

Discussion Questions

1. Define the case study approach. How is it used in political science research?
2. What is a collective case study?
3. Name five different situations when the case study approach is particularly appropriate.
4. Name four purposes for the case study.
5. What takes place during framing of the case study?
6. Why is it important to operationalize key constructs in the case study?
7. Name some typical units of analysis in case studies.
8. How are case study data usually collected?
9. Discuss the six phases through which case data analysis takes place.
10. Name the important guidelines recommended for case analyses.

Additional Reading

Marshall, Catherine, and Gretchen B. Rossman. 1999. *Designing Qualitative Research.* 3rd ed. Thousand Oaks, CA: Sage.
Van Evera, Stephen. 1997. *Guide to Methods for Students of Political Science.* Ithaca: Cornell University Press.
Yin, Robert K. 1994. *Case Study Research: Design and Methods.* 2nd ed. Thousand Oaks, CA: Sage.

25 The Explanatory Approach II: Historical Research Methods

Halfway through America's Civil War, during what may have been the greatest crisis of the nation's short history, defeat at the ballot box almost succeeded in destroying the Union where the force of arms had thus far failed. With the North and South still locked in armed conflict, President Abraham Lincoln and his supporters in Congress were dealt what Carson, Jenkins, Rhode, and Souva (2001) described as a "stunning defeat." After the votes in the 1862 midterm congressional elections were counted, the Republican Party had lost its majority in the House of Representatives. This potentially crippling political loss forced the President to forge a coalition with the Unconditional War Party, a splinter party based in the border states, in order to continue the war.

Why did Lincoln's political defeat occur? What ramifications did it hold for the future waging of the war? And possibly more important, what effect did it have on the peace that followed? What lessons might be learned from the dramatic shift in the fortunes of the majority party? The political scientists who authored this paper asked themselves these and similar questions, and embarked on a *historical research project* to find the answers. They also used the election results to test their hypothesis that modern political theories can be applied in an historical context to shed light on what otherwise might have remained hidden. They concluded that electoral district-specific events had at least as much, if not more, effect on the outcome of the elections than national events such as the horrendous loss of life resulting from the poor showing of the North's armies to that time.

This story of the congressional elections of 1862 is just one of many examples of historical research methods used in the analysis of political science phenomena. One or more historical studies may be found in nearly every issue of most of the journals in this discipline. However, not much can be found describing how to use the historical method in political science research. The purpose of this chapter is to fill that void.

Capturing the Essence of Politics in Historical Research

Speaking at a World Congress of Political Sciences, the Russian political scientist Vladik Nersesyants described the importance of an historical approach in political science research in the following terms:

The world history of political theories is a major component of mankind's non-material culture. It represents in concentrated form the vast experience of many generations; it includes the principal landmarks and findings of the many centuries of research into the theory of politics, state, law, and political power. The historical approach is thus a means of understanding and assessing the past, historically determined, significance of political theories and their present role. (Nersesyants 1988, 9–14)

The model in Figure 25.1 illustrates the evolution of emphases in historical research as suggested by such authors as Barzun and Graff (1992) and Iggers (1985), among others.

Historians and political scientists using historical research methods approach the study of history from a number of different points of view. One way of describing the different directions historians have taken was proposed by Georg Iggers (1985). Iggers identified three approaches that historical researchers have followed since history was recognized as a separate discipline in the nineteenth century. The first is the *hermeneutic* approach; the second is a

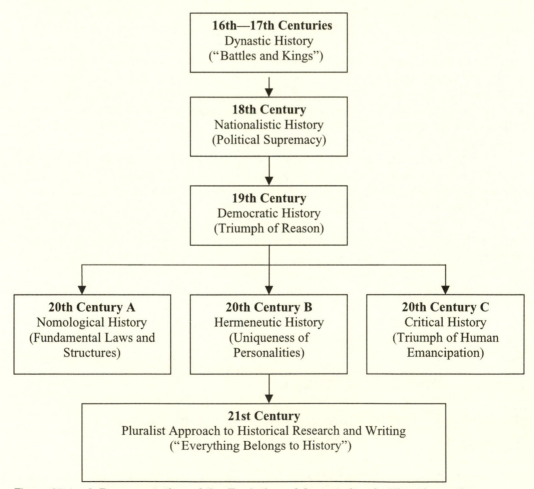

Figure 25.1   A Representation of the Evolution of Approaches in Historiography
Source: After Barzun and Graff 1992; Iggers 1985.

nomological approach; and the third is a *critical* emphasis, as exemplified by *Marxist* and *feminist* approaches.

The hermeneutic tradition of historical analysis has the longest record of use among the three twentieth century approaches. Hermeneutics is a way of interpreting historical documents and other phenomena in light of the events that took place at the time of the writing of the text, as well as approaching the interpretation from the intent and experiences of the text's author. The hermeneutic tradition has its roots in the study of religious texts from the points of view of the writers and subsequent interpreters. The objective of historians who follow the hermeneutic approach is the search for what Iggers (1985, 37) termed "the uniqueness of historical personalities." This is similar to the *Great Man* approach of the early historians.

Nomology is the science of laws, and the nomological approach to a discipline attempts to discern fundamental laws that can be used to explain and eventually predict future events. This approach seeks to make history more "scientific"; in doing so, it tries to apply the tools of the natural science to historical investigation. Nomological political scientists apply quantitative tools used in economics and the behavioralist school of the social sciences; they develop mathematical models to analyze dependent and independent variable relationships. A variation of this theme is *structuralism,* which leads historical researchers to make efforts to identify the underlying, invisible structures that form and guide societies and their institutions. The principle that guides structuralist researchers is that these structures always exist in society; if they did not, chaos would ensue. It is the job of the historian to "decode" the historical evidence in order to discover the underlying structure. The evidence exists in persistent, reoccurring events, economic records, social relationships, symbols, art forms, and other cultural artifacts; the structural historian applies quantitative methods to interpret the evidence in order to define the historical record.

The critical tradition of historical writing is one that views all social phenomena and historical events from the point of view of continually changing systems of social relationships and dependencies. Marxist and feminist historians are drawn to the idea of history as a record of social conflict leading to human emancipation. This tradition sees history as a critical social science that does not simply narrate but instead works to abet change in the human condition. For Marxists, the arena of conflict is social class; for feminists, it is gender bias.

Modern historical writing has its roots in the *Age of Enlightenment,* the intellectual and philosophical movement that shaped thought in Europe and the United States during the late seventeenth and eighteenth centuries. Prior to this change in thinking, most history consisted of interesting personal narratives written by someone with an interest in the past. It was usually the history of dynasties; it was often financed by the rulers featured in the narrative. It was, therefore, biographical history with the greatest possible bias. With the enlightenment came an unwillingness to accept dynastic rule. In its place emerged the idea that society exists as a result of a contract between the governed and those selected or allowed to govern. The ability to *reason* gave humans the power to understand the causes of and how to improve their own condition. Reason allowed humans power to gain knowledge, attain freedom, and achieve personal happiness. What emerged was a history that celebrated human progress—*democratic history.* Although the movement eventually faded, it left in its wake a secular academic tradition that saw the founding of most of the natural and social sciences that exist today.

By the nineteenth century modern colleges and universities had been formed and many of today's academic disciplines established. History was one of these disciplines. Many American historians found fault with the literary nature of history; some found an answer to their concerns in the scientific school of history that was being proposed by Leopold von Ranke at the new

University of Berlin, which was established in 1810. Ranke believed that the same scientific rigor found in the newly emerging natural sciences should be used in a systematic and scientific study of history. This meant referring only to *primary sources* to historical data gathering, and applying a value-free objectivity in the subsequent writing of the historical narrative. The primary sources referred to were the diplomatic and administrative records of governments and their administrative bodies. The proper way to investigate those sources was to use a hermeneutic approach in order to understand the source document in light of the period in which it was written, together with understanding the intent of the author at that time. The product of this approach was primarily *diplomatic* and *military* history.

The Rankean school of historical research spread rapidly across the Atlantic to quickly become the dominant approach followed by most U.S. college and university history departments. It reached its peak of influence as the eighteenth century gave way to the nineteenth. By that time, many critics of the method were charging that the demands of rapidly changing industrialized society had made irrelevant and superfluous a history that only told the story of the "great man" in diplomatic and military actions. That emphasis needed to be replaced with a history that examined and compared social and cultural forces of societies, and that did not restrict itself to a few luminaries of the time. To conduct that kind of research historians needed to adopt the quantitative tools and methods that were being applied in the social sciences. The hermeneutic approach was thus supplemented by the nomological and critical approaches to history.

Today, nearly everything is fair game for historical research, as noted by Barzun and Graff:

> Theoretically, everything we can think of has its history and belongs to History: not only kings and battles and economic forces, but costume and courtship, railroading and the game of chess, mathematics and the meaning of words, military strategy and old wine, the migration of continents and the surface of the moon . . . history is the great humanizer. (Barzun and Graff 1992, 9)

Shifting Directions in Political Science

The writing of political history has changed in a number of different ways during its several-hundred-year history. One way it has changed is in the same way that political science itself has changed. Orren and Skowronek (1995) traced the three positions of political science starting with the formal academic discipline's first fifty years, beginning in 1880 and ending about 1930. The focus of this period was on the *institutions* of politics. By institutions, they meant the fundamental formal and informal rules and agreements that made it possible for government to function and the political and economic world to survive even in the face of revolutionary change. The key institution that made that possible was the formal structure of constitutions. Therefore, the natural topics for research were constitutional arrangements. Addressing a series of contact points in society where political conflict occurs, Avery Leiserson discussed the need for a formal constitutional institution in the following way:

> The distinction [that occurs] between social and political structures in a free democracy . . . a free people, voluntarily associated in a society . . . requires a political system, a formal structure of legally coercive public offices and decision-making process based upon units of electoral organization different from those of the social and economic structures. (Leiserson 1968, 17)

During the 1950s and 1960s, adoption of the behavioralist approach by political scientists resulted in what has been described by Orren and Skowronek as a radical reorientation of the study of politics. During these two decades the focus of political science research shifted from institutions to analysis of the behavior of individuals in political groups and organizations. Except for the continuing interest of researchers on political thought, political history researchers also shifted their focus; studies that investigated changes in social structures and groups that were influenced by behavioral forces began to appear. Political scientists looked upon government as a *process* that could be defined and measured in behavioral terms. It was believed that inferential approaches could allow for the predicting of behavior in the future. The institutions of government were considered part of the larger political system that itself was a product of human creation.

The final phase of political science described by Orren and Skowronek began as a reaction to the strict empiricism advocated by behavioralists. Political scientists developed mathematical models to describe behavior in their application of *rational choice theory*. Adopted from economics, rational choice theory assumes that people make decisions, including political decisions, based upon their perceptions of achieving the greatest benefits, or *utility*, from the chosen alternative. The principles of game theory have been widely adopted by rational theory researchers, together with a renewed interest in institutionalism. Some "new institutionalist" researchers now study institutions to "make sense of institutional politics as a more or less stable game in play." Institutions—the formal and informal rules, norms, and standards of the political world—exist to bring equilibrium to the process of government.

The Nature of Political History

If history is the written record of past or current events, then political history must be the written record of past or current political phenomena (Hockett 1958; Elton 1985). This makes political history the recorded story of politics, political institutions, and the actors in the political world. Political history began with the first written records of society in Mesopotamia and continues up to and including the political activities taking place today. Politics are social phenomena; they occur in the context of society. As a result, some might describe political history as social history. Without people interacting with people, there can be no politics. In the words of Elton (1985, 6), *there is no politics without contact.* As a result, political history entails the description of the events, institutions, societies, and *individuals* that come into contact with one another, in whatever form at whatever time.

It has also been said that political history is the record of *power*—the striving for, getting, preserving, or reacting against—power over one's fellow human beings (Elton 1984; Stoker and Marsh 2002). Thus, by its very nature, the history of politics is the story of humans in conflict over power. Certainly, some of this conflict involved rational, intelligent, peace-loving diplomats sitting across from one another, negotiating in a civilized manner. But most of it has been a long and bloody record of war, famine, pillage, fratricide, regicide, genocide, and the whole litany of man's ability to do harm to his fellow man. It can make for a great read!

Much of American political science research has been concerned with the ways that voters and special-interest groups have fought for and exercised power over other groups or against one or more levels of government (Price 1985). To fight their power wars, groups and individuals have used the tools of elections, the party system, actions of organized interest groups, and the strategic use of opinion polling, among others. It is not surprising, then, that these activities are also subjects of historical research.

Political scientists often disagree in their interpretations of a historical event. A recent example of such a disagreement may be found in the *British Journal of Politics and International Relations* (BJPIR). Crowley and Norton's paper in the inaugural 1999 issue of this journal addressed issues relating to what the authors claimed was a declining cohesion among Conservative members of parliament. Three points were made in their historical analysis of the "revolt" among some Conservative Party MPs that was alleged to have occurred in 1992. They argued that (1) contrary to popular belief, Conservative MPs were not particularly rebellious in 1992; (2) the rebellions that did occur were largely over European Union issues, and did not result in the birth of damaging factions within the party; and (3) the extent of those rebellions has been overstated by earlier observers.

Several years later, however, political scientist Timothy Heppell took issue with portions of their evaluations. His alternate analysis was carried in the June, 2002, issue of BJPIR, along with a rejoinder by Crowley and Norton. Heppell stated early in his paper:

> This article intends to challenge the Crowley and Norton argument that the PCP (Parliamentary Conservative Party) remained immune to factual contagion. The methodology they employed is based primarily on behavioral factors to the virtual exclusion of attitudinal factors. (Heppell 2000, 304)

Crowley and Norton found three problems with Heppell's critique. First, they charged that the criticism "substantially misrepresents" their analysis of the behavior of Conservative Party MPs under the leadership of Prime Minister John Major. Second, the system developed by Heppell to place MPs into various categories was not an improvement upon the system created by Norton in 1990 and used by Crowley and Norton in their paper. Third, they charged Heppell with reading things in their paper that were not there.

This series of contentious articles dealt with a period that was clearly an important one to British political scientists: a major shift in the political direction of the British electorate that resulted in the return of the Labor Party to control of government. The series is included here, not for its impact upon British politics nor to remark on the conflict between authors, but rather to illustrate the use of *historical narrative* as a method in political science research—and to remind readers in passing that what is historical "truth" depends upon who is writing it. Rallings, Thrasher, and Johnston (2002), for example, also studied the same topic and era, but from a slightly different viewpoint in their historical review of the decline in fortunes of the Conservative Party in Britain. Their investigation focused on the decline in local support of the Conservatives, as measured by Conservative Party votes in local elections. They identified four key factors that they felt accounted for the decline: (1) different rates of abstention by Conservative and Labor Party votes; (2) desertion of Conservative support in rural areas, (3) opposition party concentrated attacks in selected districts, and (4) bias in the electoral systems that resulted from redistricting and restructuring.

Shifting Directions in Political History

Elton (1984) suggested that the broad, or *global,* focus of political history has also undergone a relatively slow process of evolutionary change over the past 200 years. The earliest focus of political historians—and the one with the longest record of inquiry—is the history of political thought. This type of history reached its full stride with historical analyses of the political treatises of Greece and Rome, and may have peaked with the political discourse of Machiavelli. It includes analyses of the writings of influential observers and commentators on politics and government such as Plato, Hobbes, Locke, and Marx, to mention just a few examples (Tuck 2001). Because political science was for many years a branch of philosophy, the philosophical approach to the study of politics predominated.

The second emphasis for political history was diplomatic and military history. This approach to history became popular during the nineteenth century when writing history became the province of "professional historians." As history departments appeared in colleges and universities, history professors—"professional" historians—took on the task of writing history in addition to teaching it. This history was generally written in a straightforward—some would say *dry*—manner. It focused on detailed reporting of the recorded activities of governmental institutions, important diplomats, and famous military leaders. The primary source for this history was the archival records of various branches of government, including agencies, and departments. This history is referred to as the *Great Man* or *Battles and Kings* approach to political history. In the words of Elton, this type of history is "under a cloud," but it is still being written today.

The third, and essentially a product of only the nineteenth century, is constitutional and administrative history. The historical record of these topics was considered important because they helped to explain the rules of the society from which they were drawn. In this sense, this shift in focus helped facilitate the focus of research from attention on the stories of great men and great events to the institutions that make government possible. Elton (1984) considered the writing of administrative history to be more "basic," and constitutional history to provide more information. He concluded:

> The political historian needs first to be thoroughly acquainted with what happened and could happen in the ordinary running of affairs within the society that is his concern, and thus to understand the machinery which made possible the translation of power into action; only then is he able to tell the political story both accurately and in depth. (Elton 1984, 28)

History has not seen a new guiding force emerge to replace the emphases of the past. Instead, in the words of Burke (2001), today history is concerned with nearly every activity of humanity. One new unifying thread is concerned with culture, and the idea that reality is socially or culturally constructed—the concept of cultural relativism. It is often "history from the bottom," that is, a narrative of everyday humans and their efforts to survive—the story of ordinary people and the way they cope with change in their society. The sources of this history are no longer the archives of governments or the diaries of important people, but oral histories, private letters, cultural artifacts and paraphernalia, photographs, anything that helps tell a story. These and other, related changes have not made history easier to write: "The discipline is now more fragmented than every before," according to Burke (17).

Political history today is also considered to be in a state of flux. No new all-encompassing paradigm has emerged to replace the positions of the past. Despite a renewed interest in what is called "new institutionalism," behavioralists, rational choice theorists, feminists, the narrative approaches, and postmodernists appear to be functioning side by side with little of the overt and acrimonious hostility of earlier "schools" of history, of political science, and of political history. Modern political historians have adopted a pluralistic position regarding direction and emphasis of approach (Stoker and Marsh 2002, 3). Despite the lack of a solid foundation upon which to evaluate historical research, for political science researchers, one good thing has come from the shifting philosophical ground. According to Burke (2001):

> The long-standing opposition between political and non-political historians is finally dissolving. G.M. Trevelyan's notorious definition of social history as "history with the politics left out" is now rejected by almost everyone. Instead we find concern with the social element in politics and the political element in society. On the one hand, political historians no longer confine themselves to "high" politics, to leaders, to elites. They discuss the geography and sociology of elections and the "republic" in the village. They examine "political cultures," the assumptions about politics which form part of everyday life but differ widely from one period or region to another. (Burke 2001, 18)

Conducting Historical Research

Historical research should be as systematic and intellectually rigorous as every other research design. The historical approach takes place in the same place, identifying a study problem and research questions. It then follows a logical series of distinct steps or stages. However, recommendations on how to define these steps vary from author to author. For example, Hocket (1958) claimed that historical research occurs in three steps: the gathering of data; the critical evaluation of the data; and the presentation of the facts, interpretations, and conclusions the historical researcher draws from the facts. McDowell (2002, 90–92), on the other hand, went so far as to spell out a series of twenty distinct steps for historical research. McDowell's list of twenty steps is paraphrased below, grouped into three broad categories:

I. Planning the Research
    (1) Select a subject for research
    (2) Define the subject more precisely; identify key themes; set research objectives; prepare a timetable for completion of the project
    (3) Identify source material; prepare a working bibliography; identify keywords and check bibliography of data
    (4) Identify research methods to be used: document analysis, personal interviews, artifact analysis, etc.
    (5) Begin background reading and, where necessary, refine the proposed project
II. Gathering and Interpreting Data
    (1) Prepare a draft outline of the paper
    (2) Peruse source material to prepare research notes
    (3) Review research notes and materials; prepare a list of key topic areas to subdivide the final paper
    (4) Prepare a draft outline of chapter(s); create a list of research questions for each key topic area
    (5) Prepare a detailed research proposal, incorporating chapter headings, and chapter summaries with topic organization
    (6) Form manageable subunits of work, as in chapter sections or paragraphs
    (7) Complete the survey of sources and source material
III. Writing and Presenting the Findings
    (1) Write the first draft; edit the first draft; continue editing as needed
    (2) Write the final draft

(3) Type the final draft; incorporate changes and alterations
(4) Proofread the typescript
(5) Edit the typeset draft, if to be sent to a publisher
(6) If producing a published book, check the page proofs
(7) Prepare an index from a set of the page proofs
(8) Congratulate yourself on a task well done.

Of all the tasks in the above detailed list of steps in the historical research process, the most important of all may be *preparing and indexing research notes* (McDowell 2002, 126). Notes may be entered on individual sheets of notepaper, kept in bound notebooks, written on note cards, or even entered directly into a computer. They should be organized according to topic areas and filed together. Individual notes should include the following information: a descriptive heading, the chapter and/or section in which the information is to be used, a clear distinction between paraphrased and quoted material, and a complete source identification. Detailed bibliographic information is usually kept in a separate file, but enough information to clearly identify the name of the author, date of publication, and page number of the material should be included with every note.

In terms of structure and organization of the historical report, Barzun and Graff (1970, 262–63) emphasized that historical research reports should lead the reader through a logical, chronological progression of the material. They offered the following single-case analysis of an organization as an example. The example illustrates a strategy that is followed in many, if not most, qualitative research strategies. Their example begins with the founding of an organization and ends with an outlook for its future:

1. The founding of the organization
2. Success and the first twenty years
3. Cracking at the seams (growth)
4. The big lawsuit (problems)
5. Reorganization: new management and new projects
6. Expansion through subsidiaries
7. The complete empire (the organization as it exists at the time of the writing)
8. Research and charitable enterprises (ethics considerations)
9. Present performance and outlook for the future

The key point to be taken from this list of Barzun and Graff is not that they have provided a prescription that must be followed, but instead that a *chronological order* of presentation is a logical way to present historical research findings.

Summary

Examples of historical methods used in political science research may be found in nearly every issue of the journals in the discipline. However, not much can be found describing how to use the historical method in political science research. This chapter presented information about the topics addressed and methods used by historians, defined the process of political research, and reviewed a brief history of the evolving methods and topics of political research.

Three approaches that historical researchers have followed since history was recognized as a separate discipline in the nineteenth century include (1) the *hermeneutic* approach, (2) the *nomological* approach, and (3) a *critical* emphasis, as exemplified by *Marxist* and *feminist* approaches.

The objective of the hermeneutic approach is the search for "the uniqueness of historical personalities." This is similar to the *Great Man* approach of the early historians. The nomological approach looks for fundamental laws that can be used to explain and eventually predict future events. Nomological historians apply quantitative tools used in economics and the behavioralist school of the social sciences. A variation of the nomological approach is *structuralism,* which leads historians to identify the underlying, invisible structures that form and guide societies and their institutions. The principle that guides structuralist researchers is that these structures always exist; it is the job of the historian to "decode" the historical evidence in order to discover the underlying structure. The critical tradition of history views social phenomena and historical events as continually changing systems of social relationships and dependencies. Marxist and feminist historians—two examples of schools in the critical tradition—see history as a process leading to human emancipation.

Political history is the record of past or current political phenomena. It is composed of the recorded story of politics, political institutions, and the actors in the political world. Much of American political history has been concerned with the ways that voters and special-interest groups have fought for and exercised power over other groups or against one or more levels of government.

Political history has gone through three phases. The oldest is the *history of political thought.* The second emphasis for written political history is *diplomatic* and *military history.* This has been referred to as the *Great Man* or *Battles and Kings* approach to political history. The third, and essentially a product of only the nineteenth century, is *constitutional and administrative history.*

Historical research is as systematic and intellectually rigorous as any other research design. The historical approach follows a series of distinct steps or stages. Recommendations on how to define these steps range from as few as three steps—the gathering of data; the critical evaluation of the data; and the presentation of the facts, interpretations, and conclusions drawn from the facts—to as many as twenty distinct steps. Not all projects will involve each individual step, but every project should follow some organizational structure.

Discussion Questions

1. Discuss the role of history in political science.
2. Political science has been said to be history. Do you agree or disagree? Explain your answer.
3. Describe the three approaches to historical research.
4. How has the writing of political history changed over the past several hundred years?
5. Compare the historical approach to political science research with the behavioralist approach.
6. What is meant by the new institutionalism?
7. Do you agree with the statement that political history is the record of power? Why or why not?
8. Discuss the scope of researching constitutional and administrative history.

9. Discuss McDowell's (2002) list of twenty steps for the process of writing political history.
10. How important is the idea of writing history in chronological order?

Additional Reading

Barzun, Jacque, and Henry F. Graff. 1992. *The Modern Researcher*. Fort Worth, TX: Harcourt Brace Jovanovich.

Burke, Peter, ed. 2001. *New Perspectives on Historical Writing*. 2nd ed. Cambridge, UK: Polity Press.

Farr, James, John S. Dryzek, and Stephen T. Leonard, eds. 1995. *Political Science in History: Research Programs and Political Traditions*. Cambridge, UK: Cambridge University Press.

McDowell, W.H. 2002. *Historical Research: A Guide*. London: Longman.

26 The Interpretive Approach I: Grounded Theory Methods

The *grounded theory* approach to qualitative research has, since its introduction in the late 1960s, captured the methodological interests and imagination of researchers in all the social and administrative sciences. One of its principal developers, Barney G. Glaser (1999) described it as a tool for getting from the systematic collection of data to production of a multivariate conceptual theory. The grounded theory method has been used successfully in many different circumstances, disciplines, and cultures. The fact that it is easily generalizable to many different disciplines and a variety of research topics has contributed to its increasing acceptance world-wide. Glaser noted:

> Grounded theory is a general method. It can be used on any data or combination of data. It was developed partially by me with quantitative data [which] is expensive and somewhat hard to obtain. . . . Qualitative data are inexpensive to collect, very rich in meaning and observation, and rewarding to collect and analyze. So, by default to ease and growing use, grounded theory is being linked to qualitative data and is seen as a qualitative method, using symbolic interaction, by many. Qualitative grounded theory accounts for the global spread of its use. (Glaser 1999, 842)

The grounded theory method evolved from roots in the *symbolic interactionism* theoretical research of social psychologist George H. Mead at the University of Chicago, his one-time student Herbert Blumer, and others (Robrecht 1995). Mead believed that people defined themselves through the social roles, expectations, and perspectives they acquired from society and through the processes of socialization and social interactions. Blumer added three additional concepts to Mead's thesis: (1) the meanings that people have for things will determine the way they behave toward them, (2) these meanings come from people's social interactions, and (3) to deal with these meanings, people undergo a process of constant interpretation (Annells 1996). Grounded theory was "invented" by Glaser and Strauss (1967) as a way to develop explanatory and predictive *theory* about the social life, roles, and expected behaviors of people.

From its early roots in sociology and social psychology, the method has evolved and grown in importance to become what Brian Haig (1995) has described as "currently the most comprehensive qualitative research methodology available." Also noting this increased acceptance, Denzin and Lincoln (1994, 204) called it "the most widely used interpretive strategy in the social sciences today." Recently, this method has also become an increasingly important approach in political science research.

"Grounded theory has gone global, seriously global among the disciplines of nursing, business, and education and less so among other social-psychological-oriented disciplines such as social welfare, psychology, sociology, and art," according to Glaser (1999). Miller and Fredericks added:

> It is increasingly apparent that the grounded theory approach has become a paradigm of choice in much of the qualitatively oriented research in nursing, education, and other disciplines. Grounded theory has become a type of central organizing concept that serves to both direct the research process as well as provide a heuristic for data analysis and interpretation. (Miller and Fredericks 1999, 538)

Grounded theory was first proposed as a reaction against the restrictions that its developers saw in positivist research methodology. Chief among these perceived restrictions was the requirement to conduct research for the purpose of testing preconceived theoretical hypotheses. Today, the primary objective of all grounded theory research is to develop theory out of the information gathered, rather than the testing of predetermined theories through a process of experimentation.

Beginning the Grounded Theory Process

The process begins with the researcher focusing on some area of study. This could be any phenomenon, circumstance, trend, behavior, etc. in any of the social or administrative science areas. Using such tools as observation and interviewing, among others, the researcher gathers relevant data from as many different sources as are available. Analysis of the data begins with grouping them into categories and assigning codes. Through a process of continually comparing data with other categories, theory may be generated.

Grounded theory requires the researcher to organize and apply *structure* to the data according to an eclectic set of researcher-determined groupings or *categories*. As the researcher forms categories, new data are compared across the formed categories. Linkages between categories and characteristics are also identified. The data and their linkages are assigned discrete codes that enable the researcher to identify them with their specific groupings. Similar codes are in turn assigned to other data that fit a broader category or categories. As the process continues, categories are constantly re-evaluated and changed when necessary. Only when no additional revisions are intuitively possible does the analyst form a *theory* from the collected and analyzed data. Figure 26.1 illustrates the constant comparative method of data analysis.

Importance of Grouping and Coding

Rather than function only as a matter of convenience for later reference, the actual assigning of data to their formed groupings is a critical early step in the analysis process. Strauss and Corbin (1998, 3) defined the coding process as "the analytical process through which data are fractured, conceptualized, and integrated to form theory." It is the key activity in the *microanalysis* stage of the data; it includes both the first and the second stages of coding. Grounded theory researchers conduct their studies by gathering all possible facts that pertain to a problem. These data are gathered through personal interviews, analyses of participants' diaries, and participant observation. The data are analyzed and given an initial interpretation as they are

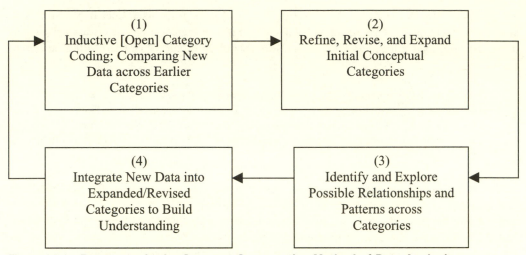

Figure 26.1   **Processes in the Constant Comparative Method of Data Analysis**
Source: Maykut and Morehouse 1994, 135.

collected by the researcher. This initial interpretation is called *open* or *substantive* coding.

The researcher applies a rigorous analytical process in order to develop theory out of the investigated social situation(s) *after* several runs through the raw data and coded categories. Thus, a key concept in grounded theory is the *continual analysis* of the data during and after they are collected.

Insights and ideas are also generated after in-depth analysis of the data. The analyst searches for commonalities and differences in the data. New data are fitted into the constructs or categories that are seen as pivotal in the data. Commonalities are compared and contrasted as the analyst weighs possible theories against other possible interpretations. Ultimately, a theory that is "grounded" in the data will emerge from the analysis.

Two Approaches to Grounded Theory

The analysis process identified by Glaser and Strauss in 1967 has been modified over time, so that today there is more than one approach to grounded theory. Locke (1996) identified two approaches as the *Straussian*—after Anselm Strauss—and the *Glaserian*—after Barney Glaser. Strauss and Corbin (1990), reporting that they observed their graduate students having great difficulty in organizing, coding, and analyzing their data, proposed that an additional coding step be added to the process. Glaser responded in 1992, taking issue with Strauss and Corbin for straying from the original emphasis on developing theory and adopting instead a process that he believed emphasized conceptual description over theory generation.

Both approaches are fundamentally similar, however, with whatever controversy that surfaces focusing on the addition of a third level of coding proposed by Strauss and Corbin. Both approaches emphasize the importance of coding as a key concept in the analysis. Glaser (1992) advocated sticking to the two steps in the coding process introduced in the original work. Glaser's two coding processes are *open* (substantive) and *theoretical*. During the first phase, coding can be relatively freewheeling, and open to continuous revision, compression, and merg-

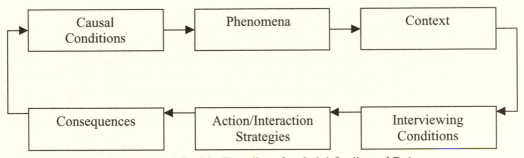

Figure 26.2   **The Strauss and Corbin Paradigm for Axial Coding of Data**
Source: Strauss and Corbin 1990; Kendall 1999.

ing. During the final, theoretical, phase of the analysis, the researcher is advised to rework the groupings as required to bring substance to any emerging theoretical conclusions.

Strauss and Corbin (1990) reported that the grounded theory process as originally proposed in 1967 made it difficult for beginning researchers to produce clear and cogent theory from the data. Retaining the open and substantive coding levels, they proposed that a third, intermediate step in the coding/analysis process be added. They called this intermediate step "*axial coding*" (Glaser 1992; Kendall 1999). This step—proposed as a way to "demystify" the grounded theory process—requires the researcher to place all the initially "open-coded" data into six categories specified by Strauss and Corbin. The six predetermined categories are: (1) *conditions,* (2) *phenomena,* (3) *context,* (4) *intervening conditions,* (5) *actions/strategies,* and (6) *consequences* (Figure 26.2).

A number of authors have objected to what they see as an artificial restriction that "axial coding" forces upon the researcher. Hall and Callery (2001), for example, concluded that the intermediary six steps resulted in a "mechanical approach" to data analysis that limited theory building. Kendall (1999) saw that "axial coding" could be advantageous for beginning researchers, but added that it forced her from the original research question when she used it in her dissertation analysis.

Kendall added that, after several years of working with her data, she found herself spending so much time trying to fit the data to the Strauss and Corbin "paradigm model" that she stopped thinking about what the data were communicating about the original study question. She added that she felt that using predetermined categories directed her analysis artificially by limiting her thinking to only the six categories.

The important thing to remember about the two different approaches is, not that the two creators of the grounded theory method disagree on how many steps there should be in the coding process, but rather that they agree on almost all other aspects of the process. Data should be continually compared with new data, coded, and placed in categories for interpretation. The researcher selects both the code and category in the first and the last steps in the analysis. Using the "axial coding" six categories is a researcher option; it is not required.

Steps in the Grounded Theory Process

A number of different models of grounded theory research have been proposed; two are presented here. The first is an eight-step model suggested by Lee (1999); the second is a seven-

STEP 1.	The researcher comes up with some ideas, questions, or concepts about some area of interest. These ideas can come from the researcher's own experience in the field, from a few key interviews, or from an analysis of the published literature.
STEP 2.	By creatively looking at the ideas, questions, or concepts, the researcher proposes some possible underlying concepts for the phenomenon and their relationships (linkages).
STEP 3.	The researcher now tests these initial linkages by comparing them with real-world data.
STEP 4.	By continually comparing the concepts to the objective world phenomena, the first step in testing a theory takes place.
STEP 5.	By continually analyzing the data and comparing new data against the concepts, the researcher works to integrate, simplify, and reduce the concepts, seeking to establish core concepts.
STEP 6.	The researcher prepares "theoretical memos" (these are simply preliminary attempts to spell out possible connections and/or theoretical explanations). This is now a continuing process, requiring the researcher to continually test and revise possible theory.
STEP 7.	The researcher continues to collect data and to code data by categories and or characteristics, while also producing theoretical interpretations of the material; this often requires the researcher to go back and repeat earlier steps in the process.
STEP 8.	The researcher prepares a final research report. In grounded theory research, this is not simply a "detached, mechanical process"; it is instead a key part of the research process.

Figure 26.3   An Eight-Step Process for Conducting Grounded Theory Research
Source: After Lee 1999.

step process developed from the work of Glaser and Strauss. The Lee model is spelled out in the series of steps in Figure 26.3.

Lee emphasizes the importance of continuous comparisons of categories in his eight-step process, but does not include the Strauss and Corbin axial coding step. In this way it is very similar to the original Glaser and Strauss model.

A Seven-Stage Model for Grounded Theory Research

Figure 26.4 is a model of the grounded theory research process reflecting the work of Glaser and Strauss; it was developed to illustrate the sequential nature of the method. The seven key steps in this process described in the following material were described in detail in Glaser and Strauss's 1967 narrative of how the method was developed, and reiterated elsewhere (Glaser 1992; Strauss and Corbin 1998).

Stage 1. Select a Topic of Interest

In political science, theories explain and predict human behavior among public employees, the citizenry, or organizations that are in some way acted upon or that influence public decisions.

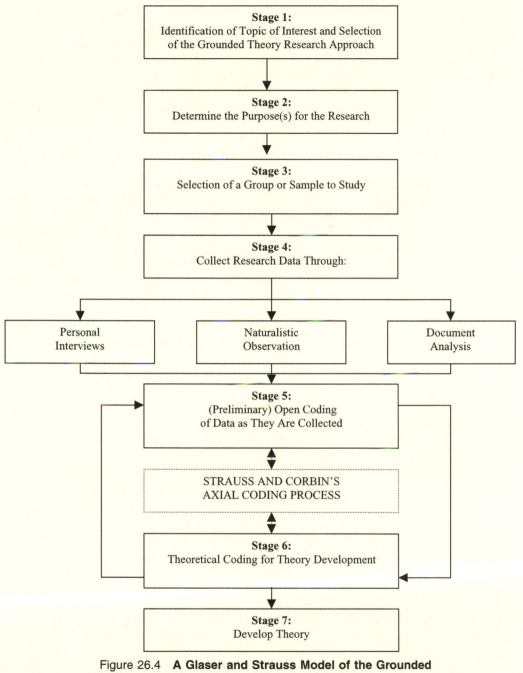

Figure 26.4 **A Glaser and Strauss Model of the Grounded Theory Data Collection and Coding Processes**

According to Glaser and Strauss, *theory is defined as the strategy for handling data in research. It provides ways of conceptualization for describing and explaining.*

Research topics—an area of interest to study—for grounded theory research are not hard to come by. They are everywhere in the researcher's field of interest, career field, and the practice of politics. The key thing to avoid in grounded theory is approaching a study area with a preconceived hypothesis.

Hypotheses *must* come from the data. Glaser, warning budding researchers to avoid the advice of others, cautioned:

> When a research problem is elusive or hard to come by a lot of people tend to give advice. . . . the researcher's search for the preconceived problem is subject to the whims and wisdoms of advisors with much experience and of colleagues. He [or she] should be careful as he may just end up studying his advisor's pet problem with no yield for him and data for the advisor. And he will likely miss the relevance in the data. (Glaser 1992, 23)

Moreover, Glaser added that it is important to remember that the identification of a research question is not a statement that clearly and succinctly identifies the topic that is going to be studied. Rather, the problem emerges from the data as they are collected. Open coding, selective (theoretical) sampling, and constant analysis of this information—these form a focus for the research study.

Stage 2. Determine a Purpose for the Research

Five main purposes or uses have been identified for grounded theory. These are:

1. To evaluate accuracy of earlier evidence.
2. To make generalizations based on experience.
3. To identify a unit of measurement for a one-case study.
4. To verify an existing theory.
5. To generate a theory.

For Evaluating Evidence. Data from additional groups are collected to compare with data that have already been collected for the purpose of evaluating whether the first evidence was correct. This often serves as a test of replicability, and can be applied for validating both internal evidence (from within the study group) and external evidence (data from sources other than the study group). This can be a powerful and important use for grounded theory because a study's categories and properties are generated from collected evidence. Collected and compared evidence is used for a defining illustration of the conceptual category. Glaser and Strauss (1967, 23) considered these categories to be the fundamental building block of theory: "In generating theory, it is not the fact upon which we stand but the conceptual category that was generated from it."

For Establishing Generalizations from the Data. If a theory is to emerge from the collected "facts," they must be generalizable to other situations, or they remain isolated bits of data—interesting but irrelevant. If they are applicable only to a single case, group, circumstance, or situation, they remain descriptors of only that specific phenomenon. In searching for generalizations, or *universals,* the researcher establishes boundaries of applicability, while at the same time attempting to broaden the theory.

For Specifying a Concept. This is the first step in a design requiring specific identification of a study sample or population for a one-case study. Grounded theory's comparative evaluations are used to clearly identify the key dimensions (i.e., key *concept or* concepts) that make the study group distinctive. It tells your readers why you chose to study one group and not another. It involves comparing the unit of analysis (individuals or groups) selected for the study with other units that are not selected. This comparison often brings to light the distinctive properties of the selected unit.

For example, a study of homeless women has many different categories of subjects from which to select for a subject sample. Alice Waterston (1999) chose to study a group of HIV-positive or possible HIV-positive homeless women residing at a shelter in a metropolitan area. Her data analysis might begin with a comparison of the characteristics of this study group with other similar groups of at-risk women. By revealing the specific characteristics of the study group that are of interest to the research, the reader will be unlikely to confuse the study group with others who are not included.

For Verifying a Theory. When conducting a grounded theory research study for the purpose of verifying an existing theory, the researcher focuses on finding information that corroborates the existing concept. In the process, the researcher generates "new" theories only for the purpose of adjusting or modifying the original theory. No new theories are sought. Neither Glaser nor Strauss says much about this potential use for the grounded theory method, emphasizing instead its role in generating new theory.

For Generating Theory. This is the primary purpose of grounded theory research; the researcher's main goal in grounded theory research is the systematic generation of new theories from the data collected. There are two broad types of theory that can be generated through this process: substantive theory and formal theory. *Substantive* theory addresses specific, empirical, or applied tasks in political science, such as police and fire department community relations, management development programs and employee training, solid-waste disposal, water purity, road construction, city planning, and similar issues. *Formal* theory, on the other hand, deals with broader, often philosophical issues. Example topic areas include public participation in the democratic process, authority and power in management situations, reward systems, etc.

Both of these applications are what Glaser and Strauss (1967, 32–33) identified as "middle-range," meaning they fall somewhere between practical working hypothesis in the everyday conduct of an administrator's job and all-inclusive "grand theories," such as global warming. It is important to note that both of these types of theories must be grounded in data if they are to be accepted as relevant.

Stage 3. Select a Group to Study

Determining where to go to get the data for a research study remains one of the major issues that confront grounded theory researchers. Researchers need to know who can provide the information that illustrates the central or core concept in the study. They call this the *theoretical sampling* problem, and define it as the process of picking the sources that can provide the most information about the research topic. The aim of theoretical sampling is described as follows:

> The aim of theoretical sampling is to maximize opportunities to compare events, incidents, or happenings to determine how a category varies in terms of its properties and dimensions. (Strauss and Corbin 1998, 202)

This suggests that the researcher must be more concerned with ensuring the representative-ness of the sample than with the concept of randomness. Researchers are encouraged to care-fully select the subjects from whom information will be acquired. This becomes even more important as the study progresses. Sampling must become more specific with time because the theory that is emerging must eventually control the sample selection. Once some categories are established, all further sampling must be focused on developing, solidifying, and enriching the formed categories. Glaser and Strauss stated it this way in their description of their inven-tion of the technique:

> The basic question in theoretical sampling is: what group or subgroup does one turn to next in data collections? And for what theoretical purpose? In short, how does the [researcher] select multiple comparison groups? The possibilities of multiple comparisons are infinite, and so groups must be chosen according to theoretical criteria. (Glaser and Strauss 1967, 47)

Stage 4. Collect Research Data

There are no restrictions to how data are collected in a grounded theory design. However, most researchers use personal interviews, simple or naturalistic observation, and narratives. They may also include some document or artifact analysis. One of the distinctive characteristics of the grounded theory method is that the data collection, coding, and interpretation stages of the research are carried out together, not as individual activities. One leads to the other, then on to the next, and back again. These steps "should blur and intertwine continually, from the beginning of an investigation to its end" (Glaser and Strauss 1967, 43).

Grounded theory methodology can be used for arriving at theories from data that are col-lected in any type of social research—quantitative and qualitative. All theories are developed for one or both of two fundamental purposes: to explain or to predict.

Stage 5. Open Coding of Data

Coding is the process of applying some conceptually meaningful set of identifiers to the con-cepts, categories, and characteristics found in the data. The key things to remember about open coding are that it is always the *initial* step in data analysis, and that its purpose is to establish (or *discover*) categories and their properties.

Open coding is the free assignment of data to what the researcher sees are the naturally appearing groupings of ideas in the data (Lee 1999). As many categories as needed are created by the researcher. These can be looked upon as the fundamental, explanatory factors that identify the central research concept. Each category contains as many bits of data that are found to fit in that category. Data bits are more or less indivisible, and intuitively fit into just one category.

The open coding process continues until one or more "core categories" are established (Strauss 1992). Then, the coding process either turns to Strauss and Corbin's *axial coding,* using preconceived categories, or proceeds directly to the theoretical coding identified by Glaser and Strauss (1967) or Glaser (1992). *Axial coding* refers to the process of assigning categories into more-inclusive groupings. Strauss and Corbin urged the researcher to use the six second-level classifications they proposed. Lee (1999), on the other hand, following the original Glaser and Strauss (1967) model, called for the researcher to propose the axial categories.

The researcher first comes up with several categories that seem to bridge all the open-coded categories. Second, the researcher examines all the open categories to see which fit within the selected second-level category. The remaining data are then compared across the second researcher-selected broader category; those categories that belong are assigned. The process continues until all the data have been compared against all the second-level categories and classified. Additional axial categories might have to be added to encompass all the data.

Determining Categories from the Data

Completion of a grounded theory research project results in the researcher identifying one or more core concepts that relate to the issue of interest, example or examples in the data that are representative of each core concept, and an indication of a set of relationships between the core concepts and their example indicators. These relationships may be illustrated in what Maykut and Morehouse (1994) called *concept maps*. Concept maps are graphic depictions of each concept category and their characteristics or indicators. The conceptual depiction also shows how, and in what direction, larger categories are influenced by or related to (1) each other, (2) lower- to upper- or broader-level concepts, and (3) higher level to lower level. This process is similar to the "bathtubs and beer barrels" semantic-network method of showing relationships developed by Kurt Lewin.

There are no hard and fast rules for coding in grounded theory research (Lee 1999). Even the inventors of the method disagree about how to go about coding and categorizing collected data. There are also many different ways to discover or establish meaningful categorical distinctions in data. Miles and Huberman (1984), for example, discuss twelve different ways to go about developing codes for raw data (Table 26.1).

An example of a code set developed for an educational site study can be found in Miles and Huberman (1984, 58–59). These five broad constructs (categories) and their codes were proposed in the preliminary coding: innovation properties (IP), external context (EC), internal context (IC), adoption process (AP), site dynamics and transformations (TR). These five constructs are the "core categories" of this study.

A different number of characteristics/dimensions were identified for each of the categories. Five of the characteristics that were determined to contribute to the innovation properties category were: objectives, organization, implied changes–classroom, implied changes–organization, and user salience.

A complete set of definitions was developed for each of the categories and the specific

---

Table 26.1

Twelve Tactics for Generating Meaning in Conceptual Categories

1. Counting	7. Particular to general
2. Noting patterns, themes	8. Factoring
3. Seeing plausibility	9. Relationships
4. Clustering	10. Finding intervening variables
5. Making metaphors	11. Chain of evidence
6. Splitting variables	12. Theoretical coherence

Source: Miles and Huberman 1984, 215.

characteristic associated with the category. For example, in the site dynamics and transformations (TR) category, the code TR-START was assigned to data that fell into the "initial user experience" category and dimension. The definition for this code was: "Emotions, events, problems or concerns, assessments, made by teachers and administrators during the first six months of implementation" (62). Similar definitions are produced for every category/dimension in the study.

Glaser is adamant that open coding and category building *not* be forced into any preconceived second-level (axial) groupings. Strauss and Corbin, on the other hand, give the researcher more leeway in this decision. As a result, both approaches to grounded theory coding are found in the research literature. There is no disagreement regarding the third (and final) coding process: selective (or *theoretical*) coding.

Stage 6. Selective (or Theoretical) Coding of Data

Selective, or theoretical, coding is the name given to the process of imposing a final structure to the data, and establishing rank-order importance of the conceptual categories (Lee 1999). Just as in the second-level coding process, the researcher proposes a small number of overarching categories. Next, these categories are ordered according to how the researcher sees their potential to contain or explain the collected data. In the third step, the researcher picks what he or she estimates is the most powerful or important category; all of the data are then judged for their fit in that theoretical category. The researcher then repeats the process, using the second most important category and all remaining data for fit in this category. The process continues until all data are categorized. The researcher is then ready to develop theory about the phenomenon.

From Core Categories to Grounded Theory

The underlying purpose of all theory is to explain and/or predict some event as phenomenon. The purpose of the theoretical coding stage is to identify the relationships between categories and their properties as they are found in the data. Theories are built in a process that moves from the *specific* (individual examples, incidences, or cases, for example) to the general. In this way, the researcher develops a *theory* that is applicable (explains and/or predicts) to more than the individual example, incidence, or case. The process occurs in the following six stages (after Miller and Fredericks 1999):

1. Preliminary (open) categories are formed from the first data collected.
2. More general or broad categories that include preliminary groupings are formed from this and new data as they are added to the analysis.
3. Categories are further refined and defined.
4. A set of *core* categories is finally accepted.
5. As data are analyzed they are assigned as *characteristics* or *dimensions* of these core categories.
6. Continual comparison may produce a revised coding scheme, which, in turn, may require revisions to the characteristics/dimensions of the codes.

Stage 7. Development of a Theory

This is the culmination of all preceding activities in the process: forming a theory that is grounded in the data. Although it is last in this process model, theory development is not "saved for last." Rather, at each stage in the process of grounded theory the researcher prepares *theoretical memos* in which he or she records ideas, conclusions, propositions, and theoretical explanations of the phenomena under study. These "memos" serve as summaries of the researcher's conclusions—recorded as they are being formed—and, as such, are the gist from which a *theory* or set of hypotheses is developed.

To qualify as a *grounded theory,* it must exhibit the following key characteristics (Locke 1996):

1. The theory must closely fit the topic and disciplinary area studied.
2. The theory must be understandable to and useful to the actors in the studied situation.
3. Finally, the theory must be complex enough to account for a large portion, if not most, of the variation in the area studied.

Often, grounded theory research results neglect to address the issue of theory in the presentation of their findings. This does not take anything away from the process, however, because in describing what was discovered from the research and proposing specific recommendations, some *derived theory* must underlie the conclusions. It is just a matter of putting it into words. The researcher would not have the confidence necessary to make recommendations regarding the findings unless he or she was sufficiently confident in the theoretical conclusions derived from the data.

A Brief Caveat about the Method

One of the reasons why Strauss and Corbin proposed their six preconceived categories for the second-level or *axial coding* step was because they saw that their graduate students were having great difficulty in conceptualizing the necessary categories for collected data. Lee (1999) has also commented on the difficulty of the method:

> Grounded theory is a long-term, labor intensive, and time-consuming process. It requires multiple waves of data collection, with each wave of data based on theoretical sampling. In addition, the iterative process should continue until a theoretical saturation is achieved. Given all this, researchers should avoid grounded theory approaches unless they can commit substantial resources to a study. (Lee 1999, 50)

Grounded Theory Research in Practice

King, Felty, and Susel (1998) used grounded theory methodology in their study of the underlying causes of public antipathy in the political process and ways to improve participation in public policy-making decisions. Using personal interviews and focus group discussions, they gathered data from private citizens and public administrators from several communities in Ohio. Focus-group participants were asked to respond freely to four broad questions: (1) How can more effective public participation be achieved? (2) What does public participation mean to the participant? (3) What are the barriers to participation? (4) What advice did they have for people trying to bring about more and more diverse participation?

Their analysis occurred in two stages. First, in the open stage of their coding the transcribed interviews were coded by each researcher working independently and using a qualitative form of content analysis. Second, the researchers synthesized the individually coded responses to come up with a set of categories and themes. These were discussed in detail in their report. Specific quotations from respondents were woven throughout their final narrative, thus providing insightful reinforcement of the thematic concepts they drew from the data.

King, Felty, and Susel identified three categories of barriers to effective public participation: (1) contemporary lifestyles, (2) existing administrative practices, and (3) current techniques for participation. The pressures and complexity of daily life, together with certain demographic factors such as class, income, education, family size, etc., and a breakdown in traditional neighborhood ties, were identified as probable causes for the lack of public participation in the communities studied. Existing administrative practices, such as abbreviated time allowed for public contribution, waiting too long to call for public input in the policy development process, and some administrators' perception of participation as a threat, also hindered the amount and quality of participation. Finally, there was widespread agreement that current techniques used to gain public participation—such as the public meeting—were inadequate and, often, entirely ineffective.

The theory generated from this research included a three-part proposal for dealing with the three sets of barriers to participation. First, citizens within the community must be "empowered," while at the same time, citizens need to be educated in ways to organize and research issues and policies. Second, public administrators must be reeducated; their traditional role of "expert manager" must be replaced with one of "cooperative participant," or "partner." Administrators must also develop their interpersonal skills, including listening, team building, and the like. Finally, the structures and processes of administration must be changed to make it easier for the public to become involved and contribute to the policy formation process.

Additional Examples

Strauss and Corbin have edited a volume of research studies—*Grounded Theory in Practice* (1999)—that illustrates a variety of applications of the grounded theory approach to research in the health, sociology, business and public administration, and social psychology fields of inquiry. Polish sociologist Kryszxtof Konecki's study of the recruiting process was done while he was attending the University of California, and enrolled in one of Anselm Strauss's grounded theory seminars. Konecki conducted a series of twenty intensive interviews with employment recruiters, one with a client employment candidate, and one with a firm that used executive search firms. He also included previously published case study descriptions of the search process.

The Konecki study is noteworthy primarily for its clear and detailed description of his application of the Strauss and Corbin third level, or *"axial coding"* of the collected data. He compared the data from different types and sizes of search firms, and wrote a number of "theoretical memos" to himself about the collected material. He then developed a conceptual matrix, subjecting the open-coded ideas to the six Strauss and Corbin established conditional categories of: (1) *conditions,* (2) *phenomena,* (3) *context,* (4) *intervening conditions,* (5) *actions/ strategies,* and (6) *consequences.*

Konecki (1997) theorized that the effectiveness of an employment search process is affected by five conditions: Internal search-work circumstances, and organization, interactional, market, and cultural conditions. He closed with the conclusion that grounded theory methodology is "a very useful tool for the reconstruction of conditions and combinations of the conditions of a category."

Other papers in the Strauss and Corbin book of example applications include studies on identity, physicians' interpretations of patient pain, abused females' self-definition, scientific knowledge about cancer, reproductive science, the evolution of medical technology, tuberculosis, and collective identity.

Grounded Theory and Public Policy

Cook and Barry (1995) used the grounded theory method to research the public policy interactions between the public and private sectors. They chose the grounded theory method because of that they saw as the "paucity of work" in the area, and because of a desire to build a rich description of the business owners' ideas and beliefs about public policy and their ability to help shape it. Over the two-year study, they conducted 31 in-depth interviews with owners in 27 firms, and three government administrators. All of the executives were owners of their firms. In addition to these in-depth interviews, Cook and Barry also attended nine trade association meetings with a government-relations focus; more than 50 additional executives participated in the meetings. Concluding their data-gathering process, they examined more than 150 public documents, papers, memos, and newspaper stories.

In what is clearly one of the major disadvantages of the method—an overabundance of raw data—Cook and Barry reported that their initial transcripts produced more than 700 individual pages of data. Before they could code and analyze the data they were forced to produce detailed abstracts of each transcript, thus eliminating some 60 percent of the original data.

Two levels of coding were then used on the remaining data: "received" coding and "emergent" coding. The first level was derived from their review of the literature in the field, from their prior learning and biases, and from categories that the interviewees themselves used. These were primarily descriptive and definitional in nature. These codes were than merged into broader codes—what they called *overarching dimensions*—that related to issues, issue characteristics, and the influence process.

In the sense of *theory,* Cook and Barry found it to be "evident" that interactions between owners of small firms and policymakers helped to create a system for interpreting and making sense of the process. These determined (1) whether a small business executive would commit to working on a policy issue, and (2) how he or she would carry out that work. Executives tended to agree to work on issues that they believed they had some possibility of influencing, and to not concern themselves with policy questions that they felt were beyond their reach.

Summary

Grounded theory is a general qualitative research method that can be used on any data or combination of data. It was developed initially for use with quantitative and/or qualitative data. However, quantitative data often are expensive and difficult to obtain. On the other hand, qualitative data are inexpensive to collect; they can be very rich in meaning and observation; and they are often rewarding to collect and analyze. So, by default to ease and growing use, grounded theory research today is linked to *qualitative* data; it is classified as a qualitative method that uses symbolic interaction.

The grounded theory research process begins with focusing on some area of study—a phenomenon, circumstance, trend, behavior, etc., in any of the social or administrative science areas. Using observation and interviewing, among others, researchers gather relevant data from as many different sources as are available. Analysis of the data begins with grouping them into categories and assigning codes. Through a process of continually comparing data with other categories, theory may be generated.

Completion of a grounded theory research project results in the researcher identifying one or more core concepts that relate to the issue of interest, example or examples in the data that are representative of each core concept, and an indication of a set of relationships between the core concepts and their example indicators. These relationships may be illustrated in what are called *concept maps,* which are graphic depictions of each concept category and their characteristics or indicators. The conceptual depiction also shows how, and in what direction, larger categories are influenced by or related to (1) each other, (2) lower- to upper- or broader-level concepts, and (3) higher level to lower level. This process is similar to the "bathtubs and beer barrels" semantic-network method of showing relationships developed by Kurt Lewin.

It is important to remember, however, that grounded theory is a long-term, laborious, and time-consuming process. The researcher should have a substantial grounding in the area of interest, and the ability to formulate a broad, meaningful conceptual interest area. This does not mean that a "study problem" must be identified in advance but rather, that the researcher be conversant enough with a phenomenon to justify an open research project in the area. Furthermore, grounded theory research requires multiple levels of data collection, each based on theoretical sampling and continual comparisons. In addition, the coding and classifying process should continue until a theoretical saturation is achieved. Researchers are advised to avoid grounded theory approaches unless they can commit substantial resources to a study.

Discussion Questions

1. In your own words, define the grounded theory research process.
2. Is the grounded theory method appropriate for conducting political science research? Explain why or why not.
3. How would you go about conducting field research for gathering the data necessary to accomplish your grounded theory research objectives?
4. Would you begin your research by developing one or more hypotheses beforehand, then using your interpretations of the data to test the hypotheses? Why or why not?
5. Do you feel that the "axial coding" paradigm, using the six categories proposed by Strauss and Corbin (1990) will be an asset in arriving at conceptual understanding of the data in this study? Why or why not?
6. Do you feel that writing conceptual memos to yourself as you code and categorize data would help you to develop a theoretical understanding of a phenomenon such as teenage drug addiction?
7. How would you handle the situation if a subject refused to be tape recorded during her interview?
8. What are the core categories of grounded theory?

Additional Reading

Glaser, Barney G. 1992. *Basics of Grounded Theory Analysis*. Mill Valley, CA: Sociology Press.

Glaser, Barney G., and Anselm L. Strauss. 1967. *The Discovery of Grounded Theory*. Chicago: Aldine Publishing.

Lee, Thomas W. 1999. *Using Qualitative Methods in Organizational Research*. Thousand Oaks, CA: Sage.

Strauss, Anselm, and Juliet Corbin. 1998. *Basics of Qualitative Research: Techniques and Procedures for Developing Grounded Theory*. 2nd ed. Thousand Oaks, CA: Sage.

———, eds. 1997. *Grounded Theory in Practice*. Thousand Oaks, CA: Sage.

27 The Interpretive Approach II: Ethnographic Methods

Ethnographic methods are not employed often in research in political science, but when they are they can provide great quantities of important information. One reason why they are not used is that these study designs typically require more time to conduct than political scientists are able or willing to devote to their research projects; in the disciplines of anthropology and sociology, ethnographic studies make take as long as six months to a year or longer to complete. However, when time and human resources permit, the approach has the power to produce powerful political science research that can provide insight into the workings of politics and political institutions.

The practice of producing notes as "thick description" is a hallmark of all ethnographic research. *Thick description* refers to research notes that exhibit great depth and detailed complexity found in ethnographic reports. An example cited by Neuman (2000) is the description of a social event that might last three minutes or less, but that takes up many pages of descriptive narrative. This use of detailed description means that ethnographic methods can be an excellent design choice when the study objective is to provide deep background information for long-term, strategic public-policy forming. On the other hand, ethnographic methods are generally not appropriate when a decision must be made immediately on the basis of the findings of the research. Despite these drawbacks, ethnographic methods have a long and important history in research in the social and human sciences.

Industrialization and the Social Sciences

A by-product of the industrialization of Western society was a belief by some observers that factory labor was dehumanizing society; unskilled workers were often seen as just another easily replaceable component in the production process. Beginning in the nineteenth century, however, concern over the deteriorating human condition in tenements and factories resulted in calls for changes in the way society treated its citizens. An increasingly educated public, the clergy, and a few in the governing elite came to recognize that the deterioration in social conditions needed to be stopped and, if possible, reversed. These early critics looked to science for solutions to the problems of the new industrialized society.

This faith in the power of science to produce answers to the problems of society encouraged adoption of a "scientific approach" to the study of the social problems and needed changes. If advances in the natural sciences and technology could be profitably applied to problems in industrial invention and innovation, it was reasoned, why couldn't they also be applied to solving social problems? If science could be used to improve production, why couldn't it also be used to improve everyone's quality of life?

The new social, or *human,* sciences that emerged out of the intellectual vitality that characterized the nineteenth century included sociology, psychology, and anthropology. Sociology emerged from early studies of the social ills that were identified as unwanted by-products of the industrialization process. At about the same time, early attempts at establishing a systematic way of explaining human behavior and mental aberrations resulted in the modern science of psychology. In each of these new scientific disciplines, curiosity about what was happening to society resulted in research that had the objective of understanding (1) why social problems occurred, and (2) what could (or *ought* to) be done to change society in order to improve the lot of the aged, the children, the working poor, and the otherwise disenfranchised.

The Emergence of Field Research

The early missionaries and adventurers who traveled with European traders and explorers on voyages to new lands encountered new and, to them strange, cultures. Early reports of these encounters became extremely popular. Often however, they were little more than lurid or bizarre tales of fancy, with little basis in reality. Despite their limited basis in fact—or possibly because of it—the tales often gained widespread distribution in books and the popular press of the time. Before long, these new "social scientists" were permitted to join in on the many voyages of discovery that were taking place. Some of these scientific expeditions were carried out specifically to study primitive cultures before they disappeared, were eradicated by disease, or were subsumed into the Western economic tradition.

A focus for much of this early research was the search for an understanding of how different societies developed. Another was searching for an explanation for how the primitive societies developed their own unique ways of coping with social phenomena. However, interpreting the coping behaviors, attitudes, and other cultural phenomena was difficult, if not impossible, with the traditional positivist methodology that was applied.

As reports of these encounters circulated in Europe and the Americas, a few of the early social scientists saw a need to apply some of what they called "scientific rigor" to the research that was being done. They turned to the research methodologies that had been emerging in the natural sciences, adopting the positivist model with its quantitative emphasis and causal focus. They modified the positivist—quantitative—approach by adding greater verbal description and explanation to their investigations and reports. This new way of doing science became what we now call *fieldwork,* and the scientific disciplines they followed became the social sciences of anthropology and sociology.

Ethnographic Research and Anthropology

The reportorial and descriptive traditions that shaped early travel stories ultimately forged a scientific way of studying indigenous cultures, and resulted in the formation of a distinct social science under which such studies were catalogued; this social science was called "*anthropology,*" after the Greek words "*anthro*" meaning "human," and "*ology,*" which refers to any kind of science (*The Random House Dictionary of the English Language* 1967).

Today, anthropology has three main themes: *cultural anthropology, physical anthropology,* and *archeology.* Of the three, the first has found a place in the research conducted in political science. Cultural anthropology includes most of the topics that were included in the earliest discipline of anthropology. The anthropologists concentrated on describing the cultures of newly discovered societies or distinct, separate groups, no matter how small, distant, or foreign. The research method they used most often is now called ethnography. Ethnographers often lived for long periods of time with the groups they studied. This approach is now called "participant observation."

The focus of cultural anthropology was originally devoted almost exclusively to the study of distant, often "primitive," cultures. It was not long, however, before it was also found to be an appropriate way of studying modern, complex, societies that remained in relative isolation from the emerging industrialized world (Alasuutari 1995). From this expanded application it was not long before anthropology and its primary research method, ethnography, took their place in the study of all aspects of modern groups and societies.

Physical anthropologists followed the lead of Darwinian ideas and began to seek answers to questions that dealt with the evolution of humankind. Examples of questions physical anthropologists are concerned with include determining the earliest primate ancestors of humans and the physical characteristics of ethnic groups. Physical anthropologists are sometimes called in to assist forensic scientists in the identification of crime and accident victims, and to aid in the design of living and work spaces, including furniture and tools.

Archeologists were at one time included under the cultural anthropology umbrella, but found their own niche by focusing on studies of ancient and unknown material cultures. Today, however, modern anthropologists can be found conducting analyses of relatively recently deposited cultural artifacts. An example is the archeological study of garbage dumps to depict trends in fashion, invention, conservation, and other descriptions of cultural artifacts.

The Involving Focus of Ethnographic Research

The traditional focus of sociology—another discipline that uses ethnographic methods in research—has also changed. Initially, the purpose of sociological research was to identify cause-and-effect relationships between the perceived ills and abuses of the new industrial society and the lives of adults and children forced to live and work in crowded, dangerous, and often-unsanitary conditions. Sociology worked hand in glove with the earliest social workers in attempts to discover how the modern, industrial society functioned, and how to discover ways that social ills could be resolved. However, as Alasuutari (1995) has noted, "many of the post-war [i.e., World War II], 'post-industrial' developments have evaded the conceptual net provided by established academic sociology, which in many countries became a tool for social engineering and social statistics" (24). As a result, the social ills rationale behind traditional sociological research is no longer the only purpose driving such research.

Because of the continually evolving nature of the focus of study for the social sciences, a new direction for ethnographic research emerged. Today, ethnographic studies are carried out in the inner cities of modern societies, in suburban and rural settings, in cross-cultural designs, in large and small organizations, and in investigations into any way that the social forces of culture and subculture impact people. More important, however, may be the focus on *interpreting* social behavior that has replaced the earlier model of simply *describing* a society. The role of the ethnographer has taken on the important task of contributing to the formation of public policy.

There is a fine line dividing sociological and anthropological ethnographic studies. Probably the easiest way to distinguish the two is to remember that sociologists are concerned with the impact of social circumstances and situations on people, whereas anthropologists tend to give greater attention to the role of culture and/or subculture on the behaviors of people. There is a place for both emphases in research.

Through an eclectic process of trial and error, anthropologists and sociologists developed a way of conducting research that allowed them to meet their study objectives in all kinds of social and cultural settings. The name they gave this method was *ethnography*—which means graphically describing a society or social group. Researchers in political science have also adopted this method of research. Ethnography is one of several important approaches for the study of *culture* as the act of governance, the formation of public policy, and the administration of diverse agencies and functions of government. The research conducted in these disciplines has often had a great influence on public policy.

Ethnographic Research Today

The direction of anthropology and sociology research has evolved and expanded during the past century. Traditional positivist methods that were originally used in the study of primitive cultures and societies were found to be unable to clearly develop the in-depth understandings needed to make sense of modern cultures and human behaviors. Anthropologists in Europe and the United States eventually supplemented traditional research methods with a new approach to the study of primitive cultures and societies that was designed to improve the way of studying humans in social settings. A key element of this new approach was its emphasis on specific ways to prepare field notes and rules for writing about cultural events. An example of a modern ethnographic study is the work of Terry Williams (1996). Writing about his ethnographic study of the cocaine subculture in New York after-hours clubs during the 1970s and 1980s, Williams defined ethnography as "a science of cultural description; more than that, it is a methodology. It is a way of looking at people, a way of looking at a culture. It is recording how people perceive, construct and interact in their own private world. It embraces the subjective realm of the individuals it seeks to understand. It defines the group the way the group defines itself" (31).

Ethnography, Ethology, or Ethnology?

Several different terms are used in modern reports of ethnographic research. Among these are ethnography, ethnology, and ethology. *Ethnography* means the descriptive study of living cultures, while *ethnology* refers to the activity of *using* the information gathered by ethnography (*Columbia On-line Encyclopedia* 2000). Thus, a political scientist might use an ethnological report for the process of framing public policy. *Ethology,* on the other hand, is a somewhat different approach to the research process; it refers to the somewhat less-intense practice of simple observation (Jones 1996).

The science of ethology is most commonly encountered in context with the study of animal behavior, although a branch seeks to apply ethological principles to human behavior as well. Ethnography involves actively observing, recording, and explaining why a culture is described in the way it is by the ethnographer; it is sometimes used as a synonym for participant observation. Ethology is used as a synonym for "simple" or unobtrusive observation. The model presented in Figure 27.1 illustrates how anthropology, sociology, and psychology, with their different but related research focuses, have each contributed to the development of ethnographic research.

Ethnographers immerse themselves into the day-to-day activities of the group they are study-

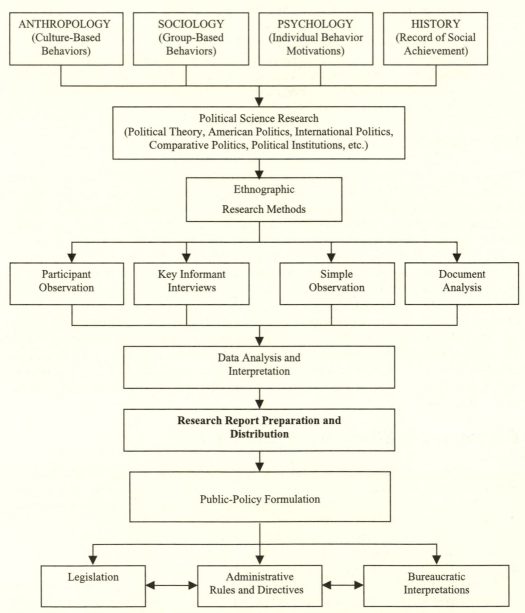

Figure 27.1   **A Model of How Ethnographic Research Is Used to Shape Public Policy**

ing. Their goal is to learn as much as they can about the behaviors and social processes taking place in the culture. They do this in order (1) to describe the setting in as much detail as possible (a process called *thick description*), and (2) to come up with some theoretical ideas that allow them to interpret and explain what they have seen and heard. Ethnographers live, work, and play with their study populations for long periods of time. Their aim is to be absorbed into the group. Their underlying objective is to be "accepted" as a nonthreatening or nonintrusive member of the group. Then, events and interrelationships will unfold as they would naturally, as if the observer were not in attendance. This process is called "gaining entry," and is the key to a successful research project. Without acceptance, without entry into the inner workings of the group, the researcher remains an outsider; he or she is then perceived as a threat and subsequently either shunned or lied to, at best.

The process of living with a social group (*doing fieldwork*) involves observing and recording individuals' behaviors. The ethnographer summarizes these field notes into a larger descriptive generalization that purported to describe the behavior of the larger society. The researcher must then develop subjective descriptions that are based on a large number of generalizations. In making these generalizations, the ethnographer moves from the specific to the general. That is, the behaviors of one or a small group are used to infer that those behaviors are also those of the larger groups in similar circumstances. The ethnographer should also develop interpretations of the observed behaviors; the question "why" should be answered to the best of the ethnographer's ability.

According to Jones (1996), one of the major attractions of ethnography for field researchers is it permits them to develop meaningful, coherent pictures of the social group and setting. Researchers get to see the phenomenon as a whole, in all of its complexity, and not just bits and pieces. Jones also suggested a way to differentiate between ethnological and ethological research involving human behavior. The key differentiating characteristic is whether the research is conducted to develop a theory or to provide background information needed to make a management decision. Figure 27.2 illustrates that, despite the different steps involved in the two approaches, the two approaches are very similar.

Modern Ethnography and Ethology

For most of the early history of ethnography, study results were often little more than simple descriptions; interpretation of the event, setting, or behavior was left to the reader. This often resulted in questioning confidence in the *validity* of ethnographic generalizations. The following statement illustrates the older paradigm: "Ethnographic generalizations are by themselves only best fit statements about the incidence or frequency of occurrences in the society. By themselves they say little or nothing about what goes with what" (Cohen 1973, 37–38). Cohen's solution to this problem was to call for more correlational or *causal* research into ethnography. This, he believed, would improve validity by improving interpretation. LeCompte has also identified a need for change in the practice of ethnography:

> Ethnography traditionally has been thought of as the investigations of the cultures of small, relatively homogeneous, natural or artificially bounded groups. However, fieldwork with such groups is nearly impossible, not only because such sites and populations no longer exist, but because even if they did, doing such work smells of an undesirable colonial legacy of exploitation and domination. (LeCompte 2002, 287)

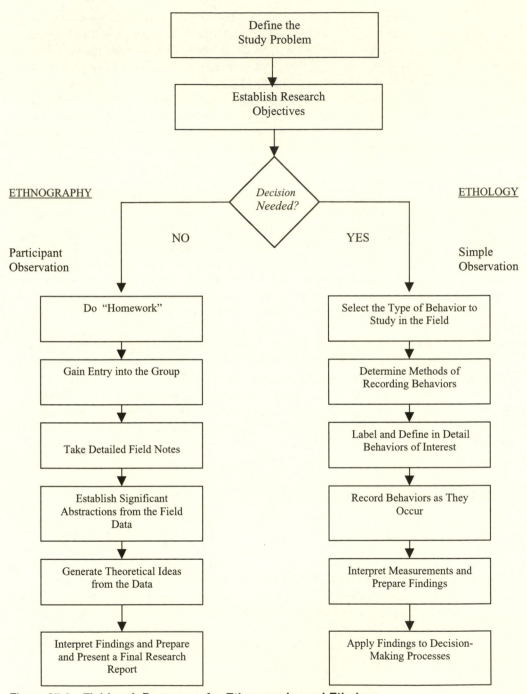

Figure 27.2 Fieldwork Processes for Ethnography and Ethology
Source: After Jones 1996, Chapter 3.

In its earliest applications, "doing ethnography" meant studying isolated, primitive cultures to develop a descriptive profile or summary of the social practices of the group of people (Naroll and Cohen 1973). Today, ethnographers are not required to seek out isolated, primitive groups for their research; rather, there are no limits to how and where ethnographic field research can be applied. Ethnography, like its parent discipline anthropology, is not restricted to the study of distant or nonliterate cultures. Few, if any, societies are left untouched anywhere in the world. Most have now been studied and restudied, to the point that little new about their "primitiveness" can be learned. The world has become smaller, and distant, diverse societies no longer live in "glorious isolation—the 'Other' have moved next door, and 'western' artifacts, television programmes [sic], and economic networks have invaded practically the entire globe" (Alasuutari 1995, 24).

Today, ethnographers are presented with few, if any, limitations in their choice of subject matter. Since the late 1980s, researchers have been using the ethnographic approach on newly defined aspects of culture that exist within what LeCompte (2002) described as the "multi-layered, multi-ethnic, highly diverse and often contentious groups that now characterize human existence."

What Do Ethnographers Do?

According to Whiting and Whiting (1973), ethnographers collect samples of types of behavior in order to understand the cognitive and social-structure *regularities* in a society. Ethnographers study the roles people adopt, economic systems, political systems, religious systems, personality, and many other aspects of any or all types of social organizations and systems.

Duveen (2000) has described the work that ethnographers do as the production of *"thick description,"* and saw it as a two-part process. First, the researcher writes down everything that he or she sees. Duveen referred to this "thick description" of events, settings, and behaviors as capturing the sense of the social actors, groups, and institutions being described.

Second, he called attention to the fact that the researcher's own interpretations of what are recorded, influence the final description. Together, the two-part process of observation-interpretation moves from one activity to the other, then backward to repeat itself again and again.

Figure 27.3 is a model illustrating the key processes involved in conducting and presenting the results of an ethnographic study. It illustrates the several different layers of observation-interpretation that characterize good ethnographic fieldwork, field notes, and final report preparation. Ethnographic methods are employed in a number of different forms. Examples of these variations are *ethnomethodology, community-based ethnography,* and *ethology.* Each of these research approaches has its own advocates and detractors, but all are considered to fall under the larger category of *field research.*

What is "Ethnomethodology"?

Ethnomethodology has been defined by Neuman (2000, 348) as "the study of commonsense knowledge." It combines themes from sociology and philosophy, and is usually seen as an application of *phenomenology* (Adler and Adler 1998). Researchers who follow this approach focus their concern on how people go about living their everyday lives. Ethnomethodologists study mundane, everyday behaviors in exceptionally close detail. They often use mechanical

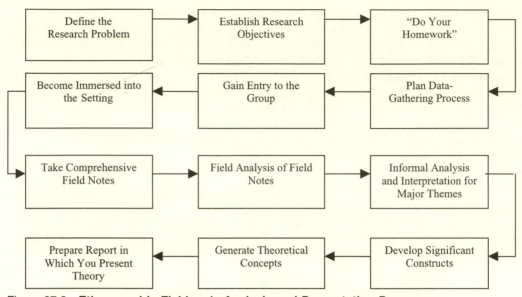

Figure 27.3 **Ethnographic Fieldwork, Analysis and Presentation Processes**
Source: After Jones 1996.

and electronic methods of recording the behavior of people. They then analyze in minute detail these audio- and videotapes, films, and other records, using what Adler and Adler (1998, 99) have described as "an intricate notational system that allows [them] to view the conversational overlaps, pauses, and intonations to within one-tenth of a second. . . . They have directed a particular emphasis toward conversation analysis."

Community-based ethnography (CBR) is closely associated with the critical approach known as *action research* (Stringer 1997), and has been used primarily in research in education. Stringer described the purpose of community-based research as a way of providing workers in professional and community groups with knowledge that is normally used only by academic researchers. As with all action research, CBR is designed to help people expand their knowledge and understanding of a situation, and on their own to come up with effective solutions to the problems they face. Everyone—researcher and researched—is involved in the process.

Stringer describes CBR as "intrinsically participatory; its products are not outsider accounts, portrayals, or reports, but collaborative accounts written from the emic—or insider—perspective of the group. Such accounts, grounded in hermeneutic, meaning-making processes of dialogue, negotiation, and consensus, provide the basis for group, community, or organization action. People can review their activities, develop plans, and resolve problems, initiate projects, or restructure an organization" (17–18).

Applying Ethological Methodology

Ethology research addresses many of the same issues addressed by traditional ethnography. Initially, the method focused primarily on animal behavior—Charles Darwin, for example, is considered to have been one of the pioneers in this field of research. Today, however, this approach is often used in organizational research, where it is employed for identifying and describing behavior in social settings.

The approach taken in an ethology study involves *simple observation,* which can be either visible or hidden (unobtrusive). Organ and Bateman (1991), discussing ethological observation in the context of organizational behavior research, referred to the method as *naturalistic observation.* They identified a number of appealing characteristics, as well as some of the shortcomings, for this approach.

Possibly the most important advantage is what Organ and Bateman call the *contextual richness* that is possible with observation (36). This includes more than the *thick description* that characterizes ethnographic field notes. It also refers to the fact that this type of research has enjoyed wide acceptance over the years, with results published in many articles, books, autobiographies, newspaper stories, conversations, and speeches.

In addition to this extensive body of available literature, the natural experience that researchers gained from working in and dealing with organizations of all types, sizes, and purposes is also an advantage. This is what is referred to as the *richness in personal insight* of naturalistic observation in organizational research. Summarizing their critique of the method, Organ and Bateman concluded:

> [Simple] observation is an attractive method of research because it confronts its subject head-on. It deals with raw, real-world behavior. Because the data are rich with the drama of human existence, it is easy to relate to accounts of these studies. (Organ and Bateman 1991, 37)

Among the disadvantages of observation is the fact that it often results in a report bias that is traceable to the natural tendency of people to exercise *selective perception* and *selective retention.* Selective perception means that from all the myriad stimuli that we encounter, everyone sees what he or she wants to see, is interested in, thinks is important. Whether they do so consciously or unconsciously, people ignore much of what else goes on.

This idea has been suggested by a number of different investigators. John Dewey, for example, noted that human perception is never "neutral." Rather, human knowledge and intelligence, what we think of as *past experience,* always influences perception. Furthermore, judgment is involved in all perception. Otherwise, the perception is nothing more than a form of what Dewey called *sensory excitation* (cited in Phillips 1987, 9).

In his *Pattern of Discovery* (1958), N.R. Hanson said that the theories, hypotheses, frameworks, or background knowledge held by researchers has the power to influence everything that is observed. Because of this power, observation cannot have a neutral foundation. The process of observation is unconsciously influenced by the ideas, theories, hypotheses, or general knowledge that the researcher holds going into the observation. Consciously or unconsciously, the investigator selectively remembers portions of what he or she observes. Psychologists call this phenomenon *selective retention.* Selective retention means that people usually remember what they *think* was said, what they *wanted* to hear, what they *believe* occurred, or what fits within their personal framing of the issue. Hence, what is remembered is inherently subjective; it should never be considered the one, the absolute "Truth."

Because observation is recorded as the field notes of one or more researchers, it will always contain what the researcher *feels* is important, or is convinced what action or actions caused or influenced a reaction. Field notes will often omit what the researcher believes to be trivial or unimportant. We are all drawn to the dramatic or exciting in situations—it makes for interesting reading, even when it has little or no bearing on the central issue or issues. Both field notes and the material that is eventually included in a report pass through a filter formed from the perceptions and memory of events held by the researcher. Therefore, researchers must always struggle with the question: Would another observer have drawn the same conclusion from these events? Researchers use *thick description* in an attempt to provide an answer.

Conducting Ethnographic Fieldwork

All variations of ethnography involve fieldwork. *Ethnographic fieldwork* includes such activities as (1) engaging in participant observation, (2) collecting genealogies, (3) recording conversations, (4) writing field notes, (5) interpreting the findings, and (6) writing up the field notes and interpretations as reports. Field notes describe events, incidents that catch the researcher's eye, in addition to anything and everything that is deemed to be relevant to the study at hand at the moment it occurs.

According to Fetterman (1989, 12), fieldwork is the key activity in all ethnographic research designs. Applying the basic concepts of anthropology, using methods and techniques of collecting and analyzing data, are the fundamental elements of "doing ethnography." Deciding on what equipment to select and use—including tape recorders, videotaping, and actual interviewing, among others—is a major decision in fieldwork. "This process becomes product through analysis at various stages in ethnographic work—in field notes, memoranda, and interim reports, but most dramatically in the published report, article, or book."

Anthropologists and sociologists who study cultures firsthand have determined that the best way to do their fieldwork is with a process called "participant observation." The early ethnographic researchers chose *participant observation* as their preferred way to function in the field for many reasons. One was the often-great distances they had to travel simply to reach the study society. That meant that they were forced to spend longer periods with the groups under study simply to justify the cost and physical hardship they were often forced to endure. Living for long periods of time in the "primitive" community, sometimes in the same huts or shelters of the members of the society under study, they were forced into being participants in order to survive—let alone understand what they were observing.

According to Bernard (1995), participant observation requires researchers to get close to people, making them comfortable enough to permit the researcher to observe and record observations about their lives. Establishing rapport with people in the new community means learning how to act in such a way that the people go about their day-to-day business when the researcher appears. Possibly most important, it means being able to retreat from the group-member role to think about what has been learned, and writing about it convincingly.

Modern Ethnography Applications

A reason for the evolution of ethnography from its former exclusive application to primitive cultures to now include research in today's settings was simply the long period of time needed to manually collect ethnographic information. Ethnographies are built on a combination of observations and extensive interviewing (Whiting and Whiting 1973), and these take time. Observation, regardless of the society or culture upon which it is focused, can be directed toward many different topics of investigation.

Whiting and Whiting have identified six topics of potential focus for research: (1) an activity of some kind, (2) a larger category of acts, such as gang behavior, (3) an object or person that is the center of attention for a larger group of persons, (4) a person who functions as a representative of a status category, (5) a pair of individuals (a *dyad*), or (6) some setting for a social event.

Ethnography in Political Science Research

When political science evolved into an academic discipline in its own light during the last decades of the nineteenth century, its own journals, professional associations, conferences, and academic departments soon followed. Bits and pieces from all the social and behavioral sciences were incorporated into its structure—and its research methodology. It is useful to remember that *all* the tools and methods used in political science research were invented for other purposes.

Ethnography has been shown to be a valuable tool for gathering information about behaviors embedded in, and specific to, cultures and subcultures. During the early decades of the twentieth century, it was often used to identify administrative options for making decisions on matters of public policy. Fetterman (1989) has defined the method and culture focus as follows:

> Ethnography is the art and science of describing a group or culture. The description may be of a small tribal group in some exotic land or a classroom in middle-class suburbia. [The] ethnographer writes about the routine, daily lives of people. The more predictable patterns of human thought and behavior are the focus of inquiry. (Fetterman 1989, 11)

Yeager has described ethnographic observation as an "old and widely used research method both in public administration and in other fields of study." In use today, it incorporates many different techniques, including simple, group, and unobtrusive observations, depth-interviewing key informants, ethnography, and controlled observation techniques. "Participant observation includes material that the observer gains directly from personally seeing or hearing an event occur. Often the participant observer establishes personal relationships with subjects and maintains those relationships over a period of time. . . . Rapport and trust are established with subjects to a far greater extent than in other methods. Typically, more exhaustive data are gathered on fewer subjects using participant observation that with other methods" (Yeager 1989, 726).

In political science, the once-traditional activity of spending long periods in the field is neither possible nor desirable. Long periods of time spent immersed in a social group are not considered to be worth the cost. Rather, the most important part of fieldwork is not the *length* of time spent with a group, but rather, of simply *being there* to observe, ask questions, and write down what is heard and seen (Fetterman 1989). Participant observation, like ethnography, has changed from its original concept of total immersion in a society under study to include new and different topics and locations of study, in addition to a wide variety of data-gathering tools and techniques.

Ethnographic field research requires the most intense connection between the researcher and the subjects of the study (Kornblum 1996); it is not unusual to see ethnographers who have lived and worked within a group for many years begin to take on a self-identity that places greater loyalty and connection to the study group over that of the researcher's prior connection.

While similar in method and analysis, ethnography as it is applied today is far different from the ethnography that evolved with the social sciences more than a century ago. "Ethnography is no longer a method used only to study foreign cultures; it has also become a method to study what is foreign or strange in our society and how social subcultures or subworlds are constructed—the adventure that begins just around the corner" (Flick 1999, 641). Ethnography has moved beyond its original focus on describing small, distant, and primitive societies, or on examining the social disruption that was rooted in communities undergoing industrialization. Today it is used to study groups in locations that its founders would never have considered. One of these is the modern city.

All facets of urban life are now considered to be legitimate targets of ethnographic research for contributing to the establishment of public policy. Studies have ranged from the public behaviors of homosexuals, ghetto dwellers, drug cultures, the urban poor and homeless, behavior at schools, and many, many more topics. There is apparently no limit to what studies can or should be carried out using an ethnographic approach.

New Directions for Ethnography

According to Fox (1977, 9), there are several different directions being taken by urban anthropologists: the anthropology of *urbanism,* the anthropology of *poverty in urban settings,* and the anthropology of *urbanization.* Despite their differences, they all appear to have the following principals in common: First, there is near-unanimous agreement among urban anthropologists that cities are important locations for research. Second, anthropologists are convinced that anthropology can make "important methodological and theoretical contributions to the study of urban place." Political scientists have followed the lead of anthropologists and now conduct research in these same directions.

Urbanism Research

Studies in the ethnology of *urbanism* are concerned with how movement from rural to urban locations has affected individuals, families, and larger groups. These major social movements are seldom seen in the industrialized West; researchers studying the rural-urban phenomenon today are more likely to focus their attentions on such locations as India, Southeast Asia, South and Central America, and other "Third World" regions.

An example of this type of modern ethnographic study is Susana Narotzky's (2000) research with a small population in rural Spain, the Vega Baja del Segura district of Valencia. Narotzky conducted intensive fieldwork in a town of about 5,000 residents. The region is an irrigated plain with a mix of agricultural and industrial economic activities, with the greatest contribution now coming from the shoemaking industry. Large shoe factories were established in the region during the 1960s and 1970s. During this period, many single men and women and young families migrated from small farms to the towns where the factories were located. Other families accepted work to be completed in their homes, for which they were paid on a piece-basis. Others work in small sweatshops that produce shoe parts and components for larger jobbers and finish factories.

Today, a mix of large factories, small family farms, unregulated workshops, jobbers, home-based workers, and migrant farm workers characterizes the economy of the region. Narotzky was interested in how the local population has come to grips with a local, specialized industrial economy that is suffering shocks owing to increased global competition. She described the region as one in which production processes are structured in diverse ways and where people tend to shift between different labor relations that vary greatly in their stability. Some people have more stable work opportunities, while others lack this stability.

A major social problem that arises from this discontinuous character of the workforce is that many workers are unable to gain access to unemployment benefits and other worker welfare legislation. She concluded that the impact upon local politics and public policy has been tremendous.

Urban Poverty Studies

Urban poverty is a global phenomenon; organizations as disparate as the United Nations, private foundations, universities, governments, and the World Bank either fund or participate in studies of its causes and effects. Ethnographers study social groups and populations in the ghetto and barrio. They study highly concentrated ethnic subcultures in urban settings. They also focus their attention on the homeless, alcoholics and other substance abusers, Native American populations, at-risk youth, and others whom Fox (1977) has identified as social groups "whose lifestyles are described as being at the furthest cultural remove from the mainstream world."

Carol Stack (1996) is an example of ethnographers conducting modern urban poverty studies. Over a three-year period she carried out participant observation in one of the poorest sections of a minority community in a large city in the American Midwest. Most of the residents of the area were unemployed; those with jobs worked in low-paying service jobs that left them little better off than those eligible for welfare. One of the key findings of her study was that families developed large kinship-based exchange networks that included many nonrelated individuals and family units. These networks provided extensive support for other members of the network, helping the residents of the area to adapt to a life of poverty, unemployment or underemployment, and welfare dependency.

Another recent example of ethnographic research in the realm of urban poverty is the 1999 work of urban anthropologist Alice Waterston: *Love, Sorrow, and Rage: Destitute Women in a Manhattan Residence*. Waterston spent two years studying the residents of a residence for at-risk women in New York City. She employed what she described as a "more interactive approach to data gathering," a practice that is apparently common among qualitative researchers. Her primary method was participant observation, although she also used informal chats, along with formal tape-recorded, open-ended interviews with both the staff and the residents of the shelter.

Waterston developed the data for her study and final report from themes that emerged from her observation and extensive interviews. Among the themes she included in her study were poverty, homelessness, work, substance abuse, sexual violence, mental illness, AIDS, family and interpersonal relationships, sexuality, race, gender, and food. She found food and preparing meals to be a unifying concept around which many of the other themes were discussed.

Research on Urbanization Issues

Ethnographic research in the anthropology of *urbanization,* while similar to that of urbanism, focuses instead on the larger process of urbanization that characterizes most modern industrial societies. How societies deal with health and safety concerns, waste management, work, play, and all the many other difficult social issues associated with urban living are the study topics addressed by these social scientists. The nature of the urban locale, cultural roles in society, its demography, class organization, and government: these are part of the greater area of interest for political scientists.

Nakano's 2000 study of volunteerism in modern Japan is an example of an ethnographic study on urbanization's effect on a society. The focus of her study was on the way some modern Japanese are achieving their self-identity by volunteering to help in the operations of government, nonprofit organizations, schools, corporations, community groups, and other social groupings. This type of study can have great impact upon public policymaking, as well as providing significant direction for managers of nonprofit organizations in a community.

In the past, Japanese society was divided into two distinct camps. The more recent camp holds that people must develop themselves through self-expression, while the older traditionalists believe that individuals must connect themselves to a social group, such as a firm or school—and define themselves through their commitment to that group. Since the 1990s, however, proponents of a third view—volunteerism—have proposed that *both* camps can be satisfied because volunteerism straddles the divide; it develops the self and contributes to society at the same time.

Nakano looked at volunteering in analysis of a densely populated middle- to lower-middle-class residential neighborhood on the outskirts of Yokohama. The community contained a variety of housing types that reflected a mix of socioeconomic lifestyles. On one end of the scale was a 1,040-household public housing project for low-income citizens. Other types ranged from rental apartments, privately owned condominium apartments, and at the top of the scale, single-family detached homes.

The practice of using volunteer activity for self-identity flourished in the area for several reasons. First, the neighborhood was aging, a trend led by the aged residing in the large public housing project, where one in four residents was sixty-five years old or older—nearly twice the average in Japan today. These older residents were both potential volunteers and the recipients of voluntary services.

Second, identifying oneself as a volunteer served as "symbolic leverage" for neighborhood newcomers. "Newcomers" was defined in the largest sense of the word; barely 1 percent of the population of the region were descendants of the original land-owning and farming families. Yet, they remained as leaders of many social groupings in the region. Some "newcomers" had lived in the community for more than twenty years.

Third, volunteerism was seen as a socially recognized activity that was particularly acceptable for middle-aged women and retired former "salary men," although volunteering was more of a social risk for men than for women. Becoming a volunteer, in fact, often resulted in a *promotion* in status for female homemakers who became quasi-public figures in their volunteer roles.

An earlier example of an urban ethnographic study is the research carried out by Ulf Hannerz (1969) among urban blacks on Winston Street in Washington, DC, and described by Fox in his 1977 monograph on urban anthropology. Hannerz's study objective was to identify and describe ways in which ghetto lifestyles and social behavior differed from what he called "mainstream America." Hannerz identified four prototypical ghetto lifestyles: *mainstreamers, swingers, street families,* and *street corner men.*

An example of sociological ethnographic research study is Alasuutari's (1995) report of research involving long hours over a period of several months socializing with drinkers in a bar in Finland. The study included a description of the role that drinking and darts playing had for regular patrons of the bar. Alasuutari's study constituted a social commentary of a pattern of behavior that was thought to contribute heavily to illness, accidents, and suicide among Finnish men. The study included some historical explanation of why Finnish men spent time in bars, tracing the practice to the erosion of Finnish traditional rural society and the immigration of farm workers to urban centers. These were explained as significant contributors to the role that alcohol consumption plays in certain segments of Finnish society.

Ethological Research

A key objective for all research in ethnography and ethology is the study of behavior in social groups. This is done through research on cultures and subcultures. As we have seen, ethnography involves participant observation, where the researcher becomes immersed in the group under study. For the ethologist, however, the process is not participatory. Rather, the researcher simply observes and records what is taking place.

Ethologists employ "simple observation" in their studies, and often conduct controlled behavioral experiments with animals and human beings. As a nonparticipating observer, the researcher is always an "outsider," on hand simply to record what is seen, and never becoming a member of the group under study. The reports of ethologists tend to be primarily descriptive or explanatory, and do not involve interpretation of the observed social setting.

Researching Organizational Culture

Every organization, whether in the public or private sector, has its own distinctive culture, as well as its distinct operating climate. The study of organizational culture owes much of its method and underlying principles to ideas produced through ethnographic research. Change-agent consultants working on organizational development projects with organizational culture are very likely to use either ethnography or ethology methodology for their data gathering. Organizational culture has been defined in many different ways, but most are similar to the definition offered by Schein in 1985:

> Organizational culture is the shared, and implicit assumptions held by a group and that determines how members of the group perceive, think about, and react to its various environments. (Schein 1985, 229)

Other definitions include those of Margulies and Wallace (1973), who defined culture as the learned beliefs, values, and patterns of behavior that characterize an organization; Peters and Waterman (1982) saw culture as the shared system of values that manifests itself through different cultural artifacts.

In addition to its culture, organizations can also be said to have a distinct *operating climate* that results from the interaction of employees, administrators, and managers functioning within that culture. Operating climate has been defined as a concept that reflects the content and strength of the salient values, attitudes, behaviors, and feelings of the people working in an organization. Lewicki, Bowen, Hall, and Hall (1988) saw operating climate as the level and form of organizational support, openness, style of supervision, conflict and conflict resolution, autonomy, and the existing quality of relationships that exist within the organization. Dastmalchian, Blyton, and Adamson (1991) were more succinct, terming operating climate as simply *the atmosphere* prevailing in an organization.

One of the principal investigators in the field of organizational studies is Edgar H. Schein, who helped to establish the field of organizational studies at MIT. Building on earlier work by such pioneers in social psychology as Kurt Lewin and Ennis Likert, Schein believed that the innate culture of an organization often serves as a barrier to planned change. Schein (1996) noted that when organizations try to alter and improve their operations, they often run into resistance that is based in the culture and/or subcultures that exist within all groups. This culture exists whether it is recognized or not. Members of the group are often not even aware of the culture of their group until they are faced with replacing it with something new and different.

Schein is critical of the positivist approach to the study of organizational culture. Traditional research has often resulted in a dependence upon abstractions about organizations and human behaviors in groups that are developed exclusively from a limited number of answers to questionnaires. These questionnaire-developed abstractions have created an artificial fabrication of reality. This has resulted in what Schein calls fuzzy theory—research findings that depend upon "massaging the data" statistically to establish significant results. His solution to this problem involves taking an interdisciplinary approach that includes ethnographic involvement in the research process.

> Concepts for understanding culture in organizations have value only when they derive from observation of real behavior in organizations, when they are definable enough to generate further study. (Schein 1996, 229)

Summary

In the new social science disciplines that emerged in the eighteenth and nineteenth centuries, curiosity was raised about primitive societies, as well as how industrialization was affecting children, families, and the working poor. This resulted in research efforts to understand (1) why social problems occurred, and (2) what could (or *ought* to) be done to change society in order to improve the lot of the poor and disenfranchised. Adding to this new curiosity was news about many strange and new societies and cultures.

Sociology evolved as a way to conduct systematic investigations into the newly emerging industrial society and the litany of social ills that was seen as an unwanted by-product of the industrialization process. Early attempts at establishing a systematic way of explaining human behavior and mental aberrations resulted in the creation of the science of psychology. Building on a tradition born from early travel stories and forging a scientific way of looking at indigenous cultures, another group of scholars created the new social science of anthropology.

Through an eclectic process of trial and error, anthropologists and sociologists developed a way of conducting research that allowed them to meet their study objectives in all kinds of social and cultural settings. The name given to this method was *ethnography*. Researchers in public administration have also adopted this method of research.

Ethnographers often live, work, and play with the members of the group under study for long periods of time. Their aim is to be absorbed into the group, with the underlying objective of becoming "accepted" as a nonthreatening or nonintrusive member of the group so that events and interrelationships unfold as they would naturally, as if the observer were not in attendance. This process is called "gaining entry," and is the key to a successful research project.

The process of living with a social group during fieldwork involves observing and recording individuals' behaviors. The ethnographer summarizes these field notes into a larger descriptive generalization that purports to describe the behavior of the larger society. The researcher must then develop *subjective descriptions* that are based on a large number of *generalizations*. In making these generalizations, the ethnographer moves from the *specific to the general.* That is, the behaviors of one or a small group are used to infer that those behaviors are also those of the larger groups in similar circumstances. The ethnographer should also develop *interpretations* of the observed behaviors; the question "why" should be answered to the best of the ethnographer's ability.

Discussion Questions

1. Do you feel that an ethnographic design is appropriate for political science research? Why or why not?
2. Describe how you would design an ethnographic study to investigate voting behavior among minority women.
3. What is thick description?
4. How has field research evolved from its early stages?
5. Define the term "ethnography." What do ethnographers do?
6. How does ethnography differ from ethnology?
7. Why are field researchers attracted to ethnography?
8. Define the term "ethnomethodology."
9. Describe how you would use participant observation in a political science research project.
10. What are urbanism studies? Cite several examples.

Additional Reading

Alasuutari, Pertti. 1995. *Researching Culture: Qualitative Method and Cultural Studies.* London: Sage.

Bernard, H. Russell. 1995. *Research Methods in Anthropology.* 2nd ed. Walnut Creek, CA: Alta Mira Press.

Fetterman, David M. 1989. *Ethnography, Step by Step.* Newbury Park, CA: Sage.

Fox, Richard G. 1977. *Urban Anthropology: Cities in Their Cultural Settings.* Englewood Cliffs: Prentice-Hall.

Neuman, W. Lawrence. 2000. *Social Research Methods.* 4th ed. Boston: Allyn and Bacon.

28 The Critical Approach: Action Research Methods

Action research is a way of initiating *change* in social systems—societies, communities, organizations, or groups—by involving members of the group in on the research process. It does this through a process that focuses first on researching the way the group functions and the problem affecting the group, and second by helping members of the group to bring about the needed change that they perceive is right for them. It has a long history of use in some subfields of political science.

The term "action research" was first used in 1946 by Kurt Lewin to describe an approach to solving practical problems in social groups. He described action research as taking place over four distinct steps: planning, executing, reconnaissance, and evaluating (Quigley 1997; Lewin 1948). His approach was characterized by a combination of research and theory building (Cunningham 1995). Lewin's perception of the change process included collaborative research between the social science researcher and the client. Lewin saw the method as *empirical research*—that is, an *applied* approach to social research, as opposed to a "pure science" or purely theoretical approach.

Lewin and his team of researchers at the University of Iowa and later at the Massachusetts Institute of Technology maintained a practical, participatory democracy focus in their research by studying citizens' participation in solving community problems. For example, early in the U.S.'s participation in World War II, anthropologist Margaret Mead invited him to do research with her for the Committee on Food Habits of the National Research Council. Lewin and his team began a series of studies to determine (1) the food consumption habits of Americans at the time, and (2) how best to get people to change their eating habits for improved nutrition together with substituting for widespread food shortages. Working under Lewin's direction, researchers at the University of Iowa had recently completed a set of behavioral studies in autocratic and democratic situations, mostly through a series of experiments with preteenage boys. Applying that methodology to the food studies, these studies became the early steps in what Lewin was to call *action research*—the experimental application of social science to advancing democratic processes. One of the most important conclusions to emerge from their research was that groups of people could do a thing better when they themselves decide on it, and they also decide on how they themselves will reduce the gap between their attitudes and actions (Marrow 1997, 130–31).

This emphasis on encouraging citizen participation is one of the reasons why action research is interesting to political scientists. Despite this interest, however, very little pure action research is conducted directly by political scientists or public administrators. On the other hand, action research has become a widely accepted research approach among social psychologists, sociologists, social workers, and educators, many of whom plan and conduct research on topics of interest to the political world, including public administrators, and nonprofit organizations.

To summarize, action research is a form of inductive, practical research that focuses on improving understanding of a social problem, and on achieving a real change or improvement in the way people function in groups through a collaborative effort (Kuhne and Quigley 1997).

Dewey's Contribution to Action Research

John Dewey was an early contributor to the development of action research, but rather than focusing on social organizations, Dewey was primarily concerned with the role of education in the process of becoming socialized. Born in 1859 and both a high school and university teacher, Dewey's concern was on improving educational processes as a tool for teaching democracy and participation in democratic living. Lewin drew upon Dewey's philosophical writings in coming up with the action research approach that is now used for research in education, psychology, sociology, and other related disciplines.

Dewey was interested in developing theory, but theory that guided the *practice* of education and learning. Dewey also believed that by participating in democratic activities in classrooms, the large numbers of children of immigrant families flooding public schools in the early 1900s could learn concepts, ideas, and skills needed for cooperative living (Schmuck 1997). The work of Dewey sparked an interest in action research among educators in the 1950s. That interest quickly waned, however, and did not re-emerge until publication in 1967 of Robert Schefer's *The School as a Center of Inquiry*, in which Schefer recommended use of action-oriented collaborative research by teachers (Quigley 1997). Today, because of its focus on early intervention and process improvement, action research has become one of the most popular qualitative research methods used in education:

> The movement has . . . grown to form a growing counterhegemony to traditional teacher preparation programs in public education and, more important . . . to traditional scientific positivism and the academic control of knowledge. (Quigley 1997, 10)

Action research in education is conducted in the same way that it is in other fields of study. For example, in their *Guide to Research for Educators*, Merriam and Simpson (1989) identified the following six-step process for conducting action research projects. It begins with analysis of the situation, getting the facts, identifying the problem, planning an intervention process, taking action on the problem, then repeating the cycle as new concepts and information emerge from the process.

Five Models of Action Research

Today, at least five different models of action research are in use by researchers in the human and administrative sciences (Small 1995): Small described four of the models in some detail: (1) traditional action research, (2) participatory action research, (3) empowerment research, and (4) feminist research. Although not discussed by Small, *action science* is a fifth

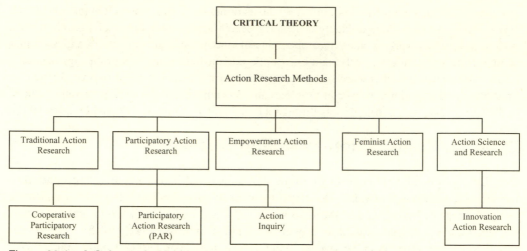

Figure 28.1   **A Schematic Model of Several Action Research Approaches**

school of action-based research. These models and their relationships are displayed in Figure 28.1.

Traditional Action Research

The *action research* model developed from the work of Lewin and others beginning in the 1940s is the most widely used model. A victim of Nazi discrimination that ended his opportunity to participate fully in an academic career in Germany, Lewin immigrated to the United States in 1933. Reflecting on his experiences in Europe, he designed a field of research that looked at how democracy can disappear under the influence of a powerful, charismatic leader. He was convinced that social science could strengthen democracy, and made searching for ways to make that happen his life's work.

In the traditional action research approach established by Lewin and his followers the researcher's primary objective is to help change dysfunctional social institutions (such as communities) while also contributing to the general fund of theory and knowledge. Lewin was convinced that researchers should be concerned with two kinds of knowledge: (a) general laws of human and organizational behavior, and (b) specific information about the institution or system that is the focus of the change effort.

Gabel (1995, 1), synthesizing Lewin, Dewey, and other early contributions that formed the approach, described traditional action research as "an informal, qualitative, formative, subjective, interpretive, reflective, and experimental model of inquiry in which all individuals involved in the study are knowing and contributing participants." He saw subject involvement in the process as a key characteristic of the research approach. Although it is usually considered to fall into a postpositivist tradition, no specific methodology is associated with action research; both quantitative and qualitative data are relevant for action research. However, the approach may be characterized by the following traditional practices.

First, data gathered in an action research study may be of any type, and can be gathered by such different methods as structured survey questionnaires, simple observation, or unstructured personal or focus group interviews. Second, because of its interventionist nature, action research is conducted in the location or setting of the social problem, and usually involves the entire group (a universe) rather than a sample. Third, action research usually focuses on a single case or organizational unit. Fourth, the researcher collaborates with subjects who are members of the group under study. The researcher brings scientific and theoretical knowledge and skills to the project, while group members add important practical knowledge and experience with the situations that frame the study. Both parts of this knowledge picture are deemed essential for the action research process to work.

Participatory Action Research

Participatory action research (PAR) is the second model described by Small (1995). Researchers employing this approach are typically concerned with three activities: research, education, and action. It owes much to the emergence of critical theory, in that a primary goal of participatory research is to effect a fundamental, emancipating change in a society. Participatory research developed from social movements among oppressed societies in the Third World, including Africa, Asia, and Latin America.

Participatory research has also gained a strong foothold in North America. For example, a four-year study with residents of the town of North Bonneville was the focus of a participatory research study conducted in the early 1970s (Comstock and Fox 1993). Groups of students and faculty from the Evergreen State College in Olympia, Washington, worked with some 450 residents of a town that was scheduled for demolition to make room for a new dam spillway and power plant.

During initial meetings with town residents, the U.S. Corps of Engineers refused to consider moving the town, and instead offered payments for residents to move to other areas. Comstock and Fox described how residents overcame a critical hurdle in their path to achieving success in their dealings with the Corps:

> Very early in the struggle, the residents discovered the contradiction between the Corps's meaning of community and their own. To the Corps the community was individuals and physical structures. This ignored the reality of community values, attachments to the land, and social networks. Through a careful description of their community, the residents gained a more articulate description of their community and vitality as a community. (Comstock and Fox 1993, 121)

Once residents learned how the Corps perceived the community and its residents and how Corps agents were using the agency's control of information as a wedge to divide citizen opinion, they moved to acquire technical information on their own. They then provided that technical information to everyone in a way that could be understood, thus breaking down the Corps' monopoly of ideas. The town eventually won in its fight to survive. The Corps of Engineers did build a new town in the location wanted by residents of the old town. The new city of North Bonneville was officially dedicated in July 1976.

Researchers using this model believe that if, through education, members of a society become aware of better ways to function, they can become politically active and able to bring about the change themselves. Thus, a key part of the research process is helping community members become active participants in their study and its action aftermath. Participants are expected to take primary responsibility for the study, including its overall design, data gathering and analysis, and eventual distribution of the findings. Thus, political activity plays the following role in the participatory action approach:

> Participatory researchers are openly and explicitly political. Their ideology emphasizes large-scale structural forces, conflicts of interest, and the need to overcome oppression and inequality through transforming the existing social order. The lack of access to useful and valued forms of knowledge by oppressed or disenfranchised peoples is viewed as a major problem that can be overcome through the research process. (Small 1995, 943)

Comstock and Fox also noted the political nature of the participatory action approach in their conclusions of how the experience changed the people of North Bonneville forever. They offered the following conclusion:

> Perhaps the most striking result of the North Bonneville experience has been the degree to which a self-sustaining political process was initiated. . . . The growth of self-direction continued as residents, no longer content with their original demand that a new town be planned and built for them, demanded (and got) control over the design of their own community. (Comstock and Fox 1993, 123)

Finally, a key distinguishing characteristic of this approach is an emphasis upon empowering the people within the group or community, making it possible for them to take control of their study. In time, the researchers are expected to back away in order to follow the lead of the participants, rather than the reverse.

Empowerment Research

The third model of action research is what Small describes as empowerment research. He defined *empowerment* as being concerned with individuals and groups who are excluded by the majority on the basis of their demographic characteristics or of their physical or emotional difficulties. The rationale for exclusion may have been experienced in the past, or may be taking place in the present.

Empowerment research is often employed in the public administration subfield of political science. Supporting this impression is the selective focus of most empowerment research that has taken place thus far. Typical questions addressed in published empowerment research include issues of mental health, citizen involvement, and community programs.

The defining characteristics of the empowerment research approach begin with (1) identifying or creating situations where a group has been silent and/or isolated—the "outsiders" of a society, an organization, or a community, (2) helping these "outsiders" gain an understanding of the underlying issues, and (3) concludes with their gaining a voice in and power over the decisions that affect them. In a word, it is a process designed to help people become *empowered*. It is collaborative in nature: researchers work with members of the group to identify group strengths and resources that may not have been recognized. As they become empowered, group members achieve a mastery over the internal and external forces that affect them.

Finally, the process focuses on bringing out the natural abilities and skills of the members of the group under study. Rather than focusing on group members' weaknesses, *empowerment research* aims at bringing their strengths to the fore, and providing guidance in the task of putting those strengths to work for the members' benefit.

Feminist Research

Feminist research is the last model of action research described by Small (1995) who defined the focus of feminist research as promoting the feminist agenda by challenging male dominance and advocating female and male social, political, and economic equality. As with all other models of action research, feminist research seeks to (1) bring about social change, (2) emancipate participants, and (3) enhance the lives of the participants.

Feminist researchers are more likely to adopt a postpositivist approach to their work, although there are no hard-and-fast rules that make it the required epistemology. Furthermore, while some have advocated that a distinctive set of feminist methods should exist, others are less convinced that a purely feminist methodology is possible. And, according to Small, a third group argues that while, indeed, no special feminist methodology currently exists, as more feminist research appears, one is slowly being formed. The following statement has been suggested as a way of summarizing the feminist model:

> Feminist researchers share the values of overcoming oppression, empowering women, and transforming society so that equality between men and women can be achieved. The purpose of knowledge is to change or transform what is considered the patriarchal nature of society. (Small 1995, 947)

An Action Science Model

Action science is the action research model seen most often in political science research; it is particularly prevalent in research that deals with public organizational settings. While it was not discussed in Small's overview of action research models, this approach clearly deserves an equal place alongside all other action research models. Chris Argyris and others developed the *action science* approach from the same contributions of John Dewey—who proposed separating science and practice—and Kurt Lewin, who contributed greatly to the field of group dynamics (an area of study in social psychology). Dewey's contributions and Lewin's separation of *diagnosis* of an organization from *practitioner intervention* became the concept of using research to bring about change (Argyris, Putnam, and Smith 1984; Schein 1995). In this model, diagnosis of a problem by research is always followed by participant-led intervention (change). Action science has been described specifically as an *intervention method* that is based on the idea that people can improve their interpersonal and organizational effectiveness by examining the underlying beliefs that guide their actions (Raelin 1997). This phase may also take the form of an evaluation of the program or entity:

> The evaluation of social situations is the point of any action theory, which strives to help actors understand their situations in a different light and to make value judgments about whether or not their situations should be changed. (White 1999, 142)

Lewin never explicitly defined action science method as such—he retained instead the label *action research.* However, his early work in developing approaches to interventions and change in social organizations led Argyris to give him credit for development of most of the techniques involved in the approach (Argyris 1985; Schein 1995). Argyris proposed the action science concept because: (1) then-current applications of action research were ignoring the theory-building element of the original approach, and (2) he believed that the practice of following traditional, positivist approaches to research was self-limiting and harmful to the growth of knowledge. Today, the two terms are usually used synonymously, together with other closely related variations such as "action learning" (Raelin 1997), "action inquiry" (Reason 1998), and "innovation action research" (Kaplan 1998).

Action Research and Critical Theory

Philosophically, action research is closely related to the *critical theory* approach to research; both seek intervention in social organizations for the purpose of helping people (clients) find better ways of living, socializing, and functioning in groups. Argyris, Putnam, and Smith (1985, 234) even go so far as to consider this approach to be a kind of critical theory. However, despite their similar roots, they are not the same. Critical theory and research evolved from the emancipatory tradition of Marx and Freud. It was ultimately refined in the 1970s by Habermas and others of the Frankfurt School. Action research, on the other hand, has its roots in Kurt Lewin's work in participatory democracy and the education systems research of John Dewey.

The *Frankfurt School* is the name given to a group of philosophers who expressed their dissatisfaction with traditional epistemology and its positivist theory by constructing a new philosophy of social science. Today, that new philosophy of science is called *postpositivism*. The name given to the new type of theory that was associated with the new postpositivist realm is *critical theory*. The Frankfurt School believed that that critical theory has three fundamental characteristics that distinguish it from traditional positivist theory (Geuss 1981, 1–2):

1. Critical theories guide human action in two ways:
   a. They enlighten the people who have them, enabling these agents to determine for themselves what their true interests are.
   b. They are inherently emancipatory; they free people from coercion, which may be partially self-imposed and based in ignorance of better ways to exist.
2. Critical theories are forms of knowledge; hence, *education* precedes emancipation.
3. Critical theories have a different epistemological basis than the theories that exist in the natural sciences: critical theories are "reflective," whereas theories in the natural sciences are "objective."

To summarize, a critical theory is a reflective theory that gives people as *change agents* a knowledge that is inherently enlightening and emancipating. Critical researchers help humans in social systems discover their own ways to change their world—i.e., to become *emancipated*—whereas action researchers *participate* with groups to bring about improvement in the way the groups function. What brings the two approaches near to one another is their focus on bringing about *social change*.

Despite their differences, the two concepts are often combined into a single research design. DePoy and Hartman (1999, 560), for example, developed what they called a "model for social work knowing founded on the tenets of critical theory synthesized with principles and practices from action research." They applied the model to a case analysis of the Maine Adolescent Transition (MAT) project. The objective of the MAT was to provide at-risk adolescents access to vital health care services. The model identifies a twelve-step process, as follows:

1. Identification of a social problem.
2. Convene a steering committee with representation from all stakeholder groups.
3. Identify (delimit) the scope of the research.
4. Select a specific set of research questions to guide the conduct of the study.
5. Determine specific change objectives for the study group.
6. Select a collaborative research team (including lay and professional researcher membership).
7. Train lay researchers in designing, conducting, and using inquiry.
8. Design the inquiry, with research questions, design, and analysis strategy.
9. Conduct inquiry and analysis.
10. Report findings in accessible formats to all stakeholder groups.
11. Submit findings to social change planning and action.
12. Steering committee identification of further areas for inquiry.

Jeffrey Glanz (1999) prepared a small but informative "primer" on action research for school administrators, in which he identified just four steps for the process. First, select a focus for the study by (a) knowing what you want to investigate, (b) developing some questions to ask, and (c) establishing a plan to acquire answers to the questions. Second, collect some data, but do so only after you have narrowed your focus onto a specific area of concern; data may be collected in either quantitative or qualitative approaches, or both. A key part of this step is to organize the data so that they can be shared with other readers after the study is completed. The third step is to analyze and interpret the data in order to arrive at some decision. Making a decision is preliminary to the fourth and final step, initiating some action. The project is not complete until this occurs; *corrective action* is fundamental to the idea of action research.

Key Themes in Action Research

In their work on the philosophical underpinnings of action science, Argyris, Putnam, and Smith (1985, 8–9) identified five key themes of the process. While these themes were applied specifically to the *action science* model, they are clearly applicable to all of the other models of action research as well. The five themes are:

1. *Collaboration in Resolution*. Action science (research) deals with processes and efforts to bring about *change* in real social systems. It targets a specific problem and then provides assistance to the (client) organization in resolving the problem.
2. *Problem Identification, Planning, and Acting*. Action research proceeds through repetitive cycles of problem identification, planning, acting, and evaluation.
3. *Educating and Re-educating*. Change in the social group or organization involves a process of *educating* and/or *re-educating* group members. This means changing the way people in the group think and act. Thus, the process works at reforming organizational culture. For re-education to work, all actors in the organization must participate in the diagnosis and fact-finding stage of the process, and contribute to identification of new ways of acting.
4. *Democratic Participation and Action*. Action research maintains a strong commitment to the idea of *democratic* action in improving group behavior and effectiveness. Thus,

the method involves questioning the status quo from the perspective of democratic values.

5. *Theory Building and Practical Application.* Two key objectives of all action research are (1) to contribute to basic knowledge in social science by developing theory, and (2) to improve action in social organizations.

Phases of Planned Change

The Dynamics of Planned Change (Lippitt, Watson, and Westley) was published in 1958, six years after Lewin's death. In that work Ronald Lippitt, a student of Lewin and collaborator on much of his research, identified seven phases of planned change (Figure 28.2). In *Phase I,* someone associated with the social group recognizes that a problem of some type exists. This could be anything from an external threat to the organization's existence to a functional barrier that hinders effectiveness and fosters frustration. An example is the diagnostic action research study for a federal supply service office conducted by McNabb and Sepic in 1995. The unit had been required to reorganize for implementation of a total quality management program. Five very different functions, with different organizational cultures and traditions, were to merge into one functioning department. Unit leaders and long-term employees were balking at making the change. The leader of one unit refused to accept the stalemate and called the researchers in to help the group find a common ground for problem resolution.

In *Phase II,* data about the situation are collected. In the federal supply office example, this began with a series of group meetings with representatives from all five units present at all sessions. This became an ad hoc research advisory team, with membership remaining constant throughout the length of the project. These sessions were tape recorded, with transcripts circulated to all members for their concurrence and approval before moving on to other problem areas. The group then agreed upon a set of nine problem areas common to the majority of the units that needed to be addressed. These problem areas served as constructs for the collaborative development of a comprehensive survey instrument. Unit leaders then administered the instrument to their own staffs.

In *Phase III,* a diagnosis of the situation is made from the collected data. In this example, the research team conducted a preliminary analysis of the combined group discussion and questionnaire data. This was shared with members of the ad hoc advisory committee, with their interpretations solicited. With all data collected and both the research team and group participants in general agreement, a composite diagnostic report was prepared. Copies were distributed downward through the organization and upward to the organizations management personnel.

In *Phase IV,* a plan of action steps to be taken to resolve organizational issues and remove barriers to change is to be made with both the researchers and participants collaborating on what is to be done and when. This step is considered to be the "heart" of the action research effort. Only action steps that address problems specifically identified in the diagnostic phase should be included in the plan. Once a set of proposed steps are agreed upon, collaborative action of setting priorities follows.

Phase V is the action phase in the action research process. Plans must be converted into actual change actions. In this example, the agency's dismal record in two broad areas of organizational climate were conceived as being absolute barriers to improving employee commitment to the organization and willingness to accept a mandated change for which they had

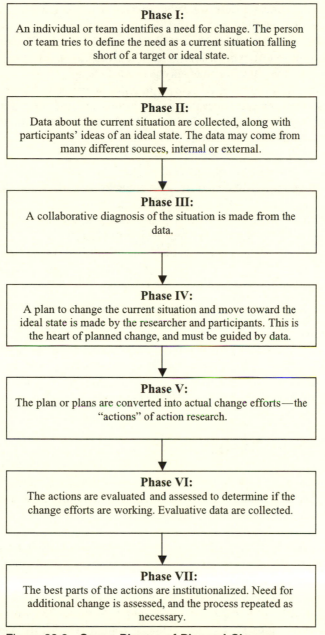

Figure 28.2 **Seven Phases of Planned Change**
Source: After Schmuck 1997, 143.

not been consulted. These barriers were the rewards and recognition and the warmth and support constructs. It is important to remember that neither the researchers nor the agency's senior management should be the ones to suggest specific changes. Rather, to succeed, these have to come from the entire organization staff. The researcher's role from this phase onward is to function only as a catalyst for internally generated change.

Phase VI is the evaluation stage; it begins with implementation of the change initiatives and continues through their complete acceptance or rejection into the organization. This often requires conducting additional research. Suchman (1967, 31) identified the following six ingredients as essential for an evaluation to be successful:

1. Clear identification of the change goals that are being evaluated.
2. Analysis of the organizational or societal problem with which the activity was designed to cope.
3. Thorough description and definition of the change activities.
4. Measurement of the degree of change that took place.
5. Determination of whether the observed change is due to the activity or to some other cause.
6. Some indication of the durability of the effects.

In *Phase VII,* the best parts of the change actions are made part of the continuing operating climate of the group. Those actions that meet with majority acceptance and approval can be expected to eventually become part of the longer-term culture of the organization; they will become accepted as "part of the way we do things around here," and passed on to the new members of the group. Where actions result in only superficial or cosmetic change, the members of the group must devise and try new change initiatives in a dynamic process of continuous evolution.

Goals of Action Research

A primary goal of action research is to help come up with the information that is needed for an action. This information is often called "practical" or "everyday" knowledge. It has particular value in the following four government applications:

1. Action research is well suited as a method of *identifying citizen needs* in a community, with the added benefit of producing potential solutions for attaining the resources necessary to meet those needs.
2. Through its ability to generate knowledge, it is an excellent way of gaining the guidance necessary to *design the most effective programs* to meet citizen needs.
3. Action research, through its interventionist nature, is a highly appropriate means of carrying out organizational development activities and programs.
4. Finally, following in the tradition of early emancipatory theory, action research can play a very important role in community development and redevelopment efforts.

Achieving the Goals

To achieve their goal, action researchers gather data in many different ways. Among the most commonly used tools are group discussions, role playing, unstructured interviews, and case discussions. Data-gathering methods identified by Argyris, Putnam, and Smith (1985) include the following tools: Observations accompanied by audiotaping, interviews, action experiments, and participant-written cases.

They noted that, most often, action researchers rely on all four methods, but may have different purposes in mind when they select one over another. Common to all of these and other data-gathering methods used in action research are the following three critical characteristics:

1. The data must be generated in a way that makes participants feel causally responsible for them.
2. Each method is structured to elicit data on how participants actually act, and on what they are thinking and feeling at the time.
3. Action experiments (such as role playing) should be used to "unfreeze" people's reasoning and reactions.

In all of the ways that data are gathered in an action research or action science project, the key to gathering the needed data is to *engage participants in free and open narrative discussions.* When people are discussing the problems of their organization, they are engaging in a cathartic activity. In this way, "talk *is* action" (Argyris, Putnam, and Smith 1985, 57).

Applying the Action Research Model

Action research takes place in a series of steps that can be grouped into three distinct phases. The first phase, *planning,* includes Steps 1, 2, and 3: identify and understand the problem, define the problem and the proposed intervention, and develop measurements. Phase II, *action,* is the critical step in the process; it includes only the fourth step, implementing and observing. Finally, Phase III, *reflection,* covers Steps 5 and 6, evaluation and transition (Kuhne and Quigley 1997). The relationships between the six steps and three phases are displayed in Figure 28.3.

Phase I involves three key preliminary steps: (1) developing an *understanding* of a problem, (2) defining and *planning* an action research project, and (3) determining the *measurements* to be used. *Developing an understanding of the p*roblem is the important first research step. It involves conducting extensive interviews with members of the group in order to bring out the subjects' perceptions on the problem and its possible cause or causes. In collaborative research such as this, the researcher's perception of the problem is not nearly as important as how the participants view it. Otherwise, the researcher may not know if he or she is a part of the problem. Gathering this information may involve brainstorming with participants and other researchers, exploring the published professional literature, and often, simple observation of the group. Finally, the researcher and group participants must decide together whether the problem is significant enough to warrant the study.

Defining and planning the project is the second step in Phase I of the action research process. The most important part of planning is deciding how to deal with the problem at hand. In a collaborative research activity, this means getting the participants to agree on the intervention program they want applied, and organizing the group for action. The end result of this step is the generation of a *readiness to accept change* among the members of the group. Finally, it also entails agreeing on how the participants are to be involved in the action phase of the process.

Determining the measurements is the third step in this phase; it is the diagnostic stage of action research. In order to know if something has been improved, if it is "better" in some

Planning Phase   **Action Phase**   **Contemplation Phase**

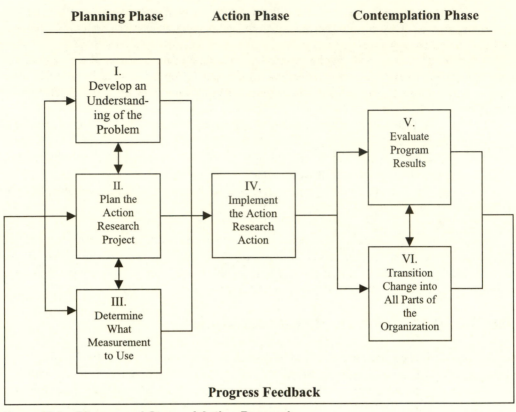

Figure 28.3   **Phases and Steps of Action Research**
Source: Kuhne and Quigley 1997, 28.

way, the researcher must have a *benchmark* from which to measure any change. A benchmark is a clear, comprehensive description of the way things are. It includes specifying what will be measured during the evaluation stage of the action research. In addition to knowing what to measure, it is also necessary to determine *when* to measure. How long should the intervention experiment run before evaluation? There is no set answer to this question; timing is a function of the severity of the problem and the degree of participatory involvement of the participants.

Lewin described this process in his 1947 paper on *Frontiers in Group Dynamics* (in Cartwright 1951, 224). He encouraged analysts to not think in terms of a goal to be reached when discussing the procedures for achieving a desired state of affairs, but instead, consider it to be an evolutionary change from the present level in the group to a desired position.

The single step that makes up Phase II, the *action phase,* of an action research project is *implementing* the change action. This is the task of the members of the group, not the researcher. The researcher's role is to function as a reference point, providing methodological advice if asked, and not as a leader or instigator of the action; action research is *participatory* research. Another important aspect of the researcher's role in this phase is to keep the group moving according to their initial plan. If the plan is not an appropriate intervention or change, the way to make sure it meets the group's objectives is to plan and initiate a second iteration of the entire system. Finally, the researcher must maintain good records of the implementation of the intervention, its effects, and how and in what form changes are generated.

Phase III is the *reflection* part of an action research project. It includes the last two steps: (5) *evaluating results,* and (6) *transitioning the change into the group or organization.* Step 5 may take as long as or longer than the actual implementation of the action. All aspects of the data collected before and during the action phase must be studied. The researcher must work closely with group participants to evaluate what the data reveal about the problem and the intervention. This means determining whether the success criteria agreed upon in Step 3 were met, and if any tangible gains have taken place. If the problem is resolved, end the project; if not, repeat a second—or more—cycle. Action research cycles should continue until the desired change is accepted and functioning. The evaluation process has been described in the following way:

> What we evaluate is the action hypothesis that defined program activities will achieve specified, desired objectives through their ability to influence those intervening processes that affect the occurrence of these objectives. . . . An understanding of all three factors—program, objective, and intervening process—is essential to the conduct of (evaluation). (Suchman 1967, 177)

The last step in the process is *reflecting on the project.* This is an in-depth interpretation of the entire project, one that includes *thinking* about what happened and what did not. It includes answering such questions as: Did the project produce promising results? Did the observed changes reflect what actually happened? Should another cycle of action research be initiated? Kuhne and Quigley (1997, 34) describe this step as a process of "analyzing outcomes and revising plans for another cycle of acting."

Step 6 also involves putting together a final report of the entire process for group participants and any other researcher/participant team planning for a similar intervention of their own. Thus, the report must be complete, produced in a form that everyone can understand, and that helps to add to theoretical knowledge of change in groups and organizations and the action research process in general.

Summary

Action research is a way of initiating *change* in social systems—societies, communities, organizations, or groups—by involving members of the group in the research process. It does this through a process that focuses first on researching the way the group functions, identifying the problem, and helping members of the group to bring about the needed change that they perceive is right for them.

An emphasis on encouraging citizen participation is one of the reasons why action research is interesting to public administrators. Despite this interest, however, very little pure action research is conducted directly by political scientists. On the other hand, the action research approach has become an accepted research approach among social psychologists, sociologists, social workers, and educators, many of whom plan and conduct research on topics of interest to public administrators and managers of nonprofit organizations.

Today, at least five different models of action research are in use by researchers in the human and administrative sciences: (1) traditional action research, (2) participatory action research, (3) empowerment research, (4) feminist research, and (5) action science or action inquiry.

Discussion Questions

1. What is action research?
2. Discuss the contributions of John Dewey and Kurt Lewin to action research.
3. Name the five different models of action research.
4. Why is the action science model seen most often in political science research?
5. How is action research related to critical theory?
6. What are the key themes in action research?
7. Discuss the seven phases of action research.
8. Name several common goals for action research.
9. Discuss how you would go about initiating an action research project.
10. How are data collected in an action research project?

Additional Reading

Argyris, Chris, Robert Putnam, and Diana McLain Smith 1985. *Action Science*. San Francisco: Jossey-Bass.

Geuss, Raymond. 1981. *The Idea of a Critical Theory: Habermas and the Frankfurt School*. Cambridge: Cambridge University Press.

Lippitt, Ronald, Jeanne Watson, and Bruce Westley. 1958. *The Dynamics of Planned Change*. New York: Harcourt, Brace.

Marrow, Alfred J. 1977. *The Practical Theorist: The Life and Work of Kurt Lewin*. New York: Teachers College Press (Columbia University).

Part 6

Analyzing Data and Writing a Research Report

29 Analysis Methods for Qualitative Data

The primary building block of all research is *data*. Data can take many different forms. In its most irreducible form, data can be quantitative or qualitative. Increasingly, and in more and more disciplines, data employed in political science research projects exists in *both* quantitative and qualitative form. In addition to different forms, data may be gathered in many different ways—by interview, questionnaire, overt or covert observation, by analysis of documents or artifacts, or by the subjective experiences of the researcher, to name only the most commonly encountered data collection methods (Martin 2000). Regardless of its form or how it is gathered, in its raw state data has little or no intrinsic meaning. Data must be *processed, analyzed*, and *interpreted* by a researcher before it takes on any rational sense.

The *analysis* processes for quantitative and qualitative research data are similar in some ways, but different in others. Similarities include (1) data are not just *there;* they must be collected in some way by a researcher, (2) when processed, both quantitative and qualitative data can be used for inference, (3) comparative analyses are used with both data types, and (4) researchers are concerned with both the reliability and validity of all data.

Quantitative data differ from qualitative data primarily in the way they are tabulated, collated, and processed. Quantitative data are typically computer-processed and analyzed with a variety of standard statistical tests. These tests are applied for one or more of the following purposes: (1) to describe a dataset, (2) to generate hypotheses through a process of association testing, and (3) to test hypotheses (Fitz-Gibbon and Morris 1987).

Qualitative data, on the other hand, exhibit greater variety in both form and context. They can also be evaluated and interpreted in a variety of ways. Qualitative data can be words, pictures, artifacts, music scores, etc. Furthermore, each of the several different analysis approaches has its own underlying purpose, and each often produces a different outcome. Software has been developed that now makes it possible to use computers for analysis of qualitative data. This chapter discusses a few of the more prevalent ways of analyzing qualitative data, and includes three separate, but similar, processing models.

What Are Qualitative Data?

Qualitative data are data that have been gathered during the conduct of interpretive or "post-positivist" research studies. They exist most often as some sort of narrative. Thus, they can be written text, transcripts of conversations or interviews, transcripts of therapeutic or consultive interviews, records of legal trials, transcripts of focus group discussions. They can exist as historical or literary documents, ethnographic field notes, diaries, newspaper clippings, or magazine and journal articles. They can also be in the form of photographs, maps, illustrations, or paintings, musical scores, tape recordings, films, or any other nonquantitative or quantitative source. Most of the time, however, qualitative research data exist as collections of rough field notes. Miles and Huberman (1998, 182) suggested that qualitative data exist as "the essences of people, objects, and situations." In their discussion, *essences* refers to the reactions and interpretations that researchers take away from the raw experiences of a research encounter or situation. A researcher must process, analyze, and interpret these essences in order to transform them into a meaningful conclusion.

All unprocessed and uninterrupted data are called *raw data*. Raw quantitative data are the set of numbers arranged according to values assigned by a researcher to optional responses to questions, or as counts of event occurrences. Raw qualitative data exist most often as a body of unorganized, unstructured field notes or narrative; that is, they exist in the form of words or other symbols, but not numbers. The following brief statement bears emphasizing: *All data must be analyzed and interpreted before they have meaning.*

Components of Qualitative Data Analysis

There are two parts to the analysis and interpretation of qualitative data. The first is *data management;* the second is *data analysis* (Miles and Huberman 1998). Data management includes three important steps. First, managing data begins with organizing the collection process. This includes preplanning, careful selection of the sample or situation to be included in the study, and making sure that entry into and acceptance by the study group is achieved. The researcher must maintain a concise record of the steps and processes taken throughout the study. A concise summary of this record must be included in the final research report under the heading of *methodology.*

The second step in this process is designing a system for storage of the collected data. In the past, this meant devising a system of index cards, preparing analytical memorandums, and careful categorical coding—in what some analysts referred to as the *clerical* portion of qualitative research. It was laborious and time-consuming. Today, however, computer software programs are increasingly taking the place of this unappealing activity. A key activity in this half of the management/analysis process is devising a system for retrieving data for comparative analyses and other interpretive activities. It is important to remember the process because some researchers still work this way:

> Only a few short decades ago, QDA (qualitative data analysis) was purely a manual process. Bits of data were copied onto cards, using the traditional technique of cutting and pasting. These cards were filed under appropriate categories generated by the researcher . . . [who] then strove to link the data and connect categories through these physical materials and manipulations, to produce meaningful reflections of the phenomena being studied. The process was a daunting one for researchers. Researchers had to manage overwhelming compilations of material, make analytical decisions that were rarely clear or simple, and work through the tedious and frustrating processes of coding, deriving themes, and building theories. (Este, Sieppert, and Barsky 1998, 138)

The second half of the interpretation process is the actual analysis of data. This phase of the interpretation process also includes three activities: (1) data reduction, (2) data display, and

(3) drawing conclusions from the data. First, data reduction is almost always a crucial stage in the interpretation process. It involves selecting the salient themes and constructs that emerge from the data. Remember: not every bit of data can be its own category; if this were true, the research report would never be written. Qualitative investigations have been known to generate thousands of pages of records. From that mass of unconnected narrative, the researcher must choose or devise a conceptual framework. This framework will be constructed of key themes, clusters, and summaries.

The next part of the analysis phase is *data display.* In the chapters on quantitative research methods, this was discussed as the use of descriptive and summary statistics, and presenting information in charts, graphs, and tables. These same graphic displays are often used to present qualitative data. Whatever research approach is followed, the objective is to be able to present findings as an organized, focused collection of pertinent information, out of which a researcher—and a reader—can draw relevant conclusions.

Finally, drawing conclusions forces the researcher to *interpret* the results of the study. It is not enough simply to present the data as they appear, even if they have been effectively organized, categorized, and structured. The research must explain what the data *mean* in relation to the study design and objectives, and in terms of their contribution to theory.

Beginning the Analysis

The analysis and interpretation of qualitative data begins with bringing the raw data into some level of order. First, the researcher identifies and selects a set of relevant *categories* or *classes* under which to sort the data. Comparing the data across categories—a step that is typically used in the testing of hypotheses—often follows the initial comparing phase of the analysis. Strauss and Corbin (1998) call this a process of *conceptualizing.* Conceptualizing means reducing the often-bulky amounts of raw data into workable, ordered bits of information that the researcher can manage with confidence. Kvale (1996) described this act of data categorization as a key qualitative research activity, and one that most distinguishes qualitative strategies from quantitative research.

Researchers can best analyze and interpret raw data if they employ some orderly process. Both a nine-step and a twelve-step data analysis process are discussed below. Figure 29.1 displays a model of the nine-step process.

A Nine-Step Analysis Process

This nine-step process for analyzing and interpreting qualitative data has its roots in the three-fold grounded theory interpretation models of Strauss and Corbin (1990), Neuman (2000), and information provided in Miles and Huberman (1994 and 1998). Each of the nine steps is discussed in more detail below.

Step 1. Preliminary Analysis for Patterns and Structure

Order and structure must be brought to all data if they are ultimately to become *information.* Miles and Huberman (1994) refer to order—the patterns or themes in textual qualitative data— as "Gestalts." This is because they pull together a variety of smaller portions of data into larger "wholes."

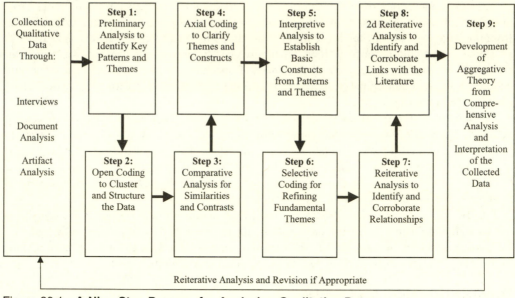

Figure 29.1   **A Nine-Step Process for Analyzing Qualitative Data**

A key task of the qualitative researcher is sorting and resorting data to identify *patterns,* from which meaning and definition can be established. Finding patterns in the data is a subjective process, and one that often comes naturally to the researcher. Miles and Huberman see this as a potential problem, however, and offer the following caveat:

> The human mind finds patterns so quickly and easily that it needs no how-to advice. Patterns just "happen," almost too quickly. The important thing, rather, is to be able to (a) see *real* added evidence in the same pattern, [and] (b) remain open to disconfirming evidence when it appears. (Miles and Huberman 1994, 216)

Step 2. Open Coding to Form Clusters and Identify Themes

A key activity in all qualitative data analysis is *clustering.* This entails putting things that are like each other together into groupings or classes. These may be pre-existing classes, although this is not the recommended way to begin. More often, the categories are groupings that the researcher creates from smaller collections of ideas that emerge from the data. Coding and categorization go hand in hand during this phase of the analysis.

Straus and Corbin (1990) and Glaser (1992) identified the coding process that occurs in the first phase of the analysis as *open* or *substantive* coding. The goal of this first, open coding process is to begin to form the raw data into meaningful categories with a structure that will guide the researcher in all subsequent analyses, and any future gathering of more data.

There are no limits to how many codes are assigned during the open coding phase, or to the inclusiveness (breadth) of each. Miles and Huberman (1994, 219) described the process as a necessary task that can be "applied at many levels of qualitative data; at the level of events or acts, of individual actors, of processes, of settings or locales, of sites as wholes."

In qualitative research, usually little or no categorization is done prior to the data being collected. The categorical codes that emerge at this time are taken from the data they embrace. However, the researcher should keep in mind that one of the goals of coding and categorization is the *reduction* of data into more manageable sets.

Step 3. Comparative Analysis for Similarities and Contrasts

Qualitative research studies usually require some comparative analysis of the collected data. In grounded theory research, comparisons are an integral part of the entire analysis process. Both Strauss and Corbin (1990) and Glaser (1992) recommended that comparative analysis should be an integral step in all studies involving qualitative data. Furthermore, they urged that previously gathered data be continuously compared with every bit of new data. Ragin and Zaret (1983) also considered comparative research to be one of the research tactics that distinguish research on social groups.

Neuman (2000) identified comparison as a "central process" to the analysis of all data. In this central role, comparative analysis has two broad objectives: the first is to find cases or evidence that belong together, based on one or more relevant characteristics. The second is to isolate anomalies in the data—events or cases that do not fit a pattern. Similarities enable the researcher to place the data within their proper category, as well as to develop new categorical codes that embrace the unclassified phenomenon. Anomalies are the distinct characteristics that are central to the research problem; finding distinctive differences in data is like a prospector finding the "mother lode."

Miles and Huberman considered the process of comparative analysis to be a part of their *drawing and verifying conclusions* step in the analysis of qualitative data. Refuting critics whom they accused of considering the act of making comparisons "odious," they responded:

> Comparison is a time-honored, classic way to test a conclusion. We draw a contrast or make a comparison between two sets of things—persons, roles, activities, cases as a whole—that are known to differ in some other important respect. This is the "method of differences," which goes back to Aristotle if not further. (Miles and Huberman 1994, 254)

They also offered the following caveats to the use of comparisons:

1. "Mindless comparisons are useless." Researchers must be sure that their comparisons are the "right" ones, and that they make sense to use them in the analysis.
2. Comparisons should also extend beyond the data alone. They should also be compared with what the researcher knows about the things being studied.
3. Researchers should pause before including a comparison in a research report to ask themselves, "How big must a difference be before it makes a difference?" and "How do I know that?"
4. With qualitative comparisons, researchers are concerned with the *practical significance* of the data; they cannot apply the statistical significance tests that are available in quantitative studies.

Strauss and Corbin (1998, 73) placed great importance on the activity of comparative analysis. In their opinion, making comparisons is an integral activity that should be used at any and all steps in the data analysis process. They define the comparative analysis process as "an analytical tool used to stimulate thinking about properties and dimensions of categories." They considered the act of making comparisons to be one of the two tasks that are essential for development of theory in qualitative research; the other essential task is *asking questions.*

Step 4. Axial Coding to Clarify Constructs and Themes

Axial coding affords the researcher a second opportunity to introduce order and structure into the initially coded data. Axial coding can use pre-established codes such as the six categories suggested by Strauss and Corbin (1990), or it can be freely employed without any imposed structure. Strauss and Corbin added their six categories when they found that the lack of structure at this point made it difficult for beginning researchers to produce clear and cogent theory from the data. Retaining the open and substantive coding levels, they proposed that a third, intermediate step in the coding/analysis process be added. They called this intermediate step "*axial coding*" (Kendall 1999). This step was proposed as a way to "demystify" the grounded theory process. It requires the researcher to place all the initially "open-coded" data into these six specified categories: (1) *conditions,* (2) *phenomena,* (3) *context,* (4) *intervening conditions,* (5) *actions/strategies,* and (6) *consequences.*

These categories require the researcher to look for antecedents that lead to the particular event or circumstance, in addition to any resulting consequences. It also forces the researcher to re-examine the strategies and processes involved in both the target organization and the research design.

Step 5. Interpretive Analysis to Establish Basic Constructs

In this stage the researcher reviews the coded data to determine whether any categorical constructs make better intuitive sense as two or more factors rather than the one originally assigned. "Unbundling" means that each major category should be re-examined to see if it is really two or more categorical constructs. If an "unbundling" is warranted, care must also be taken to apply the characteristics originally assigned to the category to each of the newly established categories.

Step 6. Selective Coding for Refining Themes

Researchers must establish categories and codes for the major and minor constructs within the data, develop meaningful ideas about the data in context, edit and make critical interpretations, and—perhaps most important—generate ideas and theories from them.

Steps 7 and 8. Reiterative Analysis to Identify Relationships

A key activity in this process is identifying *relationships* between constructs and groupings. One way to do this is to diagram the data as a set of boxes, circles, arrows, and lines. The "bathtubs and beer barrels" method can be used for this task. Bathtubs (large ovals) are used to represent key ideas, while beer barrels (smaller circles) are used to display antecedents and contributing components or factors, and to indicate effects and consequences. Lines indicate relationships, with arrows showing the direction of the influence or relationship. Diagrams such as these make it clear what sorts of relationships, if any, exist between two or more ideas, patterns, constructs, and groupings. Developing diagrams and relationship charts is an important part of the qualitative analysis procedure.

Another procedure sometimes used for this purpose is what is known as *power* or *influence analysis.* In this process, the researcher first collects data observing the way people interact or by questioning them on their perceptions of such factors as power or influence in the organization. The researcher can then draw a diagram or chart to illustrate the interactions, relationships, and responses to others within a group or other social setting. Examples of graphic displays of this type include context charts, linkage patterns and knowledge flowcharts, and role and power charts.

Step 9. Developing Theory

In this last step researchers generate theory from their analysis. It is important to remember that theory is based on the researcher's interpretation of the data, in what is a process diametrically opposed to the positivist tradition.

A Twelve-Point Scheme for the Analysis of Qualitative Data

Qualitative data gathering and analysis is carried out in a logical sequence of steps. Jones (1996) has organized this sequence into the twelve-step process shown in Figure 29.2. The twelve steps fall into two equal halves, each with six steps: the first half of the process, involving Steps 1 through 6, is the *preparatory* half, while Steps 7 through 12 constitute the *analysis and report* portion of the analysis procedure.

Part I. Preparing for Qualitative Research

Steps 1 and 2—*define the research problem* and *establish research objectives*—are the initial activities in all research designs. Step 3, *do your homework,* means becoming conversant with the full nature of the subject or topic of interest. Interviews with a few key informants and extensive analysis of the relevant literature are the activities often used in this step.

Step 4—*plan the data-gathering process*—should occur only after the researcher has developed a working familiarity with the subject and study group. The plan should include a preliminary list of the behaviors to be observed, the subjects to be interviewed, a list of the topics to be covered in the interviews, a preliminary coding scheme, and a schedule for each following step in the research process.

Steps 5 and 6—*gaining entry into the group* and *becoming immersed in the setting*—are closely related activities; in fact, they often occur simultaneously. While these are more appropriately tasks to use in ethnographic research, they are also important in other qualitative research designs. For example, researchers conducting a study of the operating climate within a government agency must first gain permission of the agency director and the support of compliance of both the managers and agency staff.

PART I:

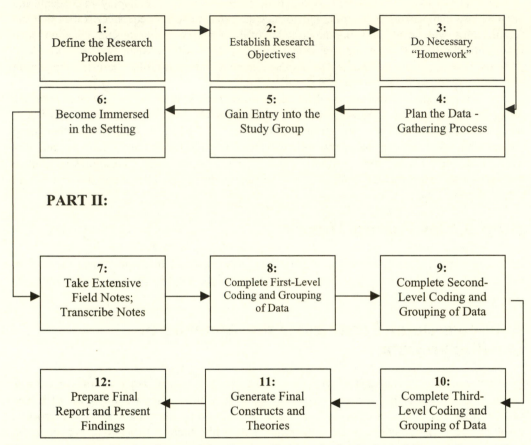

PART II:

Figure 29.2 **The Twelve Steps of Qualitative Fieldwork, Analysis and Report Preparation**
Source: Jones 1996.

Part II. Analyzing and Reporting

The first activity in the second half of the research process is Step 7, *taking extensive field notes*. *Field notes* are the notes, recordings, reminders, and other subjective reporting that the research records while observing behaviors or interviewing respondents. Not surprisingly, they are the records produced during the process of conducting *field research*. Field research is what is done when researchers want to know something about people, understanding behaviors, or describing a group of people who interact in some way (Neuman 2000). Field notes are the detailed written reports and/or diagrams or pictures of what the researcher sees and hears. The term used to describe the required detail needed in field notes is "thick description." Finally, field notes should be written down or transcribed on a regular basis, as soon as possible after the phenomenon occurs.

Taking good field notes is not an easy process; the researcher must make a conscious effort to devote the time and effort necessary to produce good notes because, without them, the final report of the research can only be second rate. Preparing field notes can be a boring, laborious task that requires self-discipline to be done correctly. The notes contain extensive descriptive detail drawn from memory. Researchers must make it a daily habit—better yet, a *compulsion*—to write their notes every day, and to begin to transcribe them immediately after leaving the field. Field notes must be neat and organized because "the researcher will return to them over and over again. Once written, the notes are private and valuable. A researcher treats them with care and protects confidentiality" (Neuman 2000, 363).

An example of how difficult it can be to listen to informants in the field (that is, to gather data) and to then transcribe those narratives into meaningful field notes can be found in Jurich's (2001) story of her lengthy field research project with Native Americans on a South Dakota reservation. She explained her methodological difficulties as follows:

> I listened to stories during the day and late into the night, often falling asleep long before conversations were ended. I learned early on that questions were likely to be considered interrogation, intrusive, and were not a frequent form of interaction. So I asked few questions. . . . The stories would get summarized in (my) notebooks. . . . I worked hard to listen and remember, to record as completely as I could the substance of what was said. More often, though, the field notes were thick descriptions of my own experiences of going places and engaging in the practices of reservation life, describing social interaction and processes that were part of my daily life. (Jurich 2001, S152)

Once field notes are transcribed into organized records of the researcher's observations or interviews, they must then be put to a preliminary, interpretive analysis. This occurs during Steps 8 through 11. Analysis is an ongoing process that begins during the first venture into the field experience, continues until a final set of codes, categories, and constructs is established, and ends with production of the final report of the research. Miles and Huberman (1994) recommend employing a series of reporting guides or work sheets to ensure that this portion of the process is complete. These include the following: (1) a contact summary, (2) a summary of each document analyzed in the study, (3) first-, second-, and third-level coding and grouping of constructs, patterns, or factors discovered in the data, and (4) a final detailed summary of the site in which the activities, behaviors, and events were studied.

Step 8, *first-level coding and grouping of data,* begins with preparation of contact summaries and a summary of each document, if any, analyzed for the study. The contact summary is usually nothing more than a single sheet that contains answers to a set of focusing or summary questions about each subject contacted in the study. It often includes demographic information, indications of relative position in the group under study, etc. It is used to ensure continuity in the treatment of responses from all contacts. The document summary is applicable only when documents of any type are acquired for analysis at the research site. The purpose of this guide is to establish a record of the document's significance and how it relates to observations, interviews, or final analysis.

First-level coding is done to develop the initial descriptive codes around which all subsequent data will be organized or grouped. These codes are abbreviations that establish descriptive categories or groupings in the data. Miles and Huberman (1994, 56) have defined a *code* as "an abbreviation or symbol applied to a segment of words—most often a sentence or paragraph of transcribed field notes—in order to *classify* the words."

Codes should be considered as *categories.* As such, they are *retrieval* and *organizing devices* that allow the analyst to spot quickly, pull out, then cluster all the segments relating to the particular question, hypothesis, concept, or theme. Clustering sets the stage for analysis.

Second-level, or pattern, coding takes place in Step 9 of the analysis process. Second-level coding involves establishing *interpretive codes.* Here, the researcher goes beyond simple description and begins to form interpretive labels for categories of behaviors. The goal at this point is to be able to read repeating patterns in the data.

Third-Level Coding, Step 10, involves *thematic development coding* of the data. This is also called *memoing.* Memoing refers to producing preliminary or partial summary reports for the personal use of the researcher or research team. These might, for example, be used to summarize a pattern or a theme in the data, and even be incorporated wholesale into the final analysis. At the third analysis level, the researcher begins to establish *explanatory* codes that link larger groups of patterns into what are called *themes.* These are the major constructs that will make up the central structure under which the final analysis will occur and be recorded.

Step 11, the final activity in the coding and analysis process, is a brief description of the events, members, circumstances, and other relevant information that can serve both as a summary of the data-gathering experience and memory jogger during the preparation of the final report.

The last step in this, as in any other type of research project, is to combine the notes, constructs, patterns, and themes, along with the researcher's analysis and synthesis, into some form of *research report.* This takes place in Step 12. This important step in the qualitative research process is not simply putting the researcher's field notes together in one cover. Rather, it involves a number of important activities:

> Assembling evidence, arguments, and conclusions into a report is always a crucial step; but more than in quantitative approaches, the careful crafting of evidence and explanation makes or breaks (qualitative) research. A researcher distills mountains of evidence into exposition and prepares extensive footnotes. She or he weaves together evidence and arguments to communicate a coherent, convincing picture to readers. (Neuman 2000, 395)

Analysis of Ethnographic Study Data

Ethnography is the study of groups of people in the settings in which they live, work, and/or play. To gather ethnographic data, researchers must gain entry into a social setting, earn and maintain the trust of members of the group, and observe and write narratives of everything that they see, hear, and feel. Ethnographic *data* are the content of researchers' field notes, while ethnographic *narratives* are researchers' descriptions of the interplay of individuals in groups, and how that interaction is influenced by the culture of the group or organization. The information contained in field notes consists of "rich descriptions" of the people, settings, and events observed by the participant researcher. They may also be tape recordings of subjects' life histories, opinions, dreams, etc. They may also be photographs, drawings, films, videotapes, artifacts, or written documents. Ethnographers use descriptions of these physical objects in their reports of social interactions.

Before an ethnographer sets a single word to paper he or she may have amassed hundreds of pages of notes, rough illustrations of relationships, and other descriptive narrative. Making sense of this mass of data, bringing order, structure, and explanation to the data, has long been the most laborious and tedious task of ethnographic research (Emerson, Fretz, and Shaw 1995). The model displayed in Figure 29.3 reveals the detailed nature of the steps followed in the analysis of ethnographic data.

The processes identified in the model are shown as individual activities. However, in actual

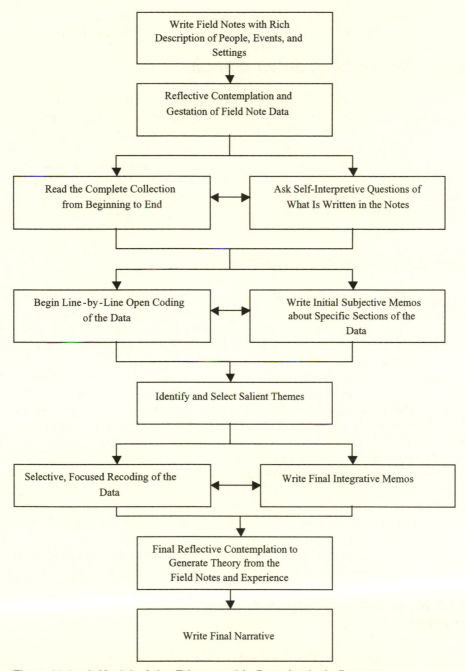

Write Field Notes with Rich Description of People, Events, and Settings

Reflective Contemplation and Gestation of Field Note Data

Read the Complete Collection from Beginning to End ⟷ Ask Self-Interpretive Questions of What Is Written in the Notes

Begin Line-by-Line Open Coding of the Data ⟷ Write Initial Subjective Memos about Specific Sections of the Data

Identify and Select Salient Themes

Selective, Focused Recoding of the Data ⟷ Write Final Integrative Memos

Final Reflective Contemplation to Generate Theory from the Field Notes and Experience

Write Final Narrative

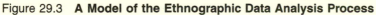

Figure 29.3 **A Model of the Ethnographic Data Analysis Process**

practice, some are best carried out in conjunction with others. Collectively, they take place in the following six analytical phases that culminate in writing of the research report.

Phase I. Reflective Contemplation

Once the data-collecting activity is complete, many researchers like to step away from their material to pause for a while and simply think about what they saw, heard, and took away from the experience. This is the act of *reflective contemplation*. During this quiet time away from the study site and data collection, ideas, insights, and preliminary interpretations are free to gestate in the mind of the researcher. After a brief period away from the data—too long and data will be lost from memory—the researcher returns to the data collection and begins a full reading of the material from beginning to end. It is likely that this experience gives the researcher his or her first "big picture" of everything that has occurred during the research study.

Phase II. Interpretive Questioning

Interpretive questioning is the process of making marginal notes or comments on separate pages for guidance in the continuation of reading and interpreting. It begins during the first complete reading of field notes that follows reflective contemplation about what has been experienced and accomplished during the data gathering. It involves writing questioning notes that help guide the development of structure and organization.

These questions can also serve as suggestions for subsequent open coding of the data. They can include any self-directive questions, suggestions for groupings, and even ideas for subsequent coding. The following sorts of questions are typical examples of questions that might be asked at this time (Emerson, Fretz, and Shaw 1995, 146):

- What are people doing in this setting?
- What are they trying to accomplish? What are they avoiding?
- How, exactly, do they go about these behaviors?
- What sorts of things do people say to each other?
- How do people understand what is going on in their group or society?
- What assumptions guide their behavior?
- What was going on here? What did I learn about them when I made these notes?
- Why did I include this information?

Phase III. Open Coding and Interpretive Memoing

This process also begins during the initial full reading of the data collection. The researcher writes identifying words or phrases to describe the portions of data that comprise relevant categories or classes of phenomena. The codes themselves should be detailed enough to inform the researcher to what they apply, without having to resort to looking up the meaning of a code in a reference file every time it appears. Also, it is important to remember that codes should emerge from the data itself; they are not artificial constructs created by the researcher.

Both quantitative and qualitative data-gathering processes are used in this phase. Qualitative methodology consists of construction techniques (stories from supplied cartoon situations), and sentence completion techniques. These projective techniques are employed to draw out the personal perceptions and attitudes of owners and managers of small businesses. These techniques—more so than quantitative methods—force the respondent to respond in a manner that reflects his or her own need/value system (Kassarjian and Kassarjian 1988).

The second part of this analysis phase is *interpretive memoing*. Memoing can be found in most research data analyses. In the open coding step, memos are written to record the insights and ideas that come to the researcher during the initial, top-to-bottom reading of the data collection. They may serve as suggestions for further analysis, references to relevant literature, personal reminders, subjective opinions, preliminary evaluations, or any such purpose. They should not be considered the final word on the data; the researcher still has much analytical work to do.

Together, initial open coding and memoing set the stage for the remainder of the analysis. At this stage in the process, however, it is important to remember that this is just the first pass through the data; changes are to be expected to occur at every subsequent phase. The need for flexibility at this stage is highlighted in the following statement:

> [I]nitial coding and memoing require the [researcher] to step back from the field setting to identify, develop, and modify the broader analytic themes and arguments. Early on [however], these efforts should remain flexible and open. (Emerson, Fretz, and Shaw 1995, 157)

Phase IV. Identification of Salient Themes in the Data

In this phase of the analysis the researcher should return to a broader view of the data collection in order to discern the core, reoccurring themes that he or she has found in the research data. At the same time, any linkages discovered between themes and constructs should be pointed out. Figure 29.4 illustrates how themes are shown to be linked to antecedent conditions and resulting consequences and transformations.

At the conclusion of this step, the researcher may elect to sort his or her field notes and/or memos into new groups that reflect the selected themes. This step can also be done during the final coding and memoing phase.

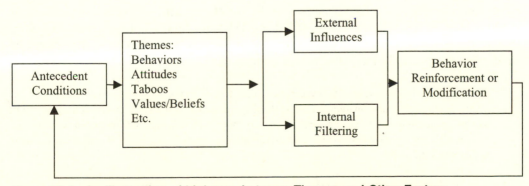

Figure 29.4 An Illustration of Linkages between Themes and Other Factors
Source: Emerson, Fretz, and Shaw 1995.

Phase V. Focused Coding and Interpretive Memoing

Focused coding—also called *selective coding*—is what Emerson, Fretz, and Shaw (1995) described as the product of a "fine-grained, line-by-line analysis of the notes." It often results in preparation of an outline of a first draft of an ethnographic narrative. As one of the last steps in the data analysis process, the purpose of focused coding is to begin to integrate the final categories into a coherent whole that addresses the central issue or issues of the study. It may include unbundling of previously formed categories, the formation of entirely new categories, or making no change whatsoever. Its purpose is to bring the researcher to a point where no new categories, characteristics, or relationships emerge from the data (Strauss and Corbin 1998).

Integrative memoing also takes place during the open coding phase. Integrative memos are the concrete manifestations of the researcher's thinking process at this stage. They are used to justify the decisions made during the selection of salient themes. Furthermore, memoing is done to provide a record of any conclusions, revisions, or insights that emerge from the second run-through of the data. Integrative memos may follow a single concept through the mass of data, connecting it with other categories as required. Or it may serve to integrate two or more concepts into a larger whole. Integrative memos that chronicle the background information of the study should also be written. These help to set the stage for analytical narrative writing, as well as providing a record of the researcher's role in the investigation.

Strauss and Corbin described three analytical tools that can facilitate the final integration process: (1) writing a story line, (2) applying diagrams and other graphic display techniques, and (3) reviewing and resorting the open memos. A *story line* is nothing more than a subjective summary of the project in the words of the researcher, without referring back to the data or memos. It should flow as a freely written narrative, much as if it were a life history of the project. At this point, details of the research are not critical; they can be inserted later. The overall purpose is to enable the researcher to take an "omniscient author" view of the experience, writing what he or she believes occurred, its meaning and its relevance. The story line is NOT the final interpretive ethnographic narrative, however. It should be considered just another interpretation guide for the researcher.

Diagrams and other graphic displays have long been important analysis tools. Miles and Huberman have offered important guidance in the use of diagrams, including descriptions and graphic examples of several different approaches. They warn, however, that diagrams and other graphic displays should never be used in an analysis without a description of the content of the display. They described the integrative capability of diagrams in the following terms:

> The display helps the writer see patterns; the first text (i.e., the first draft) makes sense of the display and suggests new analytic moves in the displayed data; a revised or extended display points to new relationships and explanations, leading to more differentiated and integrated text, and so on. Displays beget analyses, which then beget more powerful, suggestive displays. (Miles and Huberman 1998, 189)

Preparing diagrams and other graphic representations of ideas and their interrelationships is a valuable process for several reasons. First, it forces the researcher to step back from the complexity of the data to take a broader view of the study in its entirety. Second, it forces the researcher to establish collective constructs that embrace a variety of ideas and categories. And third, it forces the researcher to examine relationships between themes, constructs, and events.

Reviewing and re-sorting memos is a third way of arriving at a final integration of the data. Recall that memos are subjective notes prepared by the researcher during the review of the data. They contain the conclusions, questions, possible integrations, and perceived connections of themes and constructs as seen by the researcher. In one sense, then, they can be considered a reduced dataset. Some researchers use this opportunity to re-sort their memos into new categories that emerged from selective coding of the open-coded data. This provides a possible final structure and organization to guide the researcher in final writing of the report.

Phase VI. Final Analytical Contemplation to Generate Theory

The final step in the analysis of ethnographic research data is to reach closure by generating theory that is grounded in the study and its setting. While the concepts are similar, the theory generated by ethnographic research is not the same as the grounded theory method first described by Glaser and Strauss (1967) and modified by Strauss and Corbin (1998). Ethnographers do not "discover" theory in their data. Rather, they *create* theory during each and every step of their fieldwork and analysis. For ethnographers, theory generation occurs during the "reflexive" interplay between theory and data. Ethnographers introduce theory at every point in their studies. The key objective of this interactive process has been identified in the following way: "The goal of fieldwork . . . is to generate theory that grows out of or is directly relevant to activities occurring in the setting under study" (Emerson, Fretz, and Shaw 2000, 167).

Computer Analysis of Qualitative Data

There has been a dramatic growth in the use of computers in research and the availability of analysis software in the past several decades (Tak, Nield, and Becker 1999; Este, Sieppert, and Barsky 1998; Richards and Richards 1998; Miles and Huberman 1994; Weitzman and Miles 1995). In some research settings technology has simplified the many necessary but time-consuming and often-boring tasks of the data analysis process. However, qualitative researchers have not universally accepted this technology. As the following caveat suggests, these computers and software programs can help, but not supplant, data analysis:

> Computers and software are tools that facilitate qualitative analysis, but they do not really do the analysis. Qualitative software programs facilitate data storage, coding, retrieval, comparing and linking—but human beings do the analysis. . . . [A]nalysis programs speed up the process of locating coded themes, grouping data together in categories, and comparing passages in transcripts or incidents from field notes. But the qualitative analyst doing content analysis must still decide what things go together to form a pattern, what constitutes a theme, what to name it, and what meanings to extract from case studies. . . . While computers can play a role in qualitative analysis as they do in quantitative analysis, they cannot provide the creativity and intelligence that makes each qualitative analysis unique. (Patton 2002, 272)

Although today's computer programs are capable of processing large volumes of text material and records, sorting and indexing the data, and retrieving information from a variety of different directions, few researchers have used the qualitative-data analysis programs that are presently available (Richards and Richards 1998). Instead, most data coding, sorting, categorizing, and analysis is still done the way it has been done for more than a hundred years—by hand.

This section provides a brief introduction to the concept of computer analysis, using a single program package for an illustration. If readers seek more information about these programs they are encouraged to refer to one of several published reviews, such as *Computer Programs for Qualitative Data Analysis* by Weitzman and Miles (1995). Miles and Huberman (1994) included a valuable point-by-point comparison of a dozen or more commercially available analysis programs in their text on qualitative data analysis. Richards and Richards (1998) provided a useful introduction to the theoretical underpinnings of computer software programs for analyzing qualitative data, but without evaluating many specific programs.

In the taxonomy of analysis software suggested by Richards and Richards, software is divided into two broad classifications: (1) general-purpose software packages, and (2) special-purpose software developed specifically for data analysis. General-purpose packages include standard word-processing programs, database management systems, and text-search software. Richards and Richards identified five categories of special-purpose software:

- Code and retrieve software.
- Rule-based, theory-building systems.
- Logic-based systems.
- Index-based systems.
- Conceptual, or semantic, network systems.

Of these, the two approaches that seem to offer the most promise at this time are logic-based systems and conceptual network systems. Richards and Richards provided an extensive review of a logic-based system they authored, NUD*IST (*nonnumerical unstructured data indexing, searching, and theorizing*).

NUD*IST allows the user to code themes and categories by simply attaching labels to segments of the text (Tak, Nield, and Becker 1999). Like a majority of the systems discussed by Richards and Richards, NUD*IST is built around a code-and-retrieve facility. It has been expanded to include a number of different optional processes—a feature that may have turned out to be one of the program's greatest faults. Richards and Richards offered this caveat about their program:

> NUD*IST appears, compared with the other systems . . . as a rather awkward hybrid, containing features of code-and-retrieve, ways of handling production-rule and other types of conceptual-level reasoning, conceptual representations alternative to conceptual network systems, and database storage facilities, all interacting through interlocking tools. . . . And, perhaps most important, the software offers many ways for a researcher never to finish a study. (Richards and Richards 1998, 237)

Despite the potentially confusing complexity of NUD*IST, it has become one of the most, if not the most, popular computer software program for analysis of qualitative data. It is particularly popular in education, nursing and other medical studies, and some sociological applications. It seems to be used less often in ethnographic studies, and is hardly ever seen in political science research. Despite its slow adoption, a few innovators in political science and nongovernment organization research have started to test its capabilities.

The second software program to receive special mention by Richards and Richards was the conceptual network system ATLAS/ti, developed in Germany during the 1980s, when most of the work on analysis software was underway. ATLAS is built on a code-and-retrieve foundation, to which has been added an excellent memoing capability; codes can be assigned to memos as well as the original text. Its distinguishing feature, however, is its ability to create conceptual graphic displays that show relationships and linkages. In addition to ATLAS's sophisticated text-retrieval system is a support system of graphic tools that "support subtle exploration of text via a visually immediate interface that relates the text to the systems or theories in the [setting] being studied" (Richard and Richards 1998, 240).

In conclusion, the application of special-purpose software packages for qualitative data analysis is probably here to stay. As more and more professional researchers discover the capabilities of the packages and more students are exposed to them in their research methods classes, this growth in use should accelerate. As of today, however, owing to their complexity—due in large part to their extensive capabilities—it is likely that most researchers will still analyze their data using traditional, minimal techniques and processes.

Summary

Conducting any qualitative research is a time-consuming, complicated, and often-confusing task. One of the most problematic components of the process has been the task of analyzing qualitative data. The *analysis* processes for quantitative and qualitative research data are similar in some ways, but different in others. Similarities include (1) data are not just *there;* they must be collected in some way by a researcher; (2) when processed, both quantitative and qualitative data can be used for inference; (3) comparative analyses are used with both data types; and (4) researchers are concerned with both the reliability and validity of all data.

Quantitative data differs from qualitative data primarily in the way they are tabulated, collated, and processed. Quantitative data are typically computer-processed and analyzed with a variety of standard statistical tests. These tests are applied for one or more of the following purposes: (1) to describe a dataset, (2) to generate hypotheses, and (3) to test hypotheses.

Qualitative data, on the other hand, exhibit variety in both form and context. They can also be evaluated and interpreted in a variety of ways. Qualitative data can be words, pictures, artifacts, music scores, etc. Furthermore, each of the several different analysis approaches has its own underlying purpose, and each often produces a different outcome.

Qualitative data are data that have been gathered during the conduct of interpretive or "postpositivist" research studies. They can be written text, transcripts of conversations or interviews, transcripts of therapeutic or consultive interviews, records of legal trials, transcripts of focus group discussions. They can exist as historical or literary documents, ethnographic field notes, diaries, newspaper clippings, or magazine and journal articles. They can also be in the form of photographs, maps, illustrations, or paintings, musical scores, tape recordings, films, or any other nonquantitative or quantitative source.

There are two parts to the interpretation and analysis of qualitative data. The first is *data management;* the second is *data analysis*. Many different techniques and strategies have been developed for analyzing qualitative data; three are discussed in this chapter. The first is a nine-step process; the second follows twelve steps divided into two halves. The third was developed by anthropologists for analyzing ethnographic data.

Advances in computer software have resulted in a number of different special-purpose software packages for analyzing qualitative data. Two popular programs discussed briefly here are NUD*IST and ATLAS/ti. Researchers studying political science and NGO management topics have been slow to adopt these new approaches for analysis, but are doing so in greater numbers.

Discussion Questions

1. How do qualitative data differ from quantitative data?
2. Name the components of qualitative data.
3. What are the two parts to the analysis and interpretation of qualitative data?
4. What is the first step in qualitative data analysis?
5. Name the nine steps in the qualitative data analysis process.
6. What is open coding? What is axial coding?
7. What is the purpose of data and concept comparison during analysis?
8. What is reiterative analysis?
9. Discuss the twelve-point scheme for data analysis.
10. Describe first-, second-, and third-level coding.
11. What role does reflective contemplation play in data interpretation?

Additional Reading

Denzin, Norman K., and Yvonna S. Lincoln, eds. 1998. *Collecting and Interpreting Qualitative Materials*. Thousand Oaks, CA: Sage.

Emerson, Robert M., Rachel I. Fretz, and Linda L. Shaw. 1995. *Writing Ethnographic Fieldnotes*. Chicago: University of Chicago Press.

Jones, Russell A. 1996. *Research Methods in the Social and Behavioral Sciences*. Sunderland, MA: Sinaur Associates.

Miles, Matthew B., and A. Michael Huberman. 1994. *Qualitative Data Analysis*. 2nd ed. Thousand Oaks, CA: Sage.

Neuman, W. Lawrence. 2000. *Social Research Methods*. 4th ed. Boston: Allyn and Bacon.

Qualitative Solutions and Research. 1997. *QSR NUD*IST 4 User Guide*. 2nd ed. Thousand Oaks, CA: SCOLARI (Sage).

30 Analyzing Texts, Documents, and Artifacts

Sources of research data include people, their words and actions, publications, material culture, and any item or symbol that communicates a message of any kind. Data-gathering methods range from watching the way that people act, asking them questions about their opinions, attitudes, or perceptions, reading what they have written, watching their movements, listening to their songs and other sounds, rummaging through their garbage, examining their tools and toys, deciphering their signs, symbols, or facial expressions—the list can go on and on. This chapter discusses some of the ways that researchers go about examining textual material, cultural artifacts, body language, and similar types of written and unwritten communications, records, documents, signs, and symbols.

For convenience, these different sources of research data can be grouped into four broad categories. The first is *written texts*. These include such sources as books, periodicals, narratives, reports, pamphlets, and other published materials. Collectively, this group of sources includes most, if not all, of the *mass media*. Research using these sources is often called *library research,* or *desk research.*

The second category is *formal and informal documents;* it includes personal messages and assorted types of archival information, such as personal notes and memos, government records and vital statistics, and other informal written materials, including e-mail. The third category of sources is made up of the wide variety of *nonwritten communications.* This group includes such things as graphic displays (graphs, tables, charts), photographs and illustrations, tools and other artifacts, films and videotapes. The final category includes all *nonverbal signs and symbols.* Among these are the silent messages in body language, facial expressions, gestures, nonverbal symbols and signs, music and dance, animal sounds and behavior, and even noise.

Researchers employ a variety of analysis tools and methods in their study of texts, symbols, and artifacts. Among these are *hermeneutics, content analysis, meta-analysis, semiotic analysis, proxemics, kinesics, discourse analysis, site surveys,* and more. Table 30.1 displays the relationship between various sources of data and methods used in their analysis. The analysis approaches used most often in public and nonprofit organization research are the formal literature review; hermeneutic analysis of textual material; content, discourse, and narrative analysis; meta-analysis; archival analysis; and semiotic analysis. Each of these will be discussed in greater detail in the following pages.

Another way to categorize these research approaches might be to look at the formal literature review, meta-analysis, hermeneutics, content analysis, and semiotics as *methods,* and archives,

Table 30.1

The Relationship between Sources, Examples, and Study Methods

Source	Examples	Analysis Methods
Written Texts	• Professional Literature • Mass Media • Narratives • Books and Stories	Hermeneutics Content Analysis Narrative Analysis Meta-analysis Literature Review
Informal Documents and Other Written Records	• Archival Information • Government Reports • Vital Statistics • Records, Documents • Notes and Memos	Hermeneutics Content Analysis Archival Analysis Semiotics
Nonwritten Communications and Material Culture	• Photos and Drawings • Films and Videos • Tools and Artifacts • Graphs and Tables	Semiotics Discourse Analysis Hermeneutics Site Surveys
Nonverbal Signs, Symbols, and Other Communications	• Body Language • Gestures • Music and Dance • Nonverbal Sounds • Signs • Noise	Semiotics Proxemics Kinesics

texts, artifacts, and signs and symbols as *sources* of research data. This chapter is structured along these lines, with the discussion of textual sources first discussed in a section on the literature search process. Narrative and discourse analyses are discussed in the content analysis section.

Analysis of Texts as Data

In political science, if not all of the social and administrative sciences, library-based research draws on documents of all types as the source of data. It is in this aspect the opposite of the "field research" methods that have been discussed to this point. These types of library- or desk-research projects are common in such fields of inquiry as philosophy, social theory, law, and history, much of which relies almost exclusively upon documents as its key source (Denscombe 1998). They are also important in political science research, with many studies drawing upon legislative archives for data.

From the researcher's point of view, literature or "documentary" research can be grouped into three key classes. The first is the traditional *literature review* that is or should be a part of all scientific research. A key purpose of the literature review is to provide background information that can then be used to design a complete research project.

The second strategy is called *archival studies*. In substance similar to a standard literature review, the archival study draws upon public and private formal documents, records, and other material of a historical nature for data. They may or may not be stored in a library. When they are, they are generally not open for general access or circulation.

The third approach is what is known as a *meta-analysis* design. In this approach, researchers use other studies as subjects for analysis. Meta-analysis is a quantitative technique for summarizing other investigators' research on a topic; as such, it uses the literature as a source of data in its own right.

Reviewing the Relevant Literature

A crucial early step in the design and conduct of all research is a thorough investigation of the relevant literature on the study topic, the research question, and the methodology followed by others who have studied the same or similar problems. Called a *review of the relevant literature* or, simply, a *literature review,* the process has been defined as "a systematic, explicit, and reproducible method for identifying, evaluating, and interpreting the existing body of recorded work produced by researchers, scholars, and practitioners" (Fink 1998, 3).

The literature review serves three fundamental purposes: First, it shows those who read the research findings that the researcher is aware of the existing work already done on the topic. Second, it clearly identifies what the researcher believes are the key issues, crucial questions, and obvious gaps in the field. Third, it establishes a set of guiding signs that help readers to see which theories and principles the researcher used to shape the research design and analysis (Denscombe 1998).

Purposes for the Literature Review

Despite the critical importance of the literature review, some researchers either skip this step entirely in the mistaken belief that theirs is a "unique" study problem, or if they do look into the literature of the study topic, field, or discipline, they often take a wrong approach by just summarizing the material. The literature review is not intended to be just a summary of each of the articles and books that were read. Nor should a literature review be a list of the authors with whom the researcher agrees or disagrees. The good literature review has a greater purpose than this; it is a source of data in its own right (Denscombe 1998). Among the most meaningful strategic purposes to which the literature review can be put are the following (Piantanida and Garman 1999):

1. The review can *trace the historical evolution* of the study problem or key issues, themes, or constructs pertaining to the problem.
2. The review can provide a schematic of the *different schools of thought* that have developed or are developing with regard to the study problem.
3. The review can examine the study problem from several *different disciplines* (examples include looking at welfare reform from the point of view of social work and from an economic viewpoint).
4. The review can examine the positions of *different stakeholder groups,* such as public administrators, citizen groups, nonprofit organizations, etc.
5. The review can trace *different conceptual schools of thought* that have emerged over time, and that may be currently taking opposing or conflicting views in the literature.

These are only a few of the many approaches for a literature review; the important thing to remember about this list is that *none of the approaches or strategies is mutually exclusive.* A good literature review can achieve many goals at the same time. Lang and Heiss (1984) identified two key purposes for reviewing the related literature. First, it should help the researcher hone his or her attack on a specific study problem, and second, it provides a point of reference to use when discussing and interpreting the findings of the research. Specifically, a well-conducted literature review can do all of the following:

- Help to set specific limits for subsequent research.
- Introduce the researcher to new and different ways of looking at the problem.
- Help avoid errors and omissions in planning the study.
- Suggest new ideas.
- Acquaint the researcher to new sources of data and, often, totally different ways of looking at an issue.

A formal literature review should follow an organized series of steps. The action model portrayed in Figure 30.1 has been developed from several sources, but owes a special debt to the contributions of Arlene Fink (1998). The model begins with an encouragement to researchers to study all their options before embarking on their journey through the literature. This means that all potential sources should be considered. Limiting a literature search to a quick perusal of the Internet or a run through a single CD-ROM database is not the way to conduct a thorough, scientific review of the literature. The second step in the literature review process is made up of three equally important activities: (1) establish some basis for selecting articles (content criteria), (2) establish some methodological criteria, such as should they all be quantitative or qualitative studies, should the same size be a certain minimum, were sample members randomly selected and assigned to groups, etc.? The decision will be based on the study question and may change somewhat when the search itself—the third activity in this step—is underway.

The collected research must then be read in detail. As this occurs, relevant categories of information should begin to stand out. These categories must be coded, with the pertinent information copied onto cards or work sheets. Repeated salient themes in the literature should be recorded; these often serve as discussion points during the writing of the final research report. As this point the researcher often continues by writing interpretive memos that summarize the material and allow the researcher to comment on the content. These memos are sometimes carried into the final report with little or no revision.

During the next-to-last stage in the process, the researcher is encouraged to record all the important bibliographic information on the source documents. This usually includes information about the author(s), the discipline in which they did their research, all information about the source, and any connections to other sources that have been or might be also investigated.

Document Research Using Archival Data

Archives, long thought to be of interest only to librarians, have come to be recognized as rich sources of research material in the social sciences, including political science. They are particularly valuable as a source for cross-checking interview and narrative study data. In this way they contribute to improved validity through triangulation—using several different approaches

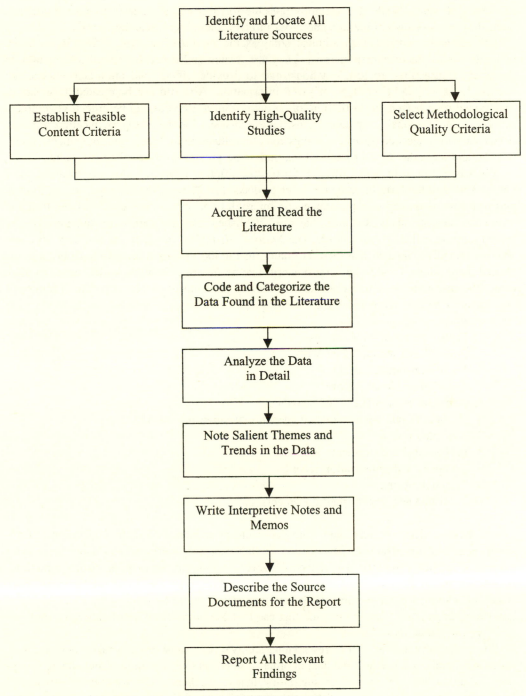

Figure 30.1 **A Model of the Literature Review Process**

in a research study. While it is certainly possible for bias and dishonesty to exist in archival data, they are less susceptible to some types of error, including researcher error.

The research element in an archival study is the *record* (Dearstyne 1993). Records are concrete extensions of human memory. They are created and stored for record information, to document transactions, to justify actions, and to provide official and unofficial evidence of events. A record can be any type of saved information. A record can be created, received, or maintained by a person, an institution, or an organization. Records can be official government reports, recorded e-mail communications, letters, diaries, journals, ledgers, meeting minutes, deeds, case files, election results, drawings and other illustrations, blueprints, agreements, memoranda, and any other type of material that has some greater or lesser historical value.

Records can exist in many different forms and different characteristics. For example, they can be stored in the form of computer tapes or disks, in electronic data storage, words, figures, and illustrations on paper or parchment, on microfilm and microfiche, cassette tape, film and videotape, among others. Records that are established and maintained by organizations or institutions are called *official records*. The *National Historical Publications and Records Commission* recently estimated that there are more than 4,500 historical record repositories in the United States alone. In addition, almost every state has its own historical society, and can often direct the researcher to sources not kept in official government archives. A few examples of specific archival records included the following:

1. Private letters and collections.
2. Political and judicial documents.
3. Voter registration lists.
4. The Congressional Record.
5. Actuarial records (i.e., vital statistics).
6. Records of quasi-governmental agencies (weather reports, etc.).
7. The mass media.
8. Professional and academic journals.
9. Company and organization records.
10. Personal histories.
11. Published and unpublished documents.

Archivists collect, organize, and store documentary evidence of events, operations, correspondence, and organizational functioning. In this way, they perform a valuable service for historians and social science researchers. However, gaining access to archives can sometimes be problematic. If the reaction of one of America's leading archivists, T.R. Schellenberg (1984), is any indication, a guiding principle of archival science might be *a place for everything and everything in its place*. One implication that can be taken away from Schellenberg is: *And that is where there they should stay.*

Researchers, by the very act of researching archival data, must often synthesize, reorganize, restructure, and condense archival data in order to interpret their meaning. Schellenberg grudgingly admitted this fact, but did so suggesting that researchers could not really be trusted to leave things the way they found them. Schellenberg blamed this on their lack of knowledge of the archival profession, but forgave them for their ignorance, as can be seen in the following comments:

If historians (and other social scientists) fail to preserve the evidential values of records by insisting on a violation of the principle of provenance, their action may be attributed to their ignorance of the archival profession, about which they are expected to know very little, and may for this reason be excused. (Schellenberg 1984, 152)

Schellenberg was indeed making a valid point—one that everyone should remember: As researchers, we all owe future investigators the same right to access to the original archival data that we expect. Therefore, researchers must always treat archives with care; they must be left in the state we would like them to be when we find them.

Types of Archives

Webb, Campbell, Schwartz, and Sechrest (2000) group the many sources into just two broad classes or types of archives: *the running record* (essentially all types of public documents, artifacts, and mass media), and the *episodic and private record* (these are discontinuous and usually not a part of the public record).

Running-record archives are the continuous, ongoing records of society. The first thing that comes to mind when we think about this source is the extensive body of vital statistics and other records kept by all levels of governments and the mass media. However, it also includes actuarial records of insurance companies, recorded votes of political office holders, government budgets, and the like. As with the second type of archive records, these data can exist as words, numbers, pictures, graphic displays, and the residue of human activity, society's refuse, and others.

Webb et al. alerted the researcher to two classes of potential bias that can creep into public records—*selective deposit* and *selective survival*. Artifacts survive in nature because they are not consumed, not eroded away, or not combined into other artifacts and thus lost to view or memory. For example, ceremonial stones, decorative stone facings, and similar components of Greek and Roman structures have been removed over the centuries to be incorporated into the baser constructions of later generations. Temples have become stables.

Changes in political administrations usually result in the filing away and delivery to archival storage of volume after volume of written records. Potentially damaging or embarrassing records somehow get misplaced, "accidentally" removed from the archival record. In other instances, well-meaning historians or social science researchers may be charged with bringing order to a body of unorganized archival records. In the process, they often "edit" the raw data, unwilling to leave the record as they found it. What survives may be what the researcher believed was important. Also, records of events tend to be grouped together, thereby blurring the real contextual time structure of events. The result is often a fictional account.

A Triangulation Example Using Archival Data

The phenomenon is visible today in the decay evident in many inner cities. Buildings are abandoned, their materials removed and used for other purposes. What remains for later generations to read is far different than the record as it was originally laid down. Researchers are encouraged in such instances to fall back on the tried-and-true practice of *triangulation,* using other sources to validate the remaining archival record. Other studies might include written records prepared by visitors from other cultures, biographies and histories, others' interpretations of the time, and for phenomena in the not-too-distant past, the remembrances of other participants in the event or events.

An example of triangulation design in which archival data played a role is the Monopoli and Alworth (2000) study involving Navaho World War II veterans. Four surviving tribal members were part of a panel who participated in a 1950s *Thematic Apperception Test* (TAT) study of attitudes and opinions of Native Americans. The surviving subjects were interviewed and the data compared with archival records of the original study. In addition to the benefits of a longitudinal design, the researchers were also able to identify some biasing errors in the earlier study results that might not have come to light with the use of the archival data in the modern study. Webb et al. also identified the mass media as an important source of archival data. Citing a number of different studies, they concluded that carefully selected media could clearly serve as a record of the values of society at a given period.

Another example of triangulation is an archival design involving a comparison of official written histories with daily reports of speeches, paid announcements, and published articles appearing in the regional mass media of the period. The study subject was the conflict between advocates of public ownership of electrical power generation and distribution, and those represented by the large holding-company forces of investor-owned utilities. The public power battle began in earnest shortly before World War I, eventually becoming one of the last great causes of the Progressive Movement in the United States (Farris and Sampson, 1973).

Political scientists are often particularly concerned with political and judicial records, another source of the public record. These include speeches by candidates and office holders, their supporters or their opponents, voting records, judicial decisions (including minority opinions), and other similar records.

Researchers may also be interested in legislators' seniority, party majorities, committee assignments, scales that measure political philosophy, events or legislative emphasis during times of economic or political stress, and many other such phenomena. For example, a study conducted in the state of Washington evaluated legislative effectiveness under stress as measured by the number and scope of bills passed during two periods when a tie existed in the lower house.

Episodic and Private Archives

Episodic and private-record archives are private data. Moreover, they are usually not as accessible as are public records. They tend to be stored for shorter periods and are often destroyed after a set period of time. This accounts for one of the major differences between the two broad classes of archives: it is often not possible to perform longitudinal analyses on private archival data.

Episodic archives can be grouped into three broad classes: company records, institutional records, and personal documents. Company information such as sales records has long been used to measure the popularity, preference, and loyalty toward a product, event, idea, or service. The data are also used to measure the effectiveness of advertising and government informational communications programs. Institutional records are the files of companies, organizations, agencies, and institutions. They can be used to measure job stress by records of absenteeism, tardiness, turnover, and labor union grievances, for example. They can also be used to evaluate agency effectiveness by measuring customer complaints and the content of suggestion programs, for example. Personal records such as letters, memos, collections, artwork, and other possessions are usually the concern of historians, and as such have little application for research in public administration.

A Word of Caution concerning Archives

Caution is advised in the use of archival materials because of the potential distortion that can exist in personal archives (Webb et al. 2000). Low-paid clerical workers often indifferently keep archives with no stake in the accuracy of their product. Because record keepers may feel that the saved material has little value, it may be stored haphazardly. It may be years, if not decades, before the material is again examined; therefore, their diligence or lack thereof seldom comes to light. When a researcher appears on the scene, however, there is a tendency for their interest to be revitalized, with the unfortunate result of some altering or even destruction of recorded data.

Archive research involves a way of looking at published or previously prepared material, and also defines the type of materials that are examined. While this approach to the investigation of archival records of all types can serve as an excellent source of pertinent data for many studies in public administration and nonprofit organization management, they are not without their disadvantages, as the following warning suggests:

> For all their gains (i.e., advantages), however, the gnawing reality remains that archives have been produced for someone else by someone else. There must be a careful evaluation of the way in which the records were produced, for the risk is high that one is getting a cutrate version of another's errors. (Webb et al. 2000, 84)

Nontextual Archives: Physical Traces

Physical evidence is another information source that might be considered to be "archival evidence," in that it was recorded for future researchers to interpret. According to Webb et al., physical evidence is probably the least-used source of data in the social and administrative sciences. However, it does hold what they called "flexible and broad-gauge potential." They identify two broad classes of physical evidence:

- *Erosion measures*—the degree of selective wear or erosion that occurs over time, such as using the rate of wear in museum floor tiles as a measure of exhibit popularity.
- *Accretion measures*—the degree to which materials collect over time. There are two subclasses of accretion measures: (1) *remnants*—only one or a few traces are available for study, and (2) *series*—an accumulative body of evidence remains.

The major advantage of physical evidence data is its inconspicuousness; it is a silent measure of change. What is measured is generated without the subject's knowledge of its use by investigators. It circumvents the problems of awareness of being measured, and removes the bias that comes from the measurement process itself becoming a part of the phenomenon. With all types of physical traces, and particularly when the phenomenon still occurs, index numbers are generated for comparisons, rather than the specific measurements themselves.

Performing a Meta-analysis of Existing Research

Examining the literature of a study topic has been shown to have many purposes and objectives. Among other things, (1) a good literature review allows the researcher to frame the study in light of what others have investigated previously; (2) it provides insights and new ideas regarding the study problem; (3) it can suggest new ways of examining the problem or conducting analysis of the gathered data; (4) a good review makes the topic under study clear to all readers; (5) it includes only studies that are substantially relevant; (6) it addresses the research on the topic from a wide range of subjects, settings, and time periods. In addition, (7) good literature reviews include a discussion of a wide range of possible explanatory variables; (8) they are also sensitive to potential bias in span of the studies examined in order to ensure that the total bias across all the studies is not more in one direction than the other. The problem is that literature reviews seldom meet all these goals. Some other approach is needed. The *meta-analysis* is one solution to this problem (Cook 1992; Lipsey and Wilson 2001).

Lipsey and Wilson (2001) defined *meta-analysis* as a type of survey research in which, instead of surveying people as subjects, previously prepared research reports are the subjects of analysis. Meta-analyses are used in order to summarize and compare the results of many different studies; other researchers have produced most, if not all, of these other studies. Meta-analysis is an excellent way of establishing the state of research findings on a subject—it provides the researcher with the "big picture," rather than simply another discussion of one or a few parts of the question, problem, or issue.

Meta-analyses can only be applied to empirical research reports—that is, studies using primary research and data gathering. The technique is not appropriate for the types of qualitative studies that summarize a set of other qualitative research studies. Although it is not necessary that the studies examined in the meta-analysis be the results of experiments, many meta-analyses have summarized experimental designs. The method uses a set of quantitative techniques that allow for synthesizing the results of many types of research studies, including, but not limited to, opinion surveys, correlational studies, experimental and quasi-experimental studies, and regression analysis (Cook 1992).

Advantages and Disadvantages of Meta-analysis

Lipsey and Wilson identified four important advantages of the meta-analysis research design. First, the complete process of establishing a coding scheme and criteria for selecting studies (a *survey protocol*), reading the study reports, coding the material, and subjecting it to a rigid statistical analysis imposes a discipline on the researcher that is sometimes missing in qualitative summarizations and comparative analyses.

Second, the process results in greater sophistication in summarizing research, particularly when compared with qualitative summary attempts. The application of common statistical tests across all the studies can correct for wide differences in sample size, for example. Third, meta-analysis may enable the researcher to find effects or associations that other comparative processes miss. Finally, it provides a way to organize and structure diverse information from a wide variety of study findings. Meta-analysis is not without its disadvantages, however. A few of the criticisms that have been cited for the method include the following:

1. The large amount of effort and expertise it requires is an often-cited disadvantage of the method. Properly done, a meta-analysis takes considerably more time than a conventional qualitative research review; many aspects of the method require specialized knowledge, particularly in the selection and computation of appropriate "effect sizes" (i.e., the statistic chosen for comparison across all the studies).
2. It may not be sensitive to some important issues, including, but not limited to, the social context of the study, theoretical influences and implications, methodological quality, design issues, procedures, and the like.
3. The mix of studies (an *apples-and-oranges* issue) combined into larger groups may hide subtle differences seen in individual studies.
4. Finally, inclusion of studies that are methodologically weak can detract from the findings in strong studies.

Lipsey and Wilson admit to validity of these criticisms, but are convinced that the strengths of the method far outweigh any such disadvantages.

How To Do a Meta-analysis

Fink (1998, 216) has recommended the following series of seven steps for conducting a meta-analysis:

- Step 1. Clarify the objectives of the analysis.
- Step 2. Set explicit criteria for including and excluding studies.
- Step 3. Justify methods for searching the literature.
- Step 4. Search the literature using a standardized protocol for including and excluding studies.
- Step 5. Devise a standardized protocol to collect data from each study, including study purposes, methods, and outcomes (i.e., effects measured).
- Step 6. Describe in detail the statistical method for pooling results.
- Step 7. Report the results of the comparative analysis, included conclusions and perceived limitations.

A slightly longer, but possibly more informative, list of steps can be discerned by combining ideas from Lipsey and Wilson's seminal manual on the method with Fink's review. This summary procedure model is shown in Figure 30.2, and the steps discussed below.

Statement of the topic or question. This step provides the framework upon which all subsequent steps in the process follow. An example question statement for a meta-analysis might be: How have mandatory sentencing guidelines affected the number of repeat arrests for crimes in which a weapon was involved?

Identify the form(s) of research relevant to a meta-analysis on the topic. The "form" aspect refers to the type of analysis conducted in the individual research studies. For example, this could be studies that report treatment/control group experiments. Or, it could be studies that focus on correlations between two or more variables. Another example is a standard two-sample comparison study. In the example proposed in the first step in this discussion, a typical form might have been studies that compare mean rates of arrests or length of sentences before mandatory sentencing, and then a repeat of the study after imposition of sentencing minimums.

462

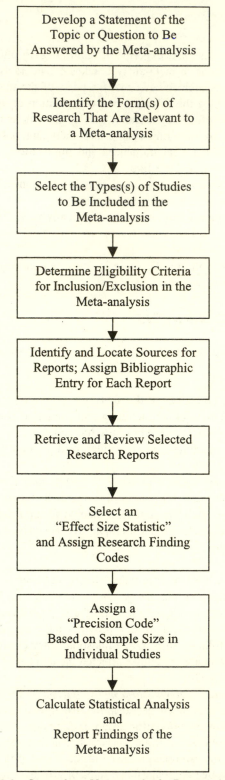

Figure 30.2 **Steps in a Meta-analysis Research Design**
Source: From material in Fink 1998; Lipsey and Wilson 2001.

This is a typical pre- and post-treatment comparison or hypothesis testing research design. The test statistic for the next step could be *t*-test scores or *p*-values of comparisons.

Select types of studies to be included in the analysis. This decision step is similar to the step above, but refers more to the statistical tests used. Four types of tests are regularly used in meta-analyses: (1) central tendency descriptions (such as mean scores), (2) pregroup/post-group hypothesis test studies, (3) other group contrasts, either pure experiments or nonexperimental grouping comparisons (for example, comparing gender or age groups, etc.), and (4) studies employing regression analysis.

Determine eligibility criteria. In this step the researcher decides which topics upon which to base a decision to include the study in the meta-analysis. Examples of types of criteria often used include (1) the distinguishing feature of a study (what made writing about it worthwhile), (2) research subjects (i.e., types or characteristics of respondents used in the study), (3) key variable(s), (4) research designs, (5) cultural and/or linguistic range, (6) time frame involved, and (7) type of publication.

Identify and locate sources of research reports. At this stage the research must apply the decision criteria established in the previous step. Researchers should develop a detailed accounting system so that each study gets its own detailed bibliographic citation, and its own identification number. Numbers are needed to facilitate future cross-referencing and to ensure that reports are assigned to their appropriate comparison group. A brief description of the subject report should also be prepared at this time.

Some sources and listings for research reports include review articles, references in other studies, computer databases, bibliographies, professional and academic journals, conference programs and proceedings, correspondence with researchers active in the field, government agencies, the Internet, colleges and universities, professional associations, and others.

Retrieve and review eligible research studies. This step involves several activities. First, researchers must find bibliographic references to potentially eligible studies. Second, a copy of the study must be obtained for screening. If it is considered to be eligible, it must be coded for inclusion in the meta-analysis.

Select an "effect size statistic" for use with the entire sample of reports. In a meta-analysis, a single research finding is a statistical representation of the relationships among the variable(s) of interest. This statistical representation is the effect size statistic that will be used in comparative analysis during the meta-analysis. Research findings in the subject reports are test statistics; each must be coded as a value on the same effect size statistic. This must be the same statistic across the entire sample of reports. For example, if the effect size statistic is the correlation between two or more variables, the variables in all the reports must have been measured at the same level (nominal, ordinal, or interval), with the same type of correlation coefficient (Pearson's *r*, Spearman's rho, the chi-square-based phi, or Cramer's V). Similar restrictions apply for other statistical measures that might be selected.

Assign a precision code for each research report. A precision code is similar to a weighting system. It is based upon the sample size employed in each subject report. For example, a study in which a sample size of 500 was tested can be expected to be considerably more precise than one in which the sample size was, say, only 5—or even 50. The statistical calculations used in meta-analysis take these precision weights into effect, thus correcting for possible error associated with small samples. The greater the perceived reliability, the greater should be the precision code value assigned to the study.

Finally, researchers must keep in mind that there are two parts to a meta-analysis coding process. The first part is the information that describes characteristics of the subject report; this is the "study descriptor" portion of coding. Study characteristics include such information as the methods, the measures, sample characteristics and size, constructs developed, treatments given, and the like. The second part of the coding protocol is the part that covers information about the empirical findings contained in the report; this is the "effect sizes" portion of the coding, together with the precision code for each study. Effect sizes, for example, are the statistical values that indicate the association between variables.

The first three sections of this chapter discussed documentary data as a source of data that researchers turn into information. The following section begins a discussion on some of the ways that researchers actually conduct analyses of texts. Texts will be shown to include such things as signs and symbols, as well as artifacts and other facets of material culture. Methods such as *hermeneutics, semiotics,* and *content analysis* will be discussed.

Hermeneutic Analysis of Text and Nontext Material

Hermeneutics is a method of analyzing all types of data (particularly written texts) according to a set of principles that requires the analyst to (1) decipher the meaning of the text through the eyes and intent of the writer or creator of the text or artifact, (2) according to the time frame existing at the time of the writing, and (3) considering the political and cultural environmental influences existing at the time of the creation of the text or artifact.

Hermeneutics owes its long history of interpretive applications to the analysis of, first, religious texts, and, second, legal documents, and written administrative rulings. (Gadamer 1975 and 1986; Bauman 1992; Alejandro 1993; and others). The term originates from the Greek word *hermeneutikós,* which refers to the act of explaining. "Explaining" refers to "making clear" or clarifying the obscure in the text (Bauman 1992).

Hermeneutic analysis requires that the researcher take a holistic, or "contextualist," approach to analysis of a problem. The meaning of a text or social phenomenon that is analyzed hermeneutically depends on the whole—that is, the text, the author(s), *and* the context. Therefore, the meaning of a text or phenomenon can only be deciphered by first understanding its context.

Hermeneutics is a way of clarifying the meaning of a text by interpreting it historically (Moore 1990, 94). It looks upon a text as the "medium which links human subjects (i.e., writers of textual material) to their world and to their past. . . . it involves identification with the intentions and situation of the [writer]." Maas (1999), writing about the hermeneutic analysis of religious texts, explained this two-part focus by describing both a *material* and a *formal* object for the process. The material object is the text or other document that is being explained; the formal object is deciphering the sense of the author at the time the text was written.

Hermeneutic analysis is particularly relevant when studying historical documents, such as past legislation, the records of discourse that occurred over legislative or administrative hearings, and similar applications. In this way, public administration hermeneutics deals with government texts or documents as its material object, with the deciphering of the intent of the framers at the time of its creation (i.e., passage or implementation) as its formal object. Thus, legislation that might seem silly today has the potential to be interpreted as logical and meaningful when considered in the light of events and circumstances at its enactment.

Principles of Hermeneutics

Several key principles underlie the hermeneutical analysis process. First, *all thought is derived from language and follows the same laws that regulate language.* A writer uses the traditions and conventions of his or her time and particular circumstances, including the rhetorical logic, the same sequence of ideas, and the same rules of grammar in use at the time of the text's creation. Therefore, if the analyst wishes to fully understand the writer and "correctly" interpret the writer's words, he or she must first understand the author's meaning *at the time and place of the writing*. The interpreter must know the writer's language, his or her train of thought or context of the text, and the writer's psychological and historical condition at the time of the writing. Hence, the first principle of hermeneutics is:

> Find the sense of a book by way of its language (grammatically and philogically) by way of the rules of logic . . . and by way of the writer's mental and external condition (at the time of writing). (Maas 1999, 3)

Several other principles follow from this first principle of hermeneutics. Among them are: hermeneutic analysis presupposes that the analyst (1) has knowledge of both the grammar and historical evolution of the language in which the work is written, (2) is familiar with the laws of logic and rhetoric, and (3) has knowledge of psychological principles and the facts of history (of the time the work was written).

Hermeneutic Analysis of Nontext Material

While it is used most often as a method for analyzing texts, hermeneutics is also considered to be a broadly based theory of interpreting all human creations. Henrietta Moore (1990), describing philosophy's contributions to hermeneutic theory and application, wrote about the nontext application in these terms:

> [The] theory of [hermeneutic] interpretation may be extended beyond the written text to encompass other human phenomena which can be said to have textual characteristics. One such phenomenon is meaningful action . . . and action is understood when it can be explained why the individual acted as [he or she] did, and thus can only be explained when a reason or motive for the action can be adduced. (Moore 1990, 99)

Richardson (1995) also commented on the application of hermeneutic analysis to phenomena other than textual materials.

> Hermeneutics has come forward as that comprehensive standpoint from which to view all the projects of human learning. For those of us who have been puzzled by the new intellectual dominance of hermeneutics, the key is that the term no longer refers to the interpretation of texts only but encompasses all the ways in which subjects and objects are involved in human communication. . . . hermeneutics or interpretation has come to be regarded as shorthand for all the practices of human learning. (Richardson 1995, 1)

Moore saw that the problem of analyzing *meaningful action* is at the very heart of much of the research and philosophical speculation in the social sciences, including public administration. She proposed that it be approached with the understanding that the social world is made up of individuals who speak and act in meaningful ways, and added that "these individuals create the social world which gives them their identify and being, and their creations can only be understood through a process of interpretation" (Moore 1990, 111).

Roberto Alejandro applied hermeneutic analysis to public administration issues in his book

Hermeneutics, Citizenship, and the Public Sphere. He described the key contributions to hermeneutics of German philosopher Hans-Georg Gadamer (*Truth and Method,* 1975). The two key principles discussed by Alejandro are: First, all humans are born into their own tradition, but, because we are all "interpretive beings," we are always working to achieve understanding and interpretation. Second, hermeneutics assumes that mankind's relation to the world is "fundamentally and essentially" made through language (Alejandro 1993, 34–35).

Meaning and Emphasis in Hermeneutics

Hermeneutics holds that there is always a plurality of meanings available for every human phenomenon. Meaning is not something that just exists; every reader must interpret it. Interpretations will vary from reader to reader, and can only be understood in the light of historical, social, and linguistic traditions:

> Interpretation is always a construction of meaning, which is what distinguishes the scientists' endeavor from hermeneutics' purpose. The scientist seeks certainty; hermeneutics seeks clarity. This clarity is anchored in the principle that the construction of meaning that interpretation makes possible is not arbitrary; it is not the outcome of the pure will of the interpreter. The construction of meaning has to consider the boundaries provided by the text (or phenomenon) itself as well as the background provided by the traditions that made it possible. (Alejandro 1993, 36)

Bauman also commented on this difference in emphasis. Social phenomena—the subject matter of public administration research—because they are ultimately acts of human beings, must be understood in a different way than by simply explaining. Men and women do what they do on purpose. True understanding can occur only when we know the purpose, the intent of the actor, his or her distinctive thoughts and feelings that lead up to an action. "To understand a human act . . . [is] to grasp the meaning with which the actor's intention invested it. . . . [this is] essentially different from [the goal] of natural science" (Bauman 1992, 12).

In terms of its importance for research on questions in public administration and nonprofit organizations, hermeneutics provides a new way of looking at public issues. The hermeneutic approach assumes that the "constant of history" exists in the mind of every individual, and that citizens' actions are inescapably influenced by their beliefs, traditions, and historical events.

The Hermeneutic Circle

The process of hermeneutic analysis is less a method than it is a philosophical approach to scientific inquiry. By this is meant that, counter to traditional scientific epistemology that focuses first on explaining and then predicting, the hermeneutic approach is concerned with *interpretation in order to understand.* Achieving understanding, according to Bauman (1992, 17), means following a circular approach "toward better and less vulnerable knowledge."

This path to understanding is called the *hermeneutic circle.* It means beginning by interpreting a single part of the whole, then reevaluating and restating the interpretation in light of information about the time and intent of the event or text. Only then does one move to the next part—again searching the context for greater enlightenment. Moon explained the hermeneutic circle as consisting of moving back and forth between the particular and the general, as the meaning and significance of specific actions, practices, texts, etc., are judged in relation to a conception of the whole, and ideas of the whole. The researcher's concept of the whole is corrected and amplified as each interpretation is compared against the parts of the text. "When we are puzzled about the meaning of a particular phrase (action, practice, or text), for example, we attempt to infer what meaning it must have in order to provide coherence to the speech or text to which it is a part. Hence, to understand the part, we must already have an understanding of the whole" (Moon 1975, 171–72).

Merrell (1982, 113) added to understanding of this process by describing the way the analysis moves from the whole to its parts and back to the whole: "When written texts are broken down into isolated segments, those segments can then be relatively easily juxtaposed, compared, and contrasted. That is, they can be subjected to analysis by means of which consciousness of condensed and embedded wholes can be increased." Understanding of parts thus builds on the greater understanding. With each of the parts assessed and reassessed in this way—in a circular analytical process that Bauman described as being "ever more voluminous, but always selective"—full understanding emerges at last.

An Application of Hermeneutic Analysis

Mercier (1994, 42) described how the hermeneutic method was used to examine organizational culture. In his opinion, a hermeneutical analysis of an organization is particularly valuable when management is considering a major shift in strategy. Mercier concluded that a good hermeneutic analysis helps members of the organization recognize that their choices are not as limited as they once believed. Mercier also proposed that hermeneutic analysis take place in the following brief sequence of steps:

1. Identification of a "spirit" or central point in an organization's culture ("spirit" refers to what might also be called the *defining characteristic* of the organization).
2. Explanation and interpretation of some of the other puzzling or contradictory elements of the organization through this central point.
3. And finally, identification of hard and/or historical elements—related to factors in the environment—that have caused or dramatically influence the defining characteristic.

Semiotics: The Analysis of Signs and Symbols

Semiotics is a relatively modern interpretive science; it emerged during the middle and last half of the twentieth century as a way of describing how meaning is derived from text, language, and social actions as symbols. The primary social action of interest was initially limited to *language*—in both its written and spoken word forms. However, it was soon applied to analysis of things other than texts, but that could be "read" as text. Social structure, ritual and myth, material culture, including art and tools: these all became the subject of research into the meaning of their signs and symbols. Today, semiotics is used as a way of interpreting all types of verbal and nonverbal signs, and symbols, regardless of the discipline.

The Meaning of Semiotics

Many definitions of semiotics have been proposed; most relate it in some way to the interpretation of signs and symbols (Morris 1967; Barthes 1968; Eco 1976; Sebeok 1976; Hodder

1982; Silverman 1983; Nöth 1990; Manning and Cullum-Swan 1998). For example, Nöth (1990) drew upon previous definitive work to give semiotics the following broadest possible definition—although later in her *Handbook of Semiotics* (p. 103), Nöth refered to semiotics as simply "the science of meaning":

> [The science of signs] has for its goal a general theory of signs in all their forms and manifestations, whether in animals or men, whether normal or pathological, whether linguistic or nonlinguistic, whether personal or social. Semiotics is thus an interdisciplinary approach. (Nöth 1990, 49)

Manning and Cullum-Swan (1998, 251–52) were just as brief in their proposed definition, but took a slightly different approach, electing to refer to semiotics simply as "the science of signs." They defined a *sign* as "anything that represents or stands for something else in the mind of someone." This definition has two parts: first, what they term an *expression* (such as a word, a sound, a symbol, or the like), and second, a *content,* which is what completes the sign by giving it meaning. Offering another interpretation, Silverman (1983) defined a sign as:

> [S]omething which stands to somebody for something in some respect or capacity. It addresses somebody, that is, it creates in the mind of that person an equivalent sign, or perhaps a more developed sign. . . . the sign stands for something, its object. It stands for that object, not in all respects, but in reference to a sort of idea, which I sometimes call the *ground.* (Silverman 1983,14)

Perhaps the most complete definition of what constitutes a "sign" was provided by Eco (1976, 16), who defined a sign as "*everything* [his emphasis] that, on the grounds of a previously established social convention, can be taken [as] *something standing for something else.*"

Components and Forms of Signs

Winfred Nöth (1990), writing on the history of the science of semiotics, identified four underlying disciplines that have contributed to the development of the Western semiotic tradition. These include *semantics* (including the philosophy of language), *logic, rhetoric,* and *hermeneutics.* Other disciplines that helped forge modern semiotics include linguistics, aesthetics, poetics, nonverbal communication, epistemology, and the human sciences in general.

Signs come in many different forms. Sebeok (1976) grouped the many different types of signs into six broad classifications: *signal, symptom, icon, index, symbol, and name.* Semiotics pioneer C.S. Peirce, however, developed the most widely used classification system, in 1962. He grouped signs into just three classes: *icons, indices, and symbols.* An icon is a sign that signifies its meaning by qualities of its own. An index communicates its meaning by being an example of its intended sign, such as a weathercock or a yardstick. Peirce considered the symbol to be a synonym for sign.

Semiotic methodology can be used for either theoretical or applied research studies. The key thing to remember is that the focus of semiotics research should always be on determining the *meaning of signs and symbols,* regardless of the form in which they are encountered. Researchers do not simply study signs; they focus instead on the *links* between the things that signs represent and the people for whom they have meaning. Symbols are not a reflection of society; rather, they play an active role in forming and giving meaning to social behavior

Table 30.2

Examples of Semiotic Research Applications

	Research Focus	Description of Content
1	Aesthetic Texts	Analysis of the aesthetic import of textual material.
2	Codes of Taste	Present in the culinary and enology fields. How tastes communicate certain images.
3	Cultural Codes	Behavior and values systems, including such things as etiquette, cultural systems, and social organization of groups and societies.
4	Formalized Languages	"Languages" of statistics, chemistry, engineering, psychology, etc.
5	Kinesics and Proxemics	Movement, gestures, special relationships.
6	Mass Communications	Coding, sending, receiving, interpreting messages.
7	Medical Semiotics	Signs and symptoms of the illness they indicate and other symbols forwarded by a patient.
8	Musical Codes	Musical "signs" with explicit denotative meanings, such as trumpet calls in the military; music that conveys selected emotional or conceptual meanings, such as "tone poems."
9	Natural Languages	Studies in such areas as logic, philosophy of language, etc.
10	Olfactory Signs	The "code of scents"; important in atmospherics.
11	Paralinguistic Sounds	Sounds without linguistic features, such as grunts, growls, etc.
12	Plot Substructure	Mythology, mass communication drama and novels, etc.
13	Rhetoric	An early contributor to the field of semiotics; includes models of oral persuasion, argument, etc.
14	Systems of Objects	From architecture to objects in everyday use.
15	Tactile Communication	Includes the communication systems of the blind, as well as such behaviors as the kiss, the embrace, slap on the shoulder, caress.
16	Text Theory	The study of text as a "macro unit"; text as a whole unit.
17	Visual Communication	Graphic displays, advertisements, brands and trademarks.
18	Written Languages	Includes unknown languages, secret codes, ancient alphabets, cryptography, etc.
19	Zoosemiotics	The communications behavior of nonhumans.

Source: Eco 1976.

(Hodder 1982). Thus, in order to really understand social behavior, one must begin by interpreting the *contextual meaning* of the signs and symbols of the society.

Political science researchers may use semiotics in any research involving verbal or nonverbal communication. Table 30.2 contains an extensive list of fields and study types that Eco (1976, 9–14) believed belong to the field of semiotics. By extension, they may be of interest to political scientists, public administrators, and managers of nonprofit organizations as well.

A Final Word of Caution about Signs

Anthropologist Christopher Tilley (1989), who identified himself first as an anthropologist and only second as a student of symbols, offered this final caveat regarding the interpretation of signs:

Meaning . . . resides in a system of *relationships between signs* and not in the signs themselves. A sign considered in isolation would be meaningless. Furthermore, the meaning of a sign is not predetermined, but is rather of cultural and historical convention. Consequently, it does not matter how a signifier appears, so long as it preserves its difference from other signifiers. (Tilley 1989, 186)

Content, Narrative, and Discourse Analysis

Content analysis is a quantitative method of analyzing the content of written documents, transcripts of films, videos, and speeches, and other types of written communication (Denscombe 1998). It has been defined as *"any technique for making inferences by objectively and systematically identifying specified characteristics of messages"* (Holsti 1969, 14). The main advantage of content analysis is that it provides the researcher with a structured method for quantifying the contents of a qualitative or interpretive text, and does so in a simple, clear, and easily repeatable format. Its main disadvantage is that it contains a built-in bias of isolating bits of information from their context. Thus, the contextual meaning is often lost or, at the least, made problematic. Furthermore, content analysis has great difficulty in dealing with *implied* meanings in a text. In these situations, interpretive (hermeneutic) analysis may be more appropriate, with content analysis used to supplement the primary analysis method.

Content analysis is best used when dealing with communications in which the messages tend to be clear, straightforward, obvious, and simple. The more that a text relies on subtle and/or intricate meanings, the less likely is the ability of content analysis to reveal the full meaning of the communication. Thus, content analysis is used most often to *describe attributes of messages,* without reference to the intentions of the message sender or effect of the message on the receiver (Denscombe 1998, 169; Holsti 1969, 27). Counting how many times in a speech a candidate denigrates the character of a political opponent is an example of application of content analysis.

The major purpose of all content analysis is to be able to make inferences about one or more variables uncovered in a text. It accomplishes this by systematically and objectively analyzing either the content of the text, the process of communication itself, or both (Sproull 1988). Content analysis takes place in the nine-step process displayed in Figure 30.3.

The content analysis process begins with establishing objectives for the content analysis research. The first step in the process should be a familiar one by now: Establish objectives for the research process. This means determining *in advance* of the research what you want to accomplish by its conduct. Next, assuming that the researcher has some familiarity with the larger issues and/or themes at stake in the phenomenon, a list should be made of what *variables* are to be counted in the text. Variables are not the same as words; rather, they tend to be constructs that can be said to describe or refer to broader complex issues of behavior or attitude. This list is clearly embedded in the study objectives.

Once the researcher has decided what to look for and where to look for it, he or she must then establish a system for first coding the content items, while also determining how they are going to be counted and recorded. The texts themselves are then collected.

Holsti (1969) recommended that at this time researchers should draw a random sample of the materials for a pilot test of the study. The pilot test will provide important clues as to the relative effectiveness of the research design. For example, since the variables of interest are established before measurement takes place, there is a possibility that the variables are not

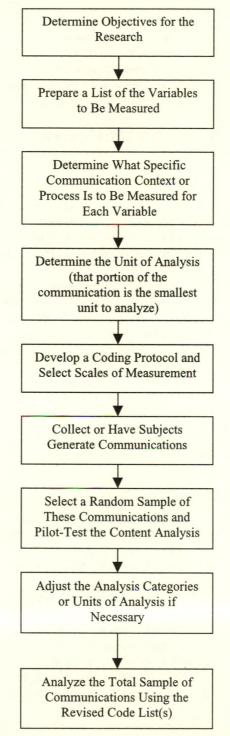

Figure 30.3 **Steps in Content Analysis Research Design**
Source: Adapted from Holsti 1969; Sproull 1988; and Denscombe 1998.

treated significantly in the sample of sources chosen. In that case, the researcher would have to go back and identify new variables for the study.

The final steps in the study involve conducting statistical analysis on the measurements. When possible, these should include correlation analysis and simple hypothesis testing, analysis tools more commonly found in quantitative research designs.

Complimentary Tools: Narrative and Discourse Analysis

Content analysis is related to several similar research designs, among which are *narrative analysis* and *discourse analysis*. A *narrative* is an oral or written exposition that typically describes the events in a person or persons' life. It is usually an exposition of a single person. A *discourse* is either an oral or written communication designed to inform, rather than entertain. The term "discourse" is often used to identify an *exchange* of communication between two or more speakers or writers.

Narratives have been formally defined as "a means of representing or recapitulating past experience by a sequence of ordered sentences that match the temporal [time] sequence of the events which, it is inferred, actually occurred" (Cortazzi 1993, 43). A *narrative analysis* is a qualitative approach to the interpretation of texts and, as such, is often used to augment a quantitative analysis of content. Noting the mutually supportive roles of the various methods, Holsti reminded researchers:

> [T]he content analyst should use qualitative and quantitative methods to supplement each other. It is by moving back and forth between these approaches that the investigator is most likely to gain insight into the meaning of his [sic] data. . . . It should not be assumed that qualitative methods are insightful, and quantitative ones merely mechanical methods for checking hypotheses. The relationship is a circular one; each provides new insights on which the other can feed. (Holsti 1969, 11)

Narratives are a record of events that have significance for both the narrator and his or her audience (a researcher, for example). Narratives are formally structured; they have a beginning, a middle, and an ending. Furthermore, they are organized according to a set of distinct structures with formal and identifiable characteristics (Cortazzi 1993; Coffee and Alkinson 1996).

Cortazzi developed the narrative evaluation or analysis model summarized in Table 30.3. The model illustrates how informal styles of narrative (speech) correlate with a number of social characteristics. The specific document selected for analysis might be newspaper stories, speeches at local service clubs, or official records such the *Congressional Record*.

Manning and Cullum-Swan (1998) have described several different approaches to the analysis of narratives, among which are, *Russian formalism* and *top-down* and *bottom-up structural methods*. Russian formalism emphasizes the role that form plays in conveying meaning in a narrative. It has been used to analyze the form that Russian folk tales follow, for example. Each tale follows a similar, simple structure. Others have used the same approach to examine myths, poetry, and fiction.

Top-down approaches analyze the narrative text according to a set of culturally established rules of grammar and exposition. These methods are used extensively in education. Bottom-up methods, on the other hand, use elements in the text to build a structure for analyzing the whole. This is the approach followed most often in ethnographic research.

Table 30.3

A Variation of the Labov/Cortazzi Six-Part Narrative Evaluation Model

Structural Element	Comment	Questions
Abstract	A 100-word summary	*What was this about?*
Orientation	Establishes the situation	*Who? What? When? Where?*
Compilation	Major account of the events that are central to the story	*Then what happened?*
Evaluation	High point of the analysis	*So what?*
Result	Outcome of the events or resolution of the problem	*What finally happened?*
Conclusion	Return to the present	*Finish of the narrative*

Karl Bühler (1934, cited in Merrell 1982) provided an early framework of narrative and discourse analysis that is still relevant today. Bühler saw three main functions for a language. First, it must be *expressive;* the message must serve to convey the emotions or thoughts of the user of the language. Second, it must serve a *signaling* or *stimulative* function. The message must stimulate an expected response by the receiver. And third, it must have a *descriptive* function. The user of the language must be able to use it to describe a particular state of affairs in ways that convey the full picture. Others have added additional functions; the most important of these is an *argumentative* or *explanatory* function, by which language users present alternative thoughts, views, or propositions to the descriptive messages (Merrell 1982, 116).

Discourse Analysis of Communications

Discourse analysis is a method of analyzing oral or written communications in order to identify the formal structure of the message, while at the same time, keeping a *use-of-the-language* purpose in mind. It can be applied to the same types of messages, texts, documents, etc. that are appropriate for content analysis, albeit for a different purpose. Discourse analysis is strongly associated with the analysis of linguistic structures in the message or text. Potter and Wetherell (1994, 48) refer to this point in their discussion of three particularly pertinent features of discourse analysis:

1. Discourse analysis is concerned with talk and texts as "social practices." It examines the linguistic content—i.e., the meaning and the topics discussed—in a message, as well as being concerned with the features of language form such as grammar and cohesion.
2. Discourse analysis has a "triple concern" with the themes of *action, construction,* and *variability* in the message.
3. Discourse analysis is concerned with the rhetorical or augmentative organization of texts and talks.

Finally, the objective of discourse analysis is to take the focus of analysis away from questions of *how* a text version relates to reality to ask instead how the version is designed to compete successfully with one or more alternative versions. These points are incorporated in the following five points that direct discourse analysis:

- Variation in theme and message is to be used as a lever in analysis.
- The discourse must be read and analyzed in minute detail.
- A key point in the analysis is the search for rhetorical organization.
- Accountability: Are points made with or without being supported?
- Finally, discourse analysis requires cross-referencing with other studies.

Examining Material Culture (Artifact Analysis)

The study of material culture—the tools and other artifacts that are created, used, or left behind by society—is closely related to the science of semiotics. While it owes a great debt to the science of archeology, it is not restricted to the search for meaning among the shards and bones of ancient civilizations. Artifact analysis is a modern science as well; modern archeologists also study the garbage dumps of modern society.

Archeologist Ian Hodder (1982) considered that artifact analysis involved a process that began with the interpretation of signs and symbols, making it a legitimate target for both hermeneutic and semiotic analysis approaches. He defined the term "symbol" as the word used to refer to an object or social situation in which a "direct, primary or literal meaning also designates another indirect, secondary and figurative meaning." Hodder (1998) identified the key problem affecting the interpretation of artifacts as the need to locate them within the contexts of their creation, while at the same time interpreting them within the context of the modern researcher. By the very act of being interpreted, the artifact is removed to a new and different context, thus bringing decisive interpretation into question. Potentially, many meanings are possible; the researcher must decide not which is best, but which is most probable. Also related to this problem is the fact that material culture, because it often lasts a long time, either takes on or is given new meanings the longer it is separated from its primary producer. While the artifacts typically retain their original form, their meaning changes: "Material items are continually being reinterpreted in new contexts" (Hodder 1998, 120).

Tilley also commented on the need to look beyond the individual "piece" of material culture itself when deciphering its meaning: "To understand material culture we have to think in terms that go beneath the surface appearances to an underlying reality. This means that we are thinking in terms of relationships between things, rather than simply in terms of the things themselves." For the public administration researcher who plans a study of material culture, Tilley (1989, 188) urged researchers to remember that "the interpretation of the meaning and significance of material culture is a contemporary activity. The meaning of the past does not reside in the past, but belongs in the present."

The Interpretation of Material Culture

The interpretation of artifacts requires that the researcher function in a scientific environment that is halfway between the past and present. Interpretation also involves comparing different examples of material culture. This makes the interpretation process problematic, at best. The physical evidence under study is often not what was expected—it has, as Hodder (1998, 121) noted, "the potential to be patterned in unexpected ways." Furthermore, because physical evidence cannot "talk" directly to the researcher, it forces the analyst to evaluate and enlarge his or her own experience and worldview. At all stages of the evaluation of material culture—from identifying categories, attributes, and what Hodder called the "understanding of high-level social processes"—the researcher must work at three levels of interpretation simultaneously:

1. The *context* within which artifacts are deemed to have similar meanings.
2. Inseparable from understanding the context is the *identification of similarities and differences* in the artifacts. By showing that people responded the same way to similar stimuli, patterns are identified.
3. While working with the first two levels of interpretation, the researcher must also establish their relevance in terms of historical theories regarding the data.

Hodder cautioned interpreters of material culture to not let themselves be locked into a theory simply because it is fashionable at the time of the research: "Observation [of material culture] and interpretation are theory laden, although theories can be changed in confrontation with material evidence in a dialectical fashion." In a final word of warning, he discussed controversies over what is seen as a major weakness of artifact analysis: The lack of a method for confirming interpretive conclusions. For all researchers working with material culture, Hodder proposed two processes to satisfy the critics of interpretation:

> Perhaps the major difficulty is that material culture, by its very nature, straddles the divide between a universal and natural science approach to materials and a historical, interpretive approach to culture. There is thus a particularly marked lack of agreement in the scientific community about the appropriate bases for confirmation procedures. . . . the twin struts of conformation are coherence and correspondence. (Hodder 1998, 122)

As has been shown, material culture interpretation methods involve the simultaneous processes of these three activities: (1) definition of the context of the artifact at its time of creation, (2) identification of patterns of similarities and difference, and (3) the use of relevant theories of social and material culture. The researcher's conclusions must present a coherent picture of the interpretation of the artifacts, while, at the same time, establishing a corresponding relationship between the artifacts, their context, and the interpretive conclusion.

Summary

This chapter discussed some of the ways that researchers go about examining texts, cultural artifacts, body language, and similar types of written and unwritten communications, records, documents, signs, and symbols. The different sources of research data were grouped into four broad categories. The first category is *written texts,* which include books, periodicals, narratives, reports, pamphlets, the mass media, and other published materials. Research using these sources is often called *library research,* or *desk research.*

The second category is *formal and informal documents;* it includes personal messages and assorted types of archival information, such as personal notes and memos, government records and vital statistics, and other informal written materials, including e-mail. The third category is the wide variety of *nonwritten communications,* including graphic displays (graphs, tables, charts), photographs and illustrations, tools and other artifacts, films and videotapes. The fourth category includes all *nonverbal signs and symbols:* body language, facial expressions, gestures, nonverbal symbols and signs, music and dance, animal sounds and behavior, and even noise.

Researchers employ a variety of analysis tools and methods in their study of texts, symbols, and artifacts. Among these are *hermeneutics, content analysis, meta-analysis, proxemics, kinesics, discourse analysis, site surveys,* and more. The analysis approaches used most often in public and nonprofit organization research are the formal literature review; hermeneutic analysis of textual material; content, discourse, and narrative analysis; and semiotic analysis.

Discussion Questions

1. In your own words, define what reviewing the relevant literature means.
2. What are archives and what is archival material?
3. Name some types of archival data, and explain how they can be important for political science research.
4. What is a meta-analysis? Can a meta-analysis be done on qualitative studies?
5. What are the steps in a meta-analysis process?
6. What is the hermeneutic approach to research?
7. What is the hermeneutic circle?
8. What is semiotics? How can political science researchers use these data?
9. What is content analysis?
10. What is measured in a content analysis?
11. What is narrative and discourse analysis?
12. What are some of the ways that researchers study material culture?

Additional Reading

Alejandro, Robert. 1993. *Hermeneutics, Citizenship, and the Public Sphere*. Albany: State University of New York Press.
Banks, Marcus. 2001. *Visual Methods in Social Research*. London: Sage.
Cook, Michael. 1986. *The Management of Information from Archives*. Aldershot, UK: Gower.
Cook, Tomas D., ed. 1992. *Meta-analysis for Explanation*. New York: Russell Sage Foundation.
Fink, Arlene. 1998. *Conducting Research Literature Reviews*. Thousand Oaks: Sage.
Hodder, Ian. 1982. *Symbols in Action*. Cambridge: Cambridge University Press.
Lipsey, Mark W., and David B. Wilson. 2001. *Practical Meta-analysis*. Thousand Oaks: Sage.
Tilley, Christopher, ed. 1990. *Reading Material Culture*. Oxford: Basil Blackwell.
Webb, Eugene J., Donald T. Campbell, Richard D. Schwartz, and Lee Sechrest. 2000. *Unobtrusive Measures*. 2nd ed. Thousand Oaks: Sage.

31 Organizing and Writing the Research Report

Once research data have been collected, tabulated, and analyzed, the researcher must then organize the information and choose a structure for presenting the findings of the study and his or her conclusions. There are many different ways to do this. One way is to use a *chronological* organization. A second approach is to use one that goes from the *general to the specific,* or from the specific to the general. The researcher could use the points in the definition of the study question or the research hypothesis as a discussion structure. This could mean starting a paragraph with a point or a hypothesis, then using material from the literature to show how the point is applied in practice. Many other approaches are also possible.

This book presents no ironclad rules to follow when deciding how to organize research findings and present ideas. However, it is recommended that the report writer avoid jumping around from one point to another with no underlying plan. Remember: A fundamental goal of your writing is that it be *read.* For that to happen, it must be interesting and readable. This requires adopting a structure and sticking to it.

How to Structure the Research Report

The key step in organizing and presenting ideas in a political science research paper is to select a *point of view.* This involves deciding how you will structure the paper so that the ideas flow smoothly from section to section. The chances of the paper being read can often be improved by following a simple, standard structure and by using a writing style consistent with the writing in that field of study. Later, if the researcher tries to publish the research report, the format *must* meet the specific structure and style requirements of the selected journal. For now, researchers should concentrate on meeting as many of the requirements as possible.

Points of View for Research Reports

Different disciplines in the social and administrative sciences and the humanities often recommend a variety of ways to structure or organize the written report. A valuable overview of some of the different directions or points of view that researchers can take when planning and writing reports of their findings has been suggested by Sorrels (1984), who lists these seven different points of view (or "patterns") that are often chosen:

1. The *indirect pattern,* which moves from factual parts to a general conclusion.
2. The *direct form,* which reverses this order. With this form you move from a general conclusion to the facts that support it.
3. A *chronological pattern.* In this organization form you take the reader through an order of events, such as a sequence of dates.
4. A *spatial pattern.* An example of this method is a paper that moves the reader from one department or location to others in a logical sequence.
5. An *analytical organization,* in which the whole is separated into its parts, with each part addressed completely before moving on to the next part.
6. A *comparative pattern.* As the name implies, parts of a whole are compared point by point.
7. A *ranked method,* where portions of the paper are presented in the order of their importance or impact; the importance may be in ascending or descending order.

Sections in a Research Report

Written research reports contain, at most, nine or ten parts or sections. These are usually organized in the manner presented in Figure 31.1. However, it is also important to remember that not all papers and reports follow this format, and not all include every one of these major components.

The following section includes a brief discussion of each of the major report components. Keep in mind that this represents a summary or compendium of many different report style recommendations. As they scan published papers and books, researchers are likely to encounter a host of variations from this list of components. This should not create problems; instead, it allows for greater flexibility in preparing the presentation. Keep in mind that most researchers and business writers in general do not regularly follow any *one* style or format for their reports. With this in mind, the format and style presented here have been designed to meet most key writing requirements and can be safely followed in most instances.

Notice that this list does not include any mention of charts, tables, graphs, illustrations, drawings, models, or other graphic communication tools. That is because these tools are not limited to any one section. Naturally, graphic items are seldom, if ever, found on the *title page* or in the *abstract* or *references.* However, there is nothing to say that they cannot be used in

I.	A *Title Page*
II.	An *Abstract*
III.	An *Introduction* or *Rationale for the Study*
IV.	A *Review of the Literature* examined for the study
V.	A discussion of the *Methodology* used for the study
VI.	A complete discussion of the *Results* or *Findings*
VII.	*Conclusions* and/or *Recommendations*
VIII.	A detailed list of the *References* and/or *Sources Cited*
IX.	Appendices

Figure 31.1 **Nine Major Components of a Research Report**

any or all of the other sections. When used correctly, graphic tools greatly improve the ability of a report to communicate. They allow the researcher to present detailed information *clearly, succinctly,* and *"at a glance,"* regardless of where they are used in the report.

The Title and Title Page

The *Title* is often one of the most important components of a paper. It should leap off the page at the reader, grabbing his or her attention. This does not mean that it should be "cute." In fact, always avoid using anything that smacks of being "cute." Never use slang in your writing. If for some reason slang must be used for special effect, for example, it should always be set off in quotation marks or in italics.

Many students and beginning researchers tend to use titles that are too general or that do not say anything about what the research or assignment involves. For example:

> "A Report in Compliance with the Research Assignment of February 2"

This is not an appropriate title, even if it is true.

Do not make the title too long; eight or ten words ought to be the maximum. Fewer is best. On the other hand, do not be terse (abruptly brief). Research papers are not newspaper stories; short, tricky headlines as titles are not appropriate—even if they are explained in the first section of the paper.

Components of a Good Title

Good titles should contain four key features. First, titles must say what the report is about. Second, they must establish the framework for the study. Third, they clearly identify the subjects about whom the study is about; and fourth, the title should say how the work was done. The components of a good title include the following:

1. The study topic;
2. The specific application or dimension of the topic you studied (examples might be *innovations, revisions, results, effects, use of, new ways of,* etc.);
3. The agency, location, people, industry, or other such relevant focus;
4. Key methodology used (such as qualitative, quantitative, etc.).

The purpose of the title is to tell the reader what the paper is about—and to capture the reader's interest so that the full-finished product is examined. For example, say that a researcher has examined the practices of a state agency accused of practices that are destructive to the environment. The research report might be titled: "Environmental Actions of a State Agency." But that's not good enough. Readers need to know what kinds of actions were studied, why they are important enough to study, and why a report has been written. Who really cares? A better approach to take with the above title, then, might be: "A Review of Reports of the Environmentally Destructive Logging Practices of the State Bureau of Water Resources."

The topic of the paper, the first component, is the "environment." The specific dimension studied is "environmentally destructive logging practices." The organization is the "State Bureau of Water Resources." The methodology is a "review" of published reports. A "review" usually refers to a secondary literature research strategy. The researcher studies the issue by reading all available information about the bureau and the topic. Then, a synthesis of that information is presented in the research report. This *qualitative research* method follows a literature review pattern. It is a good point to include the research *method* followed in the title of the final report as often as possible. Some examples of titles for reports in these types of studies include the following.

Example Qualitative Study Titles

- "An Ethnographic Analysis of Using Community Meetings to Overcome Negative Public Attitudes."
- "Using Personal Interviews as a Way of Measuring Public Confidence in Mutual Funds."

Example Quantitative Study Titles

- "A Factor Analysis of Consumer Attitudes about Banning Smoking in Tacoma, Washington."
- "A Time Series Analysis of Minority Hiring Data in Two California State Agencies."

Finally, the title page should include the title of the paper, the name of the author or authors (usually in alphabetical order based on the first letter of the last name), and any other relevant information. Examples of title pages for a typical class term paper and for a thesis for a master's degree are shown in Figures 31.2 and 31.3.

THE TITLE OF YOUR REPORT

by
Your E. Name

[Put the name of the group, team, or organization here]
[Put the name of the parent agency here]
[Put the submission date of the report here]

Figure 31.2 **Title Page for a Research Report**

THE PRIVATE vs. PUBLIC-POWER FIGHT IN SEATTLE:
1930–1934:
A study of efforts to influence public opinion

by
Your E. Name

A thesis submitted in partial fulfillment of the requirements for the degree of
Master of Arts in Communications

University of Washington
Seattle, Washington

Figure 31.3 **Title Page for a Master's Degree Thesis**

The Abstract

The *abstract* is a concise summary of the research study and report. It is placed at the top of the first page of the paper, immediately below the title and before the introduction section. While most reports are typed double-spaced, the abstract is usually typed single-spaced and indented 5 spaces on both sides of the paper. Typically, the abstract ranges from 100 to 200 words. In some journals, instructions for authors call for the abstract to be less than 100 pages. Whatever length, in this short space the abstract must inform readers what was done, how it was done, the most significant results or findings, and what readers will find when they read the entire paper.

Abstracts are found in all professional journal articles and in the long-form listing of papers included in such CD-ROM databases as *ABI-Inform* and others. Abstracts contain enough information to accurately inform the researcher of the key ideas in a paper, while also encouraging the researcher to read the full paper.

In a report prepared for internal distribution, such as a study done for management or a consultant's recommendation report, the abstract is replaced by a slightly longer summary that is called an *executive summary*. While abstracts follow normal sentence construction, the executive summary may be presented in outline or "bulleted" form. The executive summary is often made into an overhead transparency and used to guide an audience through an oral presentation of the paper. The executive summary is seldom used for classroom reports.

An Example Abstract

In the following 121-word abstract, the authors tell the audience that the paper is about a survey of the perceptions and attitudes on environmental and social issues held by students in

ABSTRACT

This paper presents findings of a cross-cultural survey of university students' perceptions of the importance of environmental and social issues, and of policies and programs to deal with the issues. Graduate and undergraduate students in Canada, Taiwan, and the United States were surveyed. The study grew out of discrepancies seen in various cultures' priorities for resolving environmental problems. The researchers developed a list of 45 environmental and/or social problems and 20 statements about how organizations deal with environmental problems. The findings supported the propositions that different countries have different ideas about global environmental problems, that more international cooperation is needed, and that management education must include more comprehensive discussions of environmental problems to prepare researchers to function in the sustainable-growth economies of the future.

Figure 31.4   **An Example Abstract for a Research Report**

Canada, Taiwan, and the United States. It explains who were members of the sample and provides a rationale for conducting the research. A brief suggestion of the results is also included (Figure 31.4).

The Introduction

In some professional journal formats, this section may be called the *background* section. In others it is referred to as the *rationale for the study*. In some journals, the section may have no label or headline; the writer just begins with the writing. Many political science journals continue to use the *introduction* label. Whether the label is used or not, the purpose of the introduction section is to explain for the reader in some detail what the study and paper are all about. Beyond this, there are few specific rules about what goes in the introduction, only suggestions. The following ideas are some of the things you might wish to think about as you write the introduction for the report or paper.

The introduction section is where readers are introduced to the full scope of the study topic. It includes background information on the topic or situation, the researcher, funding agencies, if any, and any other relevant preliminary information. It is the place to state why the topic was selected. It is also where the steps taken in developing the study are listed. The introduction section explains how or why the study was first considered, and what the researcher hoped to learn by studying this particular topic.

The introduction section sometimes includes a brief discussion of some key items of the literature so that readers can see how the research relates to other work done on this topic. Special care must be taken to avoid simply repeating what others have written, however; the researcher must *interpret* others' reports and indicate how they relate to the new study.

The introduction is the first place where writing should begin to sparkle. This section must be carefully written and rewritten. It is the first chance to "hook" the people who are in a position to judge your research and writing. The following statement from the "Information for Contributors" that appears in every issue of the *Academy of Management Review* (*AMR*) emphasizes the importance of careful presentation of your ideas:

Manuscripts submitted will be judged primarily on their substantive content, but writing style, structure, and length also will be considered. Poor presentation is sufficient reason for reviewers to reject a manuscript. Clarity and logical presentation are necessary; also, a provocative, challenging orientation that stimulates debate is appreciated, assuming professionalism is maintained. (*Academy of Management Review,* 2000)

To summarize, the introduction section should include the following:

- A brief (no more than one or two paragraphs) review of the background of the study.
- A statement explaining why the topic was selected.
- If appropriate, a brief introduction to other research on the subject.
- An indication of what will be presented in the pages to follow.
- Any additional information that logically could be considered as an introduction to the research project, study, topic, or paper.

Review of the Literature

The section that follows the introduction is the *review of the literature.* It should contain the majority of your analysis of what other researchers and authors have said about the topic. This is where results of the library and/or Internet investigation are presented. Since everything included in this section comes from the work of others, the researcher must be careful to always cite sources; if others did the work first, they *must* be given credit.

For research papers that follow a document analysis strategy, this section might more appropriately be called the *discussion section.* For example, for a paper about how elected officials exercise one or more aspects of good leadership, all data might come from already published sources, such as one or more broadly focused political science, public administration, and management journals, or similar sources on CD-ROM or the Internet. Once this is complete, the researcher might then carry out a more extensive search of the political sciences literature for specific articles on the managers in the public sector specifically. This is not as difficult as it sounds because good examples tend to get lots of attention in the media.

The researcher may include introductory paragraphs defining the topic and variables in question; in this example it means describing specific leadership traits. Then, the literature that addressed each of the traits might be examined. In this way, the researcher might do all his or her research examining already published sources. Or the researcher might be asked to prepare a more structured study that involves observing leadership traits as exhibited by managers in the researcher's own organization. The method of gathering this information may be either qualitative, quantitative, or a combination of the two research methods. In this situation, the literature search can provide suggestions about what traits might be more important than others, how leadership traits are or might be measured, and other relevant foundation material.

Research and Theory

Developing new ideas and concepts requires that a researcher first have a thorough grounding in *existing* theory. This comes from a comprehensive review of the literature on the topic. Sources may be personal interviews you conduct with "experts." They may be from the extensive body of domestic and international professional and/or occupational literature, or from current and past textbooks. Or they may be from other published materials such as newspapers, encyclopedias, yearbooks, unpublished papers, opinion pieces by other scholars, or from material prepared expressly for and carried only on the Internet.

To summarize this discussion, your review of the literature (or discussion section in a shorter paper) should do the following:

- Review earlier work done in the field.
- Explain how earlier work relates to this investigation.
- Give examples of directions being taken by other investigators.
- Give a sense of continuity or closure to your work.
- For a shorter paper, it may provide the body of your ideas and results of the study.

Methodology

Sometimes called *research methods,* or *methods and materials,* or simply known as the *methods* section, this is the part of the report where how the work was done is finally and fully explained. In research studies, this section describes in some detail how data were collected and processed. Were the data gathered completely a library study? Was the research limited to a study of Internet sources? If so, why? Was a custom-designed questionnaire developed, or was a pre-prepared questionnaire used for the survey? Why? Were the data gathered by observation? If so, was the researcher functioning as a full participant or as an unobtrusive bystander? Did the research involve conducting a series of personal interviews? Was an experiment designed and carried out? These are only a few of the many different ways to gather information. The method chosen will depend upon the nature of the study problem, the relevant study variables, and the resources available to the researcher.

Methods and Data Differences

It is worthwhile here to briefly review one of the key differences in data as it relates to study methodology. This is the *primary-secondary data* dichotomy. *Primary* data are data that the researcher generates; they can be considered to be specific to the research project at hand. An example is the collective responses to the questions in a questionnaire (also called a *survey instrument*) that are acquired from a sample of voters.

Secondary data, on the other hand, are data that were collected by someone else for a different purpose. Examples include published economic or demographic statistics. Typically, secondary data are cheaper and quicker to gather. Primary data tend to be the more reliable of the two data types. There is a place and purpose for both. If the study is a library or Internet research for a short paper, it will involve gathering secondary data exclusively. If the research study means conducting an experiment to evaluate citizens' responses to various public service announcements, it means gathering primary data.

When gathering secondary data, remember that every source of information used must be identified in the paper. This means including a complete bibliographic citation, including page numbers for actual quotes you include in your paper (page numbers should *not* be used with source citations when they are paraphrased).

Research studies can mean studying published books and articles in the library or checking sources over the Internet. They can require examining artifacts or observing behavior in the field. They can involve developing a set of questions and asking people to respond to a questionnaire. Or they can require carefully designing and conducting an experiment with human subjects. In every case, the researcher must describe exactly what was done and how it was done. That information goes here, in the *methods* section of the research paper.

The Results (Findings) Section

Once readers have been told what was researched and how it was done, it is time to tell them what the research revealed—what it accomplished. Sometimes this section is called the *discussion section;* or it is labeled simply *results* or *findings*. Whichever, this is where readers are shown the results of the effort; in the process, it explains the reasons for conducting the research in the first place.

This information must be presented clearly, factually, simply, and without editorial comment. It is not the place for the researcher to introduce opinions or reactions. This means that conclusions, judgments, or evaluations of the information should not be interjected into this section of the report. The job of the author is simply to *explain what the data reveal;* nothing more.

Do not "editorialize" about the data in this section. Remain cool and objective; simply "tell it like it is." Avoid negative opinions; don't say a manager was "really stupid." However, it is possible to describe the behavior that makes you or others think that he or she was. Let your readers make their own evaluations and conclusions; never tell them how to think.

Conclusions and/or Recommendations Section

Writing a research report can be thought to be much like writing a speech. In both cases, the writer selects a topic, finds out something about the topic, and then writes about it. The writer closes with a summary, and shares conclusions about the process with the audience. People who teach speech making have reduced this to a three-part structure: (1) tell your audience what you are going to tell them; (2) tell them; then (3) tell them what you told them.

In a sense, we have been following these directions as we moved from section to section in this chapter. In the *introduction,* readers were told what the research and report were going to be about. The *methodology* section described the way the data were gathered and processed. The *results* section presented the main body of your research findings. The *conclusions* section is the time to wrap things up by telling the audience what was learned from the research.

A good conclusions section can be one of the most valuable components of a paper (Markman, Markman, and Waddell 1989). The well-written conclusion is part summary, part interpretation, and part recommendations. This section can be used for several different purposes. First, it provides an opportunity to summarize the main ideas gleaned from the literature. It also permits repeating critical findings from any experimental research that might have been conducted. Second, it allows the researcher to *interpret* the findings and to present a subjective interpretation in his or her own words. In a good public administration paper, this may be the only place where the researcher can be "original." To this point, the writing must have remained completely objective. Only the *facts* were reported. Finally, the conclusions section gives the researcher a chance to prove to the readers that the research idea, design, and project were valid and "worth the doing."

Now, however, the research must explain what it all means. To do this well requires the researcher to finally be creative, analytical, and persuasive. At the same time, this is where the author tries to influence the audience or to convince them that the presented interpretation is the "right" one.

Tips for Preparing the Conclusions Section

Begin this section with a brief summary of the research, add your interpretation, and close the report with what you see as implications of the findings, or close with your recommendations. The conclusions section should:

* Summarize the main ideas.
* Say what these ideas mean.
* Include a personal interpretation of the findings (your *opinions*).
* Convince readers that the research was worth the effort.
* Make recommendations, if any, to the reader.

References (Bibliography)

This is where the writer identifies all sources of information used in the conduct of the research project and preparation of the research report. Typically, there are two parts to this section: (1) where in your report you locate the citations used in your study; and (2) an alphabetically listed compilation of all sources cited, studied, or examined during the study. The first part of this section is known as the *notes* or *sources cited* section and can be presented in the report as *endnotes, footnotes,* or *in-text citations*. Notes are presented in chronological order as they appear in the paper, from the first to the last. In-text citations are included in the body of the paper; they appear as the source information is used.

The second part is the *references* or *bibliography* section; it contains complete bibliographic information about all sources used in the study. Many different bibliographic styles are used in research writing. It is usually best to follow the style used by the most influential writers in the field, or to follow the style employed by the "best" journal in the discipline.

Writers may use footnotes, endnotes, or in-text citations to inform readers of the location of their information sources. "Location" information is needed for others to either replicate the study or test for flaws. For papers of approximately ten or twelve pages, authors are no longer required to follow the requirement for endnotes or footnotes. This does not mean that authors can use the work of others as their own. Doing so is *plagiarism,* and plagiarism is theft. The practice is unethical, immoral, and in most cases, illegal. At some universities and colleges, students can be expelled for plagiarism.

What it does mean is that the citations issue can be dealt with by placing the author's name and date of publication in parentheses at the beginning or end of the section dealing with that work. This is called the "in-text citations" form. The in-text citation method is growing in popularity; most publications and organizations prefer that this method be used exclusively. It is the method used throughout this book.

The *references* section of the research paper must include a complete bibliographic citation for every source used in the research. If a source has been examined for the study but not used, it is not necessary to include it in the bibliography.

References Section Summary

The information used as background for a research project can come from published books; periodicals (magazines, newspapers, journals); interviews or surveys; films; electronic sources such as the Internet; government or company brochures, reports, or pamphlets; television programs; or any other source you find. There are a variety of rules for how to list these sources, both as notes and as references.

In the past, some stylebooks called for both notes and references to be included. Today, however, in-text citations are usually substituted for endnotes or footnotes. Most periodicals still require in-text citations be used instead of endnotes or footnotes, together with a formal bibliography at the end of the paper.

Appendix or Appendices

The appendix is the last component of a research paper. This word has two plural forms: *appendixes* or *appendices;* you may use the one you prefer. The *appendix* is where to place any attachments that might relate to the paper but that cannot or should not be placed in the body of the paper itself. A brochure or advertisement is an example. Other examples include a copy of the questionnaire used in a research study, a complicated mathematical table, or a copy of an article from a magazine, journal, or a newspaper. There are no limits to what can or what should be included in the appendices.

The wide variety of materials that could qualify as appendices suggests that there is no one rule or special format to follow for appendices. Style manuals with recommendations pertaining to the appendix tend to agree with the following conclusions, however:

- Research papers for public administration, business, or economics seldom require an appendix or appendices.
- When they are used, they should be attached after the bibliography.
- While it is not completely necessary, a single title page (with the label "Appendix") should be placed before all the attached material.
- Only the number of the appendix title page is noted in the table of contents.
- When more than one appendix is used, the word "Appendices" is placed in the table of contents and on the section title page.
- More than one appendix may be labeled chronologically as follows: *Appendix A, Appendix B, Appendix C,* etc.

Style in Research Report Writing

When editors talk about "style," they mean either one or more of these writing features: (1) an author's choice of words and sentences, (2) how the author employs basic rules of grammar and punctuation, or (3) the mechanics of footnotes, endnotes, in-text citations, and various ways of recording bibliographic (reference) notation. This section is about the third component of the style concept: *notes, citations, and reference notation.* It is also a brief introduction to several of the most commonly used notation styles: the *Modern Language Association* (MLA), the *American Psychological Association* (APA), and the *University of Chicago* (Chicago style). Several discipline style references are also explained.

Style: First Person or Third Person?

Typically, quantitative reports are written in the third person, while qualitative study reports may be written in either the first person or third person. It is good to get in the habit of using the form used most often in your field of interest or study. For example, authors are strongly encouraged to avoid using the first-person approach ("I") in reports on business or economics research, whereas many political science and public administration journals include papers written in both forms. The topic and research methodology followed should dictate the form to use.

As a rule of thumb, however, it is difficult to get into trouble when always using clear, objective writing, and writing in the third-person format. Having said this, it is also important to know that many instructors require that personal opinions are included in class writing. It is believed that doing so encourages students to develop critical thinking skills. Whenever the issue comes up, it is best to comply with one of the first requirements of all writing in organizations: *Write for your audience.* To summarize, here are some key points for the *results* section of your paper:

- Third person is the preferred style for business and economics papers, political science, and public administration papers are written in either first- or third-person format.
- Unless specifically asked for your opinion, do not give it in the results section; it goes in the conclusions section.
- Try not to "editorialize" about the study results in the findings section. Remain objective.
- Avoid negative opinions; let the readers come to their own conclusions.
- Use clear, objective writing.

Is It "Style" or Is It "Format"?

The words "style" and "format" are often used interchangeably to refer to the way a paper is put together. They shouldn't be. They mean different things. *Format* refers to the way the research paper is structured or organized. It includes headlines, subheads, and the order of the components of your paper. *Style,* on the other hand, refers to the choice of words and sentences used in the report. It includes punctuation and grammar.

Format often varies from discipline to discipline, journal to journal, and according to the purpose of the paper. Sometimes, when people talk about *style* they are referring to the *writing rules* endorsed by an organization like the American Management Association or the University of Chicago. At other times, they mean the subjective, creative, artistic part of writing: selecting words that sparkle, using the active rather than the passive voice, using a variety of sentence lengths, and other style elements.

What to Avoid

What kinds of textbooks and articles do you hate to read? A volume with sentences that ramble on forever? One with huge seas of black or gray that put you to sleep because the author refused to paragraph, did not use headlines or subheads, or did not include illustrations or graphics to "perk up" the text? Those that offend you because they either talk down to you or assume you have twenty years' experience in the field and that you understand the complicated or esoteric jargon the author insists on using? Most people prefer textbooks and articles that can be read and understood. These are the examples to use as models for your own writing. Good writing *can* be learned, just as poor writing can be avoided!

Formats for Endnotes, Footnotes, and In-text Citations

Endnotes, footnotes and in-text citations are tools used to show your reader(s) where you found your information and where you locate additional material that you feel contributes to, but should not be an integral part of, the text. Endnotes are footnotes placed at the end of your paper, just before or after your bibliography. Footnotes are placed on the bottom of the page where they are introduced. An identifying number or symbol is placed at the end of the material for which the footnote applies, and repeated at the beginning of the reference information. Superscript is the preferred font for the notations.

Both endnotes and footnotes allow you to include additional or parenthetical information that is not otherwise considered part of the regular flow of your paper. They may be personal observations or comments about or questions raised about the sources. They may also be *asides*—information that adds to the understanding or fuller appreciation of a point in the paper itself. However, their primary purpose is to tell the reader the source of the ideas. Unless the ideas are exclusively yours, their source must always be cited.

Endnote and footnote entries are made in numerical order, from the first to the last. The first time a source is mentioned, a complete bibliographic entry is included. Use the same format required for a complete bibliography. If the end- or footnote is not a citation but rather additional or parenthetical information, it should be written using complete sentences with proper punctuation. With end- or footnotes, the complete citation is included in only the first note. After the first entry, all subsequent entries use only the author's last name. The Latin words ibid. and op. cit. are no longer necessary in political science—or for most social science, for that matter—research reports or any scientific writing.

Format for In-text Citations

Today, the preferred way of noting sources in the body of a paper is the in-text citation method. It is easy and quick to use. In-text citations appear as they occur in your paper—in chronological order. They consist of the author's last name and year of publication, without commas or periods, unless followed by a paper number. Page numbers are added if a direct quote is used; place a comma between the date and page number.

Say, for example, that you are writing a paper by Jones about religion and voting behavior. One of your sources discusses parables found in a political science journal. If you use an idea found in the book or article but express it in your own words (i.e., you paraphrase), you need not place your paraphrasing in quotation marks. At the end of your reference to that work, just add the following notation: (Jones 2000). Beyond this, no end- or footnote notation is required. However, if you quote from the work you must add the page number at the end of the date, thus: (Jones 2003, 243). The work itself would list in your bibliography this way (or in some other accepted form):

Jones, Pen E. 2000. "The Use of Biblical Parables in Legislative Speeches." *Journal of Religion and Politics* 6 (June): 234–52.

Use of Notes in Large Reports

For larger papers and research reports (40 pages or longer), some editors suggest that it is better to continue to use footnotes or endnotes instead of in-text citations. However, if the paper is to be published in a professional journal, the system required by the journal must be used. If it is a paper for a class, follow the instructor's requirements. Here is a good "rule of thumb" to follow: If the paper is shorter than 20 or so pages, do not use endnotes or footnotes; if the paper is longer than 20 pages, you may use endnotes or footnotes. Other than this, use them if doing so makes the paper easier to read or understand. For a report written for a college or university class, it is always best to use the approach that your instructor requires.

Style in the References Section

Most style manuals group source materials into three broad categories: (1) books, (2) periodicals (magazines, journals), and newspapers, and (3) miscellaneous, including pamphlets, brochures, annual reports, letters, interviews, films, etc. Today, a fourth category has been added: *electronic sources.* These include the World Wide Web, CD-ROMs, and miscellaneous electronically accessed databases.

A word of caution: There is a lack of agreement on which is the best or most-appropriate way to list citations. Almost every discipline has its own format. It is up to you to determine which format is accepted or preferred in the organization for which the paper is written. Follow that style. Considerable disagreement also exists on citation formats for electronic sources. Several different citation guides are listed in this guide; one is the *Columbia Guide to Online Style* (1998) published by Columbia University Press.

Political science, public administration, and economics publications usually follow format requirements established or promoted by their respective professional associations. These formats may differ somewhat from the three main style formats: *MLA, APA,* and the *Chicago* style. Communications courses also have format requirements of their own; they often follow a newspaper style established by either the Associated Press (AP) or United Press International (UPI). Citation formats for papers written for natural sciences also vary somewhat from the three major styles.

In the following pages are examples of citation styles for the MLA, APA, and for the University of Chicago's "Chicago style." These are the three "standard" styles recommended for writers. However, some academic disciplines and professions use styles that may differ somewhat from any of the three standard styles. This section also includes mention of some style requirements for government, business, and economic disciplines. Included are styles approved for management, marketing, accounting and finance, human resources, public administration, and economics. Professional societies for each of these disciplines have adopted styles that they require for all writing in their professional journals. And not all societies in the profession have identical style requirements. Book publishers often require their own style. The following is a summary of style information:

- Most style manuals group sources into three categories: books, periodicals, and miscellaneous.

- Today, a fourth category is also used: electronic sources.
- There are many different ways to cite sources: Use *one* and stick to it. Do not create your own.
- These three major styles are the standard forms in use (often with some variation): *MLA, APA,* and *Chicago.*
- Some disciplines recommend using either AP style or UPI style.
- Never mix styles within the same paper.
- Style manuals have been written for many occupations. Find the one used in your industry or discipline and use it for all your writing.

Some Standard Style Requirements

APA Style Highlights

The APA prefers that authors use in-text citations with references to an end-of-paper "works cited" section. This applies for all papers, regardless of length. All source listings should include the author(s) name, title of the work, and publication information. Page numbers are required for all direct quotes. Publication dates are placed in parentheses immediately after the author's name. APA style requires you to *underline* a title if you do not have access to an *italic* typeface. Do not indent the first line of a listing; instead, indent the second and each subsequent line three spaces. All authors' names must be listed—never use *et al.* All names must be inverted (listed last name first). If you do not have an author's name, alphabetize the listing by the first word of the title (except for short words such as *the, a,* or *an*).

Capitalize the first letter of only the first word in book, journal, and newspaper titles (except for proper nouns). Capitalize short titles like *Business Week.* Do not put quotation marks around the titles of journal articles.

Use double space or space-and-a-half for listings. APA also allows but does not require you to drop short labels such as "Press," "Co.," "Corp.," or "Inc." after the name of the publisher. Books printed by university presses are usually typed out in full, thus: Oxford University Press.

Periodical citations include the name(s) of the author(s), date of publication, title or headlines of the articles, and name of the periodical; use initial capital letters for periodical title names (examples: *Business Week, Political Science Quarterly, Journal of State and Local Government*). Volume and issue numbers, when available, are also included, appearing just before page numbers.

Other sources includes such things as pamphlets, government or company brochures, dissertations, conference proceedings, personal letters and interviews, annual reports, and the like. These are all legitimate published sources, and should be listed in your bibliography in the same way as books and periodicals.

Chicago Style Highlights

The editorial staff of the University of Chicago Press, a major publisher of works by academic authors, printed its first *Manual of Style* for writers in 1906. Since that time, the manual has gone through at least fourteen revisions, with more on the way. Possibly because it deals with the publication of books more than articles or papers, the Chicago manual recommends use of footnotes rather than in-text citations. A full bibliographic listing is required in the end-of-work references section.

When available, all listings should include the author(s) name, title of the work, and publication information. Page numbers are required for all direct quotes. Publication dates are placed at or near the end of the listing, immediately before the citation of the page numbers. Chicago style requires titles to be in *italics*. Bibliographic listings are presented in alphabetical order, single-spaced, with two spaces between each listing.

Only first-author names should be inverted (listed last name first); others are listed first name, middle initial, last name. If you do not have an author's name, alphabetize the listing by the first word of the title. All authors' names must be listed—never use *et al.* Capitalize the first letter of all words in book, journal, and newspaper titles. Put quotation marks around the titles of journal articles.

Chicago style requires these items to be listed in the following order:

1. Name of the author or authors, editors, or institution responsible for the writing of the book,
2. Full title of the book, including subtitle if one exists,
3. Series, if any,
4. Edition if not the first,
5. Publication city,
6. Name of the publisher,
7. Date of publication.

Periodical citations should include as many of the following as possible:

- Name(s) of the author(s),
- Title of the article,
- Name of the publication,
- Volume (and number) of the periodical,
- Date of the volume or of the issue,
- Page numbers of the article.

Other sources includes such things as pamphlets, government or company brochures, dissertations, conference proceedings, personal letters and interviews, annual reports, and the like. These are all legitimate published sources, and should be listed in your bibliography in the same way as books and periodicals. Some specific style examples include the following:

1. A government pamphlet brochure, no author listed:

U.S. Dept. of Agriculture. *Regulations for Applying Pesticides.* Washington, DC: U.S. Government Printing Office, 1990.

2. Company pamphlet, brochure, or annual report:

The Boeing Co. *1997 Annual Report.* Seattle: The Boeing Co., 1998.

The following data for electronic sources have been adapted to come as close as possible to Chicago style guidelines. Electronic sources must include as much of the following information that is available. For a known author, include the following:

- Author(s) name(s),
- Date it was placed on the Web,
- Title of the piece (including edition number, if not the original),
- (Type of medium),
- Producer (optional),
- If available: supplier or database identifier or number,
- Date you accessed the article.

When the author is unknown, include the following information:

1. Title (edition),
2. (Type of medium),
3. Year,
4. Producer,
5. If available: supplier/database identifier or number,
6. Access date.

MLA Style Highlights

According to the MLA, all sources included in a bibliography include three main components: author(s), title, and publication information. All other style formats are in agreement with these requirements; they differ, however, in the way and the order in which they are presented. MLA requires that this section be a separate page or pages and be titled "Works Cited." In citing books using MLA style, an entry can include most (but seldom, all) of the following information:

1. Author(s) name(s),
2. Title of the section, if a part of a book,
3. Title of the book,
4. Name of the editor, translator, or compiler, if appropriate,
5. Edition of the work,
6. Name(s) or number(s) of the volume(s) used, if a multivolume work,
7. Name of the series, if part of a series of books,
8. Place of publication (city),
9. Name of the publisher,
10. Date of publication,
11. Page numbers, if quoted or if the work is part of a compendium,
12. Any other relevant bibliographic information and/or annotation.

In addition to the above parts, as many as twelve or more types of book listings are described in the MLA style manual. These range from a single author to multiple or unknown authors. Also included are compilations by editors, various editions or volumes in a series, parts of books, the foreword or preface, encyclopedias, and dictionaries. Only a few of the most commonly encountered versions are listed here. When the name of a book's author is not known, the title of the book or journal is substituted.

MLA style calls for two spaces between citation components (for example, between the author's name and title of the work). If you do not have access to an italic typeface for the title, underline it instead. Do not indent the first line of each bibliography or note listing; instead, indent the second and each subsequent line five spaces.

Use double space or space-and-a-half for all listings. MLA also recommends that short labels such as "Press," "Co.," "Corp.," or "Inc." should not be included after the name of the publisher. An exception to this rule is for books printed by university presses: Instead of typing "Oxford University Press," use "Oxford UP." Some specific examples are shown below.

For books, include the following information:

1. Books with one author:

Aldershot, Benjamin B. *Writing for Fun and Profit.* Chicago: Winslow. 1997.

2. Books with two or more authors:

West, Barbara A. and Janet C. Lagerquist. *Principles of Qualitative Research.* London: Oxford UP. 1998.

   (Only the first author is listed last name first; separate the names of three or more authors by commas.)

3. Books with editors:

Andreeson, Elizabeth, ed. *Strategies for Competing after 2000.* Homewood, IL: Business Books. 1999.

4. Author with an editor (article in an anthology):

Marshall, Jay B. "From Cottage to Factory." *Wool and the Industrial Revolution in Britain.* Ed. James B. Galloway. Liverpool: Liverpool UP. 1990: 87–102.

   (Note that the title of the article or chapter in this book is in quotation marks; the book's editor comes after the book title, with 'Ed.' (for 'Edited by') before the editor's name; pages of the section are noted after the date, separated by a colon.)

5. Books, second or later edition:

Smith, Alfred E. *Principles of Management.* 6th ed. San Jose: Lighthouse. 1998.

6. Article in an encyclopedia.

"Ethics." *Encyclopedia Britannica.* 15th ed. 1995.

Periodicals (Magazines, Journals, and Newspapers)

Periodicals include professional and popular press magazines and newspapers that appear as often as daily or as seldom as once or twice a year. They may be of general or special interest. They may carry news of an industry, a career field, or may be about research or new developments in a discipline. Because the articles usually go into some depth on a specific idea, problem, or question, they are excellent sources of information for papers. Most, but not all, periodicals include the name of the author(s), and titles or headlines for each of the articles.

Newspapers are published daily, weekly, every one or two weeks, or monthly. Not all newspaper articles include the author's name (the author's name is sometimes called a *byline*). Newspaper articles are usually current; they include what is news *today*. However, most of the time they do not go into much depth. Exceptions are the *Wall Street Journal* and Sunday edition of the *New York Times*.

A reference listing of a periodical article must include the name of the author, the title of the article, name of the periodical, month and year of publication, and page numbers. Newspaper article citations also include the day of publication and section, if available. If the article is broken into two or more sections, say on pages 33 to 40, and continued on pages 101 to 105, use 33+, not 33–105. Following are some of the most commonly used ways to present periodical source citations:

1. Article in a weekly publication:

Serenski, Sergi V. "Cost Accounting Is Sexy." *Business Week*. 22 February 1998: 35–36.

2. Article in a monthly or quarterly journal:

Rice, Jerry B. "Tracking the Cost of Professional Football Admissions." *Journal of Accounting*. January 1991. 64–72.

(Substitute the season for the month for quarterly publications; example: Spring 1991)

3. Unknown author:

"Boeing Employment Cuts Go Deep." *Time*. 3 December 1998. 20–21.

4. Article in a newspaper:

Sorenson, Theodore X. "Microsoft Foes Throw Rocks at Windows." *Tacoma News-Tribune*. 5 October 1999. B1.

(The notation "B1" indicates that the article appeared on the first page of the "B" section of this day's paper.)

Citation information for other sources. Other sources includes such things as pamphlets, government or company brochures, dissertations, conference proceedings, personal letters and interviews, annual reports, and the like. These are all legitimate published sources, and should be listed in your bibliography in the same way as books and periodicals. Some specific MLA style examples include the following:

1. A government pamphlet brochure, no author listed:

U.S. Dept. of Agriculture. *Regulations for Applying Pesticides*. Washington: GPO. 1990.

   ("GPO" is the U.S. Government Printing Office, where most federal publications are published and distributed.)

2. Company pamphlet, brochure, or annual report:

The Boeing Co. *1997 Annual Report*. Seattle: The Boeing Co. 1998.

3. Unpublished (Ph.D.) dissertation or (M.A.) thesis:

McNabb, David E. *Segmenting the Market for Post-secondary Education*. Diss. Oregon State U. 1980.

4. A personal letter:

LeBlank, Peter A. Letter to the author. 25 June 1997.

5. A personal interview:

Jones, Edward S. Personal interview. 30 January 1996.

6. Published proceedings of a conference:

Sepic, F. Thomas and David E. McNabb. "Organization Climate and an Organization's Readiness for Change." *Proc. of Western Decision Sciences Institute*. 1994. Fullerton: Cal-State Fullerton. 1994.

Electronic Sources Highlights

Today, researchers and authors are turning to electronic sources for much, if not most, of their secondary information. Changes in these sources are occurring rapidly; the World Wide Web (www) and on-line databases are rapidly becoming preferred sources for research information. However, until recently no provision was made for citing electronic sources. Style guides still do not agree upon the preferred format(s) to use for the www and other electronic sources. The following recommendations are from James-Catalao's *Researching on the World Wide Web* (1996), Harnack and Kleppinger's (1997) manual *ONLINE! A Reference Guide to Using Internet Sources,* and Li and Crane's (1996) publication *Electronic Styles: A Handbook for Citing Electronic Information.*

A citation for a Web source must include as much of the following information as is available: author(s) name(s), title of the piece, date it was placed on the Web, address and/or other retrieval information, and date you accessed the article. The following recommendations have been adapted to comply with MLA style requirements.

1. World Wide Web sources:

U.S. Dept. of Labor. "The Occupational Safety and Health Act of 1970 (OSHA)" *Small Business Handbook: Safety and Health Standards.* November 1997. World Wide Web. 2 December 1998. http://www.dol.gov/dol/asp/public/programs/handbook/osha.htm.

Gillmor, Dan "Nader may be the true Microsoft threat." 27 October 1997. World Wide Web. 23 November 1998. http://www.computerworld.com.

2. An e-mail source:

McNabb, David E. (mcnabbde@plu.edu). *Students' Attitudes on Environmental Issues.* 4 November 1998. E-mail. Prof. Samuel Goldberg (sgoldberg@obitstateu.edu).

Other Style Manuals

Many different style manuals have been written to help you with your writing. While they all seem to vary a bit in their recommendations, they serve a common purpose. That is to serve as a guide to the "proper" way to present your written report. Some of the manuals are slim pamphlets; others are full-size books. Some manuals give suggestions and rules for all aspects of researching; others are only guides to citing sources. The following is a partial list of available style manuals; most can be found in any college or university library.

General

1. *The Complete Guide to Citing Government Information Sources: A Manual for Writers and Librarians.*
2. *Electronic Styles: A Handbook for Citing Electronic Information.*
3. *The Little, Brown Guide to Writing Research Papers.*
4. *The McGraw-Hill Style Manual.*
5. *Manual for Writers of Term Papers, Theses and Dissertations.* (Kate Turabian)
6. *A Manual of Style: U. S. Government Printing Office.*
7. *Prentice-Hall Handbook for Writers.*

Environment and Earth Sciences

1. *Suggestions to Authors of the Reports of the United States Geological Survey.*

   Originally an internal USGS document, this manual has been made available to the public and serves as a guidebook for all writing in the earth sciences.

Education

1. *Journal Instructions to Authors: A Compilation of Manuscript Guidelines from Education.*

Computer Topics

1. *Electronic Styles: A Handbook for Citing Electronic Information.*

Journalism

1. *A Broadcast News Manual of Style.*
2. *UPI Stylebook (United Press International).*
3. *AP Stylebook (Associated Press).*

Law

1. *The Bluebook: A Uniform System of Citation.*

Psychology

1. *Publication Manual of the American Psychological Association (APA Style Manual).*

Social Science

1. *Writing for Social Scientists: How to Start and Finish Your Thesis, Book or Article.*

Requirements for Political Science Journal Articles

Although most journal articles follow a format similar to that of a formal research report, articles are typically less detailed than the report. Often, they must include all the pertinent details of the study in less than twenty double-spaced typewritten pages, including illustrations and references. Huck and Cormier (1996) have provided the following outline for most journal articles:

1. Abstract
2. Introduction
   a. Review of the Literature
   b. Statement of Purpose
3. Method
   a. Participants
   b. Materials
   c. Dependent Variables
   d. Procedure
4. Results
5. Discussion
6. References

The abstract should contain enough information written in such a way as to encourage readers to delve deeper into the article. Included in the abstract must be a statement of the purpose of the study or the objectives for the research, a description of the subjects who participated in the study, a short explanation of what the subjects did as part of the study (such as complete a survey instrument, etc.), and a summary of the important findings. Abstracts for articles on theory or model building and/or testing replace the subject participant information with an explanation of how and why the theory or model was developed. Abstract lengths vary; for the *Political Science Quarterly,* for example, the abstract should be limited to no more than 200 words, whereas other journals ask that the abstract not exceed 100 words.

The results section of the article may be presented as part of the written test of the paper or summarized in one or more tables, charts, or graphs. Theory and model papers may present the results section as mathematical constructs as well as models or charts. It is important to remember at this point that the information should talk specifically to the results of the researcher's work. Often this section is exceedingly technical, and may not be fully understood by readers unfamiliar with the concepts. This problem is resolved in the next section of the article, the discussion section. The discussion section is usually written as the researcher's nontechnical interpretation of the results. It also includes an explanation of what the results or findings mean in terms of the key purpose and/or objectives of the research. Finally, Huck and Cormier note that the label "conclusion" is often used in place of "discussion," but that there is no difference in what the section includes.

Political Science Style Recommendations

Style recommendations of the *Academy of Political Science* can be found in such journals as the *Political Science Quarterly (PSQ)* and other affiliated journals. Some journals use the *Chicago Manual of Style* system for citation notations, whereas many other journals follow some form of APA style. A feature of most, if not all, political science journals is the use of in-text citations rather than endnotes or footnotes, although some journals still use footnotes for ancillary information in the text of the article. Some additional style information includes the following:

1. *Cover page:* The title of the paper, author's name, position, and organizational affiliation (for a class paper use the course number and name). At the top of the first paper only the title is repeated.
2. *Abstract:* An abstract of between 100 and 200 words should be placed on the first page between the title and the start of the paper's text.
3. *Headings:* The introduction section does not have a heading. Do not number any headings or subheadings. Headings are typically used for the *findings* and *conclusions* sections. Other headings may be used at the discretion of the author.
4. *Summary:* Papers should *not* end with a summary section. If relevant, a summary may be included in the author's conclusion section.
5. *Tables, graphs, figures:* When the paper is distributed within an organization, the tables, graphs, and figures should be inserted into the paper itself. When sending the paper to a journal for publication, tables, graphs, and figures should be attached as separate sheets.

   Authors must explain all tables, graphs, and figures in the body of the paper itself. All tables, graphs, and figures *must* be numbered and titled. When submitting the paper to a journal, tables are often numbered with Roman numerals (example: Table IX). For papers distributed within an organization, either Roman numerals or Arabic numbers may be used.

   A reference to the table *must* be included in the body of the text. Tables must have a title and a descriptive legend. Titles, column headings, captions, etc. must be clear and to the point.

Figures must be numbered with Arabic numerals (example: Figure 9). Each figure must have a title followed by a descriptive legend. The figure's title should be part of the caption.

6. *Footnotes:* Authors should avoid the use of notes as much as possible. If notes must be used, they should be numbered sequentially. A listing of footnotes typed on a separate page must be placed before the references section.

7. *Citations:* The first line of the citation should be flush left; all other lines are to be indented three spaces. Do not number the citations. In the body of the paper, use the *Chicago Manual* with in-text citations format for documentation:

> Jones and Smith (1997) found that . . .

If the in-text citation includes a quotation, the page number must be added after the date of publication, separated by a comma, as follows:

> (Jones and Smith 1997, 25).

8. *References:* The references section should include only works cited in the text. They must be typed on a separate page(s) under the heading: References. Some papers and articles include both a general bibliography and a works cited section in the references. References are listed alphabetically according to the first initial of the last name of the first author. The following hypothetical examples are typical reference listings:

A. Book citations:

Adams, Joseph M. 2002. "The Voting Behavior of Minorities Serving in the American Armed Forces." *Military Themes and Concepts.* 24 (March). 3–27.

Rouge, Anna M., and Marvin O. Johnson. 1994. *Governing the Ungovernable City.* San Bruno, CA: Mathematics Press.
For more than one work by the same author, list the works in order of publication (earliest first). Use an eight-spaced underline in place of the author's name. If subsequent works have different second or more authors, continue to list them chronologically after the first notation of the principal author. Examples:

1. Lee, Brian, and Elizabeth Chung. 1994. . . .
2. ———, and Susan H. Arden. 1996. *Training for Quick Advancement.* Tacoma, WA: University of Puget Sound Press. Note: Some journals require the use of five hyphens in place of an underline for the second and more citations by an author:
3. ———. 1997. *Development in the Central City.* Roseburg, OR: City Press.

B. Books with an editor (collective works):

Rom, Charlene D., and William D. Brown. 1997. Health programs in the inner city. In *Medical Delivery Systems Today,* Richard E. Keating and John P. MacDonough, eds. Seattle: University of Washington Press.

C. Periodicals:

Pearl, Andrew O. 1995. Measuring organizational climate in public organizations. *American Journal of Political Science.* 17 (Winter): 101–10.
Note that only the first word in the article title is capitalized; all words in the periodical title begin with a capital letter. Titles are not set apart by quotation marks. Periods separate sections. The volume number but not month of issue is included; a colon separates the volume number from the page numbers.

Finance and Economics Research Reports

The *Journal of Macroeconomics* and the *Journal of Economic Perspectives* are examples of finance periodicals. They follow style requirements established by the American Finance Association: *The Chicago Manual of Style* (14th ed.). Style requirements can be found in the *Journal of Macroeconomics.*

Organizational Management Reports

Papers written for management topics usually follow style requirements established by the *American Academy of Management,* PO Box 3020, Briarcliff Manor, NY, 10510–8020. Examples and guidelines for authors can be found in the *Academy of Management Review* and other periodicals published by the Academy.

Like all other discipline publication requirements, the Academy of Management asks that all papers be double-spaced and typed in a plain twelve-point typeface (font). If it is impossible to italicize in the paper, underlining is allowed. Boldface type should be used for the title and headings. Tables should be typed in the same font used for the body of the paper. A title page is required. An abstract of seventy-five or fewer words should be included under the title near the top of the second page. The abstract should state the purposes for the research; include any theoretical basis for the hypotheses, analyses, major results, and implications of the findings.

Summary

Today, almost all publications follow the in-text citation model. Begin with the authors' last names and the year of the reference in parentheses. For works with two authors, both names should be used every time the work is cited. For three or more authors, cite all authors the first time the reference is cited. All references used in the paper should appear in a separate section at the end of the report but before any appendices, tables, or figures. Start with a new sheet, continuing with pagination used in the body of the paper. The word **REFERENCES** should be centered in capital letters, boldfaced, at the top of the section. Double-space all references.

Citations should be in alphabetical order by the last name of the author or first author in multiple-author works or by the organization for a corporate author (example: *Seattle Times*). When more than one work by the same author or authors is used, use the most current one first. If there are two or more works with the same publication date use lower-case letters to distinguish them (1987a, 1987b, 1987c, etc.). Use the author(s)' name each time the work is cited (do *not* use the one-half-inch underline method).

Reference listings use authors' last names and initials. Additional authors of a work are also presented with the last name first followed by their initials. Use ampersand signs for additional authors. Italicize titles of publications (underline if unable to use italics). Finally, here are some tips for producing a research report that reflects favorably upon you and your work.

1. Write in the active voice.
2. Use past tense when describing the research project you have completed.

3. Arrange citations in alphabetical order according to the last name of the first author or name of the publishing organization if no author is listed.
4. List in the bibliography only the sources you have cited in the paper.
5. Use authors' initials or first and/or middle initials, following the style used in your discipline.
6. Put the date of publication immediately after the authors' name(s).
7. Capitalize only the first word of an article or book chapter title. Do not put the title in quotation marks.
8. Italicize (or underline, if necessary; not both) the title of the journal and/or book.
9. In citations for direct quotes, include the page number after the year; separate the year and page number with a comma and a space.
10. Multiple works by the same author in the same year should be distinguished by letters (1999a, 1999b, 1999c, etc.).
11. Include charts, graphs, illustrations, and tables in the body of the paper. Be sure to discuss the contents of each item in the paper, as near to the item as possible.
12. Place "Table" and its number above each table, and "Figure" and a number beneath graphs and other illustrations.

Discussion Questions

1. Select several different points of view used in research report writing. Compare and contrast the ones you are most interested in using.
2. What should you remember about the title of a research report?
3. In your own words, describe what makes a good abstract.
4. What should you include in the introduction section of a research report?
5. What are some of the important questions to answer in the methods section of the report?
6. What goes in the results section of the paper?
7. How does the conclusions section differ from the results section?
8. What is an in-text citation? How does it differ from endnote style?
9. What are some of the important features of the appendices section of the research report?
10. When should you write in the third-person style? When should you use the first-person style?

Additional Reading

Barzun, Jacques, and Henry F. Graff. 1992. *The Modern Researcher*. 5th ed. Ft. Worth: Harcourt, Brace, and World.
Baugh, L. Sue. 1995. *How to Write Term Papers and Reports*. Lincolnwood, IL: VGM Career Horizons.
Becker, Howard S. 1986. *Writing for Social Scientists*. Chicago: University of Chicago.
Williams, Joseph M. 1990. *Style: Toward Clarity and Grace*. Chicago: University of Chicago.

32 Introduction to Statistical Software: Excel™ and SPSS®

The great strides in computing power that have taken place since the appearance of the early desktop computers and electronic word processors in the 1970s have revolutionized the teaching and application of statistics and statistical analyses. This technology was once available to only a limited number of technically trained scientists and engineers with access to large mainframe computers, but today nearly everyone can use statistical software that researchers in the not-too-distant past could only dream about. Sophisticated statistical analysis can, indeed, today be carried out with just a few simple keystrokes. This chapter provides instructions on how to use two important statistical software programs that have been discussed at times in earlier chapters on quantitative methods. The statistical programs are Microsoft® Excel™ and the Statistical Package for the Social Sciences® (SPSS®).

Introduction to Excel™

Although not all users are aware of it, Microsoft® Corporation's ubiquitous spreadsheet program Excel™ has a powerful statistical processing capability built in. This program includes about eighty individual statistical functions or variations thereof, and another two dozen advanced inferential statistical processes. With the built-in Chart Wizard function and the ability to export output to the Microsoft® word processing program *Word,* Excel has become one of the most important statistical-processing and report-writing software tools available today.

Among the most important and most useful processing capabilities in Excel™ are: (1) full set of database descriptive statistics, (2) multivariate crosstabulation tables in Excel™ Pivot-Tables [sic], (3) charts, scatterplots, and area, line, and pie diagrams, (4) regression analysis, forecasting techniques with trends, (5) time-series programs with smoothing techniques, and (6) many of the most-used univariate, bivariate, and multivariate inferential statistical programs. Excel™ also contains a large number of easy-to-use algebraic and other mathematical functions that are useful for developing and solving mathematical models.

Getting Started in Excel™

All statistical processing in Excel™ begins with a spreadsheet-based dataset. The data collected for subjects or cases are entered in individual rows for each case. The values for each variable

Table 32.1

An Example of an Excel™ Spreadsheet Database

| | Party | | |
County	Dem	Ind	Rep
Adams	35	37	28
Grant	30	34	36
King	39	27	34
Lewis	42	20	38
Lincoln	44	17	39
Pierce	55	24	21
Sherman	26	31	43
Snohomish	32	32	36
Stevens	55	23	22
Thurston	23	35	42

are entered in columns. (Remember: rows = cases; columns = variables.) A typical Excel™ spreadsheet database is displayed in Table 32.1.

The data in an Excel™ file are held in two locations: a *workbook* in which files are organized and analyzed, and one or more *worksheets* that make up a *workbook*. Each workbook may contain one or more worksheets; worksheets in a workbook file are numbered consecutively from 1 upward. File tabs for each worksheet in the workbook are located at the bottom-left-hand corner of the Excel™ screen.

Most of the statistical functions in Excel™ give the researcher a choice of where the results of a statistical activity are to be located after processing. The researcher may select one or more cell addresses in an in-use worksheet, or may elect to have the test results located on a new worksheet. Although it is not a requirement, the database is typically maintained on one worksheet, with statistical process-output data directed to new worksheets. In this way, there is less possibility of contamination of the database. However, a worksheet may contain all, or any part, of the raw data file, file explanatory information, and all or any part of saved statistical information for a database.

Location of the Most-Used Functions

Most of the statistical functions used in Excel™ are found in either one of three locations: the *Function Wizard, Data Analysis* file, or the *PivotTable* tool. The first of these locations, the Function Wizard, contains individual statistical processes or variations of statistical tests. In Excel™ 2000, the Function Wizard is found on the program's main tool bar, and is accessed by pressing the lowercase f_x button. A two-pane menu option window appears when this button is pressed. The left-hand pane contains a list of twelve function categories. Researchers will use three of the options most often: *Statistical, Math* and *Trig,* and *Most Recently Used.* The statistical category will be the most important of the options for researchers. This option contains eighty separate statistical processes, from the *Average* (the mean) to the *Z-test* and most other statistical tests in between.

The second major statistical test location is in the *Data Analysis file.* This set of statistical tests is accessed from the *Tools* option. The activating button for Tools can be found at the top of the Excel™ screen. Until Windows™ 2002, Data Analysis was typically not loaded onto the computer with standard editions of Excel™. However, beginning with the 2002 version, Data Analysis is now automatically included when loading Excel™ from the CD-ROM or programs disks. To access the file if it does not appear when the Tools option is selected, the user must add it to the computer in a one-time operation. To do so, select the *Add-Ins* option in the Tools file. Check the *Analysis ToolPak* (do not load the *VBA Analysis* toolpak; the VBA set of tools are for other uses) and follow the loading instructions. You may need to refer to your program's disk to complete the installation. Once installed, Data Analysis is always accessed from the Tools option.

The Data Analysis set of statistical processes includes a short group of the more sophisticated inferential statistical processes you will need to analyze a dataset. This subset of statistical processes include a composite descriptive statistics option, several different analysis of variance procedures, three small-sample *t*-tests, regression and correlation analysis, and several different time series analysis options, among others.

The third most-used tool in the Excel™ package of statistical processes is what Excel™ calls "PivotTables," and what other statistical packages and textbooks call "crosstabulations." Click on the *Data* option located on Excel™'s main tool bar; this allows you to activate *PivotTables*. The crosstabulations produced by this tool are a category of descriptive statistics called *bivariate frequency distributions*. PivotTables are used to visually display the relationship between two or more variables.

The counts of responses and/or percentages of responses for each category may be displayed in a table. Although crosstabulations are possible with continuous data, they are typically used for categorical variables—variables that have a small number of possible responses, usually no more than five or six. Examples include demographic categories such as gender or age groups, yes-no answers, five-point agree/disagree scales, etc. Larger numbers of responses can make the resulting table too complicated or "busy" to read.

Putting Excel™ to Work

Excel™ can process statistical tests for most of the applications the political science researcher will require. In the order they are usually applied, the test results can be grouped into the following eight categories; each category has been discussed in earlier chapters; because they are used most often, instructions for the first six categories are also included here:

1. Univariate descriptive statistics (frequencies tables and other graphic tools)
2. Bivariate and multivariate descriptive statistics (crosstabulations)
3. One-sample hypothesis tests
4. Two-and-more-sample hypothesis tests
5. Association tests
6. Simple regression analysis

7. Time series, including trend-smoothing alternatives
8. Miscellaneous statistical and database management functions

Univariate Descriptive Statistics with Excel℗

The first analysis step in most research projects is the summarizing of the data for each variable. In a survey research study, for example, this involves counting and determining the percentages of all possible responses to each question. These *univariate frequency distributions* may be displayed in either a table or a graph of some kind—or both. Once the responses are counted, researchers then begin producing descriptive statistics for each variable. Researchers are typically concerned with four classes of descriptive statistics: measures of central tendency, measures of variation, measures of relative location, and measures of association.

Excel℗ produces descriptive statistics in two ways. The first is by selecting each of the desired statistics from the eighty items in the Function Wizard applications file. Examples of descriptive statistics include the average (more commonly called the *mean*), the median, and the mode; the variance and standard deviation; the range, percentiles, and quartiles; and correlation. The second way to produce most of these statistics is with the Descriptive Statistics subcommand in the Tools ⇒ Data Analysis option. Table 32.2 displays the results of three separate Descriptive Statistics commands on the raw data contained in the hypothetical party affiliation database displayed in Table 32.1.

Bivariate Crosstabulations with Excel℗ PivotTable

A crosstabulation (usually simply referred to as a "crosstab") is a bivariate or multivariate frequency distribution table. That is, it allows the researcher or analyst to present summary

Table 32.2

Three Microsoft Excel℗ Data Analysis Descriptive Statistics Examples

Democrats		Republicans		Independents	
Mean	38.1	Mean	33.9	Mean	27.9
Standard Error	3.5101	Standard Error	2.4561	Standard Error	2.1367
Median	37	Median	36	Median	29
Mode	55	Mode	36	Mode	31
Standard Deviation	11.1	Standard Deviation	7.7667	Standard Deviation	6.7569
Sample Variance	123.21	Sample Variance	60.322	Sample Variance	45.656
Kurtosis	−0.834	Kurtosis	−0.673	Kurtosis	−1.22
Skewness	0.3977	Skewness	−0.751	Skewness	−0.256
Range	32	Range	22	Range	20
Minimum	23	Minimum	21	Minimum	17
Maximum	55	Maximum	43	Maximum	37
Sum	381	Sum	339	Sum	279
Count	10	Count	10	Count	10

Table 32.3

An Excel™ Pivot Table 2 × 3 Crosstabulation Example

Count of Responses

Gender	No Opinion	Not Support	Support	Grand Total
Female	12	34	15	61
Male	6	24	29	59
Grand Total	18	58	44	120

Table 32.4

A Pivot Table 2 × 3 Crosstabulation Example, *n* = 120

Percent of Total

Gender	No Opinion	Not Support	Support	Grand Total
Female	10.00%	28.33%	12.50%	50.83%
Male	5.00%	20.00%	24.17%	49.17%
Grand Total	15.00%	48.33%	36.67%	100.00%

information on two (or more) variables together in a single table. Nelson (2002, 81) considers the PivotTable option "perhaps the most powerful analytical tool that Excel™ provides."

A PivotTable crosstabulation can display the counts and/or percentages of times that combinations of values for two or more variables occur. For example, the researcher might want to compare the responses of female candidates with responses of male candidates on one or more questions, such as attitudes toward a particular foreign policy proposal. The candidates may respond that they either support, do not support, or have no opinion about the issue; their responses can then be displayed in a 2 by 3 crosstabulation: two values for gender (either female or male) and three possible responses to the question about the policy proposal. Table 32.3 is an example of the two-variable crosstabulation prepared with Excel™'s PivotTable. Rows are cases—in this example, gender (females and males); columns are responses to the question about their attitudes toward the issue, broken down by the three possible responses (the data are hypothetical and do not represent real distributions).

PivotTable contains nearly a dozen different ways for the cell data to be displayed. It is also possible to vary the form the cell information will take. Table 32.3 displays counts of responses. However, it could also have shown sums, averages, maximum or minimum amounts, products, some percentages, etc. These PivotTable field options are accessed by (1) right clicking on one of the amounts shown in the cell, (2) selecting *Field Settings* from the shortcut menu that appears, (3) then selecting the desired option from the PivotTable Field dialog box. A second dialog box appears when *Options* is selected: a "Show Data As:" window appears in this portion of the Field box with the default setting of *Normal*. Using the scroll toggle in this window, scroll down until the desired option appears. For example, click on the "% of total" option. The values in every cell in the crosstabulation will now show the counts changed to the percentage of the total each cell total represents. Marginal totals will also change to percentages.

Table 32.4 is the PivotTable crosstabulation of Table 32.3 data, but changed to show percentages instead of counts.

One- and Two-or-More-Samples Hypothesis Tests with Excel™

Hypothesis testing is a fundamental activity in inferential statistics. In fact, hypotheses are the primary building block of all scientific research. Hypotheses are prepared in pairs. One, called the *null hypothesis,* is a statement of how things are prior to testing. The second, the *alternate hypothesis,* is the opposite of the null. The alternate hypothesis is also called the *test hypothesis.* In a one-sample hypothesis test, the researcher may want to know whether a sample is from a population with a known mean and standard deviation. If the sample has less than 30 respondents, the researcher will use a one-sample *t*-test to test the hypothesis. If the sample has more than 30 subjects—a large sample situation—the researcher will test the hypothesis using a *Z*-test. Several different applications for both of these tests are accessed in the Excel™ Function Wizard.

In a two-group example, the researcher may want to know whether female voters responded differently than male voters to a question. The null hypothesis will state that there is no difference in the way the two groups respond—the responses for females are the same as the responses for males. The alternate states that there is a difference—at some researcher-selected level of confidence—one of the groups has either a greater or lesser proportion of positive or negative responses. The researcher will use either one of the several different *t*-tests or one of the ANOVA tests—both of which are found in the Data Analysis file.

Association Tests and Regression Analysis with Excel™

Researchers use two related statistical operations when they want to describe associations between two or more variables at the same time: *correlation* and *regression analysis.* The *correlation coefficient* is used to describe the covariation between two variables—when the purpose is to show how two or more variables are related. Regression analysis is used to make predictions from an independent variable X to the dependent variable Y.

Conducting Correlation Analysis

Which statistical test to choose for correlation analysis depends upon the level of the measurement for the data—nominal, ordinal, or interval/ratio. Excel™ includes the ability to measure relationships for interval/ratio data: the Pearson correlation coefficient (r). The correlation coefficient is used to indicate the relationship between two interval or ratio variables, without stating which of the two variables, X or Y, is causal to the other (Lin 1976). Correlation is measured on a scale of -1.0 to $+1.0$; a score of -1.0 indicates a perfect negative relationship; a score of $+1.0$ indicates a perfect positive relationship; a score of 0.0 indicates no relationship whatsoever.

Excel™ provides two ways to calculate a correlation coefficient: CORREL in the Function Wizard, and *Correlation* in the Tools $\Rightarrow$ Data Analysis set of procedures. CORREL asks the analyst to identify two columns of data (X and Y), and then asks where to display the paired-variable correlation value. *Data Analysis $\Rightarrow$ Correlation,* on the other hand, permits the re-

Table 32.5

**Support for a State Income Tax
and Annual Income
Correlation, *n* = 20**

Annual Income	Percent Support
18	63
22	56
34	44
22	57
28	39
34	36
35	40
37	32
29	48
41	24
44	22
27	52
44	37
50	12
55	15
43	24
60	22
58	18
16	65
CORRELATION:	−0.9298

Source: Hypothetical data.

searcher to develop a correlation matrix in which the correlations of many variables are displayed at the same time. Excel CORREL and *Data Analysis* ⇒ *Correlation* procedures were conducted on the data in Table 32.5 and 32.6, respectively. The correlation coefficient of −0.9298 produced by CORREL is displayed at the bottom of the Table 32.5 data. The coefficient tells the researcher (1) that there is a negative correlation between family income and support for a state income tax, and (2) that 93 percent of the change in support for the income tax can be explained by income.

A second variable, Respondent's Age, has been added to the Table 32.6 database for the Data Analysis ⇒ Correlation example; the dataset now includes Income and Percent of Support. Three separate steps would have been required to establish correlations for the three variables with the CORREL function: Income and Support, Income and Age, Age and Support. However, correlations for all three (or more) variables can be calculated at once with Correlation.

Figure 32.1 is the three-variable correlation matrix produced by the Excel™ Correlations procedure. Each variable is listed twice, once in the first column and again in the first row. Correlation coefficients for each pair of variables are found where the row and column meet in the matrix. Where the variables are repeated, the value 1 appears. Income and Support have the same negative correlation of −0.9298 found in the CORREL procedure; Age and Income have a positive correlation of 0.656868; and Age and Support have a negative correlation of −0.54332.

Table 32.6

Support for a State Income Tax, Age and Annual Income Correlations, *n* = 20

Annual Income	Percent Support	Respondent's Age
18	63	18
22	56	27
34	44	42
22	57	21
28	39	26
34	36	27
35	40	41
37	32	32
29	48	66
41	24	51
44	22	33
27	52	24
44	37	36
50	12	34
55	15	52
43	24	41
60	22	68
58	18	44
16	65	19

	Income	*Support*	*Age*
Income	1		
Support	-0.9298	1	
Age	0.656868	-0.54332	1

Figure 32.1 **An Excel™ Correlation Matrix for Three Variables**

Regression Analysis

Regression analysis is the second procedure used to evaluate relationships between variables. Because it establishes the way in which two variables vary together (covary), regression is the political science researcher's primary tool for evaluating *causality*. The regression coefficient is used to make predictions about changes in the values in a dependent variable from known values of an independent variable. Six steps may be involved in the process:

1. Identification of a *dependent* variable and data.
2. Identification of an *independent* variable and data.
3. Production of a scatter diagram showing paired sets of observations. (This is an optional

step, not required for the regression procedure. However, with Step 5, which is also optional, it provides a clear visual indication of the relationship.)

4. Determination of the values for the regression coefficient:
    a. Establishment of the *Intercept* point on the *Y*-axis.
    b. Establishment of the *Slope* value to apply to *X*-axis points.
5. Plot of a regression line (Trendline) on the scatter diagram (with Step 3, an optional but desirable step in the process).
6. Extension of the Trendline for predicting future *Y* values (again, an optional step in the regression process).

Values for the two variables displayed in Table 32.5, annual income and support for a state income tax, were used for this regression example. The researcher wants to know if and by how much support is influenced by income. With this knowledge, forecasts can be made of support levels in areas where family income is known from U.S. Census data. The dependent variable Y is the percent of support shown for the new tax; annual income is the independent variable. The regression analysis can be conducted in three different ways with Excel™. The first is using the *Slope* and *Intercept* functions in the Function Wizard, and then putting the two values together to form a regression coefficient. The second method is with the Regression procedure in the Data Analysis set of procedures. This procedure is accessed from the Tools option on the main tool bar. The third method is by beginning with a scatter diagram, which is accessed through the Chart Wizard option on the main tool bar, then requesting the regression equation be added to the face of the scatter diagram. Figure 32.2 displays the results of a

SUMMARY OUTPUT

Regression Statistics	
Multiple *R*	0.9298
R Square	0.8645
Adjusted *R* Square	0.8566
Standard Error	6.2567
Observations	19

ANOVA

	df	SS	MS	F	Sign. F
Regression	1	4247.0456	4247.0456	108.4927	0.0000
Residual	17	665.4807	39.1459		
Total	18	4912.5263			

	Coefficients	Standard Error	t Stat	P-value	Lower 95%	Upper 95%
Intercept	79.8889	4.3463	18.3809	0.0000	70.7190	89.0588
Income	-1.1648	0.1118	-10.4160	0.0000	-1.4008	-0.9289

Figure 32.2 **Results of an Excel™ Regression Procedure on Income and Support Data**

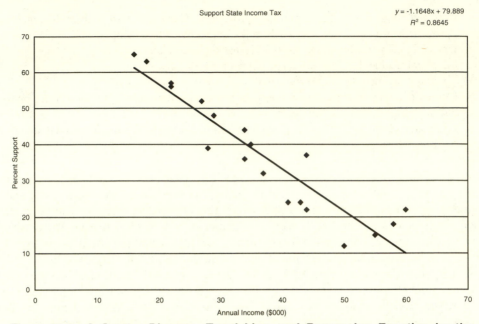

Figure 32.3   **A Scatter Diagram, Trend Line, and Regression Equation by the Excel™ Chart Wizard from Table 32.6 and Figure 32.1 Data**

Regression procedure conducted on the Income and Support data. Included in the results of the process are summary output displaying the correlation coefficient as the "Multiple R," the values for the regression coefficient (slope and intercept) as the coefficients for Intercept and Income in the first two columns of last two rows in the output. Also displayed are results of a t- test for the significance of the correlation and an F-test for significance of the predictive model; p-values for each test are also included, as are confidence intervals for the regression coefficients. Excel™ Regression also allows the researcher to request plots of the paired values and residuals; the plots are not displayed here.

The third approach to calculating a regression problem in Excel™ is to begin with the scatter diagram option in the *Chart Wizard,* adding a Trendline to the plots, and then accessing the Trendline Options to add a Regression Equation and an R^2 value to the face of the scatter diagram. It is not possible to determine the significance of the equation with this option. The results of a scatter diagram approach to the data in Table 32.5 are displayed in Figure 32.3.

Using Analysis of Variance (ANOVA) in Excel™

Table 32.7 is an extension of the hypothetical political information database introduced in Table 32.3. Four columns of data are displayed in the database: party affiliation, gender, a numeric code for gender, and the percentage supporting a state income tax. The size of the sample has been increased to thirty-three subjects. The research question in this example is whether males and females display different levels of support for the proposed tax. Because the sample size is larger than thirty, analysis of variance (Single Factor ANOVA) is the appropriate statistical test for this question. The ANOVA procedure needs numerical data for processing; therefore, categorical values of 1 and 2 have been inserted to represent female and male subjects, respectively. ANOVA is accessed in the following steps:

1. Select ANOVA: Single Factor from the Tools ⇒ Data Analysis menu options.
2. Select the data to be analyzed; indicate the spreadsheet range of the data in the **Input Range** window in the ANOVA dialog box. The data must be in adjacent columns. For example, in Table 32.7, the Gender Code was located in column C; the Percent of

---

Table 32.7

Example Four-Variable Excel™ Database for an ANOVA Procedure

Party Affiliation	Respondent's Gender	Gender Code	Percent Support
DEM	Male	2	63
DEM	Female	1	56
GOP	Female	1	44
GOP	Female	1	57
IND	Male	2	39
IND	Male	2	36
GOP	Male	2	40
GOP	Male	2	32
DEM	Female	1	48
DEM	Female	1	24
DEM	Female	1	22
DEM	Male	2	52
GOP	Male	2	37
GOP	Female	1	12
GOP	Female	1	15
GOP	Female	1	24
IND	Male	2	22
IND	Male	2	18
DEM	Male	2	65
GOP	Female	1	12
GOP	Male	2	32
DEM	Female	1	48
DEM	Female	1	24
DEM	Female	1	22
DEM	Male	2	52
GOP	Male	2	37
GOP	Female	1	12
GOP	Female	1	15
GOP	Female	1	24
IND	Male	2	22
DEM	Female	1	18
DEM	Male	2	65
GOP	Female	1	12

Support data were located in column D. The easiest way to identify the data array is to use the cursor to highlight all the data in each column, including one cell that names the variable.

3. Click in the **Labels in First Row** box if you have included a label for each column. If you have included a label and not checked this box, Excel™ will read the label as nonnumerical data and halt the process with a warning.

4. Select the level of confidence (alpha). The default value—the value that appears every time unless you change it—is 0.05, or the 95 percent level of confidence.

5. Identify the location where you want the ANOVA results to appear on a worksheet. If you want the results to appear on your current worksheet, click the radio button beside the **Output Range,** then click in the location box that will open alongside the radio button. Select a single empty cell in the spreadsheet; the results will show up beginning at the selected cell and continuing down the sheet. Figure 32.4 is an example of an Excel™ Single Factor ANOVA procedure conducted on the Gender and Support variables in Table 32.7.

6. Click **OK** in the upper-right-hand corner of the dialog box.

7. Interpret the results in the normal method for evaluating all *F*-ratios for statistically significant differences, using either the calculated and critical *F*-approach or the *p*-value approach.

Getting Started in SPSS®

The Statistical Package for the Social Sciences (SPSS®) is a powerful software package developed to perform simple and complex statistical analyses of quantitative data. The program enables users to create, modify, and analyze very large sets of data. It can also produce such graphic displays as tables, charts, and graphs. Data entry is facilitated by the use of a standard spreadsheet format; cases are in rows, and variables are in columns. A *case* is the responses or measurements of a single subject or study element. A *variable* is something that the researcher is able to measure or count in some way.

ANOVA: Single Factor

SUMMARY

Groups	Count	Sum	Average	Variance
Gender	33	48	1.454545455	0.2557
Support	33	1101	33.36363636	285.61

ANOVA

Source of Variation	SS	df	MS	F	P-value	F crit
Between Groups	16800.13636	1	16800.13636	117.54	0.00000	3.990919595
Within Groups	9147.818182	64	142.9346591			
Total	25947.95455	65				

Figure 32.4   **Results of a Single Factor ANOVA Procedure Displaying *F*- and *p*-values**

How Do I Find SPSS®?

SPSS® may already be loaded on the PCs in college and university computer laboratories, included as a Student Version with statistical or research methods texts, or purchased in several versions as add-on software. SPSS® is an easy and versatile way of processing large-sample databases; other than for the Student Version, it is essentially unlimited in the number of either subjects or variables it can process at any one time. The procedure for launching SPSS® software is the same as for any other frequently used software. At the initial Window, double-click on the SPSS® icon. The **Data Editor** window will appear on the screen (if the SPSS® shortcut icon does not appear on the main Windows screen, click on **Start**, then **Programs**, then select SPSS®). Superimposed on this opening screen may be a dialog window that asks: "What would you like to do?" Available options include:

- Run the tutorial.
- Type in data.
- Run an existing query.
- Create a new file using the *Database Capture Wizard*.
- Open an existing file.

If you have a database loaded on the hard drive or on an inserted floppy disk, you may call up that file for immediate activity. Or, you may select *Cancel,* which opens the Data Editor for data entry. You *must* have entered data in the data editor before SPSS® can perform any operations. Data can be entered directly or imported from an existing file, such as an Excel™ spreadsheet or a word-processing program.

The SPSSR® Opening Screen

The SPSS® opening screen will show two tool bars at the top of the screen and a full-screen spreadsheet (with gridlines). Along the left side of the screen are row numbers. At the top of the spreadsheet is a row for you to indicate the names of the variables in your study. Above the spreadsheet are the **Main Menu Bar** and (for all **versions lower than Version 10**, the **SPSS® Data Editor Toolbar**). Menus are named; tools are displayed as icons.

The Main Menu Bar

Look at the top line on the SPSS® screen. Running across the screen are the names for ten file menus. These menus allow you to access every process, tool, and feature contained in SPSS®. Beginning at the left and running across the screen, these file menus are:

- **File** menu: This allows you to open, close, save, and otherwise work with all types of SPSS® files.
- **Edit** menu: This allows you to cut and paste, move files, and find elements in a file or record (a *record* is all the data for a single case).
- **View** menu: This allows you to turn on or off visible features, change fonts, and show gridlines.

- **Data** menu: A key option, this allows you to define variables, indicate the type of measurements used, and assign labels to variables and values.
- **Transform** menu: This feature allows you to convert or change variable values, count responses, recode values, etc.
- **Analyze** menu: Along with the Data menu, this is the option you will use most often; it can be considered to be the *heart* of SPSS®. It allows you to name any type of analysis you want to carry out.
- **Graphs** menu: This feature allows you to select from fifteen different ways to graphically display data, including tables, graphs, and charts.
- **Utilities** menu: This allows you to call up information about your variables and your data file.
- **Windows** menu: This allows you to switch from one window to another, and back.
- **Help** menu: The standard on-line help feature that explains all features, tools, etc. as needed by the analyst.

Entering Variable Labels (Version 10 and Above Only)

Versions 10 and 11 of SPSS® employ a slightly different system for identifying variables than did Versions 9 and below. Rather than simply clicking on the first cell under the column indicator, you must now go to a separate file. When you are in this file, it is possible to define all variables in a dataset at one time. This should be done before any data are entered.

Defining Variables and Assigning Value Labels

Look at the bottom left-hand corner of the SPSS® Data Editor dialogue box. You should see two file tabs: One says "**Data View**," and the other says "**Variable View**." Click on the Variable View tab. You are now ready to define your variables and their values. In this file, all information about each variable is entered in *row* format, going across the page (this is an important distinction because data for each variable will later be entered in *column* format). The first row will hold all the information for your first variable; the second row will hold all information about your second variable, etc. SPSS will *automatically* move this information into the appropriate column for the variable.

You will have ten decisions to make about each variable in your dataset, although several will be made for you (in what is called the *default* mode). These choices are in ten columns. To enter defining information, click on the cell in the appropriate column, as follows.

Column 1:   This is where you enter the name of the variable. Names can be no longer than eight characters in length, and must start with a letter of the alphabet. On the screen, variable names appear in lowercase type.

Column 2:   This permits you to change the form of the variable data. The default is "numeric," which is the form you will almost always use. Make sure that is what appears in the cell. Move on to the next column.

Column 3:   This establishes the width of the cell. The default is eight spaces. You can widen it or reduce it in width, or leave it as the default width of eight spaces. The defining characteristic is the number of characters you use for the variable name, or the number of characters in a value for that variable.

For example, a variable name that is six characters wide (such as "Gender") will have values that are one character wide (such as the number 1 for female and 2 for male), and will require a column width of six characters—the length of the variable name. If, however, the variable name is, say, only three characters wide (such as "Inc" for Income), five characters might be required for an income amount (such as 45,000). The column width for this variable will be based on the number of characters required for the largest value, not on the three-character-wide variable name.

Column 4:   This changes the number of decimals you want to use for each variable. The *default* is two decimal points. It can be raised or lowered or left as it is. For categorical data, it is usually best to make this number zero (0).

Column 5:   This is where you may enter a longer label for the short variable name you entered in column 1. Variable values will then appear along with the shorter variable name in all printouts, making it easier for you to later remember what the statistical results apply to; this is very important with databases with many variables. Variable labels can be up to forty characters in length, including spaces and symbols.

Column 6:   This opens the box for providing *definitions* to the values of a variable. Value labels can be up to twenty characters in length, including spaces and symbols. Follow this five-step procedure to input these value labels into your data dictionary:

Step 1. Click on the blank cell in this column. Then, click on the small three-dot box that will appear at the right-hand side of the cell. This will bring up the Values dialogue box.

Step 2. Enter a number you have assigned for the value in the Values window.

Step 3. Enter a label (less than twenty characters in length) for the value in the Value Labels window.

Step 4. Click on the **Add** button. This is a critical step; you must do this after entering each value and value label!

Step 5. Repeat the process for each value of the variable. Click on **OK**.

Column 7:   This is where you can assign a value for any data missing for this variable. Follow this procedure:

Step 1. Click on the three-dot button.

Step 2. Click on the **Discrete missing values** button.

Step 3. Enter the number you want to use to signify missing data for this variable.

Step 4. Click **OK**. You can use any number or numbers that are not actual values for the variable. For most variables, the value 9 is used. THIS IS AN IMPORTANT STEP. If you leave a cell blank, it will still be counted as a zero and used in the divisor when calculating statistics for the dataset. TIP: Never leave a cell blank; never leave a row blank! (You will know if it is blank because a faint period [dot] will show up in the cell when you are in the Data View file.)

Column 8: This column allows you to specify how wide the variable name will be. The *default* is the exact width of the name as it appears. If not, change the width to match the number of characters taken by the name, but no more than eight. Most of the time you will not need to change this value.

Column 9: This allows you to specify the alignment you want for the data in each cell. You can choose from flush *right, left,* or *centered.*

Column 10: In this column you must tell the computer the type of measurement for the variable; choose from *Scale, Ordinal,* or *Nominal.*

When you have identified all variables, values, and data types, click on the Data View tab at the lower-left-hand corner of the screen. All the information you entered for each variable will be inserted in its proper location, with each variable and value now defined. Remember: you can always go back and change anything by clicking on the Variable View tab and moving your cursor to the proper cell.

You are now ready to enter data. Remember: all data for any one case must be entered in rows and inserted in the correct columns for that variable. And, remember to regularly save the data on a disk.

Entering Data into an SPSS® Data File

SPSS® is somewhat limited in what it accepts as "data." The easiest way to deal with these limits is to treat all information that is going to be processed in an SPSS® analysis as *"numeric" data.* Other than names developed for *variables* and measured or assigned *values* of those variables, only numbers should be entered for processing. Numeric SPSS® data are numbers used to signify a set of measurements or labels for a specific set of cases. The term "case" is used to mean a single entity in a dataset. Examples include one person among a group of people studied (i.e., in a *sample*), one city in an investigation of a group of cities, or one household in a group of political precincts examined for voting results. Whatever the element included in the study, the collective group of cases is usually referred to as a *sample.*

Cases are always listed in rows in an SPSS® data file. Each case in the sample is assigned its own identifying number (1, 2, 3 . . .). Each case contains a set of features that are identified and recorded as numbers. These features are the values assigned to each of the *variables.* Examples of variables include the gender of a subject (*subject* is another word for a case), the number of school-aged children in a community, or the number of citizens in a precinct who voted in the last election. Any feature or concept that can be measured or assigned a value on any one of the four measurement scales (*nominal, ordinal, interval,* and *ratio*) may be a *variable.*

Variables are always listed in columns in an SPSS® data file. The measurements or values for each variable must always be placed in the data file in the same reference order in the file. For example, if the values assigned to the variable "gender" follow the values assigned to the variable "age" in the first case entries, they must always be entered in this same order. In an SPSS® data file a complete row for an individual case is called a *record.*

It is possible to enter data in an SPSS® data file in two different ways. The one used most

Table 32.8

A Sample SPSS® Data File with Variable Labels

SNO	Gender	Age	Education	MS	State	UrbSub	Occupation
01	1	19	12	1	50	1	5
02	2	18	11	1	48	2	5
03	2	17	11	1	32	1	4
.							
.							

04–09 are omitted for this example.

.							
.							
10	1	20	13	2	47	2	4
11	1	22	10	1	33	1	3

often is called the *fixed-format* style; the other is *free-format* style. In a fixed-format file, every value for every variable is always entered in exactly the same column in the data file. Thus, every line of the data file will have the same number of columns, with the data for a variable always in the same place in the file. This is the format used by most researchers because it allows for easier editing and proofreading of a file; it is illustrated by Table 32.8 and is the only format to be discussed here.

If desired, empty spaces may be left between each variable, as in the following fixed-format example; cases 4 through 9 are omitted for this example only: If empty spaces were not used, the file would look like this (cases 4 through 9 omitted):

```
011191215015
022181114825
032171113214
04 . . .
05
06
07
08
09 . . .
101201324724
111221013313
```

In this data file, values 1 and 2 were used as database values for the two possible answers for gender, females and males. Education is answered as years of school completed; "MS" refers to number of parents at home; place of birth is by state, with each state assigned a numerical value; and the occupation of the primary wage earner parent is distinguished by a different value assigned to different types of careers.

Processing Numerical Data with SPSS®

Data (the numerical values you collect or assign to phenomena) are entered into a file using the SPSS® data editor capability. This can be done in several different ways. The most common way is to manually type the data directly into the appropriate columns in the data editor window. However, to do it this way, you must first define your variables and assign labels to all possible values of each variable.

Naming Variables

A variable is a characteristic, a concept, or a descriptive property that can take on different values or categories. Another way to say this is that a variable is something that can vary. Research deals with four broad classes of variables: independent, dependent, extraneous, and intervening variables. Definitions for these are:

- Independent variables: The characteristic that is believed to be responsible for influencing or bringing about some change in another variable. They are sometimes called "cause" or "causal" variables.
- Dependent variables: The characteristic that is altered or otherwise affected by the changes is the dependent variable. They are sometimes called "outcome" or "effect" variables.
- Extraneous variable: These are characteristics or factors that are not part of the independent/dependent variable relationship. They may increase or decrease the strength of the relationship between two variables, but have no part in whatever "causation" might be present.
- Intervening variables: Sometimes called "confounding variables," these variables serve as a link between the independent and dependent variables. Often, the relationship between the independent and dependent variable cannot occur without the presence of an intervening variable; that is, the "cause" variable will only work in the presence of an intervening variable.

Dealing with Variable Labels

It is typical to have a longer, more meaningful statement or label for the variable name spelled out in all SPSS® statistical output. This is particularly important if the name assigned to a variable is an abbreviation of two or more words or an acronym. SPSS® makes this possible by allowing you to add a longer name once during the Define Variables phase of the data entry. You can then continue to use the shorter variable name in your processing commands. The variable label can be as long as forty characters. For example, you might select this three-character name for a variable referring to subjects' date of birth: DOB. You could add this longer variable label to avoid later confusion: *Subjects' date of birth*. To add labels, follow this brief procedure:

1. To enter these new, longer labels into your program file, click on the Data box in the dialogue line. The Define Variables dialogue box should appear.

2. If you have not done it previously, type in the variable name DOB in the appropriate location.

3. Now, look at the area in the center of the dialogue box that is titled Change Settings. There should be four different choices under this heading: (1) Type, (2) Missing Values, (3) Labels, and (4) Column Format.

4. Click on the Labels box. This should bring up a new dialogue box, one that permits you to enter the longer name for the variable—and to assign labels for each of the values you must assign to variables.

5. If you do not wish to add labels for the different values possible for each variable, click on the **OK** box. You have now added a longer label for the variable name.

6. Repeat this process for each variable in your dataset. Remember: Variable names must be eight characters or less in length. Variable labels can be up to forty characters long (including spaces and/or symbols).

Dealing with Value Labels

Most of the time, adding a longer name for each variable is not enough. You will also want a name printed out for each value of your variables. For example, if the variable is "gender," you will have two possible values, one for male and one for female. If you enter only the numerical values, when the data are processed, you will get results for each numerical value, but your reader will not know that you meant "1" to signify females and "2" for males. By adding labels for each value, they will always appear with the results of any statistical analysis carried out with that variable.

As noted, the variable GENDER will have two values: "1" for females and "2" for males (and possibly a third value for a category where subjects did not respond to this question). Because you could enter only numerical data into the data file, you must now take this opportunity to tell SPSS® what each of these numerical values means. (Note: For clarity, quotation marks have been placed around numbers throughout this seminar guide, you should not use them when you enter numbers in your data files; always enter only the numbers.)

Entering value labels is as easy as entering labels for variables. It is also possible to go back later and add, change, or remove values and their labels. To add labels in a new dataset, follow this simple procedure:

1. Click on the Data box in the dialogue line. The Define Variables Dialogue box should appear.

2. If you have not done it previously, type in the variable name DOB in the appropriate location. Do the same for adding longer variable labels.

3. In the dialogue box titled Change Settings, select the "Labels" option.

4. This should bring up a new dialogue box, one that permits you to enter the longer name for the variable—and to assign labels for each of the values you must assign to variables.

5. In the Value Labels section of this dialogue box, enter the number for the first value for this variable. To return to the "Gender" example, enter the number "1."

6. Now click on the Value label box beneath this value and enter the label you wish to use. Value labels can be twenty characters or less in length.

7. Click on the Add box. The value and label assigned should appear in the larger white area alongside the Add button.

8. Click on the Value box again to add the next value and its label. Be sure to click on the Add button after entering every value and its label.

9. When you have entered all values and their labels for a variable, click on the Continue button; this brings you back to the Define Variable dialogue box. If you are finished, click on the OK button. However, you may also wish to add values for missing values. That procedure is discussed in the next section.

10. Repeat this process for each value of each variable in your dataset. Remember: Variable names must be eight characters or less in length; variable labels can be up to forty characters long (including spaces and/or symbols); and value labels can be up to twenty characters in length.

11. To change or remove values and/or their labels, such as will be necessary if you were to combine two or more values into one, click on the Change or Remove buttons in the Define Labels dialogue box and follow instruction. Length limitations still apply.

Dealing with Missing Values

Every cell in a dataset will be considered by SPSS® to have some numerical value entered—even if it is left blank. Typically, a blank cell is read as a "0." Therefore, when entering data it is a good idea to not leave any cells blank. However, you do not always have data for every cell; often subjects will intentionally or accidentally omit a response to a question. When this happens, researchers using SPSS® usually enter a value to indicate that that data are missing. These values are counted separately and not included in analysis requiring a mean (average) of the data. An example of a missing value is the number "9" entered when subjects fail to indicate their gender on a self-administered questionnaire. The number used to indicate missing data is valid for only a single variable, although the same valid number can be used for as many variables as desired. Any number other than those values specifically assigned in the dataset can be used; however, the values 9 and 0 are what are usually used.

Whatever value is assigned to represent missing data, that same number must not be used for another response in the same question. For example, if subjects are asked to indicate their rank order preference for a set of nine or ten items, the numbers "9" and "10" can be used to signify "Missing data" in the data file. To add labels in a new dataset, follow this simple procedure:

1. Click on the **Data** box in the dialogue line. The **Define Variables** dialogue box should appear.

2. In the dialogue box titled **Change Settings,** select the **Missing Values** option.

3. This should bring up a new dialogue box, **Missing Values**. Two buttons appear at the top of the box: one is titled "No missing values," if you have not already assigned a value, this button will show a black dot inside. The second option is for **Discrete Missing Values**. Click on this second button.

4. Enter the number you wish to use to signify missing data in the first of three small boxes below the Discrete Missing Values button.

5. When you have entered the missing value for a variable, click on the **Continue** button; this brings you back to the **Define Variables dialogue box**.

6. You may now select the **Value Labels** option to add a label for a number you want to use to signify a missing value. This is done in the same way as adding all value labels. First enter the value, and then enter the label "Missing Values," or "No Response," or any label you want to use. Remember to click on the **Add** button when you have entered the value and its label.

7. If you are finished, click on the **OK** button. Repeat this process for each missing value of each variable in your dataset. As always, remember that variable names must be eight characters or less in length; variable labels can be up to forty characters long (including spaces and/or symbols); and value labels can be up to twenty characters in length.

Data Types

The final option in the **Define Variables** dialogue box is a box labeled "Measurement." This box has three options: "Scale," "Ordinal," and "Nominal." These tell the statistical analysis processor what type of data it has for each variable. Different types of data (or *measurements*) require different types of statistical analyses. When you indicate to the data file editor the type of data represented by each variable, it will automatically select the correct analysis technique for each test you ask it to do.

"Scale" data consist of measurements that are considered to be at least *equidistant interval* (usually simply identified as *interval*). Statistical analyses conducted on these data types usually provide the researcher with the greatest amount of information possible. Examples are comparative rating scales, attitude scales, awareness scales, and similar question types. The key to understanding this type of measurement is that the intervals between the various points on the scale are (or are considered to be) exactly the same size; they are equidistant from one another. They are the closest things to a "ruler" that we have available in the social sciences. A second variety of "Scale" data encountered in statistical texts is called *ratio* data. In these measurements, an equal difference remains between points on the scale, but the *ratio scale* has a "fixed" or absolute zero point. The same statistical analyses are used for both variations of scale data.

Another way of defining "Scale" measurements is that the data produced are considered to be "*continuous*" rather than *discrete*. Continuous data (or data from continuous variables) are data that can be any value on the scale. For example, an "average" or mean score on a five-point attitude scale can be 2.0, 3.4, 1.7, 4.3, etc., etc.

The second option in this question about the type of measurement data gathered for a question is what is called *ordinal scale data*. The easiest way to differentiate ordinal data from "scale" or "nominal" measurements is that these measurements are ranked or ordered on some set of characteristics, but the differences between rankings are not known or are considered to be equidistant. All rank order *preference scales* are ordinal measurements.

Discrete data are data taken from *nominal scale* measurements. An example of discrete data is the values assigned to a dichotomous question such as "What is your gender?" The answer could only be female or male (i.e., 1 or 2). No mean can be calculated. Another example is a list of eight different types of occupations from which a subject might select one that applies to him or her. Frequency distributions of all responses for a sample would result in a distribution of responses across the eight options; no mean can be calculated.

The set of rules repeated in Table 32.9 should help you differentiate between the different types of measurements; prior rules also apply to higher-level data (i.e., the nominal rule also

Table 32.9

SPSS® Data Types and Their Applicable Rules

Data Type	Applicable Rules for Differentiation
Nominal	Different numbers *always* refer to different things.
Ordinal	The numbers can be *ranked* or ordered on some dimension.
Scale	The different points on the scale are *equidistant* (i.e., equal), and the scale may have a fixed or absolute zero.

applies to ordinal, interval, and ratio; the ordinal rule also applies to interval and ratio, but not to nominal, etc.).

Entering Data

Once you have indicated the type of measurement data used for that variable in the small circle alongside the data type, click on the "OK" button on the Define Variables dialogue box. You are now ready to begin entering data into your data file. This is a very simple process, much like all other spreadsheet programs. Data are usually entered across the page in rows that correspond to an individual case or subject. You can move from cell to cell using either the Tab or Arrow keys.

Table 32.10 is a classification of some of the key layers of statistical analysis seen in political science research, together with the statistical analysis tools in SPSS® and the commands for conducting those analyses. When all the variables and values are defined and all the data have been entered into your data file, it is time to save this information into an SPSS® Save file.

Putting SPSS® to Work

Assuming that you have successfully entered data to a data file, defined all the variables in that file, and established labels for variables and values of those variables, you have completed the setup phase of SPSS®. You can begin to use this powerful software to manipulate and analyze the dataset. The remainder of the guide will focus on four analytical processes: (1) developing descriptive statistics for the dataset, (2) designing and preparing graphic displays of the data, (3) transforming and recoding the raw data for refined analysis, and (4) performing some simple inferential statistical analysis on the data.

Developing Descriptive Statistics

SPSS® calculates descriptive statistics for three types of measurements: *scale, ordinal,* and *nominal.* Scale data is the label SPSS® uses to identify both interval and ratio data. Measurement data are often described in at least two additional ways. First, data may be *discrete* or may be *contin-*

Table 32.10

A Classification of Some Key Statistical Analysis Procedures in SPSS®

Analysis Level	Analysis Process	Data Type	Available Statistics	SPSS Commands
Level 1-A	Univariate Frequency Distributions	Any Data	Counts, Percentages, Chi-square	Frequencies, Explore, Descriptives
Level 1-B	Bivariate Frequency Distributions	Any Data	Counts, Percentages, Chi-Square, Phi, Cramer's V	Crosstabs, Multiple Response
Level 2-A	Bivariate Relationships Tests	Nonparametric (Nominal and Ordinal Data)	Phi and Cramer's V, Spearman's rho	Crosstabs
Level 2-B	Bivariate Relationship Tests	Parametric (Interval and Ratio Data)	Pearson's r	Correlation, Simple Regression
Level 3-A	Bivariate Differences Tests	Nonparametric (Nominal and Ordinal Data)	Chi-Square, Mann-Whitney U, or Wald-Wolfowitz runs test	Nonparametric Statistics: Chi-Square, M-W-U, W-W runs
Level 3-B	Bivariate Differences Tests	Parametric	t-Test, F-test (ANOVA)	Compare Means: t-Test One-way ANOVA
Level 4-A (Relationships)	Multivariate Association Tests	Parametric (and nonparametric with data transformations)	Multiple Regression Analysis, Multiple Discriminant Analysis, Time Series	General Linear Model: Multivariate, Classify: Discriminant, Time Series
Level 4-B (Differences)	Multivariate Differences Tests	Parametric (and nonparametric with data transformations)	Multiple Analysis of Variance	Compare Means: Means
Level 5 (Data Reductions)	Multivariate Statistics	Parametric	Cluster Analysis, Factor Analysis	Classify: Hierarchical Cluster Analysis Data Reduction: Factor

Source: SPSS® Users' manuals.

uous. Second, data may be described as *qualitative* or *quantitative*. Discrete data consist of numbers used to identify specific groups or categories, such as female and male, or undergraduate and graduate student. They are sometimes described as *categorical* data. Researchers are concerned with how many subjects fall into each category; this information can be presented either as a simple count or as a percentage of the total. Nominal data are always discrete (or categorical). Because of this nature of the data, they are also considered to be *qualitative*.

Continuous data, on the other hand, are considered to be *quantitative* because they can consist of any value within a specified or possible continuum. Values are not restricted to whole numbers. While the number of children in a family is *discrete* data because the count must be a whole number, the annual income of a sample of families is *continuous* because it can be any amount. Another example of a continuous variable is the amount of electrical energy consumed each year by households in Shelton, Washington. SPSS® considers all data from *scales* (such as questions about attitudes, beliefs, etc.) as continuous data. Ordinal data are categorical data, but in social science usage, ordinal data are often treated as continuous data.

Univariate Descriptive Statistics for Categorical Measurements

Qualitative measurements are numbers that are applied to categorical variables. The values assigned to categorical variables refer to mutually exclusive groups, categories, or classes within a variable, and have no quantitative reference. Examples include the categories used to differentiate subjects by gender, by race, by political party affiliation, by voting behavior (did vote vs. did not vote), etc. Researchers want to know how many cases fit into each category. The statistics used for these measurements are called *nonparametric*.

The SPSS® procedure used to develop descriptive statistics for categorical variables is called: Frequencies. This procedure counts the number of cases in each designated category, and identifies the mode for the variable (the mode is the category with the most cases). The mode is one type of "average" (or *measure of central tendency*); it is the only average to use with this kind of data. SPSS® Frequencies produces its results in the form of a table—called a *frequency distribution* table. Within each Frequencies table are five columns of information; moving from left to right, these are:

1. User-assigned Value Labels (such as Female–Male; Yes–No, etc.).
2. The frequency (i.e., the count) that this category occurs.
3. Percent of the total that each row represents. If any data are missing, a row will indicate what percentage of the total the missing cases represent.
4. A Valid Percent column, in which is displayed the percentages of the total minus any missing cases that are accounted for by the counts for each category. If there are no missing cases, this column will be a repetition of the third (Percent) column.
5. Finally, a Cumulative Percent column, which includes the percentages of each row plus all rows preceding this row. For example, if the percent of responses for the first category on a 5-point rating scale is 13, and the percent of the second category is 12, the cumulative percent for the first category is 13. For the second category, the cumulative percent is 25. If the percent for the third category is 10, the cumulative percent for this third row is 35. The cumulative percent column has no statistical relevance to qualitative variables, however, and should be ignored when processing this kind of data.

Using the Frequencies Dialogue Box

To carry out the SPSS® Frequencies procedure on data entered into a data file, first click on the *Analyze* option on the Main Tool Bar. Then click on the second option from the list of procedures that appears: *Descriptives*. You will have four options from which to choose: (1) Frequencies, (2) Descriptives, (3) Explore, or (4) Crosstabs. Click on the Frequencies button.

The Frequencies dialogue box contains two large windows and several different command options. All variables in the data file will appear in the large window at the left side of the box. Highlight the variable you wish to analyze by clicking on it in the list. Then click on the small arrow between the two large windows. The selected variable will now appear in the right window. To remove it, simply reverse the process. It is possible to highlight as many variables as you want to at the same time. One click on the center arrow will move all variables you select to the Analyze window.

Now click on the small window that reads Display frequency tables—it appears just beneath the main variable list. A check mark showing in the small window means that a table will be produced.

Now go to the Statistics button located near the bottom of the gray dialogue box. This will bring up the Frequencies: Statistics dialogue box. You may request percentile information, measures of dispersion (such as the standard deviation, etc.), measures of central tendency, or measures of distribution. Go to the Central Tendency section and click on the small window alongside the Mode. All you need to do to have SPSS® process your request is to click on Continue in this dialogue box, and click on **OK** in the Frequencies dialogue box that reappears after you click on Continue.

Univariate Descriptive Statistics for Continuous Measurements

Statistical analysis of *quantitative (numerical) measurements can be said to take place on two fundamental levels: descriptive* and *inferential* statistics. Descriptive statistics are used to summarize the numerical information in a dataset, to numerically describe the cases in a dataset, and to provide some sort of structure to the data. *Univariate* descriptive statistics does this one variable at a time. However, it is also possible to develop descriptive statistics for two variables at the same time; this is called *bivariate* statistical analysis (i.e., "two variables"). It is also possible to analyze more than two variables at once in what is called *multivariate* statistical analysis, but these processes are not discussed here.

Three SPSS® process can be used to produce univariate statistics for quantitative variables (i.e., variables with ordinal, interval, or ratio data). These procedures are (1) Frequencies, (2) Explore, and (3) Descriptives.

Using the Frequencies Procedure

The use of Frequencies with quantitative—nominal—data is the same as it is for qualitative data, except for the selection of the appropriate measure of central tendency. For quantitative variables, the mean and median are also calculated. The mean is the arithmetic average; the median is the midpoint in the range of possible values. Also important for quantitative measurements are measures of variation and of dispersion. To employ the Frequencies procedure, follow this set of steps:

- Select Analyze ⇒ Descriptive Statistics ⇒ Frequencies.
- Select the variable or variables desired; move them into the variables window.
- Click on the Display frequency tables button.
- Select Statistics ⇒ Central tendency ⇒ Mean, Median, and Mode.
- Next, in the Dispersion box of the Statistics Dialogue box, select Std. Deviation, Range, Minimum, and Maximum.
- Select Continue.
- Select **OK.**

How to Use the Explore *Procedure*

To calculate descriptive statistics for a variable using the SPSS® Explore process, begin by clicking on the Analyze command on the Main Menu bar. From the list of available statistical processes, select Descriptive Statistics. Then select Explore. This will bring up the Explore dialogue box. This box has four windows. The largest window displays the names of all the variables in your dataset. Highlight the variable you want to analyze. Then click on the small arrow alongside this box; the variables will be moved to the window labeled "Dependent list." When you want complete analysis for one variable at a time, ignore the other two windows (i.e., "Factor list" and "Label cases by"). Click on OK and complete descriptive statistics will be produced for each variable named.

Explore can also be used to develop descriptive statistics for different levels of a variable. The phrase "different levels" means the different categories represented in the variable. For example, the variable "gender" has two levels (also referred to as *categories* or *groups*): female and male. The variable "political party" might have three levels: Democrat, Republican, and Independent. The variable "class standing" might have five levels: freshman, sophomore, junior, senior, and graduate. Explore will quickly and easily produce descriptive statistics for each subgroup in the variable.

- Select Analyze ⇒ Descriptive Statistics ⇒ Explore.
- Select the variable or variables desired; move them into the Dependent variables window.
- Select the "grouping variable" for which you want the statistical breakdown and move it into the Factor list window.
- Click on the Display frequency tables button.
- Click on the Statistics button.
- Select Continue.
- Select **OK.**

How to Use the Descriptives *Procedure*

Descriptives is the third way to produce descriptive statistics for numerical data with SPSS®; it provides a quick list of each variable, the number of valid responses for each variable, and selected descriptive statistics. To access the program, follow these steps:

- Select Analyze ⇒ Descriptive Statistics ⇒ Descriptives.
- Select the variable or variables desired; move them into the Variables window (remember to not include qualitative variable).
- Select Options. For quantitative data, click on mean, Std. Deviation, and if desired, Minimum and Maximum.
- You can choose to have the data presented in any one of four different ways:
  - By the way the variables appear in your variable list.
  - In alphabetic order.
  - By ascending value of their means.
  - By descending order of their means.

Dealing with Bivariate Descriptive Statistics

Known as "two-way frequency distribution tables," the results of a crosstabulations table present the distribution of responses, with percentages, of two or more variables at the same time. In addition, a wide variety of statistical analyses are included in the crosstabs procedure. All types of data can be analyzed in a crosstabs table. The SPSS® crosstabs procedure is a tool for displaying the data from one variable against that of another variable or variables. The rows of a crosstabulation table (called a "crosstab" by SPSS®) represent the different values or levels of one variable, while the columns of the table represent the values of a second variable. A simple 2 by 2 crosstab will look something like Table 32.11.

Convention requires that each box in a table (except for those with labels) be called a *cell*. Thus, in the above example, the data for Females who answered Yes will fall in Cell 1, data for Females/No in Cell 2, Males/Yes in Cell 3, and Males/No in Cell 4.

Crosstab tables can have as many rows and/or as many columns as required. However, be advised that when they exceed something like five or six rows or columns, the table can become cumbersome to read and difficult to interpret. Crosstabs produces statistical information for use with interval, ordinal, and nominal (i.e., categorical) data.

SPSS® permits up to four bits of information to be displayed in each cell. These include: (1) the count of occurrences, (2) the percentage of the row total represented by the count in a cell, (3) the percentage of the column total in the cell, and (4) the percentage of the total number of counts for the variable. Row and column total counts and percentages are displayed in the table margins.

Crosstabs tables are most appropriately used when both variables are categorical (i.e., nominal data). However, there are some times when the researcher wishes to display the distribution of ordinal- or interval-level responses across the entire range of cells. In such cases, the cate-

Table 32.11

A Typical 2 × 2 Crosstabulation Table with Cells Numbered

Gender	Response	
	Yes	No
Female	(Cell 1)	(Cell 2)
Male	(Cell 3)	(Cell 4)

Table 32.12

An Example 3 × 6 Crosstabulation Table with Counts and Totals

Political Party Affiliation	Response Category					
	Strongly Agree	Agree	Neither Agree nor Disagree	Disagree	Strongly Disagree	Totals
Democrat	38	27	15	9	7	96
Republican	7	10	12	22	30	81
Independent	10	11	7	8	10	46
Totals	55	48	34	39	47	223

gorical variable is often referred to as a *grouping variable,* and its values are placed as rows. The scale data are displayed in columns. The following example uses Party Affiliation data as its row variable and the responses of a sample of subjects to a five-point rating scale. Rating scale values in columns are *Strongly Agree, Agree, Neither Agree nor Disagree, Disagree,* and *Strongly Disagree.*

From the information in Table 32.12 it is clear that this is a relatively cumbersome way to present data; the table is complex and "busy." Possibly a more meaningful way to present and analyze the information in the table would be a simple 3 by 1 table, with the means scores on the scale shown for each of the three categories of Party Affiliation. A one-way analysis of variance test could then be conducted to test for statistically significant different attitudes among the three part affiliation groups.

How to Use the Crosstabs *Procedure*

The Crosstabs procedure is bundled into the same Summarize statistics package as Frequencies, Explore, and Descriptives. In addition to this summary table, another key feature of Crosstabs is its ability to produce both association and differences test statistics for nominal, ordinal, and scale data.

How to Use Tests for Independence

The *chi-square test of independence* can be used with all data types. Its purpose is to test whether the row subgroups are independent from each other. The chi-square test is interpreted by examining the probability value produced with the chi-square value. When using a 95 percent confidence level, if this *p*-value is .05 or less, the null can be rejected and the alternative hypothesis is retained (that is, if the *p*-value is .05 or less, the responses of the groups can be assumed to be statistically different).

Dealing with Measures of Association

Statistics for Nominal Data. There are four categories of statistical tests from which to select for nominal data: the contingency coefficient, phi and Cramer's V, lambda, and the uncertainty coefficient. Of these, the two easiest statistical tests to use for testing for association are the phi statistic and Cramer's *V*. Both the phi and Cramer's *V* statistic measure association in one direction; the values produced can range from 0.0 to 1.0. Therefore, while they indicate the strength of an association, they do not indicate the direction of that association (i.e., positive or negative). The phi statistic should be consulted for 2 by 2 tables only; Cramer's *V* is applicable for all rectangular tables. These are accessed through the same selection in the Nominal Data section of the Crosstabs $\Rightarrow$ Statistics dialogue.

Statistics for Ordinal Data. SPSS Crosstabs statistics provides a variety of optional association tests for use with ordinal data. The first of these, and the one that is often considered to be most appropriate, is the *Spearman correlation coefficient,* called *Spearman's rho.* This test is accessed through the Correlations button on the Crosstabs $\Rightarrow$ Statistics dialogue box. The program produces both a Pearson's *r* correlation coefficient for use when the column variable is interval or ratio level, and the Spearman's rho when the column data are ordinal. Care must be taken in selecting the correct statistic, since the values appear in the same output box.

Both *r* and rho are interpreted in the same way—as indicators of the relative strength of an association. They should not be interpreted as measures of causation. Their values can range from -0.1 to $+0.1$.

Other ordinal-level statistical tests available in Crosstabs include Gamma, Somers' *d,* Kendall's tau-b, and Kendall's tau-c. To see examples and more detailed explanations of what these tests do and when to use them, consult *SPSS® For Windows® Base System User's Guide* (2001), or *SPSS® 11.0: Guide to Data Analysis* (2002), both by Marija J. Norusis.

Statistics Involving Interval Data. A test for association is also possible when one of the variables in a Crosstab is interval (or ratio) level and the other variable is nominal level. This is the eta coefficient. Eta is interpreted in the same way as Pearson's correlation coefficient. Eta does not assume a linear relationship exists between the two variables. When squared, the value of eta can also be interpreted as a measure of the proportion of the total variability in the interval-level variable that can be known when the values of the nominal-level variable (gender, for example) are known.

Additional Reading

Carver, Robert H., and Jane Gradwohl Nash. 2000. *Doing Data Analysis with SPSS® 10.0.* Pacific Grove, CA: Brooks/Cole (Duxbury).

Einspruch, Eric L. 1998. *An Introductory guide to SPSS® For Windows®.* Thousand Oaks, CA: Sage.

Green, Samuel B., Neil J. Salkind, and Theresa M. Akey. 2000. *Using SPSS® for Windows®: Analyzing and Understanding Data.* Upper Saddle River, NJ: Prentice-Hall.

Norusis, Marija J. 2000. *SPSS® For Windows® Base System User's Guide* (Version 10.0). Chicago: SPSS Inc.

———. 2002. *SPSS® 11.0: Guide to Data Analysis.* Upper Saddle River, NJ: Prentice-Hall.

References

Aaker, David A., V. Kumar, and George S. Day. 1998. *Marketing Research.* 6th ed. New York: John Wiley & Sons.

Abramson, Paul R. 1997. "Probing Well beyond the Bounds of Conventional Wisdom." *American Journal of Political Science.* 41 (April): 675–82.

Achinstein, Peter. 1970. "Concepts of Science: A Philosophical Analysis." In *The Way of Science.* Frank E. Egler, ed. New York: Hafner Publishing: 40–47.

Adams, Gerald R., and Jay D. Schvaneveldt. 1985. *Understanding Research Methods.* New York: Longman.

Adler, Patricia A., and Peter Adler. 1998. "Observational Techniques." In *Collecting and Interpreting Qualitative Materials.* Norman K. Denzin and Yvonna S. Lincoln, eds. Thousand Oaks, CA: Sage. 79–109.

Alasuutari, Pertti. 1995. *Researching Culture: Qualitative Method and Cultural Studies.* London: Sage.

Aldenderfer, Mark S., and Roger K. Blashfield. 1984. *Cluster Analysis.* Beverly Hills: Sage.

Alejandro, Roberto. 1993. *Hermeneutics, Citizenship, and the Public Sphere.* Albany: State University of New York Press.

Allen, K.R., and K.M. Babar. 1992. "Ethical and Epistemological Tension in Applying a Postmodern Perspective to Feminist Research." *Psychology of Women Quarterly.* 16: 1–15.

Allen, R.G.D. 1975. *Index Numbers in Theory and Practice.* Chicago: Aldine Publishing.

Allman, Dwight David. 1995. "Nietzscheanism Contra Nietzsche." *Perspectives on Political Science.* 24 (Spring): 69–76.

Ammons, David N., Charles Coe, and Michael Lombardo. 2001. "Performance-Comparison Projects in Local Government: Participants' Perspectives." *Public Administration Review.* 61 (January/February): 100–110.

Anastas, Jeane W., and Marian L. MacDonald. 1994. *Research Design for Social Work and the Human Services.* New York: Lexington Books.

Anderson, David R., Dennis J. Sweeney, and Thomas A. Williams. 2002. *Statistics for Business and Economics.* 8th ed. Mason, OH: South-Western.

Ankenman, Bruce E. 1999. "Design of Experiments with Two- and Four-level Factors." *Journal of Quality Technology.* 31 (October): 363–75.

Annells, Merilyn. 1996. "Grounded Theory Method: Philosophical Perspectives, Paradigm of Inquiry, and Postmodernism." *Qualitative Health Research.* 6 (August): 379–94.

Antony, Jiju. 1998. "Some Key Things Industrial Engineers Should Know about Experimental Design." *Logistics Information Management.* 11 (6): 386–92.

APSA Committee on Publications. 2001. *Style Manual for Political Science.* Washington, DC: American Political Science Association.

Apter, David E. 1977. *Introduction to Political Analysis.* Cambridge, MA: Winthrop Publishers.

Argyris, Chris, Robert Putnam, and Diana M. Smith. 1985. *Action Science.* San Francisco: Jossey-Bass.

Arneson, Pat. 1993. "Situating Three Contemporary Qualitative Methods in Applied Organizational Communication Research: Historical Documentation Techniques, the Case Study Method, and the Critical Approach to Organizational Analysis." In *Qualitative Research: Applications in Organizational Communications*. Sandra L. Herndon, and Gary L. Kreps, eds. Cresskill, NJ: Hampton Press: 159–73.

Aspinwall, Mark. 2000. "Structuring Europe: Power Sharing Institutions and British Preferences on European Integration." *Political Studies*. 48 (3): 415–42.

Babbie, Earl. 2001. *The Practice of Social Research*. 9th ed. Belmont, CA: Wadsworth/Thompson Learning.

Bailey, Mary Timney. 1994. "Do Physicists Use Case Studies? Thoughts of Public Administration Research." In *Research in Public Administration: Reflections on Theory and Practice*. Thousand Oaks, CA: Sage: 183–96.

Baldwin, Andrew, Alice Nakamura, and Masao Nakamura. 1966. "New Goods as a Challenge for Index Number Making." *Canadian Journal of Economics*. 29 (April): S598–S604.

Barnet, Sylvan. 1993. *Critical Thinking, Reading, and Writing*. Boston: St. Martin.

Barnett, Marva T. 1987. *Writing for Technicians*. 3rd ed. New York: Delmar Publishers.

Bartels, Larry M., and Henry E. Brady. 1993. "The State of Quantitative Political Methodology." In *Political Science: The State of the Discipline*. Ada W Finifter, ed. Washington, DC: American Political Science Association: 121–59.

Barth, Thomas. 1994. "Political Science." In *The Reader's Reader: The Best in the Social Science, History, and the Arts*, 14th ed., Vol. 3. Marion Sader, ed. New Providence, NJ: R.R. Bowker: 137–65.

Barthes, Roland. 1968. *Elements of Semiology*. Annette Lavers and Colin Smith, trans. New York: Hill and Wang.

Barzun, Jacques, and Henry F. Graff. 1970. *The Modern Researcher*. 2nd ed. New York: Harcourt, Brace & World.

———. 1992. *The Modern Researcher*. 5th ed. Ft. Worth: Harcourt, Brace & Jovanovich.

Bauer, Martin W., and George Gaskell, eds. 2000. *Qualitative Researching with Text, Image and Sound*. London: Sage.

Baugh, L. Sue. 1995. *How to Write Term Papers and Reports*. Lincolnwood, IL: VGM Career Horizons.

Bauman, Zygmunt. 1992. *Hermeneutics and the Social Sciences*. Aldershot, UK: Gregg Revivals.

Becker, Howard S. 1986. *Writing for Social Scientists*. Chicago: University of Chicago Press.

Bell, Stephen. 2002. "The Limits of Rational Choice: New Institutionalism in the Test Bed of Central Banking Politics in Australia." *Political Studies*. 50 (August): 477–96.

Bennett, Spencer, and David Bowers. 1976. *An Introduction to Multivariate Techniques for Social and Behavioral Sciences*. London: Macmillan.

Berenson, Mark L., and David M. Levine. 1996. *Basic Business Statistics: Concepts and Applications*. 6th ed. Upper Saddle River, NJ: Prentice-Hall.

Berg, Bruce L. 1998. *Qualitative Research Methods for the Social Sciences*. 2nd ed. Boston: Allyn and Bacon.

Bernard, Harvey R. 1988. *Research Methods in Cultural Anthropology*. Beverly Hills: Sage.

———. 1995. *Research Methods in Anthropology*. 2nd ed. Walnut Creek, CA: AltaMira Press.

———. 2000. *Social Research Methods*. Thousand Oaks, CA: Sage.

Bevir, Mark, and R.A.W. Rhodes. 2002. "Interpretive Theory." In *Theory and Methods in Political Science*, 2nd ed. David Marsh and Gerry Stoker, eds. Houndmills, UK: Palgrave Macmillan: 131–52.

Binmore, Ken, Aland Kirman, and Piero Tani, eds. 1993. *Frontiers of Game Theory*. Cambridge, MA: MIT Press.

Bloor, Michael, Jane Frankland, Michelle Thomas, and Kate Robson. 2001. *Focus Groups in Social Research*. London: Sage.

Blosch, Marcus, and Jiju Anthony. 1999. "Experimental Design and Computer-based Simulation: A Case Study with the Royal Navy." *Managing Service Quality*. 9 (5): 311–19.

Blyler, Nancy. 1998. "Taking a Political Turn: The Critical Perspective and Research in Professional Communications." *Technical Communication Quarterly*. 7 (Winter): 33–53.

Boskoff, Alvin. 1972. *The Mosaic of Sociological Theory*. New York: Thomas Y. Crowell.

Bottom, William P., Cheryl L. Eavey, Gary J. Miller, and Jennifer N. Victor. 2000. "The Institutional Effect on Majority Rule Instability: Bicameralism in Spatial Policy Decisions." *American Journal of Political Science*. 44 (July): 523–40.

Bowen, Elinor R., and George I. Balch. 1981. "Epistemology, Methodology, and Method in the Study of

Political Behavior." In *The Handbook of Political Behavior*, Vol. 1. Samuel L. Long, ed. New York: Plenum Press: 1–37.

Box, Richard C. 1992. "An Examination of the Debate over Research in Public Administration." *Public Administration Review*. 52 (January/February): 62–69.

Boyte, Harry C. 2000. "The Struggle against Positivism." *Academe*. 86 (July/August): 46–51.

Brase, Charles H., and Corrinne P. Brase. 1999. *Understandable Statistics: Concepts and Methods*. 6th ed. Boston: Houghton Mifflin.

Bredemeier, Harry C., and Richard M. Stephenson. 1967. "The Analysis of Culture." In *The Study of Society*. P.I. Rose, ed. New York: Random House: 119–33.

Breisach, Ernst. 1994. *Histography: Ancient, Medieval, and Modern*. 2nd ed. Chicago: University of Chicago Press.

Brewer, Gene A., James W. Douglas, Rex L. Facer II, and Laurence J. O'Toole, Jr. 1999. "Determinants of Graduate Research Productivity in Doctoral Programs of Public Administration." *Public Administration Review*. 59 (September/October): 373–82.

Brightman, Harvey J. 1999. *Data Analysis in Plain English with Microsoft® Excel*. Pacific Grove, CA: Duxbury Press.

Brooks, Arthur C. 2002. "Can Nonprofit Management Help Answer Public Management's 'Big Questions?' " *Public Administration Review*. 62 (May/June): 259–66.

Brown, Robert G. 1963. *Smoothing, Forecasting and Prediction of Discrete Time Series*. Englewood Cliffs, NJ: Prentice-Hall.

Bryant, Raymond L. 2002. "Non-governmental Organizations and Governmentality: 'Consuming' Biodiversity and Indigenous People in the Philippines. *Political Studies*. 50 (June): 268–92.

Bryman, Alan. 2001. *Social Research Methods*. Oxford: Oxford University Press.

Buckler, Steve 2002. "Normative Theory." In *Theory and Methods in Political Science*. 2nd ed. David Marsh, and Gerry Stoker, eds. Houndmills, UK: Palgrave Macmillan: 172–94.

Burke, Gibbons. 1995. "Comparing Apples to Apples." *Futures: The Magazine for Commodities and Options*. 23 (July): 50–51.

Burke, Peter, ed. 2001. *New Perspectives on Historical Writing*. 2nd ed. Cambridge, UK: Polity Press.

Burns, Tony. 2002. "Sophocles' *Antigone* and the History of the Concept of Natural Law." *Political Studies*. 50 (August): 545–57.

Button, Graham, ed. 1991. *Ethnomethodology and the Human Sciences*. New York: Cambridge University.

Carson, Jamie L., Jeffery A. Jenkins, David W. Rhode, and Mark A. Souva, 2001. "The Impact of National Tides and District-Level Effects on Electoral Outcomes: The U.S. Congressional Elections of 1862–63." *American Journal of Political Science*. 45 (October): 887–98.

Cartwright, Dorwin, ed. 1951. *Field Theory in Social Science: Selected Theoretical Papers by Kurt Lewin*. New York: Harper and Row.

Cassell, Catherine, and Gillian Symon, eds. 1997. *Qualitative Methods in Organizational Research*. Thousand Oaks, CA: Sage.

Cattell, Raymond B. 1978. *The Scientific Use of Factor Analysis in the Behavioral and Life Sciences*. New York: Plenum Press.

Charlesworth, James C. 1962. *The Limits of Behavioralism in Political Science*. Philadelphia: American Academy of Political and Social Sciences.

Chickudate, Nobuyuki. 2002. "A Phenomenological Approach to Inquiring into an Ethically Bankrupted Organization: A Case Study of a Japanese Company." *Journal of Business Ethics*. 28 (November): 59–72.

Child, Dennis. 1990. *The Essentials of Factor Analysis*. 2nd ed. London: Cassell.

Cleary, Robert E. 1992. "Revisiting the Doctoral Dissertation in Public Administration: An Examination of the Dissertations of 1990." *Public Administration Review*. 52 (January/February): 55–61.

Cochran, Clarke E., Lawrence C. Mayer, T.R. Carr, and N. Joseph Cayer. 1995. *American Public Policy: An Introduction*. 5th ed. New York: St. Martin's Press.

Cochran, William G. 1977. "Early Developments of Techniques in Comparative Experimentation." In *Experimental Design and Interpretation*. Raymond O. Collier, Jr., and Thomas J. Hummel, eds. Berkeley, CA: McCutchan Publishing: 5–21.

Coffee, Amanda, and Paul Alkinson. 1996. *Making Sense of Qualitative Data*. Thousand Oaks, CA: Sage.

Cohen, Ronald. 1973. "Generalizations in Ethnography." In *Handbook of Method in Cultural Anthropology*. Raul Narol, and Ronald Cohen, eds. New York: Columbia University Press: 31–50.

Coles, Romand. 2001. "*TRADITIO:* Feminists of Color and the Torn Virtues of Democratic Engagement." *Political Theory.* 29 (August): 488–516.

Collier, Raymond O., Jr., and Thomas J. Hummel, eds. 1977. *Experimental Design and Interpretation.* Berkeley, CA: McCutchan Publishing.

Columbia University. 1998. *Columbia Guide to Online Style.* New York: Columbia University Press.

Comstock, Donald E., and Russell Fox. 1993. "Participatory Research as Critical Theory: The North Bonneville, USA, Experience." In *Voices of Change: Participatory Research in the United States and Canada.* Peter Park, Mary Brydon-Miller, Budd Hall, and Ted Jackson, eds. Wesport, CT: Bergin & Garvey: 103–24.

Cook, Ronald G., and David Barry. 1995. "Shaping the External Environment: A Study of Small Firms' Attempts to Influence Public Policy." *Business and Society.* (December): 1–18.

Cook, Thomas D., ed. 1992. *Meta-analysis for Explanation.* New York: Russell Sage Foundation.

Cook, Thomas D., and Donald T. Campbell. 1979. *Quasi-Experimentation: Design and Analysis Issues for Field Settings.* Chicago: Rand McNally.

Cooper, Charles W., and Edmund J. Robins. 1962. *The Term Paper: A Manual and Model.* 3rd ed. Stanford, CA: Stanford University Press.

Cooper, John C.B. 1987. *Country Creditworthiness: The Use of Cluster Analysis and Discriminant Analysis.* Glasgow: Glasgow College of Technology.

Cooper, Terry L. 1998. *The Responsible Administrator: An Approach to Ethics for the Administrative Role.* 4th ed. San Francisco: Jossey-Bass.

Cortazzi, Martin. 1993. *Narrative Analysis.* London: Falmer Press.

Cozzetto, Don A. 1994. "Quantitative Research in Public Administration: A Need to Address Some Serious Methodological Problems." *Administration & Society.* 26 (November): 337–43.

Creswell, John W. 1994. *Research Design: Qualitative and Quantitative Approaches.* Thousand Oaks, CA: Sage.

Crowley, Philip, and Philip Norton, 1999. "Rebels and Rebellion: Conservative MPs in the 1992 Parliament." *British Journal of Politics and International Relations.* 1 (April): 84–104.

Cunningham, J. Barton. 1995. "Strategic Considerations in Using Action Research for Improving Personnel Practices." *Public Personnel Management.* 24 (Winter): 515–40.

Cunningham, Robert, and Lois Weschler. 2002. "Theory and the Public Administration Student/Practitioner." *Public Administration Review.* 62 (January/February): 104–13.

Dagleish, Lenard I., and David Chant. 1995. "A SAS Macro for Bootstrapping the Results of Discriminant Analysis." *Educational and Psychological Measurement.* 55 (August): 613–24.

Dastmalchian, A., P. Blyton, and R. Adamson. 1991. *The Climate of Workplace Relations.* London: Routledge.

Dearstyne, Bruce W. 1993. *The Archival Enterprise.* Chicago: American Library Association.

DeLaine, Marlene. 2000. *Fieldwork, Participation and Practice: Ethics and Dilemmas in Qualitative Research.* London: Sage.

Denhardt, Katherin G. 1989. "The Management of Ideals: A Political Perspective on Ethics." *Public Administration Review.* 49 (January): 187–93.

Denison, Dwight V., and Robert Eger III. 2000. "Tax Evasion from a Policy Perspective." *Public Administration Review.* 60 (March/April): 163–72.

Denscombe, Martyn. 2002. *Ground Rules for Good Research.* Buckingham, UK: Open University Press.

Denzin, Norman K., and Yvonna S. Lincoln, eds. 1994a. *Handbook of Qualitative Research.* Thousand Oaks, CA: Sage.

———. 1994b. "Introduction: Entering the Field of Qualitative Research." In *Handbook of Qualitative Research.* N.K. Denzin and Y.S. Lincoln, eds. Thousand Oaks, CA: Sage:1–17.

———. 1978. *The Research Act.* New York: McGraw-Hill.

———. 1998. *Strategies of Qualitative Inquiry.* Thousand Oaks, CA: Sage.

DePoy, Elizabeth, and Ann Hartman. 1999. "Critical Action Research: A Model for Social Work Knowing." *Social Work.* 44 (November): 560–70.

deVaus, David A. 2001. *Research Design in Social Research.* London: Sage.

Devine, Fiona. 2002. "Qualitative Methods." In *Theory and Methods in Political Science,* 2nd ed. David Marsh, and Gerry Stoker, eds. Houndmills, UK: Palgrave Macmillan: 197–215.

Dood, Janet S., ed. 1986. *The ACS Style Guide: A Manual for Authors and Editors.* Washington, DC: American Chemical Society.

Dovring, Folke. 1984. *History as a Social Science*. New York: Garland.

Dryzek, John S. 1986. "The Progress of Political Science." *Journal of Politics*. 48 (May): 301–20.

Dunteman, George T. 1994. "Principal Components Analysis." In *Factor Analysis and Related Techniques*. Michael S. Lewis-Beck, ed. London: Sage: 157–245.

Dusche, Richard A. 1994. "Research on the History and Philosophy of Science." In *Handbook on Research in Science Teaching and Learning*. Dorothy L. Gabel, ed. New York: Macmillan: 443–65.

Duveen, Gerard. 2000. "Piaget Ethnographer." *Social Science Information*. 39 (March): 79–97.

Easton, David. 1962. "The Current Meaning of 'Behavioralism' in Political Science." In *The Limits of Behavioralism in Political Science*. James C. Charlesworth, ed. Philadelphia: American Academy of Political and Social Science: 1–25.

Eber, Herbert W. 1975. "Multivariate Methodologies for Evaluation Research." In *Handbook of Evaluation Research*. Elmer L. Struening, and Marcia Guttentag, eds. Beverly Hills: Sage. 553–70.

Eco, Umberto. 1976. *A Theory of Semiotics*. Bloomington: Indiana University Press.

Einspruch, Eruch. 1998. *An Introductory Guide to SPSS® for Windows®*. Thousand Oaks, CA: Sage.

Eisner, Elliot W. 1997. "The New Frontier in Qualitative Research Methodology." *Qualitative Inquiry*. 3 (September): 259–74.

Elliott, Deni, and Judy E. Stern. 1997. *Research Ethics*. Hanover, NH: University Press of New England.

Elliott, Jacques. 1951. *The Changing Culture of a Factory: A Study of Authority and Participation in an Industrial Setting*. London: Tavistock Institute.

Elman, Colin, and Miriam Fedius Elman. 2002. "How Not to Be Lakatos Intolerant: Appraising Progress in IR Research." *International Studies Quarterly*. 46 (Winter): 231–62.

Elton, Geoffrey R. 1984. *Political History: Principles and Practice*. New York: Garland.

Emerson, Robert M., Rachel I. Fretz, and Linda L. Shaw. 1981. "Observational Field Work." *Annual Review of Sociology*. 7: 351–78.

———. 1995. *Writing Ethnographic Fieldnotes*. Chicago: University of Chicago Press.

Engeman, Thomas S. "Behavioralism, Postbehavioralism, and the Reemergence of Political Philosophy." *Perspectives on Political Science*. 24 (Fall): 214–17.

Este, David, Jackie Sieppert, and Allan Barsky. 1998. "Teaching and Learning Qualitative Research with and without Qualitative Data Analysis Software." *Journal of Research on Computing in Education*. 31 (Winter): 138–55.

Esterberg, Kristin G. 2002. *Qualitative Methods in Social Research*. Boston: McGraw-Hill.

Eulau, Heinz, ed. 1969a. *Behavioralism in Political Science*. New York: Atherton Press.

———. 1969b. "Tradition and Innovation: On the Tension between Ancient and Modern Ways in the Study of Politics." In *Behavioralism in Political Science*. Heinz Eulau, ed. New York: Atherton Press: 1–21.

Fagan, Patrick. *Working-Paper Sites of Political Science*, 2002. http://workingpapers.org/ (accessed June 1, 2002).

Fairweather, George W., and Louis G. Tornatzky. 1977. *Experimental Methods for Social Policy Research*. New York: Pergamon Press.

Farr, James, John S. Dryzek, and Stephen T. Leonard, eds. 1995. *Political Science in History*. Cambridge, UK: Cambridge University Press.

Farris, Martin T., and Roy J. Sampson. 1973. *Public Utilities: Regulation, Management and Ownership*. Boston: Houghton Mifflin.

Fay, Brian. 1975. *Social Theory and Political Practice*. London: George Allen & Unwin.

Fernandez, Sergio, and Ross Fabricant. 2000. "Methodological Pitfalls in Privatization Research: Two Cases from Florida's Child Support Enforcement Program." *Public Productivity and Management Review*. 24 (December): 133–44.

Fetterman, David M. 1989. *Ethnography: Step by Step*. Newbury Park, CA: Sage.

Finifter, Ada W., ed. 1983. *Political Science: The State of the Discipline*. Washington, DC: American Political Science Association.

———. 1993. *Political Science: The State of the Discipline II*. Washington, DC: American Political Science Association.

Fink, Arlene. 1998. *Conducting Research Literature Reviews*. Thousand Oaks, CA: Sage.

Fischer, Frank. 1998. "Policy Inquiry in Postpositivist Perspective. *Policy Studies Journal*. 26 (Spring): 129–46.

———, and Karl Shell. 1972. *The Economic theory of Price Indices*. New York: Academic Press.

Fischler, Raphaël. 2000. "Case Studies of Planners at Work." *Journal of Planning Literature*. 15 (November): 184–95.

Fitz-Gibbon, Carol Taylor, and Lynn Lyons Morris. 1987. *How to Analyze Data*. Newbury Park, CA: Sage.

Fleming, Michael C., and Joseph G. Nellis. 1991. *The Essence of Statistics for Business*. New York: Prentice-Hall.

Flick, Uwe. 1999a. "Qualitative Methods in the Study of Culture and Development: An Introduction." *Social Science Information*. 38 (December): 631–58.

———. 1999b. "Social Constructions of Change: Qualitative Methods for Analyzing Developmental Processes." *Social Science Information*. 38 (December): 625–29.

Folz, David H. 1996. *Survey Research for Public Administration*. Thousand Oaks, CA: Sage.

Fong, Margaret L. 1992. "When a Survey Isn't Research." *Counselor Education & Supervision*. 31 (June): 194–96.

Fowler, H. Ramsey, and Jane E. Aaron. 1995. *The Little, Brown Handbook*. 6th ed. New York: HarperCollins.

Fox, Mary F., and John M. Braxton. 1994. "Misconduct and Social Control in Science: Issues, Problems, Solutions." *Journal of Higher Education*. 65 (May/June): 373–83.

Fox, Richard G. 1977. *Urban Anthropology: Cities in Their Cultural Settings*. Englewood Cliffs, NJ: Prentice-Hall.

Frankfort-Nachmias, Chava, and David Nachmias. 1996. *Research Methods in the Social Sciences*. 5th ed. New York: St. Martin's Press.

Fredericksen, Patricia, and Rosanne London. 2000. "Disconnect in the Hollow State: The Pivotal Role of Organizational Capacity in Community-Based Development Organizations." *Public Administration Review*. 60 (May/June): 230–39.

Freedman, Paul. 1960. *The Principles of Scientific Research*. 2nd ed. London: Pergamon Press.

Gabel, Matthew J., and John D. Huber. 2000. "Putting Parties in Their Place: Inferring Party Left-Right Ideological Positions from Party Manifestos Data." *American Journal of Political Science*. 44 (January): 94–103.

Garceau, Oliver, ed. 1968. *Political Research and Political Theory*. Cambridge: Harvard University Press.

Garner, Theresa, David S. Johnson, and Mary F. Koloski. 1996. "An Experimental Consumer Price Index for the Poor." *Monthly Labor Review*. 119 (September): 32–42.

Garofalo, Charles, and Dean Geuras. 1999. *Ethics in the Public Service: The Moral Mind at Work*. Washington, DC: Georgetown University Press.

Garrick, John. 1999. "Doubting the Philosophical Assumptions of Interpretive Research." *International Journal of Qualitative Studies in Education*. 12 (March/April): 147–57.

Garson, G. David, and Samuel Overman. 1983. *Public Management Research in the United States*. New York: Praeger.

Gaskell, George. 2000. "Individual and Group Interviewing." In *Qualitative Researching with Text, Image and Sound*. Martin W. Bauer, and George Gaskell, eds. London: Sage: 38–56.

Geertz, Clifford. 1973. *The Interpretation of Cultures; Selected Essays*. New York: Basic Books.

Geuss, Raymond. 1981. *The Idea of a Critical Theory: Habermas and the Frankfurt School*. Cambridge: Cambridge University Press.

Gibaldi, Joseph, and Walter S. Achtert. 1988. *MLA Handbook for Writers of Research Papers*. New York: Modern Language Association of America.

Gill, Jeff, and Kenneth J. Meier. 2000. "Public Administration Research and Practice: A Methodological Manifesto." *Journal of Public Administration Research and Theory*. 10 (January): 157–99.

Gill, John, and Phil Johnson. 1991. *Research Methods for Managers*. London: Chapman.

Gilliam, Franklin D., Jr., and Shanto Iyengar. 2000. "Prime Suspects: The Influence of Local Television News on the Viewing Public." *American Journal of Political Science*. 44 (July): 560–73.

Glanz, Jeffrey. 1999. "A Primer on Action Research for the School Administrator." *Clearing House*. 72 (May/June): 301–5.

Glaser, Barney G. 1992. *Emergence vs. Forcing: Basics of Grounded Theory Analysis*. Mill Valley, CA: Sociology Press.

Glaser, Barney G., and Anselm L. Strauss. 1967. *The Discovery of Grounded Theory: Strategies for Qualitative Research*. Chicago: Aldine.

Glorfeld, Louis W. 1995. "An Improvement on Horn's Parallel Analysis Methodology for Selecting the

Correct Number of Factors to Retain." *Educational and Psychological Measurement.* 55 (June): 377–93.

Goddard, John, and Andrew Kirby. 1976. *An Introduction to Factor Analysis.* Norwich: University of East Anglia.

Goel, M. Lal. 1988. *Political Science Research: A Methods Handbook.* Ames: Iowa State University.

Golden, M. Patricia, ed. 1976. *The Research Experience.* Itasca, IL: F.E. Peacock Publishers.

Goss, Robert P. 1996. "A Distinct Public Administration Ethics?" *Journal of Public Administration Research & Theory.* 6 (October): 573–98.

Gottfredson, Gary D. 1996. "The Hawthorne Misunderstanding (and How to Get the Hawthorne Effect in Action Research)." *Journal of Crime & Delinquency.* 33 (February): 28–49.

Green, Samuel B., Neil J. Salkind, and Theresa M. Akey. 2000. *Using SPSS.* Upper Saddle River, NJ: Prentice-Hall.

Greeno, Catherine G. 2001. "The Classical Experimental Design." *Family Process.* 40 (4): 495–99.

Gubanich, Alan A. 1991. *Writing a Scientific Paper.* Dubuque: Kendall/Hunt Publishing.

Gubrium, Jaber F., and James A. Holstein, eds. 2002. *Handbook of Interview Research: Context and Method.* Thousand Oaks, CA: Sage.

Gummesson, Evert. 1991. *Qualitative Methods in Management Research.* Newbury Park, CA: Sage.

Gunnell, John G. 1983. "Political Theory: The Evolution of a Sub-field." In *Political Science: The State of the Discipline.* Washington, DC: American Political Science Association: 3–45.

Gurman, Pamela J., ed. 1997. *Written Communications Resources Digest.* Needham Heights, MA: Simon & Schuster.

Gustafsson, Bengt, Lars Ryden, Gunnar Tibell, and Peter Wallensteen. 1984. "The Uppsala Code of Ethics for Scientists." *Journal of Peace Research.* 21 (November): 311–16.

Gustavsen, Bjorn. 1996. "Action Research, Democratic Dialogue, and the Issue of 'Critical Mass' in Change." *Qualitative Inquiry.* 2 (March). 90–104.

Hacker, Diana. 1992. *A Writer's Reference.* 2nd. ed. Boston: Bedford Books.

Hair, Joseph F., Jr., Rolph E. Anderson, Ronald L. Tatham, and William C. Black. 1992. *Multivariate Data Analysis with Readings.* New York. Macmillan.

Hakim, Catherine. 2000. *Research Design.* 2nd ed. London: Routledge.

Hall, Wendy A., and Peter Callery. 2001. "Enhancing the Rigor of Grounded Theory: Incorporating Reflexivity and Relationality." *Qualitative Health Research.* (March): 257–72.

Hammer, Dean, Jessica Bleiman, and Kenneth Park. 1999. "Between Positivism and Postmodernism: Hannah Arendt on the Formation of Policy Judgements." *Policy Studies Review.* 16 (Spring): 148–82.

Hansen, Philip, and Alicja Muszyaki. 1990. "Crisis in Rural Life and Crisis in Thinking: Directions for Critical Research." *Canadian Review of Sociology and Anthropology.* 27 (February): 1–23.

Hanson, N.R. 1958. *Patterns of Discovery: An Inquiry into the Conceptual Foundations of Science.* Cambridge, UK: Cambridge University Press.

Hardwig, John. 1991. "The Role of Trust in Knowledge." *Journal of Philosophy.* 88 (December): 693–708.

Harnack, Andrew, and Eugene Kleppinger. 1997. *ONLINE! A Reference Guide to Using Internet Sources.* New York: St. Martin's Press.

Harrison, Lisa. 2001. *Political Research: An Introduction.* London: Routledge.

Hart, Chris. 1998. *Doing a Literature Review.* London: Sage.

Hartley, Roger E., and Lisa M. Holmes. 2002. "The Increasing Senate Scrutiny of Lower Court Nominees." *Political Science Quarterly.* 117 (Summer): 259–78.

Harvey, Don, and Donald R. Brown. 1996. *An Experiential Approach to Organizational Development.* 5th ed. Upper Saddle River, NJ: Prentice-Hall.

Hauck, Robert J. 2001. "Reforming Human Subjects Protection: The Beat Goes On." *PS: Political Science & Politics.* 34 (June): 332–33.

Hawkens, Darren, and Melissa Humes. 2002. "Human Rights and Domestic Violence." *Political Science Quarterly.* 117 (Summer): 231–57.

Hempel, Carl. 1966. *Philosophy of the Natural Sciences.* Englewood Cliffs, NJ: Prentice-Hall.

Heppell, Timothy D. 2002. "The Ideological Composition of the Parliamentary Conservative Party, 1992–97." *British Journal of Politics and International Relations.* 2 (June): 299–324.

Heywood, Andrew. 2000. *Key Concepts in Politics.* Houndmills, UK: Palgrave.

Hildebrand, David H., and A. Lyman Ott. 1998. *Statistical Thinking for Managers*. 4th ed. Pacific Grove, CA: Duxbury Press.

Hockett, Charles F. 1958. *A Course in Modern Linguistics*. New York: Macmillan.

Hodder, Ian. 1982. *Symbols in Action*. Cambridge: Cambridge University Press.

Hoddie, Mathew. 2002. "Preferential Policies and the Blurring of Ethnic Boundaries: The Case of Aboriginal Australians in the 1980s." *Political Studies*. 50 (June): 293–312.

Holsti, Ole R. 1969. *Content Analysis for the Social Sciences and Humanities*. Menlo Park, CA: Addison-Wesley.

Hoonaard, Will C. van den. 2001. "Is Research Ethics Review a Moral Panic?" *The Canadian Review of Sociology and Anthropology*. 38 (February): 19–36.

Houston, David J., and Sybil M. Delevan. 1990. "Public Administration Research: An Assessment of Journal Publications." *Public Administration Review*. 50 (November/December): 674–81.

Huberty, Carl, and Laureen L. Lowman. 1997. "Discriminant Analysis via Statistical Packages." *Educational and Psychological Measurement*. 57 (October). 759–84.

Huck, Schuyler W., and William H. Cormier. 1996. *Reading Statistics and Research*. 2nd ed. New York: HarperCollins.

Hughes, John, and Wes Sharrock. 1997. *The Philosophy of Social Research*. 3rd ed. London: Longman.

Hutcheson, Grawme, and Nick Sofroniou. 1999. *The Multivariate Scientist*. London: Sage.

Iggers, Georg C. 1985. *New Directions in European Historiography*. London: Methuen.

James-Catalao. Cynthia N. 1996. *Researching on the World Wide Web*. Rocklin, CA: Prima Publishing.

Janesick, Valerie J. 1994. "The Dance of Qualitative Research Design." In *Handbook of Qualitative Research*. Norman. K. Denzin, and Yyonna. S. Lincoln, eds. Thousand Oaks, CA: Sage: 209–19.

Jennings, Paul, Hans Keman, and Jan Kleinnijenhuis. 1999. *Doing Research in Political Science*. London: Sage.

John, Peter. 2002. "Quantitative Methods." In *Theory and Methods in Political Science*. 2nd ed. David Marsh, and Gerry Stoker, eds. Houndmills, UK: Palgrave Macmillan: 216–30.

Johnson, Janet, Richard A. Joslyn, and H.T. Reynolds. 2001. *Political Science Research Methods*. 4th ed. Washington, DC: Congressional Quarterly.

Johnson, John M. 2002. "In-Depth Interviewing." In *Handbook of Interview Research*, Jaber F. Gubrium, and James A. Holstein, eds. Thousand Oaks, CA: Sage: 103–19.

Johnson, Richard A., and Dean W. Wickern. 1988. *Applied Multivariate Statistical Analysis*. 2nd ed. Englewood Cliffs, NJ: Prentice-Hall.

Jones, E. Terrence. 1971. *Conducting Political Research*. New York: Harper and Row.

Jones, Russell A. 1996. *Research Methods in the Social and Behavioral Sciences*. 2nd ed. Sunderland, MA: Sinaur Associates.

Jorgensen, Joseph G. 1971. "On Ethics and Anthropology." *Current Anthropology*. 12 (June): 321–34.

Joseph, Sarah, Jenny Schultz, and Melissa Castan. 2000. *The International Covenant on Civil and Political Rights*. Oxford: Oxford University Press.

Jurich, Katarin. 2001. "Getting the Story Straight: Grounded Theory, Hermeneutics and the Practice of Fieldwork on the Plains of South Dakota." *Sociological Perspectives*. 43(4):S149–62.

Kalinosky, Kathy. 1997. "Action Research and Learner Participation in a Homeless Shelter." *New Directions for Adult and Continuing Education*. 73 (Spring): 52–55.

Kaplan, Robert S. 1998. "Innovation Action Research: Creating New Management Theory and Practice." *Journal of Management Accounting Research*. 10: 89–119.

Kaplan, Robert S., and David P. Norton. 1996. *The Balanced Scorecard*. Boston: Harvard Business School Press.

Kassarjian, Harold H., and Waltraud M. Kassarjian. 1988. "The Impact of Regulation on Advertising: A Content Analysis." *Journal of Consumer Policy*. 11 (3): 269–86.

Katznelson, Ira, and Helen Milner, eds. 2002. *Political Science III: The State of the Discipline*. Washington, DC: American Political Science Association.

Kaufman, Herbert. 1960. *The Forest Ranger: A Study in Administrative Behavior*. Baltimore: Johns Hopkins University Press.

Kaufman, Leonard, and Peter J. Rousseeuw. 1990. *Finding Groups in Data: An Introduction to Cluster Analysis*. New York: John Wiley.

Keller, Julia. 1998. "Cyber-Goofs Point Out Need for Fact Checking." *Seattle Times* (27 December): C2.

Kendall, Judy. 1999. "Axial Coding and the Grounded Theory Controversy." *Western Journal of Nursing Research*. 21 (December): 743–58.

Kennedy, X.J., and Dorothy M. Kennedy. 1987. *The Bedford Guide for College Papers*. New York: St. Martin's Press.

Kenworthy, Lane. 2001. "Wage-Setting Measures: A Survey and Assessment." *World Politics*. 54 (1): 57–98.

Kerlinger, Fred N., and Elazar J. Pedhazur. 1973. *Multiple Regression in Behavioral Research*. New York: Holt, Rinehart and Winston.

Kerr, Brinck, William Miller, and Margaret Reid. 2002. "Sex-Based Occupational Segregation in U.S. State Bureaucracies, 1987–97." *Public Administration Review* (July/August): 412–23.

Kidder, Louise H. 1986. *Research Methods in Social Relations*. New York: Holt, Rinehart and Winston.

Kim, Jae-on, and Charles W. Mueller. 1994. "Introduction to Factor Analysis." In *Factor Analysis and Related Techniques*. Michael S. Lewis-Beck, ed. London: Sage: 1–74.

Kim, Taeyong. 1995. "Discriminant Analysis as a Prediction Tool for Uncommitted Voters in Pre-election Polls." *International Journal of Public Opinion Research*. 7 (Summer): 110–27.

King, Cheryl S., Kathryn M. Felty, and Bridget O. Susel. "The Question of Participation: Toward Authentic Public Participation in Public Administration." *Public Administration Review*. 58 (July/August): 317–26.

King, James R. 1999. "Am Not! Are Too! Using Queer Standpoint in Postmodern Critical Ethnography." *International Journal of Qualitative Studies in Education*. 12 (September/October): 473–91.

Kiniry, Malcolm, and Mike Rose, ed. 1990. *Critical Strategies for Academic Writing*. Boston: Bedford Books.

Kirk, Roger E. 1995. *Experimental Design: Procedures for the Behavioral Sciences*. Pacific Grove, CA: Brooks/Cole.

Kitzinger, Jenny, and Rosaline S. Barbour. 1999. "Introduction: The Challenge and Promise of Focus Groups." In *Developing Focus Group Research*. Rosaline S. Barbour, and Jenny Kitzinger, eds. London: Sage: 1–20.

Klecka, William R. 1980. *Discriminant Analysis*. Beverly Hills: Sage.

Klein, Heinz K., and Michael D. Myers. 1999. "A Set of Principles for Conducting and Evaluating Interpretive Field Studies in Information Systems." *MIS Quarterly*. 23 (March): 67–98.

Kline, Paul. 1994. *An Easy Guide to Factor Analysis*. London: Routledge.

Kluckholm, Clyde. 1967. "The Study of Culture." In *The Study of Society*. P.I. Rose, ed. New York: Random House: 74–93.

Knight, Peter K. 2002. *Small Scale Research*. London: Sage.

Konecki, Krzysztof. 1997. "Time in the Recruiting Search Process by Headhunting Companies." In *Grounded Theory in Practice*. Anselm Strauss, and Juliet Corbin, eds. Thousand Oaks, CA: Sage: 131–45.

Kornblum, William. 1996. "Introduction" In *In the Field: Readings on the Field Research Experience*. 2nd ed. Carolyn D. Smith, and William Kornblum, eds. Westport, CT: Praeger: 1–7.

Krazanowski, W.J. 1988. *Principles of Multivariate Analysis: A User's Perspective*. Oxford: Oxford University Press.

Kuechler, Manfred. 1998. "The Survey Method." *American Behavioral Scientist*. 42 (October): 178–200.

Kuhne, Gary W., and B. Allen Quigley. 1997. "Understanding and Using Action Research in Practice Settings." *New Directions for Adult and Continuing Education*. 73 (Spring): 23–40.

Kuhns, Eileen, and S.V. Martorana, eds. 1982. *Qualitative Methods for Institutional Research*. San Francisco: Jossey-Bass.

Kumar, Ranjit. 1996. *Research Methodology*. London: Sage.

Kvale, Steiner. 1996. *Interviewing: An Introduction to Qualitative Research*. Thousand Oaks, CA: Sage.

Kymlicka, Will. 2002. *Contemporary Political Philosophy,* 2nd ed. Oxford: Oxford University Press.

LaFollette, Marcel C. 1994. "The Politics of Research Misconduct: Congressional Oversight, Universities, and Science." *Journal of Higher Education*. 65 (May/June): 261–65.

Laitan, David D. 2001. "The Political Science Discipline." Paper presented for delivery at the Annual Meeting of the American Political Science Association. San Francisco, CA. (August 30–September 2). http://pro.harvard.edu/abstracts. (accessed June 1, 2002).

Lan, Zhiyong, and Kathleen K. Anders. 2000. "A Paradigmatic View of Contemporary Public Administration Research." *Administration & Society*. 32 (May): 138–66.

Lance, Charles E., and Robert J. Vandenberg. 2002. "Confirmatory Factor Analysis." In *Measuring and*

Analyzing Behavior in Organizations. Fritz Drasgow, and Neal Schmitt, eds. San Francisco: Jossey-Bass: 221–54.

Lane, Ruth. 1992. "Political Culture: Residual Category or General Theory?" *Comparative Political Studies*. 25 (3): 362–88.

Lang, Gerhard, and George D. Heiss. 1990. *A Practical Guide to Research Methods*. Lanham, MD: University Press of America.

Lapin, Lawrence L. 1993. *Statistics for Modern Business Decisions*. 3rd ed. Fort Worth, TX: Dryden Press.

Laponse, J.A., and Paul Smoker, eds. 1972. *Experimentation and Simulation in Political Science*. Toronto: University of Toronto.

Lasswell, Harold D. 1953. "Why Be Quantitative?" In *Reader in Public Opinion and Communication*. Bernard Berelson, and Morris Janowitz, eds. Glencoe, IL: Free Press: 265–72.

Lastrucci, Carlo L. 1967. *The Scientific Approach: Basic Principles of the Scientific Method*. Cambridge: Schenkman Publishing.

Lathrop, Richard G. 1969. *Introduction to Psychological Research*. New York: Harper & Row.

Laurence, Helen, and William Miller, eds. 2000. *Academic Research on the Internet: Options for Scholars and Libraries*. New York: Hawthorne Information Press.

LeCompte, Margaret D. 2002. "The Transformation of Ethnographic Practice: Past and Current Challenges." *Qualitative Research*. 2 (December). 283–99.

LeCompte, Margaret D., and Jean J. Schensul. 1999. *Designing and Conducting Ethnographic Research*. Walnut Creek, CA: AltaMira Press.

Lee, Chung-Shing, J. Thad Barnowe, and David E. McNabb. 2001. "Environmental Issues in Taiwan and the USA: Public Perceptions, Attitudes and Priorities." In *Proceedings of the 2002 Pan-Pacific Conference XVIII*. Santiago, Chile.

Lee, Raymond M. 2000. *Unobtrusive Methods in Social Research*. Buckingham, UK: Open University Press.

Lee, Thomas W. 1999. *Using Qualitative Methods in Organizational Research*. Thousand Oaks, CA: Sage.

Leedy, Paul D. 1974. *Practical Research: Planning and Design*. New York: Macmillan.

Lees-Marshment, Jennifer. 2001. "The Marriage of Politics and Marketing." *Political Studies*. 49 (September): 692–713.

Lehmann, Donald R. 1985. *Market Research and Analysis*. 2nd ed. Homewood, IL: Irwin.

Lehmkuhl, L. Don. "Nonparametric Statistics: Methods for Analyzing Data Not Meeting Assumptions Required for the Application of Parametric Tests." *Journal of Prosthetics and Orthodtics* (Online Library), 1996. vol. 8 (3): 105–13. http://www.oandp.org/jpo/library/1996 (accessed May 19, 2002).

Leiserson, Avery. 1968. "Empirical Approaches to Democratic Theory." In *Political Research and Political Theory*. Oliver Garceau, ed. Cambridge: Harvard University Press: 13–36.

Leiter, Kenneth. 1980. *A Primer on Ethnomethodology*. New York: Oxford University Press.

Lenkowsky, Leslie, and James L. Perry. 2000. "Reinventing Government: The Case of National Service." *Public Administration Review*. 60 (July/August): 298–307.

Lessor, Roberta. 2000. "Using the Team Approach of Anselm Strauss in Action Research: Consulting on a Project in Global Education." *Sociological Perspectives*. 43 (Winter): S133–S148.

Lester, James D., Sr., and James D. Lester, Jr. 1992. *The Research Paper Handbook*. Glenview, IL: Scott, Foresman.

Levine, David M., Mark L. Berenson, and David Stephan. 1997. *Statistics for Managers Using Microsoft® Excel*. Upper Saddle River, NJ: Prentice-Hall.

Lewicki, R.J., R.D. Bowen, D.R. Hall, and F.S. Hall. 1988. *Experiences in Management and Organizational Behavior*. 3rd ed. New York: John Wiley.

Lewis-Beck, Michael S., ed. *Factor Analysis and Related Techniques*. London: Sage.

Li, Xia, and Nancy B. Crane. 1996. *Electronic Styles: A Handbook for Citing Electronic Information*. Medford, NJ: Information Technology Today.

Lin, Nan. 1976. *Foundations of Social Research*. New York: McGraw-Hill Book Company.

Lincoln, Yvonna S. 1997. "From Understanding to Action: New Imperatives, New Criteria, and New Methods for Interpretive Researchers." *Theory and Research in Social Education*. 26 (Winter): 12–29.

Lindzey, Gardner. 1961. *Projective Techniques and Cross-Cultural Research*. New York: Appleton-Century-Crofts.

Linz, Juan J. 1969. "Ecological Analysis and Survey Research." In *Quantitative Ecological Analysis in the Social Sciences*. Cambridge: Massachusetts Institute of Technology: 91–131.

Lippitt, Ronald, Jeanne Watson, and Bruce Westley. 1958. *The Dynamics of Planned Change*. New York: Harcourt, Brace.

Lipsey, Mark W., and David B. Wilson. 2001. *Practical Meta-analysis*. Thousand Oaks, CA: Sage.

Lipsky, Michael. 1980. *Street-Level Bureaucracy*. New York: Russell Sage.

Locher, Birgit, and Elisabeth Prügl. 2001. "Feminism and Constructivism: World's Apart or Sharing the Middle Ground?" *International Studies Quarterly*. 45 (March): 111–29.

Locke, Karen. 1996. "Rewriting the Discovery of Grounded Theory after 25 Years?" *Journal of Management Inquiry*. 5 (September): 239–46.

Long, Scott. 1983. *Confirmatory Factor Analysis*. Beverly Hills: Sage.

Loor, Maurice. 1983. *Cluster Analysis for Social Scientists*. San Francisco: Jossey-Bass.

Lowndes, Vivien. 2002. "Institutionalism." In *Theory and Methods in Political Science*, 2nd ed. David Marsh, and Gerry Stoker, eds. Houndmills, UK: Palgrave Macmillan: 90–108.

Lyotard, Jean-François. 1984. *The Postmodern Condition: A Report on Knowledge*. Geoff Bennington, and Brian Jameson, trans. Minneapolis: University of Minnesota Press.

Maas, A.J. "Hermeneutics." Janet Grayson, trans. *The Catholic Encyclopaedia, Vol. VII*, 1999. http.//www.newadvent.org/cathen/0/2/1anum (accessed August 8, 2000).

Madge, John. 1985. *The Tools of Science*. New York: Garland.

Malhotra, Naresh K. 1999. *Marketing Research: An Applied Orientation*. 3rd ed. Upper Saddle River, NJ: Prentice-Hall.

Manheim, Jarol B., and Richard C. Rich. 1995. *Empirical Political Analysis: Research Methods in Political Science*. 4th ed. Englewood Cliffs, NJ: Prentice-Hall.

Manheim, Jarol B., Richard C. Rich, and Lars Willnat. 2002. *Empirical Political Analysis: Research Methods in Political Science*. 5th ed. New York: Longman.

Manly, Bryan F. 1986. *Multivariate Statistical Methods: A Primer*. London: Chapman & Hall.

Manning, Peter K., and Betsy Cullum-Swan. 1998. "Narrative, Content, and Semiotic Analysis." In *Collecting and Interpreting Qualitative Materials*. Norman K. Denzin, and Yvonna S. Lincoln, eds. Thousand Oaks, CA: Sage. 246–73.

Marascuilo, Leonard A., and Maryellen McSweeney. 1977. *Nonparametric and Distribution-Free Methods for the Social Sciences*. Monterey, CA: Brooks/Cole.

March, James. 1977. "Administrative Practice, Organizational Theory, and Political Philosophy: Ruminations on the Reflections of John M. Gaus." *Political Science and Politics*. 30 (4): 689–98.

Margulies, N., and J. Wallace. 1973. *Organizational Change: Techniques and Applications*. Glennview, IL: Scott, Foresman.

Mariner, Wendy K. 1997. "Public Confidence in Public Health Research." *Public Health Reports*. 112 (January/February): 33–36.

Markman, Roberta H., Peter T. Markman, and Marie L. Waddell. 1989. *10 Steps in Writing the Research Paper*. 4th ed. New York: Barron's Educational Series.

Marriott, F.H.C. 1974. *The Interpretation of Multiple Observations*. London: Academic Press.

Marrow, Alfred J. 1977. *The Practical Theorist: The Life and Work of Kurt Lewin*. New York: Teachers College Press.

Marsh, David, and Gerry Stoker. 2002. "Marxism." In *Theory and Methods in Political Science*. 2nd ed. David Marsh, and Gerry Stoker, eds. Houndmills, UK: Palgrave Macmillan: 153–71.

———. 2002. *Theory and Methods in Political Science*. 2nd ed. Houndmills, UK: Palgrave Macmillan.

Marsh, David, Gerry Stoker, and Paul Furlong. 2002. "A Skin, Not a Sweater: Ontology and Epistemology in Political Science." In *Theory and Methods in Political Science*. 2nd ed. David Marsh, and Gerry Stoker, eds. Houndmills, UK: Palgrave Macmillan: 17–41.

Marshall, Catherine, and Gretchen B. Rossman. 1999. *Designing Qualitative Research*. 3rd ed. Thousand Oaks, CA: Sage.

Martin, Lana A. 2000. "Effective Data Collection." *Total Quality Management*. 11 (May): 341–45.

Maxwell, Albert E. 1977. *Multivariate Analysis in Behavioral Research*. London: Chapman & Hall.

Maykut, Pamela, and Richard Morehouse. 1994. *Beginning Qualitative Research: A Philosophic and Practical Guide*. London: Falmer Press.

McAllister, Ian. 2000. "Keeping Them Honest: Public and Elite Perceptions of Ethical Conduct among Australian Legislators." *Political Studies*. 48 (March): 22–37.

McCoy, Charles A., and John Playford, eds. 1967. *Apolitical Politics: A Critique of Behavioralism*. New York: Thomas Y. Crowell.

McCurdy, Howard E., and Robert E. Cleary. 1984. "Why Can't We Resolve the Research Issue in Public Administration?" *Public Administration Review*. 44 (January/February): 49–55.

McDaniels, Carl, Jr., and Roger Gates. 1993. *Contemporary Marketing Research*. 2nd ed. Minneapolis/St. Paul: West Publishing Co.

McDonald, Gael 2000. "Business Ethics: Practical Proposals for Organizations." *Journal of Business Ethics*. 25 (May): 169–84.

McDowell, W.H. 2002. *Historical Research: A Guide*. London: Longman.

McInnis, Raymond G., and James W. Scott. 1984. *Social Sciences Research Handbook*. New York: Garland.

McNabb, David E. 1968. "The Private vs. Public-Power Fight in Seattle, 1930–1934." Unpublished thesis. Seattle: University of Washington.

———. 1980. Experimental Methodology for Segmenting the Postsecondary Education Market. Unpublished Ph.D. dissertation. Corvallis, OR: Oregon State University.

———. 1991. "Shaping the 18th Century Consumer Society: The *London Post and General Advertiser*, 1734–1809." Paper presented at the 16th Annual European Studies Conference. Omaha, NE. (October).

———and F. Thomas Sepic. 1995. "Culture, Climate and Total Quality Management: Measuring Readiness for Change." *Public Productivity and Management Review*. 18 (July): 369–85.

McWilliam, Carol L. 1996. "Creating Understanding That Cultivates Change." *Qualitative Inquiry*. 2 (June): 151–76.

Meacham, Shuaib J. 1998. "Threads of a New Language: A Response to Eisenhart's 'On the Subject of Interpretive Review.' " *Review of Educational Research*. 68 (Winter): 401–7.

Meier, Kenneth J., and Vicky M. Wilkins. 2002. "Gender Differences in Agency Head Salaries: The Case of Public Education." *Public Education Review*. (July/August): 405–11.

Meier, Kenneth J., Vicky M. Wilkins, H.L. Polinard, and Robert D. Wrinkle. 2000. "Bureaucracy and Organizational Performance: Causality Arguments about Public Schools." *American Journal of Political Science*. 44 (July): 590–602.

Melia, Kathy M. 1996. "Rediscovering Glaser." *Qualitative Health Research*. 6 (August): 368–79.

Mercier, Jean. 1994. "Looking at Organizational Culture Hermeneutically." *Administration & Society*. 261 (May): 28–47.

Merrell, Floyd. 1982. *Semiotic Foundations:Steps Toward an Epistemology and Written Texts*. Bloomington: Indiana University Press.

Merriam, Sharan B., and Edwin L. Simpson. 1989. *A Guide to Research for Educators and Trainers of Adults*. Melbourne, FL: Krieger.

Merton, Robert K. 1967. "Research and Sociological Theory." In *The Study of Society*. P.I. Rose, ed. New York: Random House: 35–48.

Miles, Matthew B., and A. Michael Huberman. 1984. *Qualitative Data Analysis: A Sourcebook of New Methods*. Beverly Hills, CA: Sage.

———. 1998. "Data Management and Analysis Methods." In *Collecting and Interpreting Qualitative Materials*. Norman K. Denzin, and Yvonna S. Lincoln, eds. Thousand Oaks, CA: Sage: 179–210.

Miller, Delbert C. 1991. *Handbook of Research Design and Social Measurement*. 5th ed. Newbury Park, CA: Sage Publications.

Miller, Gerald J., and Marcia L. Whicker, eds. 1999. *Handbook of Research Methods in Public Administration*. New York: Marcel Dekker.

Miller, Steven I., and Marcel Fredericks. 1999. *Quantitative Research Methods: Social Epistemology and Practical Inquiry*. New York: Peter Lang.

Milner, Helen V., Ira Karznellson, and Elizabeth V. Spires, eds. 2002. *Political Science: State of the Discipline III*. New York. W.W. Norton.

Mitchell, Jerry. 1998. "Ethical Principles for Public Administration Research." In *Teaching Ethics and Values in Public Administration Programs*. James Bowman, and Donald Menzel, eds. Albany: State University of New York Press: 305–20.

Mitchell, Marilyn L. 1998. *Employing Qualitative Methods in the Private Sector*. Thousand Oaks, CA: Sage.

Monopoli, John, and Lori L. Alworth. 2000. "The Use of the Thematic Apperception Test in the Study of Native American Psychological Characteristics: A Review and Archival Study of Navaho Men." *Genetic, Social and General Psychology Monographs*. 126 (February): 43–79.

Montgomery, D.C. 1991. *Design and Analysis of Experiments*. 3rd ed. New York: John Wiley.

Moon, J. Donald. 1975. "The Logic of Inquiry: A Synthesis of Opposed Perspectives." In *Political Science: Scope and Theory*. Vol. 1. Fred I. Greenstein, and Nelson W. Polsby, eds. Menlo Park, CA: Addison-Wesley: 131–228.

Moore, Henrietta. 1990. "Paul Ricoeur: Action, Meaning, Text." In *Reading Material Culture: Structuralism, Hermeneutics, and Post-Structuralism*. Christopher Tilley, ed. Oxford: Blackwell: 85–120.

Morgan, David L. 2002. "Focus Group Interviewing." In *Handbook of Interview Research*. Jaber F. Gubrium, and James A. Holstein, eds. Thousand Oaks, CA: Sage: 141–59.

Morse, Janice M. 1994. "Designing Funded Qualitative Research." In *Handbook of Qualitative Research*. Norman K. Denzin, and Yvonna S. Lincoln, eds. Thousand Oaks, CA: Sage: 220–35.

Morton, Rebecca B. 1999. *Methods and Models: A Guide to the Empirical Analysis of Formal Models in Political Science*. Cambridge, UK: Cambridge University Press.

Mulaik, Stanley A. 1972. *The Foundations of Factor Analysis*. New York: McGraw-Hill.

Munhall, Patricia L., and Carolyn J. Oiler. 1986. *Nursing Research: A Qualitative Perspective*. Norwalk, CT: Appleton-Century-Crofts.

Myers, M.D. "Qualitative Research in Information Systems." *MIS Quarterly*. 21 (June): 241–42. *MISQ Discovery*, 1997. http://www.misq.org/misqd961/world/. *MISQ Discovery* (accessed April 28, 1999).

Naím, Moisés. 2002. "The World According to Larry." *Foreign Policy*. 130 (July/August): 31–39.

Nakano, Lynne Y. 2000. "Volunteering as a Lifestyle Choice: Negotiating Self-identity in Japan." *Ethnology*. 39 (Spring): 93–107.

Naroll, Raoul, and Ronald Cohen, eds. 1973. *A Handbook of Method in Cultural Anthropology*. New York: Columbia University Press.

Narotzky, Susana. 2000. "The Cultural Basis of a Regional Economy: The Vega Baja del Segura in Spain." *Ethnology*. 39 (Winter): 1–14.

Neef, Nancy A., Brian A. Iwata, and Terry J. Page. 1986. "Ethical Standards in Behavioral Research." In *Research Methods in Applied Behavior Analysis: Issues and Advances*. Alan Poling, and R. Wayne Fuqua, eds. New York: Plenum Press: 233–63.

Nelson, Stephen L. 2002. *Excel Data Analysis for Dummies*. Indianapolis, IN: Wiley.

Nersesyants, Vladik. 1988. "Integrating Research: The Dialectics of the Historical and the Logical." Paper presented in the 14th World Congress of Political Sciences. Washington DC: Soviet Political Science Association/USSR Academy of Sciences: 8–18.

Neuman, W. Lawrence. 2000. *Social Research Methods: Qualitative and Quantitative Approaches*. 4th ed. Boston: Allyn and Bacon.

Norris, Pippa, and Ivor Crewe. 1993. "The Reputation of Political Science Journals: Pluralist and Consensus Views." *Political Studies*. 41 (March): 5–23.

Northrop, Alana, and Kenneth L. Kraemer. 1982. "Contributions of Political Science and Public Administration to Qualitative Research Methods." In *Qualitative Methods for Institutional Research*. Eileen Kuhns and S.V. Martorana, eds. San Francisco: Jossey-Bass: 43–54.

Norušis, Marija J. 2000. *SPSS® for Windows™ Base System User's Guide* (Version 10.0). Chicago: SPSS Inc.

———. 2002. *SPSS® 11.0: Guide to Data Analysis*. Upper Saddle River, NJ: Prentice-Hall.

Nunez, Ralph. 2001. "Family Homelessness in New York City: A Case Study." *Political Science Quarterly*. 116 (Fall): 367–79.

Oakley, Ann. 2000. *Experiments in Knowing*. Cambridge, UK: Polity Press.

Office of Research Integrity. 2002. *Potential Research Topics*. Washington, DC: U.S. Department of Health and Human Services. http://ori.dhhs.gov.html/programs.potentialrestopics.asp. August 30.

Oliver, Paul. 1997. *Research for Business, Marketing and Education*. Chicago: NTC Publishing.

Oppenheim, A.N. (Bram). 1992. *Questionnaire Design, Interviewing, and Attitude Measurement*. New ed. New York: St. Martin's Press.

Organ, Dennis W. and Thomas S. Bateman. 1991. *Organizational Behavior*. 4th ed. Homewood, IL: Richard D. Irwin.

Orlans, Harold. 1967. "Ethical Problems in the Relations of Research Sponsors and Investigators." In *Ethics, Politics, and Social Research*. Gideon Sjoberg, ed. Cambridge, MA: Schenkman Publishing: 3–24.

Orren, Karen and Stephen Skowronek. 1995. "Order and Time in Intuitional Study: A Brief for the Historical Approach." In *Political Science in History.* James Farr, John S. Dryzek, and Stephen T. Leonard, eds. Cambridge, UK: Cambridge University Press: 296–317.

Oskamp, Stuart. 1977. *Attitudes and Opinions.* Englewood Cliffs, NJ: Prentice-Hall.

O'Sullivan, Elizabethann and Gary R. Rassel. 1995. *Research Methods for Public Administrators.* 2nd ed. White Plains, NY: Longman.

Parker, Robert P. and C. Brian Grove. 1996. "The Statistics Producer's Corner." *Business Economics.* 31 (July): 59–60.

Patton, Michael Q. 1980. *Qualitative Evaluation Methods.* Beverly Hills, CA: Sage.

———. 1990. *Qualitative Evaluation and Research Methods.* 2nd ed. Newbury Park, CA: Sage.

———. 2002. "Two Decades of Developments in Qualitative Research." *Qualitative Social Work.* 1 (September): 261–83.

Pechenik, Jan A. 1987. *A Short Guide to Writing about Biology.* New York: HarperCollins.

Pelto, Pertti J. 1970. *Anthropological Research: The Structure of Inquiry.* Cambridge, UK: Cambridge University Press.

Pencek, Bruce. 2000. "Internet Sources for Politics, Political Science, and Political Scientists." In *Academic Research on the Internet: Options for Scholars and Libraries.* Helen Laurence, and William Miller, eds. New York: Hawthorne Information Press: 293–334.

Pennock, J. Roland. 1968. "Political Philosophy and Political Science." In *Political Research and Political Theory.* Oliver Garceau, ed. Cambridge: Harvard University Press: 39–57.

Pernanen, Kai. 1993. "Research Approaches in the Study of Alcohol-Related Violence." *Alcohol Health & Research World.* 17 (2): 101–8.

Perry, James L., and Kenneth L. Kraemer. 1986. "Research Methodology in *Public Administration Review,* 1975–1984." *Public Administration Review.* 46 (May/June): 215–26.

Peters, Thomas J., and Robert W. Waterman. 1982. *In Search of Excellence: Lessons from America's Best Run Companies.* New York: Harper and Row.

Peterson, Karen S. 2001. "Would I Lie to You?" *USA Today.* (5 July): 8D.

Peterson, V. Spike. 2002. "Rewriting (Global) Political Economy as Reproducible, Productive, and Virtual (Foucauldian) Economics." *International Feminist Journal of Politics.* (April): 1–30.

Petrick, Joseph A., and John F. Quinn. 1997. *Management Ethics: Integrity at Work.* Newbury Park, CA: Sage.

Pfiffner, John M. 1940. *Research Methods in Public Administration.* New York: Ronald Press.

Phillips, Bernard S. 1976. *Social Research: Strategy and Tactics.* 3rd ed. New York: Macmillan.

Phillips, Denis C. 1987. *Philosophy, Science and Social Inquiry.* Oxford: Pergamon.

Phillips, John L. 1996. *How to Think about Statistics.* New York: W.H. Freeman.

Piantanida, Maria, and Noreen B. Garman. 1999. *The Qualitative Dissertation.* Thousand Oaks, CA: Corwin Press.

Plotkin, Henry. 1994. *The Nature of Knowledge.* London: Allen Lane/Penguin Press.

Poister, Theodore H., and Richard H. Harris, Jr. 1978. *Public Program Analysis: Applied Research Methods.* Baltimore: University Park Press.

———. 2000. "Building Quality Improvement over the Long Run: Approaches, Results, and Lessons Learned from the PennDOT Experience." *Public Productivity and Management Review* 24 (December): 161–76.

Pool, Ithiel de Sola. 1966. "The Necessity for Social Scientists Doing Research for Governments." *Background.* 10 (August): 111–22.

Potter, Jonathan, and Margaret Wetherell. 1994. "Analyzing Discourse." In *Analyzing Qualitative Data.* Alan Bryman, and Robert G. Burgess, eds. London: Routledge: 47–66.

Price, Alan R. 1994. "Definitions and Boundaries of Research Misconduct: Perspectives from a Federal Government Viewpoint." *Journal of Higher Education.* 65 (May/June): 286–97.

Price, Douglas. 1968. "Micro- and Macro-politics: Notes on Research Strategy." In *Political Research and Political Theory.* Oliver Garceau, ed. Cambridge: Harvard University Press: 102–40.

Prügl, Elisabeth. 2002. "Toward a Feminist Political Economy." *International Feminist Journal of Politics.* (April): 31–36.

Punnett, Betty J., and Oded Shenkat. 1996. *Handbook for International Management Research.* Cambridge: Blackwell.

Quigley, Allan, and Gary W. Kuhne, eds. 1997a. *Creating Practical Knowledge through Action Research:*

Posing Problems, Solving Problems, and Improving Daily Practice (New Directions for Adult and Continuing Education). San Francisco: Jossey-Bass.

———. 1997b. "The Role of Research in the Practice of Adult Education." *Creating Practical Knowledge through Action Research: Posing Problems, Solving Problems, and Improving Daily Practice.* 73 (Spring): 3–22.

Rabin, Jack, W. Barkley Hudreth, and Gerald J. Miller, eds. 1989. *Handbook of Public Administration Research.* New York: Marcel Dekker.

Racker, Efraim. 1997. "A View of Misconduct in Science." In *Research Ethics.* Deni Elliott, and Judy E. Stern, eds. Hanover, NH: University Press of New England: 34–51.

Raelin, Joseph A. 1997. "Action Learning and Action Science: Are They Different?" *Organizational Dynamics.* 26 (Summer): 21–35.

Ragin, Charles, and David Zaret. 1983. "Theory and Method in Comparative Research: Two Strategies." *Social Forces.* 61 (March): 731–54.

Rallings, Colin, Michael Thrasher, and Ron Johnston. 2002. "The Slow Death of a Governing Party: The Erosion of Conservative Local Electoral Support in England 1979–97." *British Journal of Politics and International Relations.* 4 (June): 271–98.

Randall, Vicky. "Feminism." 2002. In *Theory and Methods in Political Science.* 2nd ed. David Marsh, and Gerry Stoker, eds. Houndmills, UK: Palgrave Macmillan: 109–30.

Raphael, D.D. 1976. *Problems of Political Philosophy.* Rev. ed. London: Macmillan Press.

Reason, Peter. 1998. "Three Approaches to Participative Inquiry." In *Strategies of Qualitative Inquiry.* Norman K. Denzin, and Yvonna S. Lincoln, eds. Thousand Oaks, CA: Sage: 261–91.

Reisman, David. 1979. "Ethical and Practical Dilemmas of Fieldwork in Academic Settings: A Personal Memoir." In *Qualitative and Quantitative Social Research.* R.K. Merton, J.S. Coleman, and P.H. Rossi, eds. New York: Free Press: 210–31.

Reynolds, Paul D. 1979. *Ethical Dilemmas and Social Science Research.* San Francisco: Jossey-Bass.

Richards, Thomas J., and Lyn Richards. 1998. "Using Computers in Qualitative Research." In *Collecting and Interpreting Qualitative Materials.* Norman K. Denzin, and Yvonna S. Lincoln, eds. Thousand Oaks, CA: Sage: 211–45.

Richardson, Frank C., and Blaine J. Fowers. 1998. "Interpretive Social Science." *American Behavioral Scientist.* 41 (January): 465–95.

Richardson, Kurt A. "Postmetaphysical Hermeneutics: When Practice Triumphs over Theory." *PREMISE,* September 27, 1995. http://capo.org/premise/96/sep/930 (accessed Aug 7, 2000).

Roberts, Marylyn. 1992. "Predicting Voting Behavior via the Agenda-Setting Tradition." *Journalism Quarterly.* 69 (Winter): 878–92.

Robinson, Viviane M.J. 1994. "The Practical Promise of Critical Research in Education." *Educational Administration Quarterly.* 30 (February): 56–77.

Robrecht, Linda C. 1995. "Grounded Theory: Evolving Methods." *Qualitative Health Research.* 5 (May): 169–78.

Robson, Brian, Iain Deas, Michael Bradford, Cecelia Wong, and Margrethe Anderson. *The London Index of Deprivation.* London: Greater London Authority.

Rodgers, Robert, and Nanette Rodgers. 1999. "The Sacred Spark of Academic Research." *Journal of Public Administration Research and Theory.* 9 (July): 473–92.

Rohr, John A. 1998. *Public Service, Ethics, and Constitutional Practice.* Lawrence: University Press of Kansas.

Rosenthal, Cindy Simon. 2000. "Gender Styles in State Legislative Committees: Raising Their Voices in Resolving Conflict." *Women and Politics.* 21 (2): 21–45.

Rosenthal, Robert, and Ralph L. Rosnow. 1991. *Essentials of Behavioral Research.* 2nd ed. New York: McGraw-Hill.

Rothman, Jack. 1974. *Planning and Organizing for Social Change: Action Principles from Social Science Research.* New York: Columbia University.

Rubin, Jack, W., Barkley Hildreth, and Gerald J. Miller, eds. 1989. *Handbook of Public Administration.* New York: Marcel Dekker.

Ruget, Vanessa. 2002. "Scientific Capital in American Political Science: Who Possesses What, When and How?" *New Political Science.* 24 (September): 467–78.

Rummel, R.J. 1970. *Applied Factor Analysis.* Evanston, IL: Northwestern University Press.

Runyon, Melissa K., Jan Faust, and Helen Orvaschel. 2002. "Differential Symptom Patterns of Posttraumatic Stress Disorder (PTSD) in Maltreated Children with and without Concurrent Depression." *Child Abuse and Neglect.* 26 (January): 39–53.

Rutgers, Mark R. 1997. "Beyond Woodrow Wilson: the Identity of the Study of Public Administration in Historical Perspective." *Administration & Society.* 29 (July): 276–300.

Salomon, Kim. 1993. "What Is the Use of International History?" *Journal of Peace Research.* 30 (November): 375–89.

Sanders, David. 2002. "Behavioralism." In *Theory and Methods in Political Science.* 2nd ed. David Marsh, and Gerry Stoker, eds. Houndmills, UK: Palgrave Macmillan: 45–64.

Saxonhouse, Arlene. 1993. "Texts and Canons: The Status of the 'Great Books' in Political Science." In *Political Science: The State of the Discipline II.* Ada W. Finifter, ed. Washington, DC: American Political Science Association. 3–26.

Scarbrough, Elinor. 2000. "The British Election Study and Electoral Research." *Political Studies.* 48 (3): 391–414.

Schein, Edgar H. 1996. "Culture: The Missing Concept in Organization Studies." *Administrative Science Quarterly.* 41 (June): 229–40.

———. 1992. *Organizational Culture and Leadership.* 2nd ed. San Francisco: Jossey-Bass.

Schellenberg, James A. 1978. *Masters of Social Psychology.* Oxford, UK: Oxford University Press.

Schmuck, Richard A. 1997. *Practical Action Research for Change.* Arlington Heights, IL: SkyLight.

Schwab, Donald P. 1999. *Research Methods for Organizational Studies.* Mahwah, NJ: Lawrence Erlbaum Associates.

Schwandt, Thomas A. 1997. *Qualitative Inquiry: A Dictionary of Terms.* Thousand Oaks, CA: Sage.

Scott, Gregory M. 1997. *Political Science: Foundations for a New Millennium.* Upper Saddle River, NJ: Prentice-Hall.

Scott, Judy E. 2000. "Facilitating Interorganizational Learning with Information Technology." *Journal of Management Information Systems.* 17 (Fall): 81–114.

Seaman, Catherine C., and Phyllis J. Verbonick. 1982. *Research Methods.* 2nd ed. New York: Appleton-Century-Crofts.

Sebeok, Thomas A. 1976. *Contributions to the Doctrine of Signs.* Lanham: University Press of America.

Seech, Zachary. 1993. *Writing Philosophy Papers.* Belmont, CA: Wadsworth Publishing.

Selltiz, Claire, Lawrence S. Wrightman, and Stuart W. Cook. 1976. *Research Methods in Social Relations.* New York: Holt, Rinehart and Winston.

Selznick, Philip. 1949. *TVA and the Grass Roots: A Study in the Sociology of Formal Organization.* Berkeley: University of California Press.

Sepic, F. Thomas, J. Thad Barnowe, Merlin C. Simpson, and David E. McNabb. 1998. "Assessment of Organizational Climate and Commitment: First Steps toward Organizational Revitalization." *Proceedings.* Western Decision Sciences Institute. Reno, NV (April).

———. 1992. "Stressors, Moderators and Outcomes: Developing an Instrument to Measure Quality of Work Life (QWL)." *Proceedings.* Fourth Conference on Marketing and the Quality of Life. American Marketing Association. Chicago, IL.

Shahariw Kuehne, Valerie. 1998/99. "Building Intergenerational Communities through Research and Evaluation." *Generations.* 22 (Winter): 82–88.

Shaughnessy, John J., and Eugene B. Zechmeister. 1994. *Research Methods in Psychology.* 3rd ed. New York: McGraw-Hill.

Shelly, Gary B., Thomas J. Cashman, and Misty E. Vermatt. 1995. *Microsoft Office: Introductory Concepts and Techniques.* Danvers, MA: Boyd & Fraser.

Shepsle, Kenneth A. 1995. "Studying Institutions: Some Lessons from the Rational Choice Approach." In *Political Science in History.* James Farr, John S. Dryzek, and Stephen T. Leonard, eds. Cambridge, UK: Cambridge University Press: 276–95.

Shively, W. Phillips. 1974. *The Craft of Political Research.* Englewood Cliffs, NJ: Prentice-Hall.

Siblay, Mulford Q. 1962. "The Limitations of Behavioralism." In *The Limits of Behavioralism in Political Science.* Philadelphia: The American Academy of Political and Social Science: 68–93.

Siegel, Andrew F. 2002. Practical Business Statistics. 5th ed. New York: McGraw-Hill/Irwin.

Siegel, Sidney. 1956. *Nonparametric Statistics for the Behavioral Sciences.* New York: McGraw-Hill.

Sigelman, Lee. 2003. "Report of the Editor of the *American Political Science Review,* 2001–2002." *PS: Political Science & Politics*: 113–117.

Silverman, David. 1993. *Interpreting Qualitative Data: Methods for Analyzing Talk, Text, and Interaction.* London: Sage.

Silverman, Kaja. 1983. *The Subject of Semiotics.* Oxford: Oxford University Press.

Singleton, Royce A. 2002. "Survey Interviewing." In *Handbook of Interview Research.* Jaber F. Gubrium, and James A. Holstein, eds. Thousand Oaks, CA: Sage: 59–82.

Small, Stephen A. 1995. "Action-Orient Research: Models and Methods." *Journal of Marriage and Family.* 57 (November): 941–56.

Smirnov, W., ed. 1988. *Political Science: Integration of Research.* Papers presented at the 14th World Congress of Political Sciences (Soviet Political Science Association). Washington, DC: USSR Academy of Science.

Smith, Barbara L., Karl F. Johnson, David W. Paulsen, and Frances Shocket. 1976. *Political Research Methods: Foundations and Techniques.* Boston: Houghton Mifflin.

Smith, Charles B. 1981. *A Guide to Business Research.* Chicago: Nelson-Hall.

Smith, Rogers M. 2001. "Putting the Substance Back in Political Science." *Chronicle of Higher Education.* 48 (April 5): B10.

Somit, Albert, and Joseph Tanenhaus. 1967. *The Development of American Political Science: From Burgess to Behavioralism.* Boston: Allyn and Bacon.

Soni, Vidu. 2000. "A Twenty-First Century Reception for Diversity in the Public Sector: A Case Study." *Public Administration Review.* 60 (September/October): 395–408.

Sorrels, Bobbye D. 1984. *Business Communications Fundamentals.* New York: Macmillan.

Sproull, Natalie L. 1988. *Handbook of Research Methods.* Metuchen, NJ: Scarecrow Press.

Stack, Carol. 1996. "Doing Research in the Flats." In *In the Field: Readings on the Field Research Experience.* 2nd ed. Carolyn D. Smith, and William Kornblum, eds. Westport, CT: Praeger: 21–25.

Stake, Robert E. 2000. "Case Studies." In *Handbook of Qualitative Research*, 2nd ed. Norman K. Denzin, and Yvonna S. Lincoln, eds. Thousand Oaks, CA: Sage: 435–54.

Stallings, Robert A., and James M. Ferris. 1988. "Public Administration Research: Work in PAR, 1940–1984." *Public Administration Review.* 48 (January/February): 580–87.

StatSoft, Inc. *Nonparametric Statistics*, 2002. http://www.statssoft.com/textbook/stnonpar.html (accessed May 19, 2002).

Stein, Harold, ed. 1952. *Public Administration and Policy Development: A Case Book.* New York: Harcourt, Brace, and World.

Stevens, James. 1992. *Applied Multivariate Statistics for the Social Sciences.* 2nd ed. Hillsdale, NJ: Lawrence Erlbaum Associates.

Stivers, Camilla. 2000. "Public Administration Theory as a Discourse." *Administrative Theory & Praxis.* 221 (March): 132–39.

Stoker, Gerry, and David Marsh. 2002. "Introduction." In *New Perspectives on Historical Writing.* 2nd ed. Cambridge, UK: Polity Press: 1–16.

Stone, Eugene F. 1978. *Research Methods in Organizational Behavior.* Santa Monica: Goodyear Publishing.

Strauss, Anselm, and Juliet M. Corbin. 1998. *Basics of Qualitative Research.* 2nd ed. Thousand Oaks, CA: Sage.

———, eds. 1997. *Grounded Theory in Practice.* Thousand Oaks, CA: Sage.

Stringer, Ernie, ed. 1997. *Community-Based Ethnography: Breaking Traditional Boundaries of Research, Teaching, and Learning.* Mahwah, NJ: Lawrence Erlbaum.

Strunk, William, Jr., and E.B. White. 1979. *The Elements of Style.* 3rd ed. Boston: Allyn and Bacon.

Suchman, Edward A. 1967. *Evaluative Research: Principles and Practice in Public Service and Social Action Programs.* New York: Russell Sage Foundation.

Suppe, Frederick. 1988. "The Structure of a Scientific Paper." *Philosophy of Science.* 65 (September): 381–405.

Systsma, Sid. *The Basics of Experimental Design (A Quick and Non-Technical Guide)*, 2002 http://www.sytsma.com/phad530/expdesig.html (accessed May 7, 2002).

Tabachnick, Barbara G., and Linda S. Fidell. 1989. *Using Multivariate Statistics.* 2nd ed. New York: Harper & Row.

Tak, Sunghee H., Margaret Nield, and Heather Becker. 1999. "Use of a Computer Software Program for Qualitative Analyses—Part 1: Introduction to NUD*IST (N1)." *Western Journal of Nursing Research.* 31 (February): 111–18.

Taxpayers for Common Sense (TFCS). "Senator William Proxmire and the History of the Golden Fleece Award," 2001. http.//www.taxpayer.net/proxmire.html. (accessed July 7, 2001).

Thompson, Bruce. 1995. "Stepwise Regression and Stepwise Discriminant Analysis Need Not Apply Here: A Guideline Editorial." *Educational and Psychological Measurement.* 55 (August): 525–34.

Tibbetts, Arn. 1987. *Practical Business Writing.* Boston: Little, Brown.

Tranöy, Knut Erik. 1996. "Ethical Problems of Scientific Research: An Action-Theoretic Approach." *The Monist.* 79 (April): 183–96.

Travers, Max. 2001. *Qualitative Research through Case Studies.* London: Sage.

Trochim, William K. *Positivism and Post-Positivism,* 2002 http://trochim.human.cornell.edu/kb/ positivism.htm. (accessed June 10, 2002).

Tuck, Richard. 2001. "History of Historical Thought." In *New Perspectives on Historical Writing.* 2nd ed. Peter Burke, ed. Cambridge, UK: Polity Press: 218–32.

Turner, Roy, ed. 1974. *Ethnomethodology: Selected Readings.* Harmondswork, UK: Penquin.

University of Chicago. 1993. *A Manual of Style.* 14th ed. Chicago: University of Chicago Press.

Van Evera, Stephen. 1997. *Guide to Methods for Students of Political Science.* Ithaca, NY: Cornell University Press.

Velasquez, Manuel. 1998. *Business Ethics: Concepts and Cases.* 4th ed. Upper Saddle River, NJ: Prentice-Hall.

Verplanck, William S. *Fifty-Seven Years of Searching among Behaviorisms: A Memoir,* 1994. Speech given at Second International Congress on Behaviorism and the Sciences of Behavior. Palermo, Italy. http://web.utk.edu/~wverplan/bibn049 (accessed May 7, 2001).

Waddington, David. 1997. "Participant Observation." In *Qualitative Methods in Organizational Research.* Catherine Cassell, and Gillian Symon, eds. Thousand Oaks, CA: Sage: 107–22.

Walizer, Michael H., and Paul L. Wienir. 1978. *Research Methods and Analysis: Searching for Relationships.* New York: Harper & Row.

Walker, Robert, ed. 1985. *Applied Qualitative Research.* Aldershot, UK: Gower Publishing.

Wapner, Paul. 2002. "The Sovereignty of Nature? Environmental Protection in a Postmodern Age." *International Studies Quarterly.* 40 (June): 167–87.

Ward, Hugh. 2002. "Rational Choice." In *Theory and Methods in Political Science.* 2nd ed. David Marsh, and Gerry Stoker, eds. Houndmills, UK: Palgrave Macmillan: 65–89.

Wasson, Chester R. 1965. *Research Analysis for Marketing Decision.* New York: Appleton-Century-Crofts.

Waterston, Alice. 1999. *Love, Sorrow, and Rage: Destitute Women in a Manhattan Residence.* Philadelphia: Temple University Press.

Webb, Eugene J., Donald T. Campbell, Richard D. Schwartz, and Lee Sechrest. 2000. *Unobtrusive Measures,* 2nd ed. Thousand Oaks, CA: Sage.

Weiner, Norbert. 1966. *Extrapolation, Interpolation, and Smoothing of Stationary Time Series.* Cambridge: M.I.T. Press.

Weitzman, E., and Miles, M. 1995. *Computer Programs for Qualitative Data Analysis: A Software Sourcebook.* Thousand Oaks, CA: Sage.

Wengraf, Tom. 2001. *Qualitative Research Interviewing.* London: Sage.

Whelan, Robert K. 1989. "Data Administration and Research Methods in Public Administration." In *Handbook of Public Administration.* Jack Rabin, W.B. Hildreth, and G.J. Miller, eds. New York: Marcel Dekker: 657–82.

White, Jay D. 1986. "Dissertations and Publications in Public Administration." *Public Administration Review.* 46 (May/June): 227–39.

———. *The Narrative Foundations of Public Administration Research.* Washington, DC: Georgetown University Press.

White, Jay D., and Guy B. Adams, eds. 1994. *Research in Public Administration.* Thousand Oaks, CA: Sage.

Whiting, Beatrice, and John Whiting. 1973. "Methods for Observing and Recording Behavior." In *A Handbook of Method in Cultural Anthropology.* Raoul Naroll, and Ronald Cohen, eds. New York: Columbia University Press: 282–315.

Wildavsky, Arron. 1993. *Craftways: On the Organization of Scholarly Work.* 2nd ed. New Brunswick, NJ: Transaction Publishers.

Wilkenson, Sue, and Celia Kitzinger. 2000. " 'Clinton Faces Nation': A Case Study in the Construction of Focus Group Data as Public Opinion." *Sociological Review*. 48 (August): 408–24.

Williams, Terry. 1996. "Exploring the Cocaine Culture." In *In the Field: Readings on the Field Research Experience*. 2nd ed. Carolyn D. Smith, and William Kornblum, eds. Westport, CT: Praeger: 27–32.

Wilson, James Q. 1989. *Bureaucracy: What Government Agencies Do and How They Do It*. New York: Basic Books.

Winter, Bronwyn, Denise Thompson, and Sheila Jeffreys. 2002. "The UN Approach to Harmful Traditional Practices: Some Conceptual Problems." *International Feminist Journal of Politics*. (April): 72–94.

Winter, Denise Thompson. 2002. "The UN Approach to Harmful Traditional Practices: Some Conceptual Problems. *International Feminist Journal of Politics* (April): 72–94.

Wishart, David. 1999. *ClustanGraphics Primer: A Guide to Cluster Analysis*. Edinburgh: Clustan Ltd.

Woller, G.M., and K.D. Patterson. 1997. "Public Administration Ethics: A Postmodern Perspective." *American Behavioral Scientist*. 41 (1): 103–8.

Worlcott, Harry F. 1995. *The Art of Fieldwork*. Walnut Creek, CA: AltaMira Press.

Wyner, Gordon A. 1997. "Experimental Design." *Marketing Research*. 9 (3): 39–41.

Yan, Zhiyong, and Kathleen K. Anders. 2000. "A Paradigmatic View of Contemporary Public Administration Research: An Empirical Test." *Administration & Society*. 32 (May): 138–65.

Yates, Frank. 1977. "Sir Ronald Fisher and the Design of Experiments." In *Experimental Design and Interpretation*. Raymond O. Collier, Jr., and Thomas J. Hummel, eds. Berkeley, CA: McCutchan Publishing: 24–42.

Yeager, Samuel J. 1989. "Classic Methods in Public Administration Research." In *Handbook of Public Administration*. Jack Rabin, W.B. Hildreth, and G.J. Miller, eds. New York: Marcel Dekker: 683–793.

Yin, Robert K. 1994. *Case Study Research: Design and Methods*. Beverly Hills, CA: Sage.

Zeisel, Hans. 1968. *Say It with Figures*. 5th ed. New York: Harper & Row.

Zhang, Zhihai. 1998. "Application of Experimental Design in New Product Development." *TQM Magazine*. 10 (6): 432–40.

Zikmund, William G. 1994. *Business Research Methods*. Fort Worth, TX: Dryden.

Zuckert, Catherine. 1995. "The Postmodern Problem." *Perspectives on Political Science*. 24 (Spring): 78–84.

Author Index

Subject Index

Page numbers in *italic* type refer to figures or tables.

About the Author

David E. McNabb, professor of business administration at Pacific Lutheran University since 1980, is currently a visiting professor for the Stockholm School of Economics at Riga, Latvia. He recently completed a temporary MPA teaching assignment for the University of Maryland-European Division's graduate programs in Germany and the United Kingdom. He was an adjunct member of the faculty at the Evergreen State College from 1999 to 2002, where he taught quantitative and qualitative research methods, statistical analysis, and served as a graduate student advisor in the public administration Master's Degree program. He has also served as a visiting instructor in ethics and international courses at the University of Washington-Tacoma. He began his teaching career at Oregon State University, where he earned his PhD in 1980. Prior to beginning his academic career, he served as communications director for the Washington State Legislature's House of Representatives, majority caucus, and as a campaign manager for a variety of state office candidates. His municipal experience was gained as director of economic development for the City of Fullerton, California. He has served on citizen advisor boards for the cities of Seattle and Kirkland, Washington. He is the author of nearly fifty articles and conference papers. His first book, *Research Methods for Public Administration and Nonprofit Organizations*, was published by the M.E. Sharpe Publishing Company. His third book, *Management in Public Utilities*, is forthcoming. Professor McNabb is a member of the Academy of Political Science and the Academy of Management.